ENCYCLOPEDIA OF THE
YORÙBÁ

ENCYCLOPEDIA OF THE
YORÙBÁ

EDITED BY
TÓYÌN FÁLỌLÁ and
AKÍNTÚNDÉ AKÍNYẸMÍ

INDIANA UNIVERSITY PRESS • *Bloomington & Indianapolis*

This book is a publication of

Indiana University Press
Office of Scholarly Publishing
Herman B Wells Library 350
1320 East 10th Street
Bloomington, Indiana 47405 USA

iupress.indiana.edu

The paper used in this publication meets the
minimum requirements of the American National
Standard for Information Sciences—Permanence of
Paper for Printed Library Materials, ANSI Z39.48-1992.

Manufactured in the United States of America

Library of Congress Cataloging-in-Publication Data

Names: Falola, Toyin, editor. | Akínyẹmí, Akíntúndé,
    editor.
Title: Encyclopedia of the Yoruba / edited by Toyin
    Falola and Akintunde Akinyemi.
Description: Bloomington : Indiana University Press,
    [2016] | Includes index.
Identifiers: LCCN 2016010695 | ISBN 9780253021335
    (cloth : alk. paper) | ISBN 9780253021441 (pbk. : alk.
    paper)
Subjects: LCSH: Yoruba (African people)—History—
    Encyclopedias. | Yoruba (African people)—
    Civilization—Encyclopedias. | Yoruba (African
    people)—Social life and customs—Encyclopedias.
Classification: LCC DT474.6.Y67 E53 2016 | DDC 909/
    .0496333003—dc23
LC record available at http://lccn.loc.gov/2016010695

1 2 3 4 5   21 20 19 18 17 16

Samuel Àjàyí Crowther (1809–1891),
Samuel Johnson (1846–1901),
Henry Carr (1863–1945), and
Adébóyè Babalọlá (1926–2008),
in memoriam

A kì í ní ẹgbàá nílé, kí a tún máa wá ẹgbàá ròde;
Bẹ́ẹ̀ ni a kì í ní ọkọ́ nílé, kí a tún máa fi ọwọ́ kó imí.

Only the promise of a greater fortune should tempt one
to neglect what one already has.
—Yorùbá proverb

CONTENTS

PREFACE AND ACKNOWLEDGMENTS

This single volume of *Encyclopedia of the Yorùbá* is the very first to present materials on the Yorùbá in West Africa and in the African Diaspora, emphasizing the peculiarities, features, and commonalities of the people. An encyclopedia is not a dictionary, but a series of short essays, each concerned with defining a single item of information. Consequently, this encyclopedia is designed to have an integral structure, and the pieces of information are chosen to fit together so as to form a single coherent body of knowledge.

The encyclopedia comprises 285 short articles. Of these, 78 are approximately 1,000 words; 88 of them, 750 words; and 119 of them, 500 words. Many of the entries are designed to cover different aspects of the Yorùbá, including their history, geography and demography, language and linguistics, philosophy, religion, art, culture, literature, selected historical figures and authors, the Diaspora, among many others. Also, the relevance and impact of contexts such as electronic and print media, urban settings, and contemporary life in general are considered in various entries. Given the limitation of space, the volume is not absolutely comprehensive, but it is representative of the people. For now, we have succeeded in providing valuable information about the Yorùbá people in a single volume.

We chose the authors from our experience and knowledge of their abilities and promise. This careful selection has been a long and difficult task—indeed, the most difficult of any leading to the publication of the work. Our end result brings together scholars whose expertise goes back several years as well as the best minds of the upcoming generation. We have tried to balance female and male authors wherever possible, as well as authors from Africa, Europe, North America, and the remainder of the world, although their origins are no longer as relevant in today's "global" world as they used to be.

A major strength of this encyclopedia is the breadth of accomplished contributors. Nearly one-third of the scholars represented in the volume are Yorùbá, and more than one-half of them currently teach in Africa. Approximately one-half of the contributors teach in the United States, but a fairly large number of contributors also live in Europe and the Americas. In addition to geographical breadth, the volume features scholars from many different disciplines and backgrounds. The diversity in contributors' identities and fields of scholarship reflects the fact that "Yorùbá" is not an isolated and disregarded subject in scholarship but an integral part of a single world, and that there is but one image of Yorùbá that today comes from those both within Africa and outside of Africa.

Given the range and scope of the 285 entries in this encyclopedia, several tools have been employed to ensure easy navigation of the volume and access to essential information. These include an alphabetical list of all entries, thematic groupings of a large number of entries, a comprehensive index, an accompanying map highlighting major dialect groups, and extensive use of cross-references at the end of nearly every entry.

Creating an encyclopedia is an exhilarating yet exasperating project that involves many people. First, we acknowledge those colleagues who guided us and those friends who aided us in the current endeavor. In a very real sense, we thank all of our contributors not only for their excellent entries but also for their support and patience as we developed the project. The 118 authors have done so much difficult and taxing work, often at inconvenient times in their own schedules. They have truly been our partners and colleagues. We wish also to thank project staff and others at the publisher's headquarters, especially Dee Mortensen and the immense team of copy editors and researchers, proofreaders, designers, indexers, typesetters, and others working behind the scenes and invisible to us as editors.

Tóyìn Fálọlá and Akíntúndé Akínyẹmí

ENCYCLOPEDIA OF THE
YORÙBÁ

INTRODUCTION

In the interest of non-Yorùbá speakers and nonacademic readers of this encyclopedia, we highlight in the following sections some of the contexts that can guide the use of this book.

ORTHOGRAPHY AND PRONUNCIATION

It is important that readers be familiar with the orthographic guide—an English comparison, a mere approximation of the Yorùbá sounds—that we used in preparing this encyclopedia. Hopefully, this will assist users of the encyclopedia, most especially our non-Yorùbá readers, in the pronunciation of the cultural nuggets herein.

Consonants

Consonants sounds are approximately similar in pronunciation in both Yorùbá and English, except the following:

gb pronounced together with emphasis on the *b* to produce a sound like a thud—for example, *gbogbo* and *ìgbàgbọ́*

p pronounced as *kp* together to produce a forceful *p* sound as in *pátápátá*

ṣ pronounced like the *sh* in the English word *should*—for example, *òrìṣà*

y pronounced like a *y* in the English word *you*—for example, *Yorùbá*

The following letters or sounds of the English alphabet, however, are absent in the language: *c, q, v, x, z.*

Vowels

There are two types of vowels in Yorùbá: nonnasalized (oral) and nasalized vowels. The nonnasalized (oral) vowels are written as *a, e, ẹ, i, o, ọ, u.*

a pronounced like the *a* in *apple*—for example, *àṣà* and *adé*

e pronounced like the *a* in *age*—for example, *èdè* and *ewé*

ẹ pronounced like the *e* in *egg*—for example, *ẹgbẹ́* and *àjẹ́*

i pronounced like the *e* in *evening*—for example, *ilé* and *ìlú*

o pronounced like the *o* in *old*—for example, *odò* and *ìgò*

ọ pronounced like the *aw* in *awe* or the *o* in *dog*—for example, *ọmọ* and *ọ̀dọ́*

u pronounced like the *u* in *full*—for example, *Yorùbá* and *ibùdó*

Nasalized vowels are produced by adding an *n* to an oral vowel symbol (e.g., *an, ọn, in, ẹn, un*), except where such a symbol is preceded by *m* or *n* (e.g., *ọmọ* "child," or *ọ̀nà* "path").

The syllabic structure in Yorùbá language consists of either a vowel, such as *a* (we) and *i* in *ilé* (house); a consonant followed by a vowel, such as *mu* (drink) and *yo, rù,* and *bá* in *Yorùbá*; or a syllabic nasal, such as *ń* in *ń lọ* (She [or he] is going). Consequently, any word in Yorùbá having more than one syllable may be described in terms of the combination of the types of syllable above, for example, *òrìṣà = ò-rì-ṣà*, a lesser god or deity (vowel, consonant + vowel, consonant + vowel), and *àṣà = à-ṣà*, culture and/or tradition (vowel, consonant + vowel). Each syllable in Yorùbá bears one of the three tones in the language: high, acute (*ó*); low, grave (*ò*); or mid (usually left unmarked).

The following is a list of style rules that we adopted for Yorùbá and other non-English words: (1) capital letters but no italics for all proper nouns, including, but not limited to, personal names, names of cities, societies, and associations or organizations, such as Yorùbá, Wọlé Ṣoyínká, Odùduwà, Ògún, Ìbàdàn, Àgbékòyà, and Ẹgbẹ́ Àgbà ò Tán; (2) italics and tone marks (but no capital letters) for titles that are not part of proper nouns, such as *òrìṣà, baálẹ̀, àfin*, and *ọba*; (3) italics and tone marks without quotation marks for shorter samples of Yorùbá texts embedded in the body of an entry; and (4) Yorùbá text or data longer than fifty words is italicized, tone marked, and indented.

THE LANGUAGE AND ITS DIALECT GROUPS

The Yorùbá, numbering more than thirty million, are the second-largest language group in Nigeria (after Hausa) and one of the most populous and better-known African ethnic groups. They occupy southwestern Nigeria and can be found elsewhere—in the Republic of Benin and Togo in West Africa, and as members of the African Diaspora in the Americas. They speak a common tonal language, known also as Yorùbá, which belongs to the Kwa family within the Niger-Congo phylum of African languages. Speakers of the language are divided into many ethnic subgroups, each with its own peculiar dialect. A subgroup comprises many villages and towns or cities. According to Sopé Oyèláràn, the dialects of the Yorùbá can be classified as follows:

(a) West Yorùbá (WY)
   (1) Ọ̀yọ́, Ìbàdàn, Ẹ̀gbá, Ọ̀họ̀rí-Ìfọ̀hìn
   (2) Upper Ògùn
      (i) Ṣakí, Ìjìò
      (ii) Kétu, Sábẹ

   (3) Benin and Togo
      (i) Ifẹ̀ (Togo), Ìdásà, Mànígì
(b) South East Yorùbá (SEY)
   (1) Oǹdó, Ọ̀wọ̀
   (2) Ìjẹ̀bú
   (3) Ìkálẹ̀, Ìlàjẹ
(c) Central Yorùbá (CY)
   (1) Ilé-Ifẹ̀, Ìjẹ̀ṣà, Èkìtì
(d) Northern Eastern Yorùbá (NEY)
   (1) Ìgbómìnà, Kàkàǹdá, Ìgbòló
   (2) Jùmú, Búnú, Ọ̀wọ́rọ̀, Owé, Ẹ̀gbẹ̀

This classification, according to Lawrence Olúfẹ́mi Adéwọlé, is referred to as a dialect continuum because the dialects are characterized by a high degree of mutual intelligibility, which diminishes with territorial distance. As one moves from one end of the continuum to the other, some phonological, lexical, and even grammatical differences can be found in the dialects.

Thanks to missionaries and a formal school system, Standard Yorùbá, a language that all Yorùbá speakers can understand, emerged as a written language during the second half of the nineteenth century. Today, scholars point to linguistic unity and a common ancestral origin and historical experience as a strategy of uniting the Yorùbá in modern Nigeria. We shall see in some of the entries how some Western-educated elite are concerned with the issue of Yorùbá unity and how an identity has been constructed for the Yorùbá people.

The International African Institute classifies the status of the Yorùbá language in Nigeria as follows:

First language: 20 percent
Effective speaker: 25 percent
Media: P R T
Government-coordinated education: El, C2, 3
Status: N

This classification indicates that the proportion of the population of Nigeria speaking Yorùbá as a first language is about 20 percent, while 25 percent are able to speak the language regardless of whether it is their first, second, or additional language. "P R T" refers to the fact that the language is used by the press, radio, and television. With regard to government-coordinated education, Yorùbá is used as a language of formal instruction in primary schools. At the secondary and postsecondary levels, it is a curriculum subject. Finally, the "N" classification stands for the fact that the language is a national language. This means that it has a standard orthography and enjoys some measures of support or formal recognition from government at all levels, most especially from the federal government.

THE WESTERN-EDUCATED ELITE AND FORMATION OF YORÙBÁ IDENTITY

Yorùbá was not a universal concept or a general identity of all speakers of the language until sometime before European colonization. For, according to Robin Law, "the use of the word Yorùbá to refer to the whole area is surprisingly recent, dating only from the middle of the nineteenth century when it was introduced by missionaries and linguists" (5). New important centers of power, including Abẹ́òkúta, Ìbàdàn, and Ìjàyè, emerged in Yorùbáland in the first half of the nineteenth century; there was also a major population shift from the savanna in the north to the forest edge in the south and east as a result of the many wars that were fought among competing empires and kingdoms (Fálọlá and Ògúntómisìn 2001). Also during the nineteenth century, circumstances that produced a new intelligentsia began to unfold, with the abolition of the slave trade, the return of liberated slaves to Yorùbáland, evangelization by foreign missions, and the British annexation of Lagos and subsequent imposition of colonial rule. Most historians characterize the nineteenth century as an era of major changes. The intra-Yorùbá wars of the nineteenth century are reported in Fálọlá and Ògúntómisìn (2001), with groups divided between conquerors extending their frontiers and victims fighting for their independence.

The acceptance of Christianity and Western education since the mid-nineteenth century rapidly transformed the Yorùbá and created an educated elite that has played a leadership role in Nigeria (Àjàyí 1965). The first university in Nigeria was established by the colonial government in the Yorùbá city of Ìbàdàn in 1948; additional ones were later established by the federal government at Ilé-Ifẹ̀, Lagos, Ìlọrin, Abẹ́òkúta, Àkúré, and Ọ̀yẹ́ Èkìtì, and state governments in Yorùbáland established their own universities in Àgó-Ìwòyè, Adó-Èkìtì, Àkùngbá-Àkókó, Ọ̀jó-Lagos, Ògbómọ̀ṣọ́, Ọṣogbo, and Màlété. Added to these universities are other institutions of higher education (e.g., colleges of education, colleges of technology, polytechnics). Scholars based in these institutions and elsewhere have ensured the continuous study of the region, with the result that the Yorùbá are arguably the most researched group today in sub-Saharan Africa.

A vibrant writing culture exists outside the academy. This culture, in fact, dates back to the nineteenth century, before the establishment of institutions of higher learning. In Yorùbá, which had acquired a written form and standard orthography, along with the English language, a new elite began to write books, pamphlets, and essays (Ọlábímtán 1974; Ògúnṣínà 1992). Local writings began in the nineteenth century and became transformed during the twentieth century. Not all writers chose the same medium—some wrote for newspapers, others in books; and some were storytellers, others historians and chroniclers (Fálọlá 1999).

Chronicles began in the late nineteenth century as a cultural project by groups of cultural activists interested in presenting their rich heritage to the European world. Among such groups were Ẹgbẹ́ Olùfẹ́ Ilẹ̀ Ìbí Wọn, formed in 1883; Ẹgbẹ́ Onífẹ́ Ilẹ̀ Yorùbá, formed in 1907; and Ẹgbẹ́ Àgbà ò Tán, formed in 1909. These groups believed in noncolonial commerce and the recently inaugurated process of Westernization as long as it did not rob the Yorùbá of political and economic power. The defining characteristics of this new elite were Western education and claims to the knowledge of (and connection with) Western culture. The elite constituted the labor pool for the emerging government sector, consumers of imported items, readers of available books, and chroniclers of the age.

The nineteenth century witnessed the abolition of the slave trade, the liberation of many slaves, and the establishment of Freetown and Liberia in West Africa to resettle them, as well as the spread of Christianity and the European partition of the African continent. With respect to the abolition of slavery, one consequence was the return, from Sierra Leone and Brazil, of many liberated slaves between the 1830s and the 1880s to their Yorùbá homeland in Nigeria. The repatriates from Sierra Leone (known as the Sàró) had been acculturated to Western influences and had accepted Christianity, and those from Brazil (known as the Àgùdà) were familiar with Roman culture, and many were Catholic converts. These repatriates advanced the cause of Christianity in Yorùbáland by spreading it and of Western education by promoting it. In a country where the majority were not able to read and write, literacy, especially in English, was a source of power. They could communicate with foreign merchants and officers and serve as representatives of the traditional elite. Given the low number of foreign wage earners up until the late 1870s, the Western-educated Yorùbá elite had great opportunities to secure good jobs in the colonial secretariat, churches, and schools. The time was great for many who moved rapidly up the career and social ladders. A few became successful pioneers in prestigious professions of the time, notably law and medicine. In later years, others trained as engineers, surveyors, and other highly regarded occupations with good incomes. As have the elite elsewhere, the emerging Yorùbá elite invested their income and used whatever power they had to acquire more money in both legal and illegal ways.

A complement to the activities of the repatriates was the rise of Christianity, which began to spread rapidly after the 1840s. Good beginnings were made at Lagos, Ìbàdàn, Badagry, Abẹ́òkúta, and Ìjàyè, the latter of which was destroyed and evacuated in 1862. Wherever the missions were located, their aims were to evangelize and establish a major cultural presence.

The Christian elite believed in the superiority of their culture and manners. Christianity encouraged education and a writing culture.

In the attempt to participate in trade, European firms established greater contacts in Lagos and were interested in political developments in the hinterland. Trade in palm produce replaced that in slaves as the nineteenth century progressed. The goods were produced in the hinterland, and sent to the port of Lagos, both crucial centers in the import-export trade. In the late 1840s British military agents began to appear, and they bombarded Lagos in 1851. In 1861, the British established greater political control over Lagos, creating new administrative and judicial institutions, serviced by them and by educated Yorùbá. With Lagos as a base, the British penetrated the rest of Yorùbáland and established colonial control in the 1890s.

These events created consequences that gave birth to, and accelerated, intellectual development. Many ex-slaves took an interest in education, missionaries established schools, the Yorùbá language was in a written form, and the Bible was translated to Yorùbá. A tiny Western-educated elite emerged, notably in Lagos, and to a smaller extent in such places as Abẹ́òkúta, Ìbàdàn, and elsewhere where there was a missionary presence. During the nineteenth century, this elite enjoyed considerable interaction with Europeans, largely because of their ability to mediate between the foreigners and the rest of the population, over which the elite claimed superiority.

The Western-educated Yorùbá elite, possessed of the infrastructure of writing and sensitive to the European presence, gradually began to record known traditions and current events into histories. This elite initiated an intellectual production that has survived to this day. Originally dominated by the Sàró (the Sierra Leonean Yorùbá ex-slaves who migrated back to their homeland), this Western-educated elite needed history to articulate its own identity. Seeing itself as agent of change, it also had to deal with current Western intellectual traditions and the meaning of progress. It was joined by foreign missionaries, who also produced small pamphlets on a variety of issues.

The early writers tried to contend with the Yorùbá past and report contemporary events. A few struggled to invent vocabularies for the language and to write in English. Religious literature appeared quickly, in sermons and hymns. The post-1880 writers began a tradition of protest against the Europeans, for their domination of the church, politics, and the economy. This was expressed more in cultural than in political terms, especially in the search for knowledge to affirm their past and the connection to the African milieu. There were attempts by this new elite to accommodate Western civilization without rejecting the past of its own people.

The elite popularized the idea of Yorùbáness, an identity as well as an ethnic group with a common origin, a long history, and a distinct identity, although some argued that Yorùbá consciousness predated the nineteenth century, and that what the missionaries and the reduction of Yorùbá to writing contributed was merely its popularization to an outside world. If the notion of the invented Yorùbá world is problematic—more so because the Yorùbá elite thinks that it negates their efforts to build a strong Yorùbá ethnicity to compete for power in modern Nigeria—there is nevertheless consensus on the fact that the use of the term *Yorùbá* to define the people gained a wider currency only after 1850. To those who write about pan-Yorùbá issues and those who seek a Yorùbá unity, the Yorùbá are one people. Differences are recognized in dialects, food habits, drums, songs, poetry, and chants. Nevertheless, many scholars believe that the Yorùbá constitute an ethnic group and do differ from their neighbors. Historical and cultural reasons are adduced in support of this belief. The strongest of the reasons is the claim that all Yorùbá have one progenitor father, Odùduwà. Ilé-Ifè is regarded as the cradle of the race, from where most founders of dynasties and towns descended. A host of other reasons are based on cultural similarities, such as the widespread use of lineage poetry, common words in the language irrespective of dialect, the common occupation of farming, the existence of a complex political structure headed by powerful kings or chiefs, the habit of living in towns instead of little villages, the worship of common gods and goddesses (the *òrìṣà*), common dress styles, and a love for celebrations of birth, marriage, rites of passage, and funeral ceremonies.

POLITICAL INSTITUTION

There is a great deal of diversity in Yorùbá settlements and political organizations (Forde 1951; Bascom 1969; Fádípè 1970). Nevertheless, there is also significant uniformity among various cultural and social institutions. The Yorùbá live in heterogeneous cities and villages, with division of labor, social hierarchies, and diverse cultural and intellectual production. It appears that all the settlements founded by the Yorùbá, rather than being controlled by one supreme authority, initially developed independently under their own various rulers on whose ability and ingenuity they depended for their social, political, and economic organization. In light of this, we can conceive of many forms of political organization rather than an all-embracing government of Yorùbáland.

In general, among the different groups of the Yorùbá, governments are town based. Although these governments are different in form, they have certain basic similarities. At each level, an *ọba* (king) or a *baálè* (lesser ruler) is the head. The town is headed usually by the king, who, depending on the political status of the town, wears either a beaded crown (*adé*) with fringes or a beadless coronet (*akoro*). Most of the *baálè* live in villages, although some live in fairly large towns. A *baálè* is not entitled to wear a crown. The *baálè* wear caps (*oríkògbófo*) and, in exceptional cases, coronets without beaded fringe (*akoro*). Despite the differences between *ọba* and *baálè*, the two perform similar traditional functions. Sacred kingship has been the most important and popular feature of Yorùbá political organization. The *ọba* is seen as a semidivine ruler and is regarded by the people as *aláṣẹ èkejì òrìṣà*, the commander and companion of the gods. An important feature of Yorùbá kingship is that the political structure prevented *ọba* from exercising absolute power. The *ọba*'s power is constantly checked by the council of lineage chiefs. The council, given different names in different communities, is composed of the most senior lineage chiefs whom the paramount ruler could not ignore. These chiefs also have official titles by which they are identified. Among such titles are Ọ̀yọ́ Mèsì in Ọ̀yọ́ town, Ìwàrẹ̀fà among the Èkìtì, Ìjèṣà, and Oǹdó ethnic subgroups; and Ìlámùrẹn among the Ìjẹ̀bú-Yorùbá.

Before the nineteenth century, the Yorùbá lived for many years in separate autonomous kingdoms. In the central region were a few centralized states, notably Ifẹ̀, Ìjẹ̀bú, Ìjèṣà, Kétu, Ọyẹ́, Oǹdó, Ọ̀wọ̀, Òwu, and Sábẹ, with Ọ̀yọ́ being the most powerful until its collapse during the nineteenth century. The old Ọ̀yọ́ Empire, under the sovereignty of the aláàfin (king) was the largest and most powerful political unit in Yorùbáland. The empire developed a political organization that entrenched the authority of the aláàfin in all the towns and villages under his sovereignty. With the fall of the empire in 1835 and the political developments that followed, the extent of authority and power of the aláàfin reduced considerably.

In other areas, political units tended to be smaller than the towns previously mentioned, as among the Àkókó, Kàbà, Ìkálẹ̀, and Ìlàjẹ. However, a single political authority has never effectively controlled the entire Yorùbá nation. As powerful as Ọ̀yọ́ Empire was, it was unable to establish singular political control over the entire Yorùbáland. Other influences, including political imperialism, came from Benin. In historians' narration of the myths of the establishment of these states and their dynasties, they present the early phase as the golden age, when committed and military leaders emerged to establish territories or expand frontiers (Johnson 1921; Fálọlá 1999). Most mythical heroes, such as Odùduwà in Ilé-Ifẹ̀, Ọ̀rányàn in Ọ̀yọ́, Lágelú in Ìbàdàn, Lísàbi in Ẹ̀gbá, and Ọwálúṣẹ́ in Ìjèṣà, emerged during this phase.

The Yorùbá kingship institution has changed with the times. The Yorùbá internecine wars in the nineteenth century introduced many changes. The ọba were at the mercy of warriors who had become too powerful because of their participation in the long wars. The establishment of colonial rule through the British system of indirect rule eroded the power and prestige of the traditional ọba, who became answerable to the British authority. Since independence, the kingship institution has continued to experience modifications under the civilian and military governments. Although the ọba have lost or are unable to effectively exercise their powers and authority, their relevance in Yorùbá communities endures.

MYTH, RELIGION, AND BELIEF SYSTEM

The desire of the Yorùbá people for a mythical origin for their religious beliefs and their numerous deities, known generally as òrìṣà, encouraged them to formulate different kinds of myths, legends, and stories around the origin, the superhuman nature, and extraordinary powers of these objects of worship. For example, the following divinities are universally worshiped in Yorùbáland: Ifá, Èṣù, Ọbàtálá, Ògún, Òrìṣà-Oko, Ọ̀ṣun, Ṣàngó, Ṣànpọ̀nná, and Yemọja, but, Ifá is at the core of the Yorùbá religion. Existing scholarship on Ifá owes much to the efforts of William Bascom and Wándé Abímbọ́lá, who have made the most comprehensive and illuminative collections of Ifá divination poetry. Abímbọ́lá describes Ifá as "the Yorùbá god of wisdom, knowledge, and divination" who occupies a "premier position among Yorùbá divinities." He argues further that Ifá's supreme status is derived from his vast knowledge and wisdom. Ifá divination is marked by a series of chants (known as ẹsẹ ifá) from specific chapters of Ifá poetry referred to as odù ifá.

Ẹsẹ ifá verses can be treated as verbal art and as a storehouse of information about Yorùbá mythology and cosmology. The aesthetic value or merit of this poetic form, however, is, to the Yorùbá, secondary to its religious significance. The worldview of the Yorùbá can be reconstructed from information contained in the verses. This, however, needs clarification, since some evidence of the culture can be found to varying degrees in the other oral genres. While those others forms contain allusions to elements of Yorùbá culture, in ẹsẹ ifá, there is something theological and ritual about the verse; in ẹsẹ ifá are codified the origins and validation of the culture. As Bascom has noted,

"The verses embody myths recounting the activities of the deities and justifying details of ritual, and they are often cited to settle a disputed point of theology or ritual." Abímbọ́lá underlines the point that ẹsẹ ifá constitutes a compendium of information on Yorùbá worldview, when he writes that the "Ifá literary corpus is . . . the storehouse of Yorùbá culture inside which the Yorùbá comprehension of their own historical experiences and understanding of their environment can always be found. Even until today Ifá is recognized by the Yorùbá as a repository for traditional body of knowledge embracing history, philosophy, medicine and folklore."

The corpus of Ifá includes multiple genres, showing a wide variety of forms like anecdotes, wits, dilemma poems, and tales. These genres are connected in their reflection of patterns of conflicts and resolution through sacrifices. Ẹsẹ ifá verses contain statements of human problems, wishes and hopes, and testimonies of how each personage has reacted to these things. Some of these desires are universal human needs, while others are pertinent to Yorùbá life. The statistics provided by Ọlátúnjí bring out the frequency with which some of the desires occur. According to him, of the 128 ẹsẹ ifá in Abímbọ́lá (1968), 27 deal with desire for children, 20 with victory over enemies who may cause death, and 18 specifically contain attempts to escape death, while 33 of the verses deal with the desire for blessings, which also includes almost all the foregoing desires. Of the 186 ẹsẹ ifá in Bascom (1969), 36 contain the theme of death, 28 deal with desire for children, and 24 with the desire to have wives. We can use these statistics to find out the value the Yorùbá attach to the things desired or the things they wish to avoid.

Certain significant aesthetic phenomena emerge from this Ifá complex. One finds that the basic function of this oral poetry is to resolve everyday human problems. In actual divination, the Ifá priest continues to chant until the client tells the priest he or she has found the verse, which bears the story that relates to the client's own problem. The priest then prescribes the same sacrifices contained in the verse that the client has identified. Aesthetic currents still play out in the context of the sacred ritualism of divination as priest and client relate in drawing meanings from the stock of Ifá poetry.

Apart from the mythological gods and goddesses, the Yorùbá people also believe in spirits, celestial bodies, and life after death. Indeed, the dead are regarded as an integral part of one's extended family on the earth, and they maintain the right to continued involvement in their descendants' affairs. The Yorùbá thus envision a human soul after death, believing that each individual ascends skyward to take her or his proper place among the ancestors. From this belief come the sayings baba pa ipò dà (father has changed his position or status), ìyá dara pọ̀ mọ́ àwọn ará ilẹ̀ (mother has joined those who died before her), and ọbá wàjà (the king has disappeared in the attic). The Yorùbá often invoke ancestral spirits to bear witness to oaths or serve as consultants before an important family meeting. It is not unusual for family agreements to be consummated on descendants' graves.

Another key Yorùbá belief concerning death is that the human soul may ascend to heaven, and then (if it so desires) return to earth in the form of a baby, a new life. Thus, parents give commemorative names to children born shortly after the death of their grandparents—names such as Babátúndé (father comes back again) for a boy, or Ìyábọ̀ or Yétúndé (mother returns) for a girl. One critical clarification is necessary here: the Yorùbá attitude toward all those who die young, who die by drowning, hanging, or automobile accident, or by such terrible afflictions as leprosy, is different from those who die naturally. Such unfortunate individuals, whose deaths are attributed to the devil, are denied entry into heaven. This intercession by the devil prevents them from joining their ancestors in heaven, and they are barred from association with the living on earth. The only course that is open to them, according to the Yorùbá belief system, is to join a group of fairies and make their abode in giant forest trees, in the mountains, in rivers, or in outlying hills. Many Yorùbá traditional folk stories often include fearful tales about those who dwell in such places.

Moreover, beyond their belief in an afterlife, Yorùbá hold fast to the existence of other spirits that, though invisible, play an important part in daily life. These include spirits of the forest (iwin), as well as spirits associated with particular trees (ẹbọra), such as ìrókò, and those associated with anthills (ògán). A typical fairy is egbére, which is prone to tears and believed to be capable of menacing humans, especially hunters. Fairies, according to the Yorùbá, appear in a multitude of physical forms. Some are two headed, and others one legged, one eyed, or two mouthed; some have missing arms or limbs. Yorùbá believe that when these fairies decide to trick people, they can assume human form. These fairies are considered the most dangerous since they are virtually impossible to recognize. Their powers are most malevolent at night, when they come out to fetch their food.

Also, the belief in witches and in bewitchment has survived for centuries and continues to be very significant among the Yorùbá to this day (Washington 2005). Fear of witches looms large in Yorùbá consciousness and practice. Whenever reference is made to witches or to their name (àjẹ́ or àwọn ìyá), it is prudent to touch the ground with one's fingertips, saying bi a bá perí akọni, a ń fi ọwọ́ lalẹ̀ ni (if a person of violent character is mentioned, a mark is made on the ground), while those seated stand up briefly as a mark of respect and humility. The Yorùbá associate witchcraft with women and wizardry with men. Witches possess considerable superhuman, mystical powers and can perform wonders. They can hurt their victims, kill an enemy, block the fortunes of others, and cause a business failure for a neighbor. In short, they are capable of doing anything that is evil, and all with impunity. Most important, the Yorùbá believe that witches have the ability to transform themselves into birds, cats, sheep, or goats, and to congregate in the forest at night under giant trees, where they feast on the flesh and blood of their victims.

As might be expected, in a culture with strong beliefs in fairies and mystical causation, protective rituals and sacrifices are regularly performed. People must be protected from the wrath of fairies; fairy-human social relationships must be harmonized. Therefore, whenever any misfortune occurs, and the source remains unknown, both humans and invisible spirits are subjects of divination. To complete any divination process, there is always a prescribed sacrifice. Whether the prediction of the divination is good or bad, the client must always offer sacrifice. If the prediction is good, a sacrifice will quicken a positive outcome and if the prediction is evil, a sacrifice will help dispel the ill effects. Therefore, after completing the long process of divination, the diviner will advise the client specifically as to which type of sacrifice to make. The client then buys the necessary articles required for the sacrifice and brings them to the diviner. According to Wándé Abímbọ́lá, diviners believe that the psychological function of sacrifice is critically important: "They maintain that sacrifice helps to unite all the forces both natural and supernatural (including the fairy spirits) that operate in Yorùbá society."

Broadly speaking, four forces interplay in Yorùbá ritual: the gods, the ancestors, witches and other supernatural powers, and human beings. The function of sacrifice is to enlist the support of these four forces to achieve whatever ends are desired, ensuring that none of the forces work against one's purpose. It is apparent in divination texts that human beings play an essential role in making a sacrifice successful. That is why, during the offering of any sacrifice, people are invited to the shrine of the god to whom sacrifice is being made, not only to watch the ritual but also to eat part of the food used for the sacrifice.

THE DIASPORA EFFECT

The massive expansion of the Yorùbá occurred in the context of the four continents united by the Atlantic Ocean. The Yorùbá were among the African slaves drawn from Central and West Africa and tragically relocated to the Americas. When Yorùbá slaves were funneled to the Americas during the transatlantic slave period, many of the slaves carried with them a whole body of their indigenous stories, legends, poetry, songs, traditions, cultural practices, and religious beliefs. Although the arrival of the slaves in the

New World stripped them of their cultural identity, the slaves, paradoxically, refused to succumb even in their cultural nakedness. They managed to retain several aspects of their culture, which they passed on to the younger generations despite stiff opposition from their white masters. This religious survival is the most spectacular and widely studied phenomenon in the New World. Incidentally, most scholars claim that no other African ethnic group influenced the preservation of African religious practices in the New World as much as the Yorùbá.

It has not been possible to discover why the Yorùbá became the most influential group among all the African ethnic groups enslaved during the period, of which there were more than thirty. One scholar has, however, suggested that the late arrival of enormous numbers of Yorùbá indentured slaves in the Americas "ensured a strong Yorùbá character in the artistic, religious, and social lives of Africans in the New World" (Drewal et al. 1989, 13). One other important factor that probably facilitated the preservation of Yorùbá religious beliefs in the New World is syncretism. González-Wippler argues that the practice of Yorùbá religion in Latino communities "emerged as a struggle for cultural and ideological survival between the enslaved West African Yorùbá people and the Roman Catholic Church in union with the Spanish Empire. Slaves transformed the enforced worship of the Catholic Saints into the veil worship of their spirit ancestors" (182). They therefore danced before a Catholic altar with their prominently displayed lithographs and statuettes of the saints, which were in fact addressed to Yorùbá divinities. This syncretism between the Yorùbá òrìṣà and the Catholic saints permitted the slaves in the New World to continue the cult of their divinities in secret, under the cover of Christianity. Traditional Yorùbá religion is even thriving in the New World today, in contrast to the òrìṣà cult, which is declining among the Yorùbá people in West Africa. A peculiar case is that of the òrìṣà Ochosi (Ọ̀ṣọ́ọ̀sì), whose worship survives today only in the Diaspora. The deity is no longer worshipped by the West African Yorùbá because, in the words of González-Wippler, the "entire village

with its corresponding òrìshà [Ochosi] was brought over to the Americas" (12). But the deity is still one of the most important divinities in Bahia, Brazil, where he is regarded as the divinity of the hunters. There, he is symbolized by a bow and arrow and syncretized with St. Jorge.

Santería is the common name for the syncretistic religion of Yorùbá traditional religion and Roman Catholicism in Cuba. Synonymous with Santería is La Regla Lucumí (The Lucumí Rule) or simply Lucumí (a derivation of the Ifẹ̀-Yorùbá greeting olùkù mi, or "my friend"), which refers not only to the religion but to the practitioners of the religion as well. Two òrìṣà (in Portuguese, orixa) cults preserve Yorùbá traditional religion in Brazil: Candomblé and Xangô (Ṣàngó). The densest centers of Candomblé practice are in the northeastern state of Bahia, especially the cities of Recife and Salvador (the former Brazilian capital, where the religion first emerged), as well as Rio de Janeiro in southeastern Brazil. In contrast to Lucumí, which deprives women of attaining the highest level of priesthood (babaláwo), Candomblé lacks any division of gender in its religious hierarchy, and in further contrast to Lucumí, Candomblé priesthood is female dominated.

The òrìṣà Èṣù or Ẹlẹ́gbára exists in Cuba as Eleggua or Legba, and in Brazil as Exu. In Brazil Exu is equated to Satan, but Santería equates Eleggua to the Holy Child of Atocha, St. Anthony of Padua, and St. Martin de Porres, and he is protector of both home and paths. Ṣàngó (Chango), a warrior divinity, is lord of lightning, fire, drum, dance, and justice. He is highly popular in Brazil, where he is equated to St. Barbara. Ṣàngó has several wives, including Ọya and Ochun (Ọ̀ṣun), both present in the New World pantheons. Ọya is the goddess of the whirlwind and the realm of the dead in the New World, witnessed in her connection with cemetery gates. Ọya also owns the epithet ìyánsán in the Diaspora, where she is linked to St. Thérèse of Lisieux and the Virgin of Candelaria. In Cuba, the goddess Ochun (Ọ̀ṣun) is the Mother of Secrets. She is equated to the Virgin Mary in her form of Our Lady of Charity of El Cobre, Cuban's patron Virgin Mary, clearly revealing

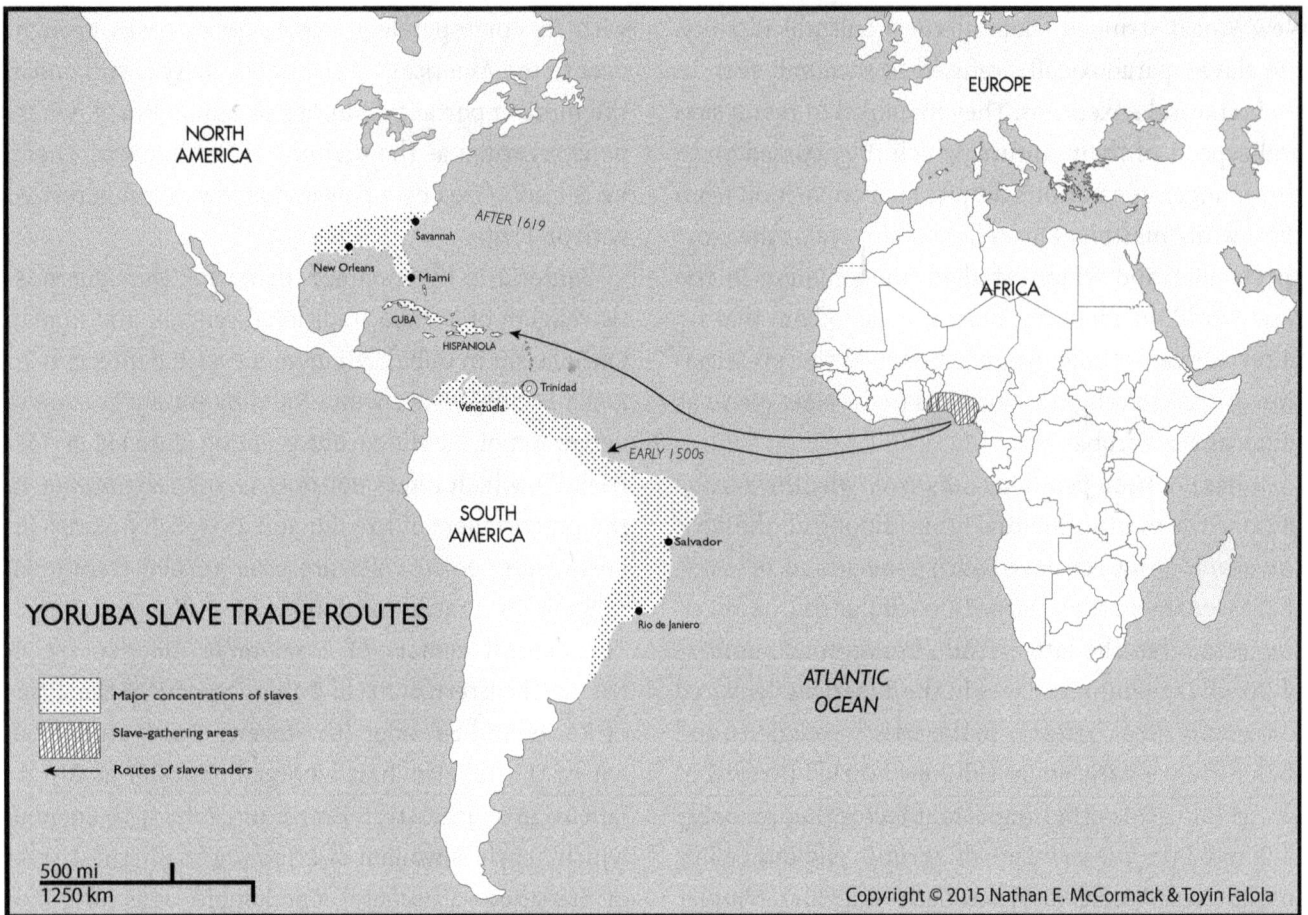

YORUBA SLAVE TRADE ROUTES

NORTH AMERICA

AFTER 1619

Savannah
New Orleans
Miami
CUBA
HISPANIOLA
Trinidad
Venezuela

EUROPE

AFRICA

EARLY 1500s

SOUTH AMERICA

Salvador

Rio de Janiero

ATLANTIC OCEAN

Major concentrations of slaves

Slave-gathering areas

Routes of slave traders

500 mi
1250 km

Copyright © 2015 Nathan E. McCormack & Toyin Falola

her popularity in Cuba. Yemaya or Yamaya (Yemọja) is also worshipped in the Diaspora in the form of the Virgin Mary just like Ọya and Ọ̀sun are. Yemaya is represented in the Catholic pantheon as Nuestra Señora de La Regla. Among the other popular òrìṣà in the Diaspora are the iron and war god Ògún (St. Peter), the god of destiny and divination Ọ̀rúnmìlà or Ifá (St. Francis of Assisi, the wise shaper and creator of human bodies Ọbàtálá (Our Lady of Mercy), the god of herbal medicine Ọ̀sanyìn or Ọ̀sanìn (St. Sylvester), the river goddess Erinlẹ̀ or Inlẹ̀ (St. Raphael), and the divine twins Ìbejì or Ìbeyì (St. Cosmas and St. Damian), who bring luck and protection against baneful magic. The Yorùbá systems of divination have also been preserved in the New World, such as the table of Ifá, Okuele, Dínlógún, and Obì or *darle coco al santo* (give coconut to the saint).

The Yorùbá cultural renaissance of the second half of the twentieth century, which was inspired initially by the Black Power Movement in the United States,

brought the practice of òrìṣà religions from South America to many North American cities. The religious wing of this movement was led by one Ẹfúntọ́lá Oseijeman Adélabú Adéfúnmi, a historical figure and the spiritual leader of African American practitioners of the Yorùbá faith and culture. Better known among religious scholars, in African cultural circles, and the Yorùbá community, he was born Walter Eugene King in Detroit, Michigan. He founded the Order of Damballah Hwedo Ancestor Priests, and he made and sold Yorùbá fabric attire, *dàṅṣíkí*, on the streets of Harlem, encouraging "Negros" to throw off the clothes of the European and take up the garments of "kings and queens." Continuing his elevation in traditional studies, King formed a unique relationship with Afro-Cubans when, in 1959, he became the first African American to be initiated into the òrìṣà-Lucumí African priesthood at Matanzas, Cuba. Back in the United States, he established the Ṣàngó Temple in 1960 and incorporated

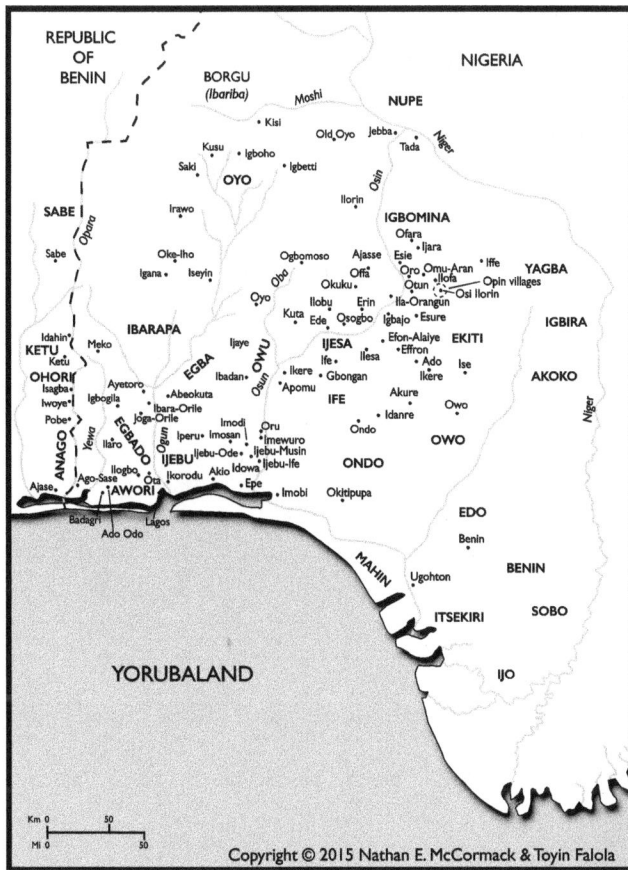

REPUBLIC
OF
BENIN

BORGU
(Ibariba)

NIGERIA

NUPE

• Kisi

Moshi

Old Oyo Jebba
Tada

Kusu • Igboho
Saki • Igbetti

OYO

Irawo

Ilorin

SABE

Sabe •

Oke-Iho

Igana • Iseyin

Ogbomoso Ajasse

Okuku •

Ofa
Offa

Oro Omu-Aran Iffe
Ilofa

Iyo
Ilobu Erin Osun

IGBOMINA

Ofara
• Ijara
Esie • Ijara

Opin villages
Osi Ilorin

YAGBA

IGBIRA

Ogbolu
Kuta Ede
Efon-Alaiye
• Effron

Ila-Orangun
Igbajo • Esure

IBARAPA

Idahin •
KETU
Ketu
OHORI
Isagba •
Iwoye • Igbogila
Pobe •

Meko
Ayetoro

Ijaye

EGBA
• Abeokuta
Ibara-Orile

Iganna-Orile

Ife
Ilesa
• Ikere
• Apomu
Gbongan

IJESA
Ado
• Ikere
Ise

EKITI

Akure

AKOKO

Idanre
Owo

Niger

ANAGO
EGBADO
Ajase •

Kewu

Ilaro •

Iperu
Imosan
Imewuro
Oru

Imodi

IFE

Ondo

OWO

OWU

Ijebu-Ode •
Ijebu-Musin
Ijebu-Ife

Ilogbo • Oru
Ago-Sase Ota Ikorodu Idowa
AWORI
Badagry Lagos
Ado Odo

• Epe

• Imobi

Okitipupa

ONDO

EDO

Benin

BENIN

MAHIN

Ugohton

ITSEKIRI

SOBO

YORUBALAND

IJO

Km 0   50
Mi 0   50

Copyright © 2015 Nathan E. McCormack & Toyin Falola

the African Theological Archministry. Later in 1970, King led a group of African Americans who rejected Yorùbá-Catholic syncretism as an outdated "compromise to a slave religion" to establish the Ọ̀yọ́túnjí African village on a twelve-acre plot of land on Highway 17 in Sheldon, Beaufort County, South Carolina (Hunt 1979). In the ensuing years, upward of five hundred people lived in the village, where they were shadowed by likenesses of African deities on Temple Row, free to practice and study Yorùbá culture and religion.

The foregoing shows that the Yorùbá have become truly global: in terms of their location in different parts of the world; the representations of various aspects of their culture in those locations; the emergence of distinctive òrìṣà traditions in the Americas; the physical presence, in various parts of the world, of the descendants of Yorùbá people taken as slaves and now as voluntary migrants in the contemporary era; and the integration of Yorùbá into African studies, Diaspora studies, the Black Atlantic, and Atlantic history.

We now invite readers to use this encyclopedia to find answers to specific questions about the Yorùbá people, as well as to formulate new questions and then seek their answers, too. We hope that, in your use of the encyclopedia, you are as excited by this material as we have been in bringing it together in this volume.

Tóyìn Fálọlá and Akíntúndé Akínyẹmí

REFERENCES

Abímbọ́lá, Wándé. *Ifá: An Exposition of Ifá Literary Corpus*. Ìbàdàn (Nigeria): Oxford University Press, 1976.

———. *Ìjìnlẹ̀ Ohùn Ẹnu Ifá (Apá Kejì)*. Glasgow: Collins, 1968.

Adéwọlé, L. O. *The Yorùbá Language: Published Works and Doctoral Dissertations, 1843–1986*. Hamburg: Helmut Buske Verlag, 1987.

Àjàyí, J. F. A. *Christian Missions in Nigeria, 1841–1891: The Making of a New Elite*. Evanston, IL: Northwestern University Press, 1965.

Àjùwọ̀n, Bádé. "Ògún: Premus Inter Pares." In *Proceedings of the First World Conference on Òrìṣà Tradition*, ed. Wándé Abímbọ́lá, 425–50. Ilé-Ifẹ̀ (Nigeria): Ọbáfẹ́mi Awólọ́wọ̀ University, 1981.

Barber, Karin. "How Man Makes God in West Africa: Yorùbá Attitudes towards the Orisa." *Africa* 51.3 (1981): 724–45.

Bascom, William. *The Yorùbá of Southwestern Nigeria*. New York: Holt, Rinehart and Winston, 1969.

Drewal, Henry John, John Pemberton, Rowland Abíọ́dún, and Allen Wardwell. *Yorùbá: Nine Centuries of African Art and Thought*. New York: Center for African Art in Association with H. N. A. Abrahams, 1989.

Fádípẹ̀, N. A. *The Sociology of the Yorùbá*. Ìbàdàn (Nigeria): University Press, 1970.

Fálọlá, Tóyìn. *Yorùbá Gurus: Indigenous Production of Knowledge in Africa*. Trenton, NJ: Africa World Press, 1999.

Fálọlá, Tóyìn, and G. O. Ògúntómisìn. *Yorùbá Warlords of the 19th Century*. Trenton, NJ: Africa World Press, 2001.

Forde, Daryll. *The Yorùbá-Speaking Peoples of Southwestern Nigeria*. London: International African Institute, 1951.

González-Wippler, Migene. *Santería: The Religion: Faith, Rites, and Magic*. 2nd ed. St. Paul, MN: Llewellyn Publications, 1994.

Hunt, Carl M. *Ọ̀yọ́túnjí Village: The Yorùbá Movement in America*. Washington, DC: University Press of America, 1979.

Ìdòwú, E. B. *Olódùmarè: God in Yorùbá Belief*. New York: Frederick A. Praeger, 1963.

International African Institute. *Provisional Survey of Major Languages in the Independent States of Sub-Saharan Africa*. Edited by Phillip Baker. New York: UNESCO, International African Institute, 1980.

Johnson, Samuel. *The History of the Yorùbás*. Lagos (Nigeria): C.M.S., 1921.

Law, R. C. C. *The Ọ̀yọ́ Empire, 1600-1830*. London: Oxford University Press, 1977.

Ògúnṣínà, Bísí. *The Development of the Yorùbá Novel c. 1930-1975*. Ìlọrin (Nigeria): Gospel Faith Mission Press, 1992.

Ọlábímtán, Afọlábí. "A Critical Survey of Yorùbá Written Poetry, 1848–1948." Unpublished PhD dissertation, University of Lagos, Lagos (Nigeria), 1974.

Ọlátúnjí, O. Ọlátúndé. *Features of Yorùbá Oral Poetry*. Ìbàdàn (Nigeria): University Press Limited, 1984.

Oyèláràn, O. O. "Linguistic Speculations on Yorùbá History." In *Department of African Languages and Literatures Seminar Series I*, ed. O. O. Oyèláràn, 624–51. Ilé-Ifẹ̀ (Nigeria): University of Ifẹ̀, 1978.

Washington, Teresa N. *Our Mothers, Our Powers, Our Texts*. Bloomington: Indiana University Press, 2005.

Introduction

LIST OF ENTRIES

A

ABÍÓLÁ, MOSHOOD KÁṢÌMAWÒ ỌLÁWÁLÉ (1937–1998)

Chief Moshood Káṣìmawò Ọláwálé Abíọ́lá was born in Gbágùrá, Abẹ̀òkúta (Ògùn State), on August 24, 1937. One of M. K. O. Abíọ́lá's names alludes to the condition of his birth. Collectively, his father's wives lost twenty-two pregnancies before he was born; the name Káṣìmawò is loosely translated as "let us wait and watch." He was a man of very humble beginnings who made the deep forests his first resource base by fetching fuel wood to sell to women in different markets. He was known to have played the àgídìgbo, a native Yorùbá guitarlike musical instrument, as a way of raising funds for his education. As if his name were a compass for his life, from his humble beginnings he became a key player in business, sports, media, and then politics.

Abíọ́lá was admitted to Nawair-Ud-Deen Primary School for his elementary education in 1944, but he later changed to African Central School, both in Abẹ̀òkúta, a year later. He obtained his primary school leaving certificate (diploma) around 1950. For the following five years, Abíọ́lá attended Baptist Boys High School in Abẹ̀òkúta and graduated in 1956. It took him just ten years to qualify as a chartered accountant at the Institute of Chartered Accountants of Scotland in February 1966.

Chief Abíọ́lá's flame started to burn brightly, and he gained notice around 1970 after assuming the leadership of International Telephone and Telegraph (ITT) as vice president for Africa and the Middle East at age thirty-three. More business successes followed, including the founding of Radio Communications (Nig.) Ltd. in 1974. His other business interests included the music recording company Decca (WA) Ltd., Wonder Bakeries, Abíọ́lá Farms, Abíọ́lá Bookshops, and finally *Concord Newspapers*, which changed the dynamics of newspaper publishing and distribution in Nigeria. Chief Abíọ́lá is also credited as the first publisher of *African Science Monitor*, a magazine that reported the scientific achievements of Africans. According to Tádé Akin Àìná, the magazine was established "as part of [Abíọ́lá's] vision and recognition of the need for a platform to challenge not only the asymmetrical power relations that constitute dominant discourses and practices in the sciences, but also to encourage and elevate Africa's self-conception of her role in the sciences and their place in the lives and cultures of her peoples" (25).

Chief Abíọ́lá's business empire spread over sixty countries and five continents, including ventures such as Concord Airlines and Summit Oil International Ltd. Chief Abíọ́lá also made it his business to inspire others by donating to different worthy causes. He contributed to the construction of sixty-three secondary schools, forty-one libraries, and twenty-one water projects across the nation (Fáyẹ̀míwò 2003). Chief Abíọ́lá was named Pillar of Sports in Africa because of his involvement at different levels. In the 1970s, he founded the eponymous football club Abíọ́lá Babes

Football Club, which was based in Abéòkúta. His philanthropy was not limited to Nigerian institutions; he also contributed to institutions of higher learning elsewhere on the African continent and in the United States. As one of the major sponsors for reparations in Africa, he established the Abíọlá Foundation for Reparation with an endowment of $500,000 and donated a large amount of money to the W. E. B. DuBois Center in Accra, Ghana.

Apart from his generosity to individuals and institutions, he was bestowed with about 150 traditional titles from different parts of the country. The most prized title was his installation as the fourteenth Ààrẹ-Ọnà-Kakanfò by the aláàfin of Ọyọ in 1988. A gap of twenty-two years separated Chief Abíọlá from his predecessor, Chief Ládòkè Akíntọlá, who was killed in 1966 during a violent military takeover. Historically, the title was bestowed on war generals in the old Ọyọ Empire. The Ààrẹ-Ọnà-Kakanfò was expected to lead other warriors to victory during wartime. Ironically, Chief Abíọlá's theater of war was the treacherous terrain of Nigerian politics.

Chief Abíọlá's first involvement with politics was in 1956 at age nineteen. When he left Baptist Boys High School, he joined the National Council of Nigeria and the Cameroons (NCNC). Not much is known about his membership in the NCNC. He joined the National Party of Nigeria (NPN) in 1980 and made an immediate impact around the country. Yorùbá people in the Southwest, the area from which he hailed, felt betrayed by his political interest because of its likely political damage for Chief Ọbáfẹmi Awólọwọ's Unity Party of Nigeria. Chief Abíọlá suffered a temporary political setback when the NPN refused him a place on its presidential ticket during the 1979 elections. He vowed to quit partisan politics but soon changed his mind after the military administration of Ibrahim Badamosi Babangida created two new political parties: the Social Democratic Party (SDP) and the National Republican Convention (NPC). Chief Abíọlá joined the SDP and eventually became its presidential candidate for the June 12, 1993, elections. Abíọlá won the election, but the results were annulled by the military

government led by President Ibrahim Babangida eleven days after the elections were concluded. As a result of this annulment, the nation was engulfed in a series of political crises and experienced a quick succession of administrations. Chief Abíọlá was arrested and detained for five years during General Sani Abacha's military administration. One of his wives, Kudirat Abíọlá, was killed on June 4, 1996, upon leaving an important political meeting. About two years after her death, Chief Abíọlá died on July 7, 1998, at the age of sixty, under mysterious circumstances while in detention.

Chief Abíọlá's death became a rallying point for many pro-democracy activists in Nigeria and others around the world who called for a return to democratic rule in Nigeria. Most states in southwestern Nigeria have immortalized him in various ways.

See also **Afénifére, Ẹgbé; Names and Naming; Royalty and Chieftaincy; Oòduà Progressive Congress (OPC); Politics and Political Parties since 1945**

REFERENCES

Àìná, T. A. "Beyond Reforms: The Politics of Higher Education Transformation in Africa." *African Studies Review* 53.1 (2010): 21–40.

Fáyẹmíwò, Moshood. *M. K. O. Abíọlá*. Tampa, FL: USAfrican Christian Publishing, 2003.

Kọléadé Odùtọlá

ACTION GROUP

The Action Group (AG) political party was the brainchild of Chief Ọbáfẹmi Awólọwọ. When the party officially launched at Ọwọ on March 21, 1951, it was already one year old, conceived over nine secret meetings that had been going on for the previous year. One reason for the formation of this political party was to bring together the progressive but divided Yorùbá people. In his 1960 autobiography, Chief Awólọwọ stated that AG's objective was to "devise plans for organizing the people of the Western Region so that they may be able to play influential and effective role in the affairs of Nigeria under the New Governor Macpherson

Constitution of 1951." In 1951, a *Daily Times* editorial hailed the formation of AG as follows:

The first, in the field of party politics, with a definite plan, for winning seats under the new Constitution. The objective of the Action Group is admirable, and deserving of support. The Convention People's Party [CPP] in the Gold Coast [Ghana] has proved that party organization pays big dividends. We therefore welcome the Action Group to the Nigerian political scene. And may other organizations follow its lead. Several strong parties are required if the new Constitution is to function effectively. (3)

Dr. Benjamin Nnamdi Azikiwe, editor of the Lagos-based *West African Pilot* newspaper, wished the AG the best of luck, noting, "Its aims and objects are laudable and in program of action is varied and wide. From all appearances it is an awakening consciousness in the West. . . . It agrees in some aspects with the Ghana Convention People's Party, in being a party organization."

The announcement of the birth of the AG took the country by storm. Those who later became covert and overt adversaries of the party also heralded its debut in glowing terms. Awólọ́wọ̀ and eight others founded the party. Despite Awólọ́wọ̀'s personal contact with sixty persons, drawn from different parts of Western Region of Nigeria, people were not interested, thus confirming the unorganized and disunited characteristics of the Yorùbá people at the time. The charter members at the party's initial meeting on March 26, 1950, at the Òkè-Àdó Residence of Chief Awólọ́wọ̀ in Ìbàdàn included Chief Ọbáfẹ́mi Awólọ́wọ̀ (Ìjẹ̀bú-Rémọ), S. O. Shónibárẹ́ (Ìjẹ̀bú-Òde), Chief Abíọ́dún Akéréle (Ọ̀yọ́), S. T. Ọ̀rẹ́dèin (Ìjẹ̀bú-Rémọ), Ọlátúnjí Dòsùmú (Ìjẹ̀bú-Rémọ), J. Ọlá Àdìgún (Ọ̀ṣun), Adéyígà Akínsànyà (Ìjẹ̀bú-Rémọ), and Ayọ̀ Akínsànyà (Ìjẹ̀bú-Rémọ).

The basic principles that brought members together were summarized in AG's motto: "Freedom for all, life more abundant." It was not only agreed that the rule of one nation by another was unnatural and unjust; the founders also believed that the people of the Western Region of Nigeria in particular and Nigeria in general would have a more abundant life when they could enjoy freedom from British rule, ignorance, disease, and want. As a political party, the AG was disciplined,

cohesive, committed, and well organized. The AG leaders' sagacity, popular appeal, and pragmatic approach to politics are indisputable.

See also **Akíntọ́lá, Samuel Ládòkè; Awólọ́wọ̀, Ọbáfẹ́mi; Politics and Political Parties since 1945**

REFERENCES

Adébámwí, Wálé. *Yorùbá Elites and Ethnic Politics: Ọbáfẹ́mi Awólọ́wọ̀ and Corporate Agency.* New York: Cambridge University Press, 2014.

Awólọ́wọ̀, Ọbáfẹ́mi. *The Autobiography of Chief Ọbáfẹ́mi Awólọ́wọ̀.* Cambridge: Cambridge University Press, 1960.

Daily Times (Lagos, Nigeria), 1951: 3, 21.

West African Pilot (Lagos, Nigeria), 1951: 3, 29.

Ọláyíwọlá M. Abégúnrìn

ADVERTISEMENT

Advertising is a form of marketing communication used to encourage, persuade, or manipulate an audience (viewers, readers or listeners, sometimes a specific group) to take or continue to take some action. Advertising as an institution tells people how to pick the best out of many materials around them. To the Yorùbá people, advertising is the "medicine" of business (ìpolówó ọjà ni àgúnmu òwò) and language its hallmark. Advertising is the soul of a business, the method the seller employs to advertise or qualify the product he or she sells in a way that will attract people. Yorùbá people have specific ways of advertising their products, and the goal of any seller is to persuade buyers, either overtly or covertly, to buy his or her goods or products. Advertising (ìpolówó ọjà) in Yorùbáland can be categorized as a form of poetry, because it follows a regular beat and is often sung. Advertisement is found all over Yorùbáland, although the names of some items, goods, or products may vary from one dialect group to the other.

When town life was still closely knit, people knew the particular house where specific items were sold. When the use of money succeeded trade by barter, when sellers no longer knew those who were interested in their items, the system of hawking came about in which the indigenous hawker goes around the neighborhood on foot to enable buyers to be aware of the fact that the seller was around.

Small-scale trading is a fashionable economic activity among women in traditional Yorùbá society. A few of the items traded include local foods—raw and cooked—traditional clothes, and daily-use items. These items are advertised through *ìkiri ọjà* (hawking) and *ìpolówó* (advertising). The hawkers also regard advertising as very crucial to their trade, and language is a very critical part of it. For this reason sellers deck their language with many traditional oral literary material, such as proverbs, idiomatic expressions, metaphors, and other devices, to strike the right chord in buyers. The essence of this is to bring the commodity being advertised to the consciousness and reach of the consumers.

As society has gradually changed in its social, political, and economic outlook, advertising has inevitably taken new shape in Yorùbáland. Instead of people advertising their goods by parading through the streets, most people now have shops and offices with signposts or banners informing others about their businesses. There are modern forms of advertising on electronic media (radio, television), print media (business card, flyer, banner, and billboard), and other media (GSM, the Internet, electronic billboards).

The following examples show how *iyán* (pounded yam) and *àgbàdo* (cooked maize) are advertised:

> *Ẹ wojú ọbẹ̀, ẹ múyán.*
> *Iyán-an re, ọbẹ̀ẹ re.*
> *Iyán-àn mi, à-jẹ-ríre.*
> Examine the soup and buy pounded yam.
> Good pounded yam, good soup.
> Eat my pounded yam, eat and experience good
>   things.

> *Láńgbé jinná o!*
> *Ọ̀sìngín àgbàdo*
> *Dandawì, olóko ò gbowo*
> Cooked maize is ready!
> Fresh maize.
> Very cheap, the farmer took no money.

REFERENCES

Akínyẹmí, Akíntúndé. "African Health on Sale: Marketing Strategies in the Practice of Traditional Medicine in Southwestern Nigeria." In *Traditional and Modern Health Systems in Nigeria*, ed. Tóyìn Fálọlá and Matthew M. Heaton, 287–304. Trenton, NJ: Africa World Press, 2006.

Ọ̀ṣúndáre, Níyì. "Poems for Sale: Stylistic Features of Yorùbá *ìpolówó* Poetry." *African Notes* 15.1–15.2 (1991): 63–72.

Olúwatóyìn M. Ọláìyá

AFÉNIFÉRE, ẸGBẸ́

Ẹgbẹ́ Afénifére is a sociocultural and political organization formed by progressive Yorùbá politicians and activists in the early 1990s. The group is built around the welfarist political and economic ideas and the egalitarian social vision of Chief Ọbáfẹ́mi Awólọ́wọ̀, the preeminent late leader of the Yorùbá and foremost Nigerian nationalist. However, the history of Ẹgbẹ́ Afénifére goes back to 1951, when the Action Group (AG) party was formed. The Yorùbá word *afénifére* was chosen as the appellation of the Action Group political party because the literal meaning of the word captures the idea and ideal of economic welfarism and social egalitarianism espoused and championed by the Action Group, which is dominated by the Yorùbá politically progressive, Western-educated elite.

The AG, led by Awólọ́wọ̀, was eager to find a name for the new political party that the largely illiterate population in the Western Region of Nigeria could relate to. It adopted the name Ẹgbẹ́ Afénifére. However, the party was not formally known by that name. When the AG was banned by the military in 1966, the name was not used to designate any political group until Awólọ́wọ̀'s death. In the immediate post-Awólọ́wọ̀ years, his political associates organized under different names.

In November 1992, Awólọ́wọ̀'s followers met in Ọ̀wọ̀ under the leadership of Chief Adékúnlé Ajáṣin, the former governor of Oǹdó State (1979–1983). Chief Bọ́lá Ìgè, the former governor of Ọ̀yọ́ State (1979–1983), formed a subgroup of his political associates and loyalists in the old Ọ̀yọ́ State, which met in his house in Ìbàdàn.

This group named itself Afẹnifẹre, which Ìgè felt buttressed his later claim that the group of Awólọ́wọ̀ associates—who later formally adopted the name—actually formed in Ìgè's house. To legitimize the new group, Ìgè claimed that the AG's 1950s group was actually named Afẹnifẹrere, not Afẹnifẹre. Surviving members of the AG dismissed Ìgè's claims by showing evidence that they used the appellation in the 1950s.

However, the group of Ìgè associates and loyalists remained part of the larger group of Awólọ́wọ̀ associates who later met in Ọ̀wọ̀ on January 18, 1993, under the banner "Awo Political Estate." The group named itself Central Working Committee. Under this name, the group adopted what it called the Ọbáfẹ́mi Awólọ́wọ̀ Creed, which reconstructed the ideological standpoint of Awólọ́wọ̀ and the programmatic exposition of same by the defunct AG and Unity Party of Nigeria (UPN), the party led by Awólọ́wọ̀ in the Second Republic (1979–1983).

Around late 1993 and early 1994, the Ọ̀wọ̀ group started to use the name Ẹgbẹ́ Afẹnifẹre. On the suggestion of Chief Anthony Enahoro, who was a member of the AG, the group became the nucleus of and the pivot in the formation of the National Democratic Coalition (NADECO), which led the pro-democracy movement in the struggle for the victory of Chief M. K. O. Abíọ́lá in the June 12, 1993, presidential election. The election was annulled by the military regime.

After Ajáṣin's death in October 1997, Chief Abraham Adésànyà was elected the leader of the Afẹnifẹre and Chief Bọ́lá Ìgè was selected as its deputy leader. The secretary-general was Ayọ̀ Ọpádòkun. Under Adésànyà's leadership, Afẹnifẹre blossomed and became the dominant political group in southwestern Nigeria. As both leader of Afẹnifẹre and deputy leader of NADECO, Adésànyà led the last phase of the battle against military rule, particularly under the brutal, self-perpetuating general Sani Abacha. Afẹnifẹre was also essential in the formation of the Alliance for Democracy (AD), a political party, in 1998. The party, which was known in southwestern Nigeria as AD-Afẹnifẹre, won the governorship election in all six Yorùbá states.

The AD also selected Chief Olú Fálaè as its presidential candidate; Fálaè later ran, unsuccessfully, under the banner of the All People's Party—which had entered into an alliance with the AD.

In the twilight of Adésànyà's life, Ẹgbẹ́ Afẹnifẹre was in the grip of internal crisis. The deputy leader, Bọ́lá Ìgè, joined President Olúṣẹgun Ọbásanjọ́'s government as a federal minister. Ìgè was later threatened with expulsion from the group. This internal crisis also led to the creation of a rival group, the Yorùbá Council of Elders, led by Venerable Emmanuel Aláyandé and Justice Adéwálé Thompson, both members of Afẹnifẹre. In 2004, because of Adésànyà's terminal illness, Chief Reuben Fáṣọ̀ràntì was selected as the acting leader of Afẹnifẹre.

The division in Afẹnifẹre also produced divisions in AD at the national level. Senator Ayọ̀ Fásanmí led one faction of Afẹnifẹre that rejected the leadership of Chief Reuben Fáṣọ̀ràntì. The Senator Ayọ̀ Fásanmí faction was supported by the faction led by Chief Bísí Àkàndé of the AD and others, such as Bọ́lá Tinúbú, the governor of Lagos State. Senator Mojísólúwa Akínfẹ́nwá led a faction of the AD that supported the Fáṣọ̀ràntì faction of Afẹnifẹre. Subsequently, the Fáṣọ̀ràntì faction announced the expulsion of Fásanmí and others, who in turn also expelled Fáṣọ̀ràntì and others from the group.

A new political party, the Action Congress (AC), was formed by the Fásanmí-Àkàndé and Tinúbú faction of Afẹnifẹre-AD. The Fáṣọ̀ràntì-led Afẹnifẹre, which included old Awoists such as Sir Ọláníwún Àjàyí and Chief Ayọ̀ Adébánjọ, continued to meet and claim the heritage of Awólọ́wọ̀, despite their greatly diminished leverage.

In October 2007, a group of young Awoists and members of Afẹnifẹre, under the rubric of Afẹnifẹre Renewal Group (ARG), brought together the two factions at a retreat held at the International Institute of Tropical Agriculture (IITA) in Ìbàdàn. Between 2005 and 2010, Bishop Emmanuel Gbónígi and Bishop Ayọ̀ Ládìgbòlù led other efforts at reconciliation, all of which failed. However, while the Fásanmí faction no longer exists, the Fáṣọ̀ràntì-led Afénifére and ARG continue to exist and to champion the position of the Yorùbá progressive camp in Nigerian politics.

See also **Abíọ́lá, Moshood Káṣìmawò Ọláwálé; Action Group; Afénifére, Ẹgbẹ́; Akíntọ́lá, Samuel Ládòkè; Awólọ́wọ̀, Ọbáfẹ́mi; Politics and Political Parties since 1945**

REFERENCES

Adébámwí, Wálé. *Yorùbá Elites and Ethnic Politics: Ọbáfẹ́mi Awólọ́wọ̀ and Corporate Agency.* New York: Cambridge University Press, 2014.

Ajáṣin, Adékúnlé M. *Ajáṣin: Memoirs and Memories.* Lagos (Nigeria): Ajáṣin Foundation, 2003.

Wálé Adébánwí

ÀGBẸ́KÒYÀ REBELLION OF 1968–1969

The Àgbẹ́kòyà rebellion of 1968–1969, in which peasants resisted class constraints, reflected Yorùbá peasants' resistance to the state's appropriation of rural surplus during a period of economic downturn in the Nigerian Civil War (1967–1970). As the civil war raged in the Eastern Region of Nigeria, Yorùbá rural dwellers rebelled against the Western State's military government in September 1968. Starting with disturbances in Ìbàdàn Division and the city of Ọ̀yọ́, rural dwellers rebelled against the state's significant increase in taxes and rates. Along with high inflation and a massive drop in the price of cocoa, the region's major export commodity, the state economic policies had a devastating effect on the masses of poor people in the Western State. Specifically, resistance was directed against the state government's flat tax of £6 levied on everyone whose income was less than £50 a year and the substantial increase in water rates imposed by the Western State Water Corporation. Àgbẹ́kòyà peasants also opposed a state government's development levy of 7 shillings and 6 pence per person, an income tax on self-employed women whose annual salary exceeded £100, and a 5 percent national reconstruction levy imposed by the Federal Military Government on all Nigerian households to remedy the devastation of the civil war in 1968.

Because of their status in local communities, the *ọba* (monarchs) and local chiefs who supported these unpopular state policies came under severe attack. For example, in Ògbómọ̀ṣọ́, the hometown of Samuel Ládòkè Akíntọ́lá, the late premier of the Western Region during the previous democratic government; the *ṣọ́ún* (king) of Ògbómọ̀ṣọ́, Ọba Ọlájídé Láoyè, his wife, and five of his chiefs were murdered in what seems to have been a well-planned assault in July 1969. Conversely, *ọba* and chiefs who distanced themselves from state agents were accorded respect and occasionally called on to participate in negotiations between Àgbẹ́kòyà leaders and the government.

Ìbàdàn Division of the Western State, where major Àgbẹ́kòyà riots occurred, witnessed the fiercest peasant resistance. Before the initial outbreak of riots in 1968, Àgbẹ́kòyà leaders had called on the state military governor Colonel Adéyínká Adébáyọ̀ to reduce the flat tax, and they expressed dissatisfaction with the performance of their local authorities. When their requests fell on deaf ears, protesters marched on the city of Ìbàdàn, demanding an audience with the Olúbàdàn, the *ọba* of the city. Failing to realize that the agitation was a formidable mass resistance, Governor Adébáyọ̀ dismissed it as the handiwork of malcontents and disgruntled politicians from the previous democratic government.

In reaction to the rebellion, which had expanded to Ẹ̀gbá, Ìjẹ̀bú, Ọ̀sun, and Ọ̀yọ́ Divisions of the state, the government appointed a High Court judge, Justice E. O. Ayọ̀ọlá, as sole commissioner to investigate the causes of the riots and make recommendations to state authorities. After two months of investigation, Commissioner Ayọ̀ọlá's report identified both economic and political causes of the riots. Although the report underscored the extreme economic conditions of the poor, it ignored Àgbẹ́kòyà demands for a significant reduction in taxes. In accordance with Ayọ̀ọlá's recommendations, Governor Adébáyọ̀ announced a number of minor policy changes, including a new flat-rate tax of three pounds and five shillings, which fell short of Àgbẹ́kòyà's demands. Adébáyọ̀'s response to the Àgbẹ́kòyà's renewed opposition was to adopt a military solution to the crisis. Confrontations between armed policemen and rural dwellers in July resulted in the death of many civilians in several rural communities. Àgbẹ̀kọ̀yà groups retaliated by attacking councilors and local chiefs who remained behind in the villages.

The impasse that ensued encouraged Ọbáfẹ́mi Awólọ́wọ̀, vice chair of the federal Executive Council and the federal minister of finance, to wade into the crisis. Embracing the cause of the Àgbẹ̀kọ̀yà, Awólọ́wọ̀ called for another inquiry and met with Àgbẹ̀kọ̀yà leaders. By obtaining the trust of Àgbẹ̀kọ̀yà leaders such as Tàfá Adéoyè, and Fọlárìn Ìdòwú, Awólọ́wọ̀ undermined Governor Adébáyọ̀'s authority in what had become the Western State's most delicate crisis since the Action Group crisis of 1962–1966. With the weight of the federal government behind him, Awólọ́wọ̀ forced Adébáyọ̀'s state government to concede to most of the Àgbẹ̀kọ̀yà's demands. Governor Adébáyọ̀ reduced the flat tax rate to £2 a year; other rates, such as parking and market fees, were suspended. With regard to local administration, Adébáyọ̀ relieved corrupt local government officials of their duties and promised to investigate their assets.

See also **Action Group; Akíntọ́lá, Samuel Ládòkè; Awólọ́wọ̀, Ọbáfẹ́mi**

REFERENCES

Beer, Christopher. *The Politics of Peasant Groups in Western Nigeria*. Ìbàdàn (Nigeria): Ìbàdàn University Press, 1976.
Fálọlá, Tóyìn. *Counting the Tiger's Teeth: An African Teenager's Story*. Ann Arbor: University of Michigan Press, 2014.
Williams, Gavin. *State and Society in Nigeria*. Idanre (Nigeria): Afroafrika, 1980.

Olúfẹ́mi Vaughan

AGE-GRADE SYSTEM

The age-grade system is a form of social organization wherein the delineating criterion of social actors is based on age stratification. The stratification allows actors to navigate the course of social practice within society. Age grade is a kind of social group that is closed to individuals outside a particular age set. Transition from one age grade to another is marked by rite of passage and initiation. Age grade is a socializing group as well as an agent of socialization.

Age grades serve a number of functions. They permit face-to-face interaction and engender a feeling of "we," as well as a sense of communality and collective assistance among age cohorts. Members of an age grade usually do many things together, wear the same attire during special festivals and when paying homage to the monarch of the community, and serve as a distinct social class to regulate social conduct of those younger than them and to serve as mentors to others. For instance, the Ìjẹ̀bú subgroup has more than twenty-four different age groups, which include Bọ́bayọ̀, Gbọ́baníyì, Bọ́bagùntẹ́, Ọbáfùwàjì, Jagunmólú, and Bọ́bakéyẹ. Age grades here are differentiated by about a three- to five-year interval.

Age groups provide assistance to members at feasts, marriages, naming ceremonies, housewarmings, and funerals. Onoge (1993) asserts that before colonialism, social conflicts were monitored, prevented, and managed through age grades and functioned as a form of social control. Fálọlá and Genova (2009) indicate that age groups of young individuals provide a reliable source of labor on farms. Children are organized into age groups, and boys are given economic, political, and military training. Fálọlá and Adébáyọ̀ (2000) affirm that age grades facilitate access to political authority, political obligations, and resources of the state. They are a kind of pressure group, as well. The generation designated as "elders" perform judicial and advisory functions. It is strongly believed that prosperity, wisdom, and experiences come with advancement in age. Therefore, seniors are revered and respected. A proverb says "a child does not have as many rags as the elderly" (*bí ọmọdé ní aṣọ bí àgbà, kò lè ní àkísà bí àgbà*). With urbanization, globalization, and the increasing complexity of society, "mechanic" solidarity is transitioning to "organic" solidarity in Durkheimian parlance—the social organization has changed. "Mechanic solidarity" in this sense refers to the associational relationship of an *àjọbí* type of bond, wherein relationship is face-to-face and diffuse, as opposed to an "organic" or *àjọgbé* kind of bond, wherein formal bonding is overstressed and anonymity is given pride of place. Some age grades have today assumed roles meant for age groups above them.

See also **Cooperative Associations; Agriculture and Farming; Festivals and Carnivals**

REFERENCES

Fálọlá, T., and A. G. Adébáyọ̀. *Culture, Politics, and Money among the Yorùbá.* New Brunswick, NJ: Transaction Publishers, 2000.

Fálọlá, T., and Ann Genova. *Historical Dictionary of Nigeria.* Toronto: Scarecrow Press, 2009.

Onoge, O. F. "Social Conflicts and Crime Control in Colonial Nigeria." In *Policing Nigeria: Past, Present, and Future*, ed. T. N. Tamuno, I. L. Bashir, E. E. O. Alemika, and A. O. Àkànó, 178–79. Lagos (Nigeria): Malthouse Press, 1993.

Fàtáì Adéṣínà Badru

AGRICULTURE AND FARMING

Iṣẹ́ àgbẹ̀ n'iṣẹ́ ilẹ̀ẹ wa;
Ẹni kò ṣ'iṣẹ́, á mà jalè.
Ìwé kíkọ́ láìsí ọkọ́ àti àdá
Kò ì pé o, kò ì pé o.

Farming is our traditional occupation;
One who doesn't work [farm] will surely steal.
Western education without the hoe and the cutlass
Is inadequate, it is incomplete.

Agriculture, *iṣẹ́ àgbẹ*, is one of four Yorùbá traditional occupations. The other three are hunting (*ọdẹ*), divining (*awo*), and designing (*ọnà*). Without question, agriculture embodies what makes and sustains society. It helps society meet its food needs and serves as the repository of Yorùbá knowledge and information regarding the weather and environment, labor relations, crop and animal life cycles, and health and wellness. Today, agriculture continues to be very important, as can be deduced from the lyrics of the above song. A World Bank publication in 2013 estimated that agriculture accounts for 70 percent of Nigeria's labor force.

Archeological and anthropological evidence suggests that agriculture emerged when humans, in their long history, learned to domesticate animals and plants. As early as nine thousand years ago, indigenous wild African cattle were domesticated. By the end of the twentieth century, cattle rearing had become a permanent feature of northwestern Yorùbáland and in the areas of Ṣakí and Upper Ògùn, which are influenced by Fulani pastoralists. Besides cattle and dogs, prehistoric West Africans who lived in the "savanna complex" (of which some of Yorùbáland is a part) were also credited with the domestication of millet, African rice, fonio, Bambara nut, and melon. In the rain forest, varieties of crops such as yam, potato, cowpea, cotton, groundnut, okra, and oil palm were domesticated. Crops cultivated by the Yorùbá are derived either from those locally domesticated in West Africa or from other parts of the world. The Colombian Exchange—or the environmental and cultural impact of the European exploration in the Americas—as well as colonialism and globalization have all have fostered the diffusion of a wide variety of crops: some are new to certain areas, and others are new species of existing crops. It is impossible to list all the food and nonfood crops cultivated by Yorùbá farmers. However, mention must be made of sugarcane, coconut, avocado, bread-fruit, mango, taro or cocoyam, banana, cotton, maize, cassava, groundnut, and various fruits and vegetables. Of the new crops, cocoa turned out to be a major success in Yorùbáland. Cocoa was introduced into the country in the early 1900s, and Nigeria is currently the fourth-leading producer in the world. Yorùbáland is still the only part of Nigeria in which cocoa is cultivated. Another produce of major regional significance is the kola nut, which has a large market in northern Nigeria, where it is consumed for its rich caffeine content. Both cocoa and kola nuts are tree crops and have been integrated into the Yorùbá rain-forest farming environment. Hence, the research mandate of the Cocoa Research Institute of Nigeria covers cocoa and kola nuts as well as cashews, coffee, and tea.

The crops that Yorùbá farmers cultivate vary according to environmental conditions. Typically, tree crops are grown in the rain forest of Yorùbáland, such as in Ifẹ̀, Ìjẹ̀ṣà, Èkìtì, Oǹdó, Ìjẹ̀bú, Ẹ̀gbá, and Òṣogbo.

They include cocoa, kola nuts, rubber, coffee, and varieties of medicinal plants. In the savanna of Yorùbáland, stretching from Ìbàdàn to Old Ọ̀yọ́ and Dahomey, tubers (like yams and potatoes) and creepers (like calabash, gourds, and melons) are grown. Yams, bananas, corn, and okra all grow widely. Along with the distinct patterns of cultivation, Yorùbá people also developed a wide variety of cuisines out of these crops. A good example is the ẹ̀gẹ́ (cassava or tapioca). Introduced from Central America, ẹ̀gẹ́ has become a major staple among the Yorùbá, and from it they derive láfún, gàrí, fùfú, animal feed, chips, and the like. New varieties have also been developed by research institutions, such as the International Institute for Tropical Agriculture (IITA), located in Ìbàdàn.

In their farming practice, the Yorùbá maintain three broad types of farms: *oko etílé* (gardens near a town or village), *oko ẹgàn* (farms on virgin lands, typically a little distance from town), and *oko àkùrọ̀* (irrigated farmlands). Broadly, *oko etílé* is where food crops are cultivated for family consumption. *Oko ẹgàn*, in contrast, is where cash crops are cultivated. There are two kinds of *oko ẹgàn*, distinguished by location: *oko igbó* (rain-forest farms) and *oko ọ̀dàn* (savanna grassland farms). While every farmer has *oko etílé*, prominent farmers are set apart by their extensive *oko ẹgàn*. Located in drained marshy lands or next to streams, *oko àkùrọ̀*, or irrigated farms, are small, and most farmers keep such farms for growing dry-season crops. Such farms result in early crops, before the full season, of maize, yams, and vegetables. These farms are usually abandoned during the rainy season.

In the past, most farming was done through peasant holdings. The family was the basic unit of agricultural labor; a farmer relied on the labor of his wife or wives and their unmarried sons and daughters. Those with large farms accessed larger pools of labor in many ways: *àáró* and *ọ̀wẹ̀* (two forms of cooperative labor supply), *ẹrú* and *ìwọ̀fà*, and *àgbàro*. *Àáró* is reciprocal labor supply by which two or three able-bodied farmers take turns working on one another's farms, usually in times of weeding. *Ọ̀wẹ̀*, in contrast, is arranged when a particular farmer needs the labor of ten to twenty men and women for a specific purpose, usually clearing virgin land or harvesting time-sensitive crops. A man may also organize *ọ̀wẹ̀* to support his in-laws. In *àáró* and *ọ̀wẹ̀*, the beneficiary of the labor provides only food for the workmen. *Ẹrú* (slavery) and *ìwọ̀fà* (peonage) were different, but they were both forms of involuntary labor supply that ended in Yorùbáland under colonial rule. *Àgbàro*, meaning literally "help with weeding," is a form of paid labor supplied by seasonal migrants from various parts of Nigeria and neighboring countries. They handle more than weeding.

Although these farming practices have continued with minimal changes, agribusiness has, with the advent of colonization and globalization, nevertheless wrought a number of changes. Today, farming in Yorùbáland presents a very complex combination of small and large holdings, livestock and animal husbandry, and mixed farming. Agricultural tools, though, have not changed significantly. The main tools are still the hoe and cutlass of varying sizes—mentioned in the lyrics in the epigraph—and the primary agricultural technique has remained largely slash and burn. However, with modernization, mechanized farming with tractors, planters, and harvesters is gaining popularity, especially in agribusiness circles. Many farmers cannot afford to buy them and so usually rent them.

Besides clearing the forest to start an *oko ẹgàn*, weeding and weed control are among the most tedious agricultural activities. Indeed, an incompetent farmer can be recognized by how much of his or her farm is overrun by weeds. The most stubborn weeds are *ẹ̀ẹ̀kan* (or *bẹrẹ*) and *eéran*, both of which are species of grass with extremely important uses. When properly dried and bundled, *ẹ̀ẹ̀kan* provides the best thatch for roofing; *eéran* is for feeding goats, sheep, and horses. Hoeing these weeds also aerates the soil, but with the introduction of herbicides, weed control has taken a very different turn. Many farmers now spray weeds, thereby introducing various chemicals into the soil. The long-term impact of these chemicals on African farming and food-crop production is yet to be fully appreciated and evaluated.

Oral traditions demonstrate the extent to which Yorùbáland and its farmers dreaded locust infestations. Even modern science finds desert locusts (*esú*) to be among the most difficult agricultural pests in West Africa. They swarm over wide distances and reproduce very rapidly—up to five generations in a year. They attack crops at periods of their greatest vulnerability: when the crops are young or mature but before they can be harvested. Many place *jùjú* (effigy) in form of *ààlè* on their farms to ward off the locusts, but the paths of swarming locusts are not only unpredictable but also uncontrollable, which led to the following saying:

Esú ò mọ̀'kà, esú ò m'olóòótọ́;
Esú ṣe bí eré ó f'oko olóore jẹ.

The swarming locust neither fears the wicked, nor respects the truthful;
In a flash, the swarming locust eats up (destroys) the farm of the beneficent.

Since the colonial era, locust destruction has been controlled through concerted international activities, from chemical destruction of locust breeding grounds to early warning systems. Occasional threats continue, such as an episode in parts of West Africa in 2005.

The type of crops determines the kind of market at which to sell them. At the village level, an okra, orange, or vegetable farmer might ask his young son or daughter to sell a part of the yield from door to door, leading to a uniquely oral advertising genre called *ìpolówó ọjà*. Larger yields are taken to periodic markets, open every fifth day (*ọrọọrún*), every ninth day (*isán*), or every thirteenth day (*ìtàlá*). Indeed, a large proportion of agricultural produce is exchanged in these periodic markets, evidence that the Yorùbá have been practicing the concept of a farmers' market long before that term entered into agricultural economics. From these periodic markets, surpluses are taken into large urban centers for consumption. In addition, food processors purchase large supplies for their trade. Kola nuts are wrapped in leaves to cure, yams are processed into *èlùbọ́*, corn is processed into *ògì*, and cassava is processed into *gàrí* or *láfún*. Furthermore, these agricultural produce enter into regional long-distance trade. Cash crops like cocoa, coffee, kola nuts, and palm oil are purchased by agents of large firms for export or for use by local industries.

See also **Advertisement; Art: Contemporary; Art: Indigenous; Communication: Nonverbal; Cooperative Associations; Divinatory System; Divination: Ifá; Food: Supply, Distribution, and Marketing; Hunting; Market; Pawning and Pawnship; Slavery**

REFERENCES

Fádípè, N. A. *The Sociology of the Yorùbá.* Ìbàdàn (Nigeria): University Press Limited, 1970.
Lawal, Adébáyọ̀ A. "Agriculture in Yorùbá Society and Culture." In *The Yorùbá in Transition: History, Values, and Modernity*, ed. Tóyìn Fálọlá and Ann Genova, 361–76. Durham, NC: Carolina Academic Press, 2006.
McIntosh, Susan Keech. "The Holocene Prehistory of West Africa, 10,000–1000 BP." In *Themes in West Africa's History*, ed. Emmanuel Kwaku Akyeampong, 11–32. Oxford (United Kingdom): James Currey, 2006.

Àkànmú Adébáyọ̀

AKÍNTỌ́LÁ, SAMUEL LÁDÒKÈ (1910–1966)

Chief Samuel Ládòkè Akíntọ́lá was born in Ògbómọ̀ṣọ́ on July 10, 1910. Akíntọ́lá's ancestors were one of the founding families of the town of Ògbómọ̀ṣọ́, and according to the history of Ògbómọ̀ṣọ́, Akíntọ́lá's family was the seventh family to settle in the town of Ògbómọ̀ṣọ́ and one of the earliest to convert to Christianity. Akíntọ́lá's grandfather Akínbọ́lá was born around 1860; he was a trader who sold various items in the northern part of Nigeria. Akíntọ́lá's father continued in the family tradition of trading; he traded mainly in textiles, and in 1914 he took his family to settle in Minna, present-day Niger State.

In 1925, Akíntọ́lá enrolled at Baptist College Ògbómọ̀ṣọ́, a teachers' college and a training ground for future deacons. In 1930, his stellar academic performance prompted his teachers to recommend that he attend the prestigious Baptist Academy in Lagos. They expected him to become a science teacher. At

Baptist Academy, he became a junior staff member and was assigned to mentoring young students. Apart from general science, he also taught Scripture. He was very strict and gained a reputation for administering corporal punishment to students.

He began dating Fadérera Awómọ̀lọ̀, the sister of one of his friends at Ògbómọ̀ṣọ́. They met when she was a nurse at Baptist Hospital in the town. Fadérera's brother gave his approval to the courtship. Fadérera's father opposed their courtship because he was an Ìjẹ̀ṣà and Akíntọ́lá was an Ọ̀yọ́. Traditionally, some members of the two groups resented one another. On August 8, 1935, without consulting their parents, Akíntọ́lá and Fadérera married; members of the staff from Baptist Academy witnessed the ceremony.

Akíntọ́lá resigned his appointment at Baptist Academy in 1942 in support of colleagues who were fired after protesting for better conditions. At the time of the crisis, Akíntọ́lá was the secretary of Baptist Teachers' Union, a branch of the National Union of Teachers. He served briefly as a railway administrator before joining the *Daily Service* as a journalist. The *Daily Service*, owned by Dr. Akinọlá Májà and many loyalists of the Nigerian Youth Movement, served as the mouthpiece of the Yorùbá nation. In addition, the newspaper was the Yorùbá answer to the *West African Pilot* and *Comet*, the pro-Igbo newspapers owned by Dr. Nnamdi Azikiwe. Akíntọ́lá was appointed editor of the *Daily Service* in 1943. He also founded and managed a Yorùbá newspaper, *Ìròhìn Yorùbá,* while he was still editor of the *Daily Service*. His cardinal aim in establishing *Ìròhìn Yorùbá* was to spread political awareness among the Yorùbá. The British Council awarded him a one-year scholarship in 1946 to study journalism in England.

He left for England to study journalism in 1946. He went to England alone, leaving his wife in Nigeria with their four children: Ọmọ́délé, Àbáyọ̀mí, Abímbọ́lá, and Ládipọ̀. The couple had a fifth child, Tòkunbọ̀, in 1951. He intended to ask his wife to join him later, in keeping with the Nigerian custom of his day. While studying in England, he wrote his friends in Ògbómọ̀ṣọ́ Parapọ̀, an organization encompassing all Ògbómọ̀ṣọ́ organizations in Nigeria and other West African countries,

about his desire to study law after completing the program in journalism. The Ògbómọ̀ṣọ́ community collected money and forwarded it to him in England. One of his former students at Baptist Academy, Alhaji S. O. Gbàdàmọ́ṣí, had become a successful businessman and also contributed money to Akíntọ́lá's training as a lawyer. Akíntọ́lá was involved in liberation politics during his student days in London, especially in the affairs of the West African Students' Union, founded by Ládipọ̀ Ṣọ́lànkẹ́ in 1925. Ṣọ́lànkẹ́ introduced Akíntọ́lá to George Padmore from Trinidad and Tobago, Jomo Kenyatta from Kenya, and Kwame Nkrumah from Ghana.

Akíntọ́lá was called to the English bar in 1949, and he returned to Nigeria in March 1950. He started practicing law in 1950. After delivering a lecture to a group of students in 1950, he was arrested for sedition. He was later reprimanded and acquitted by the Magistrate Court. He was present at Ọ̀wọ̀ on April 28, 1951, when the Action Group (AG) was formed. At that initial meeting, Akíntọ́lá was chosen as a member of the national executive board of the party and as the party's legal adviser. Also in 1951, he was elected to go to Lagos as one of the representatives of the Western Region to the new House of Representatives. A year later, in 1952, he formed a partnership with Chris Ògúnbánjọ and Michael Ọdẹ́sànyà, creating the firm Samuel, Chris, and Michael.

Shortly thereafter he became, under Sir John MacPherson, central minister of labor. In 1957, when Abubakar Tafawa Balewa took office as prime minister, he appointed Akíntọ́lá federal minister of aviation and communications. As aviation minister, he established a national airline for Nigeria, Nigeria Airways. Before then, British-owned West African Airways Corporation served Nigeria, the Gold Coast, Sierra Leone, and the Gambia. He became premier of the Western Region in December 1959, when the AG leader Chief Ọbáfẹ́mi Awólọ́wọ̀ vacated the position to participate in elections to the federal House of Representatives. His government established the University of Ifẹ̀ in 1962, built Cocoa House and Premier Hotel in Ìbàdàn, and built Western House in Lagos. There was also a significant increase in the number of scholarships awarded to the Yorùbá during Akíntọ́lá's administration. He constantly strove to bring the Yorùbá together because he believed disunity among the Yorùbá was the reason they missed out on key positions in the federal government.

Akíntọ́lá experienced problems as premier. Though Awólọ́wọ̀ was the opposition leader in the federal House of Representatives, he was still the leader of the AG, and Akíntọ́lá was answerable to him. Thus, Awólọ́wọ̀ constantly interfered in the affairs of Akíntọ́lá's government. Akíntọ́lá wanted to retain and sustain the support of conservative party elements, whereas Awólọ́wọ̀ wanted democratic socialism to be the party's policy. This resulted in the Western Region crisis of 1962, in Akíntọ́lá's removal as premier by the governor of the Western Region, and in the federal government's declaration of a state of emergency in the Western Region.

However, the Western Nigeria High Court later returned judgment in favor of Akíntọ́lá as the lawful premier of the Western Region, followed by a Supreme Court ruling that Akíntọ́lá had been wrongfully and unlawfully removed. On March 10, 1964, Akíntọ́lá and Chief Fẹ́mi Fàní-Káyọ̀dé announced the formation of the Nigerian National Democratic Party (NNDP), a party whose principles of Yorùbá unity paralleled those of the old cultural organization Ẹgbẹ́ Ọmọ Odùduwà. The *aláàfin* of Ọ̀yọ́, Ọba Gbádégẹsin II, appointed Akíntọ́lá the Ààrẹ-Ọ̀nà-Kakàǹfò in August 1964; he became only the thirteenth person to hold the title of defender of the Yorùbá nation. The NNDP formed an alliance with the ruling Nigerian National Alliance for the general elections of 1965. The elections culminated in a crisis that led to military takeover on January 15, 1966. The soldiers laid siege on the official residence of the Western Region's premier in Ìbàdàn on the night of January 15, 1966, killing Chief Akíntọ́lá in a hail of bullets. Two of his children, Yọ̀mí and Bímbọ́, served as finance ministers at various times in Nigeria's Third Republic. Also, the Ládòkè Akíntọ́lá University of Technology (LAUTECH) in Ògbómọ̀ṣọ́ is named after him.

See also **Action Group; Àgbẹ́kọ̀yà Rebellion; Awólọ́wọ̀, Ọbáfẹ́mi; Politics and Political Parties since 1945**

REFERENCES

Adébámwí, Wálé. *Yorùbá Elites and Ethnic Politics: Ọbáfẹ́mi Awólọ́wọ̀ and Corporate Agency.* New York: Cambridge University Press, 2014.

Awólọ́wọ̀, Ọbáfẹ́mi. *The Autobiography of Chief Ọbáfẹ́mi Awólọ́wọ̀.* Cambridge: Cambridge University Press, 1960.

Beer, Christopher. *The Politics of Peasant Groups in Western Nigeria.* Ìbàdàn (Nigeria): Ìbàdàn University Press, 1976.

Ṣẹ́gun Ọbasá

ALCOHOL

Yorùbá traditional alcoholic beverages have ancient origins. The preparation of these alcoholic drinks is a tradition preserved by people and passed down from one generation to another. Alcoholic drinks are used to pay fines and tributes, to appease the gods, and to pour libations. They are also used during initiations and for ancestral worship. The use of alcohol is also popular during various festivals and ceremonies such as marriage, births, deaths, circumcision, and the like.

Palm wine (ẹmu ọ̀pẹ or ògùrọ̀), tapped from oil palm or raffia palm, is an important alcoholic beverage. It is one of the most popular local drinks for relaxation. Palm wine is greatly valued because of its nutritional, medicinal, and sociocultural significance. Palm wine is high in calories and vitamins. Palm wine also contains yeast, which is essential for good vision. People believe that palm wine can prevent or cure malarial and measles. It is also used in different local occasions such as wedding ceremonies, naming ceremonies, and community festivals. As a religious drink, it is freely served to the devotees of Ògún (the god of iron and warfare) during the deity's annual festival. The creation myth of Ilé-Ifẹ̀ also emphasizes the role of palm wine in the transfer of power from Ọbàtálá to Odùduwà. As the story goes, when the former became intoxicated with palm wine, the latter simply took over and accomplished the task initially set for Ọbàtálá. Since then, it has been a taboo for any Ọbàtálá devotee to drink palm wine.

Ògógóró, a brand of liquor, is a popular derivative of palm wine. It is derived from fermented palm wine and is locally distilled. It has both social and religious functions. It also facilitates and reinforces intergroup relations, especially in southeastern Yorùbáland. *Bùrùkùtù* is another popular alcoholic beverage brewed from red or white sorghum, and it is consumed mainly in the northern region of Yorùbáland. *Bùrùkùtù* is also often consumed after communal work or meetings of village or town associations. Another traditional alcoholic drink is *ṣẹ̀kẹ̀tẹ́*. This special drink is produced by fermenting maize. During the process of fermentation, yeast and bacteria convert sugar into alcohol. The local drink *àgàdàgídí* is made of plantain; it is an established drink of the elite.

The production of traditional alcoholic beverages is an age-old tradition. Apart from its economic importance, alcohol has wide-ranging religious, sociocultural, and economic functions. The poetic rendition of *ìrèmọ̀jé* artists on the themes of birth and death also captures the importance attached to alcoholic beverages. The eighteenth line of the *ìrèmọ̀jé* chant specifically alludes to the fact that "alcohol puts humans in good form."

See also **Stimulants and Intoxicants; Libation**

REFERENCES

Fádípẹ̀, N. A. *The Sociology of the Yorùbá*. Ìbàdàn (Nigeria): University Press Limited, 1970.

Ogen, O. J. "The Ikale of Southeastern Yorùbáland, 1500–1800: A Study in Ethnic Identity and Traditional Economy." Unpublished doctoral dissertation, University of Lagos, Lagos (Nigeria) 2006.

Ògúndélé, S. A. "Understanding Aspects of Yorùbá Gastronomic Culture." *Indian Journal of Traditional Knowledge* 6.1 (2007): 50–56.

Ṣọlá Akínrìnádé and Olúkòyà Ogen

ANÍKÚLÁPÓ-KÚTÌ, FẸLÁ (1938–1997)

Fẹlá Aníkúlápó-Kútì, maverick Nigerian musician and multi-instrumentalist, was born in the city of Abẹ́òkúta in 1938. He died of illness related to HIV/AIDS in Lagos in 1997. Aníkúlápó-Kútì enjoyed a vibrant musical career despite his numerous and often brutal brushes with Nigerian law enforcement. He was also an intrepid social critic and political rebel who used his music to condemn and satirize the excesses of Nigerian military regimes.

Aníkúlápó-Kútì left the shores of Nigeria in 1958 for further studies at Trinity College of Music in the United Kingdom. After training as a classical musician in London and learning the rudiments of jazz in his free time, he made his way to Los Angeles in the late 1960s during the height of the civil rights movement. There, he was introduced to the Black Panthers. Once back in his native Nigeria, he combined these various intellectual and cultural influences into an arresting amalgam of radical politics, hypnotic rhythms (derived from a stirring brew of James Brown's funk, West African highlife grooves, and indigenous trance music), and African spirituality that he called Afrobeat.

Two of Aníkúlápó-Kútì's early bands, Jazz Quintet and Koola Lobitos, refused to play straight highlife. It took some time for him to gain an audience. He met Tony Allen, a key figure in the evolution of Afrobeat and was instrumental in incorporating indigenous Yorùbá rhythms into a highly potent mix of highlife, jazz, and funk. Around this period, Fẹlá found his voice and a new group of musicians, including Lékan Anímáṣahun, to help him pursue his musical vision.

As his fame spread, corrupt military administrations of Nigeria targeted him. Fẹlá Aníkúlápó-Kútì was also a fiery critic of Eurocentric bourgeois values, despite his own middle-class background. He was the son of a prominent educator and a far-sighted feminist. In the climate of militarism and conservative politics, he was perceived as a social gadfly. He also offended several powerful people in the country, such as Olúṣẹ́gun Ọbásanjọ́, Shehu Yar'Adua, and Moshood Abíọ́lá. As a result of his dissenting views, armed guards stormed and razed his commune, Kàlàkútà Republic, in 1977. They raped and mutilated his female singers and dancers, and they threw his aged mother out of an upstairs window. She died a year later as a result of her injuries.

Therefore, the key moments and experiences of Aníkúlápó-Kútì's life were his introduction to the thought and activities of the Black Panthers in the United States and his rediscovery of his indigenous Yorùbá music roots. Both of these influences contributed significantly to his work. Aníkúlápó-Kútì led an extraordinary life in his creation of a fresh musical idiom and in the relentless political struggles he waged against corrupt Nigerian governments.

See also **Music: Afrobeat; Music: Popular; Music: Composers of Art Music; Music: Contemporary**

REFERENCE

Moore, Carlos. *Fela: This Bitch of a Life*. Chicago: Chicago Review Press, 2009.

Sànyà Ọshá

ANIMALS IN FOLKLORE

Animals in folklore elucidate an animistic worldview that assumes animals possess souls and are accountable for their actions in the same manner as human beings are. Such stories are sometimes told to underscore the African worldview that animals were created to be in symbiotic relationship with human beings and that each can further the needs of the other. Animals in folktales may serve as agents for explaining creation stories.

In the creation myth, as recounted in Wándé Abímbọlá's *Àwọn Ojú Odù Mẹ̀rìndínlógún* (1977), when the pantheon descended to earth, they brought with them a five-legged rooster that help spread dirt over the water-filled earth to create land. This was the genesis of settlements all over the world. This story recognizes the Yorùbá insight into latter scientific knowledge that the surface of the world is predominantly made up of seas and oceans.

Animals in folktales also help explain why some animals have certain shapes or behavior. For example, one tale explains why the surface of the tortoise's shell is uneven. The most systematic collection of these explanation stories is found in *The Content and Form of Yorùbá Ìjálá* (1966), translated by S. A. Babalọlá. In this text, the behaviors and physical features of selected animals are presented through praise poems. An example is the salute to the elephant:

O elephant possessor of a savings-basket full of
     money.
O elephant huge as a hill, even in a crouching
     posture.
O elephant enfolded by honor; demon flapping
     fans of war.
Demon who snaps tree branches into many pieces
And moves on to the forest farm.
O elephant who ignores "I have fled to my father
     for refuge,"
Let alone "to my mother"
Mountainous animal, huge beast, who tears a man
     like a garment
And hangs him up on a tree.
The sight of which causes people to stampede
     towards a hill of safety.
My chant is a salute to the elephant.
Àjànàkú who walks with a heavy tread.
Demon who swallows palm-fruit branches whole,
     even with the spiky pistil-cells.
O elephant praise-named Láayè, massive animal
     blackish grey in complexion
O elephant who single-handedly causes a tremor
     in a dense tropical forest.
O elephant, who stands sturdy and alert who walks
     slowly as if reluctantly
O elephant whom one sees and points towards
     with all ones fingers.
The hunter's boast at home is not repeated when
     he really meets the elephant.
The hunter's boast at home is not repeated before
     the elephant.
Àjànàkú looks back with difficulty like a person
     suffering from a sprained neck.
The elephant has a porter's knot without having a
     load on his head.
The elephant's head is his burden which he balances.
O elephant praise-named Láayè "O death please
     stop following me"

This is part and parcel of the elephant's
   appellation.
If you wish to know the elephant, the elephant
   who is a veritable ferry-man.

Animals are also used in Yorùbá folktales for didactic reasons, to inculcate good behavior in human communities. In his explication of the Ifá figure Èjì Ogbè, Wándé Abímbọ́lá states that two types of monkey (ẹdun and àáyá) were featured in the story but that the story is an allegory about ancient times when Yorùbá people punished thieves and those who bore false witness. In explicating the Ìwòrì Méjì Ifá figure, Abímbọ́lá also showed how the bat was used to teach morals. The bat was warned to stay away from a particular tree, lest it be catapulted to death. It refused to heed the warning and suffered the consequences. The tale is meant to warn against disregarding the injunctions of Ifá priests.

The tales mentioned here are specifically associated with known guilds, such as the hunters' guild in ìjálá or the ifá divination guild. Animals also appear in universal tales, which are classified into two groups: àlọ́ àpamọ̀ (riddles) and àlọ́ àpagbè (extended tales or allegories). When a person says in a riddle adìẹ baba mi kan láéláé, owó nii jẹ kì í j'àgbàdo (my father's old cockerel that is fed only on money and not corn), the audience knows at once that the animals in the riddle are metaphors that may have nothing to do with the animal kingdom.

Àlọ́ àpagbè, in contrast, is the equivalent to the short story and novel. When performed in front of an audience, folklorists often encourage audience participation, such as inviting the audience to serve as choral background, providing call-and-response or singing along. The folklorists as well as the audience are at liberty to mimic the animals represented in the tales. The performance may use ad-lib elements or extend the plot of the tales.

See also **Literature: Oral; Urban Folktale**

REFERENCES

Abímbọ́lá, Wándé. Àwọn Ojú Odù Mẹ́rìndínlógún. Ìbàdàn (Nigeria): University Press Limited, 1977.

Babalọlá, Adéboyè. The Content and Form of Yorùbá Ìjálá. Edinburgh: Edinburgh University Press, 1966.
Ìṣọ̀lá, Akínwùmí. The Modern Yorùbá Novel: An Analysis of the Writers Art. Ìbàdàn (Nigeria): University Press, 1998.

Ọláyínká Àgbétúyì

APPRENTICESHIP

In general, apprenticeship in Yorùbá society was part of traditional education associated with learning different crafts. While learning a craft, an apprentice provides support and personal services to the master during the training period.

The apprenticeship system trains young men and women for future employment that contributes to the economic security of society. Apprenticeship usually involves a contractual agreement between the parents or guardians of the apprentice and the craftsman. Learning by doing is the most common form of apprenticeship; the apprentice acquires the necessary job skills while rendering work assistance to the master. Beyond practical skills, apprenticeship also teaches character; the apprentice is expected to respect the opinion of others, show respect for elders, and learn to speak with others and to negotiate. These qualities are necessary to prepare the apprentice to sustain himself or herself and reflect a positive public image of his or her profession after training.

Usually, masters work energetically while their apprentices cluster around them to learn. However, in the twentieth century the trend of apprenticeship changed; some apprentices were not trained as they had traditionally done in England. They worked in the colonial public works department or on large commercial farms. Traditional and modern forms of apprenticeship exist in contemporary Yorùbá society.

By the twentieth century, the duration of apprenticeship ranged from three to six years. In the first three years, the apprentice pays the master a training fee, depending on the nature of the craft. Gradually, the apprentice works for the master as a laborer. In such case, the master pays the apprentice wages based on the extent of the work done. This arrangement is common in printing, furniture, mechanic, and tailoring works. In Ìbàdàn, for example, apprenticeship in the tailoring profession involves apprentices working with London-trained Nigerian tailors in Dùgbè and environs. To aid the process of early learning, individual tailors bought tailors' guides at Kingsway Stores to use as a self-teaching manual. The guide contained modes of measurement and patterns that apprentices could use for practice to achieve desired results. In the 1960s in the interior areas of Ìbàdàn, few tailors emerged in the neighborhoods. Their prestige and popularity convinced parents to enroll their children as apprentices. The fact that they apprenticed near their residences and that the masters were from Ìbàdàn increased the confidence of the parents. In Dùgbè and environs, the Ìjèbú, Ègbá, Igbo, Lagos, and Ìjèsà people usually serve as tailoring apprentices in the trade centers.

A tailoring apprentice is expected to spend six years in training on the sewing machine, measuring, cutting and joining garments, pressing and folding garments before delivery to clients, and engaging in other activities. After six years of training, a celebratory freedom ceremony is organized for family and friends, similar to convocation ceremonies in formal schools. In some instances, the apprentice designs his or her own ceremonial robes. The apprentice places the tape rule around his or her neck and leaves it dangling in the front. The apprentice is expected to bring a number of items to the celebration, a substantial part of which are given to the master and executive union members in the branch.

In some cases, the master is expected to provide the apprentice with food, shelter, and accommodation, a practice inherited from precolonial Yorùbá society. In contemporary times, the duration of apprenticeship, depending on vocation, varies from three months to a year. This is especially the case in the Yorùbá cities of Lagos and Ìbàdàn, given the rising levels of unemployment. For instance, apprenticeship for fashion design, bag making, beauty therapy, shoemaking, barbering, bead making, and small-scale catering are undertaken within a year so as to enhance self-employment.

REFERENCE

Callaway, A. "From Traditional Crafts to Modern Industries." In *The City of Ìbàdàn*, ed. P. C. Lloyd, A. L. Mábògùnjé, and B. Awé, 153–72. Ìbàdàn (Nigeria): University Press, 1967.

Mutiat Títílopé Oládèjo

ARCHAEOLOGY

Archaeology of Yorùbáland has come of age since the German expedition of 1910–1912, which carried out amateur excavations at Ilé-Ifè. Professional archaeologists emerged in the 1930s, starting with expatriates Frank Willett, Paul Ozanne, and Peter Garlake. They were later joined by indigenous pioneers, such as Ekpo Eyo, Omótósò Elúyemí, Adé Obáyemí, Antonia Fátúnsìn, and Babátúndé Agbájé-Williams. Archaeology has followed many paths of discovery and has added new chapters to Yorùbá history. These paths take two directions: (1) Stone Age settlement history and (2) the development of social complexity and urbanism (including technology and regional interactions). Ògúndìran describes seven major periods of Yorùbá cultural history between circa 9000 BCE and 1800 CE (see table A.1).

The current evidence shows that human occupation in the Yorùbá region goes back at least to the Middle Stone Age (ca. 35,000–15,000 BCE), but it is the succeeding Late Stone Age that is better known. The oldest known Late Stone Age (LSA) site in Yorùbáland is Ìwó Elérú, a rock-shelter twenty-four kilometers from Àkúré whose lowest deposits have been dated to 9000 BCE. Other archaeological evidence for LSA occupations have been found at Itaakpa Cave in the Ifè-Ìjuùmú, the Méjiró rock-shelter at Old Òyó,

Table A.1 Historical periods in Yorùbáland

Periods	Approximate years
Pre-Archaic	9,000 BCE–500 BCE
Archaic	500 BCE–500 CE
Early Formative	500–800 CE
Late Formative	800–1000
Classical	1000–1400
Intermediate	1400–1600
Atlantic	1600–1830s

the Àyánbàndélé rock-shelter, forty kilometers from Ilé-Ifẹ̀, and the coastal areas around Badagry and Porto Novo, among others. Between 1000 and 500 BCE, in the pre-Archaic period, these LSA populations developed a subsistence culture based on the cultivation of palm oil and yam; utilization of a wide variety of plant resources including vegetables, fruits, and legumes; and hunting and fishing.

During the Archaic period (500 BCE–500 CE), there was widespread adoption of iron technology. Open-air homesteads became more common, and many of these coalesced or grew into hamlets and multifamily villages at the beginning of the first millennium CE.

Iron-using communities proliferated during the Early Formative period (500–800 CE), settlements increased in size, and many used earthen embankments to demarcate their boundaries. Many of these villages coalesced into towns and kingdoms between 800 and 1000 CE (the Late Formative period). Across the Yorùbá region, especially at Èsìẹ̀, Ilé-Ifẹ̀, and the Ìjẹ̀bú area, evidence of large scale embankment construction and individual-centered sculptures exist. The evidence demonstrates that the development of new political visions that favored the integration of multiple-lineage village complexes into centralized governments, with institutionalized social hierarchies, heralded the Late Formative period.

The Late Formative period's political gains were consolidated into sociocultural transformations across the region during the Classical period (1000–1500), when Ilé-Ifẹ̀ emerged as the leading metropolitan center in the Yorùbá region. The repertoire of material culture, technological innovations, and political institutions that have since served as the hallmarks of Yorùbá culture developed during this period. In this respect, Ilé-Ifẹ̀ led the way as the pioneer of an urban capital with concentric embankments, a royal dynasty with an elaborate network of hierarchical political and ritual officials, and the production of detailed naturalistic life-size terra-cotta and copper and bronze sculptures with idealized naturalism. Economic life was also diversified into a wide range of crafts, such as the manufacture of glass beads, iron, pottery, terra-cotta, and the like. However, only Ilé-Ifẹ̀ adopted centralized divine kingship institution. In the northeastern, southern, and southeastern peripheries of the Yorùbá cultural complex, loose political associations among villages without powerful royal dynasties and urban-based centralized government continued to hold sway.

The Intermediate period (1500–1600) marked a second wave of sociopolitical formations that were more militaristic and expansive than the preceding era. The most prominent of the states to emerge at the end of the sixteenth century was Ọ̀yọ́, and by the first decade of the seventeenth century, it had become the largest political formation in the Yorùbá region (including West Africa south of the Niger). Its imperial ambitions seemed unstoppable. The rise of Ọ̀yọ́ and other hegemonic states such as Ilẹ́ṣà and Òwu coincided with the beginning of the Atlantic Period, a new age spanning from approximately 1600 to the 1830s. During this time, Yorùbá sociopolitical and economic practices were defined by the material relationships with the Atlantic trade.

Archaeologists have concentrated their research on one or more of the foregoing temporal scales, mostly to explore and answer questions dealing with the materiality of social complexity, urbanism, regional interactions, and technology and crafts production. The attention has been mostly focused on the Classical, Intermediate, and Atlantic periods. Hence, the archaeological projects initiated by Robert Soper and Agbájé-Williams in the deserted ancient city of Ọ̀yọ́-Ilé (Old Ọ̀yọ́) were geared toward understanding the urban dynamics of this imperial capital. The archaeological survey demonstrated that, at its peak in the mid-eighteenth century, Old Ọ̀yọ́ covered an area of more than five thousand hectares, with a north-south dimension of ten kilometers and an east-west dimension of six kilometers. Agbájé-Williams, using a pioneering and innovative method of archaeological demographics, estimated that approximately one hundred thousand people were living in the city during the mid-eighteenth century.

Olú Alérù and Aríbidésí Usman have focused their interests on the north-central Yorùbá region (Ìgbómìnà), where their archaeological projects examined the question of frontier migrations, sociopolitical development, and center-periphery interactions—the center here referring to the Ọ̀yọ́ Empire, with Ìgbómìnà being the periphery. In central Yorùbáland, Akin Ògúndìran initiated two major archaeological campaigns: the Ẹ̀ka Ọ̀ṣun project in northern Ìjèṣà and the Upper Ọ̀ṣun project in the Òṣogbo and Ẹ̀dẹ areas. His goal was to explain the roles of regional interactions and migrations in sociopolitical development in internal frontier zones. He has undertaken regional comparison of the stylistic, symbolic, elemental, and contextual properties of artifacts from two or more archaeological sites and then used these to investigate questions of regional interactions, cultural and economic exchanges, and migrations.

Archaeologists are also investigating the history of crafts technology in the Yorùbá region, with emphasis on iron, primary glass production, brass and bronze, and potsherd pavement. Ilé-Ifẹ̀ seems to have played a primary role in the large-scale production of glass and brass and bronze in the eleventh and twelfth centuries. Contrary to the earlier view that glass beads were imported from North Africa and the Mediterranean through the Western Sudan and then melted and reworked at Ilé-Ifẹ̀, recent physico-chemical analyses of some of the Ifẹ̀ beads have shown that primary glass production did in fact take place in the ancient city. These studies have shown that the glass objects from archaeological sites in Ilé-Ifẹ̀ and in a forty-kilometer radius of the city have unusually high lime and high alumina contents (HLHA), higher than the proportions of alumina and lime found in ancient Islamic, European, and Asian centers of glass production. This has led to the conclusion that Ilé-Ifẹ̀ spearheaded a glassmaking technology that was unique to the Yorùbá culture.

Of comparable complexity to glassmaking is iron production; the latter is more widespread than glass manufacture. Archaeologist and geologist Akinlolú Ìgè, who conducted geochemical analysis of iron slag and iron products from Classical Ifẹ̀, noted that iron-workers enriched the primary raw materials (hematite) with ilmenite sands to produce strong titanium-rich iron tools and implements.

A long list of artifacts from scores of archaeological sites, such as potsherd pavement, spindle whorls, clay lamps, tobacco pipes, and ivory, wood, and bone ornaments and utilitarian objects, have shed new lights on crafts technologies like pottery manufacture, sea salt production, and dye and soap manufacture.

An expensive, painstaking, and labor-intensive discipline, archaeology can boast of three overlapping generations of professionals who are breaking new grounds as they direct their interdisciplinary searchlight to the deep recesses of Yorùbá's past for new discoveries of ancestral footprints.

See also **Beads; Ceramics and Pottery; Ilé-Ifẹ̀; Iron Making; Ọ̀yọ́ Empire; Political Systems**

REFERENCES

Agbájé-Williams, B. *On the Trails of Our Ancestors; Archaeology of Memory and Future.* Occasional Paper, Number 40, 2012, Institute of African Studies, University of Ìbàdàn (Nigeria).

Ìgè, O. A. *Yorùbá Iron Metallurgy: Raw Materials, Routine and Rituals.* London: Archetype and British Museum, 2013.

Ògúndìran, A. "Chronology, Material Culture, and Pathways to the Cultural History of Yorùbá-Edo Region, Nigeria, 500 B.C.–A.D. 1800." In *Sources and Methods in African History: Spoken, Written, Unearthed,* ed. Tóyìn Fálọlá and Christian Jennings, 33–79. Rochester, NY: University of Rochester Press, 2003.

——. "The Formation of an Ọ̀yọ́ imperial Colony during the Atlantic Age." In *Power and Landscape in Atlantic West Africa,* ed. Cameron Monroe and Akínwùmí Ògúndìran, 222–52. Cambridge: Cambridge University Press, 2012.

Usman, A. *The Yorùbá Frontier: A Regional History of Community Formation Experience and Changes in West Africa.* Durham, NC: Carolina Academic Press, 2012.

Akínwùmí Ògúndìran

ARCHITECTURE, CONTEMPORARY

The African environment is a product of a triple heritage: indigenous, Western, and Islamic influences. Nnamdi Elleh notes, "This triple heritage can be observed in the architecture of most African cities. These factors combine to form cities different from any other parts of the world." Western influences in Africa began with the Greeks in 333 BCE, continued through the settlement of the Romans in 146 BCE and of the Europeans in mid-fourteenth century, resulting in the proliferation of classical style influences across Africa, including Yorùbá societies. British gothic-style churches are some of the landmark churches found in Yorùbá cities today. The British also built Victorian- and English-style cottages that they predominately used for their residences during the era of colonialism. Many of these residences can still be found in the cities of Lagos, Ìbàdàn, and Abéòkúta today.

Another style of architecture, the Brazilian style, has been attributed to free men and women who returned to Africa after the abolition of the slave trade. However, some recent historians and architects argue that some features of this style predate the abolition of the slave trade. Today, Brazilian-style houses can be found in major cities. The West African Trans-Saharan trade gave Islam a route to West Africa. Today, mosques can be found in major cities. Families with Christian, Muslim, and traditional religious worshippers live together in harmony, reinforcing the notion of Mazrui's triple heritage.

In the late nineteenth and early twentieth centuries, long before most African countries gained independence from colonial rule, expatriate architects or builders who practiced in many Nigerian and African cities designed and built numerous international-style buildings. These buildings were utilized for government offices, schools, and institutions of higher learning. International-style buildings designed by various expatriate and indigenous architects dominate the skylines of major cities. The international-style is also called tropical architecture by several postwar, modernist, expatriate architects who worked in Nigeria in the early 1940s. Nickson and Borys, Kenneth Scott, Fry and Drew, Godwin and Hopwood, and Becker and Voight were some of these postwar modernists. Their work includes concrete construction, flat roofs, white walls, screen walls, minimalism, and rectangular geometry.

Olúmúyìwá was one of the first generation of architects born in Nigeria. He was trained in Manchester and worked in Europe before returning to Nigeria and opening a practice in 1958. He was involved in the formation of the Nigerian Institute of Architects (NIA). In describing Olúmúyìwá's buildings, Hannah Le Roux notes, "The buildings are generally composed of planar surfaces, arranged within a rectilinear grid, with low pitched roofs. The ornamentation of buildings is kept to a minimum." In general, most of Olúmúyìwá's buildings were predominately white, with the main structural frame constructed from reinforced concrete. He emphasized continuous fenestration, sun-shading devices, and courtyards to allow for cross-ventilation. These features were all characteristics of international-style buildings.

More recently, since the era of independence from colonial rule in the 1960s, there has been a cultural revival in many African nations, including Yorùbá spaces. Today, designers are striving to recapture elements from traditional African spaces lost since colonial rule in order to integrate them into contemporary design practices. Nigerian architect Demas Nwoko's Dominican Catholic Church in Ìbàdàn is an example. John Godwin and Gillian Hopwood note, "Nwoko's approach is deeply rooted in the Arts and craft tradition, whilst fusing the lessons of local vernaculars with modern building methods." Nwoko's architectural typology includes the courtyard (impluvium), which is derived from traditional architecture; day lighting; unfinished materials that reference nature; the roof as an edifice; and proportion and detailing with cultural influences.

See also **Architecture: Domestic; Sàró and Àgùdà**

REFERENCES

Elleh, N. *African Architecture Evolution and Transformation*. New York: McGraw Hill, 1997.
Godwin, J., and G. Hopwood. *The Architecture of Demas Nwoko*. Lagos (Nigeria): Farafina, 2007.
La Roux, H. "Modern Architecture in Post-Colonial Ghana and Nigeria." *Architectural History* 47 (2004): 361–92.
Mazrui, A. *The African: A Triple Heritage*. New York: Little, Brown & Co., 1986.

Abímbólá Aṣòjò

The traditional architecture of Yorùbáland includes rectilinear clay structures, tents, obelisks, palaces, and monumental structures. The Yorùbá trace their origin to Ilé-Ifè, located in present-day Nigeria. Archaeological and ethnographical studies indicate that traditional Yorùbá towns comprised several compounds, and each compound consisted of houses built around a series of open courtyards of different sizes, which usually contained pots to collect water from rooftops. Bessie Andah notes, "Yorùbá cities were roughly circular in shape and surrounded by some kind of defensive wall. The àfin (palace of the King) is an intricate, almost labyrinthine complex of rooms and courtyards often decorated with sculpted doors, walls, and house posts. Family and compound houses continue as it were from all sides of the palace and merge into one another." The kings were considered divine; thus, their palaces were located in the center of the city, which was the focus of economic and political activity. The kings' palaces comprised many courtyards for different economic, social, and political activities. For example, John Vlach notes:

> Since Yorùbá kings were regarded as divine, the inner core of the city was a focus for religious as well as economic and political activity. The design of palaces reflects this density of activity, for they are usually very large buildings with many courtyards. Each courtyard has a particular purpose: some are used for offering sacrifices to different deities, some for meeting between the king and the ward chiefs, and others for hearing the problems of the townspeople.

The chiefs were next in line to the king. The chief's house was smaller and simpler with about three or four courtyards. The family elder's house was even smaller, and it consisted of one or two courtyards. The family compound is very plain, with no decorations and often a single courtyard.

Towns and cities were radial or concentric in form, and the entire town was surrounded by a wall. The political and social elements of the town, such as the king's palace and market, were located at the core of the city. Painting among manifested as an extension of architecture rather than an independent medium. Traditional spaces depict extensive utilization of decorative embellishment. For example, verandah columns in ordinary houses were decorated with religious symbols, and kings' palaces had caryatids supporting the verandah roofs. Many palaces had elaborately carved entrance doors. The beams, lintels, and boards of ceilings were also carved with human, mythological, and animal figures and geometric patterns. Traditional interiors consisted of walls with murals, carved doors and columns, and geometric patterns sculpted on the walls.

See also **Architecture: Contemporary; Art: Contemporary; Art: Indigenous; Palace**

REFERENCES

Andah, B. W. *Nigeria's Indigenous Technology*. Ìbàdàn (Nigeria): University Press, 1992.

Godwin, J., and G. Hopwood. *The Architecture of Demas Nwoko*. Lagos (Nigeria): Farafina, 2007.

La Roux, H. "Modern Architecture in Post-Colonial Ghana and Nigeria." *Architectural History* 47 (2004): 361–92.

Mazrui, A. *The African: A Triple Heritage*. New York: Little, Brown & Co., 1986.

Vlach, J. M. "Affecting Architecture of the Yorùbá." *African Arts* 10.1 (1976): 48–53.

Abímbólá Aṣòjò

ART: CONTEMPORARY

Modern or contemporary Yorùbá art thrives on the revival and continuity of traditional art forms and on innovations. Traditional art, including sculpture in wood, metal, and ivory; terra-cotta pottery; and other genres, such as woven and dyed textiles and bead work have survived through the tenacity of their creators and the support of patrons and collectors who provide the resources and outlets for the artists to exhibit them. A marked transition from sacred forms to greater secularization of the arts has occurred. Patronage has shifted from traditional institutions (palaces, chiefdoms, and shrines) to public and private modern institutions (government buildings, banks, museums, galleries, and private homes). Other types of contemporary art are produced for the tourist market and for local and international collectors. Art dealers mediate between artists and buyers.

As traditional art morphs into contemporary forms, the type of media as well as scale and stylistic canons also go through processes of change. Aluminum became a new medium used in low-relief sculpture in the 1960s by some members of the Òṣogbo art school. Fiber sculpture is also a twentieth-century phenomenon. Figures, plaques, and receptacles tend to dominate the genre of wood carvings. The use of cement and stone has been on the increase since Suzanne Wenger used the media to create sculptures for the Òṣun shrine at Òṣogbo. The scale of figures in Yorùbá sculpture has also changed from former portable sizes to larger pieces, such as architectural and monumental sculpture. Stylized or idealized forms have given way to greater naturalism. Outdoor cement sculptures dot the landscapes of cities and towns, mostly depicting warlords, heroes, and heroines of traditional and contemporary history. The sculptures valorize the personalities depicted, substantiate the preeminence of towns and kingdoms, and serve as visual reminders of militarism and leadership. They also arouse pride in various Yorùbá towns, which seem to compete in creating heroic sculpture. There are also outdoor sculptures of political personalities and philanthropists.

The textile industry, from Ìṣéyìn to Abẹ́òkúta, Ìlọrin to Òṣogbo, Ọ̀wọ̀ to Ìbàdàn, remains dynamic and innovative. Indeed, weavers and cloth dyers are ubiquitous in contemporary Yorùbáland. Cloth weavers respond to new materials and generate ideas that they innovated or borrowed from the weaving tradition of their West African neighbors. The cloth dyeing industry is also vibrant given the increasing demand for àdìrẹ and batik in dressmaking, including aṣọ ẹbí for various ceremonies and for furnishings and as gifts. Níkẹ Òkúndayè, a contemporary batik and àdìrẹ artist and a product of Òṣogbo Art School, has been a game changer in the training of artisans and in the exhibition and globalization of Yorùbá textiles.

Pottery making continues in Yorùbá villages and towns. However, potters in cities and ceramicists in academic institutions have since embraced new aesthetic trajectories and modern technology. Olúṣèyí Ọláléyẹ, a ceramicist and lecturer at the Polytechnic, Èrúwà, specializes in stoneware, terra-cotta, and ceramics. He creates utilitarian ceramic wares, decorative superstructure, relief ceramics, and ceramic sculpture often decorated with beads.

Some revolutionary changes have also occurred in Yorùbá painting. In 1988 at the University of Ifẹ̀, graduate artists of Yorùbá ethnicity began to experiment with earth colors. The group, known as Ọnàists, turned to rich Yorùbá tradition—ancient and traditional sculpture and shrine paintings—for inspiration and borrowed forms and motifs to chart new creative trajectory. At Òṣogbo, more than two decades before the Ifẹ̀ experiment, Jimoh Buraimoh, under the mentorship of Ulli and Georgina Beier, had started to make bead painting.

See also **Art: Indigenous; Beadwork; Carvers; Ceramics and Pottery; Craft; Òṣogbo: Ọ̀ṣun Art School**

REFERENCES

Adésànyà, Adéṣọlá Adérónkẹ́. *The Fákẹ́yẹ Family and Contemporary Yorùbá Woodcarving*. Trenton, NJ: Africa World Press, 2013.

Adépégba, Cornelius. *Yorùbá Metal Sculpture*. Ìbàdàn (Nigeria): University Press, 1991.

———. *Nigerian Art: Its Tradition and Modern Tendencies*. Ìbàdàn (Nigeria): JODAD Publishers, 1995.

Adérónkẹ́ Adéṣọlá Adésànyà

ART: INDIGENOUS

The Yorùbá word for *art* is ọnà (design). The artist who creates ọnà is loosely called oníṣẹ́-ọnà (maker or creator of design). Thus, as a generic term, oníṣẹ́-ọnà applies to a diversity of artists working in different media. Hence, an oníṣẹ́-ọnà could be a wood carver or agbégilére (carver of wood into sculpture or images). She could be potter, amọ̀kòkò (one who molds clay into pots), which is a traditionally female profession in the culture. Others are alágbẹ̀dẹ (blacksmiths) and asúdẹ (brass casters). Similarly, many Yorùbá words that mean *indigenous* include *ìbílệ*, *ti-ìbílệ*, or *tiwa-n-tiwa* (i.e., native, aboriginal, or originating in Yorùbá society).

Alágbệdệ (Blacksmiths)

Of all the Yorùbá traditional artists, *alágbệdệ* (black-smiths) are considered the most senior, as most, if not all, other artists rely on *alágbệdệ* to make the tools they use. Hence, the saying *ẹní bá sọ pé t'Ògún kò sí, yóó sun'ṣu kò ní r'ọbẹ hó o* (whoever denigrates Ògún, god of iron, with which *alágbệdệ* smith iron tools and utensils, would roast their yam but find no knife to peel it), which is a proverbial message that every individual or profession depends on the blacksmiths. Blacksmiths' patron-deity is Ògún (the iron deity). Examples of iron tools abound. They include wood carvers' *ẹdùn* or *àáké* (adzes) and *ọbẹ-ọnà* (knives for making designs) and arrays of religious art paraphernalia, like *ọpá-Ọsanyìn*, which are iron staffs used by *oníṣègùn* (herbalists) priests of Ọsanyìn (the deity of herbal medicine); *ọpá-ọrèrệ* or *osù-babaláwo*, which are wrought-iron staffs for Babaláwo (Ifá diviners); and *agogo* (gongs), which are musical instruments played at Ifá, Ọsanyìn, Ògún, and Ọsun festivals. Most of the blacksmiths' own tools are also made of iron, including *owú* (flat-headed irons on top of which red-hot wrought irons are shaped), *ọmọ-owú* (mallets for forming red-hot wrought irons into desired shapes), and *ẹ̀mú* (iron tools for picking and holding steady on top of *owú*, the hot wrought iron). Hence, the axiom *gbogbo ohun tí ń bẹ ní'lé aró, Ògún ló ní in* (everything inside the blacksmith workshop belongs to Ògún).

Agbệgilére (Wood Carvers)

Wood carvings make up much of the indigenous art in museums and galleries around the world. As indicated by Làmídì Fákệyẹ, the late renowned Yorùbá traditional wood carver (*agbệgilére*), wood carvers are regarded as next in rank after blacksmiths. Most of the religious art used as insignia and emblems of the 401 Yorùbá *òrìṣà* deity and their priests, priestesses, and adherents are wood carvings. These include the following:

- *àgbá*, drums used by Ògbóni society
- *àgèrè*, drums used by the Ògún worshippers and the hunters' guild (*ẹgbé ọdẹ*)
- *ìgbìn*, drums used by Ọbàtálá worshippers
- *ọpọ́n-Ifá*, divination tray used by Babaláwo, priests of Ifá or Ọ̀rúnmìlà god of divination and human destiny
- *agéré-Ifá*, container used by Babaláwo (Ifá diviners) for storing sacred palm nuts for Ifá divination
- *igbá-Ṣàngó*, altar bowl with which Ṣàngó priests and priestesses store *ẹdùn-àrá* (Neolithic stones)
- *osé-Ṣàngó*, double-axe ritual staff in the form of a stylized human sculpture used by the Ṣàngó priests and priestesses
- *ère-ìbejì*, twin memorial sculptures or statuettes

In addition, *agbệgilére* also carve the household objects and utensils indispensable for Yorùbá people, which comprise *ìpọn* (wooden spoons), *àwo* (wooden bowls of different sizes used for food containers), *ọpọ́n* (wooden trays of different sizes, some used for food containers and others for washing cloths and babies), and *ọmọ* and *ìyá-odó* (mortars and pestles for pounding *iyán* yam, *èlùbọ́* yam flour, and *àgbàdo* corn flour).

Asúdẹ (Brass Casters)

Among certain Yorùbá traditional religious groups, the importance of indigenous art made in brass cannot be overemphasized. The traditional artists who work in brass (and other nonferrous metals like lead, silver, copper, and bronze) to produce the art are called *asúdẹ* (brass casters). Ògbóni, Ọṣun, and Ṣàngó society members use a variety of brass art. The items *asúdẹ* make for these society members include *ẹdan Ògbóni*, *Onílé*, and *ìpawó-àṣẹ* (staff of authority), which are the most important ones. These three art emblems are indispensable to the cult of Ògbóni (also called Ọ̀ṣùgbó), whose members worship *ilệ*, the earth goddess. Membership is open to any interested adult men and women who are morally upright. During precolonial times, Ògbóni society functioned as a town council, civic court, and body that counterbalanced the king's authority. Often worn around the neck as identification of membership of Ògbóni society, ẹdan Ògbóni (or ẹdan òlóló) is a pair of male and female brass figures held together at the top by an iron chain. On a deeper level, it symbolizes the secret pact sworn by members of Ògbóni in the presence of ilẹ̀ (the earth) on which they walk and dwell and is an allusion to the earth goddess. Therefore, the significance of the paired ẹdan figures are explained by the Ògbóni saying Ògbóni méjì ó d'ẹta (two Ògbóni become three), the third being ilẹ̀ (earth), personified as the Earth Mother goddess who witnessed the Ògbóni secret pact.

Onílé (owner of the house) is also a male and female pair made of brass; they are a larger, free-standing version of ẹdan Ògbóni. This pair is called ìyá (mother), which represents the earth goddess. It is usually placed on special altars inside the ilédì (Ògbóni lodge). On a deeper level, the pair represents both the female and male temperaments of the earth goddess. As female, she can be very soft and caring, sustaining life; as male, she can be very harsh, especially to any Ògbóni members who betrayed the society's trust. Thus, one of her oríkì (praise name) that illustrates her male dispositions is Ó pa ọ̀dàlẹ̀ túé (She killed the perfidious one with ease).

Finally, the ìpawó-àṣẹ (staff of authority), sometimes called ṣaworo-idẹ (brass rattle), is a large brass rattle usually fashioned in the form of an abstracted human head with small round bells attached on a cylinder like bottom; it jingles when shaken. Ìpawó-àṣẹ is customarily held and shaken by the Ògbóni senior titleholders, such as Olúwo, Olúrìn, and Apènà, to reply in greeting. The jingling sound produced when shaken is believed to emit àṣẹ (spiritual energy) that neutralizes the powers of evil forces.

See also **Art: Contemporary; Carvers; Ceramics and Pottery; Crafts**

REFERENCES

Fámúlẹ̀, Oláwọlé. "Ẹgbẹ́ Ògbóni: The Yorùbá Council of Elders, Its Origins and Artistic Relevance." Unpublished M.A. thesis, University of Arizona, 2003.

Lawal, Babátúndé. *Embodying the Sacred in Yorùbá Art: Featuring the Bernard and Patricia Wagner Collection, Atlanta and Newark.* Atlanta: High Museum of Art; Newark, NJ: Newark Museum, 2007.

Oláwọlé Fámulẹ̀

ASSOCIATIONS FOR PROMOTING YORÙBÁ CULTURE

Since the late nineteenth century, the Yorùbá elite formed several sociocultural organizations to promote the collection and documentation of its oral tradition. These groups include Ẹgbẹ́ Olùfẹ́ Ilẹ̀ Ìbí Wọn, formed in 1883, Ẹgbẹ́ Onífẹ́ Ilẹ̀ Yorùbá formed in 1907, and Ẹgbẹ́ Àgbà ò Tán formed in 1909. The associations for the development of Yorùbá culture and tradition were a reaction to the 1882 Education Ordinance introduced by the British colonial government. The ordinance tried to discourage teaching the mother tongue in formal schools in Nigeria. C. O. Táíwò criticized the ordinance for imitating "too closely the English Elementary Education Act of 1870 which was designed to satisfy the needs of England and was therefore unsuitable for a wholesale importation [to Nigeria]."

These sociocultural societies organized lectures and workshop for their members that coached them on collecting data from the oral tradition. They also assisted in the publication of several book manuscripts. It was not until the issuance of the 1926 Education Ordinance that the legal status of the Yorùbá language in the formal school system was finally settled. The effect of the ordinance, which lasted until 1948, resulted in a new spate of enthusiasm for the writing of Yorùbá books for use in primary schools. Three collections of regular Yorùbá riddles were published in quick succession: D. B. Vincent's (1885) Ìwé Àlọ́, with 200 riddles; E. A. Túgbiyìlé's (1948) Àwọn Àlọ́ Àpamọ̀ Yorùbá (Yorùbá Conundrums), with 434 riddles; and J. O. Oyèlẹ́sẹ's (1948) Àlọ́ Àpamọ̀: Apá Kíní, with 220 riddles. The preface to Túgbiyìlé's collection states clearly the objectives of these cultural revivalists:

> The book is meant to preserve that legacy of the invaluable casket of wisdom bestowed on us by our grandparents.

Besides, it will also serve as a drill-book which will be found useful as well as interesting, to some extent, as a substitute for the customary fire-side and moonlight education which our fathers used to impart in their children a few decades ago. . . . The desire to produce the present work has remained latent in the author for several years. But the fear that all these would ultimately fall into oblivion, impelled me to consider it obligatory for me, while I have the thought, to preserve for prosperity, this epitome of Yorùbá philosophy.

Other books published with the help of these sociocultural organizations are A. K. Ajíṣáfẹ́'s *History of Abẹ́òkúta* (1921), *Gbádébọ̀ Aláké* (1921), *The Laws and Customs of the Yorùbá People* (1924), and *Ìwé Ìtàn Abẹ́òkúta* (1924); I. B. Akínyẹlé's *Ìwé Ìtàn Ìbàdàn àti Ìwó, Ìkìrun àti Òṣogbo* (1911); D. O. Ẹpẹ́gà's *Ifá* (1908) and *The Mystery of the Yorùbá Gods* (1932); E. M. Líjàdù's *Ifá* (1897), *Ọrúnmìlà* (1907), *Àwọn Àròfọ̀-Orin ti Ṣóbọ̀ Aróbíodu àti ti Oyèsilẹ̀ Kéríbo* (1902), and *Ìwé Kejì Àwọn Àròfọ̀ Orin ti Ṣóbọ̀ Aróbíodu* (1906); J. B. O. Lósì's *The History of Abẹ́òkúta* (1924); D. A. Ọbasá's *Ìwé Kínní ti Àwọn Akéwì—Yorùbá Philosophy* (1927), *Ìwé Kejì ti Àwọn Akéwì—Yorùbá Philosophy* (1934), and *Ìwé Kẹta ti Àwọn Akéwì—Yorùbá Philosophy* (1945); T. A. J. Ògúnbíyí's *Ìwé Ìtàn Ifá, Agbigba, Yanrìn-Títẹ̀ àti Owó Ẹẹ̀rìndínlógún* (no date); M. I. Ògúmẹ́fu's *Yorùbá Legends* (1929); J. E. S. Ògújì's *Àròfọ̀ D'òwe* (1944) and *Àròfọ̀ Aláwídọ̀la* (1946); J. Òjó-Cole's *A Collection of Yorùbá Thoughts* (1931); Ṣóbọ̀ Aróbíodu's (Josiah Ṣóbọ̀wálé Ṣówándé) *Àwọn Àròfọ̀-Orin Ti Ṣóbọ̀ Aróbíodu* series (1910, 1913, 1917, 1920, 1929, 1930, and 1934); and Ṣówándé Olúṣẹ́gun's *Àwọn Àròfọ̀-Orin ti Olúṣẹ́gun Ṣówándé, ọmọ Ṣóbọ̀ Aróbíodu* (1938).

Since the 1960s, scholars have formed professional associations to promote Yorùbá language and culture. The first of such associations was Ẹgbẹ́ Ìjìnlẹ̀ Yorùbá under the leadership of the late professor Adébóyè Babalọlá. The association established the journal *Olókun* to publish short research essays and creative works in the Yorùbá language. It also published manuscripts in Yorùbá under the Yorùbá Classics Series (*Àwọn Ìwé Agbógoyọ Èdè Yorùbá*) with Collins Publishers in Glasgow, Scotland. Some of the titles published in

the series include *Àwọn Oríkì Orílẹ̀* by Adébóyè Babalọlá, *Ìjìnlẹ̀ Ohùn Ẹnu Ifá* by Wándé Abímbọ́lá, and *Ewì Ìwòyí* edited by Adéagbo Akínjógbìn.

By 1970, two other professional associations had formed: Ẹgbẹ́ Akọ́mọlédè Yorùbá, which served teachers of Yorùbá in elementary through high school, and Yorùbá Studies Association of Nigeria (YSAN), Ẹgbẹ́ Onímọ̀ Èdè Yorùbá, for scholars in tertiary institutions like the vocational schools, universities, and colleges. Both associations shared similar aims and objectives: to promote the academic development of Yorùbá studies; to initiate, encourage, and support scholarly research in Yorùbá studies; to promote and encourage the development of courses in Yorùbá studies at all levels of education in Nigeria and overseas; and to establish a learned journal in Yorùbá studies that would be published regularly. Today, many scholarly and creative works in Yorùbá by members of these associations have appeared in print; Yorùbá is taught as a subject at all levels of education; senior essays, theses, and doctoral dissertations are being written and defended in Yorùbá; and four journals, *Láàngbàsà*, *Ọpánbàtà*, *Yorùbá*, and *Yorùbá Gbòde*, appear regularly.

Since the 1980s, Yorùbá speakers in the Diaspora have also played a significant role in the promotion of Yorùbá culture and language. For instance, scholars with teaching positions in institutions of higher learning in the United States, United Kingdom, France, Germany, Japan, and other places have introduced topics related to Yorùbá language and culture into their classes. This necessitated the publication of textbooks for teaching Yorùbá language and culture to foreign learners and led to the organization of the American Association of Teachers of Yorùbá.

Similarly, Yorùbá people living in the Diaspora have formed many other sociocultural associations to promote Yorùbá culture. These include associations such as Ẹgbẹ́ Ìṣọ̀kan Yorùbá, Oòduà Foundation, Ẹgbẹ́ Ọmọ Yorùbá, Odùduwà Heritage Organization, Odùduwà Descendants Union, and others. Some of these organizations now disseminate information on Yorùbá culture worldwide through websites, online discussion groups like Tiwa-n-Tiwa, and online radio stations like Yorùbá Odùduwà Radio. For instance, the online discussion group Tiwa-N-Tiwa insists on the using Yorùbá language solely, *Fún ìsọjí, ìgbéga àti ìtànkálẹ̀ èdè Yorùbá . . . Èdè aládùn yìí nìkan ni awa tí a wà nínú ẹgbẹ́ yìí yóò máa kọ sí ara wa. A kò fẹ́ Gẹ̀ẹ́sì, Faransé tàbí èdèkédè, bíkòṣe Yorùbá* (For the revival, progress, and development of Yorùbá. This is the only acceptable language for communication by members of this discussion group. We do not want English, French, or any other language, except Yorùbá).

See also **Diaspora: Impact of Yorùbá Culture; Language: Standardization and Literacy; Literature: Oral; Literature: Written; Ọ̀yọ́túnjí: The Yorùbá Community in the United States**

REFERENCES

Akínyẹmí, Akíntúndé. *Orature and Yorùbá Riddles.* New York: Palgrave/Macmillan, 2015.

Táíwò, C. O. "Henry Carr: An African Contribution to Education." Unpublished doctoral dissertation, University of London, 1971.

Túgbiyìlé, E. A. *Àwọn Àlọ́ Àpamọ̀ Yorùbá (Yorùbá Conundrum)* Abẹ́òkúta (Nigeria): Túgbiyìlé Press, 1948.

Akíntúndé Akínyẹmí

AWÓLÓ́WỌ̀, ỌBÁFÉ́MI (1909–1987)

Chief Jeremiah Ọbáfẹ́mi Awólọ́wọ̀, the iconic leader of the Yorùbá, was on born March 6, 1909. He died on May 9, 1987. Described as Christ-like, his life and political career are cited as the epitome of the good life and a consummate example of public spiriteness. His vision of a fully empowered citizenry as the foundation of holistic social transformation is considered a cardinal principle of governance. A generation after his death, adherence to his governance paradigm has become the litmus test for the legitimacy of developmental strategies adopted by all successive administrations of the old Western Region of Nigeria. He served as premier of the region from 1952 to 1959.

Indeed, other regions of the Nigerian federation have acknowledged his visionary leadership as the single most important factor in the tremendous advances in human development and the unparalleled strides in the economic development of the old Western Region over other regions of Nigeria. In the modern era, Awólọ́wọ̀ was the first individual to be formally conferred the title Aṣíwájú Ọmọ Oòduà, which means "Leader of the Yorùbá." He is universally recognized as a significant leader. His politics were founded on the principle that a person had to be a good member of his or her immediate community to be a good citizen of the larger political community.

Chief Awólọ́wọ̀ was a stout Nigerian nationalist. He founded the Ẹgbẹ́ Ọmọ Odùduwà, a Yorùbá cultural society, in 1947 in London. The organization was a precursor to the Action Group (AG), a political party established in 1951. As Nigeria's foremost federalist, his book *Path to Nigerian Freedom* (1947) articulated a systematic federalist manifesto in which he advocated federalism as the only meaningful basis for equitable national integration. The AG stood alone in demanding the immediate independence for Nigeria based on a federalist platform. After leading the AG to victory in the Western Regional elections of 1951, he became the minister for local government and finance. He was the first premier of the Western Region when Nigeria became a federation in 1954.

Awólọ́wọ̀'s principles diverged ideologically from his deputy Samuel Ládòkè Akíntọ́lá, which led to controversy among some of Awólọ́wọ̀'s comrades. An alliance between the Akíntọ́lá and the Tafawa Balewa-led Northern Peoples' Congress (NPC) swelled into a constitutional crisis and led to the widespread breakdown of law and order in the Western Region, which led in turn to the declaration of a state of emergency in the region. Awólọ́wọ̀ and his key loyalists were arrested and jailed on charges of conspiring with the Kwame Nkrumah administration in Ghana to topple the Nigerian government. These developments sparked a military intervention in Nigerian politics and its attendant disastrous consequences, including the Nigerian Civil War. After being released from jail, Awólọ́wọ̀, acting as the de facto deputy head of the Gowon military regime, is credited with strategies that led to the defeat of the Biafra secession in 1970. In a rare honor, Odumegwu Ojukwu, the leader of the rebellion, described Awólọ́wọ̀ as "the best president" Nigeria never had.

See also **Action Group; Àgbẹ́kọ̀yà Rebellion; Akíntọ́lá, Samuel Ládòkè; Politics and Political Parties since 1945**

REFERENCES

Adébámwí, Wálé. *Yorùbá Elites and Ethnic Politics: Ọbáfẹ́mi Awólọ́wọ̀ and Corporate Agency.* New York: Cambridge University Press, 2014.

Awólọ́wọ̀, Ọbáfẹ́mi. *The Autobiography of Chief Ọbáfẹ́mi Awólọ́wọ̀.* Cambridge: Cambridge University Press, 1960.

———. *Path to Nigerian Freedom.* London: Faber, 1947.

Adémọ́lá Àràoyè

B

BARDS: OLD AND NEW

In precolonial society, bards were found mainly in the official residence, or palace, of kings. According to Samuel Johnson, the bands were "kept in royal service . . . [to] repeat daily in songs [or chants] the genealogy of the kings, the principal events of their lives and other notable events in the history of the community." These events were usually followed by verbal acclamation of the incumbent king's praises, a process that continued until very late in the night. The bard's accolades were in addition to the praises of visitors and guests to the palace, who were ushered into the palace while chanting their personal praises, which was accompanied by drumming. The bards are known by different appellations, such as *akígbe-ọba* (those who acclaim kings), *arọ́kin ọba* (chroniclers of kings' genealogy), *akéwì ọba* (the kings' poets), *apohùn ọba* (the kings' bards), and *onírárà ọba* (the kings' praise singers).

During the long Yorùbá wars from 1797 to 1893, many kings committed both human and material resources to the wars. The responsibility of chanting in honor of warlords fell on royal bards, who were renowned for praise singing. As a result of the wars, most bards were elevated to the peak of their profession. The assembly of warriors prepared to march out on an expedition became a significant time for the bards to chant and sing in praise of war leaders. Such praises were meant to encourage and spur the warriors to victory on the battlefield. After the wars, back in their villages, towns, and cities, the bards continued their traditional role of praise singing by documenting their patrons' military exploits, including reference to the patrons' journey to the battlefields, their fights, their victims, the war booty, and their homecoming.

Before the wars, stories of warriors were rarely incorporated into the performance of bards. According to Karin Barber, "It is impossible to tell whether this is because of the failure of memory, or whether the turbulence unleashed by the nineteenth-century wars threw up figures more remarkable than those who preceded them."

The intervention of the British in the administration of Yorùbá politics affected the bards. Previously, bards had relied solely on their patrons for sustenance, but the end of the wars and the transition to democracy weakened the economic base of kings and their warlords. They no longer possessed the financial means to maintain large bands of bards. Most war leaders laid off their bards, and the few powerful kings who retained their bards did so for political reasons.

As a result of this development, many contemporary bards participate in royal chanting as a part-time avocation in addition to their full-time professional engagements, such as farming, trading, driving, and loom weaving. In addition, some modern bards earn a living entertaining the general public at social gatherings such as weddings and funeral receptions.

See also **Lineages and Cognomen (*Oríkì Orílè*); Literature: Oral; Palace; Praise Poetry and Eulogy: *Oríkì***

REFERENCES

Akínyemí, Akíntúndé. *Yorùbá Royal Poetry: A Sociological Exposition and Annotated Translation*. Bayreuth (Germany): Bayreuth African Studies Series (BASS 71), 2004.

Barber, Karin. *I Could Speak Until Tomorrow*. Edinburgh: Edinburgh University Press, 1991.

Johnson, Samuel. *The History of the Yorùbás*. Lagos (Nigeria): C.S.S. Bookshops, 1921.

Akíntúndé Akínyemí

BEADWORK

Àtàtà-bí-àkún.
Ọmọ ẹni kò ṣẹdí bẹbẹrẹ,
Ká filẹkẹ sí tọmọ ẹlòmíràn;
Tẹni-n-tẹni.

He [Ọrúnmìlà] is as precious and of inestimable value as beads.
Even if one's own daughter's buttocks are not plum,
It's not an excuse to instead tie beads around someone else child's buttocks;
As that which belongs to one is what that person owns.
—Excerpt from *oríkì* praise poem of Ọrúnmìlà in Odù Èjì Ogbè

The above *oríkì* praise poem of Ọrúnmìlà (Ifá deity of divination and destiny) underscores the great value Yorùbá ascribe to both *àkún* (beads) and their deities. *Ìlẹkẹ* (stringed beads) are used as waistbands (*bèbè*) that are tied around the females' upper buttocks or hips. While *bèbè* are used primarily for enhancing and accentuating feminine beauty, it is strongly believed that it also possesses the power to entice, to arouse sexual desire.

A fine and arbitrary line exists between the use of the terms *beadwork* and *bead making*. Beadwork is any work of art made with beads. The making of beadwork entails a variety of techniques open to the artists, who choose beads as their artistic medium: threading or stringing, embroidery, beads, and knitting. The first two are commonly used among the bead workers. With threading or stringing technique, they produce an array of beadworks like *bèbè* (beaded waistbands), *ẹgbà ọrùn* (beaded necklaces), *ẹgbà ọwọ* (beaded brace-

lets), and *ẹgbà ẹsẹ* (beaded anklets). Using embroidery, they also make king's insignia and the *òrìṣà* priests' and priestesses' paraphernalia. *Adé ńlá* (conical beaded crown with veils), *òpá àṣẹ* (beaded staff of authority). *bàtà ìlẹkẹ* (beaded shoes), *ìrùkẹrẹ* (beaded horsetail fly whisks); *àpò* Ifá (beaded bag for Ifá diviners), and *apó* Udamolore (beaded sheath for Udamolore carved ivory sword among the Èkìtì-Yorùbá) are a few examples. Professor Rowland Abíọdún has noted that prominent Ifá priests may also wear beaded crowns (without veils) and beaded horsetail fly whisks (personal interview, March 3, 2014).

Bead making is the technology for making or manufacturing beads, including molded beads from powdered glass, wound beads, and drawn beads. Overwhelming evidence exists detailing the use of beads and the existence of bead-making industries in the ancient city of Ilé-Ifẹ dating back to the ninth to eleventh century. For instance, during archaeological excavations at Olókun Groove, researchers discovered glassmaking crucibles fused with glass beads, residues of mixed fragments of glass beads, tuyeres, furnaces, and stones used for grinding and polishing beads. These discoveries led Frank Willett to conclude, "Here evidently had been the center of the great glassmaking industry which had spread blue glass *ṣègi* beads across West Africa." Dating to the eleventh century, most of the Ifẹ terra-cotta, bronze, and stone human sculptures discovered in archaeological finds are carved with representations people wearing beaded clothing. This evidence confirms that bead making and use were indigenous to Yorùbá society.

Archaeological evidence and oral traditions have established at least five different bead types made in Ilé-Ifẹ and used by royalty, chieftains, and religious leaders as status signifiers. They include the most culturally valued *ṣègi* (dichroic glass beads, usually blue in reflected light and green in transmitted light), *kereú* (blue glass beads), *àkún* (red chalcedony beads), *ṣègidá* (opaque jasper beads that contain an impure variety of silica, usually in red, yellow, brown, or green chalcedony beads), and *èjìgbà* or *èjìbà* (carnelian, clear to translucent and reddish-brown chalcedony beads).

Of all beadwork, *adé ńlá* (the conical beaded crowns with veils) are the most highly esteemed emblem of kingship. According to oral tradition, Odùduwà, the first Ọ̀ọ̀ni, king of Ilé-Ifẹ̀, invented *adé ńlá* as the most important royal insignia. He then presented each of his sixteen sons with an *adé ńlá* when he sent them away to establish their own kingdoms. To this day, only the kings who can trace direct descent from Odùduwà are allowed to wear the *adé ńlá*. The characteristically conical *adé ńlá* possesses a great deal of *àṣẹ* (spiritual powers or life forces), which spiritually transform the king and wearer to *aláṣẹ-èkejì-òrìṣà* (second in command to the gods). Thus, any king who looks inside the *adé ńlá* could be afflicted with grave disasters, such as *ẹ̀fọ́jú* (blindness) or *orí-àfọ́pa* (head aching that causes death) for transgressing this *èèwọ̀* (taboo or curse-inspired mystery).

The designs of beaded crowns typically include embroidery of an abstract face or faces that represent Odùduwà, the ancestor of all Yorùbá kings, and *ẹyẹ-ọ̀kín* (African paradise flycatcher), a tiny male bird with long white tail streamers. Because of its distinctive attributes and rarity, the Yorùbá address the bird as *ọlọ́jà ẹyẹ* (king of the avian kingdom). Thus, as *ẹyẹ-ọ̀kín* rules the domain of birds, so does the king rule his entire community of townspeople. Embroidered designs of birds are commonly found on beaded crowns. The designs allude to *àwọn ìyá*, the spiritually powerful great mothers, sometimes called witches, who control the positive and negative *àṣẹ* life forces. Hence, if a king rules successfully, it is believed that he does so with the approval and protection of *àwọn ìyá*.

See also **Body Adornment and Cosmetics; Color Symbolism; Symbols and Symbolism; Words: Ọ̀rọ̀**

REFERENCES

Ògúndìran, Akínwùmí. "Of Small Things Remembered: Beads, Cowries, and Cultural Translations of the Atlantic Experience in Yorùbáland." *International Journal of African Historical Studies* 35.2–35.3 (2002): 427–45.

Willett, Frank. 1960. "Ifẹ̀ and Its Archaeology." *Journal of African History* 1.2 (1960): 231–48.

Ọláwọlé Fámulẹ̀

BODY ADORNMENT AND COSMETICS

The Yorùbá adorn their bodies using a variety of means, which can be classified into three types: body marking, dress and accessories, and cosmetics. Body marks can be permanent or temporary. Permanent body marks, or *ilà-kíkọ*, range in form from *ilà-ojù* to *kóló fínfín* and *gbẹ́rẹ́ sínsín*. The *ilà-ojú* (facial scarification) is a deep linear cut on the face. Apart from adding beauty to the body, it also serves as a form of identifying a person by his or her lineage or town of origin. Every Yorùbá subgroup can be identified by different forms of facial marks, which are known by names such as *àbàjà*, *pélé*, *gọ̀ǹbọ́*, and so on. Some body markings are made on other parts of the body, such as the chest, back, legs, or arms. They are mostly found on persons of royal blood, and their palace attendants have some variant of the mark. *Kóló fínfín* (tattoo) is a skin surface marking. Juice derived from a plant or an insect is used in the *kóló fínfín* to achieve decorative and symbolic patterns of animals or geometric shapes on different parts of the body. *Gbẹ́rẹ́* (incisions) are short, horizontal marks made on the skin that are organized into decorative rows of linear patterns.

The Yorùbá also adorn their bodies with temporary markings. Women or young girls usually paint their face or body. Cosmetics and other beautifying substances are sourced from tree plants, shrubs, and minerals; *osùn* and *ẹfun* are used most often. *Osùn* is mostly used to brighten the skin in preparation for ceremonies. Every nursing mother is expected to always have *osùn* for her and her baby's use. *Ẹfun* is often used in connection with some rites or festivals.

Dress is another prominent form of body adornment, and it includes the use of clothes and accessories as well as hairdressing. Both men and women make dress of varied styles, colors, and names. These garments are made from traditional *aṣọ-òkè* (woven fabric), *àdìrẹ* (tie-dye), or a variety of new fabrics, such as *àǹkárá*, brocade, and the like. Men's dress comprises outer garments of *dàńdógó*, *agbádá*, *òyàlà*, *gbárìyẹ̀*, and other pieces, as well as the *dàńṣíkí* or *bùbá*, which serve as *àwọ̀télẹ̀* (underwear), along with a *ṣòkòtò* (pants or trousers) made of *kèǹbè* or *sóóró*. Men often wear a coordinated cap of *òrìbí* or *abetí-ajá* in different styles. In most cases, the garments are embroidered.

The women wear *bùbá* (blouse), *ìró* (wrapper), *gèlè* (head tie or head gear), and *ìborùn*. Both *gèlè* and *ìró*, however, are worn in variety of fashionable styles that portray status and sometimes indicate a change in attitude or emotion. Accessories and jewelry are used to complement women's dress. Beads adorn women's necks, wrists, and sometimes their ankles, waist, and hips. The beads are *ìlèkè* or *iyùn* of different kinds and colors: *àkún* (mostly for chiefs), *sègi* (worn as necklace), *lágídígba* (usually worn around the waist by young girls), and *bèbè* (worn by married women around their hips). There are also *ègbà* (bangles) made of *wúrà* (gold) or *fàdákà* (silver) for the neck, hands, and legs. Some *yerí-etí* (earrings) require piercing the earlobes. Apart from adding to the beauty of the body, dress among the Yorùbá symbolizes the wearer's status, his or her wealth, and his or her position within the society.

Hairdressing is another form of body adornment practiced by women. Apart from the Ṣàngó devotees who plait their hair and the palace attendants who partially shave their heads, men generally have their hair shaved, leaving the head bald and bright. Women plait their hair in different forms, such as *bíba*, *dídì*, or *kíkó*, and wear it in variety of styles, such as *sùkú*, *pàtéwó*, *kòlésè*, *ológèdè*, *ìpàkó-elédè*, and *koróba*. The Yorùbá apply body cosmetics made from shrubs, plants, and minerals to care for their bodies and to make them look fresh, radiant, bright, and beautiful. Some examples include *àdín* or *àdín-àgbọn*, which is used as body and hair lotion, and *òrí*, which is used as body cream. *Osùn* is for brightening the skin and *tìróò* for highlighting the eyelids. In recent times, *làálì*, believed to be of Islamic influence from the north, is used for creating decorative patterns on the hands and legs.

Body adornment and the use of cosmetics are in some cases connected with rites of passage or used to attract magical or ritual connotations. However, the most common reasons for body adornment are generally beautification, status enhancement, and identity.

See also **Beadwork; Circumcision and Facial Scarification**

REFERENCES

Dáramólá, Olú, and Adébáyò Jéjé. *Àwọn Àṣà àti Òrìṣà Ilẹ̀ Yorùbá.* Ìbàdàn (Nigeria): Oníbọn-Òjé, 1975.

Fádípè, N. A. *The Sociology of the Yorùbá.* Ìbàdàn (Nigeria): University Press, 1970.

Babáṣèhìndé A. Adémúlèyá

BODY AND LANGUAGE IDIOMS

In the Yorùbá language many parts of the body are often used to describe psychological or emotional situations. Whereas the eyes, in conjunction with the adjoining facial tissue, can tell so many stories and expose our well-being to the world, other parts of the body similarly convey messages of importance. A person is said to "talk to his or her legs" (*bésè sòrò*) if he wants to depart an unpleasant situation, or to "speak to his or her stomach" (*bánúsọ*) when an issue comes to a head and someone has to take a decision. A difficult problem is said to be "convoluted to the eyes" (*díjú*). If a person is contemplating whether or not to involve himself in such an issue—particularly one that is of no immediate benefit or is even dangerous—he is said to be "poking out" (*yọjú sọ́rọ̀* or *yọnu sọ́rọ̀ tí kò kàn án*) into a business that does not concern him. "Putting one's eyes and ears down to the ground" (*fojúsílè, fetísílè*) means that one is paying utmost attention to an issue of debate, and "making sure that one stirs the brain and stomach" (*rorí, ronú*) means that one is giving that issue a full measure of contemplation. Tables B.1 through B.10 show some of the words derived by referencing various parts of the body that are used to express emotions that are otherwise not easily described.

See also **Proverbs**

REFERENCES

Abraham, R. C. *Dictionary of Modern Yorùbá.* London: University Press, 1958.

Fábùnmi, M. A. *Yorùbá Idioms.* Ìbàdàn (Nigeria): African University Press, 1969.

Julius Fákínlèdé

Table B.1 Words derived from *ojú* (eye/face)

Minor stem	Major stem	Auxiliary stem	Yorùbá word	English equivalent
Bá	ojú	mu	Bójúmu	To be appropriate
Bá	ojú	jọ	Bójú jọ	To be pleasing to the eyes
Bẹ́	ojú		Béjú	To be a impertinent
Bà...	ojú	...jẹ́	Bojújẹ́	To become sad
Dá	ojú		Dájú	To be cockeyed
Dá	ojú		Dájú	To be certain
De	ojú		Dẹjú	To be expecting (someone)
Dẹ̀	ojú		Dẹjú	To be foolish
Di	ojú		Dijú	To close the eyes; to be unconcerned
Dí	ojú		Díjú	To be confusing
Dá	ojú		Dójú	To have a mark
Dá	ojú		Dojú	To get to the point or issue
Fà	ojú	ro	Fajúro	To frown
Fà	ojú	mọ́ra	Fajúmọ́ra	To be consoled
Fẹ̀	ojú		Fejú	To open the eyes wide
Fí	ojú		Fíjú	To be lazy, to see things as difficult
Fín	ojú		Fínjú	To be clairvoant
Fò	ojú	fò	Fojúfò	To forget about something
Wẹ̀	ojú		Wejú	To use native means to see the future or somewhere
Fi	ojú	inú	Fojú inú (wo nǹkan)	To be introspective
Fún	ojú	pọ̀	Fúnjú pọ̀	To frown
Gún	ojú		Gúnjú	To be symmetrical
Gbá...	ojú	...mọ̀	Gbajúmọ̀	To be famous
Igba	ojú	mọ́	Gbájúmọ́	To mind one's business fully
Gbó	ojú		Gbójú	To be intrepid
Gbọ́n	ojú		Gbọ́njú	To become an adult
Jọ	ojú		Jojú	To be adequate
Kán	ojú		Kánjú	To be in a hurry
Kẹ	ojú		Kejú	To pretend to be angry
Kọ	ojú	(si)	Kojú sí	To pay attention to (something)
Kú	ojú		Kújú	To become dull (as in a knife); to become dull
Kún	ojú	(iwọ̀n)	Kúnjú ìwọ̀n	To be up to a task
Là	ojú		Lajú	To become civilized
Lu	ojú		Lujú	To become pierced
Mọ̀	ojú		Mojú	To become familiar (as a dog with its owner)
Mọ́	ojú		Mọ́jú (mọ́ ènìyàn lójú)	To show some kind of disrespect
Mọ́	ojú		Mọ́jú	To last till morning
Na	ojú		Najú	To take a stroll
Nù	ojú		Nujú	To stop (crying)
Pa...	ojú	...de	Pojúdé (Pajúdé)	To die
Pa...	ojú	...pọ̀	Pojúpọ̀	To close one's eyes; to become tumid
Pa...	ojú	...kú	Pojúkú	To become stale
Pé	ojú	(iwọ̀n)	Péjú (ìwọ̀n)	To be appropriate
Pọ́n	ojú		Pọ́njú	To be very poor or inprovident
Rá	ojú		Rájú	To become blind
Ran	ojú		Ranjú	To open the eyes wide
Rẹ̀	ojú		Rejú	To take a siesta
Rí	ojú		Rójú	To have time
Ro	ojú		Rojú	To be unwilling (to perform a task; to be lazy
Rọ́	ojú		Rójú	To have perseverance
Rú	ojú		Rújú	To confuse someone
Rún	ojú	pọ̀	Rúnjú (pọ̀)	To frown
Ṣí iwá	ojú		Ṣáájú (Ṣíwájú)	To lead, to be in front
Ṣẹ́	ojú		Ṣéjú	To blink
Ṣí	ojú		Ṣijú (kúrò)	To take one's mind off (something)

(continued)

Table B.1 (continued)

Minor stem	Major stem	Auxiliary stem	Yorùbá word	English equivalent
Şe	ojú	sí (ènìyàn)	Şojú (si)	To make a pass at (someone)
Şọ	ojú	(nù)	Şojú (nù)	To keep one's eyes off others business
Şọ́n	ojú		Şọ́njú	To be mean
Tẹ́	ojú		Tẹ́jú	To be plain
Tì	ojú		Tijú	To be shy
Tọ́	ojú		Tọ́jú	To take care of (someone)
Tú . . .	ojú	. . . ká	Tújúka	To become consoled
Wá . . .	ojú	. . . rere	Wójú rere	To look for another's goodwill
Wẹ̀	ojú		Wẹjú	To be clairvoyant
Wò	ojú		Wojú	To be dependent on (someone)
Yá	ojú		Yájú	To be rude (to an older person)
Yí	ojú	(padà)	Yíjú padà	To turn around
Yọ	ojú	(sí)	Yojú sí	To interfere in (another's business); to make a courtesy call

Table B.2 Words derived from *ara* (body)

Minor stem	Major stem	Auxiliary stem	Yorùbá word	English equivalent
Bú	ara		Búra	To swear
Dẹ̀	ara		Dẹra	To be easy
Di	ara		Dira	To be prepared; to be armed
Fi . . .	ara	. . . hàn	Fara hàn	To present oneself
Fẹ́ . . .	ara	. . . kù	Fẹ́ra kù	To be pregnant
Fu	ara		Fura	To be circumspect
Gi	ara		Gira	To do (something) with much difficulty
Gbá . . .	ara	. . . dì	Gbára dì	To be prepared; to be armed
Gbó	ara		Gbóra	To be strong
Kin	ara		Kínra	To be near each other
Kú	ara		Kúra	To be impotent
La	ara		Ìlara	To be jealous
Mì	ara		Mira	To show sign of life
Mọ	ara		Mọra	To have self respect
Mú	ara		Múra	To be prepared (for a journey)
Na	ara		Nara	To relax, To take a siesta
Ni	ara		Nira	To be difficult
Pa	ara		Para	To use body lotion after bathing
Ré	ara		Réra	To preen (oneself)
Rẹ . . .	ara	. . . sílẹ̀	Rẹra (sílẹ̀)	To humble (oneself)
Rí	ara		Ríra	To be irritable
Sé	ara		Séra	To show lack of congruence
Sẹ́	ara		Sẹ́ra	To be self-denying; to discipline oneself
San	ara		Sanra	To become corpulent
Sún . . .	ara	. . . kì	Súnra (ki)	To be circumspect
Şí	ara		Şíra	To make haste
Şọ́	ara		Şọ́ra	To be careful
Ta	ara		Tara	To show emotion
Ti . . .	ara	. . . ka	Tiraka	To make an attempt
Wé	ara		Fiwéra	To compare things
Yá	ara		Yára	To be quick
Yé	ara		Yéra	To have mutual understanding

Table B.3 Words derived from *orí* (head)

Minor stem	Major stem	Auxiliary stem	Yorùbá word	English equivalent
Bá	orí	sòrò	Bórísòrò	To propitiate one's maker
Bá	orí	pèrò	Bóripèrò	To promise oneself
Bẹ̀	orí		Bẹrí	To ask for favors form ones head (maker)
Bẹ́	orí		Bẹ́rí	To decapitate
Bi	orí		Bi orí	To question one's maker
Bo	orí		Borí (òtá)	To conquer one's enemies
Bọ	orí		Bọrí	To offer sacrifices to one's head
Bo	orí		Borí	To cover one's head
Bó	orí		Bórí	To shave one's head
Dé	orí		Dérí	To cover with a lid
Di	orí		Dirí	To make a hairdo (a woman)
Da (di)	orí		Dorí	To get to a particular issue
Dù	orí		Durí	To struggle (to stay alive)
Fá	orí		Fárí	To scrape a head
Gùn	orí		Gorí	To climb (a mountain, a tree) to the top
Gbà	orí	kojá	Gborí (kojá)	To pass over the top of
Gbé	orí		Gbérí	To show signs of success amongst one's peers; to show signs of aliveness
Gba	orí	lọ́wọ́	Gborí (lọ́wọ́)	To defeat (others); to become
Gbọ̀n	orí		Gbọnrí	To shake heads (in disagreement)
Já	orí		Járí	To cut off the head of (a plant)
Jù	orí		Jurí	To fling one's head
Kì	orí		Ki orí	To offer praises to one's head (make)
Kó . . .	orí	. . . jọ	Kórí (jọ)	To come together (for deliberation)
Kú	orí		Kúrí	To be a bloke
Lé	orí		Lérí	To boast
Ní (to)	orí		Lórí (torí)	As a consequence of

Table B.3 (*continued*)

Minor stem	Major stem	Auxiliary stem	Yorùbá word	English equivalent
Ní . . .	orí	. . . ire	Lórí (ire)	*Lóríire*: to be lucky; *lórí-burúkú*: be unlucky
Mì	orí		Mirí	To shake the head probably as a sign of agreement
Pá	orí		Párí	To be bald
Pè	orí		Perí	To mention someone's name (for good or bad)
Ran	orí		Ranrí	To become obstinate
Rò	orí		Rorí	To think
Rọ́	orí		Rọ́rí (ọkọ̀)	To turn back
Sà	orí		Sarí	To propitiate one's head
Ṣọ́	orí		Ṣọ́rí	To be on guard
Tẹ̀ . . .	orí	. . . ba	Tẹrí (ba)	To become subservient
Ti	orí		Torí	Because of
Wẹ̀	orí		Wẹrí	To make sacrifices for good luck
Wú	orí		Wúrí	To impress exceedingly
Ya	orí		Yárí	To be enthusiastic
Ya	orí		Yarí	To refuse (to do something)
Yẹ	orí		Yẹrí	To refuse to take responsibility for (something)

Table B.4 Words derived from *ọrùn* (neck)

Minor stem	Major stem	Auxiliary stem	Yorùbá word	English equivalent
Dẹ̀	ọrùn		Dẹrùn	To be tolerable
Rọ̀	ọrùn		Rọrùn	To be easy
Wà . . .	ọrùn	. . . kì	Warùnkì	To be impertinent

Table B.5 Words derived from *inú* (stomach)

Minor stem	Major stem	Auxiliary stem	Yorùbá word	English equivalent
Bá . . .	inú	. . . sọ	Bánúsọ	To keep one's secrets to oneself
Bí	inú		Bínú	To get angry
Dà	inú		Danú	To be stupid
Dí	inú		Dínú	To be moody
Dùn	inú		Dunnú	To be happy
Fọ́	inú		Fọ́nú	To be stupid
Gbun	inú		Gbunnú	To be oblong inside
Hó	inú		Hónú	To be really angry
Jìn	inú		Jinnú	To be moody
Mọ̀	inú		Mọnú	To know another's thoughts
Ní	inú		Nínú	To be deep; to be perceptive
Pò	inú		Ponú	To be stupid
Rí	inú		Rínú	To know the secret behind (some issue)
Rò	inú		Ronú	To think; to be sorrowful
Ru	inú		Runú	To become angry
Ṣọ́	inú		Ṣọ́nú	To have tendency for animosity
Ṣu	inú		Ṣunú	To have diarrhea
Tù	inú		Tunú	To have calming effects
Yọ́	inú		Yọ́nú	To become appeased

Table B.6 Words derived from *etí* (ear)

Minor stem	Major stem	Auxiliary stem	Yorùbá word	English equivalent
Di	etí		Dití	To be deaf
Fà	etí		Fà létí	To warn
Fi . . .	etí	. . . sílẹ̀	Fetí (sílẹ̀)	To listen attentively
Là	etí		Latí	To listen attentively
Rán	etí		Rántí	To remember
Re	etí		Retí	To be looking forward to
Tẹ́ . . .	etí	. . . sìlẹ	Tẹ́tí	To listen attentively

Table B.7 Words derived from *ẹnu* (mouth)

Minor stem	Major stem	Auxiliary stem	Yorùbá word	English equivalent
Dì	ẹnu		Dinu	To be taciturn
Fọ́n	ẹnu		Fọ́nnu	To boast
Gbó	ẹnu		Gbónu	To be argumentative, to boast
Jì	ẹnu		Jinu	To move one's mouth as if to speak
Ká	ẹnu		Kánu	To be enough to share
Là	ẹnu		Lanu	To open one's mouth (in amazement)
Ní	ẹnu		Lẹnu	To have the audacity (to speak)
Yá	ẹnu		Yánu	To open one's mouth (when a miracle is performed); *ohun íyanu*: miracle, an act that makes a person instinctively open his mouth

Table B.8 Words derived from *imú* (nose)

Minor stem	Major stem	Auxiliary stem	Yorùbá word	English equivalent
Yín	imú	—	Yínmú	To make a sign of derision at another's fortune or plight

Table B.9 Words derived from *ẹsẹ̀* (leg)

Minor stem	Major stem	Auxiliary stem	Yorùbá word	English equivalent
Bá . . .	ẹsẹ̀	. . . sọ̀rọ̀	Bésẹ̀ (sọ̀rọ̀)	To quickly depart from an unpleasant scene
Fà	ẹsẹ̀		Fasẹ̀	To move slowly
Kì . . .	ẹsẹ̀	. . . sí	Kisẹ̀ sí	To involve oneself in an issue
Kó	ẹsẹ̀	. . . sí	Kó ẹsẹ̀ sí	To use one's influence in an issue
Lò	ẹsẹ̀		Lo ẹsẹ̀	To use improper means to achieve an objective
Ní	ẹsẹ̀		Lésẹ̀	To have influence
Nà	ẹsẹ̀		Nasẹ̀	To take a stroll
Ṣì . . .	ẹsẹ̀	. . . gbé	Ṣì ẹsẹ̀ gbé	To make a mistake
Ṣi	ẹsẹ̀		Ṣísẹ̀	To make an attempt
Ti . . .	ẹsẹ̀	. . . bọ̀	Tisẹ̀ bọ̀	To look for a way into (an issue)
Yọ	ẹsẹ̀		Yọsẹ̀	To stop being part of an issue

Table B.10 Words derived from ọwọ́ (arm/hand)

Minor stem	Major stem	Auxiliary stem	Yorùbá word	English equivalent
Dá…	ọwọ́	…dúró	Dáwọ́ dúró	To stop (for a while)
Dí	ọwọ́		Díwọ́	To be busy
Di	ọwọ́		Dọwọ́	To become an issue for something or someone
Fà…	ọwọ́	…sẹ́hìn	Fawọ́ sẹ́hin	To gradually reduce (one's involvement)
Fẹ́	ọwọ́		Fẹ́wọ́	To pilfer
Gbà	ọwọ́		Gbọwọ́	To bail (someone) out
Há	ọwọ́		Háwọ́	To be stingy
Já	ọwọ́		Jáwọ́ (nínú nǹkan)	To stop being part of (an issue)
Jẹ́	ọwọ́		Jẹ́wọ́	To confess
Kẹ́	ọwọ́		Kẹ́wọ́	Fi nǹkan kẹ́wọ́: to use as an excuse
Là	ọwọ́		Lawọ́	To be open handed; to be generous
Ní…	ọwọ́	…nínú	Lọ́wọ́ nínú	To be part (of an issue)
Mú…	ọwọ́	…kúrò	Mọ́wọ́ kuro	To stop being part (of an issue)
Nà	ọwọ́		Nawọ́	To stretch a hand of help
Pa…	ọwọ́	…dà	Pawọ́ dà	To be involved in petty business
Ra	ọwọ́		Rawọ́ (ẹ̀bẹ̀ sí)	To plead with (a higher authority)
Ṣí	ọwọ́		Ṣíwọ́	To end the day's task
Yá	ọwọ́		Yáwọ́	To be nimble handed
Yí	ọwọ́		Yíwọ́	To have unexpected result
Yọ	ọwọ́		Yọwọ́ (kuro nínú nǹkan)	To leave an issue alone

BOUNDARIES: COLONIAL AND MODERN

The thirty million Yorùbá-speaking people are found in southwestern Nigeria, southeastern Benin Republic, and north-central Republic of Togo. In the Diaspora, Yorùbá communities exist in the Caribbean and in Brazil, where their distinct cultural practices have survived. Traditionally, some authorities locate the earliest home of the Yorùbá around the confluence of the Niger and Benue rivers in modern-day Nigeria. The Yorùbá heartland encompasses the seven traditional kingdoms: central of Ifẹ̀; eastern in Ìjẹ̀sà country; southern of the Ọ̀wọ̀, Itsekiri, Àwórì, and others; western of the Ẹ̀gbá; northern of the Okun Yorùbá; and subgroups of the Ìgbómìnà occupy the northeast. Yorùbáland area is approximately 225 square kilometers; it crosses 550 kilometers from the Atlantic Ocean to the south and the river Niger in the north. To the northwest, Yorùbáland extends across the Benin Republic into north-central Togo. The main neighbors of the Yorùbá are the Edo, Igbo, Ebira, and Igala to the east; the Nupe and Bariba to the north; and the Fon, Mahi, Egun, and other Ewe-speaking groups to the west. The Yorùbá share borders with the Borgu in Benin; the Nupe and Ebira in central Nigeria; and the Edo, Esan, and Afemai in midwestern Nigeria. The Igala and other related groups are found in north-central Nigeria, and the Egun, Fon, and others in southeastern Benin. Significant Yorùbá populations can be found in the north of Togo.

The traditional land area of the Yorùbá in Nigeria has been affected by the politics of British colonial era. The British extended the borders of northern Nigeria south of the river Niger. To the north, the British also consolidated control of Ìlọrin, a central Yorùbá town that was occupied by jihadists exploiting a feud between rival Yorùbá forces in the city. The situation has been compounded by successive northern-dominated military regimes that continued to gerrymander the traditional borders of the Yorùbá. Accordingly, many Yorùbá peoples have become minorities in the modern-day northern Nigerian states of Edo, Kogi, and Kwara.

As a result of all the political restructuring, in 1914 the British combined the Northern and Southern protectorates that they had created in 1900 to form Nigeria. Three culturally diverse regions were established in the north, west, and east in 1939; they were made fully autonomous units of a federation under the Richards Constitution of 1954. This federation eventually led to the creation of states in 1967, 1976, and 1991. However, these political boundaries have not satisfied the yearning or aspirations of the Yorùbá. The border manipulations have left the Yorùbá of Ogori Mangogo in Kogi state at a disadvantage. They occupy a small enclave between the Ebira and the Igala that is not contiguous with their Yorùbá brothers of Okun land.

See also **Colonial Policies and Practices; Demography: Social Characteristics; Frontier Zone; Geography and Environment; Subgroups**

REFERENCES

Akíntóyè, Adébánjí. *A History of the Yorùbá.* Dakar: Amalion Publishing Company, 2010.
Eades, J. S. *The Yorùbá Today.* Cambridge: Cambridge University Press, 1980.

Adémọ́lá Àràoyè

BURIAL AND FUNERAL

Among the Yorùbá, life does not end with death but continues in another realm. As soon as an elderly person is declared dead, his or her corpse is washed and laid out for viewing. Women of the household begin to sing funeral dirges in praise of the deceased and throughout the period of the burial ceremony. Burial rites are of great importance to the people, who believe that anyone who dies must be given a proper traditional funeral according to his or her status. If not, the dead person may become a wandering ghost, unable to live properly after death. It is also believed that giving the dead a proper burial rite helps to protect the living.

The grave is dug in the compound, sometimes in the room where the deceased lived. Burials are performed by the adult men in the family and the in-laws. After the interment (*ìsìnkú*) there is a period of feast-ing. The burial rites on the third day (*ìta òkú*), seventh day (*ìje òkú*), and fortieth day (*ogójì ọjọ́*) are very important among the Yorùbá people.

There are two types of burial or funeral rite. The first is for those who died painful death, little children, or those who died in mysterious ways, such as through suicide, auto accident, and drowning. The second is for those who lived a longer life and died at their old age, leaving behind children, grandchildren, and great-grandchildren.

The impoverished traditionally were wrapped with their clothes and buried in the grave without any ceremony. Slaves and visitors were buried in the courtyards of their owners, and the corpse of a leper, hunchback, or a person with mental illness was carried to the forest for burial so as to avert such death in the future. To the Yorùbá people, the death of a pregnant woman is a bad premonition. It is the duty of members of the *orò* cult of the concerned village to remove the fetus in the woman's womb before burying her. The widower of the dead pregnant woman then supplies the *orò* cult members a goat, a sheep, a keg of palm oil, and other things for sacrifice, to prevent a recurrence of such death in the community.

Yorùbá tradition celebrates the death of those who lived to old age, and this requires a huge financial commitment of the deceased immediate and extended family members. In precolonial times, they buried such people in one of the rooms within the person's building or home, but things have changed nowadays as corpses are buried in the family cemetery, in front of the house or in a public cemetery.

In recent times, conducting funerals for the dead requires huge financial resources: from the mortuary or morgue to an expensive coffin and burial space in a public cemetery, and organizing a befitting burial ceremony—modernization has influenced everything. Yorùbá burial rites have assumed new forms nowadays because of modernity and the introduction of Christianity and Islam into society. For instance, Christians now observe a service of songs or wake keep program just as it was obtainable in the olden days when the family women keep vigil, singing different types of songs and chanting family praise poetry (*ògbérè*) in honor of the deceased.

Another influence brought by modernization is the introduction of corpse carriers (*agbókùú*), popularly known as undertakers, who are dressed in native attires and display dexterity and dancing steps with the coffin. This really beautifies the funeral program, as popular musicians or entertainers are invited by family members of the deceased to perform at the funeral. The family members of the dead are also dressed in *aṣọ ẹbí* (a sort of party uniform commonly used by the people) to add color to the burial program and to bid farewell to the deceased. Guests are later entertained with food and drink, as well as souvenirs.

Gone are the days of the Yorùbá traditional mourning when a youngster or youth died; today, when a youth dies, he or she is given a befitting burial like an elderly person. The use of the media, newspaper, radio, and television to advertise and announce the burial program of events in honor of dead parents also colors the way the Yorùbá conduct burials and funerals in modern times.

See also **Death, Mourning, and Ancestors; Memorial Arts; Reincarnation**

REFERENCES

Dáramọ́lá, Olú, and Adébáyọ̀ Jéjé. *Àwọn Àṣà àti Òrìṣà Ilẹ̀ Yorùba*. Ìbàdàn (Nigeria): Oníbọn-Òjé, 1975.

Fádípẹ̀, N. A. *The Sociology of the Yorùbá*. Ìbàdàn (Nigeria): University Press, 1970.

Johnson Samuel. *The History of the Yorùbá*. Lagos (Nigeria): C.S.S. Bookstore, 1921.

Adékẹ́mi Adégún Táíwò

C

CARTOONS

Cartoon, a branch of satire, is a twentieth-century phenomenon in Yorùbáland. The genre has yet to gain a firm foothold in cultural and educational programs of the society. Akínwùmí Ìṣọ̀lá, playwright, actor, dramatist, and culture activist, has advocated creating cartoons of Yorùbá folktales so that the culture and language can endure and be passed on to younger generations.

Unlike cartoons, satire has a long history in the Yorùbá society. The people have a rich tradition of satire in verbal and physical performances associated with sacred and secular ceremonies. Satire was mainly performative but highly instructive. Notable examples of the verbal, visual, and performance arts in satire culture include the *alápáńsáńpá* masquerade tradition of the Ìbàdàn and the *èfè* or *gèlèdé* of the southwestern Yorùbá people, including the Kétu, Ìmẹ̀kọ, and Ẹ̀gbádò and the Yorùbá in the Republic of Benin. In the precolonial and colonial eras, such satirical performances were the main outlets through which society released tension, entertained itself, conveyed its disapproval of human misconduct, and instilled social etiquette.

With the development of printing technology and other media, other ways of engaging the public in satirical commentaries evolved, including the introduction of cartoons into newspapers, skits, and television programs, and animated cartoons on the Internet. Early newspaper publications were produced in English,

so Yorùbá cartoonists wrote in English. Among those early cartoonists were Akinọlá Láṣebìkan, a notable Nigerian artist who worked with *West African Pilot* in the colonial era; Ayọ̀ Àjàyí, who drew the *Tortoise Adventures* series for the weekly *Daily Times*; and Josy Ajíbóyè, the master of romantic subject matter typified in his pocket cartoon *Josy Ajíbóyè on Sunday* for the *Sunday Times*. Ajíbóyè also drew cartoons for the *Morning Post*. In addition, délé jẹ́gẹ́dẹ́ gained a reputation as a master of satire during the era of military dictatorship and police recklessness in Nigeria in the 1980s and 1990s.

The next generation of cartoonists of Yorùbá origin include Wọlé Lágúnjú, Bísí Ògúnbádéjọ, and Bóyè Gbénró, who drew for the *National Concord* newspapers from the 1970s to 1980s. Others include Dòtun Gbóyèga, Ọmọ Ọba, Lékè Moses, Káyòdé Tẹjúmọ́lá, Akínwálé Onípẹ̀dé, Sẹ̀indé Òbe "Obe Ess" Táyọ̀ Fátulà, Múyíwá Collins, and Yẹmí Adáramọ́dù of the *Nigerian Tribune*.

Female cartoonists include Fọláṣadé Adébáre and Adérónkẹ́ Adésànyà. Adésànyà made cartoons for a number of newspapers, specifically the *Nigerian Tribune*, *Daily Sketch*, and *Classique Magazine*. Adésànyà's longest stint was with *Vanguard Newspapers* from 1990 to the late 2000s. She sketched the *Virginia Series*, a tongue-in-cheek "freestyle" cartoon strip that centered on the life experiences and escapades of Virginia, a fictional woman living in the city. Virginia's lifestyle, experiences, and encounters reflected the reality of the lives of working-class women in a cosmopolitan city and their struggles with traditional and modern institutions.

Today, there are many newspapers published in Yorùbá, such as *Ìwé Ìròhìn* published by African Newspapers, *Gboùngboùn* published by Sketch Press, and *Aláròyé* published by World Information Agents. However, these newspapers and others have not encouraged the proliferation of cartoons in the Yorùbá language. Stories adapted from Yorùbá folklore are now available in comic form on the Internet. The trickster tales known as *ìjàpá ọlógbón ẹ̀wẹ́* and other traditional folklore appear online in the form of animated cartoons narrated in Yorùbá with English subtitles.

See also **Media: Comic Art; Media: Newsprint**

REFERENCES

Lent, John A. *Comic Art in Africa, Asia, Australia, and Latin America through 2000: An International Bibliography.* Westport, CT: Praeger Publishers, 2004.
——. "Out of Obscurity: African Cartoonists Make Pitch for Recognition." *Comics Journal* (February 2001): 16–17.

Adérónké Adéṣọlá Adésànyà

CARVERS

Ọmọ Agbọ́mátìí Ọ̀jẹ̀;
Òfùpà pagidà ó dènìyàn.
Ẹrú Ọ̀jẹ̀ ti gbẹ́nà pegbèje,
Ìwọ̀fà Ọ̀jẹ̀ ti gbẹ́nà pẹgbẹ̀fà,
Ọmọ bíbí Ọ̀jẹ̀ ti gbẹ́nà pẹgbẹ̀ẹ́dógún.

Descendant of Agbọ́mátìí, an Egúngún lineage member;
He transformed wood into human beings.
The slaves of Ọ̀jẹ̀ had carved designs and earned 1,400 cowries,
The Ọ̀jẹ̀'s indentured servants had carved designs and made 1,200 cowries,
Ọ̀jẹ̀'s own children had carved designs and received 30,000 cowries.

In the *oríkì* (praise poem) of Ọ̀jẹ̀ titled "Carvers," an Egúngún lineage member testifies that *gbẹ́nàgbẹ́nà* (carvers of designs) existed among the affluent and prestigious class in traditional Yorùbá society. The *oríkì* also affirms Agbọ́mátìí as both a renowned carver and cult member of Egúngún. Thus, Yorùbá ancestral spirits establish the interconnectedness of the Egúngún and the carvers' guild. Another version of the *oríkì* of Ọ̀jẹ̀ reveals the interconnection: Agbọ́mátìí carved archer figures for the Aláàfin Òfinràn, the eldest son of Aláàfin Onígbogí. The sculptures looked exactly like real archers. Impressed by the verisimilitude of the sculptures, the Aláàfin Òfinràn bestowed on Agbọ́mátìí the title of Ọlọ́jẹ̀ẹ́, high chief of Egúngún society.

The Yorùbá word for carver is *gbẹ́nàgbẹ́nà* (carver of designs) or *oníṣẹ́-ọnà* (one whose profession is to design). Thus, these terms are generic words that describe any artists who carve *ọnà* (designs). Examples include *agbẹ̀kùúta* (stone carvers), *agbéyín-erin* (ivory carvers), and *agbẹ́gilére* (wood carvers). In addition to the common iron tools they use to carve their respective media, be it stone, ivory, or wood, all *gbẹ́nàgbẹ́nà* (carvers) use subtractive method, a carving technique in which all the unneeded portions of the carving medium are chipped or carved away to leave behind the artist's desired sculptural form.

With the exception of ivory carvers, who use four stages in their carving process, *gbẹ́nàgbẹ́nà* typically use five stages. The first, which ivory carvers do not use, is *sísá*, in which the rough form or block is cut out from the carving medium with adzes. The second stage is *ọnà lílé*, in which the carver cuts out or defines the form of the sculpture with adzes and chisels. The third stage is *àlétúnlé*, which entails shaping the main forms and breaking them down into smaller, precise masses. For example, if carving a human face, the carver would form the eyes, mouth, ears, nose, and chin, and then use *abẹ ìdángi*, knives for smoothing the wood. The fourth stage is *dídán*, which involves putting the finishing touches on the entire sculpture and making sure all of the figure's parts are well delineated. Carvers also use the *abẹ ìdángi* in this stage. The last phase is *fínfín*, which includes cutting sharp, detailed design patterns on the sculpture, such as the eyelids, hair, facial scarifications, and the tip or cap of the penis for male figures or clitoris for female figures using *ọ̀bẹ-ọnà* (knives for making design patterns).

Unlike *agbẹ́gilére*, both the *agbẹ̀kùúta* and the *agbéyín-erin* are rarities in Yorùbá traditional society today. Stones are very difficult to carve, and few patrons commission or buy stone carvings. The elephants whose tusks are used for carving have become extinct in the once heavily forested region of Ọ̀wọ̀, where they once roamed. Deforestation for farmland and overhunting led to their extinction in the area. Cory Micots notes that hunters were required to send one of the tusks from each elephant killed to the Ọlọ́wọ̀, king of Ọ̀wọ̀; the hunter could keep the other.

Stone carvings are now found mainly in museums. Examples include the stone figure of ìdènà (watchman) housed at the Ifẹ̀ Museum in Ilé-Ifẹ̀ and the Èsìẹ́ stone sculptures presently at Èsìẹ́ Museum in Kwara State. A few examples can also be found in their original contexts where they are still ritualized, such as the Èṣù stone figure in Ìgbájọ and the Esúrẹ́ stone sculptures in Esúrẹ́-Èkìtì. As for ivory carvings, examples like ìrọ́kẹ́-ifá (ivory divination tappers used by Ifá diviners), ẹgbà-ọwọ́ (ivory ornamental bands worn by the wives of the Ọlọ́wọ̀ on their wrists or arms), and àgéré-ifá (ivory divination vessels used by the Ifá diviners) are found only at Ọ̀wọ̀ Museum and in some museums in Europe and America. Other examples, such as the Udamolore (ivory ceremonial swords usually carried by the Ọlọ́wọ̀), are seen only during important festivals, such as the annual Ọ̀wọ̀ festival of Igógo.

By contrast, Yorùbá traditional wood carvers have continued to make good money, deriving a living from their work to the present day. The main reason is that their carvings, such as the ère (masks), are indispensable parts of traditional costumes. The Egúngún, Ẹpa, and Gẹ̀lẹ̀dẹ́ masking traditions ensure high demand by members of these traditional religious groups. Similarly, art collectors throughout Europe and the Americas continue to buy Yorùbá traditional wood carvings.

See also **Art: Indigenous; Art: Contemporary; Lineages and Cognomen (Oríkì Orílẹ̀); Museums**

REFERENCES

Fákẹ́yẹ, Làmídì Ọlọ́nàdé, and Bruce M. Haight, with David H. Curl. Làmídì Ọlọ́nàdé Fákẹ́yẹ: A Retrospective Exhibition and Autobiography. Kalamazoo, MI: Oak Woods Media, 1996.

Micots, Cory. "Warrior Chiefs and Composite Animals: An Ivory Bracelet Attributed to Ọ̀wọ̀, Nigeria." Bulletin of the Detroit Institute of Arts 68.3 (1994): 16–25.

Ọláwọlé Fámulẹ̀

CERAMICS AND POTTERY

Among the Yorùbá, women traditionally exclusively specialized in pottery, while both men and women practiced ceramics. The subtle difference between pottery and ceramics comes from the finish of the product, the methods and materials employed, and the particular period when the item was produced. Pottery includes utensils, vessels, or sculptures made from clay and fired to a high temperature. Traditional pottery is porous. When pottery is coated with a particular glaze before being fired, it becomes translucent porcelain, widely known as porcelain.

A distinguishing characteristic of Yorùbá pottery is coiling. This method entails building the pottery from the bottom up using flat slabs or rolled coils of locally obtained clay (amọ̀). The coils are then kneaded and shaped into the desired form. Techniques for making pottery vary, and they depend on the size and complexity of the desired vessel. The potter may employ additive and subtractive techniques, either building up or taking away, or both. Some potters use an upturned container as a template and then build up their pots by hand. The potter faces a particular challenge when building large vessels. She walks around the stationary vessel and kneads, scrapes, and smooths the clay while circling it. Once finished but while still relatively damp, the pottery is adorned with a variety of designs. Simple instruments, such as the teeth of wooden combs or corncobs, are used to apply designs. The tactile nature of the design confers an aesthetic character to the pottery, allows for a firm grip, and serves as the potter's creative signature.

Firing finished vessels is a collective enterprise undertaken in an open space. The items are carefully arranged in a huge, circular pyre in a way that permits the circulation of air during the firing. Once they are fired to the desired temperature, at least 1,500 degrees

Fahrenheit, the items are removed with long, Y-shaped sticks before they cool off. The potter then applies the desired liquid finish at this stage; the finish bonds with the pottery and gives it its luster. The bulk of pottery items produced serve utilitarian purposes: cooking, storing, and serving. A body of items, such as containers, is created specifically for religious or sacred purposes. Such containers are often embellished with iconic and symbolic elements in high or low relief. Freestanding, three-dimensional, realistic images and abstract configurations in terra-cotta from as early as the eleventh century CE have been excavated in Ilé-Ifẹ̀.

The establishment of formal art institutions in Nigeria, which began a few years before Nigerian independence in 1960, introduced equipment and techniques that democratized the process and gave students, male and female, the opportunity to practice ceramics. The potter's wheel became standard professional equipment, as did electric kilns and assortments of glazes that could be mixed by individuals, customized, and applied to pottery after the initial bisque firing. The establishment of ceramics as a branch of specialization in art institutions spurred innovation and led to the creation of a plethora of works that have been recognized as high art.

REFERENCES

Fádípẹ̀, N. A. *The Sociology of the Yorùbá.* Ìbàdàn (Nigeria): University Press, 1970.

Lawal, Babátúndé. *Embodying the Sacred in Yorùbá Art: Featuring the Bernard and Patricia Wagner Collection.* Atlanta: High Museum of Art; Newark, NJ: Newark Museum, 2007.

délé jẹ́gẹ́dẹ́

CEREMONIAL SONGS

Ceremonial songs (*orin ayẹyẹ*) are an important subgroup of festival songs. Other types of songs include religious songs (*orin ajẹmẹ́sìn*), children's songs (*orin ọmọdé*), war songs (*orin ogun*), work-reinforcement songs (*orin amúṣẹ́yá*), folktale songs (*orin àlọ́*), proverbial songs (*orin òwe*) and invective songs (*orin èébú*). In Yorùbá tradition, almost no ceremony occurs without a corresponding song attached to it. Different rites of passage are marked with songs and dancing. Singing songs during important ceremonies is a way of life and has become an undying cultural legacy of the people. Songs are joyfully rendered at ceremonies such as marriage (*ìgbéyàwó*), the naming of a newborn child (*ìsọmọlórúkọ*), the freedom ceremony for completion of apprenticeship or education (*ìyọ̀nda lẹ́nu iṣẹ́*), housewarming (*ìṣílé*), anniversaries, thanksgiving, birthday parties, purchase of cars (*ìdúpẹ́*), funeral (*ìsìnkú*), remembrance of departed souls (*ìjáde òkú*), and chieftaincy ceremony (*ìwúyè*), among many others. The Yorùbá people, like other African communities, believe that ceremonial songs have a therapeutic effect on singers and can relieve tension if they are positively used.

Ceremonial songs are intended to explain and teach about all aspects of life. The ecstatic joy attached to ceremonial songs not only celebrates life but also shows love to celebrants as they rejoice together. Thus, there are joyful and sorrowful songs depending on the situation. The song sung at the funeral of an elderly person is called *orin Ùjàamẹ̀sẹ̀* in Èkìtì and *ìgbálá* in Ẹ̀gbá. Such songs are full of words that can make hearers burst into tears of joy. At a naming ceremony, the songs are filled with praises, joyful felicitations, advice for the mother of the newly born child, and prayers for expectant mothers. Songs rendered at *ìwúyè* (chieftancy ceremony) remind people of their past heroes and heroines and prepare the new leaders and the community to realize their collective aspirations and to experience peace together. Such songs are used to heal wounds and resolve conflicts. At a marriage ceremony, *orin ìgbéyàwó* (nuptial songs) create an atmosphere conducive for social interaction, unity, and oneness that make people experience togetherness, love, and peace and renew friendships. *Ẹkún ìyàwó* (another kind of nuptial song) is an a cappella song; it has no instrument accompaniment. Nuptial songs express the joy of marriage; the hopes and aspirations of the bride; appreciation to friends, relatives, and parents; and the sadness of the bride's separation from her parents. People share their feelings and encourage themselves through songs.

The communal nature of ceremonial songs encourages singers to adapt themselves and their performance to each ceremony. Ceremonial songs may be accompanied by instruments, improvisation, movement, and dancing. In fact, some songs derive their names from the instruments used by the singers. For instance, *orin dùndún*, *orin ṣẹ̀kẹ̀rẹ̀*, *orin àgídìgbo*, *orin agbè*, *orin sákárà*, and *orin ọ̀gbẹ̀lẹ̀* are songs that use *dùndún*, *ṣẹ̀kẹ̀rẹ̀*, *àgídìgbo*, *agbè*, *sákárà*, and *ọ̀gbẹ̀lẹ̀* as musical instruments, respectively.

Each Yorùbá subgroup has its own ceremonial songs, and such songs are performed during different social occasions, such as *orin àpíìrì* (Èkìtì); *dadakúàdà*, *bàlúù*, and *wéré* (Ìlọrin); *orin agbè* (Ìgbómìnà); *orin obitun* (Oǹdó); *orin apẹ́pẹ́* (Ìjẹ̀bú); *sákárà* and *ìgbálá* (Ẹ̀gbá); *bírípo* (Ìkálẹ̀ or Ìlàjẹ); and *ẹkún ìyàwó* (Ọ̀yọ́). These songs belong to the community; they are community property. No individual singer owns the copyright. In ceremonies where such songs are performed, the audience is an equal participant. While the lead singer leads in the singing, the audience sings the chorus. The audience serves as critic and participant at the same time. All members of the community learn ceremonial songs from childhood through participation, observation, and imitation.

In colonial and postcolonial Yorùbá society, individuals with creative ability began composing songs, forming bands, and creating new ceremonial songs. Singers and songwriters claimed the status of "originators" and "creators." Such songs include *àpàlà*, *fújì*, *wákà*, *jùjú*, and *àwúrèbe*, among others. Notable leaders among modern ceremonial singers include Alhaji Hárúnà Ìṣọlá and Alhaji Àyìnlá Ọmọwúrà (*àpàlà*), King Sunny Adé and Ebenezer Obey (*jùjú*), Alhaji Àyìndé Barrister and Kọ́láwọlé Àyìnlá Kollington (*fújì*), and Sàláwà Àbẹ̀ní and Bàtílì Àlàkẹ́ (*wákà*). The structure of the performance and content of such songs depend on economic gain. Singers produce records with profit in mind; the songs focus on the patrons' praise and use philosophical language.

See also **Insults and Ribald Language; Jokes and Humor; Literature: Oral; Music: Islamic; Music: Popular; Music:** **Traditional; Musical Instruments; Proverbs; Stories, Storytelling, and Storytellers; War Songs; Work Songs**

REFERENCES

Ọlátúnjí, O. Ọlátúndé. *Features of Yorùbá Oral Poetry*. Ìbàdàn (Nigeria): University Press, 1984.

Olúkòjú, E. O. *The Study of Yorùbá Songs*. Ìbàdàn (Nigeria): University Press, 1994.

Lérè Adéyẹmí

CHARMS

Charms within Yorùbá religious and spiritual practices constitute a broad and diverse range of materials and practice. Virtually any physical material can be used or employed in charm making. Animal parts, including bone, ivory, skin, shells, and fur, as well as vegetation, including seeds, wood, leaves, and oils, are often used to construct charms. The purpose for which an individual charm is made varies as much as the list of ingredients used in its creation. Charms are often made to protect a person from physical and spiritual harm; to protect the vulnerable, such as children and the elderly; or to meet individual needs and desires, including fertility, marriage, cursing others, attracting wealth attraction, and so on. Often the charm is carried on the body, but it may be incised on the surface of the body through scarification or by rubbing prepared powders into incisions in the skin.

Belief in charms is particularly important among *òrìṣà* practitioners, whose practice incorporates both the preparation of myriad charms and the protection from the effects of charms. Babaláwo and Olóriṣà, priests of *òrìṣà*, are trained in fashioning and activating charms. Such charms take a variety of forms and are constructed for a range of purposes. Their prescription and construction are related, through divination, to ingredients contained in *odù ifá* verses. Charm construction is accompanied by ceremonies, prayers, chants, and—at times—sacrifices to activate and empower them. Pierre Verger states that some charms are antidotes and remedies (*ìdáàbòbò*) to witchcraft and spiritual attacks (*àbìlù*). Charms may also be ingested as preparations added to food, such as ẹ̀kọ. They are given to the person either knowingly or secretly to eat.

Àdlè are physical, symbolic objects that communicate àṣẹ in visible form and are placed in prominent locations to protect land, goods, and homes. Àdlè are made of various materials, such as chili peppers, broken shoes, pieces of broom, and other materials. The materials used signal the fate of the transgressor; they warn that distress, poverty, or destitution await the person who disregards àdlè.

See also **Communication: Nonverbal; Words: Ọ̀rọ̀**

REFERENCES

Doris, David Todd. *Vigilant Things: On Thieves, Yorùbá Anti-Aesthetics, and the Strange Fates of Ordinary Objects in Nigeria.* Seattle: University of Washington Press, 2011.
Verger, Pierre Fatunmbi. "Poisons (Oró) and Antidotes (Ẹ̀rọ̀): Evil Works (Àbìlù) and Protection from them (Ìdáàbòbò). Stimulants and Tranquilizers. Money—Wives—Children." In *Seminar Series Department of African Languages and Literature,* ed. Ọlásopé O. Oyèláràn, 298–353. Ifẹ̀-Ifẹ̀ (Nigeria): University of Ifẹ̀, 1976.

Martin A. Tsang

CHILDBIRTH AND CHILDBEARING

Childbirth or childbearing has both spiritual and physical dimensions. The spiritual dimension concerns warding off tragedies such as miscarriages or difficult or life-threatening births. For example, some Yorùbá subgroups, such as the Ọ̀yọ́, followed specific procedures for warding off miscarriage. Once conception had been determined, the expectant mother would tie up her menstrual cloths and store them in a secret location that only her mother or husband might know about, and this procedure was believed to form a spiritual deterrent against miscarriage. More positively, the spiritual dimension of childbirth could involve supplications to the goddess Ọ̀ṣun, who is also known as ọlọ́mọyọyọ (one with lots of children), to show benevolence toward individuals seeking to have children.

In advance of childbirth and immediately after, special drinks and foods were reserved for expectant or new mothers. Expectant mothers were given herbal infusions that were believed to cleanse impurities from the body as well as nourish the baby and strengthen the mother. Around the third month of the pregnancy, expectant mothers were also fed a specific soup that was believed to help with the well-being of the baby. The expectant mother would consume the same soup again a few days or a few weeks before her anticipated delivery date. Immediately after delivery, new mothers were fed steaming, pudding-textured foods like ògì, believed to aid in the production of breast milk. New mothers might also be fed àmàlà with ewédú stew, a meal believed to aid in digestion for both the mother and her newborn.

In cases of normal births, the physical process of birthing followed individual preference or comfort. Women were just as likely to lie on their backs as they were to squat on their knees to deliver their babies. Things were different in cases of difficult births that required the assistance of a traditional midwife or ìyá àbíyè, who generally attended the expectant mother from the time of conception until a little bit after delivery. The ìyá àbíyè, or sometimes a male herbalist called in for the specific purpose, might make incantations (ògèdè) that were believed to call the baby to be born in a normal fashion. These incantations were combined with manual manipulations to try to ensure a healthy delivery.

A survey conducted in 1991 by this writer found that even in cities with relatively accessible clinical health facilities, only about 40 percent of women used clinics or hospitals for their childbirth needs. This meant that, counting urban and rural or modern and traditional populations together, near the end of the twentieth century, the vast majority of Yorùbá women had home births and made use of folk knowledge of childbearing. Traditionally, umbilical cords were buried in the family compound, where they were believed to link the child to that particular community and lineage. Home births enabled mothers to more easily perform this key spiritual rite tied to the well-being of their children.

The Yorùbá place significant emphasis on procreation as a condition for social adulthood, community membership, the possibility of immortality, and other valued aspects of social life. Conversely, they strongly stigmatize childlessness as an indicator of physical disease or spiritual ill health; childlessness can result in social ostracism. Men traditionally maintained significant decision-making power in determining family size, although this norm underwent transformation as government policies in the 1980s preferred small family sizes of no more than four children to each woman. The government began providing medical contraceptive methods to limit family size. More and more couples negotiated family planning. Medical methods of contraception complemented folk methods such as breast-feeding, the withdrawal method, herbal abortifacients, and the use of amulets believed to restrict conception. Even with the transition from male-determined family size to negotiated family size, twenty-first-century Yorùbá women are held accountable for childlessness in marriages just as they were in traditional societies.

Childbirth and childbearing among the Yorùbá have undergone changes over the course of the twentieth century, some dramatic and some not. The physical process of childbearing and popular understandings of childlessness have maintained significant continuity with the past, while ideas about what constitutes the ideal number of children has changed, and some methods of controlling childbirth have broken with the past. However, under the growing influence of Christianity and Islam, the traditional Yorùbá spiritual dimensions of childbirth or childbearing have become less significant.

See also **Children and Childhood; Demography: Social Characteristics; Food: Cuisines and Preparation; Medical Practitioners; Medicine: Indigenous Therapeutic System**

REFERENCES

Adéoyè, Láògún C. *Àṣà àti Ìṣe Yorùbá.* Oxford: Oxford University Press, 1979.
Fádípè, N. A. *The Sociology of the Yorùbá.* Ìbàdàn (Nigeria): University Press, 1970.

Abọ́sèdé George

The child ọmọ is the axis around which the entire life of the Yorùbá rotates. Ọmọ is the core of the people's worldview and philosophy of life and living: *Torí ọmọ la ṣe ń ṣiṣẹ́,* "we work because of children"; *torí ọmọ la ṣe wálé ayé,* "the purpose of our sojourn in life is to have children"; *torí ọmọ la ṣe ń ṣíṣẹ̀ẹ́,* "we suffer in life because of our children"; *olówó kò rí ọmọ rà,* "the rich and wealthy can get a child to buy"; *àríjó àríyọ̀ là ń rí ọmọ tuntun,* "it is with cheerfulness and joy that we welcome a newborn baby"; *ọjọ́ tí a bá kú, ọmọ ẹni ní yó wolé deni,* "and when we die, it is our child(ren) who will be our torchbearers!" There are countless ways in which the Yorùbá express the significant place and role of children in their lives.

Yorùbá beliefs and values leave no room for barrenness and impotency. To be childless is considered a curse, and the Yorùbá will do anything to remove the spell or curse to have a child. Regardless of whether their faith is Christianity or Islam, the Yorùbá consult the Babaláwo (Ifá priest) to ensure they have children. If offering sacrifices to any of the deities, especially those deities associated with childbearing (Ọbàtálá, Òrìṣà Oko, Ọ̀ṣun), couples make necessary sacrifices to appease the gods. Indeed, modern Christian pastors and Muslim leaders often have paid advertisements on radio and television inviting those who have been unable to have children to attend their prayer sessions.

Perhaps no other feature of the Yorùbá culture signifies the place and role of children than names. Names not only have meanings in the society but also tell stories about the child and his or her family: *Ilé là ń wò kí a tó sọmọ lórúkọ,* "we look at our circumstances before we name a child." Names such as Ọmọ́làjà, which means a child who has come to resolve dispute in the family; Ọmọ́boríowó, which means a child who has triumphed over riches or wealth; Ọyátóbọ, which means that most likely the woman became pregnant after making offerings to Ọya, hence Ọya River is a goddess worthy of worship; Babátúndé (Male) or Yétúndé (Female), which means a child incarnate of the deceased grandfather or grandmother, respectively; Babárímisá, which means a child whose father died immediately after he was born; Bídèmí, which means a child born while the father is away from home; and Bámidélé, which means a child born while either or both parents were away from home.

As an axis of Yorùbá life, the child belongs to the entire household and community. To ensure that the child absorbs the culture and grows to be well behaved (ọmọlúwàbí), every member of the household and community have responsibility for, and take delight in, the training and upbringing of children. Àgbà kì í wà lọ́jà kórí ọmọ tuntun ó wọ́, or "as long as there are elders in the market, the child will never be in the wrong posture at the back of the mother." Oyún nìkan ni a kì í báni gbé; tẹrú tọmọ níí báni tọ́jú ọmọ, or "it is only pregnancy we cannot help an expectant mother to carry; everyone helps to look after the baby." The Yorùbá believe that children are to be seen and not heard, but they also believe childhood is a time for learning and foundational education. It is the stage when children learn their family's trades and crafts and all the basic rules and ethics of social interactions.

See also **Childbirth and Childbearing; Deities: The Òrìṣà, Demography: Social Characteristics; Divination: Ifá; Medicine: Indigenous Therapeutic System; Names and Naming; Ọmọlúwàbí**

REFERENCES

Adéoyè, Láògún C. Àṣà àti Ìṣe Yorùbá. Oxford: Oxford University Press, 1979.

Fádípè, N. A. The Sociology of the Yorùbá. Ìbàdàn (Nigeria): University Press, 1970.

Bọ́lá Dáúdà

CHILDREN'S FOLKLORE, EDUCATION, AND DEVELOPMENT

Folklore refers to various genres that exist within or have been produced by a group of people or a particular ethnic group. Among the Yorùbá, one of the major types of folklore is that which is commonly used to educate the children in diverse ways. In preliterate society, folklore was an important means to train children. Such training usually started in the home—hence, the saying ilé ni a ti ń kó èṣọ́ rode, "charity begins at home." Children's folklore can be classified into two broad categories based on the source. The first type consists of those produced by the children themselves, and the second type consists of those produced by elders. Elders are children's primary teachers. The ultimate aim in the use of folklore is to educate children for their social and cultural development. Children learn folklore through recitation, chanting, or singing, depending on the genre of the tale. Some examples of children folklore include àlọ́ àpamọ̀ (riddles), àlọ́ àpagbè (folktales), and moonlight game songs, such as àrọ̀ jíjá, ìmọ̀ bíbú, ẹkùn mẹ́ran, bọ́kọbọ́ọ̀kọ alálọ̀ọ́mọ́tan, and ẹyẹ mélòó tolongo wáyé. A major type of children's folklore, which is solely performed by parents for their children, is orin arẹmọlẹ́kún (lullabies).

Various forms of children's folklore teach historical, moral, psychological, and sociological lessons to children apart from their aesthetic qualities. Folklore includes poetry that has an intrinsic artistic value in itself, but it also teaches lessons about kinship, politics, and nationalism. Children learn these and various other concepts through myriad different folklore stories. The goal of these stories is to prepare them for political and social engagement.

Children's folklore as an art also serves as a critique of society and as a catalyst for social transformation within society. The children are believed to be the future of the country. Therefore, children learn through folklore values that elders hope they will use to transform society and make progress in the future. The Yorùbá believe that societal values and heritage are better taught to the children while they are very young.

Children's folklore reflects various changes in the society over time. It is interwoven with various concepts, ideologies, and philosophies to reflect contemporary issues. For example, the following folk song is used to teach children the importance of formal education. It is one of the folk songs pupils sing during the morning assembly and inside their classrooms.

Ẹ̀kọ́ dára, ẹ jẹ́ ká lọ.
Ẹ jẹ́ ká lọ sílé ìwé.
Ẹnikẹ́ni tí kò kàwé
Aláàárù ni yóò ṣe lọ́la.

Education is good, let us go [to school].
Let us go to school.
Whoever is not educated
Will be a porter in the future.

Some folklore stories teach children the Yorùbá phonetic system, especially the alphabets.

See also **Dilemma Tales; Dolls and Toys; Electronic Media and Oral Tradition; Literature: Oral; Music: Traditional; Stories, Storytelling, and Storytellers**

REFERENCES

Akínyẹmí, A. "Yorùbá Oral Literature: A Source of Indigenous Education for Children." In *Forms and Functions of English and Indigenous Languages in Nigeria: A Festschrift in Honour of Ayọ̀ Bánjọ*, ed. Kọ́lá Owólabí and Adémọ́lá Dasylva, 461–81. Ìbàdàn (Nigeria): Group Publishers, 2004.

Ìṣọ̀lá, A. "The Role of Oral Literature in the Intellectual and Social Development of the African Child." In *Language in Nigeria: Essays in Honour of Ayọ̀ Bámgbóṣé*, ed. Kọ́lá Owólabí, 311–22. Ìbàdàn (Nigeria): Group Publishers, 1995.

Ọlátúndé Adéléyẹ Adéyẹmọ

CHRISTIANITY: THE ALÁDURÀ AND PENTECOSTAL CHURCHES

Christianity in Yorùbáland has witnessed phenomenal growth since its establishment in the nineteenth century. However, this growth has been characterized by the establishment of churches representing an African strand of Christianity, generally referred to as African Indigenous or Initiated Churches (AICs). Although these churches can be found in different parts of Nigeria and throughout Africa, Yorùbáland has been fertile soil for their establishment and the proliferation of their growth. Two prominent categories of AICs are the Aládurà and the Pentecostal churches. While the former emerged beginning in the 1920s, the latter emerged during the 1960s.

Although these churches differ with regard to details of doctrines, methodology, structures, and leadership styles, they seem to be united in their desire to reform the mission of Christianity. They strove to make the Christian message more relevant to the daily needs of Africans. Consequently, the churches became manifestations of historical dynamics of spiritual, cultural, political, social, and circumstantial realities of the people.

The Aládurà Churches

The Aládurà churches place strong emphasis on prayer in doctrine and practice as the fountain of blessings and success for members of the church. The word *Aládurà* means "the praying people." In addition, the churches distinguish themselves from mission churches in their reliance on divine healing, prominence of women in ministry, observance of spontaneous worship format, African cultural content, evangelism and revival campaigns, and dependence on a spiritual and loosely organized administrative structure.

Many AICs are classified as Aládurà churches. One of the earliest established and most prominent one is Precious Stone Society, founded around 1920. It started as a prayer group that broke away from the Christian Missionary Society's St. Savior's Church in Ìjẹ̀bú-Òde. The schism resulted from fallout from the bubonic and smallpox epidemics that occurred after World War I. The group believed in divine healing through the use of rainwater and prayers for the epidemics. The group gained fame after first affiliating with the Faith Tabernacle Church, and it eventually metamorphosed to the Apostolic Church and then the Christ Apostolic Church, which itself separated from the Faith Tabernacle Church. The establishment and growth of the church can be accredited to pioneering figures such as Joseph Ayọ̀ Babalọlá, Akinloyè Ògúnbánjọ, Isaac Akínyẹlé, and Joseph Sádáre (also known as Ẹṣinṣindé). The church was autonomously registered in 1943 and has grown phenomenally with the evangelical missions of T. O. Ọbádáre and Timothy Ìyàndá.

The Church of the Lord Aládurà was founded by Josiah Ọshítẹ̀lú in 1930. The Anglican Church dismissed Ọshítẹ̀lú after he was accused of introducing unacceptable rituals. With the arrival of evangelist Adélékè Adéjọbí in 1940, the church spread from its Ọ̀yọ́, Ìjẹ̀bú, Oǹdó, and Èkìtì locations to other parts of Nigeria and Africa. The distinctive characteristics of the church include use of holy names, annual Taborar crusades (annual pilgrimage festival in commemoration of an Old Testament experience of the Israelites), use of sacred objects, and rolling on the ground while praying.

Two other Aládurà churches with almost identical doctrines, and the members of which wear white garments or *sùtánà* (and so they are often called white-garment churches), are the Celestial Church of Christ (CCC) and Cherubim and Seraphim Society (C&S). The CCC was founded by Joseph Oshoffa, born in Benin Republic. He claimed to have been divinely called in 1947. The Yorùbá version of the name of the church is Ìjọ Mímọ́ Krístì Láti Ọ̀run Wá (translated literally as Holy Assembly of Christ from Heaven). It attracted many Yorùbá and spread rapidly across Yorùbáland. The C&S began as a prayer group in 1925. The church's Yorùbá name is Ẹgbẹ́ Séráfù àti Kérúbù, and it was founded by Moses Orímọládé and Christiana Abíọ́dún Akínṣọ̀wọ́n (also known as Captain Abíọ́dún). By 1929, the C&S had spread to many Yorùbá towns. It soon split. While the faction loyal to Orímọládé took the name Eternal Sacred Order of Cherubim and Seraphim Society, the faction under Abíọ́dún kept the name Cherubim and Seraphim Society. Since that time, the group has further splintered.

Pentecostal Churches

The Pentecostal AICs that have taken root in Yorùbáland are generally classified into two groups: Classical and Neo-Pentecostal. The Classical Pentecostal churches may be of foreign origin (all Pentecostal churches claim to embody the unique Pentecostal experience of the Holy Spirit, but Classical Pentecostals are distinguished by their apocalyptic doctrines that emphasize a mission of heavenly oriented salvation), they have operated in Nigeria and particularly in Yorùbáland since the 1930s. Some of them include the Foursquare Gospel Church, the Assemblies of God Church, and the Apostolic Faith Church.

The Neo-Pentecostal churches are also called Gospel churches. These churches, though still sharing the basic tenets of Classical Pentecostalism, deliberately seek a balance between the heavenly oriented focus of salvation and the existential realities of human needs as important concerns of spiritual engagements. In addition, they reflect very significant charismatic and intellectual flavor in their doctrines, structures, and mission. Also, many of them are quite recent, having being established since the 1970s. The most prominent congregations among these are the Deeper Life Bible Church, the Christian Pentecostal Mission, and the Redeemed Evangelical Mission. The Redeemed Christian Church of God, founded by Josiah Akíndayọ̀mí in 1952 and expanded by Enoch Adébóyè, has basically transitioned from a classical strand of Pentecostalism to Neo-Pentecostal as a Pentecostal mission.

Both Pentecostal churches share some common features. Principal among these are emphasis on the power and gifts of the Holy Spirit; power of prayer for healing and exorcism; literal translation of Scripture; and abstinence from immoral acts, such as smoking, premarital sex, drinking alcohol, and adultery. Unlike the Aládurà churches, these churches also condemn any form of traditional religious and cultural practices.

Over the past five decades, the Aládurà and Pentecostal churches have provided spiritual responses to the existential needs of members; they provide prosperity, marital support, health care, and promote fear of evil forces among others things. In addition, they have been able to substitute the mission churches' abstract and "other world" religious focus with emphasis on existential components of human everyday challenges and solutions. These features, as well as the general perspective that the churches have succeeded in providing an African interpretation of the Bible and liturgy, have led to the phenomenal spread of the Pentecostal churches, not only across Yorùbáland but also across Nigeria, Africa, and different parts of the globe.

See also **Christianity: Early Beginnings and Expansion; Prominent Pentecostal Pastors**

REFERENCES

Ayégbóyìn, Dèjì, and Adémólá Ìshòlá, eds. *African Indigenous Churches: An Historical Perspective.* Lagos (Nigeria): Greater Heights Publications, 1997.

Mala, Sams Babs, ed. *African Independent Churches in the 80s.* Lagos (Nigeria): OAIC, 1983.

Ìbígbóládé S. Adéríbigbé

CHRISTIANITY: EARLY BEGINNINGS AND EXPANSION

Organized Christianity arrived in Abéòkúta in 1842, and over the following forty years, it began a slow and uneven expansion among the Yorùbá, claiming only about 1 percent of an estimated two million people as coverts. By 1921, between 15 percent and 20 percent of the Yorùbá living in major cities across all social strata had become Christians, with the exception of those living in Abéòkúta, Ìbàdàn, and Òyó. In these three cities, the number of converts was less than 10 percent of the population. Many of the liberated Yorùbá slaves who returned from Sierra Leone (Sàró) had become fairly Anglicized Christians; they helped initiate the process of conversion. The Sàró had adopted a modicum of British evangelical and modernist ethos, but they retained a vibrant attachment to their local culture.

After arriving in Yorùbáland, pursued by European missionaries, the Sàró introduced Christianity in a way that resonated with the sociopolitical, economic, and philosophical values of the Yorùbá people. European missionary efforts had not been successful. Through indigenous agency, the Sàró and subsequent generations of Yorùbá Christian leaders developed the most acculturated (unorthodox) Christianity produced by Africans before the mid-twentieth century. After its introduction in Abéòkúta and Lagos during the mid-1800s, Christian missions had spread by the 1890s to the hinterland Yorùbá cities of Ìbàdàn, Ìjèbú-Ode, Ilésà, Ògbómòsó, Oǹdó, Òyó, and Ifè.

Christian beginnings among the Yorùbá occurred at the intersection of global and local currents. As part of the international abolitionist movement, Britain founded Sierra Leone as a beachhead of Victorian British culture and a place to settle liberated slaves. The resurgence in nineteenth-century European evangelical missionary work resulted in the spread of churches, schools, and clinics. The British also promoted exports to replace the previous slave trade. Meanwhile, a prolonged civil war among the Yorùbá produced major demographic and sociopolitical shifts and economic realignments, which opened the people to political, cultural, and commercial innovations.

Lagos colony, the missionaries, and the Sàró repatriates represented the European military, technological, diplomatic, and commercial resources; they created new opportunities but also perpetuated ongoing crises. In the 1840s and 1850s, Abéòkúta, Ìbàdàn, Ìjàyè, and Òyó welcomed the Sàró repatriates and their European missionary friends. In Abéòkúta and Lagos, the missionaries proselytized, and the returnees constituted the missionary churches' core membership. Samuel Àjàyí Crowther became the first ordained Nigerian Anglican clergyman, and he led one of the three Abéòkúta Anglican missions. Ìbàdàn, Ìjàyè, Òyó, and Ògbómòsó also quickly hosted Protestant missions. In 1900, the Catholics, having already established missions among Brazilian returnees in Lagos, established missions in Òyó.

Colonial Context

By the turn of the nineteenth century, fatigue from prolonged war pushed the Yorùbá to accept peace under British colonial domination, which facilitated the expansion of Christianity. Peace produced another resurgence of conversion, especially in the Èkìtì, Ilésà, Ìjèbú, and Oǹdó areas among former slaves and sojourners. Many of these converts were successful professionals and traders capable of communicating with the wider world. Equipped with a cultural package of Christianity and personal and community development ethos, they became celebrated civic leaders and promoters of community progress. Some became lay preachers to their townspeople, establishing the nuclei of Christian communities that missionaries (African and European) built upon. Urban trading and income-earning opportunities away from home allowed for religious choice and capacitated Yorùbá youths' economic independence from their senior kin, undermining elders' sociocultural dominance. Converted youths returning from the city sought to legitimate their Christian identities and establish autonomy for their church and its rituals. Consequently, they contested and challenged the local sociocultural spaces previously monopolized by local elders, who controlled the traditional religious economy through taboos and prohibitions. The empowerment on entire generation of Yorùbá youth associated with missionary education and Christianity attracted even more of them to Christianity.

In addition, early Christians in Lagos adopted and spread cocoa farming because of the affluence and progress it generated. They spread the crop to thousands of hinterland Yorùbá working on Agége plantations. These workers returned back home committed to the "package" of progressive cocoa farming and Christianity. Affluence from this package established social respectability for converts' families in the church and in the town communities. They supplied resources for building church schools, which gave their children the education the parents did not have. Before 1920, most schools were run by Christian missions, and converts' children predominated in the enrollment. Conversion to Christianity created a set of conditions conducive for upward social mobility.

Local Cultural Context

The foregoing conditions for the growth of Christianity among the Yorùbá intersected with the Yorùbá's preexisting pluralist and tolerant cultural and religious outlook. Yorùbá governments did not seek control over people's religious allegiances. Switching religions was considered philosophical and pragmatic, especially as a reaction to conditions of adversity. Family heads expressed concern about whether or not some of their converted sons would follow in their religious footsteps, thus assuring them of proper burial rites. However, evidence points to a cultural-religious disposition that allowed for experimentation. For example, barrenness and affliction justified devotees adding, subtracting, or exchanging deities in their local pantheon. Not infrequently, Ifá would prescribe either Islam or Christianity to an inquirer. A substantial minority of the Ègbá, Òyó, Òsogbo, Ìwó, Ifè, Ìjèbú, and Lagos Yorùbá were already Muslims before the Yorùbá introduction to Christianity.

Also, the indigenization of Christianity facilitated its expansion in Yorùbáland. Modeling local social organization, sex, age, and marital status-based church associations helped inscribe Christianity into Yorùbá culture and facilitated its acceptance. Other indigenization policies established the legitimacy of Yorùbá hymnody, drumming, dancing, dress culture, and—in some instances—polygamy. Even more radical was the formation of African independent churches that renounced mission tutelage, European domination, and European racism. Mójòlà Àgbébí's 1888 Native Baptist Church symbolized this development. Equally radical was the rise of the Aládurà (prophet) movement, which validated, as part of the legitimate, biblical, Christian experience, culturally resonant practices like visions, faith healing, commitment to praying, and the like.

All of these factors reconstituted Christianity as an indigenous cultural and spiritual frame of reference. They also democratized leadership and opened up participation to anyone who could receive visions or commit to praying. Praying bands within Anglicanism in the 1920s were followed in the 1930s by a number of revival movements, such as the Aládurà (now established as Christ Apostolic Church), Cherubim, and Seraphim movements. These changes led the Yorùbá to an era of mass conversion to Christianity, the likes of which only recent Pentecostal revival has matched.

See also **Christianity: Aládurà and Pentecostal Churches; Language: Government and Mission Policies; Sàró and Àgùdà**

REFERENCES

Peel, J. D. Y. *Religious Encounter and the Making of the Yorùbá.* Bloomington: Indiana University Press, 2000.

Sundkler, Bengt, and Christopher Steed. *A History of the Church in Africa*. Cambridge: Cambridge University Press, 2004.

Fẹ́mi Kọ́lápọ̀

CIRCUMCISION AND FACIAL SCARIFICATION

The cultural practice of circumcision and body and facial scarification falls under the artistic category of body marking. Circumcision is practiced on both male and female infants, and the practice has a cultural and religious basis. In traditional societies, circumcision is done by certain family lineages known as the *olóólà*. The *olóólà* profession is not gender specific. Circumcision entails certain rituals that are carried out at the family shrine. The *olóólà* uses local herbs for anesthesia. In recent times, circumcision is no longer restricted to *olóólà* families and is routinely done in hospitals. Male circumcision is popular among Yorùbá of all classes; few male children or adults are not circumcised. The issue of female circumcision, however, is more complex. It has largely declined because of the public and international outcry over "female genital mutilation." The cultural debate of tradition versus modernity and the cultural relevance of female circumcision continue to influence opinions that will determine the survival of female circumcision.

Facial and body scarification is another cultural practice that is on a steady decline. In ancient times, body marking was popular because it served two purposes: collective identification and beautification. Less than two centuries ago, marking the body and face was a cultural necessity because it tied people's bodies to their families, and families were tied to territories. The body was used as a map on which family histories and cognitive symbols were drawn. These maps provided a route of return to family members who could potentially be lost to slave raiding or scattered by war. If a great deal of time had passed after a person was lost or scattered, the person could be identified and possibly reunited with his or her family. There is a proverb that reflects this: *Tí a bàá sọnù kí a rí ara wa ni Ìbàdàn fi ń kọlà* (If we get lost, that we may find ourselves is the reason Ìbàdàn [a subgroup among Yorùbá] wear marks).

Yorùbá people also wear body and facial markings for the sake of beauty. In *The History of the Yorùbás*, Samuel Johnson indicates that this function of body scarification was discovered serendipitously: a slave punished with 122 razor cuts slashed all over his body looked beautiful when his wounds healed after several weeks. Subsequently, it was decreed that such marks should never be placed on a slave but only on royal bodies. The king decided to have his body inscribed with distinct marks of royalty known as *ẹ̀yọ̀*. Other royal families have individual marks. However, body marking is not limited to royalty; it can be done on any person or in any family that desires it. The practice has largely disappeared, and in some states in southwestern Nigeria, the practice is legally proscribed.

See also **Body Adornment and Cosmetics; Medicine: Indigenous Therapeutic System**

REFERENCES

Johnson, S. *The History of the Yorùbás*. Lagos (Nigeria): C.S.S., 1921.

Ọlájubù, O. *Women in the Yorùbá Religious Sphere*. New York: State University of New York Press, 2003.

Abímbọ́lá Adélakùn

CITIES

The Yorùbá are one of the most urbanized people groups on the African continent. For centuries they were known to live in complex, highly organized, and densely populated cities generally centered on the king's palace. This preference for city life is deeply rooted in Yorùbá creation myths. This mythology is based on the belief that the *òrìṣà* (divinities), led by Ọbàtálá were sent by Olódùmarè to come down from heaven to the earth and create the dry land out of water. Ọbàtálá, because he lacked seriousness about the mission, later abdicated his leadership position to Odùduwà. Odùduwà, the new leader, oversaw one of the first creative acts of the *òrìṣà*: the establishment of Ilé-Ifẹ̀. Thus, Ilé-Ifẹ̀ became recognized as the cradle of the human race, and it is the spiritual headquarters of all Yorùbá-speaking people worldwide. As time progressed, many of the òrìṣà intermarried with humans and began to multiply rapidly in Ilé-Ifẹ̀ until the city became too populated to sustain the inhabitants. This led to more and more people leaving Ilé-Ifẹ̀ to found other cities, far and near. Inherent in this belief is the idea that all human life began in Ilé-Ifẹ̀, and it is from this original city that all humans eventually scattered or migrated to populate the entire earth.

These cities, like the pioneering Ilé-Ifẹ̀, became the vibrant political centers of city-states—autonomous cities with their own rulers and supreme councils of elders, armies, and other communal societies. Yorùbá cities are generally surrounded by farmlands and homesteads, which make up the villages around the main cities. Since the Yorùbá were primarily an agricultural people, every city dweller used to have farmland in the surrounding villages, where he or she tilled the land and cultivated food crops such as yams, bananas, millet, beans, and other crops during the day or much of the week. The person later returned to the walled city for trade, protection, and other family or community festivities. Many festive occasions were associated with the various òrìṣà; each had its own special days of worship, either on a weekly or yearly basis. For example, special annual festivals are dedicated to the deities Ọ̀ṣun, Ṣàngó, Ògún, Ẹlẹ́gbárá, and all the numerous other deities. Egúngún festivals were also very popular annual celebrations during which people wore highly decorative masks and danced and chanted in the presence of hundreds of jubilant onlookers in festive mood throughout the city.

Before the arrival of European colonizers in the seventeenth and eighteenth centuries, the Yorùbá had lived in well-organized cities for hundreds of years. These cities, most of which eventually grew to become city-states, occasionally engaged each other in battles for supremacy. Between 1300 and 1700 CE, Ọ̀yọ́ became a dominant empire, encompassing many other city-states. Many ọba were brought under its ruling umbrella. Ọ̀yọ́ eventually unified the disparate Yorùbá-speaking peoples under its rule. This helped to homogenize Yorùbá language and culture. People came to see themselves as sharing a common ancestry and a unifying language with common cultural points of reference, and this sowed the seeds of what would later become present-day Yorùbáland. The other city-states that joined in a common Yorùbá identity included Ìbàdàn, Oǹdó, Ilẹ́ṣà, Àkúrẹ́, and several others. For instance, Ìbàdàn, founded in the eighteenth century, grew large and powerful enough to be considered, at the height of its influence, a military republic or a proto-empire. The growth of Ìbàdàn was occasioned by the influx of mercenaries, traders, and refugees because of the internecine wars waging throughout Yorùbáland at that time.

For many decades Ìbàdàn was the largest city in West Africa. Today, Lagos, another major city of the Yorùbá and Nigeria's commercial nerve center, has overtaken Ìbàdàn in population. It is the largest West African city and the second-largest city in Africa; more than eight million inhabitants live in the bustling metropolis. In fact, it is predicted that by the year 2030, Lagos, will be one of the largest cities in the world, with a projected population of around twenty-six million. Other well-known, modern cities include Ògbómọ̀ṣọ́, Ọ̀yọ́, Ìlọrin, Ilẹ́ṣà, Abẹ́òkúta, and Ilé-Ifẹ̀. Like Ìbàdàn and Lagos, these cities are all located in the forest region of southwestern Nigeria. Yorùbá cities have the largest concentration of institutions of higher learning in Nigeria, boasting some of the best and largest universities in the country.

Around the world today, it is not uncommon to find Yorùbá people living in large cities throughout the Diaspora in Europe and the Americas. In Europe, the highest concentration of Yorùbá immigrants can be found in London and in other large British cities, such as Manchester and Liverpool. In the United States, Yorùbá immigrants are concentrated in metropolises such as Atlanta, Houston, Washington, D.C., New York City, Newark, and Chicago, among other places. Thus, the Yorùbá preference for city life is not only limited to Yorùbáland and the African continent; the practice continues even as they migrate to other parts of the world for greener pastures. The concept embedded in the name of the first city of the Yorùbá—Ilé-Ifẹ̀—the place of the dispersion, continues to reverberate around the world, wherever the children of Odùduwà are found.

See also **Agriculture and Farming; Cosmology; Diaspora: Yorùbá in Europe; Diaspora: Yorùbá in North America; Deities: The Òrìṣà; Education: Tertiary; Myths**

REFERENCES

Abímbọ́lá, Wándé. "A Preference for City Life." *Calliope* 8.6 (1998): 33–36.

Àjàní, T. Tèmi. "The Rise of Ọ̀yọ́." *Calliope* 8.6 (1998): 27–29.

Timothy T. Àjàní

CIVIL SOCIETY

State-society dynamics manifested early in traditional Yorùbá societies. Societies possessed characteristics that made for strong state formation and political influence. First, societies were patrilineal, which formed the basis of political organization. Second, rampant wars and disorder led to the evolution of mostly large, centralized, and militarized political systems, with the king (ọba), who represented *aláṣẹ-èkejì-òrìṣà* (next in command to the gods), at the head. Third, the societies were kinship societies ruled by a strong seniority principle that ensured that authority did not diffuse beyond a certain hierarchical juncture.

In this context, the society necessarily must respond to the exigent dynamics of the strong state. Within the monarchical system, for instance, the people occupied the last, and hence reactive, level of political authority after the king, the chieftaincy council, and the other powerful leaders like the Ògbóni (both an association and part of the civil society) and the military class. The people's reactive "power" was represented by the various associational groups. The "civil society" (or *ẹgbẹ́*) was meant to mediate the multiple interactions and contestations between the state and the society, and to ensure that the leadership was held responsible to the most basic tenets of good governance. While the king (ọba) constituted the symbolic representative of the kingdom, the chiefs (ìjòyè) were the political representatives of the people. The civil society existed to guard the common interests of the people, which could get lost within the dynamics of political power represented by the king and the chiefs.

One of the most vibrant of these associations was age grades. For instance, the age grades that were made up mainly of youths served a variety of functions, including the enforcement of law and order in society. These age grades were also utilized in social and public works and services. Women's associations also existed, and they were usually headed by the *ìyálóde*, the chief in charge of women affairs. This associations consisted mainly of traders and artisans who made political representations to the council of chiefs for deliberation. The extent of the power of such groups is demonstrated by the strength of their leaders; for example, a case in point is Ìyálóde Ẹfúnṣetán Aníwúrà at Ìbàdàn. There were also occupational associations of artisans and craftsmen, women, hunters, and artists (artisans, painters, sculptors, chanters, jesters, poets, and singers) and trade and merchant guilds (supervised by the Pàràkòyí). The story is told of Aláàfin Jáyin, a tyrant who committed suicide because of the wrath of chanters (hence the proverb: *Ó kù dẹ̀dẹ̀ ká gbéwì d'Ákẹ̀sán, Ọba Jáyin tẹ́rí gbaṣọ*, "Just before the chanters got to the Àkẹ̀sán marketplace, King Jáyin committed suicide").

There were also mutual help associations that assisted the people in pursuing their trade and other interests. The two forms of self-help were the *àáró* (which renders collective help to individual farmers) and the *èsúsú* society (in which a group of individuals save up some amount of capital). Last are the religious associations, made up chiefly of the priests and priestesses of the òrìṣà or deities. An association was required for the political purpose of achieving uniformity in worship, propitiation, and other spiritual needs related to the welfare of the community.

See also **Age Grade System; Cooperative Associations; Government: Historical Political Systems; Kingship; Political Systems; Royalty and Chieftaincy; Succession**

REFERENCES

Fádípẹ̀, N. A. *The Sociology of the Yorùbá*. Ìbàdàn (Nigeria): University Press, 1970.

Johnson, Samuel. *The History of the Yorùbá.* Lagos (Nigeria): C.S.S., 1921.

Adéshínà Afọláyan

COLONIAL POLICIES AND PRACTICES

The imposition of British colonial rule brought tremendous transformations to Yorùbáland. After restoring peace to war-torn Yorùbá society, the British established administrative structures and put into place policies that facilitated their control and exploitation of the region. The objective of British colonialism was to exploit the raw materials or resources in Yorùbáland for the benefits of the home industries in the United Kingdom. The export of raw materials would not have been possible without the enforcement of colonial policies. British colonial policies in Yorùbáland, as elsewhere in Nigeria, can be categorized as indirect rule and economic policies.

Indirect Rule

With the formal establishment of colonial rule, the British authority administered Yorùbáland through indirect rule: a system of rule through indigenous traditional authority, such as the kings and chiefs. For reasons of expediency, the British did not administer to locals directly; instead, it allowed local authorities to govern their people as they had done previously. The goal of indirect rule was to minimize tension with the locals as much as possible. Governing the people indirectly enabled the British to gain support and minimize costs. As Fredrick Lugard reasoned, governing the locals through indigenous institutions was cheaper and unlikely to draw suspicion of the locals.

The indirect rule policy was first applied in the Northern Protectorate by Fredrick Lugard. The policy was extended to Yorùbáland after the amalgamation of the Southern and Northern Protectorates in 1914. The application of the policy in Yorùbáland differed markedly from in the north. Lagos was administered more directly, a manner different from other parts of Yorùbáland. In the mainland states, indirect rule was conducted through the council of chiefs instead of a single leader, as in the north.

The goal of indirect rule was to alter those traditional institutions and customs the British considered inimical to European civilization. Although the policy claimed to respect the traditional political institutions and to promote continuity between the traditional rulers and the colonialist, in practice, it undermined their influence and subordinated them to the European resident and district officers. Traditional authorities could not complain because, under the British rule, insubordination was a serious offense that could lead to removal from office.

Economic Policies

British colonial rule also affected the economy of Yorùbáland. The British considered restructuring the economy their primary goal. British economic policy was motivated by the need to make Yorùbáland a source of raw materials and a market for goods from Britain. Lugard stated, "It is in order to foster the growth of the trade of this country . . . that our far-seeing statesmen and our commercial men advocate colonial expansion." To further these economic goals, the British adopted different but interrelated economic policies.

The British authority monetized the economy and made it dependent on the home economy. The monetization policy abolished all existing currencies and introduced new ones to replace them. Monetizing the economy was a necessary condition for opening Yorùbáland to trade and capital from Britain. The colonial authority practically forced the new currency on people by insisting that all transactions, including payment for taxes and wages, be made in the new currency. Production of raw materials and wage labor became the only means through which the currency was obtained. Although the British claimed to have monetized the economy to remove obstacles to free trade, their economic policy damaged precolonial social relations and forced people to work for the currency. The colonial currency was first imposed in Lagos in 1881, although the old manila currency continued to be used until it was outlawed in the 1940s.

To expedite the exploitation of the raw materials for home industries, the British adopted a production policy that forced people to produce the required raw materials such as cocoa, palm oil, and rubber. The British also tightened its hold over land to make people produce the raw materials, while allowing the European firms to export them to Europe.

As a way to facilitate exploitation, the British improved transport and communication infrastructure throughout Yorùbáland. The British considered the existing transportation system inadequate to satisfy the major objectives of colonialism. The British built harbor, railway, and road systems to facilitate the transport of raw materials. The building of the railway began in Lagos in 1898, and by 1907 the mainland Yorùbá states had been connected by railway. Areas not reached by the line were connected by access roads to feed the railway traffic. The first motor road in Yorùbáland was built in 1906, and by 1914 mileage had increased considerably. In the same manner, the Lagos harbor was improved to facilitate movement of large vessels year-round. To build such large-scale infrastructure, the British adopted a policy of forced labor on construction sites.

In theory, the infrastructure was built to facilitate economic development. In practice, it expedited the exploitation of raw materials from Yorùbáland to Britain. The large-scale export of cocoa from Yorùbáland was made possible only when the railway and roads were constructed. The railway also was required for administration, military, and trade. The railway facilitated the penetration of European firms across Yorùbáland. The initiative to build the railway itself was put forward by the European commercial community.

See also **Transportation; Economic History; Economic System**

REFERENCES

Fálọlá, Tóyìn, and M. Matthew Heaton. *History of Nigeria*. Cambridge: Cambridge University Press, 2008.

Lugard, Frederick. *The Dual Mandate in British Tropical Africa*. 5th ed. London: Frank Cass & Co., 1965.

Shehu Tìjjání Yusuf

The Yorùbá organize colors according to three basic categories: white, red, and black. Each color category has an emotional and/or psychological dimension. Color categories encompass a wide array of hues, shades, and intensities. Colors often convey specific messages that are reinterpreted according to changing contexts. For example, an *òrìṣà* initially categorized as white might later be categorized as red or black, even within the same religious ceremony. Bọ́lájí Campbell underscores the dynamism of color categories, suggesting that Yorùbá colors have agency, that they "make things happen."

The first color category is *funfun*. *Funfun* is roughly translated into English as "white," and it symbolizes purity, peace, and cleanliness. *Funfun* can be any color that is considered icy and/or cold (including white, turquoise, blue, and silver). It is used to describe a person who is aloof and lacks passion. *Funfun* also signifies age and wisdom. A number of *òrìṣà*—notably Ọbàtálá—are categorized as *funfun*.

The second category is *pupa*. *Pupa* is roughly translated into English as "red," but it includes many other colors associated with heat and/or fire (including orange, dark yellow, and gold). *Pupa* describes a person who is easily angered. The *òrìṣà* Ògún and Ṣàngó are both categorized as *pupa* because of their strong associations with violence, fire, and blood.

The third category is *dúdú*. *Dúdú* can be roughly translated into English as "black" but also includes other colors like brown, blue, purple, green, brown, and dark gray. Sometimes, *funfun* and *dúdú* are opposites (e.g., *dúdú* symbolizes death and bereavement, whereas *funfun* symbolizes purity and joy). Other times *dúdú* mediates between *pupa* (hot) and *funfun* (cold). *Dúdú* is associated with pragmatic, practical people and with the restraint and tranquility of Ọ̀rúnmìlà, the founder of Ifá divination. Ọ̀ṣun is often categorized as *dúdú*. *Òrìṣà* in the New World have maintained their associations with basic color categories (white, red, black), but in many cases Yorùbá color terms (*funfun*, *pupa*, *dúdú*) did not survive.

Colors are frequently combined; for example, different-colored beads are strung together in Yorùbá bodily decoration. Associations between colors and human temperaments have implications for defining, understanding, and revealing the personalities of inanimate objects, persons, and deities. Because Yorùbá colors are grouped according to human temperaments, they evoke cognitive (visual) responses as well as sensory (feeling) responses. They create moods and motivations. *Funfun*, *pupa*, and *dúdú* also provide visual cues. They warn of forces and actions in the world for which one must be prepared.

See also **Symbol and Symbolism**

REFERENCES

Campbell, Bọ́lájí. *Painting for the Gods: Art & Aesthetics of Yorùbá Religious Murals.* Trenton, NJ: Africa World Press, 2007.

Drewal, Henry John, and John Mason. *Beads, Body, and Soul: Art and Light in the Yorùbá Universe.* Los Angeles: UCLA Fowler Museum of Cultural History, 1997.

Stephen D. Glazier

COMMERCE

It was generally believed that the Yorùbá economy was a simple subsistence one and that the "economic man," one with capitalistic tendencies, was lacking among the people. This belies the widespread economic activities that prevailed in Yorùbáland before early contact with Arabs and later Europeans. A particular subgroup, the Ìjẹ̀sà, through their òṣómàálò practice of credit (òṣómàálò literally means "squatting" and is used to recover debts), provisions to customers, and debt recovery demonstrated capitalistic tendencies before the arrival of Europeans to Yorùbáland.

Widespread exchange of goods and services prevailed among the various Yorùbá subgroups and with their neighbors, particularly to the north, the Nupe, Fulani, and Hausa groups. Goods traded included surplus farm products like maize, yam, and millet. Craft works and manufactured products were also exchanged; clothing materials, cattle, and smelted iron products were significant trade items among the various Yorùbá

groups and between them and their trading visitors from to the north of Yorùbáland. Markets for exchange existed in virtually all Yorùbá communities. Periodic weekly market days (held at five-, seven-, and nine-day intervals) were established in various communities. In addition to the exchange of goods in these markets, services such as hair and nail dressing, beautification of the body, and message handling were offered.

Barter was the common medium of exchange; people also used cowrie shells as a medium of exchange for significant trade items like woven clothing, beads, and cattle. Both male and female traders were involved in exchange transactions and services at these markets. While female traders sold farm products and rendered appropriate services to other women, male traders were involved in the exchange of luxury items, like woven clothing, beads, cattle sales, and appropriate services to other men.

The provision of credit facilities to trading partners and debt recovery were significant features of Yorùbá exchange practice. The establishment and sustenance of good relationships among trading partners was important to the average traders. However, profit making was not an insignificant consideration. In effect, capitalistic tendencies were widespread among the Yorùbá people before their contact with people abroad. When Arab and European traders came to Yorùbáland, they met their equals and traded with the people as mutual equal partners.

See also **Agriculture and Farming; Economic Systems; Market**

REFERENCES

Dáramọ́lá, Olú, and Adébáyọ̀ Jéjé. *Àwọn Àsà àti Òrìsà Ilẹ̀ Yorùbá.* Ìbàdàn (Nigeria): Oníbọn-Òjé, 1975.

Fádípẹ̀, N. A. *The Sociology of the Yorùbá.* Ìbàdàn (Nigeria): University Press, 1970.

Adémọ́lá Babalọlá

COMMUNICATION, NONVERBAL

The Yorùbá are economical with words. Speeches are often short and sprinkled with parables. A great proportion of the Yorùbá communications is non-verbal: body language, gesticulation, talking drum, and àrokò coded messages often sent as symbols and images. As part of its culture, the Yorùbá have coded nonverbal communication for all relationships and occasions. Learning to decode nonverbal communication is a lifelong process. The Babaláwo (Ifá priest) specializes in interpreting odù ifá—the nonverbal communication from the Ifá oracle. Elders are often consulted about using and interpreting advanced nonverbal communication.

As part of an elaborate process of home training, children are schooled and grounded in nonverbal communication. For example, body language such as ìfojú ṣọ̀rọ̀ (communicating with the face); ìfimú ṣọ̀rọ̀ or imú yíyin (communicating with the nose); mímọ́ni lójú (giving a contemptuous look); fífìka sọ̀rọ̀ (finger pointing), kíkọtí ikún (pretending to be hard of hearing); fẹsẹ̀fẹ́ ẹ or bẹ́sẹ̀ sọ̀rọ̀ (to take to one's heels); ìdọ̀bálẹ̀ (the male prostrating to greet); and ìkúnlẹ̀ (the female kneeling to greet) are taught from early childhood. More complex body language, such as sexual gestures, are acquired during adolescence.

The Yorùbá use more sophisticated nonverbal communication in their social interactions. For example, àalẹ̀ (a metal or palm frond) is placed on a piece of land or property as a sign to prohibit trespassers. The owners of the land could use àalẹ̀ to suspend a farmer from further cultivation of the land. For trade and commerce, a number of cowries are placed at the side of unattended merchandize to indicate to prospective buyers the appropriate price of the good.

Àrokò is a coded message; an object is sent as a symbol. For example, a king may send a sword to his neighboring kingdom to declare war. If the neighbor does not want war, he could send a dove to solicit a truce or peace. Also, the kingmakers could send a coded message in igbá, a covered calabash, to the king. On receipt of the calabash, the king would know that his people no longer wanted him as their ruler, and he would have to choose either to go into exile or commit suicide. Similarly, a groom could send an empty matchbox or a white cloth to his in-laws the day after the wedding to announce that the bride was not a virgin; a full matchbox or bloodstained cloth signaled the bride's chastity.

Overall, failure to observe nonverbal communication makes one aláìnítìjú, Kò mojú, kò mọmú, kò mọ dìde nílẹ́ẹ̀ mi, an uncultured person who can neither read the messages nor know when his or her host was telling the person that he or she has overstayed a welcome. More important, it makes one a subject of ridicule and brings shame to oneself, family, and friends.

Respect, privileges, and honor are the rewards of knowing, understanding, and observing nonverbal communication messages. The child who knows and observes nonverbal communication (ọmọ tó mojú) is parents' pride and is appreciated as a well-cultured child of high integrity and humility (ọmọlúwàbí).

See also **Body and Language Idioms; Color Symbolism; Ọmọlúwàbí; Symbol and Symbolism**

REFERENCES

Doris, David Todd. *Vigilant Things: On Thieves, Yorùbá Anti-Aesthetics, and the Strange Fates of Ordinary Objects in Nigeria.* Seattle: University of Washington Press, 2011.

Òjó, M. O. D. "Symbol of Warning, Conflict, Punishment, and War and their Meanings among the Pre-Colonial Yorùbá Natives: A Case of Àrokò." *Antropologija* 13.1 (2013): 39–60.

Bọ́lá Dáúdà

COOPERATIVE ASSOCIATIONS

In contemporary Yorùbá society, cooperative associations are set up to meet members' common economic or social needs. Such associations that are found in different cities, towns, and villages bear names like Ìfẹ́sowápọ̀ Cooperative Society, Ọ̀rẹ́dẹgbé Cooperative Society, Cocoa Farmers Co-operative Society, and Overcomers Co-operative Association.

Before contact with the Europeans, other forms of cooperative association were also formed by people of the same profession to assist one another in various works. Ọ̀wẹ̀ and àáró or àrokodóko are in this group. Ọ̀wẹ̀ is a call by any adult member of the society to request the assistance of others in carrying out specific jobs like planting, weeding, and building. Most of the time, the response a particular person gets is determined by his or her level of response to previous calls by others and whether he or she has provided enough food for people he or she invited in the past.

Àáró or àrokodóko is a practice by people who are mostly of the same gender and age helping one another on a task. They agree to work jointly for one another and in turns on allotted days. It might be farmwork, fishing, building, harvesting, and the like. Every member should be available on every assigned day, and each member is expected to finish his or her portion of the work. Unlike ọwẹ̀, food and refreshment are not compulsory during àáró, although it is always appreciated if provided.

Furthermore, the savings and investment cooperative association started as àjọ or èsúsú. People organize themselves into groups and contribute money to save for each member's financial needs. Sometimes, members may be of the same occupation, age group, religion, or locality. A member can be given financial assistance before his or her turn if in dire need. Nowadays, some people have taken up the collection of àjọ as a full- or part-time business. They collect and disburse people's saving. They also give loans or cash advances to clients. A professional collector makes his or her profit from extra contributions from each depositor and interest charged on loans.

The cooperative movement that started in Europe in the nineteenth century arrived in Nigeria in 1935 when the Co-operative Society Ordinances were promulgated. In the same year, the first cooperative registrar was appointed, and the first cooperative society in Yorùbáland, Gbẹ̀dun Cooperative Produce Marketing Society, was established at Gbẹ̀dun village in the present-day Ọ̀nà-àrà local government of Ọ̀yọ́ State. The name of the society was later changed to Ìbàdàn Cooperative Produce Marketing Society. Chief Akínpẹ̀lú Òbísẹ̀san was its founder and president, and he was ably assisted by Isaac Akínyẹlé, who, in 1952, became the Olúbàdàn of Ìbàdàn. Other early cooperative societies in the then Western Region of Nigeria were Ọ̀wọ̀ Cooperative Union founded by Chief Abólówódì and

Ifẹ̀ Cooperative Union founded by Chief Látúndé and Chief Ládìtán.

Today, cooperative and thrift credit societies or associations are registered by the government and allowed to offer saving, loan, and investment opportunities to their members. The accounts of each association are audited by government, and the election of officers is conducted annually. Each association declares profits and dividends at its annual general meeting. Yorùbá cooperative associations have extended beyond the micro-level traditional setting.

See also **Agriculture and Farming; Associations for Promoting Yorùbá Culture**

REFERENCE

Shaffer, Jack. *Historical Dictionary of the Cooperative Movement.* Lanham, MD: Scarecrow Press, 1999.

Moses Mábayọ̀jẹ́

COSMOLOGY

Cosmology is the study of the structure and constituent dynamics of the universe. In the context of the Yorùbá traditional worldview, the concept provides the proverbial window for finding answers to questions associated with the origin of the world, humans, and their relationship with Olódùmarè, the Supreme Being. Usually, these answers emanate from what Joseph Fáníran calls the root paradigms of a people culture.

Yorùbá cosmology includes mythical narratives. Ṣẹ́gun Gbádégẹsin defines myth as the conscious response of the human mind to the realities of experience. Myths help explain the world and the place of human beings in it. Yorùbá mythical narratives revolve around the three different stages of the Olódùmarè's creative engagements and developments thereafter. The first stage deals with creation of the physical world. Here, numerous myths are unanimous in describing the basic components of the creative engagements of Olódùmarè with the assistance of some principal divinities. These divinities deputized for Olódùmarè in different areas. For example,

Encyclopedia of the Yorùbá

Òrìṣà-Ńlá, also called Ọbàtálá, was placed in charge of ordering of things, Ọrúnmìlà was in charge of knowledge, and Èṣù was the inspector and enforcer of rituals. When Olódùmarè decided to solidify the watery marsh that existed below the heavens, he gave the task to Òrìṣà-Ńlá. He was assisted by a hen and a pigeon, which spread the loose earth to solidify the ground, and by the chameleon, which inspected the work and verified that it had been done properly.

The second stage describes the creation of humans. Once again, Olódùmarè assigned the task of forming the human body to Òrìṣà-Ńlá. After making the bodies, he left them in a room. Olódùmarè outwitted Òrìṣà-Ńlá, and Olódùmarè personally put living souls into the bodies, and they become living humans. The third stage explains the relationship between humans and Olódùmarè. Their cordial and affectionate relationship at the beginning of creation soon degenerated, and humans were separated from Olódùmarè. The causes of these changes are told in different myths. However, all the myths invariably lay the blame for the strained relationship with humans. Their disobedient acts culminated in the loss of harmonious union with Olódùmarè.

These mythical narratives reveal a great deal about Yorùbá cosmology. They attempt to present a harmonious, rational, and logical explanation of the origins of the world and of human life. They explain the dynamics of humans' constituent relationships with Olódùmarè to establish some basic beliefs. Principal among these are the following:

- The world was not created ex nihilo, or out of nothing.
- Olódùmarè did not create the world and humans alone.
- Humans are special to Olódùmarè because he personally put in them the living element—the soul.
- Humans are endowed with the moral freedom to enter into fellowship with Olódùmarè.

It is not quite clear the extent to which Christianity and Islam have influenced Yorùbá cosmological narratives. However, there are similarities in the general claims of God as the creator of the world and humans, the supremacy of God, human disobedience and resulting consequences, human dependency on God, and the religious search to return to God.

See also **Deities: The *Òrìṣà*; Religion and Ritual**

REFERENCES

Fáníran, J. O. *Foundations of African Communication: With Examples from Yorùbá Culture*. Ìbàdàn (Nigeria): Spectrum Books Limited, 2008.

Gbádégẹsin, S. *African Philosophy*. New York: Peter Lang, 1991.

Ìbígbọ́ládé S. Adéríbigbé

CRAFTS

Crafts among the Yorùbá were held sacrosanct as a form of occupation in the daily lives of people in precolonial society. This occupational heritage was reflected in the colonial period. By the advent of the Nigerian railway, the importance of crafts specialization was reflected in the workforce. In a 1934 survey of railway station staff, 90 percent of workers were Yorùbá, which reflects the Yorùbá's high level of skill not only in precolonial crafts but also in modern crafts.

Crafts constituted the backbone of Yorùbá indigenous economy. These crafts used indigenous technological initiatives. The type of crafts practiced and goods produced were a function of the natural resource available to various towns and communities in Yorùbáland. Crafts in traditional Yorùbá society are divided into three major forms. The first is agriculture, which include farming, fishing, and animal husbandry. The second category of craft is artworks, which include smithing, carving, and building. The third category, the most unique and specialized, includes the works of herbal medicine and priesthood.

David Hinderer, a missionary in Ìbàdàn of the 1850s, noted different sorts of crafts practices in the city; weavers, tailors, tanners, and soap manufacturers constituted thriving industries. However, the nineteenth-century transatlantic slave trade and various Yorùbá wars diminished the practice of some crafts. Twentieth-century research and observations revealed that both traditional and modern crafts coexisted in rural and urban areas. The Cooperative Department of the Ministry of Trade and Industry, organized in the Western Region in the 1950s, required craft unions to register under the Western Nigeria Cooperative Law. The Tailors Union in Ìbàdàn was the first craft group to register. In contemporary times, various craft groups are organized as associations to promote the welfare of their members.

Crafts in Yorùbáland can be divided into two types: indigenous crafts and modern crafts. Indigenous crafts are those inherited from the precolonial era, such as blacksmithing, hair weaving, wood carving, pottery, and basket weaving. Modern crafts are those crafts practiced with the use of modern tools and technologies, such as printing, dry-cleaning, tailoring, and furniture making. Learning modern crafts, though, is still based on traditional forms of learning.

The horizon of modern crafts in contemporary Yorùbáland is broadening as new vocations emerge to serve as a means of self-employment among youth. Examples of such vocations are bag making, beauty therapy, digital photography, event planning, public speaking in Yorùbá ceremonies, bead making, baking, small-scale catering, and barbering. It is important to note that both indigenous and modern crafts are practiced in contemporary Yorùbáland, but the existence of the latter has been influenced by globalization.

See also **Art: Contemporary; Art: Indigenous; Beadwork; Carvers; Ceramics and Pottery**

REFERENCES

Lindsay, L. *Working with Gender: Wage Labour and Social Change in South Western Nigeria*. Portsmouth, NH: Heinemann, 2003.
Koll, M. *Crafts and Cooperation in Western Nigeria: A Sociological Contribution to Indigenous Economies*. Berlin: Arnold-Bergstraesser-Instituts, 1969.

Mutiat Títílopé Ọládèjọ

CROWTHER, SAMUEL ÀJÀYÍ (1807–1891)

Born in 1807 in Ọ̀ṣoògùn in the present-day Ìṣéyìn Local Government Area of Ọ̀yọ́ State, Nigeria, the Right Reverend Dr. Bishop Samuel Àjàyí Crowther was captured as a slave by Fulani slave raiders in 1821 and sold to Portuguese slave traders. Fortunately for the young Àjàyí, his ship was intercepted by the British Navy's anti-slave-trade patrol, which rescued him and took him to Freetown in Sierra Leone, where he was released. At Sierra Leone, Crowther was well cared for by the Anglican Church Missionary Society (CMS). He was taught English and was converted to Christianity. He was baptized by Reverend John Raban on December 11, 1825, and named himself Samuel Crowther (after the vicar of Christ Church, in Newgate, London, one of the pioneers of the CMS).

Crowther had interest in languages. In 1826, he was sent to England to attend the school of St. Mary's Church in Islington; he returned in 1827 and enrolled at the newly established Fourah Bay College, where he studied Latin, Greek, and Temne. Upon graduating, he became a teacher in the school. Crowther became the informant of John Raban, who was a missionary very committed to the study of African languages. Àjàyí married Asano, a fellow freed slave who changed her name to Susan; their marriage was blessed with two females and a male.

In 1841, Crowther was selected to accompany the missionary Frederick Schon on an expedition along the Niger River. The objective of the expedition was to spread commerce and Christianity, foster agricultural techniques, and help end the slave trade. Following the expedition, Crowther was recalled to England to train as a minister, and on June 11, 1843, he was ordained by Charles James Blomfield, the bishop of London. When he returned to Africa that same year, he opened a Yorùbá mission in Abẹ́òkúta with Henry Townsend and C. A. Gollmer. Crowther preached his first sermon at home on December 3, 1843, in English, and in 1851 he went to London to present the cause of Abẹ́òkúta.

A prolific writer, translator, and enviable linguist, Crowther published his *Yorùbá Vocabulary* and *Journal of an Expedition up the Niger in 1841* (with J. F. Schon) in 1843, *Journal of an Expedition up the Niger and Tshadda Rivers* in 1855, and *The Gospel on the Banks of the Niger* (with J. C. Taylor) in 1859. Following the British Niger

Expeditions of 1854 and 1857, Crowther produced a primer for the Igbo language in 1857, another for the Nupe in 1860, and a full grammar and vocabulary of Nupe in 1864. He also published the Yorùbá version of the *Anglican Book of Common Prayer*. In 1864, he was ordained as the first African bishop of the Anglican Church and earned a doctorate of divinity of the University of Oxford. In the mid-1880s, the translation to Yorùbá of the Bible (*Bíbélì Mímọ́*), which he initiated and supervised, was completed.

The pioneer of Yorùbá orthography and an architect of the written Yorùbá language, Crowther was the chair of the first interdenominational linguistic conference held in St. Peters Church of the CMS Faji Mission House, Lagos, on January 28–29, 1875. The conference had a significant impact on standardizing Yorùbá writing. In 1891, Crowther suffered a stroke. He died on December 31 at about the age of eighty-two.

See also **Language: Government and Mission Policies; Language: Standardization and Literacy; Translation**

REFERENCES

Page, Jesse. *The Black Bishop: Samuel Adjai Crowther.* Preface by Eugene Stock. New York: F. H. Revell, 1909.
———. *Samuel Crowther: The Slave Boy Who Became the Bishop of Niger.* New York: F. H. Revell, 1889.

Adéníyì Àkàngbé

CULTURE

Culture is that complex whole that includes shared ideas, knowledge, belief, art, morals, law, customs, and any other capabilities and habits acquired by a person as a member of society. Culture encompasses the tangible and intangible. Culture cannot be transmitted biologically, but it can be preserved from the past and transmitted into the future by learning.

In Yorùbá culture, the family is the most important agent of culture, as it is the first social unit and the first point of contact and interaction of the individual with other members of the society. In traditional culture, the father was the breadwinner and protector. He met all the material needs of the members of his household. The mother performed domestic chores and met the emotional needs of the family. Mothers in traditional Yorùbá culture achieve fulfillment through caring for their husbands and through bearing and caring for their children and other members of their household. The family in the traditional Yorùbá culture is communal in nature, as it extends beyond the nuclear family system. It encompasses kith and kin, such as aunts, uncles, cousins, nephews, nieces, grandparents, brothers, and sisters. The extended family seems to be disappearing, with a tendency toward the nuclear family. This is as a result of cultural contact with the West. In Yorùbá society there is emphasis on equality of sexes. While this has helped to increase the status of women in modern Yorùbá society, it has its disadvantages. There are more broken homes and single parenthood because of the lack of mutual respect between parents.

In Yorùbá culture, there is traditional system of education whereby children learn traditional wisdom and knowledge that will help them become better individuals in society. Although informal, this system of education imparts attitudes and values into children and integrates them into wider society. The traditional education has today been replaced with Western education. While this has produced much positive effect in the area of science and technological development, the rich African cultural heritage and its social ethics and values have been undermined.

The social institutions of the people include greetings, naming, marriage, burial, and dress. The Yorùbá greet each other in almost every circumstance. A conversation cannot begin until rapport has been established by exchanging greetings. Greetings in Yorùbá culture establish relationship. Part of the code of courtesy is a duty to be deferential to seniors. The male must prostrate before his senior, and the female must kneel down. An extension of the greeting code in Yorùbá culture is the obligation to offer condolences to anyone who is bereaved, ill, or injured. Failure to offer such greetings may lead to bad feelings, especially among close friends and relatives. Because of modernity and foreign religion, showing respect and courtesy to an elderly one is going into oblivion. Women in modern Yorùbá society address their husbands by name as opposed to the cultural convention of addressing them by honorific pronouns. This is the result of postcolonialism and a Western concept practiced among the educated female elite.

In Yorùbá culture, names have deep meanings. The circumstances surrounding the birth of a child are always considered before giving a name. There are three categories of names given to children: a name given at birth (*orúkọ àbísọ*), a commemorative name (*orúkọ àmútọrunwá*), and an attributive praise name (*oríkì*). Today, because many people practice Christianity and Islam, they receive religious names like Samuel, Deborah, Rasheed, and Kudrat to their children. Religious-inspired names like Heritage, Goodness, Happiness, and Testimony are also given to newborn babes in contemporary Yorùbá society.

Marriage is another important aspect of the culture. It is for companionship and procreation. Basically, a Yorùbá man's purpose of getting married is for procreation. Whoever is mature enough to take a wife or marry a husband is not considered responsible until he or she does so and begins to raise his or her family. The issue of virginity for women is paramount. A would-be bride is expected to maintains her chastity and honor until her wedding night. The most common type of marriage among traditional Yorùbá is polygamy, which is preferred for economic reasons. The men's wives are to assist him with farmwork and to procreate. The strength and wealth of a man is determined by the number of wives and children he has. However, modernization and religious beliefs have been changing the Yorùbá attitude to marriage. The norm today is a monogamous type of marriage. This does not imply that polygamy does not exist. Many influential people and religious leaders practice polygamy in secret.

The Yorùbá people believe that death is inevitable. According to them, death does not mark the end of human life but is the gateway to another life. In the Yorùbá culture, man is both a material and spiritual being, possessing body, soul, and spirit. The Yorùbá believe that, after death, the soul leaves the body and returns to God the Creator while the spirit turns into a ghost or an ancestor and begins to live in the underworld. Judgment after life serves as check to those who would perpetrate evil in Yorùbá society. The Yorùbá also believe that reincarnation is the means by which departed ancestors "return to earth." This strong belief accounts for names such as Ìyábọ̀ and Yéwándé for females and Babátúndé or Babáwálé for males. In contemporary Yorùbá society people observe wakes and remembrance services for the dead, and these have undermined the traditional belief in the union and communion between the living and the world of ancestors.

The Yorùbá people are elegant, sophisticated, and fashionable. They have a rich tradition of wearing different kinds of clothes appropriate for occasions. The people believe that clothing is a covering which enhances the presentation of a person. Work clothes are not usually elaborate or colorful. A woman usually wears *ìró*, *bùbá*, and *gèlè* (wrapper, blouse, and head tie) as casual dress. A man wears *bùbá*, *ṣòkòtò*, and *fila* (top and trousers with cap) as casual dress. A man can also wear a flowing gown (*agbádá*) on top of *bùbá* and *ṣòkòtò*. Yorùbá people wear high-quality and colorful clothing for special occasions. However, with the contact of Yorùbá with other cultures, there are now different norms of dressing in society. This has blurred the need to be specifically dressed for special functions and to pay attention to respect for correctness in appearance. People now often mix casual and formal dresses, sometimes without any respect to dress code.

Governance in traditional society is hierarchical. The king is the political and spiritual ruler in the traditional society. The kings are assisted by chiefs in directing the affairs of towns and villages. The major chiefs ascend the chieftaincy stools through inheritance, while some are given titles as a mark of honor. All the chiefs, whether traditional or honorary, work together for the advancement, peace, unity, and progress of the town. The political system of the Yorùbá reflects their cultural unification. In contemporary times, the kings are at the mercy of successive ruling state governments which pay their salaries and most of which demand absolute loyalty from the kings. A king is expected not to travel out of his domain without seeking and obtaining approval from the governor of the state where he resides. Today, kings remain in the background, mostly seen but not heard.

Religion forms the foundation and the prevailing principle of life of the people. Through all life circumstances, people believe that it is God who is in control. Olódùmarè the king of heaven and earth is followed in rank and importance by divinities, then by the spirits, and finally by the ancestors. Having direct contact with Olódùmarè, for whatever reason, amounts to lack of decorum and common etiquette in Yorùbá thought. Ancestors and divinities are seen as intermediaries who convey messages to Olódùmarè. Among the Yorùbá, Olódùmarè is believed to be too mighty to be captured by any anthropomorphic, artistic, literary, or iconographic representation. With the emergence of the missionaries and their activities, Christianity and Islam were introduced to Yorùbá society. The aftermath of this is that once-valued African traditional religion came to be regarded as fetish practices.

See also **Age Grade System; Body Adornment and Cosmetics; Burial and Funeral; Children and Childhood; Dress; Education: Traditional; Festivals and Carnivals; Greetings; Marriage and Marital System; Names and Naming; Political Systems; Praise Poetry (*Oríkì*); Taboos; Worldview**

REFERENCES

Fádípè, N. A. *The Sociology of the Yorùbá.* Ìbàdàn (Nigeria): University Press, 1970.

Lawal, S. Nike, Matthew N. O. Sádíkù, and P. Adé Dọpámú, eds. *Understanding Yorùbá Life and Culture.* Trenton, NJ: Africa World Press, 2004.

Abídèmí Bọ́lárìnwá

D

DANCE: AESTHETIC AND SOCIAL MEANING

Dancing is the art of the human body in motion. Dance (*ijó*) is very different from many other artistic expressions. In many Yorùbá communities, professional drummers and singers exist, but there are fewer dancers. Thus, other art forms and artists may be rewarded and may even earn a livelihood from their art, but dance is seldom recognized as an occupation that can generate an income. Dancers receive gifts after their performances, but generally in Yorùbá culture, dancers do not charge fees like drummers do.

Dance significantly depends on other artistic forms, such as drumming, playing musical instruments, and singing songs. Without the perfection of these components, there can be no dancing. While one could engage in the other art forms without dancing, it would be considered an aberration to dance without any music.

Dance masters and choreographers teach specialized and intricate dance steps through rigorous training. Dance is a very complex art for the initiate. The complexity of dance as an art form depends on the dancer's control over his or her body and various senses. Dance borders on spirituality as dancers commune with the spirits of dance. When Yorùbá people truly dance, there can be no observers because everybody is an active participant.

For Yorùbá people, dancing is further connected to the human desire to express the self. The vibrancy of dance results from the pulsating vibrancy in the self. Through performance, dance shows an awareness of a power of the self to attain certain ends. Dance sensuously shows procreative abilities.

Attempting to identify the genesis of dance in human society is an impossible task. Scholars do not dismiss Yorùbá dance as primitive; they seriously study dance, which traditional societies consider part of their natural mode of self-expression.

Dance is often commanded or compelled by music and drums. There are specific dances associated with specific festive, religious, ceremonial occasions, and special dresses are made for special dances. This is especially so in Yorùbá society, and one must have an ear for the music to effectively dance and respond to musical performance. The dress, mistakenly called costumes by non-Yorùbá people, is distinct from other regular dress.

Dance is also a communication tool for Yorùbá people. It is a part of language for those skilled enough to understand what is being communicated. Just as dance cannot be meaningful without a keen ear for music, communication through dance cannot be effective for those who lack the ability to patiently observe and read the aesthetics and nuances in the motions. Movement is a mode of self-expression, and it fulfills the need to project the self and reach out to others and to portray images of inner visions and intentions.

Dance also serves as a critique or protest of society. As critique, dance can highlight the shortcomings of people or groups, especially leaders, in society. Thus, dance highlights issues that may be difficult to verbalize; as such, it provides the context of mutual communicative reflexivity of the art form to help correct the ills of society. Dance also can serve as protest against behavioral indulgences by the high and mighty in society.

In addition, like other art forms, there is a very significant part of dance that is mainly for the entertainment and edification of the self and the audience. This is the context in which the *alárìnjó* (a type of masquerade or a performer who dances for monetary benefit (in the form of gifts) and who moves from one place to another—the movement gives this performance the name) makes sense and is appreciated for his or her practice of dance for the entertainment of members of society. As a means of entertainment and a professional pursuit, dance helps people to assuage stress and to create fun and amusement even in the most difficult of situations. At the same time, dance can allow a person to improve his or her financial situation by generating income through voluntary cash gifts from audience members.

Notable periods when dance entertainment occurs are the periods between heavy farmwork; when other regional occupations are at a lull because of the weather, especially between late November and early February in southwestern Nigeria; and between work cycles. Consequently, dancing, drumming, singing, and the like might be diversions or recreational activities that people pick up as hobbies. This reveals the ingenuity of the people to re-create and to develop means of generating leisure in traditional and contemporary societies.

When we look at the various avenues Yorùbá people employ to dance, we see how conducive dance is to physical fitness, because people stretch different parts of their body when dancing. For instance, virtually all rituals, ceremonies, and occasions are reasons to dance. Other religions that have been introduced to Yorùbáland have had to incorporate these cultural aspects of Yorùbá society into their liturgies. The Pentecostal and revivalist churches, as well as Islamic

denominations, now incorporate these elements of Yorùbá culture into their practices—dance is one of the means of praising the gods. Sporting outings are also occasions for dancing and ululating in support of teams and individuals. Before sedentary life, when people trekked long distances, moving provided the means by which fitness was attained; now that automobiles have taken over, other aspects of cultural life have provided the means of exercise and fitness. Dietary practices have deviated from healthy ones; and so dancing in the churches and mosques constitutes a phenomenon that provides not just entertainment but also a cardiovascular workout and benefits to longevity.

See also **Dance: Types**

REFERENCES

Àjàyí-Ṣóyínká, Ọmọ́fọlábọ̀. *Yorùbá Dance: The Semiotics of Movement and Body Attitude in a Nigerian Culture.* Trenton, NJ: Africa World Press, 1998.

Bẹ́wàjí, J. A. I. *Black Aesthetics.* Trenton, NJ: Africa World Press. 2013.

John Ayọ̀túndé Ìṣọ̀lá Bẹ́wàjí

DANCE: TYPES

Dance is rhythmic movement or conscious design organized in response to sound stimulus. In Africa, dance does not exist without music or a definite form of accompaniment. Traditional African dances are more than movements or visual arts that exist in time and space. Taking this nature of African dance as a given, the Yorùbá enclave of southwestern Nigeria is not exceptional. Yorùbá myth traces the phenomenon of dance to the celestial descent of Àyàn and his drum. According to the myth, Àyàn was commissioned by Olódùmarè (Almighty God) to teach and disseminate the art of music and dance. It follows that the phenomenon of dance among the Yorùbá cannot be understood without recourse to the stringent cultural beliefs and value system of the people.

The *bàtá*, *gèsè*, and *gẹ̀lẹ̀dẹ́*, among other dances, exhibit the existential along with the social significance of dance among the Yorùbá. *Bàtá* and *gèsè* dances are named after the rhythmic choreographed movement that correlates to the musical alternation of *bàtá* and *gèsè* drums, respectively. These dances are spectacular for the embodied movements that convey the undertone of hermeneutic performance of talking drums and songs. They relay the history of significant events, figures, and lineages among the Yorùbá. These dances are dictated by the drums, which have a language of their own and a language that is effectively interpreted by the dancers. For instance, the *bàtá* dance oftentimes is attributed to the majestic performance of the god of thunder, Ṣàngó, who performed it during one of his numerous ecstatic moments. The expression *oníṣàngó tó jó, tí kò tàpá, àbùkù ara rè ni*—meaning a Ṣàngó devotee who dances without flinging his feet and legs does discredit to him- or herself—is thus often heard among Yorùbá *bàtá* dancers.

Similarly, *gèsè* dance is rendered in honor of diverse deities in Yorùbáland. For example, dance is performed with the tune of the *gèsè* drum ensembles: *ṣaworo, ìyáìlù, gúdúgúdú, kéríkérì, ìṣaájú,* and *kànnàngó*. Adorned in *aṣọ-òkè* garments, *gèsè* dancers dance in bare feet, wave fly whisks in unison, and signify the authority of divine-attested invocation of blessings upon the land. This dance is predominant among the Yorùbá people in Òkè-Igbó (Ọ̀sun State) and Ifẹ̀tẹ̀dó (Oǹdó State). *Àdàmò* of Èkìtì is similar to this, honoring not only deities but also happenstances.

Gèlèdé dance elevates the place of women. Women are commonly addressed as *àwọn ìyá wa* (our mothers); they represent the source of vitality and fertility in society. They possess the *àṣẹ* (spiritual power of life forces) that halts destruction, evil, famine, health disasters, infertility, and other vices. The myth surrounding *gèlèdé* is traced to goddesses like Yemọja or Ọya. The "dance of our mothers," as it is often called, is performed with wooden headgear or a mask that conveys a sculpted female face with three strips representing horizontal and/or vertical incisions and decorated with various images of the gods, or those of reptiles such as snakes and tortoises. It is worn on the side of the head by the male *gèlèdé* dancers. They also wear bulging wrappers that connote breasts and buttocks, which they shake vigorously as the dance takes place. The movements of the dance reflect the distinct place Yorùbá women inhabit in the ontology of Yorùbá cosmology. Women are the medium of life and breath.

Beyond the cultural symbolism of these dances, they are entertainment performed at coronations, the dedication of a band or cult, celebrations of the dead, presentations of chieftaincy titles, and other occasions. Well-known contemporary dancers such as Dúró Ládipò, Sunday Adéníyì (King Sunny Adé) and Bísádé Ológundé (aka Lágbájá) popularized traditional dances such as *bàtá, kótó,* and *gèsè*, and their popularity reflects the entertaining function of Yorùbá dances.

Dance serves both functional and symbolic, aesthetic ends; it reflects the core and periphery of the existential plane of the Yorùbá. It is also a representation of the diversity of the Yorùbá: as carvers (as in Gèlèdé), farmers, hunters, and devotees of gods and goddesses of thunder (Ṣàngó, as in *bàtá*), river (Yemọja and Ọya as in Gèlèdé), iron (Ògún), and so on. It provides visual aids and mnemonics for promoting and maintaining social cohesion, identity, and relationship patterns between humans and the gods, spirits, and deities. It also functions to entertain and instruct.

See also **Dance: Aesthetics and Social Meaning; Music: Islamic; Music: Popular; Music: Traditional; Musical Instruments**

REFERENCES

Àjàyí-Ṣóyínká, Ọmọ́fọlábọ̀. *Yorùbá Dance: The Semiotics of Movement and Body Attitude in a Nigerian Culture.* Trenton, NJ: Africa World Press, 1998.

Béwàjí, J. A. I. *Black Aesthetics.* Trenton, NJ: Africa World Press. 2013.

Ayọ̀ Fádáhùnsi

DEATH, MOURNING, AND ANCESTORS

The Yorùbá traditional thinking about death, mourning, and ancestors is fundamentally subsumed in ontological paradigms of the dual nature of humans, the circle of life, and the associated paradoxical themes of loss resulting from death and the gain of lineage sustainability through ancestry.

The Yorùbá do not regard death as the end of life. Rather, it represents a transition to the afterlife. This is why when a person dies, phrases such as *ó ti sùn* (he has slept) or *'o ti lọ ọ̀run* (he has gone to heaven) are used. Thus, burial rituals are symbolically rites of passage to assist the dead in coping with the "aches" of the journey and to provide the required "entry pass" into the ancestral world. This journey, considered a trip from known existence to an unknown one that guarantees immortality, is aptly described in the Èjì Ogbè chapter of *odù ifá* as follows: *Mo dògbògbó orósè; n kò kú mọ́; mo digba òkè; mo le gbọnin* (I am now aged *osè* tree; I no longer know death; I am two hundred hills rolled into one; I am immovable).

However, the concept of death as passage to eternity does not in any way diminish the practical experience of loss resulting from the death of a person, whether that person is old or young. Thus, mourning becomes an essential and integral part of funeral rites. The mourning process focuses on both the dead and the bereaved. Usually, the duration and intensity of mourning are determined by the age of the deceased, the cause of death, and the circumstances surrounding the death. Although the mourning rituals are designed to provide therapeutic support for the bereaved, the life of the dead person is also celebrated. Thus, expressions of mourning are usually intermixed with paradoxical messages of how the deceased will be missed, how he or she will spend the afterlife, and expectations of benevolent support from the deceased as a "citizen" of the ancestral world.

The "dual" side of the paradox of death and mourning and the resulting theme of loss for the Yorùbá is that of sustainability and continuation of a lineage. This is clearly discerned from the belief in ancestors. However, becoming an ancestor is by no means a possibility for every deceased person. Attaining such a status is usually premised on qualifications such as reaching an old age, dying a good death, having children, performing the required burial rites, and, most important, having a good moral standing. Invariably,

how the deceased participates in the afterlife depends on the quality of the life the person lived, the nature of his or her death, and the rites of passage performed. This is aptly expressed in the Yorùbá saying *kẹ́ni hùwà gbẹ̀dẹ̀gbẹ̀dẹ̀; kẹ́ni leè kú pẹ̀lẹ́pẹ̀lẹ́; k'ọmọ ẹni leè na ọwọ́ gbọgbọrọ l'éni sin* (let one conduct one's life gently and die a good death; that one's children may stretch their hands over one's body in burial).

The significance and benefits of belief in ancestors are mutually shared between the spiritual world and the world of the living. First, it is possible for the dead person to be transformed into an ancestral spirit. As an ancestor, he or she can be reincarnated in descendants and thereby continue to be part and parcel of the earthly family: actively interested and involved in the fortune of its members. In a way, the ancestor becomes an *òrìṣà* to his or her own family, receiving prayers and offerings. Second, the ancestor provides spiritual protection and serves as an adviser and consultant in different aspects of life to the living members of the family. For instance, these ancestors may be accessed through divinations, dreams, and trances.

See also **Burial and Funeral; Dreams and Dream Interpretation; Widow and Widowhood**

REFERENCES

Abímbọ́lá, K. *Yorùbá Culture: A Philosophical Account.* Lagos (Nigeria): Ìrókò Academic Publishers, 2005.

Abímbọ́lá, W. "The Yorùbá Concept of Human Personality." In *La notion de personne en Afrique Noire*, ed. Roger Bastide and Germaine Dieterlen, 73–90. Paris: CNRS, 1973.

Ìbígbọ́ládé S. Adéríbigbé

DEBT AND DEBT MANAGEMENT

Gbèsè, or debt and the debtor's debt management, is critical to the continued public perception of credibility and integrity, not only of the individual but also the family and the whole lineage. Nonpayment of debt and failing to provide restitution for outstanding debts have grave consequences for the individual and his or her family. The Yorùbá have a profound sense of history; the concept of *ọmọlúwàbí* underpins society. The *ọmọlúwàbí* concept encompasses all the good attributes and societal expectations of a community member in good standing. Thus, a debtor (*onígbèsè*) is perceived as violating the fundamental code of a good community member. Debt may be conceptualized as the stock of monetized values or service owed by a person to another. In the Yorùbá context, it can be in the form of money owed or unfulfilled service of obligations.

Because of the cultural aversion to unpaid debt, the traditional onus for the management of debt falls on the loan giver, who applies different strategies to humiliate the debtor until payment is secured. The idea of a debtor as a dishonorable person or family gave rise to the concept of *òṣómàálò*, in which the loan giver establishes a small camp prominently located in the vicinity of the abode of the debtor. The presence of the *òṣómàálò* elicits the intervention of neighbors, who urge the debtor to explore all avenues to repay the debt. It also forces family members to intervene with loans and other forms of security to pacify the *òṣómàálò* and, more important, to protect the honor of the family. So great is the aversion to debt that, as a last resort and in the ultimate humiliation, the debtor, his or her family, and his or her spouse may be indentured to service in order to repay the debt.

Ọlátúnjí Òjó observes that *panyarring*, or pawning, is another means of getting restitution for debt owed. This is one recourse to forcibly seizing the assets of the debtor. He asserts that failure to settle debts was the major cause of *panyarring*. Pawnship, or debt-bondage slavery, involves the use of family members, including children, as collateral to secure the repayment of debt. When the debt is not paid, the family members are retained and often do not return home for a long time. Slave labor is performed by the debtor or relative of the debtor, usually a child. Thus, debt management is a family affair, with implications for the continued respect of the debtor family. There is also the occasional practice of self-enslavement for debt and the sale of children. The British took a strong stance against *panyarring* when they established their administration in Nigeria and banned the practice in 1903. Also, in more recent times, Western capitalism and its emphasis on bank loans and credit for investment effectively took away the shame associated with debts in traditional Yorùbá societies.

See also **Commerce; Economic System; Ọmọlúwàbí**

REFERENCES

Fádípè, N. A. *The Sociology of the Yorùbá.* Ìbàdàn (Nigeria): University Press, 1970.

Òjó, Ọlátúnjí. "*Èmú (Àmúyá)*: The Yorùbá Institution of Panyarring or Seizure for Debt." *African Economic History* 35 (2007): 31–62.

Adémọ́lá Àràoyè

DEITIES: THE ÒRÌṢÀ

All the *òrìṣà* are said to have been either divinities that descended from the invisible world (*òrun*) and lived in this planetary world (*ayé*) like human beings or famous individuals deified as gods or goddesses after their death in recognition of their supernatural deeds, outstanding wisdom, and perseverance. The *òrìṣà* are said to be closely associated with the living and frequently involved in human affairs. Therefore, they connect humans with God, the Supreme Being. These deities enjoy a dual grouping, which is based on their personalities and modes of action. The first group includes cool, calm, gentle, temperate gods, denoted symbolically by the color white, and the second group is harsh, aggressive, demanding, and quick tempered, denoted symbolically by the colors red or black. However, this classification has nothing to do with issues of good and evil. All the deities, like human beings, are made up of positive and negative traits. Also, each *òrìṣà* has a favorite food, color, and paraphernalia, which are documented through oral tradition.

There is a commonly accepted tradition that there are 401 deities in Yorùbáland, although that figure should be viewed as a sacred metaphor and not a scientific fact. Oral traditions often give a confusing impression of the exact number of divinities; for example, sometimes they speak of *èrùnlójọ irúnmọlè* (700 divinities). We are told also that there are *igba irúnmọlè ojùkòtún, igba irúnmọlè ojùkòsì* (200

Encyclopedia of the Yorùbá

divinities of the right side, 200 divinities of the left side, for a total of 400 divinities) or ọ̀kànlénú irúnmọlẹ̀ (401 divinities). There are still ọ̀jìlélégbèje irúnmọlẹ̀ tí wọn ń lu ẹdan fún (1,440 divinities for whom metal rods are sounded).

However, there is no common saying among the people that designates a particular divinity as the most important, except for the claims in their mythological stories that some sixteen divinities descended to the earth. Having said that, however, there are certain divinities that are generally acclaimed as more important than others; these might be called the major deities. According to N. A. Fádípẹ̀, the following divinities are universally worshipped everywhere in Yorùbáland on an annual basis: Èṣù, Ọbàtálá, Ògún, Òrìṣà-Oko, Ọ̀ṣun, Ṣàngó, Ṣànpọ̀nná, and Yemọja. The issue of the order of seniority among these major deities is not very clear, and some scholars who have addressed the subject matter in their works all have opposing views. For instance, Bọ́lájí Ìdòwú holds the view that Òrìṣà-Ńlá is the "Supreme Divinity" of Yorùbáland, whereas Fádípẹ̀ sees Ifá as the "most universal . . . òrìṣà in Yorùbáland." Bádé Àjùwọ̀n presents Ògún as "first among equals" in the Yorùbá pantheon. If, however, one asks the worshippers of each of the other major divinities which is the most important of all Yorùbá deities, each will claim that his or her own deity is the more important one.

One can argue that Ifá is at the center of the Yorùbá religion and tradition, and that all aspects of this mytho-aesthetic canon are organized to explain the nature of human life and the upkeep of life itself through a divination system that is believed to be capable of offering answers to *all* human problems.

See also **Color Symbolism; Cosmology; Diaspora: Deities (The *Òrìṣà*); Divination: Ifá**

REFERENCES

Àjùwọ̀n, Bádé. "Ògún: Premus Inter Pares." In *Proceedings of the First World Conference on Òrìsà Tradition*, ed. Wándé Abímbọ́lá, 425–50. Ilé-Ifẹ̀ (Nigeria): Ọbáfẹ́mi Awólọ́wọ̀ University, 1981.
Fádípẹ̀, N. A. *The Sociology of the Yorùbá*. Ìbàdàn (Nigeria): University Press, 1970.

Ìdòwú, E. B. *Olódùmarè: God in Yorùbá Belief.* New York: Frederick A. Praeger, 1963.

Akíntúndé Akínyẹmí

DEMOGRAPHY: SOCIAL CHARACTERISTICS

The Yorùbá people occupy the southwestern geopolitical zone of Nigeria. The zone is one of the six geopolitical zones of Nigeria and houses the most densely populated state in the country, Lagos. The zone comprises the states of Lagos, Ọ̀yọ́, Oǹdó, Ọ̀sun, Ògún, and Èkìtì in present-day Nigeria. The zone shares the same boundary with the northern part of Nigeria, which includes the north-central states of Kwara and Kogi; in the east with Edo and Delta (in the southern geopolitical zone); in the west with Benin Republic; and in the south with the Gulf of Guinea. Of the six states of the zone, Lagos and Ọ̀yọ́ are the most urban states, with a 94 percent and 69 percent urban population, respectively (Nigerian Demographic and Health Survey, NDHS, 2003). None of the rest of the states falls within the least urbanized states in Nigeria.

Population, Economy, and Basic Demographic Indicators

The first officially accepted census in Nigeria conducted in 1963 revealed that the population of the Yorùbá was 7,220,074 (3,624,502 males and 3,595,572 females). However, the population of the zone is now 27,722,432 (14,081,157 males and 13,641,275 females) based on the 2006 National Population and Housing Census, which accounts for approximately 19.7 percent of the 2006 population of Nigeria.

Table D.1 Population for Yorùbá-speaking states in Nigeria

State	Area, square km	Population		
		1991	2006	2011
Èkìtì	5,887.89	Not yet created	2,398,957	2,794,575
Lagos	3,496.45	5,725,116	9,113,605	10,668,139
Ògún	16,980.55	2,333,726	3,751,140	4,412,299
Oǹdó	15,195.18	3,784,902	3,460,877	4,012,105
Ọ̀sun	8,699.84	2,158,143	3,416,959	3,999,800
Ọ̀yọ́	2,8245.26	3,452,720	5,580,894	6,596,392

Education

The southwestern zone of Nigeria is noted for the high rate of acceptance of Western education. As a result, it has produced well-known scholars in virtually all academic fields. The zone has a total of thirty universities distributed across its states. There are seventeen private universities (run or administered by individuals or corporate bodies or organizations such as Christian or Muslim missions), seven state universities (with one jointly owned by the states of Òṣun and Òyó), and six federal universities (one in each state). There are other tertiary institutions such as colleges of education, polytechnics, colleges of health technology, and schools of nursing, among others. The zone houses the first university in Nigeria, the University of Ìbàdàn, which is known as the country's premier university.

Economy

The main economic activity for the Yorùbá in southwestern Nigeria has been agriculture. The people are noted for production of food as well as agro-industrial raw materials. Major agricultural products include cocoa, cassava, yam, and kola nut. The zone is well known for the production of cocoa and is regarded as the cocoa belt of the country, accounting for about 70 percent of total annual production of cocoa in the country (242,000 metric tons) in 2008. Some Yorùbá states also house mineral resources such as gold, copper, oil, and the like.

Basic Demographic Indicators

We use the following basic demographic indicators in our discussion: fertility, mortality, and migration. Fertility is an indicator of population growth. The current and cumulative fertility is a good and essential measure. The Yorùbá zone in Nigeria has a total fertility rate (TFR) of 4.5 children per female. This is below the TFR of the whole country, which is 5.7, and also the lowest rate among the different zones of the country. The median age of women in southwestern Nigeria at first birth is 22.7 years. This could be as a result of the literacy level as well as the rate of

acceptance of contraceptive use in the zone. In 2008, the Nigeria Demographic and Health Survey (NDHS) revealed that 95 percent of women of reproductive age had heard about traditional contraceptive methods, and 94 percent had heard about modern methods. About 99 percent of men in the zone were aware of traditional contraceptive methods, and 98 percent had heard about modern methods. Thirty-two percent of women between the ages of fifteen and forty-nine reported having used any method of contraception (n = 4,366), and 21 percent had used any modern method.

Mortality

The mortality situation in the zone is best discussed using infant, child, adult, and maternal mortality. The infant and child mortality rates are used as indicators of a country's socioeconomic situation and quality of life. Infant mortality is defined as the probability of a child dying before his or her first birthday, and child mortality is defined as the probability of dying between the first and fifth birthday. The NDHS survey revealed that infant and child mortality rates in the zone are fifty-nine and thirty-two, respectively, per thousand live births, respectively. These rates are among the lowest in Nigeria. Adult and maternal mortality are major indicators of maternal health and well-being. Maternal mortality is the death of a woman during pregnancy or within forty-two days of the termination of pregnancy from any cause related to or aggravated by the pregnancy or its management that did not result from accidental or incidental causes. The zone enjoys the lowest maternal mortality rate (MMR) in the country. The NDHS reported an MMR of 545 per 100,000 live births for the country, which also represents a wide regional disparity between the different zones of the country. While the northern zones have an average MMR of 2,420 per 100,000 live births and range from 1,060 to 4,477), the southern zones have an MMR between 454 and 772 per 100,000 live births.

See also **Education: Tertiary**

REFERENCE

National Population Commission (NPC) [Nigeria] and ICF Macro. *Nigeria Demographic and Health Survey* (NDHS) 2008. Abuja (Nigeria): National Population Commission and ICF Macro, 2009.

Ṣọládoyè S. Asà

DIASPORA: DEITIES (THE ÒRÌṢÀ)

The dispersal of the òrìṣà religious culture and traditions was a direct consequence of the dispersal of Yorùbá-speaking Diaspora, first through enslavement and later as indentured workers in Latin America and the Caribbean. According to Mercedes Cros Sandoval, the first movement of the Yorùbá deities occurred with the enslavement and forced exile of initiates and priests of the diverse Yorùbá deities like Ọbàtálá, Ògún, Èṣù, Odùduwà, Aganjú, Ọya, Ọṣun, Ṣàngó, Ọbalúayé, Nàná Bùkúù, Ìbejì, Ọ̀ṣọ́ọ̀sì, Ọ̀sanyìn, Òsùmàrè, and Yemọja to different parts of the Americas, most especially to places like Brazil, Cuba, Haiti, and Trinidad and Tobago, which Alejandro Frigério has classified as places of primary irradiation of the Yorùbá religious culture in the Americas. Each of these locales was later responsible for the second dispersal of the deities, which made it possible for Afro-Brazilian, Afro-Cuban, Haitian, and Trinidadian priests and priestesses to take the diasporic Yorùbá religious traditions to new locales like Uruguay, Argentina, Colombia, Venezuela, Puerto Rico, Santo Domingo, Mexico, Panama, and, ultimately, the United States of America.

The òrìṣà (deities) were originally introduced into Latin America and the Caribbean under the guise of *santos* and *santas* (Catholic saints), because the only significant opportunity for enslaved Africans to practice their African religion openly within the slave societies in the Spanish and Portuguese Americas was to enter into a tacit agreement with the dominant Catholic religion through its belief in saints as intercessors of humans before God. This explains why some of the enslaved Africans became active members of Catholic brotherhoods known as *irmandades* in Brazil and *cofradías* or *cabildos* in Cuba and other Spanish-speaking societies.

The culture of popular saints introduced into the Americas from the brand of Catholicism of the Iberian peoples (Portuguese and Spanish) allowed enslaved Africans to surreptitiously introduce their òrìṣà as the twins of Catholic saints under a system of equivalence commonly referred to in anthropological studies as religious syncretism. This is why the religion of the òrìṣà is known as Santería in Cuba while the adherents of Afro-Brazilian òrìṣà who worship Candomblé are referred to as *o-povo-de-santo* (people of the saints). Also, the titles of ritual and liturgical leaders of a religious temple in both Candomblé and Santería orders, the *bàbálóriṣà* or *iyálóriṣà*, are generally rendered in literal translations as father or mother of the saint (*pai* or *padre* or *mãe* or *madre de santo*) in Brazil and Cuba, respectively.

Although the real implications and profound significance of syncretism continue to be highly contested within certain contemporary Candomblé and Santería circles, major Yorùbá òrìṣà continue to be associated with their counterpart Catholic saints in popular Afro-Latin religious traditions. Thus, Ọbàtálá, the deity of purity and creation, continues to be associated with Senhor do Bonfim (Our Lord of the Good End or Jesus Christ) in Brazil. Ọbàtálá is celebrated with pomp and pageantry by the *baiana de candomblé* priestesses every third Thursday after Epiphany on the *colina sagrada* (the Bonfim Cathedral) in Salvador. The Candomblé priestesses perform the òrìṣà rituals of using the sacred and perfumed "waters of Ọbàtálá" to cleanse the staircase and entrance of the Catholic cathedral.

In addition, the deity of thunder and justice, Ṣàngó (rendered as Changó in Cuba and Xangô in Brazil), is syncretized as São Gerônimo (St. Jerome) in Brazil and Santa Bárbara (St. Barbara) in Cuba. Ọṣun, the goddess of beauty and fertility, is syncretized as Nossa Senhora da Purificação (Our Lady of Purity) for the Brazilian Candomblé and as Nuestra Señora de la Caridad del Cobre (Our Lady of Charity) in Cuban Santería (Lucumí). Ògún, the deity of iron and warfare, is syncretized as St. Anthony, and Yemọja, the goddess of maternity, is syncretized as La Virgen de La Regla (Our Lady, Virgin of the Church of Regla) in Cuba and as Nossa Senhora das Candeias (Our Lady of Light) in Brazil.

Another interesting detail in the dispersal of the òrìṣà is the invention of a hierarchy or seniority. Duplicating or creating avatars of the òrìṣà is very common in Brazilian Candomblé and Cuban Santería. For example, some principal òrìṣà like Ọbàtálá and Ṣàngó are believed in Candomblé to have "older" and "younger" avatars in Brazil. Thus, Ọbàtálá or Òrìṣà-Ńlá (the Great Deity), known as Oxalá in Candomblé, is "divided" into Oxaguiã or Oxalá Velho and Oxalufã or Oxalá Moço. In other words, Oxalufã (derived from the òrìṣà Olúfọ́n) is considered the "older" Òrìṣà-Ńlá, and Oxaguiã (òrìṣà Ògìyán) is considered the "younger" Òrìṣà-Ńlá, a distinction that was not established in the personality of Ọbàtálá in the Yorùbá African homeland. The case of Ṣàngó Ogódo and Ṣàngó Aganjú is analogous in Brazilian Candomblé and in Cuban Santería or Regla de Ochá.

Ìjúbà, xirê, bembé, and wẹmílẹ̀rẹ̀ are some of the names by which the òrìṣà liturgical sessions are known in the diverse locales of the Diaspora, mainly Trinidad, Brazil, Cuba, and the United States. The sessions represent the public aspect of the manifestation of the relationship between the òrìṣà and their devotees and are held in the form of communal feasts with a lot of drumming, dancing, and eating. During such sessions, the òrìṣà are invoked in a specific order through specific drums or drum rhythms known as toques. In Cuba and its diaspora, the sacred bàtá drums are used for this purpose; in Brazil, the drums of the Candomblé ensemble include the rum, rumpi, and lê, which are accompanied by the indispensable gan or agogô. Although the same drums are used to summon the òrìṣà, the toques are specific to each òrìṣà or group of òrìṣà, as the case may be. For example, in Brazil, where the òrìṣà drum ensembles like bàtá, dùndún, and ìgbìn did not survive the restrictions on African material culture imposed by slavery, distinct rhythms or toques are used to invite each òrìṣà. Xangô is thus invited with the àlùjá rhythm, and Ogum, Oxoosi, and other hunter òrìṣà come down on the cue of the àgèrè rhythm. Oxum,

Oxalá, and other òrìṣà funfun (white òrìṣà) respond only to the ijexá toques.

The toques are accompanied by the appropriate liturgical songs for each òrìṣà, usually rendered in an ancient form of the Yorùbá language. On recognizing their specific signature tunes or toques, the òrìṣà in turn "mount" those in the assembly who have been consecrated to them during initiation. These are referred to as ìyàwó, or bride of the òrìṣà, irrespective of their biological sex. Thus, the òrìṣà momentarily takes over the body of the ìyàwó, who then dances, speaks, and acts under a complete trance, often accomplishing superhuman feats like eating fireballs, piercing his or her body with sharp objects without any sign of pain, taking on impossible tasks, or prescribing healing therapies for people afflicted with difficult ailments, who may or may not be present.

Another major manifestation of the òrìṣà identity in the Diaspora is the concept of altares, collares y colores. The altares refer to the recipients commonly used by santeros and santeras to keep the otan (Yorùbá ọta) or sacred stones and other ritual symbols of their òrìṣà. In colonial Cuba, when the practitioners of the Ochá tradition were persecuted by the state, santeros devised a way to make their òrìṣà altars inconspicuous by using porcelain dishes as their sacred recipients. The dish chosen must, however, be in the specific color of the patron òrìṣà of the individual. Thus, a son or daughter of Yemaya will use the corresponding sea-blue porcelain, whereas an ochunita—a daughter of Ọ̀ṣun—would choose a yellow one, and a devotee of Ọbàtálá would use white porcelain. These same colors are used for the collares, otherwise known as elekes, which are the ritually prepared beads that every ọmọ-òrìṣà wears from the day of his or her initiation.

Mention should also be made of the religious tradition of venerating the ancestor as egúngún and gẹ̀lẹ̀dẹ́, which was also transplanted to Latin America and the Caribbean, although on a lesser scale than the òrìṣà. This is most especially true in places like Bahia (Brazil), Trinidad, Jamaica, and Barbados. A noteworthy difference between the spread of the egúngún and the òrìṣà is that the former are not syncretized with Catholic saints, as was the case with the latter. Thus, ancestral Yorùbá *egúngún*, such as Bàbá Olúkòtún, Bàbá Aboula (Agboolá), Bàbá Bakabaka, and the like, have kept their original names and attributes in their new homes in the Ilê Axipá temple of Salvador and Amoreira on Itaparica Island in Bahia, Brazil.

See also **Deities: The Òrìṣà; Diaspora: Impact of Yorùbá Culture; Diaspora: Yorùbá in North America; Diaspora: Yorùbá in South America and the Caribbean; Lucumí; Nagô; Òyótúnjí: The Yorùbá Community in the United States**

REFERENCES

Cros Sandoval, Mercedes. *La religión afrocubana*. Madrid: Plaza Mayor, 1975.

Fálọlá, Tóyìn, and Matt D. Childs, eds. *The Yorùbá Diaspora in the Atlantic World*. Bloomington: Indiana University Press, 2005.

Felix Ayoh'Omídire

DIASPORA: IMPACT OF YORÙBÁ CULTURE

Of all the enslaved African populations whose descendants currently inhabit the diverse countries of the African Diaspora in the Americas, the Yorùbá are, without doubt, the single ethnic group whose cultural legacy is most visible in virtually all aspects of the life of contemporary Latin American and Caribbean populations. In language, religion, literature, institutions, economics, philosophy, ritual and chieftaincy titles, dress, and color codes, and the like, the Yorùbá impact continues to dominate the cultural landscape and identity formation of Afro–Latin American subjects.

One major Yorùbá legacy among Afro–Latin Americans is the *ẹbi* (family) concept. Captivity and slavery severed all sanguine family ties, and discouraged reconstituting ethnic groups and concentrating people of the same ethnic and language groups on the slave plantations as a way to avoid slave revolts. Despite these efforts, enslaved Africans were able to reconstruct the family structure in a most symbolic way. Across the Americas, the diverse religious communities within Candomblé, Santería, Vodou, Macumba, Ṣàngó, and the like are organized around the concept of a symbolic and spiritual family structure. The nomenclature used to express the diverse communities centers around the concept of the Yorùbá extended family structure and bears witness to their Yorùbá origin. Vocabularies like *ilé*, *bàbá*, *ìyá*, and *ọmọ* are intimately used by members of the religious communities in the Diaspora. For example, a typical *comunidade-terreiro* (religious temple) of Brazilian Candomblé is referred to as Ilê Axé. It is headed by a *babalorixá* or an *iyalorixá*, the initiates are called *iaô* (from the Yorùbá *ìyàwó*), and those who have completed more than seven years of initiation graduate to the rank of *ebome* (from the Yorùbá expression *ẹ̀gbọ́n mi*, or "my elder brother or sister"). It is of significant importance to note that within this concept of family ties, reconstructed through ritual initiation to the *òrìṣà*, the normal natural taboos guiding the traditional Yorùbá blood relations must also be respected. For example, no sexual relationship is allowed between a *babalorixá* or *iyalorixá* and an *ìyàwó* (male or female) initiated by him or her. The same taboo applies to *irmãos* or *irmãs de esteira*, two persons who went through initiation at the same period under the same priest, as they are both considered "blood" siblings.

The use of Yorùbá ritual titles among initiates in the diverse Yorùbá Diaspora is another strong legacy. Babaláwo, Oríàtẹ, and Oyùbọna (Ojùgbọ̀nà Awo) are some examples of functional ritual titles from Cuban Santería, and titles like *ogã* and *equede* (* èkejì*), *axogum* (*aṣògún*), *iábaxé* (head of the sacred kitchen) and *iáebe* (*iyá ẹgbẹ́*), and *iá quequerê* (*ìyá kékeré*) are given to highly respected members of the ritual hierarchy of Brazilian Candomblé. Mention should also be made of the reinvention in 1936 of the Òyó royal court in Brazil by Ìyálórìṣà Eugénia Ana dos Santos (Mãe Aninha), founder of the Ilê Axé Opô Àfònjá in Salvador, Brazil, and her Yorùbá Brazilian collaborator, Martiniano Eliseu do Bonfim (Òjẹ́làdé). The duo created what they referred to as the *mọgbà*-titled chiefs for the Candomblé temple, otherwise known in Brazilian religious anthropology as the *corpo dos obás de Xangô* (the council of Ṣàngó's ministers), complete with the Oníkòyí, Arólú, Arẹsà, and even the Àrẹ-Ònà-Kakaǹfò.

Each *olóyè*, as they came to be known, is also entitled to have his lieutenants to the right and to the left—Ọ̀tún Oníkòyí and Òsì Oníkòyí, Ọ̀tún Arólú and Òsì Arólú, and the like. The titled *ọbá* is equally an important liturgical figure in the Cuban Lucumí tradition of Regla de Ochá, otherwise known as Santería; he is responsible for the *dílóggún* (*ẹẹ́rìndínlógún*) oracular readings. This institutional legacy of the Yorùbá has been further expanded by contemporary Yorùbá religious leaders in the Diaspora through the adoption of the use of ritual insignias that bear the title of the *olóyè* on elaborately designed hats, *abẹ̀bẹ̀* (fans), pendants, and even the *bastón* (handheld ritual batons), which reflects the practice in contemporary Yorùbá homeland.

Thus, it is commonplace today to see dignitaries in Yorùbá diasporic religious practices wear engraved ritual hats bearing titles like Chief Ṣàngó-Jàkúta of Trinidad, Sárépẹgbẹ́ of Miami, or Yèyé Omi Ọ̀ṣun of Venezuela. The same importance is associated in the Diaspora with personal names that are taken by newly initiated individuals into the Yorùbá Ifá or *òrìṣà* traditions; rich-sounding names with deep meaning like Olúfọ́n Deí, Ọbá Di Méjì, Ọ̀ṣúnlétí, Iwíntọ́la, Ifátó Ọyangan, and the like are proudly exhibited and used by the new Yorùbá diasporic *ọmọ-òrìṣà* both as part of their daily lives and as part of their identity on the social network platforms like Facebook and Twitter.

French ethnologist Pierre Fátúmbí Verger and American anthropologist Ruth Landes have argued that, until the 1940s, the Yorùbá language—or at least fragments of it—was used as a lingua franca on a daily basis on the streets of Salvador da Bahia and the municipalities of the Recôncavo, like Santo Amaro da Purificação, São Félix, Maragogipe, and Cachoeira. Cuban ethnologist Fernando Ortiz confirmed that the same reality was true for Cuba through the 1950s, when a sizable population of Lucumí descendants and their *criollo* and *reyollo* offspring in cities like La Habana, Matanzas, Guanabacoa, and Santiago de Cuba used the Yorùbá language on a daily basis. In the same manner, as documented by Fúnṣọ́ Aiyéjínà, the Trinidadian ethnologist Maureen Warner-Lewis claimed that in the 1970s, when she was collecting data for her books,

there were still a number of very old Trinidadians who spoke fairly competent Yorùbá. Even today, hundreds of Yorùbá words are still present in the vocabulary of Brazilian, Cuban, Trinidadian, Haitian, and other Latin American societies.

Today, culinary references like *acarajé*, *abará*, *axoxô*, *omuluku*, *ègbo*, and *àmàlà* are fully incorporated into the Brazilian folk dictionary. The same is true of Cuba, where the legacy includes scores of Yorùbá words that have become Hispanicized and adopted as legitimate Cuban-Spanish lexis, such as *moyugbación*, *batalero*, *osainista*, *italero*, *okonkolero*, and *iyawoses*.

Throughout the African Diaspora in the Americas—from Salvador, Rio, and São Paulo in Brazil to Havana, Matanzas, Guanabacoa, and Santiago in Cuba; from Chaguana, Marabella to Tunapuna in Trinidad to Mayagüez, Cabo Rojo, and San Juan in Puerto Rico; from Maracaibo and San Juan de los Morros to Caracas in Venezuela; and from Miami to New York, Boston, and San Francisco in the United States—names of Yorùbá *òrìṣà* like Èṣù, Ògún, Ọ̀ṣun, Ọbàtálá, Yemọja, Ọ̀ṣọ́ọ̀sì, Ṣàngó, Ọya, Ọ̀ṣanyìn, Ọbà, Òrìṣà Oko, and a host of others are invoked on a daily basis by New World devotees of different racial shades within Brazilian Candomblé, Cuban Santería, Haitian Vodou, Trinidadian Ṣàngó, and other Afro-Latin religious traditions. They are referred to in the popular parlance of the Yorùbá Diaspora as the religions of the *àṣẹ*. In fact, the dual concept of *ìbà* and *àṣẹ* (Axé in Brazil and Aché in the Spanish-speaking Americas) today represents one major characteristic attribute of the Yorùbá diaspora in Latin America and the Caribbean. Used in greetings and other contexts of social interaction, the two concepts are often used interchangeably as a conscious marker of Afro-identity in the region. In concrete terms, expressions like *motumbá*, *moyubá*, and *tremendo aché* or *muito axé* have become viable substitutes to the regular doxology in intimate conversations and correspondence. Thus, these expressions have endowed these two markers of Yorùbá orality with powerful socioreligious currency in Latin America and the Caribbean where their use now transcends the confines of Candomblé, Santería, Vodou, or Ṣàngó temples and milieus.

The Yorùbá legacy in the Diaspora is evident in various other aspects of life, leading to what can be considered the power to name that gives the Yorùbá a certain cultural hegemony in the Afro–Latin American diaspora. This is evident in the names of people and places in certain regions of the Americas, where a great deal of nineteenth-century Yorùbá political history has been immortalized in the names of many locales of the New World. Names of Yorùbá towns like Abẹ́òkúta, Ìlarò, Kétu, Ọ̀yọ́, and others have been replicated in the New World. This is further complemented by the ubiquitous development of places with the Yorùbá suffix tuntun (new), such as Terreiro Tuntun in Itaparica Island, Brazil; Ilé Tuntun in Havana; and, of course, the renowned Ọ̀yọ́túnjí African Village in South Carolina, in the United States.

Yorùbá philosophy is another major area of impact in the Diaspora. Researchers on nineteenth-century Yorùbá descendants in Brazil have documented different philosophical expressions like sùúrù ni oògùn ayé, kò sí ọba kan àfi Ọlọ́run, and others inscribed on individual houses in Brazil and Cuba. In the case of Brazil, the enthusiasm of Yorùbá religious affiliation even led to the construction and official recognition of public monuments and private residential buildings that are named after or dedicated to the òrìṣà. Some good examples include the famous, larger-than-life statues of the complete òrìṣà pantheon erected on the Dique do Tororó, a lake in the heart of Salvador, Bahia, as well as houses like Edifício Ògún Onirê, Ọ̀ṣun, Yemọja, and the Orixá Shopping Centre in the commercial, cidade alta of the Bahian capital.

Throughout the New World, the powerful economic concept of èsúsú or súsú is recognized as one of the earliest forms of mutual aid associations around which enslaved Africans organized. Afro–Latin American historians and anthropologists of the slavery era have documented hundreds of individuals who were able to buy their freedom from the common èsúsú purse.

If music is one of the most significant trademarks of Latin American and Caribbean peoples, research have shown that some of their musical traits emanated from the Yorùbá-African tradition. Salsa, merengue,

son, rumba, mambo, güiro, chachachá, bolero, samba, afoxé, ijexá, axé, bembé, and the like are some of the examples of Latino musical genres with unmistakable African traits. The Yorùbá musical genres, styles, and instruments that migrated to the Diaspora found their initial outlet in Afro-Latin religious expression, where they were originally used in the liturgy of the òrìṣà. The bàtá rhythms of the aña or alubàtá and their different oro toques used distinct signature calls to the different oricha of the Cuban-Lucumí Santería, which found their way into Afro-Cuban secular dance music. This dance music was played by the world-famous conjuntos (orchestras) of the 1940s and 1950s, the orixá toques of the Brazilian alabê (ritual drummers) of the Candomblé terreiros influenced the diverse genres of Brazilian popular music, from the different subgenres of samba to the carnival rhythms of the afoxé, the Axé music of the trio elétrico as well as the samba-reggae and levada of the bloco afro like Ilê-Aiyê, Ọlọ́dún, Ará Kétu, and Muzenza, which today characterize the famous Carnaval da Bahia, a major export from Brazil to the rest of the world.

On the literary scene, the Yorùbá tradition has also left an indelible legacy in the Latin American and Caribbean societies. The different subgenres of the oríkì of the òrìṣà are preserved in the Santería, Vodou, Candomblé, and Ṣàngó traditions. They are also preserved through the myths of the different òrìṣà, referred to collectively as patakines in Santería and ìtàn in Candomblé, and these myths have been documented by scholars like Lydia Cabrera, Rómulo Lacateñere, Miguel Barnet, Fernando Ortiz, Mirta Fernández, Mãe Stella de Oxossi, Mãe Beata de Yemajá, Mestre Didi, Maureen Warner-Lewis, and many others in Cuba, Brazil, and Trinidad. They are also preserved in more secular and moralistic tales and fables of the jicotea or the trickster tortoise of the Yorùbá moonlight tales.

See also **Cooperative Associations; Culture; Deities: The Òrìṣà; Diaspora: Deities (The Òrìṣà); Diaspora: Yorùbá in North America; Diaspora: Yorùbá in South America and the Caribbean; Lucumí; Nagô**

REFERENCE

Fálọlá, Tóyìn, and Matt D. Childs, eds. *The Yorùbá Diaspora in the Atlantic World.* Bloomington: Indiana University Press, 2005.

Felix Ayoh'Omídire

DIASPORA: YORÙBÁ IN AFRICA

Historically, the Yorùbá have spread beyond their geographical and ancestral homelands in today's southwestern Nigeria. Yorùbá expansion to parts of West Africa had been going on for centuries. However, the earliest recorded presence of the Yorùbá in other parts of Africa can be traced back to the transatlantic slave trade. Between the eighteenth and nineteenth centuries, returning and freed African slaves of European, American, and West Indian descent settled in Sierra Leone and Liberia. These liberated Africans were a mixed group, but a significant number of them included Yorùbá, Igbo, and other ethnicities. Descendants of freed slaves and African Muslims, most of them Yorùbá from southwestern Nigeria, settled in Freetown in the nineteenth century. All of these peoples would become the Krio, one of the major ethnic groups of today's Sierra Leone. Even though they number some sixty thousand, or about 4 percent, of Sierra Leone's population, their language, Krio, is the national language and English is the official language. The majority of Krio people (about 80 percent) are Christians, and a significant minority of Krio are of the Islamic faith. Krio Muslims are widely known as Okú. Yorùbá middle names are common among the Krio of Sierra Leone. In Gambia, the Krio are known as the Akú.

The presence of Yorùbá in other West African nations, such as Togo and Benin Republic, is the result of cultural contiguity, the slave trade, and the migration of Yorùbá itinerant traders from the savannas of Ọ̀yọ́. The Yorùbá can be found in the coastal and central regions of these countries. They have also enriched these societies with their business acumen and acute cultural self-awareness.

A recurring theme in the creation of the African Yorùbá Diaspora is travel or movement in time and space, propelled by an intense ambition to succeed wherever Yorùbá find themselves. Thus, sojourning is part of the Yorùbá value system, and the drive to thrive is propelled by an intuitive grasp of life as a journey that must end well no matter the sojourner's circumstances. In summary, adaptability and tenacity permeate all expressions of the Yorùbá presence in other parts of Africa.

Ivory Coast and Ghana are two nations whose economies, politics, and culture have been profoundly transformed by the Yorùbá Diaspora. The Yorùbá settled in Ghana in the early decades of the twentieth century and became merchants as British colonization in the region was reaching its apogee. They rapidly filled the void left by the departing Europeans and spread not only commerce but also Christianity and Islam, especially in the hinterlands of these nations. They were often the first to establish new churches and mosques in the native towns, villages, and communities they settled. With access to huge (and pioneering) networks of mutual aid and other social organizations, the Yorùbá in these countries were able to promote and perpetuate their material culture and values across subsequent generations. Another reason the Yorùbá thrived in African lands beyond their geographic home was their race. Compared to white Europeans, they were not visibly different from the native population and were therefore not perceived as a threat.

However, over time the growing elite of these nations would come to regard the Yorùbá with suspicion as the new colonizers, and this would have repercussions for both the immigrant Yorùbá and the indigenous population. For example, in 1969, the government of Ghana under Kofi Abrefa Busia passed the Aliens' Compliance Order, which led to mass deportations of Nigerians (mainly Yorùbá) and other African nationalities from Ghana. This law was ostensibly designed to give control of the economy back to Ghanaians. The order required all immigrants in the country to have residence permits within a two-week period. Busia expelled thousands of Nigerians within a very short period. Busia died in Britain in August 1978, himself an African sojourner in a foreign land. In 1975,

Ghana would become a member of the Economic Community of West African States (ECOWAS), a regional body whose founding mission and ethos promote a pan-Africanist vision for the peoples of the region, including the Yorùbá.

REFERENCES

Fálọlá, Tóyìn, and Matt D. Childs, eds. *The Yorùbá Diaspora in the Atlantic World*. Bloomington: Indiana University Press, 2005.

Eades, J. S. *Strangers and Traders: Yorùbá Migrants, Markets and the State in Northern Ghana*. Trenton, NJ: Africa World Press, 1994.

Bíọ́dún J. Ògúndayọ̀

DIASPORA: YORÙBÁ IN CENTRAL AMERICA

The Yorùbá were part of a small group of Africans taken as slaves to work in the plantations of Guatemala, Honduras, Nicaragua, Costa Rica, and Belize. Generally referred to as Afro–Latin Americans (*afrolatinos*) in Central America, they are today part of a mixed-race heritage of Spanish, African, Afro-Caribbean, and Garífuna. The declining Amerindian population who were once used as plantation laborers during slavery led to the import of African slaves in the sixteenth century. The result was a gradual mixing of Spanish, African, and Amerindian populations, and the emergence of *mulato* and *zambo* communities, which ultimately became a mestizo population. The Yorùbá in Central America are most associated with their cultural and religious practices, of which Santería is paramount. Santería, like Candomblé in Brazil, originated from the Yorùbá people of West Africa and refers to the veneration of the deities or *orixá* (*oricha*) such as Yemọja, Ọ̀sun, Ògún, Ṣàngó, and Ọbàtálá, among others. Through syncretism, the Yorùbá worship Catholic saints and Yorùbá deities simultaneously. These religious practices constituted strategies of resistance and survival for five centuries, which has allowed Yorùbá culture to thrive in religious and popular culture in the Americas and the Caribbean today.

Working against the grain of slave owners who insisted on converting African slaves to Catholicism, these creative worshippers cultivated an alternative space to continue the growth and expansion of their Yorùbá world in spite of slavery. They initiated devotees as they had done in Yorùbáland so as to continue to reach deeper levels of spiritual growth and knowledge. Despite controversy over the use of blood, adherents believe that bloodletting signifies rebirth and the continuity of the cycle of life. By identifying similarities between characteristics of Catholic saints and Yorùbá deities, Santería devotees were able to establish some complementary practices and beliefs. Some examples are Yemọja and Our Lady of Conception (Holy Virgin Mary); Ọ̀sun, the Yorùbá goddess of the river, and Our Lady of Charity; Babalúayé, the Yorùbá healing deity, and St. Lazarus; and Ògún, god of iron, and St. Jorge. The chanting of liturgies, dancing, and drumming during ritual ceremonies make for a truly global and diasporic reenactment of a localized belief system.

The Yorùbá in Central America adapted their culture to local imperatives while minimizing conflict or overcoming bondage through strategic rebellions. Although Central America reflects less Yorùbá influence than Brazil and the Caribbean, the cultural agency remains constant. As noted by Tóyìn Fálọlá and Matt Childs in their coedited volume *The Yorùbá Diaspora in the Atlantic World*, "The massive expansion of the Yorùbá occurred in the context of the four continents united by the Atlantic Ocean. The Yorùbá were among the African slaves drawn from Central and West Africa and tragically relocated to the Americas" (4). Regardless of what they call themselves beyond the confines of Yorùbáland in West Africa, the Yorùbá of Central America have not forgotten where they came from.

See also **Deities: The *Òrìṣà*; Diaspora: Deities (*Òrìṣà*); Diaspora: Impact of Yorùbá Culture; Diaspora: Yorùbá in North America; Diaspora: Yorùbá in South America and Caribbean; Lucumí; Nagó**

REFERENCE

Fálọlá, Tóyìn, and Matt D. Childs, eds. *The Yorùbá Diaspora in the Atlantic World*. Bloomington: Indiana University Press, 2005.

Felix Ayoh'Omídire

The Yorùbá diaspora in Europe aims to encourage unity and promote their cultural heritage in Europe by passing it on to younger generations. One of the major concerns of parents and grandparents raising children in the European diaspora is how to pass on the cultural heritage to their children and grandchildren. While aspects of the cultural heritage relating to food as well as the wearing of traditional attire to weddings, naming ceremonies, birthdays, housewarmings, retirement, and funeral parties are encountered regularly, many Yorùbá in the Diaspora in Europe struggle in passing on the Yorùbá mother tongue.

Yorùbá Language in the European Diaspora

Language is one of the potent aspects of Yorùbá cultural heritage, and people in the diasporic communities in Europe belong to either those who had been proficient in the use of standard Yorùbá (and/or dialectal varieties depending on where they were raised in Yorùbáland) before arriving in Europe or those who were born and raised in the Diaspora, who have not been exposed to a Yorùbá-speaking environment in all its veracity. Various reasons have been advanced for why children born to Yorùbá families in Europe are not proficient in the language. Three of the most important follow.

First, lack of quality time spent by parents, especially mothers, because of their preoccupation with work or studies, to pass on language skills to their young children. Second, lack of a natural linguistic environment in which a child could learn Yorùbá freely and effortlessly from peers, siblings, and other members of the community apart from parents. Third, parents' erroneous attitudes of a colonial mentality, which leads them to stop speaking Yorùbá to their children at home, thinking that doing so would hinder the ability of their children to learn English, French, German, Dutch, or any other European language properly. Hence, a golden opportunity is lost: that of raising bilingual or trilingual children who are as confident and comfortable in their Yorùbá linguistic abilities as in European language abilities.

Community Groups and Associations

Several Yorùbá community groups and associations have been formed in different parts of Europe over the past six decades with the sole aim of fostering unity among Yorùbá-speaking people from the homeland and impressing the message of *ẹ má gbàgbé ilé* (don't forget the homeland) in their minds. The earliest of such groups was the Ẹgbẹ́ Ọmọ Odùduwà, formed by the late Chief Ọbáfẹ́mi Awólọ́wọ̀ and others in the United Kingdom in 1945.

Oòduà Progressive Union in Europe

Apart from pan-Yorùbá groups such as the Ẹgbẹ́ Ọmọ Ìbílẹ̀ Yorùbá or the Yorùbá Society, there are also several regional groups such as Ìbàdàn Descendants Union, Ìjẹbú Ọmọ Alárẹ̀, Ifẹ̀ Descendants Union, Ọ̀yọ́ Descendants Union, Modákẹ́kẹ́ Progressive Union, Oǹdó Descendants Union, and the like. These will not disappear, given the efforts of Yorùbá monarchs, elders' councils, and Yorùbá cultural activists who launched the Oòduà Progressive Union (OPU) in the United Kingdom, Holland, France, and Germany in September 2013.

REFERENCES

Lawal, Níkẹ, Matthew N. O. Sadiku, and Ade Dopamu. *Understanding Yorùbá Life and Culture*. Trenton, NJ: Africa World Press, 2004.

Vanguard. http://www.vanguardngr.com/2013/09/Yorùbá-monarchs-others-stormed-europe/.

Akin Oyètádé

DIASPORA: YORÙBÁ IN SOUTH AMERICA AND THE CARIBBEAN

It is perhaps important to distinguish ethnic Yorùbá, Yorùbá-speaking or Yorùbá-practicing individuals, and people of the Yorùbá worldview when discussing the Yorùbá presence in South America and the Caribbean. By "ethnic Yorùbá," one is clearly referring to people who trace their ethnic origin to the homeland in West Africa, a place geographically located between the southwestern region of present-day Nigeria (below

Encyclopedia of the Yorùbá

the Niger River); the central (Plateau) regions of the modern-day Republic of Benin and Togo; and Ghana, south of the Volta River. The ethnic origins of these people go back to the Ilé-Ifẹ̀ of the Odùduwà Dynasty (c. 800–1200 CE); the original princes were said to have dispersed and migrated mostly westward to found the principal Yorùbá kingdoms of Kétu, Sábẹ, Pópó, Ọ̀yọ́, and others. These places later served as dispersal point for newer groups like the Ìdáìsà, Mènígrì, Àjàṣẹ́, Ifẹ̀-Aña, and other Yorùbá-speaking groups as far as the Atakpamé region in central Togo.

The "diasporization" of ethnic Yorùbá into the Latin American and Caribbean regions is clearly traceable to two distinct historical moments. The first is the transatlantic slave trade; the second, which is less documented, is the movements of smaller groups of individuals and families between the Bight of Benin and diverse Latin American and Caribbean locales, either as indentured workers or as freedmen in search of employment opportunities in the post-abolition era. In the modern era of globalization, there has emerged yet a third category of diasporic Yorùbá subjects: mostly young, educated individuals who have chosen to migrate to and settle in the Americas, especially the United States. They constitute what scholars like Fálọlá and Childs would call an economic diaspora.

Concerning the first category, their exodus into the Americas became historically pronounced around the end of the eighteenth to the middle of the nineteenth centuries. This period coincided with the fall of the Ọ̀yọ́ Empire, which resulted from the rift between the aláà-fin (king of Ọ̀yọ́), his ministers (the Ọ̀yọ́ Mèsì), and his military generals, headed by the Ààrẹ-Ọ̀nà-Kakàǹfò. At the peak of this irreconcilable rift, the reigning king, Aláàfin Aólẹ̀, was forced to commit ritual suicide. However, before he obliged his powerful enemies, he pronounced some magical words and was said to have shot three magical arrows in the directions that today correspond to the New World. His actions symbolized that, consequent upon their rejection of his authority as king, his people would be carried away as slaves in the directions of his arrows.

The major entry points of Yorùbá-speaking peoples in the New World were Salvador da Bahia in northeastern Brazil and the Cuban port of Havana. From these port cities, Yorùbá slaves were moved into other locales on the South American continent and throughout the Caribbean. This explains, in part, high concentrations of ethnic Yorùbá slaves and freedmen in these two countries and regions of Latin America and the Caribbean. In Brazil, the Yorùbá became known as the nagô, a name derived from the ethnic ànàgó, which is the name the neighboring Dahomey called their archenemies, the Yorùbá-speaking people. Since most enslaved Yorùbá were sold into slavery by the Dahomean kings, (à)nàgó became the name under which they entered into Latin America, especially Brazil and Haiti. As evidenced in the material and historical culture the nagô left as their legacy in Brazil, the majority of Yorùbá-speaking people taken to that part were of Ọ̀yọ́ extraction.

In Cuba, in contrast, the ethnic Yorùbá taken to that island became known as lucumí. Historians have tried to trace this ethnic name to the Ulcamy kingdom, but a more plausible origin appears to be the term olùkù mi, which means "my bosom friend, my confidant"—a term that is still common even today in certain eastern dialects of the Yorùbá language, most especially among the Ifẹ̀ and Ìjẹ̀ṣà-Yorùbá. In the lesser Caribbean Islands of Trinidad, Jamaica, and Barbados, the ethnic Yorùbá became known as the Yarriba.

Today, it is difficult to know who is actually a descendant of ethnic Yorùbá in Latin America and the Caribbean because of the intentional strategic measures taken by slave oligarchies to destroy and obliterate the ethnic memories of enslaved Africans. However, there are exceptional cases, like that of Eduardo Ijexá, Procópio de Ògúnjá, Felisberto Sousa, the Àgùdà families of Alákìjà, Bamgboxê-Martins, and Martiniano Eliseu do Bonfim—who still communicate with their kin across the Atlantic as well as the Axipá lineage of Marcelina dos Santos, Maria Bibiana do Espírito Santo, Desocóredes Maximiliano dos Santos (Mestre Didi Alapinni), and their descendants who are prominent figures in the historiography of Candomblé (òrìṣà) tradition of Bahia, Brazil. On the Cuban side, mention can be made of the Aña (àyàn) lineages of Àtàndá, Añabí, and the legendary La Funché, as well as contemporary families and descendants of significant *santeros* and *cabildos* like Echu Bí, Pepa Herrera, and *bataleros* like Carlos Aldama, whose grandmother was a Yorùbá slave woman. Thus, today, millions of (Afro-)Brazilians, Cubans, Puerto Ricans, Haitians, Venezuelans, Colombians, Jamaicans, Trinidadians, Barbadians, Dominicans, and the like and their children and godchildren in the United States claim Yorùbá religious identity and cultural citizenship. This represents more of what can be referred to as Yorùbáness, since their affiliation to the Yorùbá cultural worldview is by choice and/or through a ritual rebirth during initiation into the Yorùbá òrìṣà or Ifá religious traditions.

See also **Deities: The Òrìṣà; Diaspora: Deities (Òrìṣà); Diaspora: Impact of Yorùbá Culture; Diaspora: Yorùbá in North America; Diaspora: Yorùbá in Central America; Lucumí; Nagô**

REFERENCE

Fálọlá, Tóyìn, and Matt D. Childs, eds. *The Yorùbá Diaspora in the Atlantic World*. Bloomington: Indiana University Press, 2005.

Felix Ayoh'Omídire

DIASPORA: YORÙBÁ IN NORTH AMERICA

The transatlantic slave trade introduced captives from Yorùbáland to the New World, where they established the initial Yorùbá Diaspora in North America. In the nineteenth century, Yorùbá slaves were increasingly transported to the Americas, particularly to Central and South America, where their descendants, such as the Lucumí in Cuba and the Nagô in Brazil, became a significant part of the Diaspora. Although fewer slaves of Yorùbá origin were brought to the Southern United States during the Atlantic trade than to other parts of the Americas, the veracity of Yorùbá culture, nevertheless, was an important strand of black cultural identity in America. One may attribute this to the desire of the few slaves of Yorùbá origin in the United States to protect their cultural identity in their new home.

The adoption of Yorùbá religious practices by some African Americans is, perhaps, the most profound expression of Yorùbá culture in the African American community, and it is expressed in a number of ways. By the mid-1950s, a small number of African Americans were already practitioners of Yorùbá religions, particularly òrìṣà worship. In subsequent years, òrìṣà adherents multiplied, leading to the opening of a number of African American òrìṣà temples in urban African American communities. Forms of Yorùbá religious practices, such as the worship of deities like Ògún (god of iron), Ṣàngó (god of thunder), Ọya (goddess of fertility), Ọ̀ṣun (goddess of the river), and Yemọja (mother goddess) and divination of Ifá, are present in the contemporary Yorùbá Diaspora.

The expression of Yorùbá culture in North America is also evident in the Yorùbá communities created by African Americans. Small in number, the best known of these communities is Ọ̀yọ́túnjí in Beaufort County, South Carolina, established in 1970 by Walter Eugene King, an African American. King became the first crown ọba (king) of the community, with the traditional title of Ẹfúntọ́lá Oseijeman Adélabú Adéfúnmi I. Named after Ọ̀yọ́, an ancient Yorùbá city in Nigeria, this community became an epitome of the practice of aspects of Yorùbá culture, especially religious ceremonies, festivals, and rituals. The community also adopted the use of Yorùbá language, music, dance, and traditional attire, especially during religious celebrations.

Outside the attempt to re-create authentic Yorùbá communities among African Americans, Yorùbá culture is expressed in the general African American community through Yorùbá attire (commonly referred to as dàṅṣíkí) and hairdos worn by women and men. It is also commonplace for many African Americans to adopt Yorùbá names, both traditional and popular.

One avenue by which Yorùbá culture has been showcased is the African street festivals popular in many American cities. One of the most popular of these street festivals is ọdúndé, an annual event in Philadelphia since 1975 that, apart from featuring cultural dances and performances, is a celebration of the Yorùbá deity Ọ̀ṣun. Named ọdúndé, a Yorùbá word translated in African American parlance as "new year," the festival was originally conceived to imitate the famous annual Ọ̀ṣun festival held in the Nigerian Yorùbá city of Òṣogbo.

The contemporary Yorùbá Diaspora encompasses not only African American devotees of Yorùbá culture but also Nigerian Yorùbá immigrants who have increasingly arrived in the United States since the late twentieth century. Incredibly proud of their culture, the Nigerian Yorùbá tend to retain their culture through traditional attire, language, and cuisine. Numerous sociocultural associations, such as the Ẹgbẹ́ Ọmọ Yorùbá, have constituted an instrument of propagating Yorùbá culture; they are also a means of promoting social identity.

See also **Association for Promoting Yorùbá Culture; Diaspora: Deities (The Òrìṣà); Diaspora: Yorùbá in South America and the Caribbean; Diaspora: Impact of Yorùbá Culture; Lucumí; Nagô**

REFERENCES

Fálọlá, Tóyìn, and Matt D. Childs, eds. *The Yorùbá Diaspora in the Atlantic World*. Bloomington: Indiana University Press, 2005.
Oyèbádé, Adébáyọ̀. "Yorùbá Culture in Contemporary America." In *Yorùbá Fiction, Orature, and Culture*, ed. Tóyìn Fálọlá and Adébáyọ̀, 321–40. Trenton, NJ: Africa World Press, 2011.

Adébáyọ̀ Oyèbádé

DICTIONARIES

The first major dictionary of the Yorùbá language, *Yorùbá Vocabulary*, was compiled by Reverend (later Bishop) Samuel Àjàyí Crowther and published in 1843. This book included an account of the grammatical structure of the language, and it is believed to be the first such work by a native speaker of the language. This dictionary, along with many other literary works, including *Yorùbá Grammar*, has been the precursor to many grammar books in Yorùbá. In 1852, the *Yorùbá Vocabulary* was greatly altered and considerably enlarged for a new edition. For many years, this book was the standard work on the Yorùbá language.

In 1911, an English-Yorùbá dictionary was published under the general editorship of the Reverend E. J. Ṣówándé, but this was intended to meet only immediate needs. This attempt, along with contributions from the Reverend T. A. J. Ògúnbíyí and Mrs. E. Fry incorporated much of the *Yorùbá Vocabulary*; it led to the publication of the *Dictionary of the Yorùbá Language* by the Church Missionary Society in January 1913. This is an English-Yorùbá, Yorùbá-English dictionary. This dictionary is still in print; the previous dictionaries are no longer in print.

The first major dictionary that did not have its roots in the church was R. C. Abraham's *Dictionary of Modern Yorùbá*, which appeared in 1958. Abraham's work highlighted all that was Yorùbá, including the indigenous religions, customs, historical events, internecine wars, and number system. This encyclopedic work continues to generate some measure of controversy among Yorùbá scholars who believe that Abraham, a foreigner, may have misunderstood or misrepresented some aspects of Yorùbá life and customs.

I. O. Délànọ̀'s *A Dictionary of Modern Monosyllabic Verbs* fills another niche among specialized Yorùbá dictionaries. The two-volume, thousand-page dictionary is designed for people who have some foundation in Yorùbá grammar and seek a better knowledge of the etymology, root, and structure of Yorùbá words. Another specialized Yorùbá dictionary is *Èdè Awo (Òrìṣà Yorùbá Dictionary)* by Chief Fama, Àìná Adéwálé-Somadhi. This publication, as its name implies, focuses on the òrìṣà language, explaining terms like *àbọrú, àbọyè, àṣẹ, eégún,* and the like.

Other specialized Yorùbá dictionaries either available in print or on the Internet include the following:

1. *A Quadrilingual Glossary of Legislative Terms*, compiled by the late Professor Adébóyè Babalọlá and published in 1991.
2. *Yorùbá Dictionary of Engineering Physics*, compiled by J. A. Ọdẹ́táyọ̀ and published in 1993.
3. *A Glossary of Technical Terminologies for Primary Schools*, by Ọlásọpé Oyèláràn and published in 1980.

4. In her doctoral dissertation, "Devising a Yorùbá Vocabulary for Building Construction," Olúbọ̀dé-Sawè, under the supervision of Professor Ọládélé Awóbulyì at Adékúnlé Ajásin University, compiled a glossary of terms that are used in the building profession.

5. Professor Yíwọ́lá Awóyalé, funded by the University of Pennsylvania's Linguistic Data Consortium, has been at work on a world dictionary of the Yorùbá language. This electronic database, entering completion at the time of this publication, compares the Yorùbá language as spoken in Nigeria, Benin, Togo, and in the Diaspora.

Recognizing that the mother tongue is the best tool for analyzing both a language and its literature, two volumes of the book *Yorùbá Metalanguage: A Glossary of Technical Terms in Language, Literature and Methodology*, edited by Professors Ayọ̀ Bámgbóṣé and Ọládélé Awóbulúyì, were compiled and published in 1981 and 1988. These volumes were meant for training teachers in content and methodology of the language.

The *Yorùbá Modern Practical Dictionary*, compiled by Dr. Káyọ̀dé Fákínlẹ̀dé and published in 2003, expands the use of the Yorùbá language into the science and technology fields. This almost seven-hundred-page dictionary contains a comprehensive review of Yorùbá alphabet and tonal system; more than twenty-six thousand word-to-word dictionary entries, including medical terms, the basic elements, and plant and animal taxonomy; a list of Yorùbá and English word roots, prefixes, and suffixes; and an appendix of scientific measurements and rudimentary mathematical terminology.

See also **Language: Government and Mission Policies; Language: Standardization and Literacy**

REFERENCE

Lieberman, M. Y., and Y. Awóyalé. "The Place of Culture in a World Dictionary of the Yorùbá Language." In *Yorùbá Creativity, Fiction, Language, Life, and Songs*, ed. Tóyìn Fálọlá and Ann Genova, 259–73. Trenton, NJ: Africa World Press, 2005.

Julius Fákínlẹ̀dé

Yorùbá dilemma tales (àrọ̀) constitute a class of tales in which a storyteller creates a problem, and then concerted efforts are made either by the storyteller or any other member of the audience to resolve the dilemma or puzzle through a narration that is presented logically. Dilemma tales are clever and popular, and they exercise the puzzle talents of the people. They are not only intellectual puzzles that sharpen the wits and promote discussion; they also highlight that, in human affairs, there are often no answers, only difficult choices that reflect conflicting moral values.

There are two types of dilemma tales: those based on the Ifá corpus and the non-Ifá-based ones. The stories may be rendered either entirely in poetry or in prose. Dilemma tales constitute a large, diverse, and widespread class of folk narratives. They leave listeners with a choice among alternatives, such as which of several characters has done the best, deserves a reward, or should win an argument or a case in court. The choices are difficult ones and usually involve arguing principles on ethical, moral, or legal grounds.

Some dilemma tales ask the listeners to judge the relative skills of characters who have performed incredible feasts. The narrator starts the story with the dilemma, often explicitly stated in the form of a question or ordinary statement that is debated by members of the audience. Here are few examples:

- Who knows how the tortoise married three princesses same day?
- Who knows how the tortoise exchanged six peanuts for 120,000 cowries before dawn?
- Who knows the home owner who resides outside the wall of the house instead of inside?
- Who knows how the dead dog can consume more food than the living?
- Who knows how a dead goat could cry louder than the living?

Sometimes the dilemma is resolved by the narrator only after the listeners have argued their conflicting points of view, but this does not occur often. Even when the tales have standard answers, they can evoke spirited discussions. Like many other types of folk narratives, their content is often didactic, but their special quality is that they train those who engage in these discussions in the skills of argumentation and debate. Thus, they prepare them to effectively participate in and to adjudicate disputes, both in the family or lineage and in formal courts of law.

It is the intellectual function and relevance to ethical standards, rather than any literary merit, that make dilemma tales interesting. No elaborate plot or surprising denouement is necessary to present a dilemma, and some examples barely qualify as prose narratives. For instance, the dilemma tale about how the tortoise married three princesses on the same day opens with the classic, generic marker of traditional Yorùbá folktales: "Long, long ago, there was a king in tortoise's native town . . ." Moreover, the five examples cited earlier are crafted in such a way as to move from a state of tension, conflict, and imbalance to resolution of the disequilibrium, which are attributes of traditional folktales. Furthermore, the central protagonist in the first two examples of tales cited here is the tortoise, the generic hero in traditional Yorùbá folktales; the tortoise is the sneaky, cunning trickster who always prevails at the end of the story. This accounts for why it has been difficult for some scholars, like William Bascom, to differentiate Yorùbá dilemma tales and folktales; he claimed that "there was no opportunity to observe the telling of dilemma tales . . . among the Yorùbá of Nigeria" (3), because he could not identify any significant difference between Yorùbá folktales and dilemma tales.

See also **Children's Folklore, Education, and Development; Literature: Oral; Urban Folklore**

REFERENCES

Bascom, William. *African Dilemma Tales.* Paris: Mouton Publishers, 1975.

Finnegan, Ruth. *African Oral Literature.* Nairobi: Oxford University Press, 1970.

Akíntúndé Akínyẹmí

DISEASE

Strictly speaking, a disease is an impairment of health or a condition of abnormal functioning that renders a person unable to perform or be active as a consequence of physical or mental unfitness. It is an abnormal condition that affects the body of an organism. In this sense, disease can mean "dis-ease": a negation of ease, disconnection, disequilibrium, or imbalance in the body system. In other words, it is the inharmonious vibration of the elements composing the human entity.

Disease conceptualization depends greatly on the worldview of a particular people and represents the core of their therapeutic principles and praxis. As a result of this, the African way of conceptualizing disease, especially among the Yorùbá, differs significantly from the Western view. While the Western conceptualization of disease is pathological, the African conceptualization is cosmological. Thus, in Africa, disease is not the problem of an individual. *Disease* refers to disorderliness in the cosmos. The presence of a disease, therefore, suggests that disequilibrium exists in the movement of the cosmos.

The Yorùbá regard disease as energies that move to occupy space in human body. In other words, disease is a hostile influence and agency that besets humans from the cradle to the grave. Consequently, the Yorùbá have developed a method to discern the causation, diagnosis, treatment, and prevention of disease. When the Yorùbá seek healing for a disease, they also seek to know both its natural and its supernatural causes to ensure a holistic healing. For this reason, they believe that diseases are often a combination of several factors: natural, supernatural, and spiritual. Divinities, ancestors, spirits, witches, and sorcerers can also cause disease if a believer fails to offer the required sacrifices. Hence, it is important to properly investigate the cause of a disease; physical observation or divination is pertinent.

On the treatment of disease among the Yorùbá, the nature of any disease determines the type of treatment. There are people who are not necessarily professional healers but who have a deep knowledge of the symptoms of and treatments for diseases. They can discern whether a disease is severe. Plants, animal parts, minerals, waters, and all that can be categorized as flora and fauna are used to treat minor diseases such as headache (èfórí), cough (ikó), and fever (ibà). However, the treatment of diseases associated with spiritual causation takes a different form. The treatment of such diseases is accomplished by combining physical and spiritual methods.

See also **Medicine; Medicine: Indigenous Therapeutic System**

REFERENCES

Jégédé, S. A. *African Culture and Health*. Ìbàdàn (Nigeria): Stirling-Horden Publishers, 1996.

Phillips, H. O. *Herbal Medical Practice: A Peripheral Exploration*. Ìbàdàn (Nigeria): Sangys Printing Company, 2000.

Obáfémi Jégédé

DIVINATION: IFÁ

Ifá is a system of geomancy, one of the divinatory techniques used by the Yorùbá to gain knowledge of their complex cosmos and understand the intellectual configuration of our human universe. It is generally regarded as a process of the pursuit of knowledge about the course of life, and it is consulted at successive stages in people's lives. Ifá divination is performed on such occasions as marriage, betrothal, childbirth, naming ceremonies, chieftaincy, burial rites, and others.

Two opposing views can be identified concerning the meanings of Ifá: the traditionalist view and the analytical view. The former recognizes Òrúnmìlà as both a human prophet and a god and that Ifá is his divination system, which conveys the impression that Ifá is nothing other than received instructions from Òrúnmìlà, the Yorùbá god of wisdom. The latter regards Ifá as a human institution, founded by Òrúnmìlà and practiced by present-day Babaláwo or diviners. The traditionalist view has generated controversy and brought about two conflicting ideas on

the meaning of Ifá. On the one hand, Ifá is used as the metonym of Òrúnmìlà; on the other, Ifá is taken to mean the apparatus or instrument used by Òrúnmìlà during divination. Textual evidence shows, however, that Ifá and Òrúnmìlà can be used interchangeably to refer to the Yorùbá deity of wisdom and divination. While the term *Òrúnmìlà* refers exclusively to the deity of wisdom or divine arbiter of Ifá divination system, the term *Ifá* refers both to the deity and his divination system.

In Ifá corpus, there are 16 basic and 256 derivative figures called *odù* that are obtained either by the manipulation of sixteen palm nuts (*ikin*) or by tossing a chain (*òpèlè*) of eight half seed shells. The 256 derivative figures are divided into two parts: the major categories are known as *ojú odù* and number 16, and the minor categories are known as *omo odù* or *amúlù odù* and number 240. Widely held to be the core of the Ifá corpus, the *odù*, or verses of Ifá, is a collection of thousands of poems, aphorisms, and riddles that the Babaláwo or diviner memorizes and passes on from generation to generation of Babaláwo. Symbols or signs, usually double vertical markings, are used to indicate each of the verses of Ifá and their respective gospels. The totality of these markings depicts all the possible combinations of the 16 principal *odù* and the 240 minor *odù*. Legends or a series of traditional stories are associated with *odù* figures, and each *odù* has diverse stories connected with it.

The Babaláwo (literally, "father of secrets") is the interpreter of the oracular message in Ifá system. The Yorùbá regard the Babaláwo as both guardians of Ifá oral text and custodians of all paraphernalia of Ifá divination. An aspiring Babaláwo is expected to commit to memory a great number of legends and stories that are associated with the *odù*, a process that may take many years. Thus, some people have always insinuated that the office of a Babaláwo necessarily suggests an elderly person. However, young men have been found to be good practitioners of Ifá divination; if a Babaláwo is regarded as a man of sagacious intellect, he merits that compliment not because of his age but because of his resourcefulness.

Paraphernalia of Ifá Divination

- *Ikin* refers to the sixteen sacred palm nuts that are generally held to be the most important objects of Ifá divination and ritual. The Yorùbá regard *ikin* as the first and the most ancient divination instrument. The use of *ikin* is becoming unpopular among diviners, who are often reluctant to employ them in divination because of the considerable amount of time spent when they are used. To expedite the process of divination, therefore, most diviners now resort to the use of *ọ̀pẹ̀lẹ̀*, or the divining chain.

- *Ọ̀pẹ̀lẹ̀* consists of eight halves of seed shells or pods joined together by short sections of chain three to four inches long. The Yorùbá believe that the fall of the seeds during divination is always occasioned by the divine intervention of Ọ̀rúnmìlà, the Yorùbá god of wisdom. In other words, the diviner is not regarded as the author of the figure that emerges after the cast of the *ọ̀pẹ̀lẹ̀*. Hence, this idea about divine intervention removes the suspicion that the diviner gathers gossip about his client.

- *Ọpọ́n Ifá* refers to the divining tray, usually with *ìyẹ̀rosùn* (yellow powder of divination) sprinkled on it.

- *Àgèrè* is used for storing the sacred palm nuts and other Ifá materials. Hence, the Yorùbá saying *a kì í kọ́fá tán l'àgèrè* (no one can divest the *àgèrè* of Ifá, that is, *ikin*).

- *Ìrọ́kẹ́*, the rattle or tapper, is rattled or tapped against the divining tray to invoke the presence of Ọ̀rúnmìlà (Ifá) during the process of divination.

- *Ìbò* refers to a pair of cowrie shells tied together and a piece of animal bone. The *ìbò* involves the use of specific alternatives of yes and no by the Ifá priest to arrive at answers to the client's questions. The Ifá priest poses the answers in terms of two statements: the first affirmative, the second negative.

- *Òsùn-awo* refers to the Ifá staff, The Babaláwo ensures that the *òsùn-awo* is brought to and erected at *igbódù* (initiation grove) during Ifá initiation rites. It is taboo for the staff to lie on its side. Hence, the saying *òrógangan lòsùn ń sùn sí* (the *òsùn* must always stand in erect position).

- *Àpò Àbìrà* refers to the Ifá bag, which is part of the Babaláwo's outfit, where he keeps some of his Ifá objects.

Today, many scholars have shown that Ifá is not a completely esoteric system or a mere religious and mythic discourse. The system is appreciated as a Yorùbá traditional body of knowledge that embraces history, science, medicine, folklore, and philosophy. As a complete Yorùbá philosophy, for instance, Ifá oral text is a repository of such fundamental philosophical issues as existence, nature of reality, knowledge, and human conduct.

See also **Divinatory Systems**

REFERENCES

Adégbindin, Ọmọ́tádé. *Ifá in Yorùbá Thought System*. Durham, NC: Carolina Academic Press, 2014.

Abímbọ́lá, Wándé. *Ifá: An Exposition of Ifá Literary Corpus*. Ìbàdàn (Nigeria): Oxford University Press, 1976.

Ọmọ́tádé Adégbindin

DIVINATORY SYSTEMS

Divination is a universal phenomenon among several peoples of the world and is practiced in different forms. Divination is a prominent practice among the Yorùbá people of southwestern Nigeria and in the Diaspora. The Yorùbá people opine that the world in which they live is very complex, and they believe that there are forces behind various incidences and experience. As a result, they employ various forms of divinatory systems to decipher the causes, effects, and cure of incidences. Likewise, the Yorùbá employ divinations to live peaceful lives, given their belief in the chaotic nature of the cosmos. Yorùbá beliefs about the nature and structure of their cosmology and cosmography inform the importance they attach to divination. They believe a person is born with a particular destiny. Thus, determining his or her success or failure is paramount in the hearts of the Yorùbá people. Divination knowledge reveals what can be done to change a bad destiny to good one. This is why people are anxious and curious to know and possibly try to alter their future, such as the day of their death and their destiny. They also try to avoid calamities.

They use various divinatory systems to discover things such as the causes and cures of illness; the causes of death; what to do to avert evils; and knowledge about when and how major decisions should be taken in important choices, as for a future partner, king, chief, career, or leader. A diviner, therefore, can be regarded as a consultant.

There is no traditional cult among the Yorùbá that does not have its own divinatory system. However, there are purely divinatory institutions whose main function is to make inquiry. The major and most prominent divinatory systems among the Yorùbá are Ifá, Ẹ̀rìndínlógún, Ọ̀sanyìn, and Agbigba. It has been observed that each of the mentioned divinatory systems combines specific oratory with the divinatory materials to decipher the issue at stake on each occasion.

There are several divinatory items used in Ifá divination that range from the use of ọ̀pẹ̀lẹ̀ chains, sixteen palm nuts (ikin), and cam powder (ìyẹ̀ròsùn). The Ẹ̀rìndínlógún involves casting sixteen cowries on the ground. With Ọ̀sanyìn divinatory system the deity speaks to the diviner, and it is only the diviner who can interpret the thin voice uttered by the Ọ̀sanyìn. The Agbigba system employs a set of four separate strings of agbigba seeds with four markers in which the diviner reads the pattern formed by the cowries or the markers in advising his or her clients.

In other divination practices, a client whispers his or her problem secretly into a coin or paper currency and either puts it on the divinatory object or holds the coin or paper currency. First, the diviner holds the chain in the middle and throws it on the divining mat. A single throw of the ọ̀pẹ̀lẹ̀ divining chain can lead to having an odù. The ọ̀pẹ̀lẹ̀ is made of eight half nuts of the ọ̀pẹ̀lẹ̀ seeds or pods, tied together with a string. When the inner rough surface faces upward, it represents a mark, but the outer smooth surface represents a double mark. The ọ̀pẹ̀lẹ̀ is used more often because it is easier to carry and to manipulate, especially when the client asks questions to clarify his or

Table D.2 Principal Odu in Ifá, Agbigba, and Ẹ̀rìndínlógún

	Ifá	Agbigba	Ẹ̀rìndínlógún
1	Èjì-ogbè	Òsíkà/ Ogbè	Ọ̀kànrànṣodè
2	Ọ̀yèkú Méjì	Ọ̀yèkú	Èjì-Òkò
3	Ìwòrì Méjì	Ògòrì/Ìwòrì	Ògúnda Méjì
4	Òdí Méjì	Òjì/Òjí/Èdí	Ìrosùn Méjì
5	Ìrosùn Méjì	Òro sùn/ Ìrosùn	Ọsẹ́ Méjì
6	Ọ̀wónrín Méjì	Ògá/Ọ̀wónrín	Ọ̀bàrà Méjì
7	Ọ̀bàrà Méjì	Ọ̀bàrà	Òdí Méjì
8	Ọ̀kànràn Méjì	Ọ̀kànà/Ọ̀kànràn	Èjì-Ogbè
9	Ògúndá Méji	Ògúntá	Ọsá Méjì
10	Ọsá Méjì	Ọsá	Òfún Méjì
11	Ìká Méjì	Ọyínkán	Ọ̀wọ́nrín Méjì
12	Òtúúrúpọ̀n Méjì	Ọtaru	Èjìlá-asẹ́bọra
13	Òtúá Méjì	Òtúá méjì	Ètẹ̀là/Ẹ̀tàlá
14	Ìrẹtẹ̀ Méjì	Ìrẹtẹ̀	Ẹnírániníṣẹ́
15	Ọsẹ́ Méjì	Ọkín	Odù-ẹni-tí-àá-fàbọ̀-fún
16	Òfún Méjì	Òfún	Odù-ẹni-to-ṣojú-rẹ̀

her doubts with the ìbò "symbols of specific alternatives," according to W. Bascom. The Ifá priest may use ikin, the sixteen sacred palm nuts Ọ̀rúnmìlà is believed to have handed over to his children as a way to hear his predictions.

Ifá, Ẹ̀rìndínlógún, and Agbigba are closely related but have some differences. They all have sixteen principal odù, as listed in table D.2.

In addition, many differences exist in naming and positions of odù.

It must be noted, however, that Yorùbá divination has not given itself to civilization and modernism. The attitude of Yorùbá people toward their quest in knowing the future has not changed. The Yorùbá traditional, Islamic, and Christian divinatory systems are intermingled. Some Yorùbá people approach Muslim diviners who practice sand cutting, or iyanrìn-títẹ̀, which is believed to have been introduced to Yorùbáland by some Islamic clerics. Some Yorùbá consult Christian diviners, or aríran (the one who sees the future). Likewise, there are Christians and Muslims who consult the Yorùbá traditional diviners either openly or secretly. This development is an indication of the space that divinatory system occupies among the Yorùbá people.

See also **Divination: Ifá; Spirit Possession**

REFERENCES

Abímbọ́lá, Wándé. *Ifá: An Exposition of Ifá Literary Corpus,* Ìbàdàn (Nigeria): Oxford University Press, 1976.

Bascom, W. *Ifá Divination: Communication between Gods and Men in West Africa.* Bloomington: Indiana University Press, 1969.

Táíwò Olúnládé

DOLLS AND TOYS

In the past, a child growing up in Yorùbá communities seemed to have much leisure. Leisure time was spent playing in the home and outside of it. Even before the advent of institutional schooling and education, leisure occurred for stretches of time during the dry season when the harvest had been taken in and the land waited for the preparation and planting for the coming season. The growing child fashioned playthings either alone, with the help of older siblings, or under the guidance of uncles with the contribution of parents. As a result of these collaborative efforts, the growing child possessed toys such as òkòtó, bobbins used as wheels, pawpaw stock trumpets, banana-stem gunshots, wheeled scooters and boxes on wheels, bicycle wheels, and many others. Before describing these toys, it is necessary to say that there were a few toys and dolls that were part and parcel of the Yorùbá home environment.

One of the toys for infants was ṣaworo, a small gourd filled with pebbles that made sounds at the least touch. Once a baby began to stand up and take his or her first steps, there was the wooden walker (kọ́mọnírìn), made to measure by the neighborhood carpenter. There was a special wooden doll made for twins. Twins are the kings and queens of children as far as the Yorùbá are concerned. If one of them were to die, a doll was made as a replacement for the surviving twin to play with. Sometimes these dolls are no more than a flat piece of wood, marked with a mouth, eyes, ears, and nose, for the baby to play with and sleep with. At other times, wooden dolls are well carved, elaborate, fine wood statuettes, some of which have become collectors' items for those who invest in African Yorùbá art.

Òkòtó is more than a mere spinning top. Made of discarded tin with a pointed spinning point, it could be spun for the mere fun of watching the spinning top dance. Among older children, it became a fighting instrument, with the spinning point used to hit anyone who failed to turn it so that the spinning point comes up tops.

The wooden bobbins discarded by tailors did double duty as wheels for various toys. All that needed done was to attach the bobbins to a base, and one would have a moving carriage. To create a trumpet, the leaves on pawpaw stalks were cut off and a hole was opened toward the end of the stalk and covered with the white membrane used by spiders to protect their eggs. The midrib of the banana leaf can be made to sound like gunshots by running the hand over flaps cut out of it. A bicycle rim led along with a piece of stick made a long journey endurable. All of these toys were fashioned out of materials that were at hand. They were never monetized or turned into marketable objects, with the exception of elaborately carved dolls coveted by collectors.

REFERENCES

Adéoyè, Láògún C. *Àṣà àti Ìṣe Yorùbá.* Oxford: Oxford University Press, 1979.

Lawal, Níkẹ, Matthew N. O. Sadiku, and Ade Dopamu, eds. *Understanding Yorùbá Life and Culture.* Trenton, NJ: Africa World Press, 2004.

Kọ́lé Ọmọ́tọ́ṣọ̀

DRAMA

Dramatic arts are one of the most important and enduring aspects of Yorùbá culture and tradition. The first written description of Yorùbá drama appeared in the diaries of nineteenth-century British explorers Hugh Clapperton and Richard Lander. The diarists witnessed a three-act command performance of an aláràjó troupe at the palace of the aláàfin of Ọ̀yọ́ on February 22, 1826. The first act consisted of dancing and acrobatic displays, followed by a revue in which one performer caught a boa constrictor thrown to him. The final act was an enactment of a satire of the explorers, who were described as "the white devil." Choral songs were also produced by women and the audience. However, oral evidence dates *alárìnjó* theater to more than three hundred years before the explorers' visit.

Alárìnjó Theater

Alárìnjó theater is one of earliest important Yorùbá dramas. Others include Egúngún festivals, the Àdìmú-Òrìṣà (Èyò) funeral rites, the Gèlèdé, and other festivals that use dramatic elements such as song, dance, and costumes. The different varieties of drama include heroic drama, burlesque, satire, and ribald comedy. The *alárìnjó*, or traditional traveling theater, is also known as *eégún aláré* (the masked performer). It is one of the most reliable aesthetic formats of the Yorùbá theater. The *alárìnjó* itinerant professional theater includes three developmental stages of ritual, festival, and theater. It dates from about the fourteenth century, when, according to oral history, Ṣàngó, the deified *aláàfin* of Ọ̀yọ́, founded the Egúngún festival to honor his departed father. The festival was formalized two centuries later into a lineage seasonal festival of specialized dance displays. These were then refined into purely entertainment guilds as professional Yorùbá theater.

Alárìnjó's association with Egúngún is part of the Yorùbá dramatic heritage. The group took part in the annual Egúngún festival and became variously known as *òjè* or *egúngún apidán* (magic-performing masquerade). Gradually, through the involvement of Olúgbẹrẹ Àgan, the son of the cymbalist to the *aláàfin*, Ológbìín Ológbojò, *alárìnjó* performers started wearing costumes and wooden masks to disguise the identity of the performer. By the first half of nineteenth century, troupes such as Ayélabọ́lá, Agbégijó, Àjàngìlà, and Ajó-féèbó had been organized. In addition, the repertoire of the troupes had become more professionalized. The troupes still participated in the annual Egúngún festival, but they increasingly geared their performances toward entertaining people on nonfestival days, particularly at secular ceremonies like child naming, funerals, and weddings. They also became itinerant.

With this development, *alárìnjó* became a theatrical art and the increased professionalism improved the troupes' performances.

Performance Mode

The troupes' methods of presentation in the first of half of the nineteenth century became defined. A performance usually started with songs, drumming, and acrobatic displays, which heralded the troupe to a town. On the day of performance, the drummers would sing and chant while accompanying the actors around the town. They ended up at the market square, where the performances were usually staged. The performances were generally spectacles rather than sketches, because the main intention of a troupe was to entertain first before making social or political comments. This mode of performance influenced modern Yorùbá traveling theater in the early twentieth century, and it was made popular by the trio of actor-impresarios Hubert Ògúndé, Kọ́lá Ògúnmọ́lá, and Dúró Ládipọ̀.

Modern Yorùbá Drama

Hubert Adédèjì Ògúndé (1916–1990) formed the African Music Research Party in 1945 and produced *Tiger's Empire* the following year. *Tiger's Empire* attacked colonial rule and set the tone for subsequent plays, which were politically and socially relevant. He produced more than forty plays, including *Yorùbá Ronú*, *Aiyé*, and *Jáyiésimi*. Elijah Kọ́láwọlé Ògúnmọ́lá (1925–1973) formed his troupe in 1947 and was the first to link the traditional traveling theater with popular literary theater by becoming the first "student" and resident artist of the University of Ìbàdàn School of Drama in 1962. He adapted Amos Tutùọlá's *The Palmwine Drinkard* into an opera entitled *Lànkẹ́ Ọ̀mùtí*, which was performed at the First Pan-African Cultural Congress in Algiers (1969). The third dramatist, Dúró Ládipọ̀ (1931–1978), started Mbárí Mbáyò Club in Òṣogbo in 1961 and produced plays based on myths and legends of Yorùbáland. These include *Ọbamọrọ̀* (1962), *Ọba kò so* and *Ọba Wàjà* (1964), and *Mọrèmi* (1968).

Dramatic Form

The dramatists have two basic modes of performance or enactment: musical and nonmusical. In musicals, the text or dialogue is structurally dependent on the music for narrative continuity and dramatic impact. In nonmusical dramas, the drama is dependent on dialogue and action. Although there is no definitive form, structure, or format for modern theater, the format often adopts the tripartite structure established by the *alárìnjó* tradition and the *ewì* poetic chants of the Egúngún. Before a performance, there is the publicity element, which is adopted from the *alárìnjó* tradition. There is a campaign around town or village in the company's lorry, with loudspeakers announcing the evening's performance to the accompaniment of vocal and instrumental music played by the company's orchestra. A performance usually started with the ritualistic *ìjúbà* (opening glee) in which the *oríkì* of the troupe is recited; it reveals the relationship between the performer's art and the drama. This is followed by the dance, which is divided into two parts: ritual dance, to honor the notable deities and divinities worshipped in the town, and social dance, to feature the dance steps in current fashion. Next, the drama is performed, and it reflects both genres of spectacle and revue. The end of the performance, or the finale, consists of a valedictory song and dance, or a closing glee.

Modern Literary Drama

In 1968, Ọlá Rótìmí began the Orí Olókun Theater at the University of Ifẹ̀, Ilé-Ifẹ̀, around which a strong literary theater culture developed. The members were drawn from the traveling theater and university staff and students. Some of the plays the group produced include Akínwùmí Ìsọ̀lá's *Madam Tinúbú*. Ìsọ̀lá also wrote contemporary and historical plays such as *Kòṣeégbé* and *Ẹfúnṣetán Aníwúrà*.

Film Tradition

In recent years, Yorùbá traditional traveling theater practitioners have collaborated with literary dramatists to convert their stage plays into film or to create new stories for films. The foremost practitioners are Tádé Ògìdán, Túndé Kèlání, and Délé Odùlé, who all grew out of the old tradition and worked with the pioneer dramatists Ògúndé, Ládipọ̀, and Ògúnmọ́lá.

See also **Ládipọ̀, Dúró; Nollywood: Films and Cinema; Ògúnde, Hubert Adédèjì**

REFERENCES

Clapperton, Hugh. *Journal of a Second Expedition into the Interior of Africa from the Bight of Benin to Soccatoo*. London: J. Murray, 1829.
Ògúnbíyì, Yẹmí. *Drama and Theatre in Nigeria: A Critical Source Book*. Lagos (Nigeria): Nigerian Magazine, 1981.

Ṣọlá Adéyẹmí

DREAMS AND DREAM INTERPRETATION

Two types of dreams are important to the Yorùbá: dreams of prophecy and dreams of intrusion into one's psychic space. Yorùbá perceive both the earthly world and the extraterrestrial world as warring universes in which humans constantly and continually battle against both feasible and unseen enemies. These enemies could be within one's family, household, neighborhood, and community; and they are often disguised as close friends and family. Such enemies go at any length to exact revenge or avenge perceived wrongs. They employ the services of supernatural agents, including witches, wizards, and soothsayers, and the evil forces of deities, such as Èṣù, Ṣàngó, and Ògún.

The world of dreams, or *àlá*, signifies the connection with Yorùbá beliefs in reincarnation, unbroken communication and relationships between the dead and the living; extrasensory perception; diabolic power of enemies, evil, and the people of the underworld; and the extraterrestrial (spirit) world—perhaps more than any other element of Yorùbá culture. Among the Yorùbá, dreams constitute a window for the living to view the spirit world: *ọrun*, the real home, the home of those who have passed on—especially since ancestors continue to control and direct the affairs of their progeny. *Ayé lọjà, ọrun nílé*: the earthly world is a marketplace that humans only visit and then permanently return home (to *ọrun*) after shopping.

Dreams play an important part in the material wealth, emotional health, and spiritual balance and well-being of the Yorùbá, not only because a dreamer is most vulnerable and helpless when in the dream state but also because the Yorùbá literally interpret what happens in dreams as portents: prophesy or warning of things to happen. Dream interpretation relies on the symbols and symbolism in dreams. For example, many snakes are poisonous and their bite can often be deadly. Therefore, to see snakes in a dream means an enemy is about to attack. Should one successfully kill the snake in the dream, it implies that one has conquered one's enemy. In contrast, a defeat in such an encounter would require consulting with and seeking the help of "elders," the Babaláwo (Ifá priest), or Adáhunṣe (the traditional doctors), who are perceived to have greater power than one's enemy. They are presumed to know what to do, and they are required to take necessary action to avert the imminent danger. Depending on what transpires in a dream, the appearance of masquerades in pursuit could mean that one's ancestors or enemies are out to settle a score! A child's nightmare could mean the child is engaged in ominous battles with the evil spirits. "Wet" dreams could mean the spouse of the spirit world is in competition with the living spouse. Being presented with food in a dream may mean that an enemy is using the dream to poison the dreamer.

Because the Yorùbá often perceive dreams as forewarnings of what is to come, no one ignores the omens in dreams, whether a pleasant or a bad dream. Consequently, different religious groups (e.g., Muslim, Christian, traditional) now make a living from the Yorùbá fundamental beliefs in the power of evil forces, taking advantage of the naïveté and vulnerability of the ignorant and superstitious dreamers!

See also **Cosmology; Divinatory System; Sacrifice**

REFERENCE

Empson, J. *Sleep and Dreaming*, 3rd ed. New York: Palgrave/ St. Martin's Press, 2002.

Bọ́lá Dáúdà

Dress, as generally conceived, describes any item used by humans to cover their nakedness or to adorn their bodies. These include items such as cloth, jewelry, and other forms of adornment. Among the Yorùbá people, dress is considered not only an item but also a process. As an item, dress includes clothes, jewelry, coiffed hair, facial marks, pierced ears, scented breath, as well as an equally long list of garments, accessories, and other categories of items added to the body as supplements. As a process, dress includes the semiotics, or meanings, associated with presenting the human body, both to oneself and to others. This includes the values Yorùbá people place on dressing and dressing well. As an item, dress covers the body, preventing it from the vagaries of nature and from unauthorized visual intrusion. It is a microenvironment that interfaces with the body. As a process, dress espouses values, identity, and position. It helps in creating, establishing, and reinforcing Yorùbá individual and collective identity. Dress reveals the body, the values associated with the body or a person. In other words, dress alters the body and serves as a canvas on which values, identity, position, and the like are inscribed both to oneself and to the public. It is on account of these rather complex conceptualizations that Yorùbá people invest so much time and resources to how they dress.

In folk songs, everyday sayings, and cultural practices, Yorùbá people demonstrate that dress is a sine qua non of human existence. For instance, a few lines from the *oríkì* of the Òpómúléró describe a popular Yorùbá family and eloquently testify to the value of dress among the people: *kẹ̀kẹ́ ta dídùn, aṣọ l'èdìdì ènìyàn; bí kò sí aṣọ, bí kò sí èjìgbà ìlẹ̀kẹ̀; onírúurú ìdí là bá rí* (the spindle spurns beauty; cloth beautifies the human body, if not for cloths, if not for the big beads, we would have seen varying sizes of buttocks). In addition, Yorùbá people liken dress in human existence to birds' wings: *àdàbà tí kò l'ápá; kí ni yó fi fò? Ọlọ́mọge tí kò l'áṣọ, kí ni yó fi lògbà?* (A wingless dove—with what will it fly? A lady without dress—how will she survive the season?) By comparing dress to wings, Yorùbá people believe that just as a wingless bird cannot fly, a person without dress is naked. Here, *dress* refers to a process. Hence, a nuanced interpretation of the above extends to possession of children, people, good morality, and the like.

A careful reading of the previous saying shows that, to the Yorùbá people, dress must also conform to fashion and seasonal changes. Season here has little or nothing to do with planting seasons or seasonal changes in weather but instead with occasional swings in fashion. In other words, a Yorùbá person, as part of his identity as an individual and a member of a group, is expected to possess a wardrobe of fashionable clothes and other items of dress. A young lady must wear not only whatever is in vogue at any point in time but also a hairdo that follows with the fashion. A young man's dress sense is regarded as faulty and unacceptable if he lacks whatever dress items or fashion items his mates are wearing.

In a paradoxical manner, the people also say *aṣọ ńlá kọ́ ni ènìyàn ńlá* (a well-dressed person is not necessarily a well placed or highly reasonable or remarkable person). With regard to the first position, this second position serves as a caveat that dress differs markedly from identity and that one should make efforts to separate a person's accouterment from his or her real identity. Compared to the earlier position, which demonstrates the people's reference for dress and dressing, this latter position subsumes a paradox. This paradox is made more pronounced in contemporary society by clerics of religious organizations who loudly admonish their followers to make sure their mode of dressing is culturally acceptable in the society.

Unarguably, the society makes distinctions between dress and existential values espoused by dress, such as identity. In the praise names of the *ọba*, the political head of Yorùbá kingdoms and states, people reference the *ọba*, *kábíyèsí*, *alase èkejì òrìṣà*, *kí adé pẹ́ lórí*, *kí bàtà pẹ́ lẹ́sẹ̀* (royal majesty, commander, and vice-regent of the gods—may the crown and the royal shoes last long). In this particular instance, the personality of the *ọba* and his dress are fused, as an *ọba*'s crown is both a dress and a symbol of authority. For instance, the presence of the *ọba*'s staff (or any of his instrument of office) in an occasion signifies the *ọba*'s approval and his presence at the occasion. *Ọba*, chiefs, and notable individuals in Yorùbáland dress to reflect their positions and wealth just as the commoners also dress to reflect their stations in life. From the foregoing examples, dress among Yorùbá people is both a measure of self-preservation and a process of communication.

Dress communicates age, sex, occupation, social status, and religion affiliation. The meanings associated with dress are shared across Yorùbáland. The process of learning these shared meanings starts from the family and children are taught to dress and conduct themselves in ways that bring glory, not shame, to their families.

There are different types of dress among Yorùbá people. These include *kíjìpá, pẹtùjẹ, sányán, ẹtù, àlàárì*, and *òfì*, which are known collectively as *aṣọ-òkè*. Also included are *yẹrí-etí* (earrings), *ẹgbà-ọwọ́* (bangles), and *ẹgbà-ọrùn* (necklaces). Others are *ilà-ojú* (facial scarification), *ara-fífín* (body scarification), *làálì* (the use of henna), *sọjú* (incisions), and all kinds of hairstyles. It must be noted that some of these items of dress are permanent additions to the body, while others are not. For the most part, fashion, social status, political affiliation, and religion play fundamental roles in how and when these items are used. However, there are three broad categories of dress among Yorùbá people: *aṣọ ìyílẹ̀* (play dress), *aṣọ iṣẹ́* (work dress), and *aṣọ-ìmúròde* (occasional dress).

Specific dress patterns and modes give some Yorùbá communities their identities. For instance, Abẹ́òkúta is notable for *àdìrẹ* (tie and dye); Ọ̀yọ́, Ìṣẹ́yìn, Ọ̀yọ́-Ilé, Ìlọrin, and the Iléṣà are notable for *òfì* or *aṣọ-òkè*; while Oǹdó is notable for *àlàárì*. In the same manner, groups within societies have their dress patterns. The Ògún (god of Iron) worshippers, for instance, are famous for wearing *gbérí*, a traditional shirt. In state, religious, and secular matters, different occasions require different dress and dress tradition.

While *aṣọ ìyílẹ̀* and *aṣọ iṣẹ́* are used every day either at home or at work, *aṣọ-ìmúròde* is worn occasionally. Unlike other items of dress, *aṣọ-ìmúròde* are divided into two categories: *aṣọ-ẹbí* (family ceremonial dress) and *aṣọ-ẹgbẹ́-jọ-dá* (well-wishers' ceremonial dress). Males and females have their respective style of dress. While males mainly wear *ṣòkòtò* (trouser), *bùbá* (shirt), *agbádá* (male's flowing gown), and *fìla* (cap), females wear *ìró* (wrapper), *bùbá* (blouse), *gèlè* (headgear), and *ìpèlé* (shawl).

The incorporation of Yorùbáland into the vortex of global commerce from the era of the transatlantic slave trade through colonial rule and post-independence introduced all kinds of sartorial cultures to Yorùbáland and Yorùbá people. Some of these new dress cultures, for instance, use African wax-print textiles and others were introduced to Yorùbáland during the colonial period and have become part of the sartorial makeup of Yorùbáland today. The same also goes for the use of European or Western dress.

See also **Body Adornment and Cosmetics**

REFERENCE

Fádípẹ̀, N. A. *The Sociology of the Yorùbá.* Ìbàdàn (Nigeria): University Press, 1970.

Bùkọ́lá Oyèníyì

DRUMS

Generally, a drum is a musical instrument made of a hollow, round frame with plastic or skin stretched tightly across one end or both ends, and it is played by hitting it with drumstick(s) or the hands. Drums include any of the various types of percussive musical instruments that consist of a hollow cylinder or hemisphere of wood, metal, or other material usually with a skin stretched tightly over the end or ends struck to produce a sound. Wherever they are found in Africa, either as instruments of communication, dance, or musical performance, drums are made of skin. Drums known as *ìlù* among the Yorùbá are made of hides and skins of different kinds tightly stretched across a hollow wooden surface held round the wood by thread or sharp stick and beaten with hand or stick.

Among the Yorùbá, drums serve many useful purposes. They are used for communication and entertainment. They are featured during observances and performances of different types. They are beaten at ceremonies for naming children, marriages, and funeral rites. Drums also are featured during coronations, festivals, and religious solemnities. Depending on prevalent norms or conventions held sacrosanct in a particular Yorùbá community, drums can be beaten in private or publicly. They are beaten at markets, palaces, religious shrines, or groves.

When drums are used for the purposes of communication, they are beaten with embedded meaning by the source to the destination. Although most drums communicate one thing, only a few of them "talk" in discernible manner. Drums are beaten by the *àyàn* to communicate with those who are gifted or trained to understand the drum verse. Other drums are beaten with noncommunicative intent. When they are beaten, they act as support or accompaniment to those that do "talk" or communicate meaning. These categories of drums are played mostly for entertainment and during religious ceremonies.

There are different categories of drums in Yorùbáland. Categories of drums are usually informed by a number of factors. Among the usual determinants of drum types are the functions a particular drum performs and the occasions on which it is used. Drums can be classified into two broad categories: communicative or talking drums and noncommunicative or nontalking drums. Drums, irrespective of their classificatory paradigms, are identified by different names.

Yorùbá communicative drums fall into three categories: the "talking" drums called *dùndún*; the dialect-speaking, stammering talking drum called *bàtá*; and other Yorùbá drums like *sákárà, apíntì, bàtákoto, ìpèsè, àgèrè, gbẹ̀du,* and *ìgbìn.* The *dùndún* is made of a piece of carefully carved *apá* wood to form hourglass-like frame with two ends covered by membranes of young goat skin, which is carefully joined by strings made of goat skin. It is beaten with a curved drumstick. When beaten, the *dùndún* can imitate the tones of Yorùbá speech and can be used to communicate insults, praises, admonition, and even proverbs. There are six types of *dùndún* drums: *ìyá ìlù dùndún, kẹríkẹrì, gángan, ìṣaájú, kànàngó,* and *gúdúgúdú.*

Bàtá drums form part of the Yorùbá music ensemble that are prominently featured during Ṣàngó worship and Egúngún performances. They are also performed on other occasions. Like the *dùndún,* the *bàtá* drum set is made from *apá* wood, which is shaped into cones with two ends (big or small) and covered with skin. The *bàtá* drums are usually hung on the neck and beaten by the *alubàtá.* They are beaten with two leather straps. The *bàtá* ensemble consists of *ìyá-ìlùu bàtá, omele-abo bàtá, omele-akọ bàtá,* and *kudi.*

See also **Communication: Nonverbal; Musical Instruments**

REFERENCES

Olúga, Samson Ọlásúnkànmí, and Halira Abẹ̀ní Latini Babalọlá. "Drummunication: The Trado-Indigenous Art of Communicating with Talking Drums in Yorùbáland." *Global Journal of Human Social Science, Arts, and Humanities* 12.11 (2012): 1–23.

Dáramọ́lá, Olú, and Adébáyọ̀ Jéjé. *Àwọn Àṣà àti Òrìṣà Ilẹ̀ Yorùbá.* Ìbàdàn (Nigeria): Oníbọn-Òjé Press, 1975.

Túndé Babáwálé

E

The metamorphosis of Yorùbá society from a primitive to a complex and highly organized one reflected the group's historical circumstances and experiences. Precolonial economic activities in Yorùbáland were complex and diverse. The totality of the social and economic processes produced changes that constantly defined and redefined social and economic investments. By the nineteenth century, Yorùbáland had developed a high degree of urbanization, with about a dozen towns with populations of more than twenty thousand. Ìbàdàn was considered the largest of these towns, with an estimated population of seventy thousand.

The rise of kingdoms and the development of an economic system formed the basis of an integrated and innovative process of change, with agricultural production at its apex. A range of manufacturing industries also revealed the long-established capacity of the people for technical know-how. Knowledge of iron working existed before contact with Europe, and a complex of highly specialized mining villages had flourished around Ọ̀yọ́ during the precolonial period. Other occupations existed either as full-time or part-time activities.

The internal and external trades of Yorùbáland assisted in the task of economic expansion. Networks of markets were created to perform economic, religious, political, and social functions. Yorùbáland was also linked to the outside world by the Atlantic Ocean and by a network of trade routes that passed through Ọ̀yọ́ and other towns to Kukawa and Kano in northern Nigeria.

Centuries of Turmoil and Economic Decay

The disruptiveness of combat, raids, rapine, and civil wars between the seventeenth century and the last decades of the nineteenth century significantly affected the economy and society of Yorùbáland. Contact with Europe had induced strong linkages between the domestic economy and external trade. During the period of the transatlantic slave trade, Yorùbáland was implicated in the trade. Ọ̀yọ́, the most powerful of the kingdoms, sold its slaves in the late seventeenth and early eighteenth centuries through the ports of Whydah and Allada. By the nineteenth century, the ports of Lagos and Badagry had become the most important areas of exportation of slaves to the New World.

In the interior, the breakup of the Ọ̀yọ́ Empire in 1817 inaugurated a cataclysm of events that negatively affected the economy of Yorùbáland. The empire crumbled under the combined stress of internal friction and the activities of Fulani jihadists. By the middle of the 1830s, the whole of Yorùbáland had dissolved into crisis. The mass exodus of people from the savanna in the north to the forest area in the south created pressure on the land in the forest zone and affected the landscape of western Nigeria as deforestation started to set in.

As Ìbàdàn, Ọ̀yọ́'s most powerful successor state, began to extend its control over the towns in the southern part of the old Ọ̀yọ́ Empire, its vassal states comprising the Ìjẹ̀sà, Èkìtì, and other eastern groups in the late 1870s established a confederacy known as the Èkìtìparapọ̀ to resist Ìbàdàn domination and exploitation. Until the negotiated settlement of 1886, the towns along the war zones were subjected to harassment by belligerent warriors, who often despoiled the farms and communities for their own sustenance and amusement. The British, who had seized control of Lagos in 1861, used the war with the Ìjẹ̀bú in 1892 to extend their "protection" to most of Yorùbáland. By 1900, all of Yorùbáland had come under British rule.

The Colonial Economy

The nineteenth century represented a change in the structure of the economy and society. The relationship with Europeans became the main channels of the commercialization of indigenous forest products and the diffusion of European goods and foreign crops. The spread of New World crops such as cocoa and tobacco affected the economy in new ways. During the early nineteenth century, the British withdrew from the slave trade, blockaded the waterways, and instituted legitimate commerce allowed under the law of the land. The era of legitimate commerce saw the introduction of goods and services that began to generate additional income in legitimate ways. While the import trade aided the consumption of cheap, mass-produced consumer imports, the export trade in palm products, which became the main staple export of the nineteenth century, yielded good returns and mass participation. It was estimated that the new legitimate enterprise brought about fifteen million palm trees into production for the export market in Yorùbáland.

The end of the civil wars and the institution of colonial rule further expanded the new economy. Many Yorùbá began to engage in migrations to seek economic opportunities. They gravitated toward areas of administrative and commercial activity, commercial agriculture, jobs, and new opportunities for trade.

Others moved to coastal towns or to rural areas such as Agége, Ìjan, and Ọ̀tà, where farmers were beginning to produce foodstuffs for the new urban markets and to experiment with crops. Many also sought employment in the railways lines being constructed.

Colonialism and the Cash-Crop Economy

During the first fifty years of British colonialism in Nigeria, the burden of development was laid upon the cultivation and processing of raw agricultural materials for export. This was a major development that modified and transformed the economy and society of western Nigeria. The replacement of indigenous currencies with the sterling as the legal tender modified the structure of the indigenous economy by creating new relationships based on money. Successive British administrators and agricultural experts therefore devoted their time to persuading peasants to produce crops for the world market. Commercial agriculture succeeded in producing the raw materials needed by European industries and, as a consequence, furnished the peasants with the means for satisfying their newly developed tastes for European goods. Cocoa, which had become a part of the Yorùbá economy by the 1850s, dictated the pace and pattern of the economy well into the twentieth century.

The need for modern means of transport to evacuate agricultural produce served as an early stimulus to the building of roads, rail lines, and wharf facilities. The modern means of transportation, most especially roads and railways, had their early beginnings among the Yorùbá, and these have remained vitally important to the modern economy of Nigeria. The construction of rail lines began in Lagos in 1896; road transport development in Nigeria began in 1906 with the construction of Ọ̀yọ́-Ìbàdàn road. The transport infrastructure became economically important for the movement of agricultural and other goods during the colonial and postcolonial periods. Spurred by the oil boom prosperity of the 1970s, the economy and society of Yorùbáland expanded geometrically. The city of Lagos is today regarded as the economic capital of the country.

See also **Economic Systems; Ọ̀yọ́ Empire; Slavery; Transportation**

REFERENCES

Akínjógbìn, I. A., and S. O. Ọ̀ṣọbà, eds. *Topics on Nigerian Economic and Social History*. Ifẹ̀ (Nigeria): University of Ifẹ̀ Press, 1980.

Ẹkúndáre, R. O. *An Economic History of Nigeria, 1860–1960*. London: Methuen, 1973.

Olútáyọ̀ C. Adéṣínà

ECONOMIC SYSTEM

The evolution and sustenance of a dynamic and coherent economic system has been a tribute to the skill, capacity, and adaptability of the Yorùbá people of southwestern Nigeria. Decisions about the commodities to be produced and distributed, and for and to whom, have been part of the economic processes for millennia. An economic system requires the skills and input of men and women, states, and communities, all of which serve as mechanisms of growth for the domestic economy and export production. The interaction of the human and natural resources of the region resulted in occupational and regional diversities in production and distribution.

The Economic System: From Production to Exchange

The vitality of Yorùbá society historically depended to a large extent on a vibrant agriculture, which became the mainstay of the economy. Apart from keeping domestic animals and engaging in subsistence and commercial fishing, the sector depended on numerous small-scale farmers (*àgbẹ̀*) who produced the foodstuffs, cash crops, and a variety of fruits and vegetables distributed and consumed every year from small plots of land either located near their domains (*oko etílé*) or farmsteads (*oko iwájú*).

For a long time, hoes, cutlasses, and planting sticks remained the main tools for crop production. The period of planting became one of the busiest periods in agriculture. Each farmer relied on the services of his biological family and dependents, mostly male members of his household, to till the field, plant, and harvest. The periods of planting and harvest promoted the concept of reciprocal labor exchange known as *ọ̀wẹ̀* and *àáró*. Agricultural production also relied on the availability of suitable land, a factor that was seen in many ways as the basis of economic existence, as a prominent symbol of unity, and as the basis of socioeconomic interdependence within and between lineages. The abundance of land had an important consequence: it allowed a sustainable system of cultivation. Land that had already been cultivated and became less productive could be exchanged for a virgin piece of land or a land that had been left fallow for years to regain its fertility.

Several crafts developed across the land, with many places identified by their specializations. The mat-weaving culture, for instance, became quite significant in Ìjèṣà areas, where a specific type of local long grass occurred. Thus, the Ìjèṣà people became quite renowned for their mat-weaving proficiency, to the extent that a group nickname evolved for them. They were known as *ọmọ ẹlẹ́ní ẹwẹlẹ* (children of those who weaved fanciful mats).

The distributive system fostered the growth of trade, commerce, currencies, and credits over a widely dispersed area. This created and relied on the domestic and regional network of markets, trade, traders, and trade routes. Palm oil and kola nut traveled from the forest to the savanna in the long-distance trade that radiated from south to north. The main channels of distribution were the markets and trade routes that dotted several areas of Yorùbáland. The trans-Saharan trade connected Kano in the north with the interior and coasts of Yorùbá territories. From the coast of Lagos, these routes passed through Abẹ́òkúta, Ìbàdàn, Ọ̀yọ́, Ìṣéyìn, Ìgbòho, Ìgbétì, Ògbómọ̀ṣọ́, and Ìlọrin to Kano. All these also facilitated the reception of imported consumer goods such as meat and dairy products, leather goods, grains, onions, peppers, natron, salt, potash, and several other goods. Commercial transactions were multilateral and widespread. The commercial system depended on the trust system through the concept of *àwìn* (credit). Goods were advanced toward a future payment. The *ọ̀ṣómàálọ́* trading system of the Ìjèṣà advanced the processes of trust, credit, and debt recovery in very significant ways.

The transport sector oiled the wheels of the economy. Two modes of nonmechanical transport were prevalent in the economy of the region. These were human porterage and canoes. Pack animals never thrived in the forest region, but those who participated in trade with the north from the savanna region adopted their usage in the caravan trade.

Minor occupations such as hunting, trapping, and palm-wine tapping complemented activities in the major sectors of the economy. The capacity of the economic system to expand and redirect the economy at particular epochs through the agency of the indigenous people is one of the most publicized achievements of the Yorùbá people.

See also **Agriculture and Farming; Commerce; Cooperative Associations; Debt and Debt Management; Economic History; Transportation**

REFERENCES

Adébáyọ̀, A. G. "Money, Credit and Banking in Pre-Colonial Africa: The Yorùbá Experience." *Anthropos* 4.6 (1994): 379–400.
Akínjógbìn, I. A., and Ọ̀ṣọbà, S. O., eds. *Topics on Nigerian Economic and Social History*. Ile-Ifẹ̀ (Nigeria): University of Ifẹ̀ Press, 1980.

Olútáyọ̀ C. Adéṣínà

EDUCATION: ELEMENTARY

Elementary and secondary school systems have evolved from the humble beginnings of Ilé-Ìwé Awólọ́wọ̀, the postindependence free education introduced by the Western Region government under the leadership of Chief Ọbáfẹ́mi Awólọ́wọ̀, to the free universal basic education, initially known as universal primary education. Elementary education is often referred to in Nigeria by its British name, "primary school." The Yorùbá use the nickname *ilé-ìwé alákọ̀ọ́bẹ̀rẹ̀*, literally, "school for beginners," or beginners' education. It is indeed the beginning of formal Western education. It is at the elementary level that children are first exposed to formal curricula.

Before 1960, during the colonial era, grade levels were classified in standards form. For example, a child would begin in standard 1 and end in standard 6. Each class ran through the calendar year (January through December). The curriculum was rigorous, and the completion of standard 6 automatically guaranteed a teaching job in an elementary school or decent civil service employment. The subjects taught included English language, Yorùbá language, arithmetic, Bible knowledge, social studies, and sometimes nature studies and hygiene. In fact, anyone who successfully completed any aspect of the standards, even if unable to complete schooling because of financial strain, family, or other commitments, could still land a fairly decent job as a produce clerk, civil servant, or even teacher. Many elementary school teachers of the 1950s and 1960s never went beyond standard 6. Many village headmasters were standard 6 certificate holders.

Today, elementary school curricula include the study of Nigeria's three major languages, Hausa, Igbo, and Yorùbá. Private schools may also run curricula in basic computer education, French, Spanish, and fine arts. Students have to take a battery of tests to transition from one grade level to another and to seek admission to secondary schools, whether such schools are private or public. After experimenting with the British model of K–12 and postsecondary education, in which a child spends six years in elementary, five years in high school, two years in postsecondary school, and three years in university education, Nigeria dropped this system for what it called the 6-3-3-4 system, which means six years of elementary education, three years of middle or intermediate school, three years of senior high school, and four years of college (university) education. A fairly modified form of the same system is what is used in today's school system.

In the 1980s, apart from the regular elementary school system, the federal government introduced some new forms of nontraditional schooling for nomadic Hausa-Fulani all over the country, the *al-majiri* (street children and beggars), and disabled, itinerant people.

See also **Awólọ́wọ̀, Ọbáfẹ́mi; Education: Modern; Education: Preschool; Education: Tertiary; Education: Traditional**

REFERENCES

Aliu, S. "The Competitive Drive, New Technologies and Employment: The Human Capital Link." Unpublished paper presented at the Second Tripartite Conference of Manpower Planners, Chelsea Hotel, Abuja, 2001.

Ito, Ismaila. "Nomadic Education and Education for Nomadic Fulani." http://www.gamji.com/fulani7.htm.

Michael Ọládèjọ Afọláyan

EDUCATION: MODERN (JUNIOR AND SENIOR SECONDARY)

The secondary education system comprises three years of junior secondary school (JSS) and three years of senior secondary school (SSS). The two combined used to be known as high school. This almost fits snugly with the American school system, except that in the American school system, students spend four years in senior high school, not three. Secondary education is critical in Nigeria, as it is the bridge to achieving a highly valued university education. Transitioning from a three-year junior secondary school requires a standardized examination administered by a national testing body. If and when a child successfully completes the three years and passes the examination, he or she can transition into SSS. The SSS curriculum comprises the arts, sciences, mathematics, and Nigerian languages. Failure in English language or mathematics would deny a student the grade average required to enter university, regardless of how well he or she performed in other subjects.

Students are encouraged to take the General Certificate Examination (GCE) Ordinary Level around October and November in the second year of the senior secondary school. Students must participate in the Senior Secondary Certificate Examination (SSCE) in the last year of secondary school, which takes place in June and July. Students must take at least seven and up to nine subjects. Mathematics and English language are required. In order of superiority, the grades are A1, B2, and B3 (distinctions); C4, C5, and C6 (credit grades); D7 and E8 (passing grades); and F9 (failing grade). University admissions require a minimum achievement of credit grades. An independent regional examination body, the West African Examination Council, in collaboration with National Examination Council, conducts both the GCE and the SSCE.

State and federal governments manage secondary education in Nigeria. Private individuals also own some schools but must conform to government regulations. Some secondary schools are called colleges in Nigeria, in line with the British system. The federal government established two colleges in each of its thirty-six states and the Federal Capital Territory of Abuja. They are funded and staffed through the federal Ministry of Education. Those sponsored by individual states derive their funding from the states.

Teachers in state-owned institutions are expected to have a baccalaureate degree or a National Certificate of Education (NCE). Teachers are not licensed in Nigeria; they do not have teacher certifications. They only have academic qualifications without the legal mandate of a license. Anyone with a degree in a content area can teach the subject. For example, an individual with a bachelor of arts, bachelor of science, or NCE diploma in physics can teach physics at any secondary school.

Immediately after the end of colonial rule, a new form of secondary education known as the "modern school" began; in reality, it belonged in no particular educational category. There was nothing modern about the modern school: it was a three-year experience borne of the misguided adoption of the British junior vocational high school system. However, in Nigeria it became an outlet for several categories of students. The first category included those who were very talented and had completed elementary education but whose parents had no means of paying for them to attend high school.

A second category of students included those who were academically challenged and could not make it through the competitive common entrance examinations that led to high school. If members of this group completed the modern school, they were most likely able to attend the grade 3 teacher training college or find jobs as menial workers. A third category comprised students who had no access to a high school within their immediate proximity, and so the modern school education became an adequate substitution for high school education. It would not be until the late 1970s and early 1980s that this educational system was eradicated for its redundancy.

See also Education: Elementary; Education: Preschool; Education: Tertiary; Education: Traditional

REFERENCES

Schultz, T. P. "Why Governments Should Invest More to Educate Girls." *World Development* 30.2 (2002): 207–25.
Nussbaum, Martha. "Women's Education: A Global Challenge." *Journal of Women in Culture and Society* 29.2 (2003): 325–55.

Michael Ọládèjọ Afọláyan

EDUCATION: PRESCHOOL

The Yorùbá are among the most educated ethnic groups in Nigeria. Many were beneficiaries of various educational schemes that politicians at the national and regional levels instituted. Literally, from womb to tomb, the Yorùbá person is exposed to one form of education or another. It is for this purpose that even preschool education is ingrained into the social functioning of the Yorùbá child.

For the most part, preschool education is informal in Nigeria because it is an arrangement of convenience, partly due to the modern-day professional engagement of both parents. In those days when mothers would remain home, preschool was not an issue, but in today's Yorùbá society, where mothers often work outside of the home, it has become more pervasive. In the past, when a child attended preschool, it was called *ilé-ìwée jẹ́lé ó sinmi*, or school for those who needed to "let the household be in peace." The presupposition was that a child was sent to the preschool program primarily so that adults could have peace at home. It was intended to serve the purpose of babysitting rather than formal education. More important,

it was intended to keep the child in a safe, nursery school environment, not an environment for learning. The corollary is that there does not have to be any moderated or government-mandated curriculum in preschool. However, it is not uncommon that children receive some basic education, like learning the alphabet or memorizing numbers.

Under normal circumstances, a child would start school around age five or six. In the colonial period, when there were no birth registries and birth records were kept only by a very few educated parents, one way people determined the child's readiness to attend school was for the child to touch his or her left ear with the middle finger of the right hand stretched across his or her head. If the middle finger touched the left ear, then the child was determined to be of age for school. Therefore, children who failed that test, even if they were of school age, were forced to attend preschool. While most elementary schools were government sponsored, preschool education had always been a private business for the privileged few. Most children who attended preschools are often far beyond their peers in terms of educational development when they eventually start elementary school.

See also Education: Elementary; Education: Modern; Education: Tertiary; Education: Traditional

REFERENCES

Ogbaa, K. *Carrying My Father's Torch: A Memoir.* Durham, NC: Carolina Academic Press, 2014.
Togun, Philip A. *Victoria's Son: A Memoir.* Kearney, NE: Morris Publishing, 2012.

Michael Ọládèjọ Afọláyan

EDUCATION: TERTIARY

Nigeria has more than five hundred institutions of higher learning, including universities, medical schools, polytechnics, schools of nursing, colleges of education, advanced teacher-training colleges, colleges of technology, colleges of agriculture, schools of forestry, theological seminaries, technical colleges, military colleges, police academies, and cooperative colleges. Nigeria might have more educational institutions than all other African countries combined. For the most part, federal and state governments own these institutions, although private proprietary individuals own some. Of those institutions, a large majority are located in the Yorùbá southwestern part of the country. There is hardly any major Yorùbá city where institutions of higher learning are not found; they are located in Lagos, Abẹ́òkúta, Ìjẹbú-Òde, Ìbàdàn, Ilé-Ifẹ̀, Òṣogbo, Ẹdẹ, Ìlá-Ọ̀ràngún, Ìréè, Ìrẹ̀sì, Gbọ̀ngán, Ìwó, Èjìgbò, Iléṣà, Èsà-Òkè, Ògbómọ̀ṣọ́, Ọ̀yọ́, Ìṣéyìn, Làǹlátẹ̀, Èrúwà, Oǹdó, Àkúrẹ́, Adó-Èkìtì, Ọ̀fà, Ìlọrin, Ọ̀wọ̀, Òró, and so on.

Most privately owned proprietary institutions of higher learning are universities. They came into existence after being created by a 1993 federal law. Such institutions mushroomed into a barrage of substandard higher education institutions, with a few exceptions. Most Nigerians love to have university degrees and tend to look down on nonbaccalaureate academic diplomas.

Federal government universities are classified by their dates of establishment; they are often referred to as first-, second-, and third-generation universities. First-generation universities are those institutions founded between 1948 and 1965; they are University of Ìbàdàn, University of Nigeria, Nsukka, University of Ifẹ̀ (later renamed Ọbáfẹ́mi Awólọ́wọ̀ University), University of Lagos, and Ahmadu Bello University, Zaria. The second were founded between 1970 and 1985; there are twelve of them. In the third category are those founded between 1985 and 1999. A large number of state-run universities and private ones exist.

In 2011, the federal government established nine new universities: Federal University, Lafia, Nasarawa State (in the North-Central geopolitical zone of Nigeria); Federal University, Lokoja, Kogi State (North-Central); Federal University, Kashere, Gombe State (North-East); Federal University, Wakari, Taraba State (North-East); Federal University, Dutsin-Ma, Katsina State (North-West); Federal University, Dutse, Jigawa State (North-West); Federal University, Otuoke, Bayelsa State (South-South); Federal University, Ndufe-Alike, Ebonyi State (South-East); and Federal University, Oyé-Èkìtì, Èkìtì State (South-West). These new sets of universities were created purely for political expediency rather than for any functional or logical purpose. As a result, they have drawn a great deal of criticism from Nigerian educators, especially those in the already-established but poorly funded universities, which have long been in a deplorable state.

For the most part, university education in Nigeria follows the pattern of the U.S. higher education system, using the semester model in which schools start in September for the fall semester and the spring semester begins in January. Instructors are generally known as professors in the United States; in Nigeria, following the British model, instructors at the universities are referred to as lecturers.

See also Education: Elementary, Education: Modern, Education: Preschool; Education: Traditional

REFERENCES

Onyepere, Eze. "The Three New Universities." *Punch Online*, January 28, 2013. http://www.punchng.com/opinion/the-three-new-federal-universities/.
UNESCO. *Education for All*. Oxford: Oxford University Press, 2008.

Michael Ọládèjọ Afọláyan

EDUCATION: TRADITIONAL

The indigenous form of knowledge production among the Yorùbá, which was often passed from one generation to another by the word of mouth, predates Western education. Vocational training, or learning a trade, was achieved under the tutelage of a master practitioner, following a strict curriculum and unfettered pedagogy. The home-based, social, purely observational mode of knowledge acquisition was always availed of by the patient, observant child (*ọmọ t'ó fojú sílẹ̀*). Ẹ̀kọ́ ilé (home training) is distinct from ẹ̀kọ́ òde (lessons learned from the outside, "street smarts"). To the Yorùbá, the former is free, but the latter is costly, often accompanied by hardship, insult, and stress; it is acquired through regret, agitation, and contestation. It is for ọmọ aláìgbọràn (the obstinate), olóríkunkun (the stony hearted), oníwọ́nranwọ̀nran (the restless, impatient)—ọmọ tí kò gbọ́n nílé, òde ni wọ́n ti ń kọ́ ọ wá'lé (a child who resists home training will learn his or her lesson from the outside).

The benefit of good home education includes the tendency to preserve the socioeconomic dignity of the family (bá-n-kọ́lé ọmọ). On the contrary, the family may be disgraced in the hand of the bá-n-túlé ọmọ. The Yorùbá thus say, ọmo tí a kò kọ́ ni yóò gbé ilé tí a kọ́ tà (a child left untrained will sell off the house that is built). Notice the play on the word kọ́, which means "to teach (to train)," "to learn," and "to build."

Learning to respect both human and nature is a significant part of traditional education. There is grave expectations of a child to respect elders, most especially one's parents. It is an imperative injunction, a nonnegotiable filial duty, to pay homage and give adequate honor to one's parents. Anything to the contrary is considered sacrilegious. Children are taught to do anything humanly possible to find the favor of elders and be acceptable to them so as to be granted close proximity, acquiring secrets of life from them, as they are repositories of knowledge and custodians of the secrets of life and tradition. The child must do everything and anything to earn their trust: ọmọdé tó bá mọ ọwọ́ọ́ wẹ, á bá àgbà jẹun (a child who knows how to wash his hands will eat among the elders), which means that a child who follows the rules of proper behavior will earn the trust of elders. Ìyá ni wúrà, baba ni díńgí; l'ọ́jọ́ tí ìyá bá kú ni wúrà bàjẹ́; l'ọ́jọ́ tí baba bá kú ni díńgí ẹni wọmi (mother is golden, father is crystal; on the day the mother dies, the gold is spoiled; on the day the father dies, the crystal drowns). Ìyá ni wúrà iyebíye tí a kò le fowó rà (a mother is the precious gold, which money cannot buy). Elders teach children to recite the following:

Yí, yí, yí ẹsẹ̀ rẹ sí apá kan.
Má ṣe tẹ kòkòròo nì.
Kòkòrò tí ìwọ kò nááńí,
Ọlọ́run ni ó leè dá wọn.
Watch, watch, watch your steps.

Do not trample on that insect.
The insects that you so much despise,
Only God can create them.

Traditional education has a universal quality, and it is cyclical: ọgbọ́n ọlọ́gbọ́n ni kì í jẹ́ ká p'àgbà ní wèrè (borrowing the wisdom of others is what makes the elders wise), and àgbà wá búra b'éwe ò bá ṣe ọ́ rí (let the elders swear if they've never been youth).

See also Children's Folklore: Education and Development; Ethics; Ọmọlúwàbí

REFERENCE

Fádípẹ̀, N. A. The Sociology of the Yorùbá. Ìbàdàn (Nigeria): University Press, 1970.

Michael Ọládèjọ Afọláyan

ÈKÌTÌPARAPỌ̀ WAR

Èkìtì has existed since time immemorial as a collective name for the land of a subgroup division of the Yorùbá. A panoramic view of Èkìtì in about 1800, a few years before the ravage of Benin, Nupe-Fulani, Ìlọrin-Fulani, and Ìbàdàn invaders and slave raiders was likely to present a land of many medium-sized towns and villages. Before 1878, each kingdom and city-state in Èkìtì had maintained its own corporate existence and managed its own affairs in peace and in wartime as best as its leaders and citizens could, given the available human and material resources. The nineteenth-century Yorùbá wars threw Èkìtì into political and social turmoil. No part of Èkìtì was spared the agony of imperialist invasion.

The rapacity of Ìbàdàn war chiefs and the burdensome tributes they and their consuls and agents exacted from their Èkìtì, Ìjẹ̀sà, and Ìgbómìnà subjects disrupted the usual peaceful coexistence that had prevailed in these kingdoms. In the 1870s, the repatriated ex-slaves of Ìjẹ̀sà and Èkìtì extraction in Lagos, Abẹ́òkúta, and other places came together and formed the Ìjẹ̀sà Association. The association was renamed Èkìtìparapọ̀ (Èkìtì United Front) in 1876.

The source of the Èkìtìparapọ̀ liberation struggle and war against Ìbàdàn grew out of an event that occurred in mid-1878 at the Fábùnmi compound in Igbó Odò (known as Òkè Ìmèsí since the 1900s). The occasion was the new yam festival. Celebrants and visitors who milled about the lineage compound were in a festive mood, eating and drinking. The Ìbàdàn resident consul, Oyèpẹtun (aka *agùntáṣọọ́lò*), and his aides arrived, but they had hardly settled in when the consul reportedly fancied the breasts of Òní, one of the lineage wives, and straightaway fondled them. Fábùnmi is said to have reacted to this affront by beheading the consul and some of the aides he brought in tow.

The murder of the consul and his entourage was obviously a breach of a powerful Yorùbá convention, which forbade physical attack or assault against envoys, consuls, and official messengers. Igbó Odò authorities knew that Ìbàdàn authorities would be deeply affronted by the murders, and they decided to involve their immediate neighboring communities in any inevitable conflict that might ensue. Igbó Odò (Òkè Ìmẹẹ̀sí) envoys reported to the various main and subordinate towns and called for large-scale rebellion against Ìbàdàn hegemony.

The killing of Ìbàdàn consul and Ọ̀yọ́ settlers jolted Ìbàdàn authorities into the realities of the revolt of their Èkìtì subjects. Early in September 1878, the armies of the confederacy assembled at Ìmèsí Ìpólé, each army led by its Balógun. It was an exceedingly large army compared to those of Ìbàdàn in the Ìkìrun camp. The sheer size of Èkìtìparapò hosts caused Ìbàdàn to make urgent calls for reinforcements.

The war began in October 1878. Èkìtìparapò recorded heavy casualties. In early November, Èkìtìparapò brought in more men to reinforce the armies, but Ìbàdàn repeated their earlier successes, and the armies of the confederacy suffered great reverses. The reverses of these early encounters forced Èkìtìparapò leaders to look farther afield for assistance. They mounted greater pressure on Ògèdèngbé, then at Ìdóàní. He finally arrived at Ìmèsí Ìpólé at the end of November 1897. The battles raged, and the war dragged on between the hills and ravines at Ìgbórókò between Èkìtìparapò's camp at Ìmèsí Ìpólé and Ìbàdàn's camp at Ìgbájọ. The scope of hostilities

widened in 1882, when Ifẹ̀ and Ìjẹbú authorities joined Èkìtìparapò. In the early 1880s the Èkìtìparapò society in Lagos began to provide logistic support by procuring for the fighters sophisticated weapons. The unusual sound made by the discharge of those guns, *kí-rì-jì*, was adopted as popular name for the wars.

Efforts to mediate peace between the major belligerents Èkìtìparapò and Ìbàdàn were intensified in the middle of the 1880s. On September 23, 1886, two British government commissioners visited both Ìmèsí Ìpólé and Ìgbájọ camps; they supervised the peace process and signaled the commencement of a truce. The governor completed the peace process and ordered the combatants and their supporters to return to their respective homes. Finally, the governor proclaimed a general emancipation of slaves by which those who wished to return to their former homelands or birthplaces were granted the liberty to do so.

REFERENCES

Johnson, S. *The History of the Yorùbás.* Lagos (Nigeria): C.S.S., 1921.

Ọ̀lọ́mọ́là, I. *Èkìtìparapò Aspirations Since 1890s.* Ilé-Ifẹ̀ (Nigeria): Andkolad Ventures Nigeria Limited, 2005.

Olúwatóyìn M. Ọláìyá

ELECTRONIC MEDIA AND ORAL TRADITION

The Yorùbá have several oral traditions, including those associated with the life cycle—birth, growth, and death; the economic cycle of agriculture, industry, tourism, and the market; the political institutions of chieftaincy and the monarchy; the polytheistic religious institutions of God, deities, and ancestors; the literary genres of poetry, prose, and drama; and the gender institutions of men and women. With colonialism, modernity, and globalization came writing and the process of documenting various Yorùbá traditions. Colonizers and early literate people played prominent roles in writing down the history and traditions of various Yorùbá societies. Just as colonialism, modernity, and globalization led to the writing down of various Yorùbá traditions, they, along with the technological revolution of the past four decades or so, particularly the invention of the computer and the Internet, have moved Yorùbá traditions forward to allow for their preservation electronically.

Traditions that were available previously in only oral and written forms are now available electronically, and they can be stored on tape recorders, compact discs, video recorders, and computers, and they are available for production on radios, televisions, and films. Four of the institutions directly related to the electronic preservation of oral traditions are music, Nollywood films, the Internet, and the Global System for Mobile (GSM) communications revolution.

Regarding music, there have always been exceptional music and musicians in Yorùbáland. Some of the musical practices include rituals, chants, and festivals. The most popular is recorded music in the forms of highlife, popularized by Bobby Benson and Dr. Victor Ọláìyá; *jùjú* music, championed by I. K. Dáiró, King Sunny Adé, and Chief Commander Ebenezer Obey; *fújì* music, developed by Ààrẹ Síkírù Àyìndé Barrister and Alhaji Kollington Àyìnlá; *wákà* music, promoted by Alhaja Bàtílì Àlàkẹ́ and Sàláwà Àbẹ̀ní; and various subethnic Yorùbá musical forms, such as Èkìtì dialect music, Ìkálẹ̀ dialect music, Oǹdó dialect music, and the like. In churning out release after release, initially on LPs and later on cassettes and CDs, musicians and the various traditions they represent earn a great deal of money for themselves, and they promote and preserve various Yorùbá cultures and traditions using different formats. The concentration of people in urban centers, particularly Lagos and Ìbàdàn, and the oil boom of the 1970s provided resources that allowed for the flowering and electronic preservation of these different musical traditions.

Like the electronic preservation of music in audiocassettes and CDs, oral theatrical traditions are preserved in Nollywood films. Nollywood refers to the popular Nigerian video and film industry and its Yorùbá part, arguably one of its strongest segments, goes by the same name. It grew out of several preexisting oral Yorùbá theatre traditions and festivals, such as the traveling theater group with principal actors like Chief Hubert Ògúndé and Moses Ọláìyá (a.k.a. Bàbá

Sàlá), television series, early writings such as the works of D. O. Fágúnwà, and later celluloid films. Over the years, Nollywood has preserved various Yorùbá oral traditions and made them available in electronic formats, including video compact disc and video home system (VHS) forms. In these newer formats, we see not only oral literary activities like chants, tales, and dramatic presentations but also virtually all aspects of traditions like religion, marriage, monarchy, agriculture, clothing, market, industry, the Diaspora, and globalization represented.

Like Nollywood, the Internet is a contemporary electronic preservation avenue for oral traditions. The use of the Internet for electronically preserving oral traditions takes various forms, including storage of musical and dramatic performances online, especially on YouTube. A cursory search of Yorùbá traditions on YouTube reveals various music, video, oratory, and other traditions. They are also preserved on social media platforms, such as Facebook, especially representations of various traditions, such as the *oríkì* or panegyric form, in which people describe themselves and their cultures. There are also various social media groups dealing with religion and other sociocultural activities and societies. In addition, there is an increase in the use of Yorùbá for written communication in social media and for text messages to communicate ideas and words that have no direct translation in English.

Finally, telephone technology, particularly the GSM revolution of the past decade, has been very instrumental in preserving Yorùbá oral traditions. Before this revolution, only the elite had access to telephones, but with GSM, almost everyone has one form of mobile telephone with audio- and video-recording capability. It is very common for people to use their cell phones, tablets, iPads, and other mobile devices to record Yorùbá traditions at various ceremonies, including festivals, parties, and meetings. In this way, traditions are spread and preserved beyond what was previously limited by oral dissemination.

In addition, the GSM technology allows people to leave voice mail for others in Yorùbá, and these recorded messages can be in the form of chants, songs, and prayers that they were not able to preserve or retransmit. An equally important dimension to this phenomenon is the welcoming song, chant, *oríkì* (praise poetry), prayer, or music that welcomes a caller when making a phone call. All these traditions that were only available orally before are being preserved electronically by the GSM format. They can be listened to over and over again and spread among the population.

See also **Fágúnwà, D. O.; Language: Standardization and Literacy; Media: Radio and Television; Nollywood Films and Cinema; Music: Islamic; Music: Modern Composers; Music: Popular; Ògúndé, Hubert Adédèjì; Oral Tradition**

REFERENCE

Barber, Karin. *The Anthropology of Texts, Persons and Publics: Oral and Written Culture in Africa and Beyond.* Cambridge: Cambridge University Press, 2007.

Adétáyò Àlàbí

ELITE

Elite structure is an integral part of the Yorùbá unwritten constitution for effective and efficient governance. The political culture of the people includes an unwritten constitutional monarchy, hierarchy, age deference (indeed, elders require that children be seen and not heard), and a seeming male chauvinism; it is complex and deceptive. To a stranger, the system is autocratic and elitist. But in practice, it is democratic and more plebiscite, classless, and republican than aristocratic.

The king is, and operates solely as, the king-in-council of chiefs and elders. Democratic institutions for the rule of law are built in to check any abuse of power and to reward compliance to norms and mores. No member of the household, village, or town leadership has absolute power, even to veto, without regard to precedent and the will of the people. Although the Ifá oracle may choose a slave to become king, the political system also allows the kingmakers to dethrone the king. The king, too, has the power to sanction

the chiefs. No citizen is above the law or untouchable within the constitutional authorities of any Yorùbá community.

Bearing in mind the intricacies of the political system, it becomes easier to understand the status, role, and limitations of the elite within the Yorùbá nation-state. Every group in society has its elite, and there are names for different categories of the elite, such as *gbajúmò* (a prominent person), *sànmòrí* (the famous), *omo àgbà* (the one who has learned from the wisdoms of the elders or the humble and wise child of the elders), *ọlọgbón* or *olóye* (the wise), *akin* (the courageous), *olówó* or *ọlọ́rọ̀* (the rich or wealthy), *olójú àánú* (the kind and generous), *elẹ́rú* or *oníwòfà* (the slaves' or pawns' owner), and *ọmọlúwàbí* (the one of worthy character).

There are perhaps two very significant features of elitism among the people. First, becoming elite is a choice of priority: *ohun t'ó wuni níí pọ̀ lọ́rọ̀ ẹni, ológún ẹrú kú, aṣọ rè jẹ́ òkan*—it's what we cherish that we choose to acquire; thus, the owner of an army of twenty slaves died and had a legacy of only one garment! In other words, an individual's elite status lies in the number of slaves acquired, not in the possession of garments.

Second, becoming elite is more of an earned and achieved status rather than an ascribed or inherited one based on heritage, position, or status. One works not only to become elite but also, more important, to sustain that status. Elite status is more accurately an honor and privilege that the society bestows on an individual, and they could withdraw the title anytime if one fails to live up to expectations of the position. The people say, *a ti rí ẹrú tó jọba; a sì ti rí ọmọ ọba tó dẹrú rí; bẹ̀ẹ ni a ti rí ìjòyè tó di ìwòfà; kò sí ohun tójú kò rí rí*, there is nothing new under the sun; we have seen a slave becoming a king; and we have seen a prince who became a slave; and we have also seen a chief who became a pawn.

The highest elite position a person could aspire to is that of *ọmọlúwàbí* (a paragon of humility and trustworthiness). Hence, Òṣun State uses the title as its slogan: *Ìpínlẹ̀ Ọmọlúwàbí* (the state of people of worthy character). It is interesting and paradoxical to note that while it might appear that there is societal endorsement for corruption in contemporary Nigeria, the Yorùbá do not really have any respect for the *newly rich* corrupt politicians and businesspeople. They tend to believe it will be a matter of time before they lose it and are ridiculed. The people say, *a kò lè fi owó ẹkún ra ẹrín; bí irọ́ lọ lógún ọdún, ọjọ́ kan ni òtítọ́* [or *òdodo*] *yóò bá a:* you cannot use fraudulence or blood money to buy joy or happiness; and if falsehood is on the run for twenty years, one day, the truth will catch up with it.

See also **Education: Traditional; Ethics; Ọmọlúwàbí; Political System**

REFERENCE

Fádípẹ̀, N. A. *The Sociology of the Yorùbás.* Ìbàdàn (Nigeria): University Press, 1970.

Bọ́lá Dáúdà

ETHICS

Ìwà as ethics is the unwritten constitution for the everyday running of both the public and private affairs of the Yorùbá society. At home and in the workplace, and in any relationship, there are codes of behavior for everyone (children, youths, and adults). *Ọmọ tí ó bá mọ ọwọ́ wẹ̀, á bá àgbà jẹun*—only the child who knows how to keep his or her hands clean is allowed to eat with the elders. *Ẹnì kan kì í kí ọba ní ìbẹ̀rẹ̀, a kì í kí ọba ní ìnàró, ìdọ̀bálẹ̀ ni à ń kí ọba*—no one bows or stands to greet the king; we prostrate to greet the king. *Ẹni tó sọ òyìnbó nílé àna, ni yó túmọ̀ rẹ̀*—a groom who is rude enough to speak English at his illiterate in-laws' house would have to do the translating himself.

Consequently, to reinforce compliance, Yorùbá have names that describe all ethical behaviors: *olódòótọ́*, the truthful; *olódodo*, the upright or one with integrity; *onírẹ̀lẹ̀*, the humble or modest; *ọmọ ọkọ*, the legitimate son; *ọlọgbọ́n*, the wise one; *olófintótó*, the one who follows the rules to the letter; *eni tí ó mọ àá-tií-gbọ́*, the one who would not do anything secretly that he would be ashamed if disclosed in public; and *ọmọlúwàbí*, the one of high integrity and probity or the paragon of all ethical behavior. There are also names for all unethical behaviors: *oníró*, or *opùró*, the liar; *jàǹdùkú* or *ipáǹle*, the hooligan or hoodlum; *olè*, thief or rogue; *aláìnítìjú* or *kò mọ àá-tií-gbọ́*, the one who knows no shame; and *ọmọ àlè*, the bastard. Because ethical behaviors create harmony and peace, the people say, *ilé tí ó tòrò, a jẹ́ pé ọmọ àlè ibẹ̀ ni kò tíì dàgbà*—when there is peace in a home, it means the bastard child in the family is still young!

Yorùbá have a treasury of taboos, fairy tales, and legends either to create fear of repercussions for any violation of the ethics or to promise rewards for total compliance with them. For example, because a chili pepper could easily enter the trachea while eating, children are warned that it is forbidden to talk while eating. Because sitting in the doorway could create an obstruction, children are often warned that they will never feel satiated if they sit at the door while eating. Because it is unhygienic to use one's bare hand to clean up after using the restroom, people are admonished that they will have shaky hands if they use their bare hands to clean up.

Perhaps the most powerful ethics enforcement practice in the society is *ìbúra*, taking an oath. Hardly would anyone take an oath invoking his or her *orí*, life or honor, unless he or she is absolutely truthful and honest. When a Yorùbá invokes his or her life, the life of his or her children, or the spirits of his or her ancestors or the gods—especially the god of iron (Ògún), the god of thunder and fire (Ṣàngó), or the god of smallpox (Ṣànpọ̀nná)—one can be certain he or she is innocent or speaking the truth and nothing but the truth.

However, in the culture, *ìwà* is more than ethics, moral principles, or codes of conduct. *Ìwà l'ẹ̀sìn*—it is *the* religion. *Ìwà l'ẹwà*—it is *the* yardstick to measure the beauty or fine character of a person. *Ìwà niyì ọmọ ènìyàn*—it portrays *the* probity and dignity of a person. *Ìwà l'ọba àwúre*—it is *the* greatest secret of generating wealth or making a fortune. *Èéfín ni ìwà*—in life, it is as a smoke that goes along with the smoker. *Ìwà níí bání dé sàréè*—in death it follows us into grave and lives after us.

See also **Education: Traditional; Ọmọlúwàbí; Taboo**

REFERENCE

Fádípè, N. A. *The Sociology of the Yorùbá*. Ìbàdàn (Nigeria): University Press, 1970.

Bólá Dáúdà

ETHNICITY

As a social group of people with common cultural traditions, ethnicity among the Yorùbá has gone through five historical phases. First, all the primordial Yorùbá settlements have ancestral claims to Odùduwà and his children: Olówu, Alákétu, Ọmọ N'ọba, Ọ̀ràngún, Onísábẹ, Olúpópó, and Aláàfin. Thus, the precolonial civil unrest in Yorùbá kingdoms was presented as royal sibling rivalries and animosities that deteriorated into civil wars.

Second, at the turn of the twentieth century, the secretary of state for the colonies, Joseph Chamberlain, literally and metaphorically imported British ethnicity into Nigeria through his appointment of English army officer Sir Fredrick Lugard as head of the protectorate of Northern Nigeria. Much of the area was already under a form of military conquest and under formal rule of the emirates. A Scottish medical doctor, Sir William MacGregor, and an Irish police officer, Sir Ralph Moor, were the administrators of the predominantly Yorùbá and "unhealthy" Lagos and the "unruly" Southern Protectorate, respectively. The divide-and-rule policy constituted the covert, imperial policy; the posting of these men was not coincidental and reflected the uneasy political relationship among the British polities of Ireland, Scotland, and England. The differences in these officers' personalities, attitudes, and interpretations of colonialism have had and continue to have far-reaching effects on the Nigerian religious and ethnic geopolitics. Their rule over Nigeria certainly not only reinforced the tense ethnic politics in Nigeria but also reflected the contentious nature of British politics.

Third, at the end of World War II, there was a wide gap in the socioeconomic, educational, and political development of the three regions in Nigeria. In 1920, Sir Hugh Clifford, who succeeded Sir Lugard, lamented, "After two decades of British occupation, the northern provinces have not produced a single Native of these provinces who is sufficiently educated to enable him to fill the most minor clerical post in the office of any government department." This assessment was patently untrue. Herbert Macaulay, for example, founded the Nigerian National Democratic Party (NNDP) as a platform for elective representative government in the Legislative Council for the colony of Lagos in 1922. The political culture of direct rule in the Yorùbá Western Region not only put in place the political institutions but also prepared the political elite, under the leadership of Ọbáfẹ́mi Awólọ́wọ̀, for self-government. The Yorùbá never missed any opportunity to participate in the politics of ethnicity between themselves and with other Nigerian ethnicities. For example, in the 1951 Legislative Council election for the colony of Lagos, the Yorùbá used their ethnic electoral majority to edge out Dr. Nnamdi Azikiwe. Yorùbá Western Nigeria was granted self-rule in 1954.

Fourth, at the time of independence in October 1960, the public service of the Western Region, including the colony of Lagos, was fully dominated by Nigerians. In addition, just as the north was not self-governed until 1959, the attempt to dominate the public services came two years after independence. The fact that the north held 54 percent of the Nigerian population but only 1 percent of the federal civil service positions at the time of independence continues to fuel the nation's ethnic politics.

Finally, rather than bridging the educational gap between the north and south, which would have helped address the issue of imbalance of ethnic representation in the public sector, the 1979 Constitution of the Federal Republic of Nigeria introduced a quota system (diplomatically coded as "federal character") for the three tiers (local, state, and federal) of government. It also established the Federal Character Commission. Ironically, the adoption of the quota system for admission into university is not consistent with merit system, but merit favors the educationally advanced Yorùbá.

Consequently, there is no other issue that threatens Nigerian nationhood more than the geopolitics of ethnicity and religion. Ethnicity, euphemistically referred to as political zoning or federal character, and the issue of imbalance of representation in the public service positions are akin to the policy of derivatives (compensation for the producing source) in the sharing of the revenues from natural resources. In the 1950s, with regions operating more like a confederation than a federation, the Yorùbá benefited from the revenues from cocoa production in the same way the contemporary oil-producing states now benefit from oil revenues. Since politics is all about who gets what, when, and how, ethnicity among the Yorùbá, as with the rest of Nigerian politics, is no more than a shared value or common interest. This is reflected especially in the Yorùbá's agitation for the creation of states and protest for the readjustment of revenue-sharing ratios among the federal, state, and local governments. Ethnicity is a weapon for mobilization to get a fair share of the national cake of revenue, power, and positions.

See also **Colonial Policies and Practices; Politics and Political Parties since 1945; Subgroups**

REFERENCES

Nicolson, I. "The Machinery of the Federal and Regional Governments." In *Nigerian Government and Politics*, ed. Johns P. Mackintosh, 138–52. London: George Allen and Unwin, 1966.

Dáúdà, Bọ́lá, "Fallacies and Dilemmas: The Theory of Representative Bureaucracy with Particular Reference to the Nigerian Public Service, 1950–86." *International Review of Administrative Sciences* 56.3 (1990): 467–95.

Bọ́lá Dáúdà

ETHNOMUSICOLOGY

Musical concepts and practices among the Yorùbá are based in ethnicity and, as a result, heterogeneous. Categories of Yorùbá music include traditional classical (found in kings' palaces), traditional folk (used in day-to-day activities), traditional sacred (music of the gods), neo-traditional (traditional music recontextualized in a modern context), popular music (hybrid Western and African musical elements), pop music (Yorùbá version of Western pop), art music (contemplative music), and contemporary religious music (various Christian and Islamic forms). Musical sound is organized along vocal, instrumental, or both; the vocal, however, predominates. Vocal music includes a variety of song forms and chants, both of which may be arranged in solo, chorus, or call-and-response forms. Audience participation and improvisation are chief characteristic features of vocal music.

Musical Forms

Song forms are named after their functions, such as *orin ogun*, *orin eré ìbílẹ̀*, *orin eré ọ̀ṣùpá*, and the like. Chants can be divided into two broad categories. First are the universal ones: *ìyẹ̀rẹ̀ Ifá*, *iwì* or *ẹsà*, *ìjálá*, and *òrìṣà pípè*. The second category consists of localized forms because of the variation in ethnic and linguistic characteristics, geographical surrounding, and social conventions of traditions. In the coastal and southern part of Yorùbáland, the *igbe*, *ike*, and *igbe-olorì* predominate, and the *ègè*, *ìgbálá*, *agbè*, and *ike* are the predominant forms in the western part of Yorùbáland. In the central and northern Yorùbá, *rárà*, *ẹkún ìyàwó*, *àjàgbó*, *orò*, and *ẹ̀kà* are prominent, while *àdan*, *àsíkò*, *ògbérè*, *alámọ̀*, *ayúù ọ̀ṣírìgí*, *olele*, *ọ̀sàré*, and *rẹ́sọ̀* are prominent in the eastern Yorùbá area. Some of these forms are accompanied by musical instruments while others are performed a cappella.

Instruments and Instrumental Music

Instrumental music, in practice, is controlled by the text and also accompanied with the voice. A good example is *dùndún-ṣẹ̀kẹ̀rẹ̀* music. Membranophones or musical instruments that feature any kind of stretched skin over a resonating body, of different types dominate the musical instrument typology. Idiophones or musical instruments that create sound primarily by vibrating the whole instrument rather than using strings or membranes, are also used. Popular instrumental ensembles include *àgèrè*, used for the worship of Ògún; *ìgbìn*, for the worship of Ọbàtálá; *ìpèsè* or *àràn*, for the worship of Ọ̀rúnmìlà; and *bàtá*, for the worship of Ṣàngó. The *agogo* ensemble is also used for the worship of Ọ̀rúnmìlà, while *dùndún* is meant for sociopolitical functions. *Bẹ̀ǹbẹ́* drums are used in *ìgunnukó* festival.

Roles

Music in Yorùbáland is essentially functional, as it permeates the entire life circle of an individual from birth to childhood, adolescence, adulthood, marriage, and death. All initiation rites and rites of passage from one stage to the other are carried out with music. In addition, music plays prominent roles in traditional festivals, such as the Gẹ̀lẹ̀dẹ́ festival and the Adámú-Òrìṣà play in Lagos; Ọbàtálá, Ọ̀ràǹfẹ̀, and Ọlójọ́ festivals in Ilé-Ifẹ̀; the Egúngún festival celebrated throughout Yorùbáland; and the Ọbalógun festival at Ìlokò. In these and similar festivals, music plays various roles, including the symbolic; communicative, as signal and announcement; accompaniment, as in the processions and outings; evocative and invocative; panegyric; historical; satirical; entertainment; and dramatic.

See also **Ceremonial Songs; Music: Christian; Music: Contemporary; Music: Islamic; Musical Instruments; Music: Popular; Music: Traditional**

REFERENCE

Adédèjì, Fẹ́mi, ed. *Essays on Yorùbá Musicology*. Ilé-Ifẹ̀ (Nigeria): IMEF Music Publishers, 2012.

Fẹ́mi Adédèjì

F

FÁDÍPẸ̀, NATHANIEL AKÍNRẸ̀MÍ (1893–1944)

Nathaniel Akínrẹ̀mí Fádípẹ̀, the oldest son of Reverend L. O. Fádípẹ̀ of the Baptist Mission Òkè-Sàjẹ́ near Abẹ́òkúta, produced the monumental 1,012-page PhD dissertation "The Sociology of the Yorùbá" in 1944, which was later published in 1970. Fádípẹ̀ experienced many firsts. He was the first Yorùbá scholar to combine the systematic, macroanalytical data-gathering method with the comparative and holistic ethnographic anthropological method of participant observation. He was the first to recognize the limitations of the "Cartesian methodic doubt" *cogito ergo sum*, "I think, therefore I am," which forms the foundation of Western ethnocentric, radical individualism. He learned in Europe that Cartesian distinctions between the past and the present, the sacred and the profane, and the living and the dead are inadequate analytical tools for deciphering the complex and relational symbolisms of the Yorùbá. The Yorùbá do not submit to such neatly bipolar, exclusive terms. For example, items that may be considered profane in quotidian activities may assume sacred dimensions on specific occasions.

In his thesis, Fádípẹ̀ criticized scholars and existing scholarly works on the Yorùbá. Fádípẹ̀'s analysis of Yorùbá political institutions identified four monarchical types: (1) the Ọ̀yọ́ model, deriving from Old Ọ̀yọ́; (2) the Ifẹ̀, Ìjẹ̀sà, Èkìtì, and Oǹdó model, deriving from Ilé-Ifẹ̀; (3) the Ìjẹ̀bú-Òde model; and (4) the Ẹ̀gbáland model. More important, through combining quanti-

tative and qualitative methodologies, he was able to use the knowledge gained from one model to solve the problem of the other. As a case in point, he saw monarchy as constantly changing to respond to the chaotic circumstance in which it was implicated. The first example of this was the revelation that the trauma of the Old Ọ̀yọ́ Empire arose out of institutional arrangements that had become outdated. The conflict between the military chiefs and the king grew from the military chiefs' lack of constitutional rights and inability to participate in state councils even though they were often the first to die for the state. This accounted for the intergenerational hostility between the Ààrẹ-Ọ̀nà-Kakàǹfò, or field marshals, and the Ọ̀yọ́ king (*aláàfin*). Upon succession to the throne, the new *aláàfin* inaugurated some reforms that reflected the rights of the individual. A more pragmatic change with repercussions for the field marshals and the *aláàfin* was the decision to do away with the practice that allowed the *aláàfin* to lead the army in fighting in the battlefront. This occurred because an *aláàfin* was killed in the battlefront. Fádípẹ̀ has, through his sacrifice, become the reference point in Yorùbá studies.

See also **Prominent Scholars**

REFERENCE

Fádípẹ̀, N. A. *The Sociology of the Yorùbá*. Ìbàdàn (Nigeria): University Press, 1970.

Emmanuel Gbádébọ̀ Babátúndé

FÁGÚNWÀ, DANIEL OLÓRUNFÉMI (1903–1963)

The realm of African indigenous writers undoubtedly has evolved because of the unprecedented roles of some notable writers, who, despite the harshness of their times, were able to tell the world the story of their people using the people's language instead of European languages like English and French that were being promoted by the colonialists. One such indigenous writer was Daniel Olórunfémi Fágúnwà. Fágúnwà was a folklorist, educator, and animal rights advocate. Fágúnwà was born in 1903 (the precise date of his birth is not known) to Joshua Akíntúndé and Rachael Òsúnyomí Fágúnwà in the town of Òkè-Igbo, in present-day Oǹdó State, Western Nigeria. He completed his early education at St. Luke's Primary School, Òkè-Igbó, in 1924. He started his teaching career as a pupil teacher because of his academic prowess. Fágúnwà went to St. Andrew's Teacher's College, Òyó in the late 1920s. He left for St. Andrew's Demonstration College, becoming the head of the Department of the Primary Section.

In the 1930s, he began to write short poems and plays, such as Òjó Asòtàn, Ìwé Kínní, in the Yorùbá language for schoolchildren at Òyó. In 1936, a writing competition organized by the Ministry of Education of colonial Nigeria brought the first novel of D. O. Fágúnwà to the public eye. The submitted manuscript of his first novel, titled Ògbójú Odę Nínú Igbó Irúnmalè, was bought and published by the Church Missionary Society Press in 1938. It was an immediate success. He also wrote a travel memoir, which was very successful. He received public acclaim for his narrative style in the later works Ìrìnàjò, Apá Kínní (1949) and Ìrìnàjò, Apá Kejì (1951).

In the late 1950s, he worked as an administrator and educator with the publishing arm of the Ministry of Education in Western Nigeria. In 1959, he was honored as a Member of the Order of the British Empire (MBE) in recognition for his work as chief official translator for Oba Adésojí Adérèmí (the Òòni of Ifè) and the queen of England. He was also the Bógunbólú of Òkè-Igbó.

Fágúnwà's fiction written in the Yorùbá language aimed to reveal the historical and cultural complexities and beauty of black Africa. Some of his other prominent works are Igbó Olódùmarè (1949), Ìrèké Oníbùdó (1949), Ìrìnkèrindò Nínú Igbó Elégbèje (1954), and Àdììtú Olódùmarè (1961). He also wrote collections of short stories, including Àsànyàn Ìtàn, and he coauthored, with L. J. Lewis, Táíwò àti Kéhìndé, a pioneer text for the teaching of the Yorùbá language in primary schools. Fágúnwà's fictional stories are adventure stories in which a hero or group of heroes sets out on a mission against many obstacles. His writings earned him the Margaret Wrong Prize in 1955.

His works have gone through numerous editions and translations in English and French. His uniqueness as a writer lies in his dexterity with the Yorùbá language, in which he particularly reveals the beauty of the language. Fágúnwà has had a great influence on most Yorùbá authors who writes in Yorùbá or English, including Amos Tutùolá, Wolé Sóyínká, Olá Rótìmí, and others. He is the Nigerian equivalent of such indigenous writers as Gao Xingjian of China and Wisława Szymborska of Poland. Fágúnwà died in an accident on December 7, 1963, when he fell in the Niger River after the bank gave way under his feet.

See also **Folklore; Narration Techniques; Prominent Scholars; Sóyínká, Wolé; Stories, Storytelling, and Storytellers; Translation; Tutùolá, Amos; Writers**

REFERENCE

Bámgbósé, Ayò. *The Novels of D. O. Fágúnwà*. Benin City (Nigeria): Ethiope Publishing Corporation, 1974.

Tèmítópé C. Fágúnwà

FAITH

Faith is a word with several interrelated meanings, and a word that is used in a number of ways. Faith is usually associated with religious beliefs (ìgbàgbó), belief in the Supreme Being or in the doctrines or teachings of a religion based on spiritual trust rather than proof or evidence. The typical Yorùbá person, like the adherents of Islam and Christianity, believes in the existence of a self-existent being called Olódùmarè (the Almighty) who is responsible for creation and maintenance of heaven and earth, men and women, and all animate and inanimate objects. Olódùmarè also created the deities and spirits, who serve as his functionaries in the theocratic world and as intermediaries with humankind. These deities are referred to as òrìṣà. Whoever wishes to reach Olódùmarè must have faith in these deities and rely on them for beneficial assistance of all kinds. The use of intermediaries to access Olódùmarè stems from the belief that Olódùmarè is too great to deal with directly, and he has delegated the care of man to the deities.

One of these deities is Ọbàtálá, the great goddess who shapes the human body in the womb. Ọbàtálá worshippers believe she has power to prosper them by making them increase and multiply through material blessings. Ọrúnmìlà, also called *agbáyé-gbọ́run* (one who lives both on earth and in heaven) and *ẹlẹrìí ìpín* (one who bears witness to fate), is believed to be in the best position to plead with Olódùmarè on behalf of human beings. His status derives from the belief that he was present when humans were created, and his fate is bound up with humans. One seeks his intercession to avert or rectify unpleasant circumstances. Other deities include Èṣù, the trickster god or divine enforcer; Ṣànpọ̀nná, the god of smallpox; and Ògún, the god of war and iron. Like Ọbàtálá, Ògún is believed to be capable of providing prosperity for his devotees: *onílé owó, ọlọ́nà ọlà, onílé kángunkàngun òde ọrun* (the owner of the house of money, the owner of the house of riches, the owner of the innumerable houses of heaven), and the like.

See also **Deities: *Òrìṣà*; Divinatory Systems; Divination: Ifá; Religion and Communication; Religion and Ritual**

REFERENCE

Awólàlú, Ọmọ́sadé F. *Yorùbá Beliefs and Sacrificial Rites.* London: Longman Group, 1981.

Kazeem A. Ọmọ́fóyèwá

FÁLỌLÁ, ỌLỌ́RUNTÓYÌN ỌMỌ́YẸNI (1953–)

Fálọlá Ọlọ́runtóyìn (Tóyìn) Ọmọ́yẹni is a distinguished university professor and holder of the Jacob and Frances Sanger Mossiker Chair in the Humanities at the University of Texas at Austin. His outstanding career as a scholar of African history spans more than three decades, and he has generated an incredible output of scholarly works, including more than a hundred books. He is a leading contemporary historian of Africa and one of the most prominent since the academic study of African history began in the post–World War II period.

Tóyìn Fálọlá was born on January 1, 1953, in the historic city of Ìbàdàn, then the capital city of the defunct Western Region (now Ọ̀yọ́ State) of Nigeria. He completed elementary school at the age of thirteen and proceeded to attend high school, first at Òkèbàdàn High School in his hometown, Ìbàdàn, and subsequently at the famous Molúsì College in Ìjẹbú-Igbó, in the present-day Ògùn State of Nigeria.

Fálọlá's insatiable desire for learning ensured that he would pursue higher education. In 1973, at the age of twenty, he matriculated at the University of Ifè (renamed Ọbáfẹ́mi Awólọ́wọ̀ University in 1987), a world-class institution located in the ancient city of Ilé-Ifè to pursue a bachelor of arts degree in history, graduating in 1976 with honors. After a one-year stint as a high school teacher at the Government College, Makurdi, in fulfillment of the National Youth Service Corps (NYSC), a program mandatory for new college graduates, he returned to his alma mater in September 1977, to commence graduate studies in history.

For his doctorate, Fálọlá studied Nigerian history with specific focus on precolonial Yorùbáland. In 1981 he completed his dissertation, "The Political Economy of Ìbàdàn, c. 1830–1900." The first extensive study of the history of Ìbàdàn from the political economy perspective, this groundbreaking work examines the rise of the city-state as a military power, the British imperial interventions, and its eventual subjugation by and incorporation into the British Empire. The dissertation soon appeared as *The Political Economy of a Pre-Colonial*

African State: Ìbàdàn, 1830–1900, published by the University of Ifẹ̀ Press in 1984.

With his doctorate in hand, Fálọlá transitioned from a graduate assistant to full-time permanent faculty at Ifẹ̀'s history department, thus beginning a remarkable career in academia. By 1985 he had attained the rank of senior lecturer (associate professor), before assuming a full professorship position in the department of history at York University, in Toronto, in 1989. A new chapter in his academic career began in 1991 when he joined the Department of History at the University of Texas at Austin as professor of African history.

A versatile scholar, teacher, and researcher, Fálọlá's most noted contribution to the development of academic history is his unparalleled scholarly output covering virtually all areas of historical enquiry relating to the history of Africa and the black Diaspora. Through books, book chapters, journal articles, reviews, conference presentations, and public lectures, he has greatly affected African historiography. His widely acclaimed works are many, including his award-winning first memoir, *A Mouth Sweeter Than Salt*, and a second memoir, *Counting the Tiger's Teeth: An African Teenager's Story*.

Through wide-ranging public service, Fálọlá has also significantly contributed to the expansion and visibility of African studies. He has served on the boards of numerous national and international academic and civic bodies: president of the Nigerian Studies Association, general secretary of the Historical Society of Nigeria, president of the African Studies Association, vice president of the UNESCO Slave Route Project, and member of the Scholars Council of the US Library of Congress. He has also served as editor of many academic journals and scholarly book series, including Greenwood's Culture and Customs of Africa, University of Rochester's Rochester Studies in African History and the Diaspora, Carolina Academic Press's Africa and the Black World, Palgrave's series African Histories and Modernities; and Cambria's series Africa: Nations, Nationalities and Development.

Fálọlá is a recipient of more than twenty awards, including five honorary doctorates. In recognition of his distinguished service to African history, several festschriften have been published, including Adébáyọ̀ Oyèbádé (ed.), *The Foundations of Nigeria: Essays in Honor of Tóyìn Fálọlá* (2003); Adébáyọ̀ Oyèbádé (ed.), *The Transformation of Nigeria: Essays in Honor of Tóyìn Fálọlá* (2002); Akínwùmí Ògúndìran (ed.), *Precolonial Nigeria: Essays in Honor of Tóyìn Fálọlá* (2005); Níyì Afọlábí (ed.), *Toyin Falola: The Man, the Mask, and the Muse* (2010), and Nana Akua Amponsah (ed.), *Beyond the Boundaries: Tóyìn Fálọlá and the Art of Genre Bending* (2014). Also, an international annual conference, the Tóyìn Fálọlá Annual International Conference on Africa and the African Diaspora (TOFAC), is named after him. In April 2014, Fálọlá was honored in his hometown with a chieftaincy title—Bọ́bapìtàn of Ìbàdànland—conferred by the city's traditional ruler, Ọba Samuel Odùlànà, the Olúbàdàn.

See also **Prominent Scholars**

REFERENCES

Níyì Afọlábí, ed., *Tóyìn Fálọlá: The Man, the Mask, the Muse*. Durham, NC: Carolina Academic Press, 2010.

Abdul Karim Bangura, *Tóyìn Fálọlá and African Epistemologies*. New York: Palgrave Macmillan, 2015.

Adébáyọ̀ Oyèbádé

FESTIVALS AND CARNIVALS

The indigenous Yorùbá universe is holistic and has been—and largely is still—determined and defined by the gods, goddesses, and deities. This rather inclusive worldview comprises both tangible and intangible "worlds" that are distinct yet interrelated. These worlds coexist together: the world of the living, the ancestral world (including gods and goddesses, the deities, and deified heroes and heroines), and the world of the unborn. The worlds depend, in degree, on one another. Therefore, the tangible world of the living is obligated to always ensure maintenance of spiritual equilibrium. The world of the living tries to achieve this by reaching out through prescribed sacrifices to the ancestors, gods, goddesses, and deities. Therefore, the world of the living offers regular or periodic appeasements, the scope and quality of which determine the approval (or, in their absence, disapproval) of the intangible world.

Indigenous festivals constitute a major effort on the part of the world of the living to ensure continuity between the worlds, to elicit blessings and fruitfulness, to banish sicknesses and calamities, and to promote peace, development, and social cohesion. Festivals are periodic communal rituals or observances—some festivals are secular. The two categories of indigenous festivals are hegemonic and nonhegemonic. Hegemonic festivals acknowledge the sovereignty of the monarchs and their unquestioned authority over the lives of their subjects. All the "crown towns" founded by the seven children of Ọ̀kànbí and their descendants celebrate hegemonic festivals. The monarchs are the central figures of the festival; the purpose of the ritualized festivals is to elevate the monarch to the status of deity. In some cases, by the virtue of their sacred office, the monarchs are required to play the role of the deified founding fathers of their domains. Hegemonic festivals are intended to promote societal cohesion and peace, township development, peer progress, and cooperation. They are usually conducted in a convivial, celebrative, and carnival-like atmosphere. Examples are Udi'Rókò in Adó-Èkìtì, Ọlọ́jọ́ in Ilé-Ifẹ̀, Igógo in Ọ̀wọ̀, Ojúde-Ọba in Ìjẹ̀bú-Òde, and Ọ̀rànyàn in Ọ̀yọ́ town.

Nonhegemonic festivals are religious in nature and form. Èyọ̀, or Adámú or Adímú Òrìṣà, in Lagos is primarily a funerary festival. Its purpose is communal cleansing and purification, and shown by the symbolic sweeping of the land to usher in a clean and fruitful new year or the installation of a new king. Ìwẹmọ in Adó-Èkìtì, ushers in the "new yam"; the monarch must taste the yam before any of his subjects in the kingdom can begin to eat the new yam. Edì in Ilé-Ifẹ̀ is an annual purification ritual meant to cleanse society of all iniquities accumulated over the previous year. The scapegoat motif foregrounds the ritual. For example, a complete stranger is required to be the sacrificial scapegoat and convey the sacrifice across the Esimirin River. Similarly, Òkè'Bàdàn in Ìbàdàn is a communal purification ritual; it is also meant to usher in a brighter and fruitful new year.

Both the Edì and Òkè'Bàdàn festivals are characterized by orchestrated merriment and wild dancing. They include daring performances by young men and women that border on obscenity, as well as a secret list of nobles who are guilty of misbehavior, based on their conduct over the previous year. On the day of the festival, celebrants publicly highlight their "crimes" through satirical songs. The humiliated nobles might choose to go into self-exile if they find the public shame unbearable—this is a mechanism that the indigenous Yorùbá societies put in place to check the excesses of morally reckless nobles in the society.

Ùjòyè-Juṣu in Òde-Ìrèlè is a fertility rite similar to that of Luperca in ancient Rome. The nobles identify with the poor, fools, and clowns by deliberately becoming laughing stocks and the butts of satire and jokes. They put on rags and outrageous costumes made of everyday materials. People laugh and boo at them. They are ridiculed as a necessary sacrifice to redeem and cleanse society of all impurities. At the same time, they usher in the new year.

Other festivals in the nonhegemonic category include those dedicated to ancestral cults: Ògún, Ṣàngó, Ọya, and Ọ̀sun, among others, who were human beings before they became deities. They were progenitors and founders of towns and war heroes and heroines. In the case of Ọdún Ọbalógun in Ilésà, the members of the towns the deities helped found or helped the towns overcome challenges celebrate the respective deities. The Ọbalógun and Agẹmọ festivals in Ìjẹbú-Òde share similar traits and concepts. Both parade powerful and fearful masquerades during the festive gathering and are characterized with a public demonstration of charms and magic to affirm the potency of their progenitors. Ògún in Oǹdó and Ilẹ̀-Olújì, Ọ̀sun in Ọṣogbo, Ọlọ́sunta in Ìkéré-Èkìtì, Ọlọ́fin in Ìlawẹ̀-Èkìtì, Olúa in Òsì-Èkìtì, Òkóróbò in Ìfàkì-Èkìtì, and Semúregede in Òde-Èkìtì are ancestors whose towns celebrate festivals to periodically appease the deities. The Ògún festival in Oǹdó and Ilẹ̀-Olújì, the Èyọ̀, or Adámú or Adímú Òrìṣà festival in Lagos, Ùjòyè-Juṣu in Òde-Ìrèlè, and Ọlọ́fin in Ìlawẹ̀, among others, take the form of carnivals as people of different professions and occupations parade and dance in their professional clothing and uniforms.

See also **Ceremonial Songs; Deities: The** *Òrìṣà*

REFERENCE

Ọlátúnjí, O. Ọlátúndé. *Features of Yorùbá Oral Poetry.* Ìbàdàn (Nigeria): University Press, 1984.

Adémọ́lá Dasylva

FOOD: CUISINE AND PREPARATION

The Yorùbá are an agrarian people. Their worldview acknowledges that food is essential to life. In their estimation, if a person has food, she or he is not totally impoverished. The types of crops that thrive in the geographical (tropical) location of the Yorùbá determine the local cuisine. Since most people still use crude implements like cutlasses and hoes for farming and nonmechanized tools for household chores, they need to eat energy-rich meals filled with carbohydrates and fiber. These energy-rich foods are eaten with soups and stews that are rich in protein, vitamins, fats, and oils.

With the exception of fruits, the Yorùbá rarely eat their meals raw. Food items are either boiled, fried, steamed, dried, or roasted for consumption or preservation. *Iṣu*, or yam (dioscorea), is the most common source of carbohydrates. *Iyán*, or pounded yam, is popular among all the Yorùbá subgroups. Indeed, a popular aphorism goes

> *Iyán loúnjẹ,*
> *Ọkà loògùn;*
> *Àìrí rárá làá jẹkọ.*
> *Kẹ́nu ó má dìlẹ̀ ni ti gúgúrú.*

> Pounded yam is the real food,
> Yam flour meal is just like medication;
> Cornmeal is only eaten if there is no alternative.
> Popcorn is nothing but a snack.

Àmàlà, also called *ọkà*, is another popular meal made from *èlùbọ* (yam flour). Other popular meals are *àsáró*

or *ẹbẹ*, which is made of mashed yam mixed with peppers, tomatoes, and onions; *iṣu sísè*, or boiled yam; *dùńdú*, or yam fried in oil; *iṣu-sísun*, or roasted yam; and *ẹpípá*, or yam that is diced, dried in the sun, and boiled like rice).

Ìkọ́kọrẹ́ is another meal made from *ewùrà* (water yam). It is made by grating raw *ewùrà* into small pieces and cooking it in boiling soup prepared with peppers, *ògìrì* (fermented melon), and lots of fish and meat. *Ìkọ́kọrẹ́* is a very special dish among the Ìjẹbú and Rémọ Yorùbá subgroups, but it is also eaten by other subgroups, especially during festivals and special occasions. *Èbìrìpò*, a meal common among the Rémọ and Ìjẹbú-Àgọ́-Ìwòyè subgroups, is made from grated and stemmed cocoyam. *Èsúrú* and *ọ̀kùnkún* or *kùnkúnndùkún* are other species of yam that are eaten boiled, fried, or roasted.

Cassava (*ẹgẹ́/gbágùúdá/pákí*) is another root vegetable the Yorùbá rely on for carbohydrates. Some species of this tuber are edible if eaten boiled or roasted, but most are poisonous if not well processed before consumption. *Gààrí*, which is grated, fermented, and dehydrated, is the most consumed cassava product. Others are *láfún* (grated, fermented, and sun dried); *púpurú* (smoked after grating, fermented, and shaped into large balls); and *fùfú*. To prepare *fùfú*, cassava is fermented, strained through a sieve, and cooked by constant stirring over fire until its consistency is solid enough to be formed into morsels that can be chewed and swallowed.

Maize (*Zea mays*) or *àgbàdo/ọkà* is also consumed in various ways. It can be eaten boiled as *lángbé* or roasted as *àgbàdo sísun*. It can also be dried, fermented, strained, and prepared with hot water as *ògì*, which can also be wrapped in leaves and left to cool as *ẹkọ tútù* (solid pap). Maize can also be fermented, dried, and milled into flour, and be made into *túwó*. Rice, another carbohydrate source, can be boiled and consumed with soup or stew. In modern times, it can be made into jollof, fried, or curried fried rice. The indigenous species of rice among the Yorùbá is a short-grain rice with a unique texture and aroma, popularly known as *ọ̀fàdà* or *ìgbèmọ*.

Beans and black-eyed peas are the primary sources of plant-based protein. The Yorùbá also rear goats, pigs, sheep, and fowl and poultry. They also hunt and trap wild game, snails, fish, and shellfish. Beans can be boiled and eaten as *ẹwa-wooro*, or they can be boiled, seasoned, mashed, and mixed with oil as *ẹwà rírò*. They can also be boiled with fresh maize and eaten as *pẹkulẹ*, or have peppers, onions, and oil added to become *àdàlú* or *ẹwà alágbàdo*. The taste of beans can be muted if soaked in water and then strained; the beans can be used to make other bean-based meals. If soaked beans are milled, that is, ground into a paste; wrapped with leaves (*ewé eéran*); and steamed, they become *èkuru* or *ofúlójú funfun*. When pepper, onions, oil, and other spices and seasonings are added to milled beans that are then boiled or steamed, it becomes *mọ́ínmọ́ín*, *ọ̀lẹ̀lẹ̀*, or *ọ̀ọ̀lẹ̀*. If one adds raw pepper pieces, especially *ata wẹẹrẹ* (small dried pepper) to milled beans, then fry the mixture in oil, it becomes *àkàrà* (bean cakes).

Carbohydrate-rich meals like *iyán*, *ẹbà*, *fùfú*, *àmàlà*, *ẹkọ tútù* (solid pap) *èbìrìpò*, *púpurú*, and *láfún* are never eaten alone but with soups (*ọbẹ̀ ata*) and stews that combine stock with vegetables, meat, and water, which is immediately consumed. These soups are eaten before the main meal or as an appetizer. *Ọbẹ̀ ata* is usually a combination of assorted ground peppers, tomatoes, onions, and other spices and seasonings; meat, such as beef, pork, fish, or snails, is added. The soup can be consumed alone or with rice, yams, or plantains. However, stews made with boiled okra (*ilá*), *ewédú*, or vegetables are served with *ọbẹ̀ ata*. Morsels of *fùfú*, *ẹbà*, *àmàlà*, and *iyán* are dipped (using the bare fingers) into the stew or soup then eaten.

Ọbẹ̀ ẹfọ́ ẹlégùúsí (stew made from vegetable, *ẹfọ́*) and *ẹgùsí* (melon seeds) is often eaten with *iyán* and *fùfú*. Raw vegetables, like *ilá, ewédú* and *ààpọn*, go well with *àmàlà, ẹkọ tútù*, and *láfún*. *Gbẹgìrì* (bean soup) is made from milled and sieved beans to which pepper meat, fish, pork, or chicken is added. It is eaten particularly with *àmàlà* but also works well with *ẹbà, fùfú*, and *iyán*.

Traditionally, Yorùbá do not eat meals in sequential courses. It is not unusual to take more than one type of food at meals. For instance, *mọ́ínmọ́ín* is taken with *ògì* and *ẹkọ tútù*. The people do eat snacks and refreshments between meals, including *ìpékeré* (fried, unripe plantain), *wàrà* (cottage cheese), *ẹpà* (groundnuts), *ọ̀jọ̀jọ̀* (grated and fried water yam or cocoyam), *gúgúrú* (popcorn), *àádùn* (maize flour mixed with pepper, palm oil, honey, and salt), *kọ́kọ́ró* (made from fried corn paste), and *róbó* (milled melon seeds that are seasoned and shaped into small balls, then fried in vegetable oil).

See also **Agriculture and Farming; Food: Supply, Distribution, and Marketing**

REFERENCE

Fádípẹ̀, N. A. *The Sociology of the Yorùbá*. Ìbàdàn (Nigeria): University Press, 1970.

Olúfadékẹ́mi Adágbádá

FOOD: SUPPLY, DISTRIBUTION, AND MARKETING

The supply, distribution, and marketing of food have been activities since centuries before the colonial era. The need to eat necessitated the commercialization of food distribution and a robust trade network of food business became associated with the trans-Sahara and transatlantic slave trade. Supply and distribution of food commodities were determined by the forces of demand and supply among different towns and villages. Both imported and locally produced food commodities were transported along the network of the Saharan and Atlantic trade routes. One important factor that aided food supply and distribution was agriculture. The Yorùbá age-old agricultural practices combined with forest vegetation resulted in a constant supply of food commodities.

The strategic operations of the Saharan and Atlantic trades led to the prominence of some towns. Thus, markets developed to facilitate the processes of supply distribution and marketing. These markets are referred to as *ọjà*, an institutionalized activity where people meet at a definite place and at particular point in time. *Ọjà* represented the convergence of food distribution and marketing at intervals or in daily markets. The markets are strategically located and linked. Before the 1950s, periodic markets were very popular, occurring on the third, fifth, ninth, and seventeenth days of each month. These periodic markets served as points of convergence for the supply and distribution of food commodities. Within the markets, associations specialized in certain commodities. Associations or guilds such as ẹgbẹ́ aláta (association of pepper sellers), ẹgbẹ́ ẹléja (association of fish sellers), ẹgbẹ́ ẹléfọ́ọ́ (association of vegetable sellers), and ẹgbẹ́ elélùbọ́ (association of yam-flour sellers) coordinated prices and monitored the supply of food commodities in the markets.

This system has persisted through contemporary times and has served as a vital and reliable trade network for female retailers in the markets. Virtually all markets are centers for the supply and distribution of foodstuffs. By the twentieth century, supply to these markets determined the historical association of food commodities. Many of the markets are strategically located in proximity to farms, which enhanced supply and distribution. For instance, the Elékùrọ́ market in Ìbàdàn was noted for its abundance of palm oil because of its proximity to palm-oil-producing areas. An important feature of supply and distribution in the twentieth century was the movement of lorries bringing goods in and out of markets of major cities in Yorùbáland.

The prices of foodstuffs are normally fixed by the head women sellers of each commodity. In Badagry (Lagos), Ọjàa'Ba (Ìbàdàn), and almost all other markets in other places, market women are major players in the process of supply, distribution, and marketing of food commodities. Market women control prices to protect consumers from high prices and regulate the goods farmers supplied to the market. Supply and distribution of foodstuffs are determined by geography and seasonal variations. The period of availability for all foodstuffs depends on the season; thus, each commodity seller operates in different, periodic markets when a commodity is available. This kind of marketing still exists in the rural areas; markets in urban areas are conducted daily.

See also **Agriculture and Farming; Market**

REFERENCE

Hodder, B. W., and U. I. Ukwu. *Markets of West Africa.* Ìbàdàn (Nigeria): University Press, 1968.

Mutiat Títílọpẹ́ Ọládèjọ

FRONTIER ZONE: GEOGRAPHY AND CULTURAL IMPACT

Three main types of cultural frontiers have been identified in precolonial Africa. The first is the frontier of contact, where distinct political and cultural groups occupied adjacent territories and operated as neighbors. Second, there is the frontier of separation, where societies or politics were separated by a buffer zone. The third type is the frontier of transition, where diverse cultures overlap so much that it is impossible to maintain any clear demarcation between the sociopolitical units.

The frontiers of contact and of transition appear to have been the most common between the Yorùbá and its non-Yorùbá neighbors. Frontiers of contact were present between the Yorùbá and Hausa and between the Yorùbá and Dahomey. Frontiers of transition were prevalent all over Africa, especially in the peripheries of major culture areas. This included the zones between the Yorùbá and neighboring groups such as the Aja in the west; the Edo in the east; the Nupe, Ebira, and Igala in the northeast; and the Bariba in the northwest. The frontiers between the Yorùbá and other, non-Yorùbá groups lacked any major or conspicuous physical barriers. Natural resources, means of subsistence, mobility patterns, and climatic conditions are similar on either side of the frontier.

There were three clearly discernible geographical frontier zones: the western frontier, the eastern frontier, and the northern frontier. In the western frontier, the Yorùbá people (e.g., the Kétu, Ìdásà, Sábẹ, and Ọ̀họrí) lived with a group called the Aja (e.g., Egun, Allada, and Fon). Since the tenth or eleventh century, settlements of the Yorùbá and Aja were interspersed, which led to strong cultural affinity between the two groups. The expanding Yorùbá population had a significant impact on the Aja in language, religion, and social and political institutions. As a result, the Yorùbá and Aja became fused into almost a single cultural area, and the Yorùbá language became the dominant tongue for the two groups. The Aja kingdoms of Savi, Weme, Allada, and Dahomey formed in the sixteenth century and harbored large populations that were closely patterned after Yorùbá kingdoms. The political elite of the Dahomey kingdom were made up of Aja and Yorùbá. The expansion of the Dahomey kingdom by the late seventeenth century posed a major threat to the Yorùbá. The decline of Ọ̀yọ́ Empire from the late eighteenth century further gave Dahomey opportunity to threaten all the kingdoms of western Yorùbáland in the nineteenth century.

In the eastern frontier zone, the Yorùbá shared boundaries with the Edo (Benin) and other related groups, like the Àkókó-Èdó, Afenmai, and Ishan. The thickly forested southeastern region was a melting pot of intensive culture contact and interactions leading to mixed populations, related languages, cultural exchange, intermarriage, trade, and migration. Even though the Ọ̀wọ̀ Yorùbá and the Edo were separated from each other by at least fifty miles, strong cultural influence between the two still took place. For example, the Ọ̀wọ̀ Yorùbá dialect had a strong impact on the Edo language. The Yorùbá-Edo region is considered one of the oldest and busiest trade routes in southern Yorùbáland. Ọ̀wọ̀ was the major center of this frontier zone and was well known for its artistic transmission between ancient Ifẹ̀ and Benin. The Yorùbá and Edo political institutions and royal regalia exhibited a preference for use of beads. The Yorùbá kingdoms of Ọ̀wọ̀, Àkókó, and Èkìtì borrowed some Edo traditions, royal festivals, chieftaincy titles, as well as architectural styles for palaces.

On the northern frontier, the Yorùbá shared boundaries with non-Yorùbá groups such as Nupe, Bariba, Ebira, and Igala. The Yorùbá, Bariba, and Nupe are closely related in their sociopolitical evolution and remained neighbors throughout their histories. The Yorùbá and Bariba occupied the same villages in the western parts of the Middle Niger, and Yorùbá and Nupe also lived side by side in some areas to the east of the Niger River. From the beginning of the sixteenth century and throughout the seventeenth and eighteenth centuries, the Yorùbá traded with the Nupe people to the north and the Igala people to the east. The Nupe traders sold cloth, rice, pottery, and beads. The Nupe living on both the northern and southern banks of the Niger have great influence over the river crossings beyond the Niger. Trading allowed for the exchange of ideas, traditions, and customs.

Oral traditions dating back to at least the sixteenth century provide historical evidence of extensive cultural interactions and influences. The Ìgunnu masquerade of the Nupe was said to have been borrowed by the Yorùbá (Ìgbómìnà) through descendants of Nupe who settled among them or were captured as slaves, and the Nupe must have borrowed the Ifá divination system in turn from the Yorùbá. There are remarkable similarities and sometimes differences in the language, purpose, and apparatus of their divination systems. The vernacular word for divination occurs among the entire Yorùbá as Ifá, as well as among the Ebira and Igala. From a linguistic standpoint, there is a very close affinity in the words for masquerade. For example, Egúngún or Eégún is the word for masquerade among the Yorùbá. The word manifests as *eku* among the Ebira, *gugu* among the Nupe, and *egwu* among the Igala. Among the Igala, red cloths (òdòdó) were the special preserve of adult males and of royalty. The Okun Yorùbá improvised the Igala òdòdó for their Yorùbá masquerade by weaving the cloth on a large scale. The improvised òdòdó was then called *upo* by the Yorùbá.

As Yorùbá kingdoms emerged in the Niger area, they were immediately challenged by the Bariba and Nupe. For example, the Òwu was first located in the north in the Ògbòrò area, but it later pushed to the south by the Bariba. In addition, the Kétu kingdom was first established in the territory to the west, where Ọ̀yọ́-Ilé was later founded. Bariba forced Kétu to give up that location and moved south. The Nupe aggression at the Yorùbá northern frontier is mentioned in many of the Yorùbá traditions. The expansion of Ọ̀yọ́ into the northern frontier since the sixteenth century contributed to the displacement or partial absorption of the Nupe. The incessant friction between Nupe and Yorùbá during this time (which most often resulted in military incursions into Ìgbómìnàland) has been described by Cornelius Adépégba as "frantic efforts by the Nupe to regain the territory" (98). The Ọ̀yọ́ were challenged on how to defend themselves and protect their newly established frontiers and peripheries from intermittent Nupe incursions. In the Jebba-Mokwa area, the main corridor of Ọ̀yọ́ Yorùbá and Nupe economic, cultural, and political interactions, there is evidence of Yorùbá or Yorùbá-related communities that were driven across to the right bank of the Niger River by the Nupe or were "Nupe-ized" as Gbedegi communities. By the second half of the eighteenth century, Ọ̀yọ́'s power began to decline, and the Nupe became more aggressive in their attack on the Yorùbá. The Nupe invaded many Ìgbómìnà towns, forcing inhabitants to abandon their settlements. The Okun Yorùbá territory was not spared, and lacking centralized polities, the population there became an easy target for slave raiders, which culminated in the displacement of many settlements.

See also: **Geography and Environment**

REFERENCES

Adépégba, Cornelius. "Ifẹ̀ Art: An Enquiry into the Surface Patterns and the Continuity of Art Tradition among the Northern Yorùbá." *West African Journal of Archaeology* 12 (1982): 95–109.

Olúsànyà, G. O. *Studies in Yorùbá History and Culture.* Ìbàdàn (Nigeria): University Press, 1983.

Aríbidésí Usman

G

GAMES

The term *eré* or *iré* (play or game) is often a prefix to the actual name of a game. Some examples are *eré ayò* (mancala board game), *eré àgbáàrín* (*àgbáàrín* seed game), *eré ìdárayá* (physical games), and *eré òṣùpá* (moonlight games). Games are meant to keep children and adults fit, mentally and physically. A number of games have ancient origins and are still played; others are dying or have died out.

Games can be categorized into two types: games of wit and training games. Games of wit engage the player's intelligence through maneuvers, quick thinking tactics for self-protection, and attacks on the opponent. Training games combine the use of the aforementioned skills with physical fitness. The games in the first category include *ọpọ́n ayò*, a popular board game similar to the Egyptian and Asian mancala games. Other games of wit include *Àgbà tí ò dájú dánu* (An elder who is not quick thinking or fast speaking—tongue twister), *Wòrú o, Kín ní ń léjẹ̀?* (What does have blood—riddle song), and *ẹnà* (code language). These games are designed to teach and to test mastery and accuracy in the pronunciation of words and phrases. Children and adults play these games. The games trip up even skilled, indigenous speakers because they require speakers to say the phrases quickly.

Ayò is a popular game with children and adults alike and is still very much in use. However, it tends to be played by males more than females. *Àgbáàrín* is also a popular game common with younger children, but the *ààrín* seeds used in playing it are not as readily available as they used to be. *Bojúbojú, gbádìígbádìí, idìndijú, kò-sóló́ko-ló́ko*, and *ijàkadì or ẹkẹ* are examples of children's popular games still in use.

Some games, such as *olookotobé, ìtórò, òkòtó*, and *òǹgo*, are becoming extinct. One reason is that knowledge about how to play them is not passing on to children. One way to preserve the games is to incorporate them into the school curriculum so that children can play them during recess and use them during school physical education lessons.

See also **Children's Folklore: Education and Development; Dolls and Toys; Sports**

REFERENCE

Adéoyè, C. L. *Àṣà àti Iṣe Yorùbá.* Oxford: Oxford University Press, 1979.

Akin Oyètádé

GANGS, GANGSTERS, AND GANGSTERISM

In Yorùbá culture as in other cultures, people often organize into groups, clubs, or associations for various purposes, and various terms are used to describe the aggregations of members of society. Because of the sophistication of Yorùbá society and culture, organizations along specialized and nonspecialized lines are not uncommon, depending on the reasons that bring the people together. In some instances, age, gender, skills, vocation, and social roles, among other factors, may determine the groups to which individuals belong. In most cases, groups are formed for progressive reasons: to perform various roles in the maintenance of the community, to protect the community, to maintain law and order, and to encourage and sustain professional knowledge. These kinds of groups are known as *ẹgbẹ́*, *ọgbà*, *ìgbìmọ̀*, *àkójọpọ̀*, *awo*, *ọmọ-ilé*, and the like.

People with nefarious motives, poor upbringing, or moral decadence can band together to form gangs, become gangsters, and engage in gangsterism. People regard such persons and groups as reprobates who are up to no good, and their antisocial activities have a negative impact on collective survival. As a consequence, they must be watched closely, and other members of society, especially the weak and vulnerable, must be protected from them. There are various ways such groups are described; the names are descriptive and sometimes euphemistic, such as *ìgárá*, *jàndùkú*, *jàgùdà páálí*, *agbódegbà*, *ẹgbẹ́kẹ́gbẹ́*, *àwọn ọmọ ìsọta*, *ọlọ́sà*, and *adigunjalè*.

In the culture, the formation of gangs is due to a number of factors, such as poor home training (*àbíìkọ́*), falling into bad company (*àkọ́ọ̀gbà*), inherent deviance in human nature (*ọmọ tó ya'wọ́*, *ìpánle*, or *dìgbòlugi ọmọ*), laziness (*ọ̀lẹ*), and greed (*aláìnítẹ̀ẹ́lọ́rùn*). These factors drive like-minded people to form gangs that perpetrate dastardly acts against other persons and against society. When such individuals are identified, people treat them with hostility, and they bring shame (*ìtìjú*) and disgrace (*ìbànújẹ́*) to themselves and to members of their family and community.

Gang members are usually discrete and seldom admit their nefarious activities, which constitute evil to society and an abomination to ancestors. The opprobrium they garner reaches beyond them to those who failed to raise them properly as youth (family, community,= and society). Therefore, gangs are derided and shunned by all well-meaning and properly cultured members of society (*ọmọlúwàbí*). To behave like an uncouth individual (gangster) is nothing to be proud of. The gangster is aware that because of the nature of moral norms and conditioning that society imposes on individuals, a gangster cannot promote or openly disclose his or her activities or the identities and activities of other members of his or her gang.

Thus, while fraternities (e.g., professional guilds, academies, priests) are encouraged for the good they do for society and for their members' contributions, gangs (e.g., criminal groups, cults, secret societies) are not encouraged. The fraternities may be able to assist society in governing and maintaining public order and security for society. Gangs, by contrast, prey on vulnerable members of society and are agents of disruption of the moral order (*ọ̀bàyéjẹ́*, *agbódegbà*, *ẹni ibi*). Yorùbá people believe that "the walls have ears," and consequently, there is very little one can embark on in secret that does not become public knowledge, no matter how careful one is. A life of gangsterism, therefore, is frowned upon. Where the good order of society has been compromised by gangs, gangsters, and gangsterism, efforts must be made to return the society to a state of social, economic, and moral equilibrium through purgative, religious cleansing, fines, and—in extreme cases—the complete expulsion, ostracism, and excommunication of such individuals. The responsibility for restoring order falls on all adults in society, but it is primarily the responsibility of the parents (*òbí*), community heads (*baálè*), leaders (*sọnmọ̀rí ìlú*), chiefs (*ìjòyè*), and kings (*ọba*) to restore order and enforce the laws in various communities. If they fail to act, then they will encourage the festering of evil to the point that it may consume everyone: *bi ara ilé ẹni bá ń jẹ kòkòrò búburú, a kò gbọdọ̀ dáké, tori hẹ̀rẹ̀ huru rẹ̀ lóru kò níjẹ́ á sùn* (when one's neighbor is eating something dangerous or poisonous, one should not keep quiet, because when he or she is unable to sleep in the night, it becomes a problem for everybody in the home).

In recent times, gangs, cults, and secret societies have proliferated in institutions of higher learning in Nigeria. Members of these gangs could not go home to their families and celebrate their membership in such organizations. If parents and guardians heard that their sons, daughters, and wards were members of gangs, they would have been distraught and inconsolable. The majority of parents expect their children to go do school to learn, not to become miscreants and gangsters.

See also **Age Grade System; Insults and Ribald Language; Ọmọlúwàbí; Social Control**

REFERENCE

Oyènéyẹ, O. Y., and M. O. Shórẹ̀mí, eds. *Nigerian Life and Culture.* Ìbàdàn (Nigeria): Ògùn State University Publications Committee, 1985.

John Ayọ̀túndé Ìṣọ̀lá Bẹ́wàjí

GENDER

As in most patriarchal societies of the world, a Yorùbá woman is socialized into a culture of female subordination, male superiority, and domination. A major feature of most traditional societies is the patriarchal structure, that is, a structure of a set of social relations with material base that enables men to dominate women. Yorùbá was a gendered society prior to colonialism; evidence of this abounds not only in contemporary social reality but also in the oral history that has been passed down.

The images of men and women in oral history are important sources of cultural knowledge and understanding of gender issues. The study of images of a social or gender group in a society's oral art reveals cultural and social codes in that society. This not only reveals certain conventional traits that are characteristic of genres of literature but also reflects underlying social relations and worldviews specific to gender, social class, and—perhaps—religious groups. By implication, an analysis of such cultural and ideological images has relevance for issues of socioeconomic development. Solutions to gender-related problems in a largely nonliterate rural society might be reached by analyzing both the personal and the public life that defines the values, attitudes, and behaviors through which women are perceived. Texts are social facts, and they are used to do things: they are forms of action, and they are central to understanding what it means to be a person in every culture. Issues relating to

gender, social status, and sexuality should be properly addressed to promote people's sexual and reproductive health, especially in rural areas.

Language, with all its complexities and diverse avenues of meaning, will forever be necessary for development. Without language, the discourse of gender would not even be considered for discussion; power relations would be vague, and identities would be neither fashioned nor categorized. Elucidating gender is crucial to understanding how and why people, especially women, face particular risks. Also, improved knowledge about gender will help devise effective prevention and treatment strategies. There are no gender restrictions in the healing sphere, where both men and women occupy a central space.

The problems associated with widowhood practices and inheritance are gender sensitive, as women tend to be at a disadvantage in most cases. The wall of patriarchy that encourages male dominance and property inheritance through the male line has further assisted to devalue and pauperize women. Consequently, the achievement of sustainable development and gender equality becomes more a figment of the imagination than a reality if issues such as abhorrent widowhood practices in the name of culture and property disinheritance are not addressed. When a woman is murdered, her death is often attributed to natural causes such as sickness, accidents, or old age without pointing an accusing finger at any suspect. Even when a query is made into suspicious deaths, the culprit is sought among the victim's contenders, such as co-wives or neighbors. Her husband is not usually seen as responsible.

On the contrary, the death of a man is viewed from various dimensions. The widespread belief is that his wife must have been responsible for his death. This idea is encapsulated in a proverb among the Yorùbá: *obìnrin bímọ fúnni kò pé kó má pani* (that a woman gave birth to children for a man does not prevent her from killing her husband). The culture of patriarchy tends to favor men in issues relating to widowhood and property inheritance essentially because, instead of suspicion and accusations, the husband receives more sympathy and support upon the death of his wife. For instance, in some communities in southwestern Nigeria, arrangements are made for a woman to sleep with the widower for a night so that he is not haunted by the spirit of his dead wife. Hence the saying *opókùnrin kì í dá sùn nítorí ìyàwó ọrun* (the widower does not sleep alone because of the dead wife's spirit). While both wife and husband experience emotional trauma at the loss of a spouse, the man is usually given more social support to cope and eventually readjust to a new life.

In the traditional religious space, gender issues are visible. Male and female deities exist, and male and female adherents exist in all religious cults. It is rare to see a particular traditional Yorùbá cult without the involvement of both genders. This is because society is constructed on the principle of binary, complementary essences. However, there are male- and female-dominated cults.

In naming practices, gender is equally visible. Many names given to children, including their personal praise names (*oríkì*), clearly show gender differentiation.

See also **Deities: The *Òrìṣà*; Inheritance; Widows and Widowhood**

REFERENCE

Oyèwùmí, Oyèrónké, ed. *Gender Epistemologies in Africa: Gendering Traditions, Spaces, Social Institutions, and Identities.* New York: Palgrave Macmillan, 2010.

George Olúṣọlá Ajíbádé

GEOGRAPHY AND ENVIRONMENT

The geographic location of present-day Yorùbáland is in southwestern Nigeria, west of the Lower Niger River. This area was formerly the British colonial demarcated Western Region. Today, Yorùbáland falls primarily within the political state boundaries of Èkìtì, Kwara, Lagos, Ògùn, Oǹdó, Ọṣun, and Ọ̀yọ́ states; Yorùbá are also found in the states of Kogí and western Edo (Àkókó Ẹ̀dó). The Itsekiris of the Niger Delta are descendants of Yorùbá. These states do not exactly coincide with the historical Yorùbá kingdoms that

existed between the eleventh and early eighteenth centuries. These historical kingdoms include Ifè, which is the oldest; Ọ̀yọ́; Abéòkúta; Ìlọrin; Ìbàdàn; and the smaller kingdoms of Òwu, Kétu, and Pópó. In the eighteenth century, Ọ̀yọ́ was an extensive and powerful empire founded on agriculture, with trade networks extending westward into what is now the neighboring state of Benin (formerly Dahomey). The city of Ìbàdàn is the administrative center of present-day Ọ̀yọ́ state, and Lagos is the original federal and state capital of Nigeria. The Yorùbá make up approximately 21 percent of the Nigerian population. Culturally, there are several ethnic subgroups of the Yorùbá with slight variations in dialect, such as the Àkókó, Àkúré, Awórì, Ègùn, Èkìtì, Ìbọló, Ifè, Ìgbómìnà, Ìjẹbú, Ìjẹsà, Ìkálẹ̀, Ìlàjẹ, Oǹdó, Ọ̀wọ̀, and Ọ̀yọ́. In addition, there is a significant Yorùbá Diaspora, and descendants include, for example, the Akú of Sierra Leone, the Lucumí of Cuba, and the Nagô of Brazil, who have retained several aspects of Yorùbá cultural heritage.

Much of Yorùbáland lies in two of Nigeria's five physical geographic regions, namely the low coastal zone along the Gulf of Guinea and the Atlantic Ocean and the hills and low plateaus to the north of the coastal zone. Dome-shaped granite hills of the Precambrian basement complex, ranging in height from 500 meters to 1,219 meters above sea level, rise above ancient plains. These highlands have prominent inselbergs, such as Ìyámọ̀pó. Agbele Hills are the source of rivers such as the Ògùn, Ọṣun, Ọba, Ọyán, Ọtìn, Òfikì, Saàsá, Ọni, and Erinlẹ̀. Other rugged, hilly terrain occurs in eastern Yorùbáland in Èkìtì State, including Ìkẹ́rẹ́-Èkìtì, Ẹ̀fọ̀n-Aláayè, Adó-Èkìtì, and Ọlọ́sunta Hills. The Ìpólé-Ìlọ́rọ̀ (Arinta) waterfalls are an important natural feature in Èkìtì.

Vegetation varies from coastal ecologies comprising freshwater swamps and brackish mangroves along the Atlantic Ocean to the south, to tropical rain forest with distinct wet and dry seasons and mixed woodlands and savanna to the north. Those ecologies lying within the tropical climatic zone that have high rainfall are suitable for the production of a variety of food crops, such as root crops like yams and cereal crops like millet, which are widely grown in the savannah woodland. Oil palm, kola nut, and cocoa thrive in the forest zones. The forest zones of Èkìtì are rich in a variety of timber and are the heart of Nigeria's cocoa-producing industry. Wildlife is abundant and includes monkeys, crocodiles, snakes, leopards, and hippopotami. Some states, like Kwara, are rich in mineral resources, such as gold, iron ore, and phosphate, and rich in economically valuable building stones like limestone, marble, and granite.

With respect to livelihoods, some states are more urbanized than others, such as Èkìtì and Oǹdó in the east. Large urban centers are Ìbàdàn, Ifẹ̀, and Ògbómọ̀ṣọ́. Lagos is the commercial capital of the nation, with manufacturing and industrial estates such as Àpápá, Ìkẹjà, Yábà, and Mushin. People in urban environments serve in such jobs as politician, accountant, entrepreneur, academic, medical doctor, and lawyer. Traditional subsistence livelihoods are primarily farming and fishing, but hunting and trading are also practiced. In addition to the bush fallow cultivation carried out by the majority of the population, there are also export cash-crop farmers (cocoa, palm produce, and rubber), some large-scale government sponsored farms, and cattle ranches on suitable grazing lands on the savanna. Fishing is an important livelihood near rivers, creeks, and lagoons of the coastal zones, which also serve as important means of transportation. Other traditional water-based livelihoods are collection of riparian resources, such as building poles and gathering raffia for matting, roofing, and basket weaving, as well as cultivating riverine or swamp rice.

Because the majority of the people practice subsistence livelihoods and depend on wild flora and fauna as resources, there is a close attachment to and respect for the earth. Similar to other indigenous groups around the world, resource use and management strategies have evolved from perceptions rooted in spirituality, esoteric knowledge, and technological innovation and adaptation. Hills, rock features, forests, and water bodies such as rivers, lagoons, springs, and the sea are customarily sacred sites or *ojúbọ* and

igbó (forest grove) where community ceremonies, worship, and their accompanying rituals take place. There are numerous sacred places in Yorùbáland that are considered inhabited by deities, spirits, or divinities known as *òrìṣà*.

One example is Yemọja of the Ògùn River. Also, the Ọ̀ṣun River is home to the goddess of the same name (Ọ̀ṣun), wife of the thunder god Ṣàngó. She is revered among the Yorùbá. Her shrine is along the riverbanks within the Ọ̀ṣun Òṣogbo Grove at Òṣogbo, which was declared a UNESCO World Heritage Site in 2005. Every August, an annual religious festival is carried out at the shrine. Another sacred forest grove is Iwinrin in Ilé-Ifẹ̀. Shrines in riverine areas include one to Ọlọ́sà, the lagoon spirit, and another for Olókun, the spirit of the sea. Hills and rock features are revered for serving as safe havens for people during past intertribal wars. Annual religious festivals are carried out at such shrines, as at Òkè'Bàdàn. Certain tree species are considered the abode of spirits also, such as the ìrókò (*Chlorophora excelsa*) and osè (*Adansonia digitata*).

The practice of one's daily livelihood is often accompanied by rituals and special prayers at shrines. For example, at the Ọlọ́fin Festival in Ìlawẹ̀ Èkìtì, the community offers special prayers for success with cocoa cultivation, a major economic activity. Sacred forests like the Ọ̀ṣun Òṣogbo Grove are preserved and protected from pollution because priests, acting as guardians, prevent activities such as hunting, logging, and fishing in the river.

See also **Frontier Zone: Geography and Cultural Impact**

REFERENCES

Awólàlú, J. Ọmọsadé. *Yorùbá Beliefs and Sacrificial Rites*. London: Longmans, 1979.
Udo, K. Reuben. *Geographical Regions of Nigeria*. Berkeley: University of California Press, 1970.

Fenda A. Akíwùmí

GLOBALIZATION

The Yorùbá, by their very nature and history, are itinerant people for whom the questions of dispersal, displacement, migration, movement, and return to their source is as fortuitous as it is a way of life, despite the complexities of globalization. As the most historically prevalent ethnic group in Nigeria, the Yorùbá have participated in their own cultural and political survival across the globe. In the face of various modes of external impositions, such as transatlantic slavery, Christianity, Islam, and colonialism, Yoruba religion and culture have remained resilient and dynamic, as shown by how the Yorùbá people of West Africa reinvented their religious practices and core cultural values. They have endured in Africa but also in the Americas, Asia, Europe, and Australia.

Through internal migration and transatlantic crossings (forced or voluntary), the Yorùbá are in a state of constant and shifting transition, both physically and spiritually, through the intricate relationships between the worlds of the living, the ancestors, and the unborn. In their shrines, belief systems, rituals, ceremonies, festivals, museums, and overall expressive cultures that translate to vivid visual, oracular, and profane metaphors, they have preserved, reinvented, and hybridized their age-old religious traditions in the New World—especially in Brazil (Candomblé), Cuba (Santería), Trinidad (Ṣàngó), and the United States (Santería).

Recent waves of globalization include first-generation Yorùbá Westerners, such as Yorùbá Americans, Yorùbá Brazilians, Yorùbá Trinidadians, and Yorùbá French, among many others. Their parents, once self-declared exiles, must face the reality of creating a new community abroad, even as their children are caught between the Yorùbá culture they are alienated from and the new Western culture in which they are raised. The challenges of globalization for the Yorùbá are, therefore, multiple. Their children, some of whom were born abroad are caught, as their parents are, in the enchanting power of assimilation and "recolonization" in the West, given economic and political expediency. As challenging as the reality of migrating fathers, mothers, and their children born in exile or raised in exile is, there is room for consolation in the crossover appeal of such young musicians such

as Fẹ́mi Kútì, Lágbájá, Ṣeun Kútì, Davido, among many young talents who are trying to merge the diasporic and global with the local.

Perhaps one lesson learned from globalization is that "charity begins at home." As hybridized as Yorùbá religious practices and cultures are in the many corners of the globe, the process of so-called glocalization, without losing indigenous values to the global, must be a worthwhile compromise, even as traditional values are being constantly eroded by the enticing power of capital and exoticized, commercial diffusion. The pioneering works of Abímbọ́lá, Herskovits, Rodrigues, Ortiz, Bastide, Cabrera, Verger, Bascom, and Mason, among others, are instructive reminders that, despite globalization, many elements of Yorùbá culture remain significant. Ifá divination in Nigeria; Candomblé and Santería in Brazil and Cuba, respectively; Yorùbá revivalism in the United States; and gender dynamics in these sacred (and even profane) manifestations and rituals are lasting legacies of the impact of Yorùbá culture as a globalized phenomenon.

See also **Diaspora: Yorùbá in Africa; Diaspora: Yorùbá in Europe; Diaspora: Yorùbá in North America; Diaspora: Yorùbá in Central America and the Caribbean; Diaspora: Yorùbá in South America; Diaspora: Impact of Yorùbá Culture**

REFERENCE

Fálọlá, Tóyìn, and Matt D. Childs. *The Yoruba Diaspora in the Atlantic World.* Bloomington: Indiana University Press, 2005.

Níyì Afọlábí

GOSSIP AND RUMOR

Aláròká kò gb'ẹgbàá, ibi ọpẹ́ ló mọ (no one is compensated for gossip or rumormongering) and *b'étí ò gbọ́ yìnkìn, inú kì í bàjẹ́* (rumormongering creates disaffections) are two proverbs that sum up Yorùbá beliefs with regard to gossip and rumormongering. Gossip is regarded as *ẹjọ́ ẹlẹ́jọ́, gbéborùn, tẹnubọlẹ̀, àròká,* or *àròyé,* and it is a product of idleness, mischief, or a bad mind. It is understood that responsible persons, with proper cultural grounding (*ọmọlúwàbí*), will not engage in such behavior because it ruins the lives and integrity of people. Such habits, once formed, are capable of destroying families, societies, associations, and the happiness of people in society.

Yorùbá society insists on strict moral codes regarding discretion in how one carries the burden of knowledge, regardless of age, gender, or position in life. In some instances, for the overall good of social living and good community existence: *bójú bá rí, ẹnu a dákẹ́,* or *gbogbo ohun tójú rí kọ́ ni ẹnu ń sọ* (when the eye sees, the mouth must exercise discretion in telling). There are also instances when, in virtue of the positions that individuals occupy in society, either as religious leaders or as political functionaries, the following is said: *ọbẹ̀ kì í mì ní ikùn àgbà* (the soup does not move around in the elder's stomach).

Does this mean that Yorùbá people are averse to telling the truth? Not in the least. For when there are important issues that have to be decided, the eyewitness account and truthful testimony are highly valued and rewarded. This is because telling the truth is not rumor mongering or gossiping. A gossip bears tales without being solicited. Whereas, the witness to the truth bears the responsibility of aiding the cause of justice in society, and hence his or her service or testimony is highly valued. In some instances it takes a lot of courage to tell the truth, and Yorùbá society places a premium on the contributions of those who would risk personal pleasure or opprobrium to help the cause of justice.

Gossips and rumormongers often cause incalculable harm to society, communities, associations, friendships, and families. Often such gossips and rumormongers believe that they are helping, that they will gain acceptance, or that they will be praised for letting people know what others think and say behind their backs. However, the story of Ìjàpá, who, because of gossip, found himself in a situation where the king decided that his fate and punishment should suffer capital punishment, is told to youth with relish to let them know that gossiping and rumormongering is disdained by Yorùbá society.

There is a paradox, though. Yorùbá also believe that *eti ọba ní'lé, etí ọba l'óko, ènìyàn níí jẹ́ bẹ̀ẹ̀* (the ears of the king are at home and on the farm, because there are persons bearing tales for the king). This is because there is need for society to be in equilibrium and for the leaders and rulers to have access to needed information. *Ọ̀tẹlẹ̀múyẹ́* (spies) are sometimes employed to ensure that there is justice, conformity, and balance in society. Overall, there must be balance in all situations: when there is truth waiting to be told to advance the cause of justice, then courage must be summoned to speak the truth, but when one's speaking could cause damage to individuals and communities, then discretion is most valued.

REFERENCES

Oyènẹ́yẹ, O. Y., and M. O. Shórẹ̀mí, eds. *Nigerian Life and Culture.* Ìbàdàn (Nigeria): Ògùn State University Publications Committee, 1985.
UNESCO. "Tangible Cultural Heritage." http://www.unesco .org/new/en/cairo/culture/tangible-cultural-heritage/.

John Ayọ̀túndé Ìṣọ̀lá Bẹ́wàjí

GOURDS: USES AND DECORATIONS

Gourds are the Yorùbá person's best inanimate friend—one almost unseen and unappreciated but dutifully performing the various tasks for which it is called upon and without complaint. From the moment it is disemboweled, relieved of its contents, and prepared for its specific task, gourds of different sizes serve people as calabashes. They accompany them in their journey through life, in peace or in war, in happiness or sadness, from infancy to old age, when things are smooth or when sacrifices are needed to appease their maker. Such interactions have resulted in many stories, songs, and rhymes about calabashes, for example:

Ọjọ́ itọ́rọ́, ẹmu ni.
Ọjọ́ isísì, ẹmu ni.
Ǹ bá ti l'áya,
Kèrègbè ni ò jẹ́.

Some days, I spent three pence on palm wine.
Some other days, I spent six pence on palm wine.
I should have been married,
But the [palm wine] in the gourd prevented that.

This balladeer blames the lowly gourd for his misfortunes in life, since the calabash held the palm wine that led to the man's self-inflicted woes.

In one story, Tortoise had used a gourd to collect all the wisdom of the earth; his aim was to deprive humankind of its wisdom. He had planned to hang his loot on top of a palm tree. However, the gourd slowed down his ascent to the top of the tree because he carried it at his front instead of his back. Hare, passing by and seeing Tortoise's predicament, advised him to shift his load to his back. This advice revealed to Tortoise that he had failed in his mission to collect all the wisdom on earth. Had he succeeded, there would have been no advice for Hare to offer him. Therefore, he smashed his load on the ground for all wisdom to escape.

Gourds come in various shapes, forms, and sizes. The smallest of these, àdó is one of the receptacles of the native healer, the Babaláwo. The tip of a small gourd is cut and carefully emptied of its natural contents, then cleaned and dried, which leaves a small space for storing powdered medications and charms. The àdó served as the receptacle that followed the ancestors to the battlefield, and hunters used it for storing antidotes to various poisons they encountered in the forest.

In times past, the ahá, which resembles a modern-day cup, was used extensively for drinking palm wine. A slightly bigger version, the ìkéèmù, rested on every water pot in many households. All members of the family used it as a utensil to dip water from the water pot.

A ṣ́ę́ę́rę́ is obtained when a long-necked gourd is cut vertically into two halves, cleaned out, and dried. This implement is used as a ladle. Other kitchen utensils constructed from gourds, include the ìgbakọ, a small piece of broken calabash shaped like a scoop and used mainly for dishing out hot ògì-ẹ̀kọ or àmàlà from the pot. The beauty of these utensils compared with many modern-day ones is that they do not conduct heat.

A long-necked gourd carefully cleaned out through a hole at the top and filled with beads is called ṣèkèrè. This serves as a hand percussion instrument in many musical forms. Ṣèkèrè may also come as a bigger, more rounded calabash with a net of shells or ìlèkè very loosely covering it. Beating the ìlèkè against the calabash produces a rattling sound. This instrument is much favored by sákárà and àpàlà musicians. Another musical instrument from the calabash is the flute called ekùtù in the eastern part of Yorùbáland. This is formed from a much slimmer and longer calabash than the ṣèkèrè. Just like a regular flute, it has a hole on the side of the narrow neck and a bigger opening at the other end. This instrument features prominently in many festivals.

The agbè or akèǹgbè is the object of riddles and folklores in Yorùbáland. It is the preferred container for palm wine or bùrùkùtù. It is a large, short-necked, roundish calabash used for transporting palm wine by ordinary men and kings alike. The akèǹgbè can be said to be an equal-opportunity server. The akèǹgbè accompanies all celebrations, from those as mundane as naming a newborn child to those as exalted as the coronation of kings. It is believed that no Yorùbá worth his or her drink would accept palm wine poured from any other receptacle than the akèǹgbè.

The koto is a very deep, basket-shaped calabash used for transporting and peddling foodstuffs ranging from ògì-ẹ̀kọ to dried pepper. The broader and less deep igbájẹ̀ is used for household chores like washing clothes or storing dried foodstuff. A smaller and beautifully carved and decorated igbájẹ̀ is often used for presenting gifts to important personalities or potential in-laws. It might carry kola nuts, bitter kola, fruits, and other items that accompany the celebrations of the day of marriage.

Calabash carving is a profession almost as old as the Yorùbá nation itself. The Western part of Yorùbáland is especially known for traditional gourd use and art. These dried gourds ranging in size from a doorknob to a big bowl are carved and used for different purposes, including serving food and for storage. Many of these find their ways into living rooms all over the world, where they are used for decoration. Nowadays, carved calabashes have taken the form of mementos presented to those celebrating birthdays, retirement, and the like. They also serve as art, hung on walls. It is not uncommon to find some of these items being sold at galleries and international airports to foreigners who would like to take a piece of Yorùbáland home with them. In spite of modern life, gourds, either for decorative purposes or in service to the Yorùbá person, have remained part of the people's culture.

See also **Music: Islamic; Musical Instruments; Music: Traditional**

REFERENCE

Abraham, R. C. *Dictionary of Modern Yorùbá.* 2nd ed. London: Hodder and Stoughton, 1958.

Julius Fákínlèdé

GOVERNMENT: HISTORICAL POLITICAL SYSTEMS

The primordial Yorùbá nation-state evolved seemingly simple cultural beliefs and values, but it also developed sophisticated and complex political systems and democratic institutions for governance. The Yorùbá political culture and governance, especially the hierarchy of authorities, are derivative of beliefs in Olódùmarè, Elédùmarè, or Olórun (the almighty God, the owner of the universe of heaven and earth). Power and authority, therefore, flow from Olódùmarè through the *irúnmolè* or *òrìsà* (deities), such as Ògún, Sàngó, Obàtálá, and Òsun, to the *oba* (the king). The *oba* is *aláse* (the approved authority and true representative of the Olódùmarè on the earth), *èkejì òrìsà* (the next after the deities), and *ògbóni* or *alàgbà* (the elders).

As a hierarchy, the elders traditionally ruled within a seemingly simple but rather sophisticated separation of powers among the ruling functionaries: the Babaláwo (Ifá priest), the Ògbóni (elders), the kingmakers, the village head or town ruling king-in-council, and the general populace. No one dared cross the line of his or her place within the hierarchy. Sanctions and penalties were swift and severe; even the king could be dethroned. Household members and groups deferred to, and were responsible to, the household head. The heads of households were responsible to the *baálè*, the village head, while the village heads were responsible

to the *oba*, the town head. Household members and groups, village members, and town members have clearly defined functions and duties, just as with modern bureaucratic organizations. There are also rules binding on all members of the community. The unwritten constitution also provides for due process in the succession of leadership positions.

There are unified political systems among the Yorùbá because they all have shared cultural values and beliefs as well as ancestral links with Odùduwà and his seven children: Olówu, AláKétu, Omo N'Oba, Òràngún, Onísàbè, Olúpópó, and Aláàfin. With Odùduwà at Ilé-Ifè, and the seven children in the earlier town settlements, any slight variations in political system can be traced to the personalities of the founders. In all the Yorùbá towns, there is a hierarchy of executive chiefs, for example, Balógun (the commander of the army), Ìyálóde (the head of the women affairs), Ìyálájé (the head of the market women), and Olúwo (the chief Ifá priest). There are trade associations, which all have their own rules and systems of political governance. These systems and institutions are fueled by and operated with an unwritten constitution of fables, proverbs, ethics, and verbal and nonverbal communications for governing the public and private affairs of the three tiers of the Yorùbá settlements: households, villages, and towns.

The Yorùbá possess a holistic worldview of cooperation between heaven and earth. Consequently, their beliefs in cooperation between dead ancestors and the living, in the responsibilities of the deities in the public and private affairs of the people, in reincarnation, and in the continuity of life all worked together to make for the smooth running of the historical political systems. The child joins this system at birth; his or her parents consult the Babaláwo (Ifá priest) to know which deity the child is obliged to worship and from whom he or she is to seek protection and assistance from the evil machinations of the world. The Ifá's choice of the god for the child sometimes determines not only the child's personal god but also his or her career or occupation.

The political culture of the Yorùbá's unwritten constitutional monarchy, hierarchy, deference to age—

indeed, *alàgbà* and *ògbóni*, or the rule of elders in which children are to be seen and not heard—and seeming male chauvinism is complex and deceptive. To a stranger, the system is autocratic and elitist. But in practice, it is democratic, and indeed more plebiscite, less classist, and more republican than aristocratic. The king operates solely as the king-in-council of chiefs and elders. Democratic institutions for the rule of law are built in to check any abuse of power, and to reward for compliance to the norms and mores. No member of the Yorùbá household, village, or town leadership has absolute power, even to veto, without due regard to precedent and the will of the people. While the Ifá oracle may choose a slave to become king, the political systems also allow kingmakers to dethrone the king. The king, too, has the power to sanction chiefs. No citizen is above the law or untouchable by the constitutional authorities of the Yorùbá nation-state.

A significant and integral part of the historical political systems is the role of the Yorùbá deities and the seasonal cultural festivals. The deities and the festivals have their roles in the smooth running of the Yorùbá communities. Because the Yorùbá believe not only in reincarnation but also in ancestors who have passed on, the ancestors continue to have a say in the affairs of their living progenitors. Egúngún festivals are celebrated every year in all towns and cities. Similarly, Orò, Ṣàngó, Ọ̀ṣun, Gẹ̀lẹ̀dẹ́, Òrìṣà-Oko, Ògún, and others are important deities and festivals in which the people accord a place of importance in their everyday life and political systems.

Contemporary leaders face a dilemma and conflicting issues with the colonial and postindependence political systems. On the one hand, they cherish the historical political systems and would like to promote and create a place for it within the modern political systems. On the other hand, the historical political systems were workable within the small communities of individuals of a common primordial ancestry with shared cultural values and beliefs. While most of the Yorùbá historical political systems are adaptable to the modern political economies and government practices, the historical political systems are, in reality, somewhat anachronistic and problematic in today's world for five main reasons. First, most people have embraced either Islam or Christianity, and both religions are overtly incongruent with the Yorùbá deities. Second, the Yorùbá as a nation-state are part of the modern Nigerian federation of more than 250 ethnic groups, all with different cultural values and beliefs. Third, the modern Yorùbá are also now a part of the global village, with a new worldview of what is acceptable good practice for governance. Fourth, the Yorùbá nation-state is no longer a homogeneous ethnic group with shared cultural values and beliefs; things such as economic migration, interethnic and interreligious marriages, Western education and Western ideologies, evangelical and fundamental orthodoxies, and the like have infiltrated the previously unified Yorùbá political culture. Fifth, the modern Yorùbá are acculturating and bringing up their children without their language, values, and beliefs, which represents perhaps the greatest threat to the historical political systems.

See also **Deities: The *Òrìṣà*; Kingship; Political Systems**

REFERENCE

Fádípẹ̀, N. A. *The Sociology of the Yorùbá.* Ìbàdàn (Nigeria): University Press, 1970.

Bọ́lá Dáúdà

GREETINGS

The verbal art of greetings is known as *ìkíni*, from the verb *kí*, which means "to greet." The verb *kú*, which is very prominent in a multiplicity of Yorùbá greetings, derives from the verb *kí*. Greetings are one of the main pillars of Yorùbá cultural heritage. A child brought up by responsible parents and extended family relations is expected to become an *ọmọlúàbí*, a well-bred adult, and must know how to greet and respond appropriately to greetings for various occasions.

The elaborate pattern of Yorùbá greetings is born of communal living in traditional agricultural and trading environments, where people are closely interested in and concerned about the welfare of extended family relations and neighbors. The people have specialized greetings for virtually every kind of situation conditioned by their everyday living experiences. This kind of elaborate system of greetings is usually witnessed among people engaged in communal existence. It is difficult to maintain such a system in fast-paced individualistic communities of emerging urban centers and sprawling cities.

There are several greetings for different times of the day, the most prominent being *ẹ kúùdájí* (greetings for the dawn), *ẹ káàárọ̀* (greetings for the morning), *ẹ kúùyálẹ̀ta* (greetings for midday), *ẹ káàsán* (greetings for the afternoon), *ẹ kúùrọ̀lẹ́* (greetings for early evening), and *ẹ káalẹ́* (greetings for late evening). Apart from times of the day, there are several other greetings, such as *ẹ kú ìrójú* (greetings for your fortitude in the face of bereavement), *ẹ kú ewu ọ̀nà* (greetings on your safe return from your travels), *ẹ kú ewu ọmọ* (congratulations on the birth of your baby), *ẹ kúùyèdún* (congratulations on your anniversary), and *ẹ kú àtijọ́* (greetings and glad to see you after so long!). For all these greetings, there are appropriate responses.

Urbanization and fast-paced individualistic lifestyles in big cities are killing off the elaborate greeting styles, as people no longer have the time and space that they had in rural communal societies. It is inevitable that some of the elaborate greeting styles will diminish in relevance and usage in busy industrialized commercial centers. However, older people who are knowledgeable in the greeting styles should use them regularly and pass them on to the younger generation.

REFERENCE

Adéoyè, C. L. *Àṣà àti Ìṣe Yorùbá*. Oxford: Oxford University Press, 1979.

Akin Oyètádé

H

HEALING

Among the Yorùbá, as in many African cultures, healing is always approached holistically. This is based on the concept that sickness or illness implies a combined physiological and spiritual condition that results from an imbalance between the metaphysical and the human world. The imbalance disturbs the expected normal flow of life. In addition, the interaction between the physical and the metaphysical world is central to Yorùbá theology. In this context, ritual dynamics of divination, spirit possession, offering, and sacrifice play central roles in the Yorùbá response to issues of illness and healing. This is particularly true in the employment of spirit possession as a key element in the process of health care and healing.

The sources and methods of healing manifest in different ways. To begin with, healing is regarded primarily as a gift from the Supreme Being. This notion vividly demonstrates the Yorùbá conviction that traditional healers possess knowledge of healing from Olódùmarè and exercise their knowledge through the agency of Ifá. Thus, the employment of Ifá in the process of determining the cause and cure of illnesses becomes paramount. The central figure is the Babaláwo (Ifá priest), who is widely consulted as a diviner and healer concerning all kinds of ailments and their cures. The Babaláwo are believed to possess a wide variety of ways to communicate with the supernatural, which they rely on to determine both the source and the method of healing. The involvement of the supernatural beings is concretized by the belief that traditional health practitioners are inspired by òrìṣà such as Ọ̀sanyìn, who is regarded as the special consultant deity of medicine and the ancestors.

However, there are different categories of traditional healers. In addition to the category of the Babaláwo, who uses divination, there is also the category of oníṣègùn, healers who employ the use of herbs, charms, and incantations. Usually, the decision of which category of healers to approach is determined by the nature of the illness and the role to be attributed to supernatural agents in curing illness.

Perhaps the greatest evidence of the Yorùbá subscription to the inseparable and ultimate connection between the natural and spiritual realms in healing is spirit possession. This process largely involves the healer's employment of rituals associated with invoking spirits, not only for diagnosing the cause or source of illness but also for curative procedures. Such healing sessions are characterized by specific songs and dance steps that invoke the spirits; the healer eventually enters a trance state. Sometimes during the trance, the spirit mounts the healer or devotee, and he or she alternates between full alertness and a complete absence of personal awareness. Healing takes place either by exorcism, driving away the notorious spirits that "endanger" the life of an individual, or by prophetic pronouncements of necessary offerings, sacrifices, and herbal prescriptions.

See also **Charms; Deities: The Òrìṣà; Disease; Divination: Ifá; Divinatory Systems; Health Care; Plants; Spirit Possession**

REFERENCES

Fálọlá, Tóyìn, and Matthew Heaton, eds. *Traditional and Modern Health System in Nigeria.* Trenton, NJ: African World Press, 2006.

Walker, Sheila. *Ceremonial Spirit Possession in Africa and Afro-America.* Leiden: Brill, 1972.

Adépéjú Johnson-Bashua

HEALTH CARE

Both health and life are seen as being on a single continuum by the Yorùbá. Thus, the need to maintain life in its wholeness is paramount in the society. Sound health is interpreted as a harmonious relationship between a human being and all the organs of the body, soul, and spirit, coupled with a corresponding harmony with the cosmic totality. On the basis of this premise, ill health is seen as affecting the person, not the body—that is, both the physical and the spiritual parts of a person and not just certain parts of the body, as with the practice in orthodox medicine. This explains the close relationship that exists between the people's health system and religion and the reason health-related issues, such as diagnosis and healing, are always approached holistically.

In the culture, there are three different dimensions of health. The first is *ìlera*, which comes from a fusion of the prefix *ì* with the words *le*, which means "strong," and *ara*, which means "body." *Ìlera* is a practical approach to health that is synonymous to possessing the physical strength to perform daily activities. This is usually expressed in the statement *Ṣé ara le?* (How is your health?) Second, *sàn*, meaning "well," is the opposite of *àìsàn*. *Sàn* implies attaining the ideal health standard. Finally, *àlàáfíà* means general well-being and usually implies wellness in both body and soul for an individual. An individual is regarded as healthy when he or she has a combination of the three

dimensions. This belief is concisely expressed in the adage *ìlera lọrọ̀*, meaning "health is wealth."

In traditional society, health-care delivery is the sole responsibility of the medicine men and women (*onísègùn*), who are regarded as professionals. Among them are priests of Ọsanyìn (tutelary deity of medicine), diviners, herbalists, and Ifá priests. Proficient medicine by Yorùbá standards consists of knowing the nature of the disease as well as the things that will cause it to go away. Thus, traditional health practitioners are trained and skilled individuals who treat any kind of ailment, disease, and misfortune with physical, psychological, and spiritual procedures based on the belief that the causes of disease and sickness may transcend natural factors. Thus, a medicine man or woman doubles as a psychiatrist, physician, pediatrician, and performer of rituals, to mention a few. Traditional doctors often claim to have been taught the art of medicine by deities and other spiritual beings in dreams, trances, and divination, or through inheritance from their parents who were healers in the past.

Today, traditional healing homes abound in different communities; they have multiple duties as consultation centers and clinics. They are most often the preferred option for patients because patients believe that the healers are dealing with their misfortunes spiritually, as compared to orthodox practitioners. In addition, high rates of poverty make access to modern pharmaceutical and medical treatment difficult. As a result, traditional healing homes are people's first choice for health care. In many government hospitals today, traditional and orthodox health-care services are integrated. Traditional health care remains an integral part of the people's cultural belief.

See also **Charms; Deities: The Òrìṣà; Disease; Divination: Ifá; Divinatory Systems; Health Care; Plants; Spirit Possession**

REFERENCE

Walker, Sheila. *Ceremonial Spirit Possession in Africa and Afro-America.* Leiden: Brill, 1972.

Adépéjú Johnson-Bashua

HERITAGE, CULTURAL: PRESERVATION AND MANAGEMENT

Cultural heritage is a function of human memory manifesting in the tangible and intangible accoutrements of existence. Especially for human beings, memory and the retention of things of practical, emotional, and spiritual value that take the form of cultural materials are critical to our existence. According to UNESCO, cultural heritage is the legacy of physical artifacts and intangible attributes inherited from past generations, maintained in the present, and bestowed for the benefit of future generations. They include buildings and historical places, monuments, artifacts, archaeological materials, architecture, science, and/or technology of a specific culture.

Cultural heritage is one of the most important ways our histories animate, inform, and give meaning to our current actions and experiences. It is a source of knowledge that must not be allowed to be destroyed, especially as it relates to the preservation of Yorùbá civilization. The issue here is that the incursion and spread of Christianity and Islam threaten the validity and provenance of the ancestral cultures of the people. This process is further compounded by the globalizing effects of popular culture and the waves of technology. As a result, much ancestral cultural heritage has been ignored, abandoned, or destroyed in the name of it being vestiges of superstition, primitive society, or idolatry. Bearing in mind how difficult it is for any society to develop without proper use of its traditions and heritage, the danger of the destruction of cultural heritage alluded to here becomes obvious.

Some of the elements of Yorùbá cultural heritage include the creation story or origin of the universe from Ilé-Ifẹ̀, the cradle not just of Yorùbá people but of humanity. The religion consolidates this, with its many deities under the direction and supervision of Olódùmarè, the Supreme Being. The organization of society dovetails with this order, which is preserved through a hierarchical system that is natural and human. Stories (ìtàn) and fables (àálọ́) are constructed to preserve these ideas for the memory of the members of society;

they chronicle the deeds of Olódùmarè, the deities, heroes and heroines, and ancestors. Even more significant than these chronicles is the Yorùbá religion's holy scripture, Ifá, as well as various forms of discourses on the metaphysics of existence in àyájọ́, ọfọ̀, and ògèdè incantations.

Ifá has been transported globally as the foundation of Yorùbá religion to the Americas, and it is preserved as a distinctly Yorùbá heritage in these parts of the world. The works of D. O. Fágúnwà, J. F. Ọdúnjọ, Amos Tutùọlá, Hubert Ògúndé, Fẹ́mi Ọ̀ṣọ́fisan, Dúró Ládipọ̀, Moses Adéjùmọ̀, Akin Ìṣọ̀lá, and Wọlé Ṣóyínká, among many others, have been critical in preserving the heritage of Yorùbá people. In some instances, intangibles are memorials, as in naming people after ancestors, poems, songs, stories, histories, scriptures, mysticisms, myths, legends, and the like. For example, the stories about tortoise (àlọ́ ìjàpá) constitute remarkable philosophical discourses consolidating the moral principles that the people consider important to impart to youth. Yorùbá people have done well globally in preserving their cultural heritage in language, music, dress, family values, sociopolitical organization, body adornments, tattoos, and culinary heritage.

Memorials are the physical, material, or tangible preservation of cultural heritage. In modern society, memorials attract tourists, even when the original meanings of these items may have been lost to the external visitor. As part of the cultural heritage, Yorùbá people have done well historically to preserve memorials as external objects or instruments (material or otherwise) that serve as foci for preserving heritage. Popular memorials include landmark buildings, sites, objects, and art objects such as sculptures, pictures, busts, statues, fountains, and even entire parks and groves. Examples abound in different towns and cities, such as Ọ̀pá Ọ̀rànmíyàn, Orí Olókun, Ọ̀wọ̀n Ògèdèngbé, Ọpọ́n Ifá, Egúngún, Orò, Ààfin, shrines, groves, and the tradition of kingship.

It is hard to imagine a society without memorials documenting their cultural heritage like the Yorùbá people. The documentation and commemoration of past significant events in the lived experiences and historical epochs of individuals and societies include dirges, elegies, poetry, documentaries, fiction, myths, chronicles, histories, monuments, obelisks, building names, structures, infrastructures, holidays, and the commemoration of specific days after events or persons, heroes, and heroines.

There is a grave danger that Yorùbá people may lose their cultural heritage unless urgent steps are taken to preserve endangered aspects of the cultural heritage. So much damage has been done through the denial and destruction of cultural heritage as a result of colonization from the West and the East, and that has been cemented by globalization and popular culture. Yorùbá people need to be wary of becoming the proverbial ọmọ àlè, as "it is only the bastard who disrespects his or her parents." Deliberate efforts must be made to preserve the rich cultural heritage of Yorùbá people for posterity, and modernity should not be used as cover for its destruction—otherwise, others will come to teach the Yorùbá their language, their games, and their value systems.

See also Art: Indigenous; Heritage, Cultural: Sites; Tourism and Leisure; Travel and Exploration

REFERENCE

Béwàjí, J. A. I. *Black Aesthetics*. Trenton, NJ: Africa World Press, 2013.

John Ayọ̀túndé Ìṣọ̀lá Béwàjí

HERITAGE, CULTURAL: SITES

Cultural heritage is the legacy of tangible and intangible attributes of a group or society that are inherited from past generations, maintained in the present, and preserved for the benefit of future generations. Tangible cultural heritage is physical items such as buildings, monuments, landscapes, books, works of art, and artifacts. Intangible cultural heritage includes folklore, traditions (marriage, naming, and burial ceremonies), language, knowledge, and festivals. Natural heritage includes culturally significant landscapes such as rock shelters, waterfalls, caves, and biodiversity.

Tangible cultural heritage is generally split into two groups of movable and immovable items. Immovable heritage includes buildings, which themselves may include artwork such as carved house posts, statues, and the like, and historical places and monuments, such as the Ọ̀rànmíyàn staff in Ilé-Ifẹ̀. Movable heritage includes documents, artwork (terra-cotta, wooden objects, bronze work, and the like), clothing (masquerade dress or ẹkú eégun), and other cultural artifacts depicting the ancestors, heroes or heroines, and professions that are considered worthy of preservation for the future. These include objects significant to the archaeology, architecture, science, or technology of a specific culture such as the *lúwó* potsherd pavement in Ilé-Ifẹ̀ and other Yorùbá towns.

The Yorùbá people are known for their well-established culture and cultural heritage. They are also blessed with numerous natural heritage sites, such as the Olúmọ rock shelter in Abẹ́òkúta, Òkè'Bàdàn in Ìbàdàn, the Olúmirìn waterfall in Ẹ̀rìn Ìjẹ̀ṣà, the Ìkọgòsì spring in Ìkọgòsì Èkìtì, and a host of others. Most of these sites have served humans in their effort to survive in the environment. For instance, remains of the earliest recorded hominid were found in Ìwó Elérù near Ìsàrun in southwestern Nigeria.

Unfortunately, tangible cultural heritage is threatened by many factors: environmental pressure, uncontrolled urban development, globalization, religion, warfare, communal conflicts, poverty, lack of political will, lack of awareness of the value of heritage, low levels of funding, inadequate expertise and equipment, political instability, illicit trafficking, uncontrolled and unprofessional excavation, and outright looting. Intangible heritage, in contrast, is threatened mostly by religion, foreign culture, and the colonial administration that encouraged the abandonment of Yorùbá ways of life for European ways of life. As noted by Webber Ndoro and Herma Kiriama:

> The custody of both the tangible and intangible heritage of African societies are vested in the elders, special custodians, chiefs or and king. With the coming of colonization, however, the African Customary legal system were destroyed and replaced with the European legal system

which unfortunately only recognized and therefore protected tangible heritage to the exclusion of the intangible heritage.

Before the coming of the Europeans, the Yorùbá people appreciated, understood, and cherished their heritage. They adored their heritage and imparted it on their young ones. As early as the age of one year, through different forms of learning and teaching such as storytelling and play, children were taught the rudiments of their culture. Masters handed down, through apprenticeship, the skills for producing objects of importance to Yorùbá heritage. Heritage is also preserved and expressed when masqueraders are brought out or when certain objects come out once a year for festivals. For instance, the cherished *arè* crown, reputed to have been worn by Odùduwà himself, comes out once in a year during the *olójó* festival in Ilé-Ifè town.

The fundamental role of cultural conservation is to preserve and restore, as appropriate, cultural property for present and future generations. We have a lot to learn from the experiences and events of people who have gone before us. However, we cannot learn much from the past if we do not have a record of it. The significance of physical artifacts can be interpreted against the backdrop of socioeconomic, political, ethnic, religious, and philosophical values of a particular group of people. In Yorùbáland, most of the tangible heritage is preserved and conserved in the shrines and groves where houses are built for statues, including terra-cotta, stone, metal, and wooden objects of worship and reference. Monuments are often surrounded by forest; the preservation of these monuments also helps preserve and protect the environment around them. Such forests are referred to as sacred forest (*igbó àìwọ̀* or *igbó àìkò*). The forests are so because they need to be protected from destruction and unauthorized encroachment and to allow easy access for harvesting medicinal herbs.

The management of cultural heritage is vested in the hands of every member of society. Children are taught to pass down the legacy from one generation to the other. Mothers teach their daughters housewifery and home management, praise songs, how to weave their hair, and all other practices associated with females. Male children are taught the family trade and traditions such as hunting, carving, smelting or smithing, molding, and the like.

Tangible heritage is protected by the community through the priests or devotees attached to a monument or practice. It is the daily routine of the priest to see to the protection and preservation of such objects and practices. Festivals are held annually (*ọdọọdún*), weekly (*ìje*), or bimonthly (*ìtàdógún*). Preceding a festival, objects and sites are well kept, and any damaged portions or parts are repaired and preserved against further damage. In the Yorùbá political tradition, the spiritual group plays a prominent role because the Yorùbá place significant emphasis on preserving their heritage.

Unfortunately, with the arrival of foreign culture and religion, the Yorùbá tangible and intangible heritage is facing destruction. With regard to language, most people speak English rather than Yorùbá. Most of the festival groves have been destroyed. In fact, in Ilé-Ifè, as in other urban centers, groves have been demolished to pave the way for building constructions. Festivals are fading away because they are regarded as "satanic" or "uncivilized." A revolution must take place to reawaken and to sensitize the public on the importance of preserving and practicing Yorùbá heritage for future generations.

See also Art: Indigenous; Heritage, Cultural: Preservation and Management; Tourism and Leisure; Travel and Exploration

REFERENCE

Ndoro, Webber, and Herma Kiriama. "Management Mechanisms in Heritage Legislation." In *Cultural Heritage and the Law: Protecting Immovable Heritage in English Speaking Countries of Sub-Saharan Africa*, ed. Webber Ndoro, Kiriama Herma, and George Abungu, 53–64. ICCROM Conservation Studies 8. Rome: International Centre for the Study of the Preservation and Restoration of Cultural Property, 2008.

Àdìsá Ògúnfọlákàn

HERO, HEROINE, AND HEROISM

The Yorùbá concept of heroism is premised on a person's ability and confidence to display exceptional abilities. Heroes and heroines are characterized by their bravery, tactics, smarts, agility, and great enduring spirit while they undertake challenging endeavors. Usually, the concept of heroism is linked to a person's great performance in war, on the job, and in philanthropic deeds. The names *akin* and *akíkanjú* are for hero, heroine, and heroism. Both words can refer to a hero and a heroine.

The concept of heroism can be easily understood from the panegyrics of leading warriors like Ààrẹ-Ọ̀nà-Kakàǹfò, Baṣọ̀run, and Balógun and from the eulogies of kings, chiefs, and other important people. In addition, lineage praise poetry also presents family heroes and their brave deeds; they are ingrained in the historical poetry of men and women who have done what other people in the communities were unable to accomplish.

The concept also refers to the acts of any person who has offered him- or herself as a sacrifice so that his or her people could make progress or have peace. In other words, a hero is a person who is tough, determined, courageous, and adventurous; such a person usually treads on a path filled with danger or serious challenges, a path that other people fear or do not have the courage to pursue or follow to the end. A hero or heroine is not afraid to face obstacles as long as he or she makes up his or her mind on an issue of interest. A hero or heroine is a leader with exemplary tactics, actions, and courage. Such a leader is usually aggressive in the pursuit of his or her mission or public interests and is tactical in his or her approach. The leadership role of a hero or heroine is captured in the Yorùbá saying *olórí-ogun, kò gbọdọ̀ kẹ́hìn ogun; jagunja-gun ní ń bọ̀*—a war commander is never led by anyone; he (or she) leads the warriors.

Most heroes are male warriors. Apart from a few women and religious priests or leaders, most of the heroes (heroines included) are associated with hunting and war. Such leaders include Oníkòyí, the first military leader of the Yorùbá army. He attained this status before Ààrẹ-Ọ̀nà-Kakàǹfò was considered the most powerful person among the ẹ̀ṣọ́, the warriors. The Oníkòyí family and Ààrẹ-Ọ̀nà-Kakàǹfò titleholders are known to be fearless and battle ready.

A few women who have shown bravery in their lives include the mythological Mọrèmi Àjàṣorò, who surrendered herself for sacrifice so that Ilé-Ifẹ̀ could have peace; Fúnmiláyọ̀ Kútì, who led women in Abẹòkúta to challenge tax imposition in the first half of the twentieth century; and Kudirat Abíọlá, who fought valiantly for democracy in Nigeria in 1993 and was murdered for her activities.

There are also regional or local heroes and heroines. For example, among the Ìjẹ̀ṣà, Ògèdèǹgbé Agbó-gungbórò is a hero; in Ìbàdàn, Baṣọ̀run Ògúnmọ́lá and Àjàyí Ògbóríẹfọ̀n are heroes, Ẹfúnṣetán is a heroine; and in Ilé-Ifẹ̀, Mọrèmi is a heroine. Besides local heroes, there are national heroes and heroines. These are heroes and heroines whose veneration covers the entire Yorùbáland. The Ààrẹ-Ọ̀nà-Kakàǹfò titleholders are good examples. Fúnmiláyọ̀ Kútì, the first female to drive a vehicle in Nigeria and the first woman to lead a group of women against the tax imposed on women, belongs to the group of national heroes. The implication of Mọrèmi Àjàṣorò's sacrifice for the Yorùbá race also qualifies her as a national heroine.

Today, the words *hero*, *heroine*, and *heroism* apply to every endeavor of the Yorùbá. Besides war, they extend to politics, economy, science, religion, sports, and other aspects of life. For example, Moshood Káṣìmawò Abíọ́lá, whose free and fair presidential election was annulled in 1993, became a national hero of democracy in Nigeria after his sudden death in 1998. Chief Ọbáfẹ́mi Awólọ́wọ̀'s successful political career made him a political hero, and Wọlé Ṣóyínká's great achievement in creative writing made him a literary hero. They are just few examples to illustrate modern-day Yorùbá heroes.

See also **Abíọ́lá, Moshood Káṣìmawò Abíọ́lá; Awólọ́wọ̀, Ọbáfẹ́mi; Deities (The Òrìṣà); Lineages and Cognomen (Oríkì Orílẹ̀); Praise Poetry and Eulogy (Oríkì); Ṣóyínká, Wọlé**

REFERENCE

Ládélé, T. A. A., Oyèbámijí Mustapha, I. A. Awórìndé, Oyèdèmí Oyèrìndé, and Ọlátúnbọ̀sún Ọládàpọ̀. Àkójọpọ̀ Ìwadìí Àṣà Yorùbá. Ìbàdàn (Nigeria): Macmillan Nigeria Publishers, 1986.

Báyọ̀ Ọmọlọlá

HISTORIOGRAPHY

Archaeological and historical findings at Ìwó Elérù by Thurtsan Shaw, at Ifẹ̀ by Frank Willet and William Fagg, at Ọ̀yọ́ by Garlake and Agbájé Williams, and in other places, confirm that human habitation in Yorùbá country dates back to prehistoric times. For most of history in a nonliterate society, the Yorùbá preserved and transmitted their history through oral traditions, myths, folklore, verbal and plastic arts, as well as rituals and ceremonies. The copious and extensive Ifá literary corpus (odù); the wide variety of oríkì or praise poems of individuals, lineages, and communities; and proverbs, songs, and poems (àròfọ̀) are veritable sources of history.

The most historically oriented of these sources, such as the oral traditions, are subject to distortion, embellishment, and rationalization for political and other gains. Ensuring validity will require internal analysis to check for consistency and accuracy; to collect, compare, and analyze variants of the same traditions; and corroborate and crosscheck with linguistic, archaeological, and written sources. However, many of these traditions have been collected and written down, of which the earliest and the most comprehensive was Samuel Johnson's The History of the Yorùbás (1921). Although focused mainly on early Ifẹ̀ and Ọ̀yọ́ history, Johnson's book remained the most widely referenced sourcebook on Yorùbá history. Johnson's example was followed by others, such as Adéyẹmí and Ọ̀jó Badà on Ọ̀yọ́ and Ṣakí, Akínyẹlé on Ìbàdàn, Ògúntúyì on Adó Èkìtì and Ìkéṛé, Ashára on Ọ̀wọ̀, Ajíṣafẹ́ and Lósì on Abẹ́òkúta, Lósì on Lagos, and Abíọ́lá on Ìjẹ̀sà.

Written sources on the Yorùbá before the mid-nineteenth century were extremely limited. The earliest glimpses appeared in Arabic scripts composed by the Yorùbá's Hausa Muslim neighbors to the north.

More extensive references to the Yorùbá began to appear in European travelers' accounts beginning from the early sixteenth century and increasing steadily during the nineteenth century due to European Christian missionary and commercial penetration into the interior. While these accounts and reports were often tendentious and quite limited because the writers visited only a few places, the information provided proved quite valuable for contemporary history of the time. European colonial rule also generated a written historical record. The practice of indirect rule required knowledge of the history of the community, resulting in colonial commissioned reports, dubbed "intelligence" or "assessment" reports, that documented the basic political history of the community and provided information that have proved useful to historians.

The achievement of independence and the rise of a new class of Western-educated elite led to the development of nationalist and modern academic historiography. Yorùbáland benefited, which resulted in a sustained effort to produce academic works on different areas and themes of Yorùbá history. In 1957, Sàbúrì Bíòbákú wrote The Ẹ̀gbá and Their Neighbours, 1842-1872. Bíòbákú's work was followed by others, such as I. A. Akínjógbìn's Dahomey and Its Neighbours, 1708-1818 (1967) and other works. In modern times, important works have focused on various subjects, such as the fall of Ọ̀yọ́ Empire; the Ìjẹ̀bú; the causes, course, and consequences of the Yorùbá wars; the rise of Ìbàdàn; slavery and the slave trade; Christian missionaries; the Yorùbá intelligentsia; Islam and Ìlọrin; kingship; women and gender; Lagos; and the different regions in Yorùbáland.

See also **History; Oral Tradition**

REFERENCES

Bíòbákú, S. O., ed. Sources of Yorùbá History. Oxford, UK: Clarendon Press, 1973.

Fálọlá, Tóyìn, ed. Yorùbá Historiography, Madison: University of Wisconsin, 1991.

Fúnṣọ́ Afọláyan

The primacy of Ilé-Ifẹ̀ in the origin, life, and history of the Yorùbá is widely acknowledged. Regarded as the cradle of the race, the source or *orírun* of the people and their civilization, Ilé-Ifẹ̀ was the earliest or one of the earliest centers of sociopolitical development in Yorùbá country. At the center of these developments was the personality of Odùduwà, widely regarded as the founder of the Yorùbá race, its first crowned ruler, and the ancestor of the principal royal dynasties. On arriving at Ifẹ̀, Odùduwà fought, defeated, and eventually incorporated the aboriginal groups into his new kingdom. After a long and successful reign, demographic expansion, drought, diseases, personal ambition, and other factors precipitated a series of migrations and dispersals led by scions of the Odùduwà family from Ilé-Ifẹ̀ to other parts of Yorùbá country. New states and kingdoms emerged and claimed dynastic connection with the Ilé-Ifẹ̀ royal family and thus the right to wear the beaded crown with fringe. Much remains unknown about Ifẹ̀ history. However, by the thirteenth century, it was a well-developed state, noted for its social, economic, political, aesthetic, and artistic sophistication, evident in its uniquely specialized and incomparable bronze and terra-cotta sculptures. Many of these sculptures can be found in leading museums all over the world.

Beyond Ilé-Ifẹ̀, kingdoms flourished in many parts of Yorùbá country. One of the earliest, and certainly most powerful, of these was Ọ̀yọ́. Located some two hundred miles to the north of Ile-Ifẹ̀ and founded by Ọ̀rànmíyàn, a descendant of Odùduwà, Ọ̀yọ́ gained many advantages from its location in a fertile region, participation in the trans-Saharan and transatlantic slave trades, and succession of a line of able leaders; it emerged as the most powerful state in the West African Niger-Volta region. By the sixteenth century, Ọ̀yọ́ had incorporated into its expanding empire central and western Yorùbá groups as well as much of Nupe-, Borgu-, Fon-, and Aja-speaking peoples.

At the center of this empire was the *aláàfin*. Regarded as a sacred king and saluted as *ọba aláyélúwà* (the king and lord of the world and of life), the *aláàfin* ruled with the advice of his chiefs, most especially the seven-member council known as Ọ̀yọ́ Mèsì. The Ọ̀yọ́ Mèsì included representatives of the principal lineages in the capital town. To the east of Ifẹ̀ and Old Ọ̀yọ́, in the wooded hills of Ìjẹ̀ṣà and rocky landscapes of Èkìtì and Ìgbómìnà, several kingdoms proliferated. The most notable of these were the kingdoms of Iléṣà, ruled by the Ọwá; Oǹdó, ruled by the Òsemàwé; the numerous Ìgbómìnà kingdoms, of which the most notable were Ìlá, ruled by the Ọ̀ràngún, and Àjàṣẹ́, ruled by the Olúpo; the sixteen kingdoms of Èkìtì; and Ọ̀wọ̀. Beginning in the fifteenth century, proximity ensured that several of these kingdoms came under increasing military, economic, and political pressure and influence of the Ọ̀yọ́ Empire and the Edo kingdom of Benin.

To the west, the Yorùbá world extended beyond the present boundary of Nigeria to the Republic of Benin, where kingdoms flourished in precolonial times, of which the most notable were Kétu, Sábẹ, and Ìdásà. Ruled on and off by the Ọ̀yọ́ Empire, these kingdoms became a buffer zone in the imperial struggle between Ọ̀yọ́ and Dahomey during the eighteenth and early nineteenth centuries. To the south and southwest of Ilé-Ifẹ̀ were the kingdoms of Ìjẹ̀bú, noted for their exclusivity, hostility to strangers, and intense local patriotism; the state of Òwu, noted for its early militarism; the numerous but federated towns of Ẹ̀gbá before their unification and liberation from Ọ̀yọ́ under Lísàbi during the last decade of the nineteenth century; and the decentralized states and towns of Ẹ̀gbádò, Ànàgó, and Àwórì, of which the most notable were Ìlarò, Ìjànnà, Ọ̀tà, Badagry, and Lagos. Commercial and imperial pressures from Ọ̀yọ́ and Dahomey, and later from the European slave traders and imperialists, especially over control of the slave and palm trade at the coast, constantly threatened the autonomy and integrity of these states.

While it lasted, Ọ̀yọ́ was a source of order and stability for much of Yorùbá country. Its decline started during the late eighteenth century, and it eventually collapsed early in the nineteenth century, arising from internal squabbles between the *aláàfin* and his principal chiefs. These squabbles weakened the military balance and effectiveness of its army; accompanied by revolts of the Nupe, Borgu, and Ẹ̀gbá vassal states and the Fulani Jihadist invasion from Ìlọrin, Yorùbá country was thrown into a vortex of civil wars which lasted until the end of the nineteenth century. The defeat of Ọ̀yọ́ and the sacking of its capital led to a demographic exodus to central and southern Yorùbáland. Depleted of its population, previously important old towns, such as Ìkòyí and Òwu, disappeared from the map. To the south, refugees of war augmented old towns like in Ile-Ifẹ̀ and Oǹdó.

Of the new towns, the most notable were New Ọ̀yọ́, the military republican state of Ìbàdàn; the autocratic state of Ìjàiyè; and the military-dominated but loosely federated Ẹ̀gbá state of Abẹ́òkúta. All of these new towns competed with one another for power and dominance. The defeat and elimination of Kúrunmí's Ìjàiyè by Ìbàdàn in 1862 left the latter fighting on many fronts against Ìlọrin, the Èkìtìparapọ̀ in the north, and the Ẹ̀gbá and Ìjẹ̀bú in the south. The stalemate was eventually broken by the imposition of British rule.

British rule enhanced the prestige and authority of traditional rulers and institutions. It encouraged the planting of cash crops such as cotton and cocoa. It resulted in improved and newly built roads, railways, telegraphs, and harbors. New religions such as Islam and Christianity spread, and a new class of Western-educated elite emerged. Many of these elite became prominent in the nationalist struggle for independence and active in the social, economic, and political developments of postindependence Nigeria.

See also **Historiography; Ìbàdàn Empire; Ifẹ̀ Kingdom; Oral Tradition; Ọ̀yọ́ Empire**

REFERENCES

Smith, Robert. *Kingdoms of the Yorùbá*. Madison: University of Wisconsin Press, 1988.

Akíntóyè, S. A. *A History of the Yorùbá*. Dakar: Amalion Publishers, 2010.

Fúnṣọ́ Afọláyan

HOMAGE (ÌBÀ)

The word for homage is *ìbà*, which comprises of two morphological components: *ì* (the act or fact of) and *bà*, which refers to fermenting; perching or marking something for future possession; or hitting a target, all of which evoke an assumption of focused humility, intentionality, sobriety, helplessness, vulnerability, and more. *Jíjúbà* means the act of paying homage and *júbà* is to pay homage. The Yorùbá take this as a very important aspect of their sociology of interaction. It connotes humility on the part of the individuals who honors it and uses it in its appropriate context.

Comprehensive Nature of *ìbà*

Homage is paid to everyone and everything in the culture. There is an expression of comprehensive totality in the way this aspect of the culture is constructed. A chant artist, for example, may start the performance by rendering the following lines:

Mo júbà ọmọdé;
Mo júbà àgbà;
Mo júbà ọkùnrin,
Mo júbà obìnrin.
Ìyá arúgbó eléyín wẹlẹmu.
Ìbàa rẹ!

I pay homage to the youngsters;
I pay homage to the elders;
I pay homage to men;
I pay homage to women.
The aged woman with no teeth left in the mouth,
Homage to you!

Natural and Supernatural Phenomena

Homage is paid to the gods and other supernatural forces, unforeseeable to the naked eyes. Thus:

Mo júbà akọ́dá.
Mo júbà aṣẹ̀dá.
Mo júbà Ọlọ́jọ́.
Mo júbà Arẹ̀sà.
Mo júbà ọ̀kànlénirinwó irúnmọlẹ̀—
Tó ti ìkọ̀lé ọrun bọ̀ wá sí tayé.

Mo júbà àwọn ìyáa mi òṣòròǹgà—
Ajojú-jẹmú
Ajèfun èèyàn má bì.

I pay homage to the primordial creation or first to
    be created.
I pay homage to the creator.
I pay homage to the owner of the day.
I pay homage to the owner of the lagoon.
I pay homage to 401 divinities—
Who descended from the heavens into the earthly
    plane.
I pay homage to the vindictive spirit of witches—
Those who eat the eyes and the noses,
Devouring human entrails without throwing up.

The popular *jùjú* musician King Sunny Adé rendered a similar version of the same utterance when
he sang:

Ìbà akódá
T'ó dá tiè sórí ewé;
Ìbà aṣèdá
Tó dá tiè sílè pèpè
Mo ṣe'bà èyin alayé
Ẹ jé kí n jayé orí mi.

I pay homage to the primordial creation or first to
    be created
Whose creation took place on the surface of the
    leaf.
I pay homage to the creator of humans;
Whose creation took place on the bare surface of
    the earth.
I pay homage to you powers that be
So you may let me live out my full destiny.

Clearly, homage is paid to natural and supernatural
phenomena and is used as a celebration of entry—
physically and metaphysically. For example, it is common to hear artists chant:

Onílé,
Mo bodè kí n tó wọlé;
Àgùàlà,
Mo bodè oṣù

Ajá òṣùpá,
Mo bodè f'Ọlọrun Ọba

Owner of the house,
I pay homage before entering;
Venus,
I pay homage to the early moon;
Dog constellation,
I pay homage to the King of the Sky.

The Human Anatomy

From head to toe, homage is paid even to body parts. It
is said, for example:

Mo júbà pélébé ọwó
Mo júbà pèlèbè ẹsè;
Mo júbà àtélẹsè
T'ó d'orí kodò tí kò hurun.

I pay homage to the bare hand
I pay homage to the bare feet;
I pay homage to the underfoot
That stays flat to the ground without the hair.

The Power and Sacredness of *Ìbà*

The people believe that when homage is paid, impossible acts are made possible. This is why it is often said,
b'ékòló bá júbà ilè, ilè a lanu (if the earthworm pays homage to the ground, the ground will split asunder).

    Not paying homage incurs heavy cultural sanctions
on the person of the perpetrator because it implies
deliberate violation and desecration of a sacred cultural
norm, an oppositional deviance that is viewed with dis-
paragement in the context of oral discourses. Thus:

Ewúrẹ wọlé kò kágò
Ó di mímúso;
Àgùntàn wọlé kò kágò
Ó di mímúso.
Àgbébò adìẹ tó bá wọlé tí ò kágò
Omitooro níí ṣe síni lẹnu

A goat that enters the house without paying homage
Opens itself to entrapment (leashing, tethering) to
    the post.

A sheep that enters the house without paying
   homage
Opens itself to entrapment (leashing, tethering) to
   the post.
A rooster that enters the house without paying
   homage
Becomes a condiment for the tasty stew.

To underscore the sacredness of paying homage and the extreme polarity of the consequences of not paying homage to those to whom it is due, tradition has it that Ọ̀rúnmìlà, the oracular divinity, once had eight sons, all of whom were appointed royal kingships of traditional Yorùbá kingdoms—Alárá, Ajerò, Ọlóyẹ́mọyin, Alákégi, Oṅtagi-Ọ̀lẹ́lẹ́, Ẹlẹ́jẹ̀lúmọ̀pé, Ọwáràngún Àga, and Ọlọ́wọ̀. It was the tradition of Ọ̀rúnmìlà to hold an annual feast for all his young monarchs. All his children would pay homage to him at the outset of the occasion. One year, the youngest of them all, Ọlọ́wọ̀, refused to pay homage to the grand patriarch on the audacious assumption that it was below the dignity of a royalty to pay homage to another. While the older brothers received rewards from their father, the audacity led to a major altercation, which prompted the disrobing of the discourteous son and the mythical withdrawal of the oracle from the earthly plane. In addition, Ọ̀rúnmìlà took along with him all elements of peace and normalcy. The consequence was devastating as the sociology and ecology of the human race turned upside down, and there was utter pandemonium, which almost resulted in a complete annihilation of the human race—but for the timely intervention of the gods. All this underscores the place of homage among the Yorùbá, for whom the concept is of great magnitude in traditional society.

See also **Words:** Ọ̀rọ̀

REFERENCE

Abímbọ́lá, Wándé. *Ifá: An Exposition of Ifá Literary Corpus.* Ìbàdàn (Nigeria): Oxford University Press, 1976.

Michael Ọládèjọ Afọláyan

In the colonial era and for part of the twentieth century, the Yorùbá lived in communities where the primary unit was *agbo-ilé*, a compound of extended family groups. The communities had two layers of settlements: the village (farm) and the town (commercial or market). In times of peace, the villages and towns evolved as families, grew larger, and expanded their farming landholdings and commercial activities. A number of *agbo-ilé* made up a village or town, which often comprised the same ethnic subgroup, with a common ancestry. Most Ìjẹ̀bú villages and towns followed this pattern. However, in times of war, town settlement comprised many *agbo-ilé* of allies in war. Hence, in Abẹ́òkúta, Òwu households exist alongside Ẹ̀gbá households. In Ìbàdàn, Ìsàlẹ̀-Ìjẹ̀bú exists side by side with the Ọ̀yọ́ at Ọjà-Ọba in the center of the city.

Each *agbo-ilé* was often named after the occupation of the founder or the head of the household. For example, *agbo-ilé* Jagun or Balógun was the household of a warrior or head of the army; *agbo-ilé* Olóólà was the household of the tattooist, or surgeon who specialized in circumcision and tribal marks; *agbo-ilé* Ọlọ́na was the household of the fine artist; *agbo-ilé* Ìyálájé was the household of the head of women traders; *agbo-ilé* Aláró was the household of the dyers; and *agbo-ilé* Olúọ́dẹ was the household of the head of hunters.

Each *agbo-ilé* has many domestic groups, including *àwọn àgbà ilé*, elders of the household; *àwọn ìyálé ilé*, first wives of the members of the household; *àwọn ìyàwó ilé*, junior wives of the household; *àwọn ọmọ ilé*, children of the household; *àwọn ọmọ ìyá (iyèkan)*, children of the same mother; *àwọn ọmọ baba (ọbàkan)*, children of the same father; and *àwọn mọlẹ́bí*, relatives. Some households had *àwọn ẹrú*, slaves, and *àwọn ìwọ̀fà*, pawns or bondsmen.

Each domestic group performed functions and duties that ensured the smooth running of the household. For example, elders were often responsible for settlement of domestic disputes, dispersing the assets of the deceased, choosing spouses for the young adults, and arranging weddings and funerals. While children ran errands for the elders, junior wives did the cooking, laundry, and cleaning. For example, Tóyìn Fálọlá in his first memoir reported that he grew up in an *agbo-ilé* and could not identify his biological mother among the four wives in the household until he was ten years old.

Only two features of the elaborate old household structure and function of the domestic groups persist in modern times. First, kingship and chieftaincy succession and the accompanied political rites and benefits are based on the old households' positions within the hierarchy of village head (*baálẹ̀*) and town or city king (*ọba*). Second, there is a growing industry of events and ceremonial functionaries who earn their livelihood from organizing various events, including funerals of household dignitaries; conferment ceremonies and celebrations of *oyè ìdílé* household chieftaincy and kingship titles; and society weddings, especially the traditional introduction of the bride's and groom's families.

See also **Kinship**

REFERENCE

Fálọlá, Tóyìn. *A Mouth Sweeter Than Salt: An African Memoir.* Ann Arbor: University of Michigan Press, 2004.

Bọ́lá Dáúdà

HUNTING

In traditional society, hunting was one of the most revered professions. Hunters occupied a high position because of the several crucial roles they performed. They were brave and strong men and women of valor who possessed arms and ammunitions, earned a living from hunting, enforced laws, provided security, protected kingdoms, hunted game, and supplied meat to society. They fought in all Yorùbá wars, including Ọ̀yọ́ Empire wars, the Àgbẹ́kòyà uprising, and the Èkìtìparapọ̀ wars. They also participated actively in the social and literary life of Yorùbá communities as poets and artists producing and performing oral poetry or *ìjálá* and the *ìrèmòjé* dirge, which celebrated the death of their colleagues.

Hunters are typically the subject of *ìjálá* poetry, and they use the genre as a panegyric tool for self and communal promotion, to contest individual and collective representations, and to teach history. One of the most popular *ìjálá* call-and-response songs often rendered at hunters' gatherings for entertainment and didactic purposes is about a proverbial Ògúndélé who defiantly rejected pounded yam (the most cherished Yorùbá meal) and ate plantain (a less desirable food) for supper: *ọjọ́ Ògúndélé kọyán ọ̀gẹ̀dẹ̀ ló jẹ sùn, yíyó ló yó.*

Hunters participate in various festivals to showcase their roles and activities. Most, if not all, of them are adherents of polytheistic traditional religion and worship Ògún, the god of iron, because they work with iron. Since they are Ògún worshippers, Ògún is a common prefix to their names, such as Ògúnwọlé (Ògún, the god of iron, has arrived at home), Ògúngbèmí (Ògún, the god of iron, protects me), and Ògúntóyìn (Ògún, the god of iron, is enough to be praised). Since the Yorùbá word for hunters is *ọdẹ*, it also functions as a prefix to many hunters' names, such as Ọdẹlọlá (hunting is wealth), Ọdẹ́wálé (the hunter has returned home), and Ọdẹ́jídé (the hunter has been resurrected).

Hunters feature prominently in early Yorùbá writings, such as those by author D. O. Fágúnwà, who writes of hunters' diplomacy and bravery. Most of Fágúnwà's books deal with the forest, and hunters are protagonists, heroes, and diplomats. The literal translation of Wọlé Ṣóyínká's *Ògbójú Ọdẹ Nínú Igbó Irúnmalẹ̀* (*The Forest of a Thousand Daemons*) is "the brave hunter in the forest of Irúnmalẹ̀." Other translated works that prominently feature hunters include Ṣóyínká's *Igbó Olódùmarè* (*In the Forest of Olódùmarè*) and Dàpọ̀ Adéníyì's *Ìrìnkerindò Nínú Igbó Elégbèje* (*Expedition to the Mount of Thought*).

Hunters must undergo rigorous training and learn codes of behavior—and the punishment for breaking these codes—as part of their guild requirements. Part of hunters' ethics is the requirement that they respect their weapons and not use them irresponsibly. They must also be circumspect in their choice of animals to kill. It is, therefore, unusual for a hunter to kill baby animals, even in the wild; they are usually released to grow into adulthood.

See also **Translation, Wildlife: Preservation, Hunting, and Destruction**

REFERENCES

Àlàbí, Adétáyò. "'I Am the Hunter Who Kills Elephants and Baboons': The Autobiographical Component of the Hunters' Chant." *Research in African Literatures* 38.3 (Fall 2007): 13–23.

Ṣekoní, Olúrópò. "Mechanism and Meaning in Yorùbá *Ìjálá*." *Ba Shiru* 8.1 (1977): 31–36.

Adétáyò Àlàbí

ÌBÀDÀN EMPIRE

Ìbàdàn is one of the ancient towns founded by eminent adventurers who dispersed or migrated from Ilé-Ifẹ̀ to found other lands. It was established almost at the same time as its Ẹ̀gbá neighbors: Ìdó, Ọ̀jọ́ọ̀, Ìká, and Òwu town of Ẹ̀rùnmu.

Oral tradition revealed that the Ọ̀yọ́ army destroyed the first Ìbàdàn. This was the time of Lágelú, one of the founding figures. Ìbàdàn, at this time, comprised areas around Òkè'Bàdàn Hill near Àwòtan Market to as far as Orí-Iyangí. The fall of the first Ìbàdàn was not unconnected with an incident that occurred during an annual Egúngún festival, where the secret of the masquerades was exposed. Ọ̀yọ́, consequent to this unfortunate incident, deployed its army against Ìbàdàn and the town was sacked. On account of its war, Ìbàdàn people fled in different directions, then returned to Orí-Iyangí after the war.

The reconstitution of Ìbàdàn notwithstanding, it had no specific importance other than as a roadside market until the internal crisis in Ọ̀yọ́ and the marauding activities of its chiefs, especially Baṣọ̀run and Tóyèjẹ, the *baálẹ̀* of Ògbómọ̀ṣọ́. These individuals formed a band of marauders, called the *ògo-wẹẹrẹ*, who terrorized the different communities under Ọ̀yọ́'s suzerainty. Many fled from these Ọ̀yọ́ communities and settled at Ìbàdàn and other relatively unknown towns and villages. A large number of people came from Ìjẹ̀bú, Ilé-Ifẹ̀, Ìṣẹri, Old Ọ̀yọ́, and Òwu. The *baálẹ̀*,

Olówu Akínjọbí, led the Òwu people. Máyẹ̀ Okùnadé and Lábọ́sìndé, an elderly man of great intelligence, grace, and military experience, led the band of migrants from Ilé-Ifẹ̀, while Lákanlẹ̀, also a brave, but young, warrior, led the Ọ̀yọ́ group.

This development radically transformed Ìbàdàn. On the one hand, the population increased to such a point that Ìbàdàn could defend itself. On the other hand, the different migrants brought to Ìbàdàn different skills and expertise that, under strong leadership, became of great importance to Ìbàdàn. For instance, with Máyẹ̀ Okùnadé, Lábọ́sìndé, and Lákanlẹ̀, Ìbàdàn successfully built a standing army and attained importance by sending a contingent of warriors, led by Okùnadé, to the Ìpẹ́ru front.

A major problem with this development was that Ìbàdàn evolved to become a composite town, especially as each of these migrant groups was allowed to settle in different parts of Ìbàdàn, each governed by its different leaders. The leaders of Ìbàdàn achieved a balance and were able to maintain peace by diplomacy. For instance, in an effort to foster security and cultivate a healthy relationship with the immigrant population, which had far outstripped the proto-Ìbàdàn people, the leader of Ìbàdàn gave his daughter in marriage to Olówu Akínjọbí. Okùnadé and Lábọ́sìndé (both from Ilé-Ifẹ̀) controlled the army. However, the precarious nature of this administrative style led to destruction. Akínjọbí was not pleased, and civil war ensued. Okùnadé led the army to quell the internal crisis and

159

sacked the indigenous leadership, becoming the first effective *baálè* of Ìbàdàn. Lábósìndé was the Baba-Ìsàlè, and Lákanlè was recognized officially as the leader of the Òyó group. The different migrant groups occupied different parts, and leaders were appointed among them to keep the peace. These leaders regularly met with the *baálè* in the general administration of Ìbàdàn. While the Òyó and Ifè migrants settled at Ojà-Ọba, the Ìjèbú migrants settled around Ìsàlè-Ìjèbú, and the Ègbá migrants at Yéọsà.

The emergence of Ìbàdàn as a strong power and successor to the Old Òyó Empire began in 1841, when Ìbàdàn successfully conquered the Fulani Jihadists at Òsogbo. It soldiers went on to conquer Ìjàyè, and in 1860, it crushed the Iléṣà Revolt. Over the following ten years, Ìbàdàn developed into an empire. Having conquered Ìjàyè, Ìbàdàn consolidated its power by conquering towns and cities in Àkókó, Èkìtì, Ìgbómìnà, and Ìjèṣà areas between 1847 and 1870. In addition, many towns and cities voluntarily came under Ìbàdàn's control. For instance, Òsogbo, Ìwó, and many other towns and cities in the Òsun areas voluntarily sought protection from Ìbàdàn given their closeness to Ìlọrin, the seat of the Fulani Jihadists.

Although Ìbàdàn's war of expansion was largely successful, it met stiff opposition from the Ìjèṣà areas. However, Iléṣà, the fulcrum and lever of the opposition fell to Ìbàdàn in 1870, which marked the zenith of Ìbàdàn's power. Expansion, however, came with requirements, especially the need to administer a very large area. Like the Old Òyó before it, Ìbàdàn also adopted the use of resident officials, *ajélè*, in the subordinate towns. The system required that a resident official be appointed for each town or village. This resident official was controlled by a chief and representative of the Ìbàdàn *baálè*—hence, the name *baba kékeré*. In this way, Ìbàdàn chiefs distributed these subordinate towns and villages among themselves and derived income and loyalty from them on behalf of Ìbàdàn.

Quality of administration depended on the resident official and the chief. Leaders relied on harsh methods to obtain material wealth and keep the peace. Most of chiefs and resident officials abused their positions. Very soon, Ìbàdàn gained a reputation for oppression and arrogance, especially in the Ìjèṣà areas and other areas along the eastern corridors of Yorùbáland. The Ìjèṣà and Èkìtì allied together as the Èkìtìparapò, and they resisted the highhandedness of Ìbàdàn chiefs and resident officials.

The Ìbàdàn Empire developed and gained a reputation not only because of its warfare, prosperity, and brutality of its chiefs and resident officials but also because of its social mobility. It was the place where even a slave could rise to the top of the social hierarchy. Just as Ìbàdàn chiefs and lords enslaved others, especially along the eastern corridor of Yorùbáland, slaves who distinguished themselves in warfare and in commerce gained independence, socioeconomic importance, and political influence. Many slaves even had slaves of their own.

In this way, Ìbàdàn gained fame as a community where a commoner could rise by sheer enterprise. This fame played a fundamental role in bringing more and more people to Ìbàdàn. The empire was, however, short lived; it was defeated in 1876 during the Kírìjì War while the Ààrè Mómòh Látòsísà was on the throne.

See also **Èkìtìparapò War; Òyó Empire**

REFERENCE

Fálọlá, Tóyìn. *Politics and Economy in Ìbàdàn, 1893-1945*. Ìbàdàn (Nigeria): Modelor Press, 1989.

Bùkólá Oyèníyì

ILÉ-IFÈ

Ilé-Ifè is widely regarded as the ancestral homeland of the Yorùbá people and their religious headquarters. The city symbolizes the genesis of the totality of Yorùbá ethnicity, and that is why the town is popularly referred to as *orísun*, the source. As such, particularly in matters of traditional belief systems and mode of worship, the town is a common referent and rallying point. Ifè-Ifè is located in the heart of Yorùbáland. In the present time, Ilé-Ifè has remained the stronghold of indigenous religious worship; only one day is said to be free of traditional ceremonies and rituals. Worship and celebration through festivals commemorate the 401 gods and deities; the *ọ̀ọni* is the sole living legend.

Strategically positioned on the border of the northern forest region and close to trade routes, Ilé-Ifẹ̀ was an important urban center before the arrival of the Portuguese in West Africa in the fifteenth century. The origin of Ilé-Ifẹ̀—the acclaimed cradle of Yorùbá people and its founder, Odùduwà—was lost in antiquity and remains cloudy. It has generated a lot of controversy and debate between and among oral traditional and academic historians. However, from numerous historical and archaeological investigations, it has been well established that people migrated out of Ilé-Ifẹ̀ to establish many other Yorùbá towns and cities. This is evidenced in the discovery of archaeological evidence, especially potsherd pavements, popularly known as *àpáàdìi lúwó*, in almost all notable towns and in the Diaspora, such as Benin Republic, Togo, and Ghana.

Ilé-Ifẹ̀ was and is the source and center for kings of numerous kingdoms, including Ọ̀yọ́ (the present *aláàfin* of Ọ̀yọ́ took his sword of office from Ọ̀rànmíyàn Grove), Benin, Kétu, Ìjẹ̀bú, Ẹ̀gbá, Èkìtì, Àkókó, and others. Ilé-Ifẹ̀ still confers legitimacy on these rulers. The fact is still evident today, as many Yorùbá rulers across West African trace the source of their beaded crowns to Ilé-Ifẹ̀.

Before the advent of Odùduwà administration, the autochthonous rulers in Ilé-Ifẹ̀ were scattered all over the region. Ọ̀ràńfẹ̀, Ọrẹlúere, and Ọbàtálá were among the paramount leaders. The physiography of the Ifẹ̀ region encouraged interactions among her inhabitants. The settlements were within a spherical valley encircled by steep-sided hills. No wonder, then, that Odùduwà centralized the political administration and government by placing the palace (*ààfin*), the seat of power, at the center of the town. Although the lineage settlements were bound together in what seemed like formal political alliances or confederacies, each of them was somewhat independent. The basis for forming any confederation was an element of cooperation, but the political integration of the communities only

extended so far. The confederacy was not considered a single indivisible unit; each of the component parts continued to retain its political autonomy.

The alliance was thus a loose one. There was no central chieftaincy system, leadership was vested in an individual, and leadership rotated among leaders of the component settlements. For instance, the first leader of the confederacy was the head of the Òkè-Ọ̀rà lineage-community, Ọ̀ràńfẹ̀ (*ọ̀rà tí ó ni Ifẹ̀*, the Ọ̀rà who owns Ifẹ̀). The reign of Ọ̀ràńfẹ̀ was dated to the time of creation (*igbá ìwáṣẹ̀*), and he was succeeded by Ọbàtálá, the head of the Ìdíta community. The confederacy was also elastic enough to accommodate settlements that accepted the idea of mutual cooperation. However, membership in the confederacy was voluntary, and it was presumed that any settlement could pull out of the alliance when its leader so wished.

With the coming of Odùduwà, the administration was centralized, and Odùduwà assumed leadership. In addition, those who followed Odùduwà settled near the palace. Àgbọnnìrègún (Baba Ifá) relocated from Òkè-Ìgẹ̀tí to Òkè-Ìtasẹ̀, whose name changed to Òkè Àgbọnnìrègún. Ògún, the pathfinder, also settled at Òkè-Mògún near Òkè-Àgbọnnìrègún. Other rulers or leaders of the autochthonous communities relocated to the center: Ọbàtálá left Ìdíta-Oko for Ìdíta-Ilé, and Ọbàlọràn led the people of ìlọràn to the present-day Ìlódè area. Ọbàlarà, Ọbameeri, Ọbaláayẹ, Ọbaléèjùgbẹ̀, and others also relocated to their present area. This resulted in the clustering of the settlements around that of Odùduwà and in the formal emergence of Ilé-Ifẹ̀ as a cosmopolitan city.

A major innovation of this era was the building of a wall to encircle the cluster of settlements. The transformation of the loose alliance of the pre-Odùduwà era into a permanent one established the first dynastic state or kingdom in the region. Unlike the pre-Odùduwà period, the leadership was not rotated among the heads of the predynastic groups but was monopolized by the Odùduwà group, which set itself up as the ruling dynasty. The monopoly of symbols of royalty and political authority lay in the hand of Odùduwà group. They reserved exclusive rights over the use of the *are* crown, which was a symbol of superior authority.

One problem beset the successions to the Ifẹ throne from the beginning: the system left the choice of successor from among members of the royal family open. Unlike in Benin, where succession to throne was by primogeniture (succession by only the first son of the king), Ifẹ had chosen to give the highest chiefs the power to choose the new ọọni from among princes of the royal family, including sons and grandsons of former kings. The system became the abiding Ifẹ system and later the typical Yorùbá system.

Ifẹ is widely recognized as the oldest dynastic state formed by the Yorùbá. Ilé-Ifẹ, the capital city, has the reputation of being one of the longest continuously inhabited centers south of the Niger River. Three major groups—Àgbà Ifẹ, Modéwá, and Ìsòrò—held the kingship or palace administration, or the Ìhàrèfà. In Yorùbá politics, spiritual and secular affairs were intertwined. No major political or economic decision was taken without adequate consultation with the Ìsòrò. Members of the Ìhàrèfà or Àgbà Ifẹ were the civil chiefs through whom the ọọni ruled the town. The uniqueness of Ilé-Ifẹ in divine, aristocratic, and art traditions finds expression in stone, terra-cotta, bronze heads, and wood carvings that attested to the centuries of old tradition of artistic prowess and civilization between 500 BCE and 1400 CE. Long before the arrival of the Europeans, the Ifẹ built impressive roads. In fact, while Europe struggled to make roads, as early as the eighth century in Ilé-Ifẹ, people had been constructing roads with pottery sherds (potsherd pavement or àpáàdìi lúwó). The discovery by Leo Frobenius in 1910 of Olókun beads in Gao, an ancient city of Mali, confirms the extent of trade links between Ifẹ and other African countries. Frobenius learned about the ancient city of Ilé-Ifẹ, well known for its knowledge of beads, iron, bronze, and terra-cotta artworks. Since the early twentieth century, the ancient urban center has gained international recognition. The fame of Ilé-Ifẹ was based on its fascinating figures in copper alloy, terra-cotta, and stone, which Frobenius attributed to a lost "Greco-Roman empire."

In the modern political arena, Ilé-Ifẹ has been the political center of Yorùbáland as the first governor of the region late Ọba Adésọjí Adérẹmí came from Ilé-Ifẹ. In addition, late Ọba Adérẹmí was one of the Nigerians who went to the meeting called by the then colonial masters in London for the Nigerian constitution in 1948. Before that, the colonial government had invited Olúbùṣe I to Lagos in 1903 to settle a chieftaincy dispute in Ìjẹbúland. To demonstrate the primacy of the ọọni, all the kings on his route to Lagos vacated their palaces and worked for the safe return of the ọọni before returning to their thrones. Today, the economic nerve of Ọṣun State is in Ifẹland, where farm products like cocoa, palm oil, and kola nut are well cultivated and exported.

See also **Ifẹ Kingdom**

REFERENCE

Johnson, Samuel. *The History of the Yorubas*. Lagos (Nigeria): C.S.S., 1921.

Àdìsá Ògúnfọlákàn

IFẸ KINGDOM

The kingdom of Ifẹ was an ancient Yorùbá urban center located in present-day Ọṣun State in southwestern Nigeria. Ifẹ is the oldest Yorùbá center, and it is from where, according to tradition, the Yorùbá originated. In fact, it is believed that the creation of the universe started in Ifẹ. Ilé-Ifẹ is the capital of all Yorùbá kingdoms, and it is rich in traditions. The rich Ifẹ tradition and its sustenance to the contemporary period is in part due to the dynastic kingship that founded classical Ifẹ between the eleventh and fifteenth centuries that still exists in the city.

Many sources have attested to the supremacy of Ilé-Ifẹ both within and outside of the Yorùbá region. For example, some historical sources have documented the strength, political influence, and affluence of Ilé-Ifẹ since the fourteenth century. The first mention of Ilé-Ifẹ in the historical record was by the Moroccan-born Arab traveler Ibn Battuta, who described Yufi (Ifẹ) in the fourteenth century as one of the biggest countries of the Sudan. He went further to describe the king as one of their greatest sultans (king or ruler). In the fifteenth century, Pereira Pacheco, a Portuguese sailor, wrote about the king of Ifẹ and equated his power to that of the pope. Having been fascinated about the artworks of Ilé-Ifẹ̀, Leo Frobenius, a Germany anthropologist, erroneously described Ifẹ civilization as remnants of the Greek culture. All these historical records point to the greatness of the Ifẹ kingdom. However, the Ifẹ kingdom predated the fourteenth century.

Oral tradition and numerous archaeological investigations in Ilé-Ifẹ̀ and other surrounding towns and villages have helped to bring the trajectory to Ifẹ civilization into the limelight. A careful examination of these sources delineates the social complexity of Ifẹ kingdom in three main phases: preclassical period (before the eleventh century), classical period (eleventh to fifteenth centuries), and the postclassical period (after the fifteenth century). Although, the sociopolitical structure of the preclassical Ifẹ is uncertain, oral traditions has it that the kingdom of Ifẹ started as scattered villages and hamlets, which consisted of thirteen settlements: Ìdó, Idẹ̀ta Òkò, Ìlọràn, Ìlóròmù, Ìjùgbẹ̀, Ìmọ́jùbí, Ìráyẹ̀, Iwinrin, Ọdun, Òkè-Awo, Òkè-Ọjà, Ọmọlógun, and Parakin.

During this period, the inhabitants were mostly farmers with a few artisans. Archaeological evidence has revealed that limited crafts were in place at about tenth century CE. Politically, each of these settlements was ruled by either a priest king or a chief priest. Although the system of government was flexible and lacked centralization, it fostered mutual cooperation among clans, which is best described as confederacy. Akin Ògúndìran describes this early political structure in Ifẹ as "a loose political alliance short of political integration, with no central chieftaincy hierarchy, powerful royal dynasties, centralized governments, or urban capital." However, by the late tenth and early eleventh centuries, a complex sociopolitical structure began to emerge at Ifẹ. Historians have linked this period to the time of the emergence of Odùduwà in the history of Ilé-Ifẹ̀, who, according to tradition, laid the foundation of social complexity in Yorùbáland

and became the first ọ̀ọni (the supreme ruler or king) of Ifẹ.

This epoch of Odùduwà marked the beginning of the classic Ifẹ kingdom, which was characterized by state formation, associated with political upheaval and the establishment of a new dynasty and a new political culture based on religious cult. The political organization in Ifẹ became centralized and hierarchical, founded on a sacred kingship system that venerated the power of the ruling elite as that of the gods. Indeed, the Ifẹ kingdom established a political structure that became the source of the greatest movements in the spiritual and cultural life of Yorùbá people as well as the Edo speakers. Many of the political and religious figures of Ifẹ were elevated to the position of gods, goddesses, and deities. For example, according to tradition, Ọ̀rúnmìlà (priest of Ifá or god of wisdom and knowledge), Ògún (god of iron), and Olókun (goddess of the sea) were at one time political and religions personage in Ifẹ kingdom, but they were soon venerated as gods and deities across Yorùbáland.

The political system and religious power of Ifẹ kingdom are directly readable from its material culture. Various archaeological investigations and chance discoveries in Ilé-Ifẹ have revealed several artworks in bronze and terra-cotta. Dated to between the twelfth- and fifteenth-century Ifẹ kingdom, many of these artworks often depict the political rulers in their full royal regalia and other paraphernalia of office. The most important symbol of power in Ifẹ kingdom was beads, which became the distinctive material component of royal grandeur. The political ideology of Ifẹ kingdom emphasized the place of beaded crown as a symbol of power and authority. This ideology was not only in place at Ilé-Ifẹ̀; it also became the rule across Yorùbáland. As Akin Ògúndìran has written, "These preciosities and symbols [beads] were crucial in the development of Ilé-Ifẹ as the primate center that many harbingers of dynastic institutions in the region visited and allied with to establish and validate their political power and ideology."

As Ilé-Ifẹ succeeded in making beads, the most important emblem of political royal dynasty, the kingdom was equally swift to establish and monopolize glass bead industry. Prior archaeological investigations in Ifẹ̀ and current research on the Ilé-Ifẹ̀ glass industry revealed materials suggestive of a massive glass-bead industry in Ifẹ̀ between the twelfth and fifteenth century. These materials included crucible fragments, glass beads, cullet, and abundant production debris. Detailed studies of these materials have shown that glass beads were locally produced in large scale at Ifẹ̀, which also monopolized the process for making local glass. The Ifẹ̀ kingdom was not only producing glass beads but also supplying other Yorùbá kingdoms, mainly as a commodity for paraphernalia of political and religious office. The supply of glass beads soon transcended the Yorùbá region, and the object became a valuable trade good.

By the fifteenth century CE, the Ifẹ̀ kingdom had developed intercontinental contacts through long-distance commerce. The Ifẹ̀ kingdom traded beads, kola nut, and other valuable objects. Archaeological investigations revealed that Ilé-Ifẹ̀ glass beads must have been traded further afield among the Sahel and Sudan kingdoms. These goods were, at the same time, exchanged for other commodities, especially copper alloy materials, which were used in bronze casting in the Ifẹ̀ kingdom. Lead isotope analysis of Ilé-Ifẹ̀ bronze figurines has revealed that the copper alloy used was sourced from across the Mediterranean in southern Europe. This further affirms the active involvement of the Ifẹ̀ kingdom in the trans-Saharan trade in the second millennium CE. This external contact and participation in trans-Saharan commerce revolutionized the economy of Ilé-Ifẹ̀, which made the kingdom much more prosperous than other African kingdoms of its time. Thus, the location of Ifẹ̀ at the northern bulge of the forest and its proximity to the Niger River presented it with the opportunity to participate in early north-south trade networks.

It is not surprising, however, that the decline of political power and economic prosperity of the Ifẹ̀ kingdom in the centuries preceding the classical era was in part tied to the loss of the trade routes to both the north and the south. Oral traditional, historical,

and archaeological sources have indicated a massive population movement out of the Ifẹ̀ kingdom. Overpopulation and the quest to be a founder have been suggested as part of the reason for this mass migration. Obviously, among the immigrants, political and religious elites and craft specialists left to found new kingdoms. Some joined existing small settlements and helped them to grow. Thus, the empire of Ọ̀yọ́ to the north and Benin kingdom further south gained prominence and control of the trade routes.

The Ifẹ̀ kingdom did not only lose the trade routes; it also witnessed a major decline in its craft industries, a main source of its economic power. However, migration resulted in the spread of craft production in Benin, Ilésà, Ọ̀ṣogbo, Ọ̀wọ̀, and other places. Similarly, the Ifẹ̀ kingdom became politically weak. It was sacked twice by its neighbor Modákẹ́kẹ́ in the nineteenth century. Although by that time the Ifẹ̀ kingdom had lost almost everything that made it the most prosperous Yorùbá kingdom between the eleventh and fifteenth centuries, Ifẹ̀ still holds on to its religious power, for which it is accorded the title of the spiritual homeland of the Yorùbá.

See also **Beads; Ilé-Ifẹ̀**

REFERENCES

Akínjógbìn, I. A., ed. *The Cradle of a Race: Ilé-Ifẹ̀ from the Beginning to 1980*. Port Harcourt (Nigeria): Sunray Publication, 1992.

Ògúndìran, Akínwùmí. "Of Small Things Remembered: Beads, Cowries, and Cultural Translations of the Atlantic Experience in Yorùbáland." *International Journal of African Historical Studies* 35.2–35.3 (2002): 427–45.

Abídèmí Babátúndé Babalọlá

INHERITANCE

Inheritance is an integral part of the Yorùbá custom relating to the sharing of the property of the deceased. Before the intervention of Euro-American and Western education, N. A. Fádípẹ̀ notes, "the principal beneficiaries of the deceased person are his mother's children, male and female." The Yorùbá believe that deceased siblings are immediate blood-related family members and have all access to property.

Inheritance could be classified as wealth materials and nonwealth materials. Wealth materials are shared on the basis of the acquired property of the deceased. Nonwealth materials are the widow(s) and slave(s) of the deceased, who could also be "shared" along with wealth materials. Fádípè explains that widows are believed to be "at the disposal of their husband's siblings. . . . [E]ven half-brothers inherited whenever there was a sufficiently large number of widows available." This idea is based on the belief that surviving relations of the deceased should continue where the deceased stopped.

Modernization, Christianity, Islam, and Western education have neutralized the old system of inheritance. Now only the "legal" widow and children of the deceased have all access to the deceased's property without any consideration for the children born out of wedlock, unless there are instructions by the deceased through a will. This effort could be truncated if the legal wife refuses the idea. If the deceased's family member wanted to enforce any illegal decisions, the legal wife and children could take necessary steps to assert their rights by taking them to court. The inclusion of other widows in sharing the property is seldom practiced today, especially among the elite. Some widows prefer to remain single mothers. However, if the family members of her late husband decide to force a man on her, the concerned widow may decide to reject and leave her husband's house.

In Western law, inheritance can take place before the death of the owner. The property owner may decide to donate his or her property to a church or mosque, charitable institutions, or for government use. But in Yorùbá society, when a woman dies, her property belongs to her children or her husband.

See also **Widows and Widowhood; Succession**

REFERENCE

Fádípè, N. A. *The Sociology of the Yorùbá.* Ìbàdàn (Nigeria): University Press, 1970.

Ayọọlá Ọládùnkẹ́ Àránsí

Dìrọ̀ m'ẹ́gbẹ́,
Kóo má bàa j'ìyà;
Ẹgbẹ́ ní ń gba'ni.

Hold on tight to your initiation society members,
So that you'll not suffer;
As initiation society is one's best savior.

The foregoing Ilé-Ifẹ̀ song is explicit about the importance of initiation in Yorùbá society. Initiation rites fall into two main categories: rites of passage (birth, marriage, adulthood, eldership, and afterlife or *ẹ̀hìn-ìwà*) and traditional religious rites related to initiation groups, such as the Ògbóni society, Ifá priesthood, and Orò cult. Owing to limited space, this entry defines initiation and provides an overview of just two examples, initiations to the Ògbóni society and Ifá priesthood.

What Is Initiation?

Initiation is a process through which the *ọ̀gbẹ̀rì* (novice) is formally accepted into a society to start a new phase in life after completing certain required activities and undergoing certain rites pertaining to that society. As it applies to rites of passage, initiation marks the passing from one phase of life to the next, a more mature one. On death from old age, passage to *ẹ̀hìn-ìwà* (the afterlife) upgrades the deceased's status to ancestor.

Initiation to Ògbóni Society

The Ògbóni (also called Ọ̀ṣùgbó) is an initiation society whose members worship *ilẹ̀*, the earth goddess. During the precolonial period, Ògbóni society functioned as a town council, the civic court, and the body that counterbalanced the king's authority. Technically, membership was open to any adult in good moral standing, but in reality, the requirements for initiation to Ògbóni extend beyond this. First, the candidate must be what the people refer to as *àgbàlagbà*, someone who is old enough for his or her eldest child to have become an adult. The reason this requirement is stressed is that tradition attributes great experience, wisdom, knowledge, and understanding needed to function well in society with old age. Interestingly, the society's names, Ògbóni and Òṣùgbó, translate to "he or she is old" and "he or she has grown gray hair," respectively. The eligibility requirement gives preference to individuals who are patrilineal descendants of Ògbóni. Thus, many Ògbóni family lineages' praise names (oríkì) often include ọmọ Ògbóni (descendant of Ògbóni).

Having met these two requirements, the ògbẹ̀rì (novice candidate) is summoned for initiation at the ilédì (Ògbóni lodge or meeting house). He or she is required to bring certain animals for sacrifice at the initiation. The initiation convener (usually a senior Ògbóni member) places the society's emblem, ẹdan Ògbóni (also ẹdan òlóló), on the floor: a pair of male and female brass figures. The leader smears or soaks the emblem with animal blood. The novice kneels before the ẹdan Ògbóni, bends forward, and touches the blood-soaked emblem with his or her forehead and then lips, which prompts the Ògbóni members present to say, "Hail the Earth Mother! Powerful, old!" The Olúwo conclude the rite with a prayer. As a sign that this first phase of the initiation is complete, a string adorned with three cowries is tied around the candidate's left wrist.

The candidate returns to ilédì on the third day to complete the final phase of the initiation, which includes the removal of the three cowries previously tied around his or her wrist. In addition, the Olúwo teach the candidate the society's secret pacts and taboos. After the Olúwo's final lesson, the initiation is concluded, and the initiate-elect is presented with the ẹdan Ògbóni, which identifies his or her membership as Ògbóni and symbolizes the Ògbóni pacts and taboos that he or she has sworn to uphold.

Initiation to Ifá Priesthood

Ifá priesthood is reserved largely for men; the Ifá priest is called Babaláwo. He divines for his clients by consulting the deity of divination, Ọ̀rúnmìlà (also Ifá), to find out the Odu Ifá that oversees and reconciles the client's dilemma. To become a member of the highest grade of practicing Ifá priests, àwọn-tí-a-tẹ̀-ní-ifá (those whose Ifá nuts have been trampled on or consecrated) first requires apprenticeship to an established Babaláwo and then two expensive and extensive initiations. The apprenticeship period could take at least ten years, during which time the apprentice learns enough to consult the Ifá oracle (dá ifá) for his future clients. The apprentice maintains continuous contact with his teacher-Babaláwo to learn all of the divination activities required for clients who come to inquire about their affairs.

On completion of his apprenticeship, the teacher-Babaláwo asks the candidate to pay for all the required initiation items. The two-phase initiation lasts for seven days. The first day includes the rite of ìtẹ̀-ní-ifá, in which the novice tramples with his right foot two sets (or thirty-two) ikin ifá (Ifá nuts) that have been immersed in a lump of corn-flour pudding. His teacher-Babaláwo and other senior colleagues form a circle round him as the candidate performs this first initiation rite, which earns him the accolade àwọn-tí-a-tẹ̀-ní-ifá (those whose Ifá nuts have been trampled on or consecrated). The accolade is an allusion to the teaching and knowledge of the Babaláwo. Next, the candidate collects all the trampled ikin ifá and buries them in the mud for three days. He exhumes the darkened ikin ifá on the third day, washes and consecrates them in omi ifá (Ifá water), and wraps them with ewé ifá (Ifá leaves), which he delivers to the officiating Babaláwo for further consecration.

The second and last phase (or second initiation) is held on the seventh day and is called the giving and receiving ceremony. The community's Babaláwo (Ifá priests) surround the kneeling candidate. The candidate kneels with his or her eyes closed and his hands raised, palms open. The officiating Babaláwo stretches forward in a receiving gesture. He calls the candidate's name three times, to which the candidate responds each time. The Babaláwo then places the packet containing the consecrated ikin ifá on a plate and solemnly lays the container on the candidate's palms. Sensing the content on his palms, the candidate gladly accepts the package of consecrated ikin ifá. He touches his forehead and chest with it and exclaims joyfully, "May my head, or the divinity of my destiny, or my Creator accept it! My own heart accepts it."

Upon completing the ceremony, a band of the initiate-elect's teacher-Babaláwo, friends, and senior colleagues leads him to a river, where the officiating Babaláwo properly washes and purifies him and ties a parrot's red tail feather to his forehead. This signifies that he has been consecrated and duly initiated and belongs to the strata of àwọn-tí-a-tẹ̀-ní-ifá (an allusion to the versed and knowledgeable Babaláwo). He is then escorted home with an unending ìyẹ̀rẹ̀ or ọ̀yẹ̀rẹ̀ ifá (the praise songs of Ifá).

See also **Apprenticeship; Divination: Ifá**

REFERENCE

Fámulẹ̀, Ọláwọlé. "Ẹgbẹ́ Ògbóni: The Yorùbá Council of Elders, Its Origins, and Artistic Relevance." Unpublished M.A. thesis, University of Arizona, 2003.

Ọláwọlé Fámulẹ̀

INSULTS AND RIBALD LANGUAGE

An insult results when one fails to use polite language with the intention to hurt the feelings of another person or makes an action, remark, or rude expression that injures the dignity of another person. In the precolonial period, the male had to prostrate himself before his senior, and the female had to kneel down to greet her husband and other senior persons. Failure to offer such greetings would be regarded as insult. It was an insult to call elderly persons by their names. Ẹ̀yin ("you" plural) was used to address elders in authority. It was also an insult to offer anything to someone using the left hand. It was an insult for a younger person to refuse to answer when a senior person called him or her to send him or her on errand. When one spoke to or was addressed by an elder or person in authority, he or she must lower his or her eyes or keep them averted; to make eye contact was to show disrespect.

Today, people are always careful to avoid situations that warrant insults against the elderly, kings, diviners, priests, medicine men, and physically challenged people. These interactions are managed through social control mechanisms like taboos, instructions, advice, persuasions, reward, and punishments. However, insults are commonly used among children, youths, and cowives mostly through proverbs, folktale songs, and the like.

Ribald language, in contrast, is vulgar or indecent speech (ọ̀rọ̀ èfè, àsé, yèyé, ìsọkúso, and ọ̀rọ̀ ẹ̀gbin) characterized by obscenity, coarse jesting, and rude, licentious, or unrefined humorous words. Ribald language is humorously vulgar and sexual. Codes of proper conduct among the Yorùbá discourage the use of vulgar, filthy, sexual, and obscene language in day-to-day social interactions. For example, sexual organs and matters concerning sexuality are considered sacred and should not be openly discussed. However, acceptable use of ribald language is permitted during some festivals as a form of social control over certain groups of people. The annual Òkè'Bàdàn festival in Ìbàdàn, òrògbo festival in Erínmọ̀pé Èkìtì, and ọpèlú in Ọ̀wọ̀ allow ribald sexual vocalizations and graphic sexual demonstrations with props that resemble genitalia. This provides the people with a liminal space for otherwise forbidden performances as respite from their highly regulated lives. Ribald language is also common among èsà, ìjálá, and èfè chanters. Modern comedians also use ribald language for entertainment and satire.

See also **Jokes and Humor**

REFERENCE

Fádípẹ̀, N. A. The Sociology of the Yorùbá. Ìbàdàn (Nigeria): University Press, 1970.

Lérè Adéyẹmí

INVESTMENT

Investment can be defined as an addition to the stock of capital goods in the public or private sector over a given time period, or the purchase of a financial asset. Thus, investment involves putting money to work to generate more money, stock, or capital goods, such as houses, cars, tools, and instruments.

Before the advent of stocks and bonds in the capital markets, Yorùbá society was aware of the concept of investment. In other words, the idea of investment was not foreign to them, and the people made investments with the future in mind. Although Yorùbá society was fundamentally agrarian, people made investments in sectors beyond agriculture.

One form of investment still practiced today is *àjọ*, a system by which several individuals living in the same geographic area contribute money. *Àjọ* is given to each person who contributed on the basis of the order of their registration or by ballot. Collection of *àjọ* occurs on a rotational basis determined by the group of contributors. The time could be weekly, monthly, bimonthly, every four months, every six months, annually, or some other time frame. At some point, everyone gets back his or her own share of the contributed money, which is continually replenished through various contributions.

Before modern-day banking systems for saving money and other valuables, Yorùbá people saved money in a wooden or clay box called *kóló*. Wall caves were also used to keep money safe until enough was saved for whatever need arose. Accumulated money from the safe box can be used to buy agricultural produce during the season when there is a surplus and prices are low. Produce is then preserved and sold in a season when it is scarce and prices are high. For example, palm oil is bought in different-sized barrels every March when there is a surplus, then sold in other seasons when scarcity drives the price up. Kola nut is another agricultural product that people invest in. Kola nuts are purchased and sold in baskets. They are purchased and preserved with chemicals to prevent damage until the price rises and profits increase for the investor. Corn and yam can be purchased and preserved in silo and ban, respectively, during surplus and sold during scarcity. Some people even invest in fruit, for example, oranges, mangoes, pineapples, and the like, before they mature. The buyer or investor waits until the fruit matures and is then plucked or harvested for sale.

Furthermore, some invest their money in buying mature crops to harvest and sell in different quantities.

For example, one can buy cassava stands and harvest later when the price rises. Tubers can also be sold in baskets to flour mills that process different products such as *láfún*, *gàòrí*, or *fùfú*. In contrast, the person may not sell the cassava raw but process it him- or herself into *gàòrí* or *fùfú*, which will be sold with a measuring bowl or in bag.

Furthermore, some people invest their money by purchasing farm implements that they rent out to others. These farm implements include cutlasses, hoes, herbicides, fungicides, and insecticides. An investment of 5,000 units of local currency, for instance, may be sold for 8,000 or 10,000 with an agreement that the buyer will pay back immediately after harvest of farm produce.

Some invest cash in property leases. For example, a cocoa or palm-tree plantation owner may need money for his or her children's school fees, hospital bills, funerals, or wedding ceremonies, and the only available way to get money is to lease out part or all of his or her farmland. Also, some lend out money as an investment. The borrower makes an agreement with the lender to pay back the money at a specific rate of interest. If a borrower refuses to pay the money back, his or her land, farm, and/or property may be claimed by the lender.

Since the abolition of slavery, laborers (*oníṣẹ́-ọdún*) were employed to work on farms (*oko-olúwa wọn*). They were provided accommodation, food, and sustenance by the farm owner, who acted as their employer (*ògá*). They received payment at the end of each year. The master (*olúwa*) of these laborers could contract them out to another person for a period when they had less work to do on their lord's farm. At the end of the year, the laborers could renew the contract with their masters (*ògá*) or go back to their hometowns or villages.

People also earn money through cooperative societies known as *alájẹṣẹ́kù*. Members of these societies lend each member double the amount of his or her contribution to the societal purse. Members who borrow can make investments with the money. Additionally, the societies' loans are investments: borrowers pay back the loans with interest. All members eventually share the accrued interest.

Today, people invested in tools, equipment, cars, houses, canopies, event tables and chairs, and other ventures and assets that can be rented or leased out. Those who need these kinds of items but cannot afford to buy them can rent them and pay the owners hourly, daily, weekly, monthly, or yearly. Furthermore, Yorùbá people also invest their time in endeavors that will bring more money or returns in the future. A farmer can join his fellow farmers on their farm to work with them, with the agreement that the same group of workers will join him when he is in need of labor on his farm. This pattern of investment is called àáró. This pattern of investment is common in an environment with little knowledge of stocks and bonds. It is common in agrarian societies and in developing countries in Africa where there are high rates of dependency on agriculture and illiteracy.

See also **Agriculture and Farming; Cooperative Associations; Economic Systems**

REFERENCE

Junanker, P. N. *Investment: Theories and Evidence*. London: Macmillan, 1972.

Gabriel Ayòọlá

INVOCATION

Traditional Yorùbá believed that the world is made up of two connected realms: the visible world of the living, called ayé, and the spiritual world of the òrìṣà, the ancestors, and spirits, called òrun. Àṣẹ (the power of authority) is the life force that is given to everything by the Olódùmarè, the Creator of the universe. Àṣẹ is in everything: plants, animals, people, prayers, songs, rocks, and rivers. Existence is dependent upon àṣẹ, because àṣẹ is the power that makes things happen. In the preparation of medicine, for example, each ingredient is invoked and activated separately, thus contributing its own inimitable innate ability or power to concertedly bring them into actual existence, to marshal them, and set them into action. For instance,

the Yorùbá use certain medicines for business prosperity such as àwúre (something that wakes, digs out, or bring out one's goodness), awòrò (something that pulls crowds or customers to the trader), and the efficacy of such medicines depend mainly on invoking the life force (àṣẹ) of the various ingredients combined together to prepare the medicine.

Invocation occurs during the worship of the òrìṣà (the deities). It is a means of communion and communication with the deities, ancestors, and supernatural powers and spirits. Pouring of libations and making sacrifices to the deities are also means of invoking them, especially during time of worship. One major weapon of invocation among the Yorùbá is oríkì (praise poetry) and oríkì-orílẹ̀ (praise descriptive poetry). The adherents of various deities believe that the spirits of their deities reside at the shrine (ojúbọ)—private or public. Both verbal (oríkì and other related genres) and visual rituals are germane in invoking the spirits of the deities. In other words, invoking the spirits is gaining access to the deities, ancestors, and the spiritual forces, for deeper communion. Oríkì unlocks the inner or hidden powers of the deities, ancestors, or spiritual forces to stimulate their vital forces for the support of the person invoking their spirits. Oríkì are felt to capture and evoke the essential characteristics of the subject: to have the most profound and intimate access to its inner nature (orí inú). When uttered, therefore, oríkì evoke the subject's power and arouse it to action. The performer of oríkì always establishes an intense, one-to-one bond with the addressee. Thus, oríkì constitute a channel of communication between devotee and deity through which reciprocal benefits flow. Through the performance of oríkì the deities and spiritual beings are empowered; their powers are revived and galvanized into furious activity by intensive chanting of oríkì. In this kind of exercise, the inner head of the deities are appealed to in order to call them into action. The dead may be empowered to return to the community of the living by intensive performance of their oríkì at the grave-shrine. The Yorùbá people also believed that there are ways they can invoke the spirit of the dead person to make certain inquiry from them, especially about the cause of their death in case they died prematurely. This is what they called *bíbá òkú sòrò*—communicating with the dead (the dead person's spirit). Likewise, somebody's sprit could be called through certain magical words, which is popularly referred to as *pípe elédàá eni*, literally, calling one's inner head.

During the festivals of many deities, intensive chanting of *oríkì* arouses them and creates path or opens the way for them to enter the human community by possessing their principal priest, who is similarly translated from his normal state into a receptive trance. In this regard invocation attracts the attention and goodwill of the deity.

It is conventionally believed that the truthful performance of *oríkì* in honor of progenitor or the ancestors gladdens the progenitor and ancestors in the world of spirits and induces them to shower blessings on the people who invoke them on earth. A priest or priestess invokes the spirit of his or her deity to descend on the altar by chanting the *oríkì* of such deity, and it might be accompanied by certain musical or sound-producing instruments like drums or gongs. Invocation of the deity's spirits can instigate spirit possession, which is a symbol of the deity's imparting his or her power on the devotee. The deities are sometimes invoked by dancing and singing of songs in their honor. As already mentioned, both verbal and visual arts are important in invocation, and whenever this is done to either the deities or the ancestors, the good things of life are bestowed upon the people invoking the deities and the ancestors through sacrifice, pouring of libations and/or *oríkì* and songs. The Yorùbá people also believe that the person invoking the deities or the ancestors can receive inspiration to perform things that go beyond his or her ordinary ability.

In traditional medical practices, invocation is highly regarded. It is believed that every object is infused with the innate power to make things happen; thus, the user of traditional medicine usually invokes the power of different types of ingredients combined in a particular medicine to call them into action. It could be likened to an act of waking someone who is sleeping. Before invocation through incantation, the powers of the herbs in such medicine are inert, but they are made active through invocation. Invocation brings the person invoking into a deeper relationship with the invoked and puts the latter in a good and generous mood through which the will of the person invoking can be established.

See also **Homage (Ìbà); Libation; Linages and Cognomen (Oríkì Orílè); Names and Naming; Praise Poetry and Eulogy (Oríkì); Words: Òrò**

REFERENCE

Barber, Karin. *I Could Speak until Tomorrow.* Edinburgh: Edinburgh University Press, 1991.

George Olúsolá Ajíbádé

IRON MAKING

Iron making or metallurgy is the science of the properties of metals or the art of extracting metals from ores. Broadly speaking, iron making is the art of refining metals and of adapting them to use. One of the oldest arts, metallurgy or iron making gave rise to the steel industry that today is the spine of our civilization. Hence, such moving masses of metal as automobile, ships, aircraft, railroads, and almost everything in today's world depends on metal, from tools and machines to construction and manufacturing.

Iron making is the occupation of those referred to as *alágbède*, blacksmiths, or iron smelters. Smelting is carried out at a worksite called *ebu*, which is usually constructed not too far from where people live. Smelters go through the rigor of collecting iron ore called *òkúrú*, washing the ore, and burning trees for charcoal. The Yorùbá associate all iron implements with Ògún, the god of war, metal, and iron. Therefore, occupations and industries making use of iron are indebted to him. In this sense, iron or iron tools are the universal symbols of Ògún, who is acknowledged in indigenous beliefs as the most indispensible deity. Many scholars have assigned dates to the discovery of iron-making technology and place a premium on the idea of deification popular among the West African people. The

Yorùbá deified Ògún as a cultural hero. Some scholars believe that the concept of Ògún probably arose from certain sacred rituals and the process of iron making.

Thus, the discovery of iron and its attendant ideology led to the deification of Ògún as deity or divine being. Yet there are those who believe that Ògún, as deity among the Yorùbá, should be traced to the sixteenth century because objects made of iron were in good supply at the time. But all these dates, if accepted, would destroy the religious and the mythological basis for the worship of Ògún as a god whose origin, the Yorùbá believe, is traceable to the creation of the universe. Hence, they hold him as a primordial being, existing from the beginning of time. Contrary to the suggestion that iron making preceded Ògún as deity, the Yorùbá, especially the devotees of Ògún, hold tenaciously to the belief that Ògún was the inventor of iron or the divine smith. This underscores the relationship the Yorùbá often see between the material and the spiritual.

The sense that the origin of ironwork should not be dated is considered by non-Africans, especially European anthropologists and archaeologists, as preposterous and unacceptable. These researchers fail to see any connection between the material and the spiritual. They do not believe in any primordial history that sources its material from mythology. However, it is noteworthy that these anthropologists and archaeologists are in conflict regarding the dates and origins of iron technology. Some contend that ironworking technology originated in Africa and that Europe borrowed it from Africa. Other researchers suggest that it was imported to Africa from the Middle East.

The Yorùbá do not have a materialistic conception of the universe; there is a hallowed separation between the spiritual and the material. For them, a universal life force or spirit exists that unites all that there is. Therefore, it is not superfluous to see iron making as symbolizing the unity of two seemingly opposing realms: the material and the spiritual. The blacksmiths and iron smelters believe that at the base of iron making, a material activity, lies a spiritual ordering. Iron making is the function of Ògún, a demonstra-

tion between spirit and matter. As a primordial being, Ògún is believed to have been the first to discover and work with iron and the first to have fashioned such tools as shaft hammers, billets, adzes, and tongs and to make implements of war as swords, knives, cutlasses, and iron tips for arrows. Ògúndá Meji, a chapter in the Ifá corpus, attests to this:

> Ògún ló dá irin wọnran-wọnran sílé ayé.
> Ògún ló dá bàbà wọnran-wọnran sílèẹ Sòkòrì.
> Ògún ló dá idẹ wọnran-wọnran s'óde Ìjùmù.
> Ògún náà ló rọrin tí-tíí-tí
> Tó fi dó'de ọrun.
> Níbi tí Ajagunmàlè gbé tẹ Ọrúnmìlà n'Ifá.

It was Ògún who introduced iron with a ringing sound to the world.
It was Ògún who introduced bronze with a ringing sound to the land of Sòkòrì.
It was Ògún who introduced brass with a ringing sound to the town of Ìjùmù.
It was Ògún who forged iron continuously,
Till he reached the expanse of heaven.
Where Ajagunmàlè initiated Ọrúnmìlà in the casting of Ifá.

The devotees of Ògún rely on this excerpt to support the claim that ironworking started with Ògún, who is variously described as the god of war, the god of iron, the patron of the smiths, and so on. For this reason also, all smiths are believed to imitate Ògún by participating in this art, whereby the artistic and the spiritual come together.

The Yorùbá believe that metals possess certain benevolent or malevolent powers depending on how they are handled and which rituals associated with iron making are observed. That is why people often lick iron or drink water in which certain metals are submerged as a form of oath; whoever swears falsely by a metal will incur the wrath of Ògún (for Ògún "resides" in the metal) and bring upon him- or herself some imprecation.

Unlike in the industrial world, where technologies are explained and comprehended scientifically, the processes of iron making among the Yorùbá are made comprehensible by analogy to other natural or social processes like interference by ancestral spirits and by acts of sorcery from fellow mortals. Certain secret rituals, rules, and taboos are therefore observed by the blacksmiths to overcome the dangers involved in the processes of iron making. They range from the use of cutlasses for clearing the bush, pickaxes for digging up the soil, and ladders for descending into and climbing from inside the mines, to the collection of òkúrú stone (ore) and the smelting of iron ore.

REFERENCE

Adéníji, David, and Robert G. Armstrong. *Iṣẹ́ Irin Wíwà àti Sísun ní Ilẹ̀ Yorùbá (Iron Mining and Smelting in Yorùbáland)*. Ìbàdàn (Nigeria): University Press, 1977.

Ọmọtádé Adégbindin

ÌSHỌLÁ, HÁRÚNÀ ADÉBÁYỌ̀ (1919–1983)

Alhaji Hárúnà Adébáyọ̀ Ishọla, fondly called Bàbá-ń-Gàní-àgbà and Eégún Mọgají, is a native of Ìgbàire, Òkè-Sòpín, but he spent much of his life in Ìjẹbú-Igbó, Ògùn State, Nigeria. Ìshọlá was born in 1919 to a father who was a singer and traditional doctor. Ìshọlá's *àpàlà* musical career started during the World War II, in 1944 more precisely with his band Hárúnà Ìshọlá and His Àpàlà Group. His musical themes cut across culture, political, history, philosophy, economics, social issues, and religion awareness in Nigeria. He had numerous records to his credit, such as *Punctuality, Omítanikókó, Gbọtí Ọlọtí lẹ̀, Late Ọba Adébóyè (Orímolúsì of Ìjẹbú-Igbó), Iná Ràn, Òròkí Social Club, Pàlùdà, On My Way to London, Àdìsá Aláago, Bàbá Ń'Jẹbà, Late Muritala Muhammed, Mary Awólọ́wọ̀, Onísẹ́ Ńṣiṣẹ́, Ẹgbẹ́ Ọmọ Ẹlẹ́ran Àgbáyé, Ògún ló Nílé Arọ́, Àpàlà Disco, Late Owónifáàrí, Ẹyin Tí Ńperí Wa S'áìda, Nínú Ẹsẹ̀ Méjì, Alh. Làmídì Arówólò Àpàlà Messenger, Ìshọlá Ọmọ Dàda, Ìròhìn Mecca, Ẹgbẹ́ Parkers, Òwe Lẹsin Ọ̀rọ̀*, and a host of others.

He made his first record, titled *Late Ọba Adébóyè (Orímolúsì of Ìjẹbú-Igbó)*, in 1948, but the record did not sell as expected. Seven years later, Hárúnà Ìshọlá made another record and dedicated it to the same *ọba*.

As destiny would have it, the record brought Ìshọlá fame as a talented *àpàlà* musician, and he became a household name. His first album, titled *Òròkí Social Club*, was released in 1971. He sold more than five million copies of the record between 1971 and 1983; it became a turning point in his musical career. Ìshọlá established a record company called Star Records in Lagos State in collaboration with *jùjú* music master I. K. Dáiró in 1969. They were the first African musicians to embark on such task.

Ìshọlá produced music to propagate the aforementioned themes for four decades. By reaching a vast audience and exerting considerable social influence, his music has helped sustain Yorùbá philosophy, tradition, and cultures. He sings in the Yorùbá language but also incorporates words, concepts, and phrases from English and other Nigerian languages, such as Hausa and Igbo. He toured and performed around the world in countries such as the United States, United Kingdom, Italy, Sweden, France, Saudi Arabia, Czechoslovakia, Yugoslavia, Germany, Ghana, Benin Republic, Ivory Coast, Liberia, Guinea, and a host of others.

The first executive president of Nigeria, Alhaji Shehu Shagari, conferred the national award Member of the Order of Niger (MON) on him in 1981 in recognition of his contributions to the social, cultural, political, and economic awareness of the country. Ìshọlá died on November 9, 1983. Despite his physical disappearance from the earth, his music legacy lingers on. His colleagues in the *àpàlà* music industry were the late Alhaji Àyìnlá Ọmọwúrà, Yusuf Ọlátúnjí, and Kásúmù Àdìó. His innovations in the music industry tremendously influenced the *fújì* music of the late Síkírù Àyìndé Barrister, Wàsíù Àyìndé KWAM 1, Àyìnlá Kollington, his son Muslim Hárúnà Ìshọlá, and others. They added more percussion, adapted the talking drums, and imitated the bass lines they heard from overseas with the goal of increasing the tempo of *àpàlà* music to match the frantic pace of social life of the Yorùbá. However, *àpàlà* music has undergone changes in both concept and practice, as might be expected of any dynamic musical style. These changes came about through cultural contact and creative musical innovations, and through social, political, cultural, and economic changes in Nigeria. Ìshọ́lá succeeded in telling the general audience that the Yorùbá have contributed significantly to world music.

See also **Music: Islamic**

REFERENCES

Adébáyọ̀, R. Ibrahim. "The Utilization of Music for the Dissemination of Islamic Message in Yorùbáland." *Journal of Religion and African Culture* 1.2 (2006): 151–64.

Adépọ̀jù, Dàpọ̀ A. "Some Yorùbá Social Realities in Selected Songs of Hárúnà Ìṣọlá." In *Yorùbá Creativity: Fiction, Language, Life, and Songs*, ed. Tóyìn Fálọlá and Ann Genova, 291–310. Trenton, NJ: Africa World Press, 2005.

Nurudeen Ọlátóyè Arógundádé

ISLAM

Islam (*ẹ̀sìn ìmàle* or *ẹ̀sìn mùsùlùmí*) is one of the world's major religions. It is one of the main religions adhered to by a good number of Yorùbá people who have denounced traditional religion and converted to Islam. Although it is difficult to state precise numbers of Yorùbá who are Muslim, statistics indicate that about 50 percent of the population is Muslim, with the overwhelming majority following the Sunni order. The main Sufi orders among the people are Tijjaniya and Qadirriya. It is not unusual for members of the same family to practice Christianity, Islam, and traditional religion.

Islam first came to Yorùbáland in the late fourteenth century through the activities of Malian traders and scholars, hence the reference to it as *ẹ̀sìn ìmàle* (religion of the Malian). Islam entered through the trade routes. Islam did not meet a nonreligious society; it confronted traditional beliefs and religions, which coexisted with Islam until it overwhelmed the former. The movement of traders, scholars, soldiers, and slaves into Yorùbáland from the Islamized areas of Ìlọrin, Nupe, Hausaland, and Borno, as well as the French Republic of Benin, facilitated the penetration and spread of Islam in Yorùbáland. Muslim immigrants from those areas kept the light of Islam alive until it was embraced by the traditional religious community.

Until the eighteenth century, Islamic worshippers were a minority in Yorùbáland and were mostly Muslim immigrants. In its infancy, Islam appealed mostly to the elite and royal courts, members of whom became the principal agents of its spread. The activities of two Yorùbá monarchs, most notably the King Kòsọ́kọ́ of Lagos (1775–1780, 1832–1834) and Aláàfin Àjàgbó of Ọ̀yọ́ (1600–1658), were most important for its spread. The two tolerated Islam and permitted Muslims in their courts and palaces. King Kòsọ́kọ́ lost his throne in 1780 because he tolerated Islam. Because of the influence of the Muslim community, relations between Muslims and the adherents of traditional religion are marked by tension and confrontations.

The increased activities of Muslims from the Islamized areas and locals enhanced the position of Islam in Yorùbáland. Muslim clerics and scholars propagated Islam and built mosques and schools. By the end of the century, Islam had attracted considerable followers who helped spread the faith across Yorùbáland and as far as Porto Novo and Dahomey. Yorùbá traditional religion tolerated Islam, which facilitated its spread and acceptance. Islam appealed to traditionalists because it adapted itself to Yorùbá elements of the culture, such as polygamy and amulet use. Most of the early Islamized centers in Yorùbáland before the nineteenth century were in the Ọ̀yọ́ Empire.

By the nineteenth century, the position of Islam in Yorùbáland was mixed. The emergence of Ìlọrin as stronghold of the jihadists and as a center of learning in the early part of the century was marked by persecution of Muslims by the traditionalists because of their attacks on the Ọ̀yọ́ overlords. This development undermined the position of Islam. Islam made a resurgence in the mid-nineteenth century. It reestablished itself despite conflict with Yorùbá traditionalists. Muslim refugees were reintegrated into society and helped organize and reenergize the scattered Muslim communities. The newly founded towns of Ìbàdàn, Abéòkúta, and Ọ̀yọ́ and the refugee towns of Ìlarò, Ìwó, Ẹdẹ, Ògbómọ̀ṣọ́, Ṣakí, and Òṣogbo emerged from the crisis as centers of Islam. The Muslim community increasingly expanded. For instance, the Muslim community in Lagos increased from 800 in 1862 to 10,600 in 1871 to 14,295 in 1891. Accompanying the expansion of the Muslim community was an increase in places of worship and education. For instance, the number of mosques in Ìṣéyìn increased from twelve in 1875 to seventeen in 1878. In 1877, Ìbàdàn had no fewer than twenty-four mosques; Lagos had thirty-six in 1887.

However, despite the religious ferment that swept across Yorùbáland, some of the states were untouched by Islam. The eastern Yorùbá countries of Èkìtì, Oǹdó, Ìjẹ̀ṣà, Àkúrẹ́, and Ọ̀wọ̀ were unaffected by Islam until the 1870s given a lack of contact with the Islamized areas. The reopening of trade routes with the Islamized areas facilitated the penetration of Islam to those parts of Yorùbáland after the 1870s.

The return of liberated Yorùbá Muslim slaves from Liberia and Freetown from the mid-nineteenth century onward further enhanced the position of Islam in Yorùbáland. These returnees were literate, and they helped propagate the faith and changed Yorùbá Muslims' perception of Western education. Because of its strategic location, Lagos was the main attraction of these returnees and became a center of activity. As the Muslim community expanded, the pace of evangelism increased and the number of new converts, mosques, and Islamic schools also expanded. The earliest recorded Muslim pilgrimage from Yorùbáland occurred in the 1860s. The increased demand for Islamic teachers and amulet makers during and after the civil war enhanced the position of Islam in Yorùbáland. During this period, Islam competed with Christianity for followers, but Christianity did not appeal to the locals because it was perceived as a white man's religion.

However, despite its increasing influence, Islam did not become a state religion in Yorùbáland as in the north. The imposition of British rule, starting with Lagos in 1861 and then the inland states in the 1890s, undermined the position of Islam in Yorùbáland. Although Muslims were represented in the colonial administration and the Native Courts, their power was constrained by their limited number and by the native and customs laws. Because of resistance to control of Western education by the Christian missions, coupled with a reformist tendency, Muslim organizations established schools for Muslim children in the 1920s. Islam has enriched Yorùbá culture in many ways, such as language and dress.

See also **Islamic Medicine; Pilgrimage: Islamic**

REFERENCE

Farias, P. F. "Yorùbá Origins Revisited by Muslims: An Interview with the Arokin of Ọ̀yọ́ and a Reading of the Asl Qaba'il yuruba of Al-Hajj Adam al-Iluri." In *Self-Assertion and Brokerage: Early Cultural Nationalism in West Africa*, ed. P. F. De Moraes Farias and Karin Barber, 109–47. Birmingham University African Studies Series 2. Birmingham, UK: Center of West African Studies, Birmingham University, 1990.

Shehu Tìjjání Yusuf

ISLAMIC MEDICINE

For two reasons, it is difficult to draw any line between the Yorùbá cultural concept and perception of òògùn medicine and the religious—or rather the ritual—practice of medicine among Yorùbá Muslims. First, the Yorùbá have been in contact with Islam for centuries; hence, the saying *ayé la bá'fá, ayé la bá'màle, òsán gangan nìgbàgbọ́ wọlé*, which means "Ifá divination has been part of Yorùbá culture for ages." Christianity is a relatively recent phenomenon for the Yorùbá. Second, and closely related to the first reason, Islam, unlike Christianity, with its attendant Western education, individualism, and monogamous family rules and restrictions, is more congruent and consistent with Yorùbá communal traditions, values, mythical or metaphysical monotheism, and beliefs and superstitions in the supreme God. As in the making of offerings to the Olódùmarè, the God of heaven and earth, through the Babaláwo, the Ifá priest, the almighty Allah could be worshiped and appeased with prayers and sacrifices through the *alfa*, the learned one.

Consequently, Islamic medicine is little more than a branded and differentiated Yorùbá medicine with a tweak of Islamic scholarship and mysticism. For example, incantation is a primary belief among the

Yorùbá. Thus, with a bit of ingenuity, Muslim scholars have adopted and acculturated the Yorùbá mystical and magical power of words to create special prayers, mantras, and invocations, and to create charms for wealth and good luck, for protection against enemies and evil spirits, for victory in battles and war, for overcoming difficult times, for blessings and success in life, and for healing. Charms can be worn as pendants (necklaces, bracelets, and loin guards or ìgbàdí). Syrup or powdered medicine can be taken as drinks, cooked, or mixed with food, while aromatic herbs are used as protective perfume or tùràrí, incense that are burned to dispel evil spirits.

While Islamic medicine seemed rooted in Yorùbá beliefs, there are four distinct strands of Islamic medicine: (1) hànntú (special prayers written on tablet, which is later washed with water to produce a syrup drink); (2) charms wrapped in leather as pendants; (3) the chanting of mantras, especially the ninety-nine holy names of Allah, certain powerful verses and phrases in the Holy Qur'an, and the like; and (4) fasting and prayer, especially tahajud (night vigil), in particular during the fasting month of Ramadan. A significant feature of Yorùbá culture is àyànmọ́ destiny, also called kádàrá in Islam. However, while the Yorùbá believe there is no antidote for destiny—àyànmọ́ kò gbóògùn—Islam has a different view. The Holy Qur'an stipulates that there is an unknown or unspecified Glorious Night of Destiny (lailatulqadri), most likely in the last ten days of the month of Ramadan. During that night, the almighty Allah could shower abundant blessings and forgiveness on the faithful and, more important, grant them the grace of changing their destiny for good.

Perhaps the most distinctive Yorùbá feature of Islamic medicine in practice is in the consultation and use of the services of the alfa, the learned Muslims. Because many Muslims only learned a few verses of the Holy Qur'an in Arabic, just enough to enable them to say their daily prayers, they resort to consultation and delegation of the learned alfas. In oral and written principles and precepts of Islam, simply as a way of life, there seems to be nothing to show that Islamic medicine required an intermediary between the Muslims and the almighty Allah.

See also Islam; Pilgrimage: Islamic

REFERENCE

Farias, P. F. "Yorùbá Origins Revisited by Muslims: An Interview with the Arokin of Ọ̀yọ́ and a Reading of the Asl Qaba'il yuruba of Al-Hajj Adam al-Iluri." In *Self-Assertion and Brokerage: Early Cultural Nationalism in West Africa*, ed. P. F. De Moraes Farias and Karin Barber, 109–47. Birmingham University African Studies Series 2. Birmingham, UK: Center of West African Studies, Birmingham University, 1990.

Bọ́lá Dáúdà

J

JOHNSON, SAMUEL (1846–1901)

The Reverend Samuel Johnson (Àyìnlá Ògún) was a Christian minister and a clergyman of the Church Missionary Society (CMS). He was born on June 24, 1846, in Freetown, Sierra Leone. Though born a creole, he was by descent a blue-blooded prince from the ancient city of Ọ̀yọ́ and scion of the *aláàfin* from the royal lineage of Aláàfin Abíọ́dún Adégoólú. A foremost Anglican priest, Reverend Samuel Johnson was educated at the Church Missionary Society Training Institute and served as a teacher during the period of the Yorùbá civil war. He was ordained a deacon in 1880 and in 1888 made a priest.

The contribution of the late Reverend Johnson to the resolution of the Yorùbá civil war in the late nineteenth century was immense. Together with Charles Phillips, a fellow CMS priest, he worked to negotiate a cease-fire during the Èkìtìparapọ̀ War in 1886 and also arranged for a treaty that granted independence to the Èkìtì towns and villages. From 1881, Johnson's ministry was largely based in Ọ̀yọ́, where he contributed significantly to the spiritual, social, and political progress of his people. A proud Yorùbá man, Johnson loved his race so much that he was bothered by the fact that his people, particularly the educated, were becoming so versed in and highly acquainted with the history of England, Rome, and Greece but diminished in their own (Yorùbá) history. It was this fear that prompted him to embark on writing his masterpiece, *The History of the Yorùbás*, a feat that established him as a pioneer in the field of Yorùbá studies. This book remains the most authoritative, comprehensive, and prized reference source on the origin, qualities, and historical antecedents of the Yorùbá people.

Johnson completed the work in 1897, but regrettably, misfortune befell the original manuscripts and the author never lived to see his work in print. His British publisher lost the manuscripts. Reverend Johnson died unexpectedly on April 29, 1901, at age fifty-five. His younger brother, Dr. Obadiah Johnson (Àjàgbé Ògún), who had served as editor of the publication and as a collaborator on the project, took it upon himself to see that the invaluable work was published. The resulting publication was *The History of the Yorùbás: From the Earliest Times to the Beginning of the British Protectorate*, which was rewritten based on Reverend Johnson's copious notes and rough copies he left behind. Some chapters were completely rewritten, some were shortened, others were amplified, and some new ones were added where necessary. Since 1921, when *The History of the Yorùbás* was published by C.S.S. Limited, in Lagos, the title has remained sought after by scholars who desire an original account of the Yorùbá race. To this date, Reverend Johnson remains a leading historian on the Yorùbá race.

See also **Èkìtìparapọ̀ War; Fádípẹ̀, Nathaniel Akínrẹ̀mí; Scholars**

REFERENCE

Johnson, Samuel. *The History of the Yorùbás.* Lagos (Nigeria): C.S.S. Ltd., 1921.

Adéníyì Àkàngbé

JOKES AND HUMOR

Jokes and humor are purposeful acts of communication created for amusement. Whether in written or spoken form, the ultimate goal of both is to create amusement. Humor is a quality that is expressed in speech and in writing. Humor is also perceived as a person's ability to appreciate or express forms of amusement, and possessing this ability, or not, is traditionally thought to determine a person's natural gift. Jokes are an expression of humor: either statements made to create amusement or witty actions or tricks played for fun. Jokes are also described as jape, jest, quip, wisecrack, and gag—all of which suggest that joking necessarily involves some sort of action that can be humorously carried out.

Laughter evoked by jokes remains the subject of critical and academic study. Laughter is often perceived as creating a ripple effect, be it coincidental or premeditated, that dissolves a tense mood into nothingness. Laughter is, therefore, the expected human response and reaction to humor and jokes. One concurs that laughter indeed is the best medicine and that moderate reaction to jokes and humor promotes health. Science has proved that laughter releases endorphins, natural chemicals that stimulate good feelings into the brain. Many people also consciously employ contextual jokes as a coping mechanism to get through difficult and challenging periods. This therapy is described as "survivor humor," which purposely designs jokes for those who have suffered extreme tragedies. Nations that have suffered psychological effects and realities of disasters or war promote comical forms as a tool to rehabilitate their peoples.

Both elements are woven into the cultural fabric of the people. There are festivals and periods in the year when humor, jokes, and ribaldry are celebrated in palaces and in society. Court jesting remains a major form of entertainment in the court of Yorùbá kings. For instance, jesters (*asa*) in the *aláàfin* of Ọ̀yọ́'s palace perform age long universal forms of jesting that are simultaneously therapeutic and entertaining. Festivals promote humor and joking at specific periods of the year. The Òkè'Bàdàn festival is an example; it is a day entirely dedicated to ribaldry, jesting, and joking.

Contemporary responses to the needs of the twentieth- and twenty-first-century Yorùbá gave rise to other comical forms, particularly stand-up comedy, whose pioneer was Gbénga Adébóyè. This stand-up is different from the comedy of the *alárìnjó* professional theatrical group for which Moses Adéjùmọ̀ (or Bàbáa Sàlá) is known. Stand-up comedy evolved as an intricate combination of humor and jokes in a most unusual and hilarious form. It has, in recent times, become a standard professional form, and comedians very often play to a full house. This comedy is included in formal and informal settings, particularly programs held at all arms of the government, which attracts exceptional financial reward.

See also **Insults and Ribald Language**

REFERENCE

Ògúnpolú, I. B. "Pathos and Humor in Some Yorùbá Folktales." *Fabula: Journal of Folktale Studies* 16.1–16.2 (1975): 1–18.

Doyin Àgúorù

K

KINGDOMS

Kingdom founding was a common event in Yorùbá antiquity. Ilé-Ifẹ̀ is purported to be the oldest kingdom. Its dynasty was established between the eleventh and twelfth centuries, yet the founding of new kingdom, or conglomeration of existing settlements, continued from the twelfth century through the nineteenth century. As a result, historians, anthropologists, archaeologists, and ethnographers have identified, described, and narrated sociopolitical situations of the Yorùbá both in the past and in the present. These studies have demonstrated that Yorùbá kingdoms were founded consistently from the twelfth through the nineteenth centuries. The prolonged civil war in the eighteenth and nineteenth centuries displaced many people from their original homeland and was a significant factor in the development of the kingdoms.

Historians have grouped the kingdoms into major geographical locations. The northern kingdoms include the Ọ̀yọ́ Empire, Ìlọrin, and the Okun territory of the Ìgbómìnà kingdoms. Among the significant kingdoms of Ìgbómìnà are Ìlá, Gbẹdẹ, Apatéki, Okegi, Èsìẹ, Ìgbàjà, Ìdọ̀fin, and Àjàsẹ́ Ìpo. The western kingdoms consist mostly of the Ẹ̀gbá Forest kingdoms. The central kingdoms include the ancient urban center of Ilé-Ifẹ̀, Ilésà, Ìmẹ̀sí-Ilé, Ìgbájọ, Ìpetu, Ọtan, and Òwu. In the east are Àkókó and Èkìtì kingdoms. Other kingdoms within Èkìtì province are Adó, Ìkàrẹ́, Àkúrẹ́,

Ẹ̀fọ̀n, Emùré, Ọyẹ́, Òbó, Òmùò, and Ìrè. The southern kingdoms include Ọ̀wọ̀, Ìkálẹ̀, Oǹdó, Ìjẹbú, and Àwórì. By the end of first three decades of the nineteenth century, changes in the Yorùbá political landscape resulted in the birth of new kingdoms. Abẹ́òkúta, Ìbàdàn, and New Ọ̀yọ́ are some of the significant newly formed states.

Despite the multiplicity of old and new kingdoms, all share a common denominator in terms of their tradition of origin and sociopolitical structure. Most of the kingdoms trace their origins to Ilé-Ifẹ̀. Consequently, most kingdoms claim that their founder originated from Ilé-Ifẹ̀. For example, the tradition of Ọ̀yọ́ says that Ọ̀rànmíyàn, one of the grandsons of Odùduwà, founded the dynasty of Old Ọ̀yọ́. However, some of the later kingdoms claim origin from Old Ọ̀yọ́. This is true of most of the kingdoms in the northern frontiers. There, traditions claim that their founders were warriors or group of migrants from Old Ọ̀yọ́. It is not surprising that many of the kingdoms continued a centralized political system, similar to the one that existed in their mother kingdom. This political structure places the ọba, the king, at the apex of the political hierarchy. The council chiefs are the ministers in charge of various businesses of the kingdoms. This form of political system was instituted at Ilé-Ifẹ̀ during the era of revolution.

Ilé-Ifẹ̀ was the oldest and the most prominent kingdom in antiquity. Traditions at Ilé-Ifẹ̀ and throughout

Yorùbáland suggest that Odùduwà founded Ilé-Ifẹ̀ and established the first dynasty in the kingdom. Archaeological, historical, and oral traditional sources revealed that the Ilé-Ifẹ̀ kingdom was a product of the combination of several agricultural settlements. By the ninth and tenth centuries, Ilé-Ifẹ̀ witnessed a transformation that amounted to a revolution. According to Akíntóyè, the revolution not only transformed Ilé-Ifẹ̀ but also triggered a movement of profound change throughout the whole of Yorùbáland. Archaeological evidence has dated the urban center's classical period to between the late eleventh and fifteenth centuries. The classical period at Ifẹ̀ witnessed a change in the city's spatial construction and urban landscape, which resulted in the construction of a city wall to accommodate the booming population during this period. The population of Ifẹ̀ at this time was estimated to be between seventy thousand and one hundred thousand people. Similarly, classical Ifẹ̀ was associated with major political transformations and the growth of industries, which were represented in the material culture (e.g., bronze and stone figures, terra-cotta, potsherd pavement, burial materials, glass and glass beads, domestic pottery).

The development of the institution of sacred kingship was the most significant transformation at Ifẹ̀. This new religio-political system emphasized a centralized political structure that places the king as the central of not only political operations but also economic, religious, and social functions. A crown crafted of glass beads became the symbol of political and religious power. The ideology of the divine kingship system was the most significant institution developed at Ifẹ̀, and it came to be seen as the natural order of sociopolitical organization at the regional level. Thus, the system was and is still being practiced in many contemporary Yorùbá societies.

In terms of prominence and influence, Old Ọ̀yọ́ ranks second behind Ilé-Ifẹ̀. As mentioned earlier, Old Ọ̀yọ́ kingdom was located in the northern Yorùbáland. Northern Yorùbáland directly faced the lower Niger River and extended to the fringe of forest belt of the southwestern Nigeria. Its boundary separated Yorùbá speakers of the south from non-Yorùbá speakers of the north. Archaeological evidence reveals that, during the Iron Age, people occupied northern Yorùbáland as far back as the early first millennium. However, there was no evidence of an established kingdom in the northern Yorùbáland until the emergence of Old Ọ̀yọ́ in the fifteenth century.

The power of Old Ọ̀yọ́ lay in its cavalry army, which aided expansion of the empire. By the seventeenth century, Old Ọ̀yọ́ had extended to virtually all parts of the Yorùbá region, and its political and military influence was felt in kingdoms such as Ẹ̀gbá, Ẹ̀gbádo, Ìgbómìnà, and Ìjẹ̀bú, as well as in some Nupe and Ìbàrìbá kingdoms in the northern Niger River. Also, Old Ọ̀yọ́ captured other kingdoms outside of present-day Nigeria, including Kétu, Porto-Novo, and Sábẹ in present-day Republic of Benin. Furthermore, the location of Old Ọ̀yọ́ was an advantage, as the empire controlled the passage of trans-Saharan trade from south to north. Old Ọ̀yọ́ controlled this trade route and became rich from taxing other kingdoms and settlements that used the route. This trade corridor also encouraged Old Ọ̀yọ́'s participation in the trans-Saharan and, later, transatlantic slave trade. All the Ọ̀yọ́ Empire's subject kingdoms and settlements were sources of Ọ̀yọ́ slave raids. However, in the nineteenth century, Old Ọ̀yọ́'s political power began to wane as a result of massive immigration and internal political rancor, which opened the door for external aggression and the eventual collapse of the empire in the beginning of the 1840s.

Old Ọ̀yọ́'s military strength allowed it to expand into the frontier kingdoms and establish colony settlements. Archaeological and historical data reveal that Ẹdẹ-Ilé was established as the first Old Ọ̀yọ́ colony in the seventeenth century. Those early kingdoms established in the thirteenth and fourteenth centuries became prominent under the influence of Old Ọ̀yọ́ during the fifteenth and the seventeenth centuries. Many of the Ìgbómìnà kingdoms followed the same political structure as that of Ọ̀yọ́. Others relied solely on the protection of Old Ọ̀yọ́ and developed an internal political system. Archaeological evidence has further proved the association of the Ìgbómìnà kingdoms with that of Old Ọ̀yọ́ in form of similar defensive mechanisms and other material culture, such as pottery.

In the south, the Ẹ̀gbá Forest kingdoms were among the kingdoms where the influence and eventual collapse of Old Ọ̀yọ́ was most keenly felt. The inhabitants of Ẹ̀gbá Forest are referred to as forest dwellers because of their location in the rain-forest belt of southwestern Nigeria. Ẹ̀gbá kingdoms are believed to have occupied the region as far back as the fourteenth century. Tradition has it that Ẹ̀gbá Forest was founded by a prince from Ilé-Ifẹ̀. However, according to Samuel Johnson, most of the rulers of Ẹ̀gbá Forest were warriors from Old Ọ̀yọ́. Johnson argued that, after the collapse of the Ọ̀yọ́ Empire, many of its inhabitants took refugee in Ẹ̀gbá kingdoms and others formed new towns. As a result, many kingdoms grew in Ẹ̀gbá Forest.

According to A. K. Ajísafẹ́, more than three hundred towns were in the territory of Ẹ̀gbá Forest, including the present city of Ìbàdàn, Ìjàyè-Orílé, and others. The towns constituted three main kingdoms: the Ẹ̀gbá Àgùrá in the northern section of the forest; the Ẹ̀gbá Òkè-Ọnà on the bank of Ọnà River; and the Ẹ̀gbá Agbẹyin in the western part of the forest. The Ẹ̀gbá Forest kingdoms were ruled as federated kingdoms by kings with beaded crowns from the capital of each of the kingdom provinces. For example, Ìlúgùn was the capital seat of Ẹ̀gbá Àgùrá, Ọṣilẹ̀ or Olókò of Òkò was the principal king of Ẹ̀gbá Òkè-Ọnà, and Aláké of Aké was the paramount ruler of Ẹ̀gbá Agbẹyin or Aláké. Aláké was the most powerful among these major kings of Ẹ̀gbá forest kingdoms.

The Ẹ̀gbá kingdoms' proximity to the Atlantic provided opportunities for settlers to actively partake in the transatlantic slave trade. Ẹ̀gbá has received the appellation of "The Gateway City," which it holds to this day. In fact, tradition has it that it was through the Ẹ̀gbá Forest kingdoms that maize, an indigenous America crop, came to Yorùbáland. Oral tradition in Ẹ̀gbá has it that Ojoko, the ruler of Ẹ̀gbá Agbẹyin before Aláké ousted him, became prosperous from supplying corn to other Ẹ̀gbá towns and kingdoms until Aláké

broke his monopoly and overthrew him. Hence, the trade routes that linked Ẹ̀gbá Forest to other kingdoms in the north and parts of the south and the profitability of cash-crop farming enabled the Ẹ̀gbá forest to gain economic prominence.

However, economic prosperity and increasing military power was cut short in the early nineteenth century by an outbreak of war, which resulted from political rivalry and greed among rulers. As a result, Ọ̀yọ́ warriors who coveted Ẹ̀gbá forest attacked the kingdom and sacked its inhabitants. The people of Ẹ̀gbá Forest lost in the battle. They were forced to relocate further south and founded Abẹ́òkúta ("under the rock") around 1830s, which became the new metropolis of all the Ẹ̀gbá.

Ìbàdàn is another important kingdom of the south founded by Ọ̀yọ́ immigrants in the nineteenth century. It was one of the newly founded states following the aftermath of the decline of Old Ọ̀yọ́ Empire. The early history of Ìbàdàn is connected to the collapsed of the empire of Ọ̀yọ́, further north of present-day Ìbàdàn. It was in the wake of violence occasioned by the fall of Old Ọ̀yọ́ that Ìbàdàn was founded at about the same time as Abẹ́òkúta. The Ifẹ̀ and Ìjẹ̀bú allies fought against Òwu in this war with the help of Ọ̀yọ́ refugees, and they defeated Òwu. The same allied forces that destroyed Òwu destroyed Ẹ̀gbá and occupied the land around the Màpó Hill in present-day Ìbàdàn as a temporary war camp. From this war camp the kingdom of Ìbàdàn was established in the late 1830s. The young war camp quickly established itself as a large polity. People across Yorùbáland moved into Ìbàdàn because of the security it offered against the depredations of the Hausa-Fulani jihadist. Prominent among the new refugees were the Ọ̀yọ́ Yorùbá, the Ìjẹ̀bú, the Ifẹ̀, and the Ẹ̀gbá.

From a small war camp under the leadership of Baṣọ̀run Olúyọ̀lé, Ìbàdàn soon became the most militarized state in the nineteenth century. The military capability of Ìbàdàn and its openness to immigrants attracted more exiles, refugees, and the most talented warlords of the era from across the Yorùbáland. Within the span of four decades, Ìbàdàn grew in power and political influence over many northern and eastern Yorùbá cities such as Òṣogbo, Ẹdẹ, Ìwó, Ògbómọ̀ṣọ́, Ilẹ̀ṣà, Òwu, Ifẹ̀, and Adó Èkìtì. As a result, Ìbàdàn assumed the position of the most powerful kingdom. By the mid-nineteenth century, Ìbàdàn had become an influential kingdom; it assumed the role of Old Ọ̀yọ́ in providing military protection for other militarily weak kingdoms and settlements.

See also: Ìbàdàn Empire; Ifẹ̀ Kingdom; Ọ̀yọ́ Empire

REFERENCES

Akíntóyè, A. S. *A History of the Yorùbá People*. Dakar: Amalion Publishing, 2010.

Smith, R. *Kingdoms of the Yorùbá*. 3rd ed. London: James Currey, 1988.

Abídèmí Babátúndé Babalọlá

KINGS AND CHRONOLOGIES

The traditional ruler of a Yorùbá town is referred to as the *ọba* (king), a tradition that many people trace back to Ilé-Ifẹ̀, regarded as the home origin of all the Yorùbá people and Odùduwà as the first Yorùbá *ọba*. All other kings trace their roots back to Ilé-Ifẹ̀. Yorùbá *ọba* are ordered by class. The first class consists of the kings who are the direct descendants of Odùduwà and are entitled to wear beaded, fringed crowns. The second-class kings are those who have historical or traditional links with Ilé-Ifẹ̀, and they also wear these crowns. Other classes of kings are sometimes referred to as *baálẹ̀*, or the head of smaller villages. In the past, they did not wear crowns but caps. These traditions have since changed in many places because of several sociopolitical, economic, and cultural changes among the people. Despite these changes, the Yorùbá still recognize some *ọba* as very prominent, and their position not contested. Among these are the *ọọ̀ni* of Ifẹ̀, *aláàfin* of Ọ̀yọ́, *awùjalẹ̀* of Ìjẹ̀bú Òde, *aláke* of Ẹ̀gbáland or Abẹ́òkúta, and a few others. Today, nearly all Yorùbá towns and settlements have a king, and the list is almost endless as new ones are created and established. The following list is of the titles of kings in different towns and cities, including kings in Ilé-Ifẹ̀ and Ọ̀yọ́ from inception to date:

List of Kings in Ilé-Ifẹ̀ (Ọọ̀ni of Ifẹ̀)

1.	Odùduwà	31.	Ọlọ́jọ́
2.	Ọ̀sángangan Ọbamakin	32.	Òkìtí
3.	Ògún	33.	Lúgbadé
4.	Ọbalùfọ̀n Ògbógbódirin	34.	Aríbiwọsọ
5.	Ọbalùfọ̀n Aláyémọrẹ	35.	Ọ̀sínlàdé
6.	Ọ̀rànmíyàn	36.	Adágbá
7.	Ayétiṣe	37.	Ọ̀jígìdiri
8.	Lájàmìsán	38.	Akínmóyèró (1770–1800)
9.	Lájódoogun	39.	Gbanláre (1800–1823)
10.	Láfogídò	40.	Gbégbáajé (1823–1835)
11.	Òdìdìmọdè Rógbẹṣin	41.	Wunmọnijẹ (1835–1839)
12.	Àwòròkọlọkin	42.	Adégúnlẹ̀ Adéwẹlá (1839–1849)
13.	Ẹkun	43.	Dégbinsòkun (1849–1878)
14.	Àjímudá	44.	Ọrarigba (1878–1880)
15.	Gbóóníjìò	45.	Dérin Ọlọ̀gbéńlá (1880–1894)
16.	Ọ̀kanlájósìn	46.	Adélẹ́kàn Olúbùṣe I (1894–1910)
17.	Adégbálù	47.	Adékọ́lá (1910–1910)
18.	Ọ̀sínkọ́lá	48.	Adémilúyì Ajagun (1910–1930)
19.	Ògboòrú	49.	Adésọjí Adérẹ̀mí (1930–1980)
20.	Gíẹsì	50.	Okùnadé Ṣíjúwadé Olúbùṣe II (1980–2015)
21.	Lúwoòó	51.	Adéyẹyè Ẹnìtàn Ògúnwùsì, Ọ̀jájá II (2015–)
22.	Lúmọbi		
23.	Agbẹdẹgbẹ́dẹ̀		
24.	Ọ̀jẹ́lokunbìrin		
25.	Lágùnjà		
26.	Lárùnnká		
27.	Adémilú		
28.	Ọmọgbogbo		
29.	Àjílà-Oòrùn		
30.	Adéjinlẹ̀		

List of Kings in of the Ọ̀yọ́ Empire (Aláàfin of Ọ̀yọ́)

1.	Ọ̀rànmíyàn (892)	8.	Onígbogí (1497)
2.	Àjàká Dàda (1042)	9.	Òfiràn (1512)
3.	Ṣàngó (Àfọ̀njá) (1077)	10.	Egungunojú (1534)
4.	Aganjú (1137)	11.	Ọ̀ròmpọ̀tọ̀ (1554)
5.	Ìyayùn (Regent) (1300)	12.	Ajíbóyèdé (Sópàsán) (1562)
6.	Kọ̀rí (1345)	13.	Àbípa (1570–1580)
7.	Olúàso (1357)		

14. Ọbalókun (Àgànná Erin) (1580–1600)
15. Olúodò (1600)
16. Àjàgbó (1600–1658)
17. Ọdàrànwú (1658–1660)
18. Kánran (1660–1665)
19. Jáyin (1655–1670)
20. Ayibi (1676–1690)
21. Òsíyàgo (1690–1698)
22. Òjígí (1698–1732)
23. Gberu (1732–1738)
24. Amúniwáyé (1738–1742)
25. Onísílé (1742–1750)
26. Lábísí (1750)
27. Awọ́nbíojú (Odùbóyè) (1750)
28. Agbólúaje (1750–1772)
29. Májéógbé (1772–1775)
30. Abíọ́dún (1755–1805)
31. Aólẹ̀ (Àsàmú Aróga-nagan) (1805)
32. Adébọ̀ (1811)
33. Máku (1811)

Interregnum 1812–1817
34. Majotu (1817)
35. Amode (1818)
36. Olúewu (1818 deposed; 1833–1834 reappointed)

Interregnum
37. Abíọ́dún Àtìbà (Atóbatẹ́lẹ̀) (1829–1859)
38. Adélù (1858–1875)
39. Adéyẹmí I (Alówólódù) (1876–1905)
40. Láwànì Agogoòjà (1905–1911)
41. Şiyanbọ́lá Ládìgbòlù (1911–1944)
42. Rájí Adániran Adéyẹmí II (1945–1955)
43. Bello Gbádégẹsin, Ládìgbòlù II (1956–1968)
44. Làmídì Ọláyíwọlá Adéyẹmí III (1971–)

Titles of Yorùbá Kings

Ọọ̀ni of Ifẹ̀
Aláàfin of Ọ̀yọ́
Ààrẹ of Àgọ́
Ààrẹ of Òfikì
Àjàláyé of Ìpetu Ìjẹ̀sà
Àjàlọ́run of Ìjẹ̀bú Ifẹ̀
Ajerò of Ìjerò
Ajoríwin of Ìràwọ̀
Akíbio of Ìlọrà
Akínlà of Ẹ̀rin Ìjẹ̀sà
Akran of Badagry
Aláyégún of Ọdẹ Òmu
Aláké of Ẹ̀gbá

Alákétu of Kétu
Alámọ́dù of Àgọ́ Àmọ́dù
Alápatẹ of Ìgbòho
Alárá of Ìlárá Mọ̀kín
Alokò Ìlokò Ìjẹ̀sà
Amúníjìò of Ìjìò
Apetu of Ìpetumodù
Aṣẹ́yìn of Ìṣẹ́yìn
Àtáọja of Òṣogbo
Attah of Ayédé Èkìtì
Jẹgun of Ilẹ̀ Olújì
Olúbarà of Ìbarà
Ọṣinlẹ̀ of Òkè Ọnà

Olówu of Òwu
Onísábẹ of Sábẹ
Àgùrá of Gbágùrá
Olómù of Òmù Àrán
Àyángbùrẹ́n of Ìkòròdú
Olú of Ifọ
Ọlọ́tà of Ọ̀tà
Alayé of Ayétòrò
Alárá of Arámọkọ
Arígbámú of Àgbámú
Awújalẹ̀ of Ìjẹ̀bú-Òde
Balùfọ̀n of Sẹ̀pẹ̀tẹ̀rí
Déjì of Àkúré
Elérò of Ìlerò
Eléruwà of Èrúwà
Ẹrínmọpé of Ẹ̀rìn Ọ̀sun
Èwí of Adó Èkìtì
Iba of Kìsí
Olú of Igbóọrà
Ọba of Lagos
Ọdẹmọ of Ìṣarà
Ògòga of Ìkéré
Ògúnsúà of Modákékè
Òkèrè of Şakí
Ọlọ́gbàgì of Ògbàgì
Ọlọ́jẹ̀ of Ọ̀jé Owóde
Ọlọ́kàákàá of Ọ̀kákà
Ọlọ́wọ̀ of Ọ̀wọ̀
Olúbàdàn of Ìbàdàn
Olúbaka of Ìkàrẹ́ Àkókó
Olúbọ́sìn of Ifẹtẹ̀dó
Olúfi of Gbọ̀ngán
Olúigbó of Igbójàyè
Olúmòro of Mòro
Olúpópó of Pópó
Olúwòó of Ìwó
Àkárìgbò of Rémọ
Onídèrè of Ìdèrè
Onídìko of Ìdìko Àgọ
Onígbòho of Ìgbòho
Onílàlá of Lànlátẹ
Oníró of Kọmu

Oníro of Òtu
Onísanbó of Ọ̀gbọ̀ọ̀rọ̀
Onísẹmi of Ìsẹmi-Ilé
Onítàbó of Ìtàbó
Ońjò of Òkèihò
Ońwéré of Ìwéré-Ilé
Ọ̀ràngún of Ìlá
Ọ̀ràngún of Òkè Ìlá
Òsemàwé of Oǹdó
Ọwá Obòkun of Ìjẹ̀sà
Ọwámìrán of Ẹ̀sà-Òkè
Ọwaòyè of Òkè Mẹsí
Sábigànná of Ìgànná
Sàlú Ẹdún Àbọ̀n
Şòún of Ògbómọ̀ṣọ
Tìmì of Ẹdẹ
Oníkòyí of Ìkòyí
Òòrè of Ọ̀tùn- Èkìtì
Ẹlẹ́kòlé, Ìkòlé-Èkìtì
Alárá of Arámọkọ-Èkìtì
Èfọ̀n of Ẹ̀fọ̀n Aláayè
Olójùdó of Ìdó-Èkìtì
Ọlóyé of Ọyé-Èkìtì
Ọlọ́gòtún of Ogòtún-Èkìtì
Arìnjalẹ̀ of Ìsẹ-Èkìtì
Onítaji of Ìtaji-Èkìtì
Onísàn of Isàn-Èkìtì
Elémùré Emùré-Èkìtì
Olómùò of Òmùò-Èkìtì
Olósì Òsì-Èkìtì
Olójùdó of Ìdó-Ilé
Arájàká of Ìgbàrà-Odò
Aláwẹ̀ of Ìlawẹ̀-Èkìtì
Olúyìn of Ìyìn-Èkìtì
Alárè of Àrè-Èkìtì
Onígèdè of Ìgèdè-Èkìtì
Ọbańlá of Ìjẹ̀sà-Isu
Oníyè of Ìyè-Èkìtì
Ọbaléo of Ẹrínmòpé-Èkìtì
Olúkóro of Ikóro-Èkìtì
Alárá of Ará-Èkìtì
Aláwó of Awó-Èkìtì

Aláyétòrò of
 Ayétòrò-Èkìtì
Elérìò of Èrìò-Èkìtì
Olóhan of Èrìnjiyàn-Èkìtì
Olúfàkì of Ìfàkì-Èkìtì
Oníkùn of Ìkùn-Èkìtì
Alásà of Ìlasà-Èkìtì
Owálogbò of Ìlogbò-Èkìtì
Obańlá of Ìpaò-Èkìtì
Olúpotì of ìpotì-Èkìtì
Oníre of Ìrè-Èkìtì
Owátàpá of Ìtàpá-Èkìtì
Owá of Òbó Ayédùn
Olówá of Odò-Owá-Èkìtì
Olósàn of Osàn-Èkìtì
Olúsì of Ùsì-Èkìtì
Olúsin of Ùsin-Èkìtì
Apalúfin of Àísègbé-Èkìtì
Aláayè of Àayè-Èkìtì
Aláayè of Àayè- Oja-Èkìtì
Aláfàò of Àfàò-Èkìtì
Aláráròmí of
 Aráròmí-Èkìtì
Olójà of
 Aráròmí-Òkè-Èkìtì
Òdòlófin of Aráròmí-Òbó
 Èkìtì
Alásín of Asín-Èkìtì
Owá of Ayébodè–Èkìtì
Owá of Ayégbajú-Èkìtì
Owá of Ègbè-Èkìtì
Eléwú of Ewú-Èkìtì
Eléyió of Eyió-Èkìtì
Elédà of Edà-Ilé Èkìtì
Elépè of Èpè-Èkìtì
Elesùré of Èsùré-Èkìtì
Elésùn of Èsùn-Èkìtì
Owá of Òkè-Orò-Èkìtì
Onífisìn of Ìfisìn-Èkìtì
Olúgbolé of Ìgbólé-Èkìtì
Lókè of Ìgbònà-Èkìtì
Oníjan of Ìjan-Èkìtì

Oníjèsà of
 Ìjèsàmodù-Èkìtì
Eléjèlú of Ìjèlú-Èkìtì
Olójà of Ìkogòsì-Èkìtì
Níkòsùn of Ìkosùn-Èkìtì
Oníkòyí of Ìkòyí-Èkìtì
Oníkùn of Ìkùn- Èkìtì
Elerí of Ìkùnri-Èkìtì
Aláfòn of Ìlafòn-Èkìtì
Alámoò of Ìlamò-Èkìtì
Obadú of Ilémèsó-Èkìtì
Lógun of Ìlogun-Èkìtì
Eésàlókun of
 Ìlokunò-Èkìtì
Ajagun of Òmù-Èkìtì
Onípere of Ìpére-Èkìtì
Olúmojo of Ìmojo-Èkìtì
Olúpólé of Ìpólé-Ìlórò
 Èkìtì
Oníràre of Ìràre-Èkìtì
Onírèlè of Ìrèlè-Èkìtì
Olúroyè of Ìroko-Èkìtì
Onírò of Ìrò-Èkìtì
Arómirò of Ìrò-Èkìtì
Obasàóyè of Ìsà-Oyè-Èkìtì
Onísin of Ìsínbòdé-Èkìtì
Olú of Ìyémèrò-Èkìtì
Obalémò of Odò-Orà Èkìtì
Owá of Òkè-Ako Èkìtì
Olóòjèbú of
 Òkè-Ìjèbú-Èkìtì
Olórà of Òkè-Orà Èkìtì
Obalojà of Olójè-Èkìtì
Owájùmú of Òmù-Èkìtì
Olórìn of Òrìn-Èkìtì
Olówúrò of Òrùn-Èkìtì
Olósìn of Òsìn-Èkìtì
Oníkùn of Tèmídire-Èkìtì
Amúrò of Tèmídire-Èkìtì
Eísà of Irá-Èkìtì

See also **Kingship**

Olómolà, Ìsòlá, Bádé Àjùwòn, and Dayò Omótóso, eds. *Prominent Traditional Rulers of Yorùbáland*. Ilé-Ifè (Nigeria): Celebrity Publications Limited; Ìbàdàn (Nigeria): Obáfémi Awólówò University Press, 2003.

Stephen Folárànmí

KINGSHIP

Settlements consist of towns and villages. At each level, an *oba* (king) or a *baálè* (lesser ruler) is the head. The town is headed usually by the *oba*, who wears either a beaded crown with fringe (*ade*) or a beadless coronet (*akoro*), depending on the political status of the town. Most of the *baálè* live in villages, although some lived in fairly large towns. A *baálè* is not entitled to wear a crown. The *baálè* wears caps (*oríkògbófo*) and, in exceptional cases, *akoro* without beaded fringe. Despite the differences between *oba* and *baálè*, the two perform similar traditional functions.

Sacred kingship has been the most important and popular feature of Yorùbá political organization. The *oba* is seen as a divine ruler and is regarded by the people as *aláse èkejì òrìsà*, the commander and companion of the gods. An important feature of kingship is that the political structure prevents *oba* from exercising absolute power. The *oba*'s power is constantly checked by the council of lineage chiefs. Each *oba* or *baálè* has a title, though this is more common with the *oba*. Examples are the *awùjalè* of Ìjèbú-Òde, *aláàfin* of Òyó, * òoni* of Ifè, *àtáója* of Òsogbo, *òràngún* of Ìlá, *olúpo* of Àjàsépò, *olú* of Owode-Òfàrò, *olúbàdàn* of Ìbàdàn, the *déjì* of Àkúré, and the *alówá* of Ìlówá-Ìjèsà. In the administration of the town, the *oba* is assisted by a council of lineage chiefs and some other institutions.

The office of the *oba* is hereditary and confined to particular lineages, most especially those of the founders of settlements. The accession of a new *oba* is marked by elaborate rituals. During a period of seclusion, the selected candidate is initiated and instructed in the new position. Succession rules vary from place to place. Usually the royal family is divided into a number of ruling houses that occupy the stool in turn. In some places, the tradition is to consider candidates only among males born to a reigning king; in other places the new ruler from the ruling house whose turn it is to present a candidate must not have any physical deformity. When there is more than one candidate, the elders of royal descent make a preliminary selection and senior chiefs make the final choice in consultation with the Ifá oracle. However, selection is rarely easy or free of dispute. In Ọ̀yọ́, primogeniture was the normal succession rule until about 1730, after which the aláàfin's eldest son, the àrẹ̀mọ, was expected to die with his father, a practice that ended in 1859.

The kingship institution has changed with the times. Internecine wars in the nineteenth century introduced many changes. The ọba were at the mercy of Yorùbá warriors who had become very powerful because of their participation in the long wars. The establishment of colonial rule through the British system of indirect rule also eroded the power and prestige of the traditional ọba, who became answerable to the British authority. Since independence, the institution of kingship has continued to experience modifications under the civilian and military governments. Although the ọba have lost some or most of their ability to effectively exercise their power and authority, their relevance continues to endure.

See also **Kings and Chronology; Succession**

REFERENCES

Òjó, G. J. A. Yorùbá Palaces. London: University of London Press, 1966.
Rájí, A. O. Y., and H. O. Dánmọ̀le, H. O. "Traditional Government." In Understanding Yorùbá Life and Culture, ed. N. S. Lawal, N. O. Sádíkù, and Adé Dọ̀pámú, 259–70. Trenton, NJ: Africa World Press, 2004.

Aríbidésí Usman

KINSHIP

Kinship relationships are based on shared descent, coresidence, and marriage. In the nineteenth century, towns and cities were made up of compounds (agbo ilé) in which extended patrilineal lineages lived with their wives and other followers or dependents. Compounds were important units of social and political organization because they held collective rights to land, chieftaincy titles, and other resources, such as traditional deities (òrìṣà). They were also collectively responsible for one another. Members of the family who could trace their descent to the founder of the compound were referred to as ọmọ ilé, or "children of the compound or house." The most senior male member of the ọmọ ilé was the baálé, or head of the compound. The ọmọ ilé formed the core of the compound's corporate identity. Although descent was primarily reckoned through the male line, the children of female ọmọ ilé were sometimes accepted as members of the patrilineal lineage, especially in parts of eastern Yorùbáland, including Rẹ́mọ, Ìjẹ̀bú, Oǹdó, Ìkálẹ̀, and Ìlàjẹ. Over time, coresidents, bondsmen or pawns, and even slaves could become assimilated into the ọmọ ilé.

As people left their rural compounds to move to the cities during the twentieth century, kinship relations shaped rural-urban links. Although compound membership has declined in many areas, the claim to membership of a compound remains key to maintaining rights to corporately owned land or titles. To maintain access to these resources, many migrant members of families remain in regular contact with those who have stayed in their old compounds or hometowns. Sending remittances and supporting infrastructural development in the rural areas, they receive agricultural products and may even confirm their achievements by building houses or accepting chieftaincy titles in their (family's) hometowns.

Marriage is exogamous for kin by descent and coresidence, and it constitutes a bond between corporate groups as well as individuals. Women are expected to leave their fathers' houses or compounds upon marriage to become obìnrin ilé or ìyàwó ilé, women or wives of their husband's house or compound. The status of a wife among her new kin is measured by the length of her marriage. Polygamous marriages are declining but still prevalent, and the first wife expects respect from the younger wives. In compounds, all ìyàwó ilé form a corporate group under the leadership of the most senior wife. Every *ìyàwó ilé* considers all male and female relations of her husband to be "husbands," and she may in turn be a "husband" to her brothers' and uncles' wives. Women in urban areas often join the other *ìyàwó ilé* for activities during weddings and funerals.

The corporate nature of kinship has also enabled many families to negotiate the growth of religious difference as family members converted to Islam or Christianity during the twentieth century. Where family members of different religions live together, wives and dependents generally accept the rights of husbands and senior members of the household to determine collective religious practices. As a result, some Pentecostal and Islamic groups have issued warnings to members of their congregation not to keep ties with extended family members, in order to avoid possible spiritual attacks from them.

REFERENCES

Eades, Jeremy Seymour. *The Yorùbá Today.* Cambridge: Cambridge University Press, 1980.

Nolte, Insa. *Ọbáfẹ́mi Awólọ́wọ̀ and the Making of Rẹ́mọ: The Local Politics of a Nigerian Nationalist.* Edinburgh: Edinburgh University Press, 2009.

Insa Nolte

KOLA NUT

Kola nut is a tree in the tropical rain forest. It requires a hot humid climate but can withstand a dry season on sites with a high level of groundwater. It may be cultivated in drier areas where groundwater is available. Kola nuts can be harvested mechanically or by hand; they are plucked off the tree branch. When kept in a cool, dry place, kola nuts can be stored for a long time. Kola nut is a flavoring ingredient and source of caffeine. Kola nut is an important cash crop, and many farmers rely on it.

There are two important species of kola nut: *obì àbàtà* and *obì gbàǹja*. *Obi àbàtà* is commonly used for religious rituals, and *obì gbàǹja* is commonly used for social rituals. Nevertheless, either one can be used for religious and social rituals. From experience and observation, sacredness is more attached to *obì àbàtà*, which is the reason many people call it *obì òrìṣà* (kola nut of the deities).

Kola nuts are an important part of the traditional spiritual practice of culture and religion. They are used as a religious object and sacred offering during prayers, ancestor veneration, and significant life events, such as naming ceremonies, weddings, and funerals. They are also used in the traditional divination system. In this context, only kola nuts divided into four lobes (*obì olòjú mẹ́rin*) are suitable. They are cast upon a special wooden board or the ground, and a trained diviner reads the resulting patterns. A trained diviner can foretell the future or outcome of a journey or a particular enterprise. This portends that kola nut has imbued spiritual essence or trait. The spirituality that the Yorùbá attach to kola nut means it occupies a central place in their concept of vitality.

It is a popular folk belief that witches use kola nut to initiate people into their cults. For example, when a charmed kola nut is given to a person the witch would like to bring into his or her cult, the person will be compelled to show his or her willingness to join the cult. In addition, kola nuts can be used as poison. The idea of using kola nut to perform these functions connects with its social functions. It is one of the seeds used in social gatherings and entertaining people, especially visitors.

It is believed that there is a vital force (*àṣẹ*) embedded in kola nut that makes it work, which is why it is a material used during various rites and rituals. For example, kola nut is used during the traditional naming practice. On such an occasion, the person conducting the naming takes a piece of kola nut, touches the baby's head, and prays, *Obì nìyí o. Obì níí bi ikú, obì níí bi àrùn. Bá wa gbá gbogbo ibi tó bá fẹ́ dojú kọ ọmọ yìí lọ o* (This is kola nut. It is kola nut that sweeps off death and diseases. Sweep off all evils that may contend against this child). Kola nut is used to ward off impending evils. In many instances, the people make use of the kola nut as a prayer element because of the meaning associated with the ending syllable of *obì—bì*, which means "to ward off."

Similarly, during the traditional marriage ceremony, kola nuts are used at different stages of the ritual. Most significantly, purple kola nuts (*obì àjóòpá*) symbolize virginity. After it has been confirmed that a particular bride is a virgin, the groom's family will send plenty of red kola nuts to the bride's family in appreciation of the good training they believed has been given to their daughter. They sing, *àjóòpá lobì oge* (the red kola nut is the symbol of the virgin).

During the actual traditional marriage ceremony, kola nut is used to seal or bind marriage ties between the bride's and groom's families. When the marriage is consummated, the elders from both families share kola nut as the seal of covenant. Reference to this act of sharing kola nut is usually made whenever there is any form of threat to the marriage; hence the saying *èyin àgbààgbà tí ẹ jẹ̀ṣẹ́bì, ẹ pera yín jọ* (you elders who ate pieces of kola nut, gather yourself together). This connotes that the elders from the bride's and groom's families entered into the marital bond through the eating of kola nut, and they must come together to solve the quarrel between the couple. This practice underscores the important space that kola nut occupies in the culture of the people.

Research has shown that the ritual significance of kola nut forms an important part of the ritual material attributed to almost all deities in the land. Kola nut is one of the favorite items offered to Ṣàngó, the Yorùbá god of thunder and lightning. Hence, he is praised, *olójú orógbó ẹlẹ́ẹ̀kẹ́ obì* (the one whose eyeball is like bitter kola, who has cheeks of kola nut). Ifá priests note that when kola nuts are part of a sacrifice to be offered, it signifies that Ṣàngó is one of the recipients of such a sacrifice. Of all fruits in the land, the space and place that the kola nut occupies cannot be overemphasized. It functions in almost every area of people's life.

See also **Stimulants and Intoxicants**

REFERENCE

Fádípè, N. A. *The Sociology of the Yorùbá*. Ìbàdàn (Nigeria): University Press, 1970.

George Olúṣọlá Ajíbádé

L

LABOR: CHILD

The concept of childhood as a social principle emerged around the sixteenth century. It is difficult to say exactly when street trading started among children in Nigeria. Initially, a few were found on the streets. Later, they became conspicuous, then a menace, and now a social problem. In the past, as now, a child is considered a blessing and an addition to human capital in the process of survival and social interdependence. From a sociocultural angle, children are gifts and result from the consummation of marriage. From political and economic angles, children are economic assets for labor and material wealth, and they are the basis for possession and wealth. In the Yorùbá culture, children are expected to serve their parents and provide for them. They are also social insurance against future uncertainty.

Child labor includes agriculture labor. Traditionally, the Yorùbá are agrarians, and children as young as five years old weed, plant, harvest, and sell farm products for their parents. Children also engage in street trading or hawking. Hawking was common in rural economies, and this has translated to street trading in urban communities for family sustenance and for commission.

Domestic labor is another form of child labor. It dates back to traditional times, when children of impoverished families were sent to wealthier family members for training or discipline. Urbanization and changing roles and increasing employment of women have brought about an increase in need for domestic labor. Pawning and bonded labor known as ìwòfà under the Yorùbá traditional culture was a pre-nineteenth-century practice of child labor in which children were given out as security for loan, and their labor served as payment for interest of the loan.

Some reasons for child labor include support for family production, skill acquisition and training, socialization into the culture, community integration, and survival. Work for children is not necessarily detrimental. It should, however, not be abusive, oppressive, exploitative, or hazardous. Some laws have been promulgated to protect the rights of every child. These include laws at state, national, regional, and international levels such as the Sharia Penal Code Law of Zamfara State (2000), the Child Rights Act (2003), the Criminal Code Act (2004), the Constitution of the Federal Republic of Nigeria (1999, as amended), the African Charter on Human and Peoples Right (Ratification & Enforcement) Act (1990), the African Charter on the Rights and Welfare of the Child, and the UN Convention on the Rights of the Child.

REFERENCES

Bámgbóṣé, Olúyémisí. "Child Labor and Effects of the Economic Climate on the Rights of a Child in Contemporary Nigeria." *Journal of School Health Education* 5.1–5.2 (1998): 1–21.
Lovejoy, P. E., and Tóyìn Fáló̩lá. *Pawnship, Slavery and Colonialism in Africa.* Trenton, NJ: Africa World Press, 2003.

Olúyémisí Bámgbóṣé

As an aspect of human migration, labor migration describes any human movement from one location to another, over long or short distances, in large or small groups, and with the intention of making a permanent settlement in a new location. The history of Yorùbá people cannot be told except in relation to migration. For instance, two accounts of Yorùbá origin noted that the people migrated to Ilé-Ifẹ̀. In the first account, they were said to have migrated from the heavens; in the second, the place of origin was said to be somewhere in the Middle East. Irrespective of where they migrated from, some of them left Ilé-Ifẹ̀ later to settle in their current locations. Consequently, migration is an age-old phenomenon among the people.

In precolonial times, labor migration was one of the various ways people solved population and employment problems. A cursory look at Yorùbá history shows that three migratory trends have occurred in their history. The first is movement within Yorùbáland. The second deals with the movement of non-Yorùbá people into Yorùbáland. The third describes the movement of Yorùbá people into places other than Yorùbáland. These movements were driven by trade, conquest, and insecurity.

Odùduwà's sons migrated from Ìta-Ajamọ at Ilé-Ifẹ̀ to found different kingdoms. For example, one son founded the Benin Kingdom, and Ọ̀rànmíyàn founded Ọ̀yọ́-Ile. Others founded Pópó, Kétu, Ìlá-Ọ̀ràngún, and other places. Movements such as these abound in Yorùbáland before, during, and after colonial rule.

The most enduring periods of internal migration were perhaps those during the transatlantic slave trade, the nineteenth-century war, and the period of colonial rule. During these periods, a large number of people were compelled to migrate from one part of Yorùbáland to another in search of safety or employment opportunities. The slave trade and civil war forced people to migrate; most ended up as slaves, housekeepers, and laborers in different parts of Yorùbáland and beyond.

During the colonial period, migration was essentially for labor. This development relates primarily to the incorporation of Yorùbáland vis-à-vis Nigeria into the vortex of global trade. During this period, the colonial government built roads, railways, and harbor ports, telecommunication systems, and the like. In addition, employment opportunities arose in government service and with European merchants. One impetus for migration was necessitated by the push and pull of trade and commerce. Included in these migrations were educated elite, unskilled youth, native administrative staff, and others in the European trading firms. Another impetus was the abolition of the slave trade, human sacrifice, and pawnship. Included in these migrations were mostly former slaves and bondsmen or pawns. These migrants, as a result of precolonial developments such as the slave trade, domestic slavery, and civil wars, became residents in communities other than original homes. They were set free after the establishment of colonial rule. Many of these people returned to their original homes or migrated to other places where they were at liberty to pursue their desires.

The three major trends in labor migration in colonial Yorùbáland are rural-to-urban, urban-to-rural, and rural-to-rural migration. The first deals with movements of people from rural areas of little or no economic activities to urban areas of greater economic activities in the region. The second relates to the effect of climate. In areas where absence of rainfall freed the people from their regular activities, Nigerians used such freedom to travel for pleasure, commerce, training, skill acquisition, education, and the like. In some communities in Nigeria, peasant farmers, whether on a seasonal or permanent basis, moved across regional frontiers. Nomadic cattle herders migrated from northern Nigeria to southern coastal areas of Nigeria. Cocoa-producing areas of western Nigeria, especially during the late 1940s and the 1950s, also benefited from this trend when there was an unprecedented boom in the cocoa trade. There were also labor migrants from the land-starved Hausa lands and overpopulated Igbo lands to the cocoa-producing areas of Oǹdó, Ọ̀yọ́, Èkìtì, Ilé-Ifẹ̀, and others during the period.

The third and most popular trend relates to rural-to-urban migration. From 1893, there was a massive drift from rural areas and the lesser towns and villages to urban centers, where new opportunities had sprung up for commerce and for employment in colonial services and Euro-Asian trading companies. Peasant children, educated villagers, peasant farmers, craftsmen, and freed slaves thronged urban centers in search of wage-earning opportunities.

REFERENCE

Johnson, Samuel. *The History of the Yorùbás.* Lagos (Nigeria): C.S.S., 1921.

Bùkọ́lá Oyèníyì

LABOR: TRADE UNIONS AND ASSOCIATIONS

Trade unions and associations are collective alliances based on membership in a profession. Their major focus is the representation and protection of interest and goals of members at the workplace and in the wider society. The major roles of trade unions and associations include economic emancipation, social welfare, and political functions. In fact, they possess economic power and influence the labor market. They affect workers' identities, and they build a sense of connectedness and solidarity. With their economic power, trade unions and associations address substantive issues such as wages and salaries, service conditions, job security, and respect and dignity in the profession.

Trade unions and associations serve as social movements underpinning local democracy; they influence government reforms at the national level. They constitute a formidable pressure to enhance bargaining power; they influence local and state governments' decision through lobbying, demonstrations, and petitions. Trade unionism has also launched some members into political careers; they have gone on to become representatives in government. Trade unions and associations are characterized by a spirit of togetherness and discipline. They recruit and exchange apprentices as well as tools and instruments among themselves. They meet regularly to discuss their professional challenges and ways to meet those challenges.

Trade unions and associations build solidarity and facilitate local democratic political participation by providing members with information that helps mitigate the problem of rational ignorance around political issues and lower individual costs of active participation. In electoral campaigns, they help parties mobilize members for electoral campaigning, both as voters and as volunteer campaign workers. This role, however, helps strengthen voter participation and influences public policies to serve the wider interests of ordinary citizens rather than just the elite.

Trade unions and association create industrial democracy in the workplace. Members have the opportunity to elect their management committee members through the ballot. Through industrial democracy, trade unions are fertile institutions for the furtherance of participatory democracy and rights such as the freedoms of assembly, speech, and choice. In addition to collective bargaining, trade unions and associations also develop valuable services for members. They develop housing and land-lease schemes, transport and service stations, and credit unions for the benefit of members. At social functions, attendance is mandatory and members wear the same outfit (*aṣọ ẹgbéjọdá*).

Trade unions and associations also provide regulatory roles by setting standards in relation to terms and conditions. These include issues such as discipline, job evaluation, work changes, technological use and improvement, and safety and health. They inform and train members on the development and use of new technologies to enhance their output. They agree on a common price and on service policies for customers. They disseminate useful social and economic information among themselves. They serve as jury and negotiate between members and customers.

REFERENCE

Fájánà, S. *Functioning of the Nigerian Labour Market*. Lagos (Nigeria): Lobofin and Co., 2000.

Tósìn Akínjọbí-Babátúndé

LÁDIPỌ̀, DÚRÓ (1931–1978)

Dúró Ládipọ̀ represented the top of the popular traveling theater tradition with roots in both indigenous and Western performance traditions. He was an unparalleled cultural ambassador who displayed the grandeurs of Yorùbá traditions through theatrical presentations before international audiences in Europe, North and South America, and the Middle East. He was born Timothy Dúródọlá Àdìsá into the family of Joseph Òní and Dorcas Tọwọ́bọlá Àjíké Ládipọ̀ at Òṣogbo. His grandfather, a veteran drummer, was originally from Èrìn-Ọ̀fà but settled in a Balógun Ọdérìnlọ compound at Òṣogbo after the Jálumi War of 1878. Though from a Ṣàngó and Ọya familial worship background, Dúró's father converted to Christianity and became a clergyman in the Anglican Church. This afforded Dúró easy access to Western education and culture through the church. He had his elementary education and childhood experiences at Ọ̀tan Ayégbaju, Ìlá Ọ̀ràngún, and their environs, where his parents served in the church.

After earning his Government Middle Two Certificate in 1942, Dúró began a teaching career, which lasted eighteen years in the old Western and Northern Regions. He took in-service trainings and had his Teacher's Grades III and II Certificates in 1955 and 1958, respectively, and he took drama and theater courses at the University of Ìbàdàn from 1963 to 1964. Dúró expressed an interest in the theater, which manifested while in elementary school. Those who encouraged his interest were A. J. Ọdúnsì and Alex Peters, two head teachers he worked with. Other notable personalities who collaborated with and encouraged him include Ulli Beier and Georgina Beier, Peggy Harper, Suzan Wenger, and Dennis Williams.

Dúró Ládipọ̀ was reprimanded by church authorities for introducing traditional drums into his Easter cantata in 1961; they were regarded as fetishes. Beier, however, arranged for a performance of the cantata on the Western Nigeria Television channel, and that marked the beginning of his television performances. A Christmas cantata followed at the end of that year, and several other television plays came after. With the help of Beier and financial assistance from a £200 grant received from a friend, Dúró remodeled the Popular Bar in Òṣogbo, an old apartment in his father's house. Dúró turned it into a cultural center with a performance space and a gallery, similar to the Mbárí Club at Ìbàdàn. Dúró named the space Mbárí Mbáyọ̀. It was there that many of Dúró's plays were produced and had their premiere.

Dúró specialized in producing plays that were derived from folktales, histories, myths, and legends. They heavily used folk music and other folkloric materials. The plays include *Ọba Mọ́rọ̀* (1962), *Ọba Kò So* and *Ọba Wàjà* (1963), *Mọrèmi* (1965), *Ewé Ayọ́* (1967), *Béyìí ò Ṣe* (1968), *Ọbàtálá* (1969), *Ọ̀rúnmìlà* and *Ọ̀ṣun* (1971), and *Ajagun Ńlá* (1973). He also adapted plays from biblical stories and other sources, such as William Shakespeare and Hugo von Hofmannsthal. Examples include *Kọ bí Ìdì* (David and Goliath), *Olúorogbo* (Nativity), *Afọláyan* (Joseph the Dreamer), *Jáléyẹmí* (Samson and Delilah), *Ọ̀tún Akọgun* (Macbeth), *Káróunwí* (Hamlet), and *Ẹ̀dá* (Everyman). Dúró distinguished himself in the role of Ṣàngó in *Ọba Kò So*, his most popular play, which tells the story of the conflicts that led to Ṣàngó's deification.

See also **Òṣogbo: Ọ̀ṣun and the Art School; Prominent Scholars**

REFERENCE

Beier, Ulli. *The Hunter Thinks the Monkey Is Not Wise . . . A Selection of Essays*, ed. Wọlé Ògúndélé. Bayreuth African Studies Series 59. Bayreuth (Germany): Bayreuth University, 2001.

Philip Adédọtun Ògúndèjì

LÁMBÒ, ADÉOYÈ THOMAS (1923–2004)

Dr. Adéoyè Thomas Lámbò was the first Nigerian to become a psychiatrist in the European medical tradition. He was internationally renowned for his work in cross-cultural psychiatric epidemiology and for his clinical innovations at the Arò Mental Hospital (later Arò Neuropsychiatric Hospital) in Abẹ̀òkúta, Nigeria. He also served as deputy director general of the World Health Organization (WHO) for most of the 1970s and 1980s.

Born in Abẹ̀òkúta on March 29, 1923, Lámbò undertook missionary schooling, graduating from the Baptist Boys' High School before studying medicine at the University of Birmingham, United Kingdom. Upon graduation from medical school in 1948, Lámbò practiced in Birmingham before returning home to Nigeria for a brief period in 1951. While in Nigeria, Lámbò was briefly stationed at the Yaba asylum, one of only two mental asylums in all of Nigeria at the time. His work at Yaba convinced him to specialize in psychiatry. In 1952, he returned to England for further study at the Maudsley Hospital in London. Lámbò returned to Nigeria in 1954 to take up the position of medical superintendent at Arò Mental Hospital, the first medical hospital for the treatment of mental illness in Nigeria.

At Arò, Lámbò began to develop a significant research agenda into the epidemiology of mental illness among Nigerians. He produced several works indicating that the incidence of schizophrenia and depression was likely higher in Nigerian populations than had been previously assumed. Along with Tọ́lání Asúni, Lámbò oversaw the participation of Arò Mental Hospital and the University of Ìbàdàn as a catchment area for the World Health Organization's International Pilot Study of Schizophrenia, among other important projects.

Lámbò also oversaw the development of Arò Mental Hospital into a full-fledged treatment center. While the hospital provided some inpatient care from the late 1950s, Lámbò's greatest legacy perhaps was the establishment of the Arò Village Scheme, which sought to treat rural Nigerian patients on an outpatient basis. Patients came to Arò Village, located near the hospital, with a relative. They lived with a local family and received a variety of medical and therapeutic treatments during their stay. Lámbò even incorporated indigenous healers into the village system, believing that they understood a great deal about mental illness in their communities and, as such, could provide care to patients in culturally appropriate terms. The Arò Village scheme became a model of outpatient care adapted in many different African countries.

In 1963, Lámbò left Arò Mental Hospital to become chair of the Department of Psychiatry at the University of Ìbàdàn. In 1971, he left the university to work full-time for the WHO, first as an assistant director general with oversight of the divisions of mental health, noncommunicable diseases, therapeutics, and prophylactic substances. In 1973, he became the deputy director general, a position he held until 1988. Lámbò passed away on March 13, 2004. Over the course of his career, Lámbò had become, as one eulogizer put it, "the recognizable face of African psychiatry."

See also **Prominent Scholars; Psychiatry**

REFERENCE

Fálọlá, Tóyìn, and M. Matthew Heaton, eds. *Traditional and Modern Health System in Nigeria.* Trenton, NJ: Africa World Press, 2006.

Matthew M. Heaton

LAND TENURE AND REFORM

Land tenure flows directly from the patrilineal social organization of lineages, towns, and communities. An individual belongs to only his father's descent group, and membership of the paternal lineage is exclusive. Rights to property, land, and titles are inherited within these exogamous corporate descent groups, which hold them in trust for its members. This lineage is the land- and title-holding unit in the town and communities. The male members of each lineage typically reside together, along with their wives and children, in the *agboolé* (a compound).

Distinctions may be made between the cognatic and agnatic systems of land acquisition. In the cognatic system typified by the Ìjẹbú, a man could claim land from a number of different descent groups. As the lineage grew including through the acquisition of large numbers of wives and slaves by powerful chiefs, members could move to ease pressure on land available to the lineage. This practice allowed boundaries of the ìlú (the town) to remain the same for a long period.

In the agnatic system, a man could claim land only from his father's descent group. Among the Oǹdó, land is held by descent groups on behalf of the community. A man is entitled to farm only the land of his descent group. Increased demand for land often resulted in war and the conquest or absorption of surrounding settlements. In this traditional system, the right of disposal belonged only to the community, which acted through traditional authorities. Property rights are exercised in accordance with customary law. While the principles of land ownership in the traditional setting are fairly established, the influence of Westernization created serious tensions with traditional modes of land acquisition and ownership.

The tensions have occurred mainly along two fronts: the human rights challenge to traditional practices of inheritance regarding girls and women and the emergence of the modern state's seeking to control the totality of national real estate. The land reforms instituted by the state were justified as required for developmental purposes. In the south of Nigeria, including in Yorùbáland, colonial authorities introduced the concept of individual ownership of property. Various laws and ordinances conferred on the government the power of statutory landholdings in return for compensation. In March 1978, the Federal Military Government promulgated the Land Use Decree to establish a uniform system for all of Nigeria. A 1979 decree nationalized all land by the state's acquisition of the authority to issue certificates of occupancy, and the payment of rent on land to the state. However, anyone who could prove effective occupation of land and developed it continued to enjoy the right of occupancy. He could sell or transfer his interest in the development of the land.

REFERENCE

Lloyd, P. C. Yorùbáland Law. London: Oxford University Press, 1962.

Adémọ́lá Àràoyè

Translating the Yorùbá language to the written word was the first contribution of the missionaries to the development of Western education in western Nigeria. Subsequently, they translated several books of the Bible into Yorùbá. A Southern Baptist missionary, Reverend Thomas Jefferson Bowen, produced *Grammar and Dictionary of the Yorùbá Language* in 1858. Other missionary groups, such as the Church Missionary Society (CMS) and the Methodists, also produced textbooks, primers, and dictionaries that enabled the missionaries to teach their converts to read the Bible in Yorùbá. They produced the first widespread literate class of people in southwestern Nigeria. In 1852, the CMS and Reverend Henry Townsend established the first printing press in Nigeria; it published newspapers in Yorùbá. Some of the first local printers and journalists emerged. In 1859, Ìwé Ìròyìn fún àwọn Ẹ̀gbá àti Yorùbá was established. In 1875, the CMS and Reverend Àjàyí Crowther coordinated a conference at Ìta Fájì in Lagos. The representative missionaries standardized the language's orthography, which facilitated a steady flow of religious and educational literature over the following seventy years.

In 1922, a Phelps Stokes Commission Report recommended the use of vernaculars (Yorùbá) for instruction in schools in the Western Region. With the establishment of many primary and secondary schools there during the 1940s, instruction occurred both in English and in Yorùbá. In 1963, UNESCO set up an ad hoc committee to review Yorùbá orthography. The late J. F. Ọdúnjọ chaired the committee. In 1966, the Western Region accepted the report of the Yorùbá Orthography Committee, which reviewed 1875 and 1963 editions of the orthography. In 1974, a Joint Consultative Committee on Yorùbá orthography in the Federal Ministry of Education reviewed and came up with best practices for writing the language.

In 2012, the Federal Ministry of Culture established the Unified Standard Orthography for Yorùbá language clusters in Nigeria, Republic of Benin, and Togo. Section 55 of the Nigeria Constitution states: "The business of the National Assembly shall be conducted in English and in Hausa, Ibo [Igbo], and Yorùbá when adequate arrangements have been made therefore." Also, section 97 of the same constitution states: "The business of a House of Assembly shall be conducted in English, but the House may in addition to English conduct the business of the House in one or more other languages spoken in the state as the House may by resolution approve." In 2001, the National Policy on Education required that every child learn the language of his or her immediate environment and that every child who did not know how to speak Yorùbá learn the language. The policy states further that, in early childhood and preprimary education, the language of instruction should principally be in the child's mother tongue. In secondary school, Yorùbá is one of the core subjects that students are required to pass.

REFERENCE

Àjàyí, Adémólá. "Christian Missions and Evolution of the Culture of Mass Education in Western Nigeria." *Journal of Philosophy and Culture* 3.2 (2006): 21–40.

Harrison Adéníyì

LANGUAGE: SOCIOLINGUISTICS

Sociolinguistics is the descriptive study of the effect of any and all aspects of society, including cultural norms, expectations, and context, on the way language is used. It also involves the effects of language use on society. There is a strong relationship between language and culture in the Yorùbá language. One is the respect for elders and superiors during interactions, which clearly shows the way the language is used. For example, elders are addressed with honorific plural pronouns by young people. In a conversation between a child and mother or between a supervisor and his or her subordinate, the plural pronouns *ẹ*, *ẹ̀yin*, and *yin* are used by the child or subordinate instead of *o* and *ìwọ*. This practice shows respect for elders and superiors.

In addition, kinship terms reflect the way language is used. In Yorùbá, only five words show kinship terms: *bàbá* (father), *ìyá* (mother), *ẹ̀gbọ́n* (elder sibling, male

or female), *àbúrò* (younger sibling, male or female), and *ọmọ* (child). Therefore, there is no description *ẹ̀gbọ́n bàbá mi*—my father's elder brother—rather, it is *bàbá àgbà*, which literally means "senior father." Nor is there such a description as *àbúrò ìyá mi*—my mother's younger sister—rather, it is *ìyá kékeré*, which literally means "younger mother." Any child whom one is old enough to have given birth to is referred to as *ọmọ mi* (my child). Any woman in the family who is old enough to give birth to a child is referred to as *ìyá* (mother). Any older child in the family who is not young but is not old enough to give birth to someone is referred to as *ẹ̀gbọ́n*. If the person is addressed by his or her personal name, members of society interpret that to mean that the speaker is overtly expressing the wish to distant him- or herself from the addressee. It is a subtle denial of any intimate relationship. The implication of the usage is that it invariably causes a breakdown of harmonious relationship within an extended family.

Yorùbá also have two types of dialects: regional and social. Examples of regional dialects are Ọ̀yọ́, Ọ̀nkò, Àkúré, Èkìtì, Ifẹ̀, Owé, Àwórì, Ẹ̀gbá, Ikale, Ìgbómìnà, Yewa, Ìjẹ̀sà, Kétu, Ìjẹ̀bú, and Ànàgó. These dialects are mutually intelligible. However, the more distance between the dialects, the less they are mutually intelligible, so much so that they become a distinct language. Social dialects are spoken by different social groups, such as profession, sex, age, or occupation. Examples include bus and cab drivers and conductors who have words such as *faíbà* (fifty naira), *wàsó* (twenty naira), *párò lọ* (please move on), and *wọlé kanlẹ̀* (exit to the fastest lane).

Students in tertiary institutions use slang such as *ẹfikòó* (studious), *gúnṣẹ́ lọ́bẹ* (absent from class), *gbéégún nínú ìdánwò* (cheat on the examination), *àlútà ni Ṣọlá* (Ṣọlá [a fictitious name] is committed to human rights struggle). Traders have words such as *wòsìwósì* (petty wares to sell), *onífàyàwọ́* (smuggler), *èènì* (extra), and *alájàpá* (petty trader).

See also **Language in Contact; Linguistics: Morphology; Linguistics: Semantics; Linguistics: Syntax**

REFERENCE

Abíọ́dún, M. "Ìmọ̀-ẹ̀dá èdè ajẹmáwùjọ." In *Ilò-èdè àti ẹ̀dá-èdè Yorùbá: Apá kejì*, ed. Harrison Adéníyì and Akinloyè Ọ̀jó, 78–91. Trenton, NJ: Africa World Press, 2005.

Harrison Adéníyì

LANGUAGE: STANDARDIZATION AND LITERACY

Codification of the Yorùbá language has undergone different stages in the past four centuries. The earliest attempt to develop a written form of the language was initiated with the Ajami (also known as Ajamiyya) script, which is a seventeenth-century adaption of a modified Arabic script. The system was developed by Islamic scholars to document biographies, diseases and illnesses, poetry, administrative correspondence, and so on. Thus, speakers were able to write their thoughts in the Ajami script. This was a great leap from centuries past, in which Yorùbá existed only in the oral form. Some of the works in the Ajami script survive today. An example of the Yorùbá-language materials written in the Ajami script in 1891 is the *waka* poetry attributed to Badamasi Bin Musa Agbaji. The introduction of Christianity, colonization, and Westernization to the people systematically led to the decline in the use of the Ajami script and its eventual demise in the Yorùbá writing system.

Christianity was introduced to Nigeria from the fifteenth to nineteenth centuries. Western education was subsequently introduced by the missionaries. Efforts to write Yorùbá in the Latin alphabet accompanied the introduction of Western education. Bishop Àjàyí Crowther was the leader in using the Latin alphabet to write Yorùbá. This includes his work on the Yorùbá Bible and on Yorùbá grammar, starting in the 1840s. Some of the unique features of the Yorùbá language in the Latin alphabet include the use of diacritic marks on vowels and under certain letters. The grave symbol is used to mark the low tone in the language. *Ìmọ̀* (knowledge) has two low tones. Also, the acute symbol is used to the high tone. *Díńgí* (mirror) has three high tones. The middle tone is left unmarked. *Oorun* (sleep) has three middle tones. Three letters have diacritics below them (ọ, ẹ, and ṣ). This differentiates them from their counterparts that do not have the marks and are pronounced slightly differently (o, e, and s). Also, two of the eighteen Yorùbá consonants (/p/ and /gb/) are produced with coarticulations. The consonant /gb/ is a labial and velar sound.

Yorùbá has many dialects that are divisible into about five groups: southwestern Yorùbá, southeastern Yorùbá, central Yorùbá, northeastern Yorùbá, and northwestern Yorùbá. There is a need to standardize the language because of its many dialects. Efforts to standardize Yorùbá written with the Latin alphabet were initiated by the missionaries around 1848 and 1849 in Britain and in 1875 in Nigeria. Native scholars continued these efforts in 1966, 1974, and—more recently—with the publication of *Modern Yorùbá Writing Manual* by the Yorùbá Cross-Border Language Commission. Some of the features of the current standard Yorùbá include the nonoccurrence of consonant clusters, codas (i.e., syllable final consonants), vowel /u/ initial words, nasal vowel initial words, and high-toned initial-vowel disyllabic words in the language.

Several foundational Yorùbá grammar and history books were produced by Àjàyí Crowther, J. T. Bowen, Samuel Johnson, Ida Ward, and others. Many literary books were also produced in the language based on the evolving Yorùbá orthography. Some of the foremost authors of Yorùbá literature include I. B. Thomas, who was credited with the first Yorùbá novel, *Ìtàn Èmi Ṣẹgilọlá Ẹléyinjú Ẹgẹ́*; D. O. Fágúnwà, who wrote five timeless Yorùbá novels, including *Ògbójú Ọdẹ Nínú Igbó Irúnmọlẹ̀*, which was translated by Wọlé Ṣóyínká into English as *The Forest of a Thousand Daemons*; Mójọlà Àgbébí, who wrote *Ìwé Àlọ́* (1895); and Sóbọ̀ Aróbíodu, who wrote many poems. Hundreds of Yorùbá literature and grammar books have been produced with the Latin alphabet. And dozens of institutions that award bachelor's degrees in Nigeria have Yorùbá studies programs, some of them up to the doctorate level.

See also **Colonial Policies and Practices; Fágúnwà, D. O.; Language: Government and Mission Policies; Translation; Writers**

REFERENCE

Ògúnṣínà, Bísí. *The Development of the Yorùbá Novel c. 1930–1975.* Ìlọrin (Nigeria): Gospel Faith Mission Press, 1992.

Olúṣẹ̀yẹ Adéṣọlá

LANGUAGE IN CONTACT

Language in contact occurs when two or more languages or varieties interact. In this case, the Yorùbá language interacted with languages in its environs (Edo in the east, Ebira in the northeast, and Ogu in the west) as well as with distant languages such as English and Arabic. Because of its strength as a major language and its higher social position, the language has assumed a "superior" role in the sociolinguistic lives of the speakers of these minority languages. Most speakers of these minority languages are not only bilingual but also believe that speaking Yorùbá is more fashionable. Apart from this, they code switch and code mix. They have imbibed Yorùbá sociocultural practices such as naming practices and ceremonies, greetings, marriage ceremonies, and others. The speakers of the Yorùbá language, in contrast, do not attach much prestige to these neighboring minority languages. In fact, speaking any of them confers a low social status on the speakers. Nonetheless, the Yorùbá language also borrowed some lexicon from some of these neighboring minority languages, though in peculiar ways. For instance, *dẹ̀pẹ̀* in the Ogu language means "a handsome fine guy"; however, in Yorùbá, it refers to a stupid person. *Ìkẹ̀bẹ̀* in the Edo language means "buttocks," and it has the same meaning in the Yorùbá language, but the tones are different (*ìkébè*).

Languages borrow from other languages that they interact with. Borrowing is not suggestive of weakness; it is linguistic self-preservation. Any language that stops borrowing will sooner or later die. To this end, Yorùbá borrowed extensively from English, because of the long history of colonialism in Nigeria, and it borrows from Arabic because of the religious connection with the Arabs and Hausa. Most Arabic words in Yorùbá did not come through direct borrowing; they came through the Hausa language. Hausa speakers have had extensive trade and cultural relations with the Yorùbá since the fifteenth century. Arabic loanwords started to appear in Yorùbá at the peak of trans-Saharan trade.

Some borrowed Arabic words include *ìwàásù*, derived from the Arabic *waz*, which means "admonition" or "sermon"; *fìtílà*, derived from *fatil*, which means "any kind of lamp"; and *àdúrà*, derived from *du'a*, or "prayer." Borrowed English words include *kámẹ́rà* from *camera*; *sẹ́nẹ́tọ̀* from *senator*; and *ẹ́m̀básì* from *embassy*. Yorùbá speakers also code switch, change from one sentence in English to another in Yorùbá, and code mix, or mix English and Yorùbá words in the same sentence. An example of code mixing is *mo ti spend owó yẹn*, meaning "I have spent the money."

See also **Language: Sociolinguistics**

REFERENCE

Crystal, D. *The Cambridge Encyclopedia of Language.* 2nd ed. Cambridge: University of Cambridge, 2007.

Harrison Adéníyì

LANGUAGE PEDAGOGY

Yorùbá is a dialect continuum including distinct dialects in terms of pronunciation, grammar, and vocabulary. A standard has evolved for language pedagogy. Developments in linguistics since the 1980s have allowed for more sophisticated study and teaching of the language to natives and nonnatives in Nigeria (as part of the national language policy), in the African Diaspora (as part of African heritage), and universally (as part of foreign-language education). Yorùbá is a viable medium of instruction in education and has a significant amount of instructional materials available.

In Nigeria, Yorùbá is the language of instruction during the first three years of public primary schooling. Instruction in English occurs in primary 4, and Yorùbá is offered as a required subject. In secondary schools, Yorùbá is offered as a subject for native speakers. With instruction in Yorùbá, the curriculum is divided into language (core) and literature. Yorùbá is also offered as a second language to nonnatives. At the college level, Yorùbá is the primary language of instruction in Yorùbá courses offered in linguistics and African languages departments. Graduates of these programs produce their writings in Yorùbá. Interestingly, teacher-training colleges are the dominant institutions for Yorùbá as second-language programs in Nigeria. Many Yorùbá instructors belong to the professional organizations Ẹgbẹ́ Akọmọlédè Yorùbá and Ẹgbẹ́ Onímọ̀ Èdè Yorùbá.

In Europe, two prominent institutions for the study of Yorùbá are the School of Oriental and Africa Studies (SOAS) in London and the Institut National des Langues et Civilisations Orientales (INALCO) in Paris. In America, the National African Language Resource Center (NALRC) identifies eighteen established Yorùbá language programs, and other centers report thirty-nine institutions offering some Yorùbá courses. The American Association of Teachers of Yorùbá (AATY) serves as the professional platform for Yorùbá educators in the United States. The formalization of the methodology for Yorùbá L2 teaching has developed and grown as a field. A dominant methodology is the goal-based approach, which focuses on the student and emphasizes the interrelationship between L2 pedagogy and knowledge about language, culture, learning strategies, and communication strategies.

REFERENCE

Òjó, Akinloyè. "A Global Evaluation of the Teaching and Learning of Yorùbá Language as a Second or Foreign Language." In *Selected Proceedings of the 36th Annual Conference on African Linguistics*, ed. Ọláọba F. Arásanyìn and Michael A. Pemberton, 116–20. Somerville, MA: Cascadilla Proceedings Project, 2006.

Akinloyè Òjó

LAW: CUSTOMARY

Before colonial rule, customary law governed the Yorùbá people in southwestern Nigeria. Simply put, customary law refers to those customs generally accepted by a particular community as binding, the breach of which results in customary sanction. A rule of conduct is customarily recognized, adhered to, and applied by the inhabitants of a particular community in their relationship with one another within or outside their particular community. This conduct has obtained the force of law, in that noncompliance with the rule or custom in question results in adjudication and possible sanction.

A custom is different from a customary law. According to Remigius Nwabueze, a custom is a rule of conduct. When it attains a binding or obligatory character, it becomes customary law. There are sanctions for breach of customary law. Sanction under customary law includes banishment, compensation, excommunication, restitution or restoration, corporal punishment, death penalty, ridicule and humiliation, and apology.

Some of the characteristics of customary law include that it is unwritten, flexible, and generally accepted. D. O. Ibekwu stated:

> Regrettably enough, our own customary law is unwritten. It was handed down the ages, from generation to generation. Like a creed, it seems to live in the minds of people. This explains why so little was really known at the beginning about the vast body of laws which had always governed the affairs of our ancestors from time immemorial.

Because customary law is unwritten, it is part of the informal education of children from birth. Proof in the modern court of law is by expert witnesses grounded in customary law.

Customary law is flexible. It is a mirror or a reflection of acceptable usage. This was stated in the case of *Lewis v. Bánkọ́lé* (1909). Customary law remains flexible, evolutionary, and capable of adapting to changing circumstances. In addition, it is a generally acceptable norm by the people subject to it, as illustrated in *Èshúgbàyí Elékòó v. Government of Nigeria* (1931). Assent is supported by sanction, and the sanction is enforceable. Parties to a dispute subject to customary law are usually not strangers to each other. There is usually a social, marital, or tribal tie that binds them. Changes in customary law usually evolve from usage and are not declared by a repeal or amendment.

See also **Law: Modern**

REFERENCES

Ibekwe, D. O. "Conflict of Cultures and Our Customary Law." In *African Indigenous Laws*, ed. T. O. Elias, S. N. Nwabara, and C. O. Akpamgbo, Proceedings of Workshop, 7–9 August 1974 by Institute of African Studies, University of Nigeria, Nsukka, 283–99. Enugu (Nigeria): Government Printer, 1974.

Nwabueze, Remigius N. "The Dynamics and Genius of Nigeria's Indigenous Legal Order." *Indigenous Law Journal* 1 (Spring 2002): 1–16.

Olúyẹmisí Bámgbóṣé

LAW: MODERN

Modern Nigeria dates to 1914. This was when the then Protectorate of Southern Nigeria was amalgamated with the Protectorate of Northern Nigeria to form the Colony and Protectorate of Nigeria. As a result of Nigeria's historical link with Great Britain, English law has become a major source of Nigeria's modern law. The Common Law of England, the doctrines of equity, as well as Statutes of General Application in force in England on January 1, 1900, form an integral part of Nigerian law. In addition, certain English statutes that have been received into the laws through local legislation are important parts of Nigerian law. Other modern sources of Nigerian law include local legislation, case law, the Constitution, and laws from various courts.

Local legislation consists of enacted laws that emanate from the major legislative arm of government: either the National Assembly, comprising the Senate and House of Representatives, or a state House of Assembly serving the federal and state legislative interests, respectively. Case law has been defined by John Asien as "that body of principles and rule of law which over the years have been formulated or pronounced upon by the courts as governing specific legal situations." Thus, the principle of judicial precedent is a fundamental part of Nigeria's legal system. The modern legal system in operation in Nigeria is the adversarial system of court proceedings, which is similar to other common law countries. However, the jury system is not used in the Nigerian system of administration of justice.

The 1999 Constitution of the Federal Republic of Nigeria, which is the supreme law of the country, is binding on all authorities and persons in Nigeria. It is another source of law. The Constitution makes provisions for the establishment and constitution of courts, thus making a hierarchy of courts a fundamental part of the Nigerian legal system. The courts provided for by the constitution are the Supreme Court, the apex court in the hierarchy of courts, and the Court of Appeal, with judicial divisions that sit in various states for administrative conveniences. There are judicial divisions in some major cities in Nigeria, such as the Federal High Court and judicial divisions in different states of the federation for administrative convenience. The High Court is present in each of the thirty-six states as well as the Federal Capital Territory. The Sharia Court of Appeal has appellate and supervisory jurisdiction in civil proceedings involving questions of Islamic personal law. The Customary Court of Appeal has appellate and supervisory jurisdiction in civil proceedings involving questions of customary law. The Magistrate Courts, District Courts, Area Courts, and Customary Courts are established in various states by state laws.

See also: **Law: Customary**

REFERENCE

Asein, John Ohireme. *Introduction to Nigerian Legal System.* Ìbàdàn (Nigeria): Sam Bookman Pub., 1998.

Olúyẹmisí Bámgbóṣé

LIBATION

Rituals of libation have gained a permanent place in the Yorùbá culture. It is a significant aspect of the traditional religion; it is customary that libations be offered to deities. Oral tradition claims that there are 401 deities in Yorùbá traditional religion, and each requires daily or weekly libations, depending on the deity. Libation is the offering of blood, water, or liquor to deities and sometimes food to ancestral spirits.

The two most common types of libations in the culture are water and liquor. The water libation usually involves complete submergence of the deity's symbols, which represent the deity, or sprinkling water on them annually. Liquor is often poured into the mouth and spat out three or more times to the deity. Ọ̀rúnmìlà is the god of wisdom and the first among the deities; he has been said to have witnessed the creation of all beings and to have been present when everyone chose their fate (ìpín). When anyone is experiencing problems, Ọ̀rúnmìlà always has the solution because he was there at the beginning. A Babaláwo is a priest of Ọ̀rúnmìlà; he is believed to have a direct link with the god. When Babaláwo wakes up in the morning, he salutes Ọ̀rúnmìlà. Thanking the god for the blessing of the past days, he pleads with the god to bring clients that day and then performs liquor libation as a form of inducement to force the deity to give blessings. After the first libation, liquor libation is done every time divination is cast for a client. The same procedure occurs for the other deities.

Libation with blood applies to all the deities, much like water and liquor libations. The blood libation mostly involves sprinkling an animal's blood—birds, goats, cows, and the like—on the deity. This form of libation happens only when it is crucial. For example, it is customary for devotees of Ògún the god of war and metal—hunters, farmers, blacksmith, and drivers—to decapitate a dog annually for the deity to thank him for the years past and in the hope that he would continue to bless them in the years ahead. In this act of libation, only the blood of the dog is needed at the shrine, which is often poured on the deity. Synecdoche comes into play here as the blood of the dog represents the dog so that the shrine is not defiled by rotten dog's flesh.

Food libation is not reduced to a particular group of people; anyone can do it. It is done to feed ancestral spirits. It is believed that the spirits of the ancestors never leave the people they truly care about, which provide the motive behind food libation. When a person eats, a handful of the food is thrown to the side, after which the eater says, "That is for you, ancestral spirits," before he or she continues eating. Another scenario involves a person throwing the handful of food to keep malicious spirits busy with the food so that he or she can enjoy the meal in peace without fear of attack. Food libation is also used to teach children etiquette: if they accidentally drop their food, malevolent spirits lurking would have already eaten out of the food, so it is no longer considered safe to eat. It is just meant to teach them that eating dirty food is not healthy.

See also: **Deities: The** Òrìṣà

REFERENCES

Adéoyè, C. L. Àṣà àti Ìṣe Yorùbá. Ìbàdàn (Nigeria). University Press, 2005.
Iléṣànmi, T. M. Àwọn Nǹkan Abàmì Ilẹ̀ Yorùbá. Ilé-Ifẹ̀ (Nigeria): Ọbáfẹ́mi Awólọ́wọ̀ University Press, 2009.

Tọ́pẹ́ Olúwabùnmi Akíndípẹ̀

LINEAGES AND COGNOMEN (ORÍKÌ ORÍLẸ̀)

Oríkì orílẹ̀ is descriptive poetry about origins. It is all about the place of origin and the distinctive attributes of that place and its people. It is one of the principal means by which groups of people who regard themselves as kin recognize one another and assert their unity. Oríkì orílẹ̀ alludes to illustrious men and women among the ancestors of the group, but these allusions are attached only to the notion of the town of origin.

Karin Barber argues that oríkì orílẹ̀ do not trace genealogies or revolve around the notion of a lineage founder. Rather, they tell each individual where he or she belongs in the community. They establish the individual on the social map and give him or her a background without which he or she would scarcely exist as a social being. According to Barber:

> People from the same place of origin—the same orílẹ̀—say, "we are one." When they meet . . . they recognise an obligation to help each other, and observe a prohibition on intermarriage. They have a number of things in common. They share certain food taboos, special funeral custom, a particular òrìṣà or a specialised occupation . . . all of which are traced back to the town or origin. But the most important thing they have in common is the oríkì orílẹ̀ themselves.

Oríkì orílẹ̀ is the basis for a variety of named chants or chanting modes, some very localized and others in widespread use. Among the most widespread and best known are *ìjálá* (hunters' chants), *iwì* or *èsà egúngún* (ancestral masquerade chants), *ekún ìyàwó* (bridal chants), and *rárà sísun* (*rárà* chants). When *oríkì orílè* is performed by an *ìjálá* artist, for instance, the verbal salutes become *ìjálá* chants proclaiming information about particular lineages and ancestors. Although no two minstrels would give the *oríkì orílè* of a particular lineage in exactly the same words, a common core of constantly recurring information exist in such *oríkì*, no matter by what expert minstrel they are performed. The items of information usually given are, according to Adébóyè Babalolá, a multitude of alternative names for the progenitor being saluted; narratives (*ìtàn*) of several incidents connected with the progenitor and doing him either credit or discredit; and remarks about the progenitor's claims to distinction, about his favorite sayings, and about and his likes and dislikes.

The most important lineages—Olúfè, Oníkòyí, Olú-Òjé, Arèsà, Olówu, Ológbìín, Òpómúléró, Elérìn, Olómù, Òkò-Ìrèsé, and Olófà—are notable for the length of their *oríkì orílè*. Consider the lineage of the Arèsà as a representative sample. The *oríkì orílè* Arèsà focuses on two distinguished full brothers: the elder is dark skinned, and the younger light skinned (*dúdú lègbón, pupa làbúrò*). However, both are of similar temperament and were born and bred in the town of Àlò. The younger Arèsà (Arèsà *pupa*) became a wealthy man, and he founded and ruled a new town he named Ìrèsàapa (*Ìrèsà pupa*). He wore a beaded crown. The elder Arèsà (Arèsà *dúdú*) suffered a great deal of misfortune. Although he also ruled over a town of his own called Ìrèsàadú (*Ìrèsà dúdú*) and wore a beaded crown, he was forced by his comparatively poor circumstances to hand over all his young children to his younger brother for upbringing.

During a war, Ìrèsàadú fell into enemy hands, and its inhabitants fled to the town of Ògbómòsó, where their king was allowed to retain his title Arèsà, although as a mere subordinate chief to the king of Ògbómòsó. With the return of peace, their old town of Ìrèsàadú became a homestead where one member of the Arèsà family

later set himself up as a chief bearing the title Arèsà. Hence, the Arèsà gained a reputation for being fond of bearing three chieftaincy titles.

The Arèsà were renowned for their tall stature, strength, and energy-intensive work in producing in palm oil. Palm oil forests abounded around their original hometown of Àlò. They always had an abundance of homemade palm oil in their personal stores and never needed to go to the marketplace to buy it. They were highly talented in the arts of singing, drumming, and dancing, and they were knowledgeable in performing ceremonies pertaining to Ifá worship. The honor of their lineage was said to have been tarnished solely by the notoriety of their Arèsà princesses because of their sexual immorality.

Oral poets attach a great deal of importance to *oríkì orílè*, and it is believed that the correct performance of the *oríkì*, according to Babalola,

> in honor of a progenitor gladdens that progenitor in the world of the spirits and induces him to shower blessings on his offspring on earth. The reciting or chanting of the appropriate *oríkì orílè* in honour of the ancestors of a particular family causes the members of that family who hear the performance to feel very proud of their pedigree, and, if they are then away from home, they also feel exceedingly homesick. (24)

This is probably why oral artists pay great attention to *oríkì orílè* in their repertoires. Through impressive chanting of these verbal salutes to the progenitors of and distinguished persons in a family, an artist easily prevails on the members of that family, as they listen to his or her performance, to offer gifts in cash or in kind.

Even today, contemporary poets rely more on *oríkì orílè* when entertaining the general public. Generally, *oríkì orílè* is more stable than other types of *oríkì* and hence easier for poets to memorize and recite. It has a core set of images and references that are considered unchanging. They formed the basic building blocks in the eclectic and flexible performances that also draw on personal *oríkì*, prayers, blessings, proverbs, and topical comments. There is no doubt that *oríkì orílè* is highly valued even today. As a result of its popularity, texts of *oríkì orílẹ̀* are being collected and published. They also feature prominently in print and electronic obituary advertisements.

See also **Bards: Old and New; Literature: Oral**

REFERENCES

Babalọlá, S. A. *The Contents and Form of Yorùbá Ijala*. Oxford (United Kingdom): Clarendon Press, 1966.

Barber, Karin. *I Could Speak until Tomorrow*. Edinburgh: Edinburgh University Press. 1991.

Akíntúndé Akínyẹmí

LINGUISTICS: HISTORICAL

Historical linguistics is concerned with the description of and accounting for observed changes in particular languages and other changes associated with the sounds and words of the language. The Yorùbá language is classified as a member of the Defoid category of the Benue-Congo subgroup of languages, part of the Niger-Congo language family. The Defoid group of languages includes two main subgroups: the Àkókóid cluster and the Yoruboid cluster. The Àkókóid cluster includes four languages, and the much-larger Yoruboid cluster includes Yorùbá, Igala, and Itsekiri, among others. In the seventeenth century, Yorùbá was written in the Ajami script, a form of Arabic. However, in the later part of the nineteenth century, the Latin alphabet was adapted to represent the sounds of Yorùbá by using the digraph *gb* and a few diacritics, including a dot under the letters ọ, ẹ, and ṣ. The Latin letters *c, q, v, x,* and *z* were not used.

Early efforts to standardize written Yorùbá were initiated by English missionaries and priests who visited the region. Some of the books produced at that time in which the language featured prominently include *Mission to Asante* (1817), *Specimen of Languages Spoken in the Colonies of Sierra Leone* (1828), and *Outline of a Vocabulary of the Principal Languages of Western and Central Africa Compiled for the Use of Niger Expedition* (1841). In 1843, Bishop Àjàyí Crowther wrote *The Vocabulary of Yorùbá Language.* He noticed the following sounds in the language: /b/, /d/, /e/, /ẹ/, /f,/ /g/, /h/, /I/, /j/, /k/, /l/, /m/, /n/, /o/, /p/, /s/, /t/, /u/, /w/, /y/, and /gb/. Reverend Henry Townsend published the newspaper *Ìwé Ìròyìn fún Àwọn ará Ègbá àti Yorùbá* in 1859. This newspaper, the first monolingual newspaper in West Africa, did not take seriously the issue of tone marking. Instead, the paper proposed the use of double consonants; instead of ṣ, it used *sh*, and instead of ọ it used *aw*.

However the foundation for a modern orthography of the language was laid in 1875 at Church Missionary Society Ìta Fájì, where all those involved in the writing of the language came together to agree on a uniform way of writing. After this meeting, many modifications still took place. In 1965, Ayọ̀ Bámgbóṣé proposed major modifications in his monograph *Yorùbá Orthography: A Linguistic Appraisal with Suggestions and Reforms.* In 1974, the federal government of Nigeria set up a committee to review the orthography of the language, and the majority of their submissions were based on Bámgbóṣé's suggestions.

In the Benin Republic, where Yorùbá is also spoken, the speakers use a different orthography. The Yorùbá alphabet was standardized along with other Beninoire (Republic of Benin) languages in the National Languages Alphabet by the National Language Commission in 1975 and revised in 1990 by the National Center for Applied Linguistics. In 2010, the Centre for Black and African Arts and Civilization in Lagos set up a committee to harmonize the orthography of the language among the three West African countries of Nigeria, Togo, and Benin Republic. Examples of changes observed in the lexicon of the language over a period of time include *alàààmù* to *aláǹgbá* (lizard); *akọ́dà* to *ọlọ́pàá* (police); *rìbá, àbẹ̀tẹ́lẹ̀,* or *owó-ẹ̀yìn* to *ẹ̀gúnjẹ* (bribe); *àbú* to *àlejò* (visitor); *oòrè* to *ẹ̀mí* (heart); and *ọkinni* to *abẹ́rẹ́* (needle).

See also **Language: Government and Mission Policies; Language: Standardization and Literacy**

REFERENCE

Crystal, D. *The Cambridge Encyclopedia of Language*. 2nd ed. Cambridge: University of Cambridge, 2007.

Harrison Adéníyì

Standard Yorùbá nouns typically have the structure vowel-consonant-vowel (VCV). That is, they usually consist of at least two syllables beginning with a vowel followed by another consonant vowel sequence, such as *omi* (water) and *apá* (arm). Among the major word classes, only nouns can begin with vowels. However, nouns can also begin with consonants, such as *rárà* (dirge), *gèlè* (head tie), and *gẹ̀gẹ̀* (goiter). Simple nouns are, in general, not longer than four syllables, such as *ìkarahun* (big snail shell), *ìjímèrè* (brown monkey), and *àjànàkú* (elephant). When simple nouns are four or more syllables, they are often ideophonic, such as *ògúlúǹtu* (sand block or clod of earth).

The initial vowel of a noun cannot be a nasal vowel, and it cannot be the vowel /u/. Therefore, there are no nouns like *inlé** or *ulé**; standard Yorùbá uses *ilé* (house) instead. The word *ulé* (house) occurs in some eastern dialects such as the Oǹdó dialect, but a word like *inlé* does not occur in any dialect. The third restriction on initial-vowel nouns is that they cannot begin with a high tone. So, initial vowels of nouns have either a low or a middle tone.

Verbs are minimally and typically consonant-vowel (CV). That is, the simple verb in Yorùbá consists of a consonant followed by a vowel. Except for a few disyllabic forms like *pàdé* (meet), all Yorùbá verbs have the CV structure. Other major word classes begin with consonants and are disyllabic or longer.

Morphological Processes

Word formation in Yorùbá is the result of three derivational processes: prefixation, reduplication, and compounding. Nouns and verbs are not inflected for case, person, number, or gender. Nouns may be formed from verb stems or from verb phrases by adding prefixes. Various kinds of nouns (e.g., abstract, agentive, instrument) are formed in this way. For example, the prefix *ì* or *à* may be attached to a verb, to a verb plus object, or to serial verbs to form an instrument nominal.

ì-lu	opener	(< *lu* "make a hole")
ì-ránṣọ	sewing instrument	(< *rán* "sew," *aṣọ* "cloth")
à-lòkù	used material	(< *lò* "use," *kù* "remain")

Abstract nominals and agentive nominals may be formed the same way, using other prefixes. Furthermore, negative nominals are formed by prefixing both *à* and *ì* to a verb or a verb phrase:

à-ì-sàn	illness	(< *sàn* "be well")
à-ì-lọ	(act of) not going	(< *lọ* "go")
à-ì-tètèdé/	(act of) not arriving early	(< *tètè* "quickly," *dé* "arrive")

Finally, possessor nominals are formed by adding the prefix *oni* to a noun or to a noun phrase:

| aláṣọ | owner of cloth or seller of cloth | (< *oní* + *aṣọ* "cloth") |
| oníṣẹ́ ọba | government worker | (< *oní* + *iṣẹ́* "work," *ọba* "king") |

Nouns are also formed through reduplication, which may be partial or complete. Several forms of reduplication exist. The most productive partial reduplication is one that forms gerundive nominals from verbs or verb phrases by copying the first consonant of the stem followed by a "prefix" *í*:

lílọ	going	(< *lọ* "go"),
jíjẹ	eating	(< *jẹ* "eat"),
ríránṣọ	sewing clothes	(< *rán* "sew" *aṣọ* "clothes")

Second, the first VCV of a noun may be reduplicated to form a word meaning "all" (noun). The first tone of the stem is spread onto the reduplicant, and the initial vowel of the stem assimilates the last vowel of the reduplicant:

ọṣooṣù	every month	(< *oṣù* "month"),
ìr̀ìrọ̀lẹ́	every evening	(< *ìrọ̀lẹ́* "evening"),
ìt̀ìtàdógún	every fifteen days	(< *ìtàdógún* "fifteen days")

One form of complete reduplication similar to the above takes various lexical classes, including verbs, adverbs, adjectives, and numerals as input and produces an intensified output, or forms with "group" meaning:

kíákíá	very quickly	kíá	quickly
burúkúburúkú	very bad	burúkú	bad
dáradára	good (adjective)	dára	good (verb)
mẹ́rinmẹ́rin	four by four	mẹ́rin	four

Another form of complete reduplication takes verb phrases as input to form agentive nominals:

woléwolé	sanitary inspector	(< wò "look at," ilé "house")
panápaná	fireman	(< pa "kill or put out," iná "fire")

Finally, reduplication may be combined with affixation. The formatives kí and ni may be inserted between a reduplicated noun base. The kí forms a nominal with the meaning "any" or "bad." Note that the n of ni changes to l in the last two examples:

ọmọkọ́mọ	any child, bad child	(< ọmọ "child")
èròkérò	any thought, bad thought	(< èrò "thought")
àgbàlagbà	oldish or middle age	(< àgbà "adult," literally middle-aged person)
ọ̀pọ̀lọpọ̀	abundance	(< ọ̀pọ̀ "many")

Ideophonic reduplication constitutes a special class of reduplication in Yorùbá. These reduplications have three additional features:

1. They can be suffixing instead of the usual prefixing reduplication elsewhere in the language:

Wọ́ọ́rọ́	quietly	wọ́ọ́rọ́wọ́	of withdrawing quietly
tààrà	straight	tààràtà/ tààràrà	of going straight ahead

2. They can involve more than one repetition of the base"

Wógó-wògò-wógó	of clumsy movement
hábá-hàbà-hábá	of slow, clumsy movement
gọ́lọ́-gọ̀lọ̀-gọ́lọ́	of difficult movement

3. They are sometimes accompanied by fixed tonal pattern that have morphological content. In the forms below, which all have the pattern high tone, mid tone, low tone, and mid tone, (HMLM) the tone pattern connotes a pejorative meaning:

wérewère	of abnormal behavior
wúruwùru	of being disorganized
kátikàti.	of being confused

See also **Linguistics: Phonology; Linguistics: Semantics; Linguistics: Syntax**

REFERENCES

Awóbulúyì, Ọládélé. *Essentials of Yorùbá Grammar.* Ìbàdàn (Nigeria): Oxford University Press, 1978.

Bámgbóṣé, Ayọ̀. *A Short Yorùbá Grammar.* Ìbàdàn (Nigeria): Heinemann Educational Books, 1967.

Akínbíyì Akinlabí

LINGUISTICS: PHONOLOGY

Yorùbá has seven contrastive oral vowels (*i, e, ẹ, a, ọ, o, u*); replacing one of these vowels with the other will change the meaning of the word, as exemplified by the words *kí* (greet), *ké* (cry), *kẹ́* (pet or pamper), *ká* (fold), *kọ́* (build), *kó* (pack or carry), and *kú* (die). The orthographic vowels (*ẹ, ọ*) are phonetic /ɛ/ and /ɔ/, respectively, and roughly correspond to the vowels in the words *bet* and *bought* in American English. All seven oral vowels are pronounced nasalized after nasal consonants. In this context, the mid vowels /ẽ/ and /õ/ are perhaps the least nasalized: *mĩ* (breath), *mẹ̃́rĩ* (catch elephant) (from *mú* "catch" and *erin* "elephant"), *mẹ̃́rĩ* (four), *mã́* (don't), *mọ̃́* (be clean), and *mówo* (take money) (from mú "take" and owó "money"), *mṹ* (catch or take). Predictable nasalization, as in these examples, is not marked in the orthography.

Yorùbá also has four inherently nasal vowels, orthographically spelt with a consonant /n/ after the vowel (in, ẹn, ọn, un), or phonetically /ĩ/, /ɛ̃/, /ɔ̃/, /ũ/. These vowels can occur following oral consonants; as in ikin (palm nuts for Ifá divination); ìyẹn (that one); ìbọn (gun) and ikún (type of squirrel).

Two of these vowels, /ọn/ and /ẹn/, require comment. The vowel /ọn/ is written as an following non-labial consonants, such as ikán (white ants), and as /ọn/ following labial consonants, such as ìbọn (gun). The nasal vowel /an/, however, occurs contrastively in some dialects such as Ìkálẹ̀. The remaining nasal vowel /ẹn/ is severely restricted, occurring only in a few related items: ìyẹn (that one) and yẹn (that). Although long vowels occur phonetically in Yorùbá, vowel length is not contrastive. Long vowels occur most commonly as a result of vowel assimilation, as in: egúngún ~ eégún (masquerade), òrùka ~ òòka (ring), and òrìṣà ~ òòṣà (deity).

Yorùbá has eighteen consonants. They are listed here as written in the orthography, with the International Phonetic Alphabet symbol indicated where both notations differ. The consonant /g͡b/, written as gb in the orthography, is a doubly articulated voiced labiovelar plosive and not a consonant cluster. Its voiceless counterpart, /k͡p/ is written as p in the orthography, since the voiceless bilabial plosive /p/ does not exist in the language.

Some Yorùbá consonants have two variants, depending on context. First, Yorùbá sonorant consonants are pronounced as oral /l, r, w, y, h/ before oral vowels, and as nasal /n, r̃, w̃, ỹ, h̃/ before nasal vowels (*indicates unacceptable pronunciation): */lũ̀/ ~ /nù/ (feed), */rĩ̀/ ~ /r̃ĩ̀/ (walk), */wĩ́/ ~ /w̃ĩ́/ (lend), */yṹ/ ~

/ỹṹ/ (dispense), and */hũ/ ~ /h̃ũ/ (weave). Except for the /n, l/ alternation, nasalized variants of sonorants are not indicated in the orthography.

Second, when the nasal /n/ is syllabic (i.e., a syllable on its own), it has six variants that are pronounced at the same point in the mouth with the next consonant. Therefore, it is pronounced as bilabial /m/ when next to /b, m/, as a labiodental /ɱ/ before /f/, an alveolar /n/ before /t, d, s, n, r, l/, a palatal /ɲ/ before /ʃ {ṣ}, ɟ {j}, j {y}/, a velar /ŋ/ before the consonants /k, g, w, h/ and the vowel /o/, and a labiovelar /ŋm/ before /k͡p, p, g͡b/. This variation is not symbolized in Yorùbá orthography, except that /m/ is written before /b/, and /n/ is written before other consonants, as indicated in the rightmost column:

/òrom̀bó/	orange	òrom̀bó
/bóńfò/	short skirt	bóńfò
/pañla/	stockfish	pañla
/ɲáɲá /	small piece (of meat)	ìjáǹjá
/ògòǹgò/	ostrich	ògòǹgò
/gbaŋmgba/	an open space	gbañgba

Finally, Yorùbá has three contrastive tones—high (H), mid (M), and low (L)—that are generally realized on vowels and sometimes on nasal consonants when they form a syllable by themselves. Tones carry a heavy functional load in Yorùbá, since they distinguish the meanings of words like consonants and vowels do:

kọ́ (H)	build
kọ (M)	sing or crow
kọ̀ (L)	reject

Except for this minor restriction, tones occur freely in lexical representations, without apparent restrictions

Table L.1 Consonant chart

			Labial	Alveolar	Palatal	Velar	Labiovelar	Glottal
Obstruents	Stops	Voiceless		t		k	p /k͡p/	
		Voiced	B	d	j /ɟ/	g	gb /g͡b/	
	Fricatives	Voiceless	F	s	ṣ /ʃ/			
Sonorants	Nasals		M	n				
	Approximants	Lateral		l				
		Central		r	y /j/		w	h

on word melodies. For example, there is a restriction on the distribution of the high tone; the high tone does not occur in word-initial position except in (marked) consonant-initial words. Thus, in vowel initial words, while it is possible to have forms like ọkọ̀ (ML) (vehicle) and ọ̀kọ̀ (LL) (spear), it is impossible to have a form like *ọ́kọ̀ (HL) with a high tone on the initial syllable.

Yorùbá words result from a very simple syllable structure. Using the symbol C to stand for consonants and V to stand for vowels, Yorùbá has only two types of syllables, V and CV (a hyphen marks syllable division):

V: àlá   /à-lá/   dream
CV: wá   /wá/   come

Other than pronouns, which can be single vowels and so are representative of the V syllable, this syllable type is largely found as the initial vowel of nouns. Yorùbá disallows consonant clusters within a syllable. Thus, it is impossible to have a combination like /krim/ (the pronunciation of the English *cream*), which has the cluster /kr/ at the beginning, or /sɪlk/ (the pronunciation of the English *silk*) which has the cluster /lk/ at the end.

Major Phonological Processes

Yorùbá has vowel occurrence restrictions known as vowel harmony. In simple nouns, the last vowel of the word determines rest of the vowels in the word. If the last vowel is produced with retracted tongue root (RTR) /a, ẹ, ọ/, then all the preceding vowels are pronounced RTR as well. However, in standard Yorùbá only M vowels /e, o, ẹ, ọ/ are fully involved in the harmony. The H vowels /i, u/ do not participate in the harmony at all; that is, the high vowels can occur with any vowel. The following are examples of permitted and nonpermitted M vowel sequences:

Permitted		Permitted		Not Permitted
ọ...ọ	ọjọ́ day	ẹ...ẹ	ẹsẹ̀ leg or foot	*o...ọ
ẹ...ọ	ejọ́ case	ọ...ẹ	ọsẹ̀ week	*e...ọ
ẹ...a	ẹja fish	ọ...a	ọjà market	*ẹ...e
				*ọ...e

o...o	òjò rain	e...e	ètè lips	*e...a
e...o	ejò snake	o...e	olè thief	*o...a

Another major phonological process is vowel assimilation. Vowel assimilation is most commonly observed when two nouns are next to each other, one ending in a vowel and the other beginning with a vowel. In general, the first vowel of the second noun completely assimilates the preceding vowel, except when the second vowel is /i/, in which case it becomes completely assimilated to the first vowel:

owó	adé	→	owáadé	Ade's money
owó	ẹmu	→	owẹ́ẹmu	wine money
owó	epo	→	owéepo	oil money
owó	ilé	→	owóolé	house rent

Finally, the most documented phonological phenomenon is vowel deletion. Vowel deletion is most commonly found when words, other than two nouns, occur next to each other; such as when a noun occurs after a verb (i.e., verb + object). Leaving well-documented exceptions aside, it is the first vowel in the sequence that gets deleted, except if the second vowel is /i/:

wá (H) + look (for)	ẹ̀kọ́ (LH) education	→	wẹ́kọ́ (HLH) look for education
wá (H) + look (for)	owó (MH) money	→	wówó (HH) look for money
wá (H) + look (for)	ọkọ̀ (ML) vehicle	→	wọ́kọ̀ (HL) look for a vehicle
wá (H) + look (for)	ọkọ (MM) husband	→	wọ́kọ (HM) look for a husband
wá (H) + look (for)	ilé (MH) house	→	wálé (HH) look for a house

The stability of tone in the processes of vowel assimilation and vowel deletion is of crucial importance. When a vowel gets assimilated or deleted, its tone remains behind on the surviving vowel, except when it is a mid tone.

See also **Linguistics: Morphology; Linguistics: Semantics; Linguistics: Syntax**

REFERENCES

Awóbulúyì, Ọládélé. *Essentials of Yorùbá Grammar.* Ìbàdàn (Nigeria): Oxford University Press, 1978.

Bámgbóṣé, Ayọ̀. *A Short Yorùbá Grammar.* Ìbàdàn (Nigeria): Heinemann Educational Books, 1967.

Akínbíyì Akinlabí

LINGUISTICS: SEMANTICS

Semantics deals with the study of meaning, changes in meaning, and the principles that govern the relationships between words, sentences, and their meanings. Questions that have been agitating the minds of scientists from time immemorial is, What is a word? What does it represent? And what is its relationship to reality? For instance, consider the word *ilé* (house), with its various meaning in the following expressions: *ilé Yínká dára* (Yinka's house is good), *ilé ayé gbẹgẹ́* (the world is delicate), *kí Kẹ́mi di ilé rẹ̀ mú* (Kemi should keep her home), and *ilé-ọlá ló ti jade* (he is from a wealthy home). *Ilé* in the various constructions only means what has been generally agreed upon by the native speakers of the language, and any meaning given to it by individual speakers remains invalid. There are several semantic features that are noticeable in Yorùbá at word level, such as homonymy, synonymy, antonymy, and polysemy.

Homonymy refers to a lexical item that has the same form but different meaning. For example, *kẹ́ran* may mean *kí èèyàn kó ẹran sí ibì kan* (to pack meat into a plate) or (to be in trouble) and *fẹ́* may also mean *fẹ́ ìyàwó* (to marry), *fẹ́ iná* (to fan a light), or *fẹ́ ojú* (to blow a particle from one's eye). Likewise, *jẹ* may mean *jẹ oúnjẹ* (to eat), *jẹ ayò* (to win a game), or *jẹ gbèsè* (to be in debt).

Synonymy refers to a situation where two lexical items may have a similar meaning. For example, *ọmọdé* and *aròbó* mean "child or kid," *aya* and *ìyàwó* mean "wife," and *ọkà* and *àmàlà* mean "yam flour." We also have some words that are near synonymous, such as *abà* and *ahéré*, where *abà* may or may not be built with thatched roof. However, *ahéré* is always built with a thatched roof. In addition, *èwù* and *aṣọ* mean "cloth."

Antonymy refers to the relationship that holds between words that are opposite in meaning. It is restricted to gradable expressions that usually correlate with opposite members of a scale. For example, *gbóná* (hot) and *tutù* (cold), *wọlé* (enter) and *jáde* (exit), and *àgùtàn* (sheep) and *àgbò* (ram).

Polysemy refers to an expression having two or more meaning with some common features that are usually derived from a single basic meaning. While the meanings of homonyms can be traced to different etymological roots (thus, different words are involved), the semantic variants of polysemic expressions go back to a single root. For instance, *ojú* (eye) means different but related things in the following phrases: *ojú-ara* (eye of the body, i.e., vagina), *ojú ìríran* (eye that we see with), *ojú ọ̀nà* (eye of the way, i.e., road), and *ojú abẹ́rẹ́* (eye of the needle).

At the sentence level, ambiguity refers to a word that has more than one interpretation. For example, *lawọ́* may mean "to open one's hand" or "to be generous." Contradiction refers to a sentence that is false on the basis of its logical form, such as *òkú náà ṣe àṣìṣe nínú ìdánwò rẹ̀** "the dead made a mistake in his examination," an illogical sentence.

See also **Linguistics: Morphology, Linguistics: Phonology** and **Linguistics: Syntax**

REFERENCE

Adéníyì, Harrison, and Akinloyè Òjó, eds. *Ilò-èdè àti ẹ̀dá-èdè Yorùbá: Apá kejì.* Trenton, NJ: Africa World Press, 2005.

Harrison Adéníyì

LINGUISTICS: SYNTAX

Yorùbá words can be broadly classified into nouns and verbs. Most nouns begin with a vowel initial and are disyllabic, such as *orí* (head) and *ìbàdí* (waist). All verbs have a consonant initial and are mostly monosyllabic, such as *gé* (cut) and *gbé* (carry). A few verbs are disyllabic, such as *dòtí* (dirty) and *patì* (abandon). A few nouns start with a consonant, such as *bàtà* (shoe) and *pátá* (panties). Prepositions derive from verbs and all have the same forms as verbs, such as *ní* (at, on, or in), fún (for), sí (to), pẹ̀lú (with), and ti or láti (from). Each of the possible lexical categories can project phrases such as verb phrases and noun phrases.

Every sentence is expected to have a verb. It is the core of the sentence. A sentence can also have a subject. It may also have an object. In *Adé pa ejò* (Adé killed a snake), *pa* is the verb. The subject is *Adé*, and *ejò* is the object. The basic word order of the language is subject, verb, and object. Of these, only the verb is required to form a sentence. It can have a direct or an indirect object. In *Olú ra iwé fún Adé* (Olú bought a book for Adé), the direct object of the verb *rà* is *ìwé*, and its indirect object is *Adé*. Thus, the indirect object of the verb is the direct object of the preposition, in this instance *fún*.

Yorùbá sentences can be divided into simple, compound, and complex on the basis of their structures. Simple sentences contain just one clause: *Olú rí Adé* (Olú saw Adé) is a simple sentence. Compound sentences can have two or more coordinate clauses. The sentence *Olú rí Adé ṣùgbọ́n Òjó kò rí i* (Olú saw Adé but Òjó did not see him) is a compound sentence with two clauses that are conjoined with *ṣùgbọ́n* (but). Complex sentences have one or more main clauses and one or more subordinate clauses: *Olú sọ pé Òjó fẹ́ràn Adé* (Olú said that Òjó likes Adé). On the basis of how they are used, Yorùbá sentences can be broadly divided into declarative, interrogative, and imperative: *Mo ránti ilé* (I remember home) is declarative, *Ta ni ó ránti ilé?* (Who remembered home) is interrogative, and *Ránti ilé* (Remember [your] home) is imperative.

The three sentence constructions that are unique to Yorùbá and other languages in its family are constituent focusing, speakers' perspectives, and the use of several verbs in monoclausal sentences without conjunctions. Constituent focusing occurs when a sentence is a complement of the predicate head *ni* (be) in Yorùbá. In *Adé ni Olú fẹ́ràn* (It is Adé that Olú likes), the embedded sentence *Olú fẹ́ràn* is in the complement position to the predicate head *ni*, and *Adé* is the subject of the main clause.

Logophoricity describes the perspectives of the speaker. A distinction is marked between weak and strong pronouns in this construction. The strong pronoun can be used to express the views or perspectives of the speaker: *Adé sọ pé òun fẹ́ràn Òjó* (Adé said that he likes Òjó). The strong pronoun *òun* (he) picks the same referent as *Adé*, the subject of the matrix clause. In comparison, the weak pronoun *ó* (he) in *Adé sọ pé ó fẹ́ràn Òjó* (Adé said that he likes Òjó) is not required to pick the same referent as *Adé*. The type of construction in which several verbs are used in a monoclausal sentence without conjunctions is usually called serial verb constructions. Two or more verbs share the same subject and perhaps the same object: *Àdìò pa eja jẹ* (Àdìò killed a fish and ate it.) *Àdió* is the shared subject in this sentence; he does the killing and the eating of the fish. In addition, *eja* (fish) is the shared object.

See also **Linguistics: Morphology; Linguistics: Phonology; Linguistics: Semantics**

REFERENCES

Awóbulúyì, Ọládélé. *Essentials of Yorùbá Grammar.* Ìbàdàn (Nigeria): Oxford University Press, 1978.

Bámgbóṣé, Ayọ̀. *A Short Yorùbá Grammar.* Ìbàdàn (Nigeria): Heinemann Educational Books, 1967.

Olúṣèyẹ Adéṣọlá and Akínbíyì Akinlabí

LITERATURE: MODERN AND WRITTEN

The emergence of Yorùbá written literature can be closely linked to Western civilization and Western education. The efforts of the Church Missionary Society and linguists like Hannah Kilham and Samuel Àjàyí Crowther led to the commitment of Yorùbá to writing. The development of the written tradition was facilitated by the Ministry of Education in the then Western Region and others that supported Yorùbá writing, such as the organizations Ẹgbẹ́ Àgbà ò Tán, Ẹgbẹ́ Onímọ̀ Yorùbá, and Ẹgbẹ́ Akọ́mọlédè Yorùbá. Broadly, written literature is classified into three types: poetry, play, and prose. The Yorùbá written tradition started in 1848 with the Henry Townsend poem "Taní ṣe Jésù." Since its inception, the main phases that the composition of poems has gone through are the following:

Encyclopedia of the Yorùbá

1. Translation of English poems into Yorùbá: Henry Townsend's "Taní ṣe Jésù" (1848) and "Jẹ́ Òtítọ́" (1861)
2. Adaptation of English poetic style, church hymns, and hymnal rhythm into Yorùbá: Afọlábí Johnson's couplets, triplets, quatrain, and rhymes, notably "Ara líle loògùn Ọrọ̀," "Ìgbàgbọ́" and "Àṣírí Ọlọ́run"
3. Transposition of the traditional poetic form, style, and rhythm, such as Ṣóbọ̀ Arobíodu's and Oyèṣílé Kẹ́ríbo's transposition of àrùngbè to originally created poems
4. Admixture of the oral poetic forms and the original composition: Dẹ́ńrelé Adétìmíkàn Ọbasá's Àwọn Akéwì 1-3
5. Straddling of the oral poetic forms and structure and themes in the composition of poems: Adébáyọ̀ Fálétí's and Akínwùmí Ìṣọ̀lá's poems

The first attempt at writing a play started in 1923, with E. A. Akíntàn's short play Rẹ́rìín Díẹ̀ or Pa-mí-n-kú. However, the first plays, Adébóyè Babalọlá's Pàsán Ṣìnà and J. F. Ọdúnjọ's Àgbàlọ́wọ́méèrí Baálẹ̀ Jòntolo, were published in 1958. The latest trend is the adaptation of written plays into films and home videos. Examples include Adébáyọ̀ Fálétí's Baṣọ̀run Gáá (1970) and Akínwùmí Ìṣọ̀lá's Ẹfúnṣetán Aníwùrà.

The novel emerged in 1930 with I. B. Thomas's epistolary novel Ìtàn Èmi Ṣẹgilọlá Ẹ̀lẹ́yinjú Ẹgẹ́ Ẹlẹ́gbẹ̀rún Ọkọ Láyé, which portrays the moral degeneration in Yorùbá society of that time. Fágúnwà followed with the publication of Ògbójú Ọdẹ Nínú Igbó Irùnmalẹ̀ (1938) and four others novels. Other novelists in this category are J. O. Ògúndélé's Ibú Olókun (1956) and Olú Owólabí's Orí Adé Kì í Sùnta (1974). Works that address the fears, hopes, and aspirations of Nigerians are now the trend in Yorùbá novels. Examples of such are Ọládèjọ Òkédìjí's thrillers Àjà Ló Lẹrù (1969), Àgbàlagbà Akàn (1971), Atótó Arére (1981), and Ká rìn ká pọ̀ (2007) and Akínwùmí Ìṣọ̀lá's Ó le Kú (1974), Ogún Ọmọdé (1990), and Ṣaworoidẹ (2008).

Written literature can be classified into didactic, protest, historical, propagandist, and satirical. Thematically, Yorùbá written literature centers on cultural belief, sociopolitical structure, economic situation, and religious and socioethnic conflicts.

See also **Literature: Oral; Translation**

REFERENCES

Ògúnṣínà, Bísí. The Development of the Yorùbá Novel c. 1930-1975. Ilorin (Nigeria): Gospel Faith Mission Press, 1992.
Ọlábímtán, Afọlábí. "A Critical Survey of Yorùbá Written Poetry, 1848-1948." Unpublished doctoral dissertation, University of Lagos, Lagos (Nigeria), 1974.

Àrìnpé Adéjùmọ̀

LITERATURE: ORAL

Oral literature as a concept is used by scholars to depict those rich and varied oral traditions such as folklore, proverbs, narratives, chants, poetry, songs, and riddles that are transmitted orally within a society. Yorùbá oral literature, therefore, is a collection of verbal text forms that represent the experiences of the people and present a form of literary language that fulfills aesthetic and educative functions. It is an orally creative text that enriches the social and moral life of the people and ensures the continuity of Yorùbá culture. Oral literature is also used to express the ideals and values of society and to teach the younger generations the history and culture of their ancestors.

Oral literature comprises oral narratives such as stories, myths, legends, folktales, fables, riddles, tongue twisters, proverbs, songs, and chants. These various types of oral literature live through performance by a performer and an audience or spectators. This performance can be in religious or social settings or in various workplaces. In addition, there are some types of oral literature that need no physical audience for its existence. In Yorùbá oral literature, there is no claim to authorship.

Most types of oral literature are learned during childhood. The apprentice listens to, observes, and imitates the master in all aspects, with the exception of àlọ́ (riddles), òwe (proverbs), and some songs. These three genres are not formally taught.

The major challenge confronting the study of oral literature is the issue of data collection. A lot has been done in this direction but not much in the area of publications. Second, the issue of transcription has endangered oral literature. In addition, it has become increasingly difficult to obtain authentic performances of the various genres of oral literature because the source text is generally polluted. Regarding analysis, a lot is often neglected or overlooked. To achieve a good analysis of any oral literature, the context has to be considered: what happens during the performance, the cultural views, and the performers. These elements are usually underestimated; only the words of the texts are often considered.

However, the varying types of oral literature play an important role in the society. They are full of revelations of the historical past and exposition into the sociology of life of people. They enrich the social and moral life of the people and ensure the continuity of Yorùbá culture. In addition, the various genres of the oral literature express the ideals and values of the communities, teach young generations the history of their ancestors, and help them improve their self-awareness.

The various genres of Yorùbá oral literature fall into three classes: poetry (ewì), narratives (ìtàn àròsọ), and drama (eré-oníṣe). However, each of these classes can further be classified into the following subgenres:

- Oral poetry (ewì alohùn)
- Narrative poetry (àrángbọ̀): oríkì (praise poetry), ẹsẹ-ifá (ifá verse), ọfọ̀ (incantation), òwe (proverbs), àlọ́ àpamọ̀ (riddles), and the like
- Chants (Ìsàré): religious chants, such as ìjálá, ẹ̀ṣà or iwì egúngún, rárà, ìyẹrẹ̀-ifá, ẹkún ìyàwó; various orìṣà pipe, such as Ṣàngó pípè, Èṣù pípè and Ọya pípè, all among the Ọ̀yọ́; entertainment chants such as ègè among the Ẹ̀gbá and èfẹ̀ among the Ẹ̀gbádo; alámọ̀ and àsamọ̀ among the Èkìtì; olele among Ìjẹ̀sà; àdàmọ̀ and ọ̀sàrè among Ifẹ̀ and Ìjẹ̀sà; àsíkò among Oǹdó and Ìkálẹ̀; and résọ̀, ọ̀sẹ́ghẹ̀, lághálogho among the Ọ̀wọ̀

- Songs (orin), which go with clapping, drumming, and dancing of various types:
  ○ Native or festival songs (orin ìbílẹ̀): orin Edì in Ifẹ̀; orin ọdún Igógo in Ọ̀wọ̀; and orin ọdún Òkè'Bàdàn in Ìbàdàn
  ○ Children's songs (orin ọmọdé): orin arẹmọ (lullabies), orin erémọdé/eré-òṣùpá (pastime or moonlight recreation songs, orin àlọ́ (folktale songs), and orin ìwéréǹde (occasional recitations)
  ○ Recreational and entertainment songs (orin ìdárayá): àpàlà, etíyẹrí, àgbè, wákà, and sákárà
  ○ Proverbial songs (orin òwe): Abusive songs like orin èébú and orin ọ̀tẹ̀.
- Oral narratives (ìtàn àròsọ) that consists of the following:
  ○ Myths (ìtàn ìwáṣẹ̀), stories with elements of the sacred and divine that give meaning to existence, and ensure that the communities do not lose hold of their rationale for existence; stories common among elders who are truthful to the original stories
  ○ Legends (ìtàn ọjọ́un): stories about the exploits of heroes and heroines; stories of their origin or account of their migration and conquest of one group by another; usually narrated among the elders.
  ○ Folktales and fables (àlọ́ àpagbè or onítàn): stories with no historical purpose that serve as entertainment; occur in more relaxed atmosphere, especially at evenings; no age limit for the narrators, but children usually serve as the audience; narratives full of abstractions, such as a dilemma tale or trickster tale with human or animal characters; start with riddles (àlọ́ àpamọ̀) and are followed by a short dialogic poetic verse; usually rendered with songs accompanied by clapping, drumming and dancing
  ○ Proverbs, riddles and tongue twisters
  ○ Drama (eré-oníṣe): enactments during various traditional festivals (ọdún ìbílẹ̀) and masquerades (eégún aláré); elements include imitation, actors, stage, spectators, props, and regalia.

See also **Literature: Modern and Written**

REFERENCE

Ọlátúnjí, O. Ọlátúndé. *Features of Yorùbá Oral Poetry.* Ìbàdàn (Nigeria): University Press, 1984.

Láídé Sheba

LITERATURE: TRANSLATION

The application of Yorùbá sociocultural belief is pivotal to the translation of Yorùbá literature. Yorùbá is a language that uses tonal counterpoint and pun, which may be lost when translated. Moreover, the use of metaphor, euphemism, and repetition may not be captured in translation. Translators of Yorùbá literature make use of both the denotation and connotation methods of translation. In using the denotation method, translators may use definitional, literal, obvious, or commonsense meanings to describe a word, as seen in the following:

Ojú mi relé ò dénú ilé o.
Ojú mi roko ò dóko.
Ibi ojú mi dé, ẹsẹ̀ mi ò rè.
Bí ojú mi lo sódò Aládìgún-un mi.
Yẹ́ẹ̀s, bẹ́ẹ̀ náà ni,
Ojú mi lọ sọ́dọ̀ Aládìgún mi.

My eyes desire to go home but could not get home.
My eyes desire to go to the farm but could not get to the farm.
Where my eyes desire to go my legs refuse to go there.
My eyes go to my Àdìgún.
Yes, that is it.
My eyes go to my Àdìgún.

Connotation depends largely on the translator's knowledge of the culture, the understanding of the situational and verbal context in which lexical items are used, and a thorough understanding of the voice, reference, inference, and relevance of each word. Redundant and repetitive words are usually disregarded when translating Yorùbá literature to English.

Extended meanings are also given to words. Some words are not translatable; hence, they are retained or changes are made. Below are examples of different forms of translation:

Ìtarúkú awo ìtarúkú,
Ìtarùkù awo ìtarùkù

Ìtarúkú (N1) the priest of *ìtarúkú* (N1)
Ìtarùkù (N3) the priest of *ìtarùkù* (N4)

Ìtarúkú and *Itarùkù* are not translatable, hence they are retained. Also (N1) and (N3) are names, and (N2) and (N4) are locales. Also:

Ọya wọlẹ̀ nílé Irá.
Ṣàngó wọlẹ̀ ni Kòso.
Ọba Adéfowópè tilẹ̀ Ògèrè tẹ́rígbaṣọ,
Ó rẹ̀wàlẹ̀ àsà.

Ọya died at Ira.
Ṣàngó died at Kòso.
King Adéfowópè of Ògèrè is dead,
He is gone to the world beyond.

The word *ikú* (death) is not mentioned, but the translation is based on the shared cultural belief that kings do not die but go to meet with their ancestors.

The following example shows the extension of meaning and the discarded redundant lexical items:

Sílífa àti Kọ́láwọlé mo rí wọn ríre
Ọkọ ń lo Mẹ̀sí-ọlọ́yẹ́ ayọ́kẹ́lẹ́

Sílífá and Kọ́láwọlé are progressing
The husband rides a Mercedes Benz car

Mẹ̀sí-ọlọ́yẹ́ is an invention that describes a Merceeds-Benz car with an air conditioner in the translation, the qualifier *ọlọ́yẹ́* (air conditioner) is removed.

In summary, the issue of fidelity to both the original and target language is paramount to Yorùbá literature translation. Getting a perfect and exact translation may not be possible all the times. This necessitates retaining some lexical items in their original forms and creating near-perfect variations.

See also **Translation**

REFERENCE

Ọṣúndáre, Níyì. "Yorùbá Thoughts, English Words: A Poet's Journey through the Tunnel of Two Tongues." In *Kiss and Quarrel: Yorùbá/English Strategies of Mediation*, ed. Steward Brown, 15–31. Birmingham University African Studies Series 5. Birmingham, UK: Birmingham University, 2000.

Àrìnpé Adéjùmọ̀

LITERATURE: WOMEN WRITERS

Yorùbá women are not unknown to the oral poetic genres, many of which are composed and performed by women, while others are exclusively for women. Although Yorùbá written literature began in 1848, female writers did not emerge until the late 1970s because of the sociocultural milieu of the society. Traditionally, women are relegated to the background; hence, many of them could not acquire Western education as early as their male counterparts did.

In 1979, the first novel appeared written by a female writer, Ọmọsùnlọ́lá Johnston's *Ìyábọ̀ 1* and its sequel, *Ìyábọ̀ 2*. Johnston published *Kúsoró* in 1983. Other novels appeared: Délé Adégbèmí's *Ta La Rí Báwí?* (1990), Olúyẹmisí Adébọ̀wálé's *Walé* (1990) and *O Sèyí Tán* (1995), and Àrìnpé Adéjùmọ̀'s *Eyin Àparò* (1998). The first published female poet is Olúyẹmisí Adébọ̀wálé, who published *Ìgbà Lónigbà Ń Kà* (1998). She was followed by Àrìnpé Adéjùmọ̀'s *Rò ó o Re* (2002).

Most female writers published poetry and plays. Janet Ọláídé Sheba has asserted that, because women talk more than men, playwriting is more convenient for women because of the dialogue nature of plays. Second, the centrality of domestic work in women's lives does not allow sufficient time to engage in longer creative works; plays and poems may be more convenient. However, in recent times, many female writers engage in novel writing. Examples include Olúfúnláyọ̀ Akínọdé's *Ọmọ́ládùn* (2004) and *Àpínkẹ́ Onígàngan* (2005), Nikẹ Adésànyà's *Ọdún Á Yakọ* (2007), Ọládiméjì Bọ́láńlé's *Àbẹ̀bí* (2007), Adùnọlá Àmọ̀ọ́'s *Ọlẹdàrùn* (2008), Múbọ̀ Adéríbigbé's *Òkété* (2008), and Yínká Adébóyè's *Ó Ṣojú Mi* (2010).

The themes many Yorùbá female writers touch upon include motherhood, parenthood, domestic issues, and cultural issues like marriage, childbearing and child rearing, dressing and modesty, sexual chastity, and power relations between men and women. However, the theme of gender inequality has a predominant space in their discourse. From the presentation of female characters and plot arrangements in the works of female writers, female characters can be broadly categorized into three types: the liberal feminist, as in Yinka Adeboye's *Ó Ṣojú Mi* and Nikẹ Adésànyà's *Ọdún Á Yakọ*; the womanist, as in Adébọ̀wálé and Adéjùmọ̀'s poetry, and the macho, as in Jọláádé Fáwálé's *Kúsóró* and Adùnọlá Àmọ̀ọ́'s *Àbẹ̀bí*.

See also **Writers**

REFERENCE

Sheba, Janet Ọláídé. *Ìṣẹ̀tọ́fábo Nínú Iṣẹ́ Òǹkọ̀wékùnrin Yorùbá*. Cape Town: Centre for Advanced Studies in African Society, 2000.

Àrìnpé Adéjùmọ̀

LIVESTOCK: DOMESTICATION AND SPECIES

To the average Yorùbá, a home without domesticated animals is prone to physical or spiritual attack. This belief is rooted in the saying *ẹní kú túẹ́ bí aláìní-nǹkan ọ̀sìn* (the person without domestic animals is the one who dies mysteriously). This hinges on the belief that livestock serve as a protective measure for their owner. Animals die the death that was meant to claim their owner's life. Domesticated animals are reared free to range around the house or around the compound.

One of the most common domesticated animals among the Yorùbá is the dog (*ajá*). Dogs are reared for home security. For instance, if no one is at home, the dog watches over the compound and the house and chases away any unfamiliar or threatening individual. Dogs are used as watchdogs during the day and at night. Dogs are used for hunting as well. People rear and train their dogs to hunt game, which can be sold or consumed by the hunter-owner. The cat (*ológbò*) is another common domesticated animal that is used to protect foodstuff from mice and rats.

Some family traditions (*orò-ìdílé*) do not permit domesticating or breeding certain types of animals while other traditions encourage it. For instance, it is believed by some families that bred cats may die mysteriously or run away from home. Some of these animals are domesticated based on personal affinity or love for such kind of animals on the part of the owner.

Moreover, goats (*ewúrẹ́*) and sheep (*àgùntàn*) are also domesticated for consumption. Goats, especially females, may be reared for the purpose of dowry payment, which is part of the marriage contract between two families. The groom's family, as a matter of tradition, is expected to include a mature she goat among the items presented to the bride's family. This is a symbol of fruitfulness in the marriage. It is believed that the wife will never be barren as long as the female goat is also procreating. Additionally, sheep (*àgùntàn*) and ram (*àgbò*) may be reared on the basis of affinity or family tradition. For instance, Ọya, Ṣàngó, and Egúngún worshipers breed them for sacrifice during their festivals. More important, these animals serve as good sources of protein.

In addition, the horse (*ẹṣin*) is also an important domesticated animal, but only few own one. Horse ownership is particular to kings (*ọba*), high-class chiefs (*olóyè*), and wealthy people (*bọ̀rọ̀kìnní*). In fact, horse ownership has become so prevalent among some of wealthy families that it has become part of their praise poetry *oríkì* or family encomium. Some families are called *ajíbẹ́ṣinró*, the one who wakes early to tender horses, or *alẹ́ṣin-ńlá-lágbàlá*, meaning, literally, the one who has horses in its courtyard. These animals are also sold for profit as reflected in the saying, *títà lèrè ẹ̀sìn*, that is, selling is the gain for rearing the horse.

Furthermore, people rear animals to protect themselves from spiritual attack. Yorùbá typically rear domestic animals in the name of themselves or their children. If a person wants to thwart an evil enchantment through spiritual media, an animal that has been given the name of its owner suffers the attack instead. For instance, one might say, "This is Olújídé's goat," even though Olújídé is a baby and did not buy any goat. Sometimes, the person who claims to be the owner of the animal might not even live in the same village or community. As a child, however, the parent bought the animal and raised it on his or her behalf to serve as a kind of shield and protection against evil attack for the child.

Yorùbá naming practices regarding domestic animals such as goats, sheep, dogs, and fowls include names like *Tañfẹ́-á-ní* (nobody wants us to have peace, happiness, wealth, house, children, and the like) or *Tẹlẹ́gàn-ló-ṣòro* (the oppressor is the one who has trouble). These names serve as reminders to the people that they live among enemies; therefore, they make fun of or humiliate the oppressing neighbor who always fights or bemoans others.

Naming domestic animals is also a form of security for the animals themselves; in situations where thieves steal these animals away, the owner can easily locate where the animal is kept (if it has not been killed). As soon as the animal's name is called, it responds by bleating and follows its owner home. Sometimes, when the animal falls into a trap and the owner is looking for it by calling its name, the animal will respond so as to be rescued. In addition, some great hunters domesticate wild animals to show their people that they are spiritually powerful and as a symbol of pride. People will also fear the animals and hunters.

See also **Hunting; Names and Naming; Wildlife: Preservation, Hunting, and Destruction**

REFERENCES

Jẹ́bọ̀dà, Fẹ́mi. *Yorùbá Gbayì (Ìwé Karùn-ún)*. Ìbàdàn (Nigeria): African Universities Press, 1982.

Ọdẹ́tókun, Adémọ́lá. *Yorùbá Gbayì (Ìwé Kẹfà)*. Ìbàdàn (Nigeria): African Universities Press, 1982.

Gabriel Ayọ̀ọlá

LUCUMÍ

Lucumí was a term generally assigned to Yorùbá-speaking slaves arriving from ports in the Bight of Benin to the Spanish Americas, most especially Cuba, between the sixteenth and nineteenth centuries. The term derives either from the phrase *olùkù mi* (my friend) or from an Edo phrase *oluku mi* (that young animal, or simply foreigner). By the nineteenth century, colonial authorities and slave owners often made distinctions among different types of Lucumí using subclassifications indicative of different Yorùbá kingdoms and subgroups, including Ọ̀yọ́, Ẹ̀gbá, Ìjẹ̀bú, Òwu, Ànàgó, and Ẹ̀gbádò. At other times, Lucumí subclassifications referred not to Yorùbá speakers but to non-Yorùbá ethnolinguistic groups from the Bight of Benin hinterland, such as Bariba, Benin, Nupe, and Hausa, among others. By the mid-nineteenth century, there were well more than one hundred Lucumí subclassifications in use in Cuba, all of which were representative of the diversity of the migration from the Bight of Benin to the Americas.

Lucumí is still used in Cuba today and generally refers to one of the most popular Afro-Cuban religions, commonly known as Santería or the Religión Lucumí (Lucumí religion). Its liturgical language, which is also known as Lucumí, can be considered a dialect of Yorùbá. The term *Santería* refers to the syncretization of *òrìṣà*, such as Ṣàngó, Yemọja, Ọ̀ṣun, and Ifá, with Roman Catholic saints, such as St. Barbara, Nuestra Señora de La Regla and Nuestra Señora de la Caridad, St. Francis of Assisi, and so on. The Lucumí religion has other syncretic ties to other Afro-Cuban religions, African belief systems, and indigenous American traditions.

Both Santería and Lucumí consist of two intertwined belief systems based around the *òrìṣà* pantheon called the Regla de Ifá (Rules of Ifá) and Regla de Ochá (Rules of Ochá). The main differences between the two distinct religions relate to initiations, priesthood, and divination practices. The former involves only male priests and initiates called *babaláwo* who are skilled in Ifá divination, and the latter priests or priestesses called *babalórìcha, ìyálórìchas, olórìchas*, and/or *ọbá-oriaté*, who consult the oracular system *dilogún*. Another defining characteristic of the two religions is that Regla de Ifá is viewed as a more unified system centered on the authority of Ifá divination, whereas Regla de Ochá seeks to challenge Ifá by granting cosmological primacy to the many other gods in the *òrìṣà* pantheon. The Lucumí religions have much iconography, music, and dance revolving around *òrìṣà* worship, some of which is clearly linked to West Africa, while others are not and are unique to these cultural beliefs and practices.

Lucumí culture is mostly found in the Americas, and most notably the Caribbean Basin, including but not limited to Cuba, Puerto Rico, Dominican Republic, Panama, Colombia, Venezuela, Mexico, and the United States. The Lucumí religions spread out from Cuba to elsewhere, especially following the migration of people in the aftermath of the Cuban Revolution of 1959. As a result, there are many Lucumí communities to be found elsewhere in Europe, North and South America and, to a much lesser extent, Africa and Asia.

See also **Deities: The Òrìṣà; Diaspora: Deities (The Òrìṣà); Diaspora: Yorùbá in North America; Diaspora: Yorùbá in South America and the Caribbean; Diaspora: Impact of Yorùbá Culture; Nagô; Ọ̀yọ́túnjí: The Yorùbá Community in the United States**

REFERENCES

Brown, David H. *Santería Enthroned: Art, Ritual, and Innovation in an Afro-Cuban Religion.* Chicago: University of Chicago Press, 2003.

Fálọlá, Tóyìn, and Matt D. Childs, eds. *The Yorùbá Diaspora in the Atlantic World.* Bloomington: Indiana University Press, 2004.

Law, Robin. "Ethnicity and the Slave Trade: 'Lucumí' and 'Nagô' as Ethnonyms in West Africa." *History in Africa* 24 (1997): 205–19.

Lovejoy, Henry B., and Ọlátúnjí Òjó. "'Lucumí' and 'Terranova' and the Origins of a Yorùbá Nation." *Journal of African History.* 56 (2015): 353–72.

Henry B. Lovejoy

M

MAGIC

In the Yorùbá worldview, the existence of supernatural powers and forces cannot be overemphasized. Human beings and life itself are full of mysteries. Among these powers and forces, magic is prominent. The belief in magic and medicine is one of the cardinal structures of Yorùbá religion. Therefore, we cannot discuss magic without a clear understanding of religion. The African world is an agitated world. Since the dawn of consciousness, humans have been confronted with a need to control their circumstances. Magic is one way that people self-determine their lives. It is an attempt to tap into and control the supernatural resources of the cosmos for personal advantage. It is also an attempt to influence people and events by supernatural means. It is connected with a belief in supernatural powers and the method of obtaining assistance from these powers to support the affairs of people. Hence, magic is an act that is not easily explainable to common reasoning because it involves mysterious agency or power.

The supernatural force in magic is associated with *mana*, an impersonal power or authority operating on principle similar to electricity. If harnessed, one can control *mana* to serve his or her will. Magic serves the human ego and is a shortcut to divine ecstasy. Egocentricity or ethical egoism is the theory that the pursuit of one's own welfare is the basis of morality. Magic is a supernatural device employed to gain an advantage through the help of spirits, gods, or other entities in the spiritual realm. One might suggest that the common motto for those practicing magic is "my will be done."

Among the Yorùbá people of southwestern Nigeria, magic is used to meet the nontherapeutic needs of men and women, such as *àwúre* (good luck), *awọ̀rọ̀* (attracting customers), and *ìsọ̀yè* (aiding one's knowledge or memory). To the Yorùbá, any magic that does not involve the loss of life or the killing of human being is good or legitimate magic. Bad or illicit magic is known as sorcery. Black magic signifies evil, and white magic signifies good. Therefore, magic can be used for social and antisocial needs.

Sorcery is feared because it can be used to kill or destroy lives and properties. A person who uses bad magic is called a sorcerer. The sorcerer often works in the darkness because his or her deeds are evil, and his or her goals always focus on destruction. One example of sorcery is sending poisonous animals such as snakes, scorpions, or other dangerous animals to attack a victim. Victims of such attacks seldom recover from such attacks. Another technique of sorcery is called *mágùn* (literally "do not mount"). For example, a jealous husband secretly puts *mágùn* on his wife without her knowledge. Anyone who has sex with her, including her husband, will die a shameful death. Even if the husband meets with his wife believing that someone else has carried away the *mágùn*, he himself will fall into the trap that he sets for others. Cursing an enemy is another form of bad magic called *èpè* (curse). With èpè, a person can become insane or mad and be made to commit suicide. However, it is believed that a more powerful èpè can be used to remove the evil effects of the previous èpè. The Yorùbá say, èpè la fi ń wo èpè (curse is what is used to expunge another curse).

Magic falls into two categories: private and public. It is private when used for specific personal purposes, and public when used to protect or provide for the peace and security of a house, compound, or city.

See also Sorcery; Witchcraft; Words: Ọ̀rọ̀

REFERENCE

Edgerton, Robert, and L. L. Langeness. *Methods and Styles in the Study of Culture.* San Francisco: Candler and Sharp, 1983.

Ọbáfẹ́mi Jẹ́gẹ́dẹ́

MÀMÍ-WÀTÁ

In Yorùbá cosmology and worldview, Yemọja is known as Mami-water or Màmí-wàtá. Yemọja is the goddess of the sea. She is known by different names: Yemọja Okun is known as Olókun. Yemọja Ọ̀sà is known as Ọlọ́sà, and Yemọja Ọ̀sun is Ọlọ́sun. This means not that there are as many Yemọja as there are seas and oceans, but that the universally acclaimed goddess inhabits all the seas and oceans in the world. She is a universal goddess. Each river, ocean, or sea is named along with Yemọja. The Niger River possesses her own Yemọja; her name is Ọya. The Yorùbá believe that Yemọja is half human, half fish. She is human from her head to the waist, and below the waist she is a fish. She controls the movements of the seas and all that inhabits them. She is believed to have a large body with large hips and breasts. She is the epitome of beauty.

Yemọja is worshipped along with other deities like Ṣàngó, Ògún, and Ọbàtálá. She is the mother of many children. The name Yemọja is etymologically derived from *yèyé ọmọ tó lọ jàrá* (mother of many children). Other sources for her name include *yèyé ọmọ eja* (mother of fishes) and *yèyé máa já a* (mother continues to cut it [her devotees' problem] into pieces). Regardless of the source of her name, the Yorùbá see Yemọja as a mother, and this is why they revere and worship

her. In the Yorùbá city of Ìbàdàn, for example, Yemọja is popular; a fairly large part of the town, called Pópóo Yemọja, is named after her. Her temple is located in this area, and her yearly festival begins in this area.

Devotees of Yemọja believe that she comes out from the sea once a year during the festival. This is when she listens to the supplications of her adherents. Women are mostly devotees of Yemọja. Items used in the worship of Yemọja are *èkuru* (steamed black-eyed peas), *ọ̀sọ̀sọ̀ ẹ̀wà* (a type of bean), *àádùn* (grinded roasted corn mixed with palm oil), *ẹ̀pà* (peanuts), *ìrèkè* (sugarcane), *oyin* (honey), *ẹ̀wà síse* (cooked beans), *ẹran ewúrẹ́* (female goat), and *obì* (kola nut). Yemọja has dominion over all kinds of creatures living in the sea; she sees to their well-being.

People worship Yemọja for the same reason they worship all other gods and goddesses. They look to her for healing, prosperity, and knowledge. Above all, Yemọja is said to have the power to give children to barren women, as her name connotes "mother of many children." It is believed that Yemọja can, through her benevolence, open the womb of a barren woman and put a child there. Yemọja is believed to be able to give children to her many children in the seas, and these children go into the wombs of women who beseech her intervention at her shrine.

When Odù Ifá Ọ̀sẹ́ Méjì or Òdí Méjì is revealed during Ifá consultation by a client, it means the client would have to make sacrifice to the goddess Yemọja. People usually sacrifice to a river goddess, which means that they sacrifice to Yemọja.

See also Deities: The Òrìṣà; Divination: Ifá

REFERENCE

Drewal, Henry John, ed. *Sacred Waters: Arts for Mami Wata and Other Divinities in Africa and the Diaspora.* Bloomington: Indiana University Press, 2008.

Paul Olúwọlé Àsáwálé

MARKET

Markets (*ọjà*) exist and have continued to exist as an integrated and organized framework of exchange, production, and services. The general spatial diffusion of markets is an important element of the domestic and regional economy of a people. The Yorùbá are considered one of the most highly industrious and sophisticated people in Africa because the flow of goods and services in society occurs through a large variety of redistributive mechanisms. Markets are categorized on the basis of their size, structure, location, and period. The development of the distinctive marketplace, which operates according to well-organized schedules, is distinguished from international trading systems and from ceremonial exchanges and obligatory gift giving. These markets facilitated intra- and interregional trade between different geographic and ecological zones. Because food supply varied seasonally with harvest cycles, markets in particular areas coexisted with agricultural production. Specializations also existed on the basis of geographical location. For example, in precolonial times, the Ìjẹ̀bú port of Ìkòròdú had a lagoon where fishing and trade along the waterway flourished, and it was a place where natives sold fine cloth to Europeans along the coast. Beginning in the 1400s, the Ìjẹ̀bú acted as intermediaries between the European traders on the Atlantic seaboard and other Yorùbá groups in the interior. The emergence of Lagos as the premier port in the Bight of Benin for the transatlantic slave trade also marked it as a notable market.

Market Services

The markets in Yorùbáland were established as distinct places where buyers and sellers of goods and services interacted at regular intervals for business and other sociocultural transactions. Each market offered different services to consumers, and markets became a distinctive feature of the society from the precolonial period and to the present. These galvanized a productive system that linked the rural and urban regions in several ways. Markets gave rise to a group of people who engaged in the buying and selling of commodities according to the principles of market transactions using the currencies available at that time. In many cases, marketing activities encouraged rudimentary urban places to evolve from their rural matrix.

Features of Yorùbá Markets

Markets have, over time, been divided into different categories based on their spatial, behavioral, and institutional attributes. These ranged from the periodic markets, daily markets, night markets, rural markets, junction markets, and house markets. Goods and services provided ranged from foodstuffs to products of craft industries, barbering, smithing, and repairs. The periodic markets, as distinct from daily or continuous markets, were markets that operated in an integrated sequence and met at intervals according to a set schedule of market days. This developed as a function of the volume and spatial distribution of the purchasing power of the population. The periodic markets operated in a ring system that enabled each community or individual to gain regular access to goods and services while keeping the costs of collection and distribution low. The size of the cycle or ring and the density of the markets depended, to a large extent, on the population density of any given area. The frequency with which these markets operated also depended on the number of markets in a particular ring. Market cycles included two-, four-, seven-, eight-, and sixteen-day cycles. The seven-day markets appeared to be the most common.

In the city of Ìbàdàn, the Bodè (Ìbúkọ̀) market located on the southern edge of town became a veritable center for foodstuffs. Òjé market in the city also developed into a collection and distribution center for food crops and the products of craft industries. Today, the market, which takes place every sixteen days, has become a specialized indigenous cloth market. Like Ìbàdàn, different areas of Yorùbáland also developed a system of markets that created a collaborative system that ultimately fused them together in commercial relationships that have lasted for a long time. Among the Ìjẹ̀bú, there were, for instance, a ring of market towns from Orù through Ajeregún and Ajégúnlẹ̀ to Màmu.

The daily markets were numerous and vibrant. These operated in both the rural and the urban centers. They were noted for retail trading. While many of the daily markets were located in different parts of urban centers, the ones known as the king's markets were usually located at the center of the town. Ìbàdàn, Dùgbẹ̀, Mọ́kọ́lá, Gbági, Agbeni, Gẹ́gẹ́-Orítamẹ́rin, and Ọjà-Ọba were prominent daily markets frequented by buyers and sellers. In smaller towns, daily markets were located in front of the palace, and these are known as Ọjà-Ọba (the king's market). The night markets (ọjà alẹ́) existed in almost every Yorùbá town. Like the daily markets, these are usually situated at the center of the town near the palace of the ruler. They commence operations at dusk and end shortly before midnight.

There were, however, specialized daily markets such as the Gẹ́gẹ́-Orítamẹ́rin foodstuff market in Ìbàdàn, where food products such as yam, yam flour, cassava flour, beans, corn, peppers, onions, and palm oil were collected and dispersed to other points of sales in the city. The kola nut market site at Ọjà-Ọba market, the Ṣàngó cattle market, and the Mọ́níyà cattle and pepper markets, all in Ìbàdàn, were notable for the overwhelming influence of Hausa traders who controlled the goods to and from the northern parts of the country.

In rural markets, alájàpá, traveling merchants who formed a chain of intermediaries known for their wholesale buying, provided space for farm produce that was dispersed throughout Yorùbáland and beyond. They collect foodstuffs in bulk from producers in rural markets and transported them to periodic markets in other market centers.

Numerous ad hoc places for trade included compound markets and house markets, where goods were sold in small lots to consumers. A distinct feature that grew out of the house market was the hawking of small goods in the neighborhood.

Administration of the Markets

Groups, individuals, and the state are actively involved in the efficient running of the markets. The markets are well organized and have various guilds and officers who operate under the direction of their officers. A variety of traders' organizations exist in the markets. These are known as the ẹgbẹ́ (association) and are organized according to the commodities they deal in, such as Ẹgbẹ́ Aláṣọ (Association of Cloth Sellers). Traders dealing in similar commodities occupy particular sections of the market. These guilds or traders' organizations try to exert a measure of control over prices and competition. Traders' organizations have greater success in representing the interests of their members in negotiations with state authorities and in helping enforce regulations regarding weights and measures and laws governing debts, contracts, and access to bank loans.

The ìyálójà (mother of the market) not only sees to the day-to-day running of the markets but also represents the interests of the traders in the traditional ruling council in the town. The rulers in the precolonial period were known to also develop a group of trading chiefs to oversee trade and commerce in and out of their domains. The Awùjalẹ̀, the traditional ruler of Ìjẹ̀búland controlled the trade in his kingdom through the Pàràkòyí (the trade chiefs). They were supported by the Pámpá, a group of commoners who supervised markets in peacetime. Two or more of its members were present in the market on market days to ensure that the market was kept clean and to settle minor disputes among the traders. Today, local governments are in charge of the day-to-day running of the markets. However, the traditional administrative structures have remained in place. With the imposition of colonial rule and the spread of Western ideas, important shopping and trading centers based on Western models began to develop. Despite the intrusion of the modern supermarket and chain stores, the traditional market system has remained resilient, vigorous, and progressive.

See also **Agriculture and Farming; Economic System**

REFERENCES

Eighmy, Thomas H. "Rural Periodic Markets and the Extension of an Urban System: A Western Nigerian Example." *Economic Geography* 48.3 (July 1972): 299–315.

Smith, Robert H. T. "Periodic Market-places and Periodic Marketing: Review and Prospect." *Progress in Human Geography* 4 (January 1, 1980): 1–31.

Olútáyọ̀ C. Adésínà

Marriage is the most celebrated event in Yorùbáland. According to N. A. Fádípè, a man or woman who has reached marriageable age but remains single is living against the mores of Yorùbá. Men get married even when they are sexually impotent in order to save their reputation. Marriage is not an affair between husband and wife alone but a relationship between the families of both sides. In addition, most marriages in Yorùbáland are polygamous, for a man's importance is based on the number of children and wives he has.

Before a marriage system can be established, a marriage broker, or *alárinà*, usually negotiates between a man and woman who propose to become husband and wife. The *alárinà* gracefully backs off after arranging the meeting between the potential husband and wife. Investigations are done into the individual families before a formal introduction. Divinations are performed to seek the advice of Ifá and to prevent unforeseen circumstances in the union.

Marriage system occurs in stages. The first stage is *ìtọrọ*, proposal, when members of the two families get to know themselves. This may occur before the conception of a girl child or immediately after a girl is born. She is marked for a man without her consent, *ba ọmọbìnrin sílẹ̀*. However, if a man's family had not "marked" a girl child for their son, the family will have to look for a suitable spouse. This is termed *ìfojúsóde*, which is achieved only after thorough investigations by both sides. In ancient times, the parents and families, not individuals, look out for suitable spouses.

When satisfied with the proposal, an exchange of gifts occurs between the two families, beginning with the girl's family when she is young. Ifá divination (*ifá ìfọmọfọ́kọ*) is consulted again by the girl's family, and representatives of the groom's family attend, which encourages a bright future for the relationship. The next stage is *ìṣíhùn* (voicing out), a ceremony of parents' formal consent. Various food items are sent to the girl's family as a token of thanksgiving for a positive response from Ifá after consulting with an oracle (*ẹbọ ìyàwó*).

The next stage is *ìdána*, commonly known as the engagement ceremony, or formal betrothal. It starts with the occasional presentation of gifts of various types through the chosen *alárinà* to the girl's family until she is of age. The groom's family gives the girl's family a list of items to ensure that their daughter is not marrying into a family that cannot afford to take care of her. On the appointed date, the in-laws come with the specified engagement items, such as yam tubers, kola nuts, bitter kola, wine, dried fish, alligator peppers, traditional dresses, and the like. The dowry or bride price, an amount that varies from family to family, is also paid. The dowry legitimizes the union so that the man can lay claim to any children that result from their union. The bride starts the performance of the bridal nuptial poetry (*ẹkún ìyàwó*), which eulogizes her parents and expresses her happiness and fears about the journey she is starting.

The bride goes to her husband's house early in the morning. The groom's sisters-in-law, accompanied by the bride's friends, take the veiled bride to the groom's house. It is mandatory for the groom to leave the house before the bride arrives. On arriving at the groom's house, the ritual washing of the bride's feet is performed at the doorstep. The groom comes in to greet and welcome the bride into his family after she has settled in. Merriment continues until the evening when the breaking of the maidenhead is performed.

Virginity is important in the Yorùbá marriage system. If the husband meets the maidenhead "intact," gifts are sent to the bride's family the following morning. The wife is honored. Brides without an intact hymen are punished and disgraced for losing their virginity before marriage. Nevertheless, the birth of a child seals the bond between the two families.

There are other types of marriages. There is *ìyàwó òrìṣà* (the deity's wife), when an oracle specifically marks a girl to marry a devotee. Another type is marriage to a divorcee. Although divorce is rare, when it happens, such women can remarry to become new wives elsewhere. Another type is wife inheritance (*opó ṣíṣú*), in which a brother-in-law inherits the wife of a deceased elder brother. For these other forms of marriage, the husband must satisfy the demands of his in-laws and pay certain sums of money as dowry before the relationship is recognized.

It is important, however, to note that the marriage system differs among subgroups of the Yorùbá. For instance, while the Yorùbá from the states of Ọ̀yọ́, Ọ̀sun, Èkìtì, Lagos, and Kwara share the same marriage system as explained above, those from the state of Oǹdó have some differences. In Àkókóland, for instance, marriage takes place annually during each community's traditional festival. In Ọ̀kà-Àkókó, there is *òdeèsán* marriage, whereby a married woman replaces herself in her father's house with her first daughter. The first daughter is expected to marry her maternal uncle. However, if the woman is not interested in marrying her maternal uncle, this uncle has to give his consent to whomever the woman likes before the marriage can be consummated.

Today, other forms of marriage exist, but each is preceded by the traditional processes explained already. Registry or court marriage can be combined with either church or mosque marriage. The registry marriage is strictly monogamous and is performed for couples who are at least eighteen years of age. Church marriage is for Christians and involves the exchange of rings. The Islamic marriage known as *yìgì síso* is for Muslims in accordance with Islamic injunctions, but in Nigeria it is polygamous, as in the Yorùbá marital system.

Therefore, Yorùbá marital status can be described in different terms. When single and unmarried, it is *ọmọge/wúńdíá/ọ̀dọ́bìnrin* for girls and *ọ̀dọ́kùnrin/ọ̀sọ́ọ́rọ́* for boys. For married women, the term is *ìyáálé* for the senior wife and *ìyàwó* for the junior wife. Married men are *baálé*. The widows are *opó*. A married woman not living under a husband's roof is *adálémosú*.

See also **Deities: The *Òrìṣà*; Diaspora: Deities (*Òrìṣà*); Divination: Ifá; Literature: Oral; Widows and Widowhood**

REFERENCE

Fádípè, N. A. *The Sociology of the Yorùbá*. Ìbàdàn (Nigeria): University Press, 1970.

Láídé Sheba

Masks

Masks are important artifacts among the Yorùbá people. They are used for various reasons: by traditional healers to drive away evil spirits or perform some healing acts; by masquerades in their performances; and by actors for other theatrical purposes. Masks are usually carved from wood and are decorated with various materials, such as fabric, leather, shells, colored glass, plant fibers, animal horns, and metal pieces. Sculpted and carved masks are placed on shrines dedicated to the gods and the ancestors. In essence, masks serve many purposes among the Yorùbá people, including functionality and performance artistry. Functionally, they are used for ceremonies, rituals, initiations, celebrations, and secret organizations such as masquerades. Some of the masks are believed to be imbued with the essences of the gods and ancestral spirits that may possess the wearer of the mask during performance. Such masks bear images of animals, human beings, and abstract forms. During the mask ceremony, a dancer goes into a deep trance when he or she communicates with the spirits or ancestors. During initiation ceremonies or rituals, for instance, the mask enhances the process of unifying the initiate with the gods or the ancestors, and it enhances the masquerade performances, as in Egúngún or Gẹ̀lẹ̀dẹ́.

Masquerades

The Yorùbá people believe in reincarnation, and the concept of transcendental existence is primal to Yorùbá life. The ancestors, along with the gods, aid people at transition points during life and in the afterlife, particularly in crossing the space that separates the living from the ancestors. These ancestors are revered and venerated through masquerade performances. Egúngún, which could be ritual or for entertainment, is popular among the Ọ̀yọ́ Yorùbá, Agẹmọ, and Agbo. Ekine is practiced by the Ìjẹbú, and Gẹ̀lẹ̀dẹ́ is found in the Ẹ̀gbádò area. These are some of the main types of Yorùbá masquerades or masked, costumed figures.

Egúngún

The belief is that those who are dead are still very close to the world of the living, particularly to their relatives, whom they protect from evil forces and misfortunes. Special days are reserved for the veneration of these ancestors, represented by masks, in the form of Egúngún masquerades. They refer to the Egúngún as *ará òrun* (the inhabitants of heaven). Masquerade refers both to a performance given by masked characters and to the masked performer, the "masker" or Egúngún. *Mask* is the face or body covering. The human performer who dons the mask represents the embodied spirit and is accorded the same respect as the ancestors.

Egúngún is a performance that is ritualistic in intent and purpose or as a performative ritual. There are various types of Egúngún, including satirical masks, elegant masks that exhibit the beauty and elegance of costumes and dance, and masks that dramatize masculine strength. However, the most significant among the Egúngún are the ancestral masks. Egúngún is performed for ancestral veneration and ritual purposes, but the entertainment function is also important. This is evident in choice of maskers. A performer has to be a good poet or orator and attuned to different styles of music to entertain and educate the spectators and to help them treasure memorable aspects of the performances.

Ancestral masks are recognized by their moral and mystical authority, attributes that serve as embodiments of the ritual importance of the ancestors. These ancestral Egúngún perform various functions, from officiating during burial ceremonies, when they are assumed to take the soul of the departed to the land of the ancestors, to performing at night to maintain societal equilibrium. Some Egúngún use songs or proverbs to ridicule people whose habits or behaviors are considered undesirable in the community. Yet others adjudicate difficult cases or perform oracular roles.

In a typical Yorùbá town, each household has its own Egúngún, and a household may have more than one Egúngún or even different kinds of Egúngún.

Usually, the spirit of the most powerful or the most benevolent individual in the household is invoked into the mask of the more important Egúngún.

There are Egúngún who represent powerful ancestors who were either great medicine men or chiefs in their past existence on earth, known for great feats like waging wars, curing diseases, making sacrifices, executing decisions, and dispatching convicted criminals. They are regarded as the elder Egúngún. Most communal rites are performed by the elder Egúngún. There are also dancers, poets, acrobats, satirists, praise singers, and *láyèwú*, the hunter masqueraders famous for their imitations of wild animals in mime and dance.

Gèlèdé

The Egúngún is not dissimilar to Gèlèdé and Agẹmọ performances, which take place between March and July every year at the beginning of a new agricultural season. They also take place at funerals and during times of drought, famine, or epidemic. The purpose of the Gèlèdé performance is to pay tribute to the special power of women, both elders and ancestors, who are known affectionately as "our mothers." Women can use a spiritual life force (*àsẹ*) creatively for the benefit of the society or for destruction, in which case the women are regarded as *àjẹ́* with the ability to affect the well-being of individuals or the community.

The masquerade has an elaborate and bulky costume, emphasizing the female forms of the woman it represents; unlike Egúngún, the identity of the wearer is not secret. He can be seen through the transparent cloth worn over the face, and he can unmask in public. The dancers are men, although they represent both men and women in the performance. The name of the dancer may be used in the song that accompanies his act—making him the subject of praise or criticism, depending on the skill and rhythm of his performance. Drumming and singing are also essential components of the performance. Because Gèlèdé is a "woman" cult, the brightly painted headdress of the mask comes in two parts: a lower mask depicting a woman's face, which expresses the qualities of femininity, patience, and responsibility desired in women, and the upper part, which shows women's inner powers for all to see, thus pleasing "our mothers" and ensuring the well-being of the community. One of the most repeated adornments of the upper part of Gèlèdé mask is that of two fighting animals.

Masquerades can be used as a form of social control. Masquerades are regarded as having the power to avert any evil, danger, or fear that may befall a Yorùbá lineage or community.

See also **Carvers; Media: Comic Art; Memorial Arts; Sculpture; Witches**

REFERENCE

Drewal, Henry J., and Margaret T. Drewal. *Gèlèdé: Art and Female Power among the Yorùbá*. Bloomington: Indiana University Press, 1983.

Ṣọlá Adéyẹmí

MEDIA: BOOK PUBLISHING

Books are an important form of print media. Newspapers, magazines, and journals are extensions of books; they are closely associated with the evolution of printing and publishing. Christian missionaries started the first Yorùbá newspapers, and their efforts extended to book publishing. Pioneer authors include Daniel Ọlọ́runfẹ́mi Fágúnwà, who wrote what is believed to be the first novel published in Yorùbá, *Ògbójú Ọdẹ Nínú Igbó Irúnmalẹ̀*. Amos Tutùọlá did not write in Yorùbá but is widely credited with publicizing Yorùbá culture and folklore in his celebrated *The Palm-Wine Drinkard*, published in 1952. Chief Joseph Ọdúnjọ's *Aláwìíyé* series taught Yorùbá at the primary and secondary school level to children. Ọdúnjọ later became minister of education in the Western Region. Also worthy of note is Adébáyọ̀ Fálétí, famed broadcaster, poet, and dramatist, who wrote several books, including a book of Yorùbá greetings and *Ẹ̀dá kò Láròpin*.

The publications of scholars further promoted Yorùbá culture, such as Professors Afọlábí Ọlábímtán, Akínwùmí Ìṣọ̀lá, Ọlátúndé Ọlátúnjí, and Samuel Ọlánipẹ̀kun Èṣan. Èṣan was a classics scholar who wrote several

Yorùbá books and plays. Interestingly, the first convocation lecture to be given in the Yorùbá language was delivered in 2013 by Professor Akínwùmí Ìṣọ̀lá at Adékúnlé Ajásin University, Àkùngbá Àkókó, Oǹdó State.

Many of the early books were published by overseas institutions such as Oxford University Press, Longman, Collins, and Nelson. Very early on, however, Yorùbá publishers began to make their mark. Oníbọnòjé Publishers, located in the Mọlété area of Ìbàdàn, was founded by Gabriel Ọmọ́táyọ̀ Oníbọnòjé. This remarkable indigenous publishing house celebrated its fiftieth anniversary in 2009, illustrating the rising and dwindling fortunes of several Yorùbá publishers. Started as a one-man business with only eight employees, Oníbọnòjé blossomed into a moderately sized business employing as many as 150 workers. Economic problems, such as the high cost of printing papers, sporadic electricity, and a poorly developed reading culture limited the company's growth. Other notable Yorùbá publishers include Fágbàmígbé Publishers, based in Àkúrẹ́ and owned by the late Honorable Albert Ọláìyá Fágbàmígbé, renowned for making the thoughts and popular sayings of Chief Ọbáfẹ́mi Awólọ́wọ̀ available to a mass Yorùbá audience through several books and publications.

Since the mid-1980s, publishing has struggled with setbacks because of the harsh economic climate. A few notable Yorùbá publishers, located mainly in Ìbàdàn, such as Bánkọ́lé Ọláyẹbí of Bookcraft and Táíwò Owóẹyẹ of College Press and Publishers Limited, continue to struggle against the odds.

See also **Fágúnwà, D. O.; Tutùọlá, Amos; Writers**

REFERENCE

Abímbọ́lá, Wándé. *The Study of Yorùbá Literature: An Assessment.* Inaugural Lecture Series 24. Ifẹ̀ (Nigeria): University of Ifẹ̀ Press, 1977.

Dàmọ́lá Àyánṣọlá

MEDIA: COMIC ART

Art is produced for religious and secular purposes. Comic art falls within the secular realm and is found mostly in sculptures. It is different from Western culture where cartoons and pictorial illustrations are used. Traditionally, comic art satirizes, lampoons, derides, abuses, entertains, or informs. Three dimensional in form, rather than the two-dimensional art used for decoration and aesthetics, comic art is used in textiles design, shrine and wall paintings, mat weaving, calabash carving, decoration, and other art forms. Because art performs a role in the culture, the comic arts advertise events or comment on social issues.

Yorùbá comic art is best illustrated with sculptural masks worn by the performers, who have the sole aim of passing information to the audience and for their entertainment. The best example of Yorùbá comic art is illustrated by Gèlèdé masks, usually worn by women performers. Gèlèdé masks have an elaborate aesthetic and symbolic system. In this system, the concept and image of women in African society and women's spiritual and social roles in the culture are explored. The art forms that constitute Gèlèdé comic art comment on society both independently and collectively to produce a complex multifaceted phenomenon. Gèlèdé masks are worn by women to entertain the public on topical issues in order to pass information, praise achievement among women, amuse, or deride.

A Gèlèdé mask is a headdress created for a particular purpose. The headdress takes the form of a human head, with motifs on top that are intended not only to entertain onlookers but also to address social concerns expressed in songs that are part of the performance. The acts performed in the female masquerades are comical, entertaining, and satirical—unlike the typical masquerades in which the followers beat themselves with sticks and sometimes use incantations and charms. Some forms of Gèlèdé masks may depict a protruding male penis symbolic of manhood, which is worn purposely to mock or deride promiscuous behavior among men or women. The act is usually accompanied with appropriate songs and different dance steps. The artist carves different mask forms that illustrate different issues among women. The visual illustration of different forms is supported with performance and songs to drive home the message to the public. The dance steps, songs, and drums illustrate womanhood.

Another related Yorùbá comic art is omolángidi, carved wooden dolls children play with. Some dolls were carved for children born shortly after the death of an older sibling (àbíkú). The child plays with the doll to ward off death. The Yorùbá believe that if the àbíkú child continues to play with the carved doll, he or she will not die at tender age.

See also **Carvers; Dolls and Toys; Mask and Masquerades; Memorial Arts; Sculpture**

REFERENCES

Adépégba, C. O. *Yorùbá Metal Sculpture*. Ìbàdàn (Nigeria): University Press, 1991.

Drewal, Henry J., and Margaret T. Drewal. *Gèlèdé: Art and Female Power among the Yorùbá*. Bloomington: Indiana University Press, 1983.

Wahab Adémólá Azeez

MEDIA: JOURNALISM

There are two types of journalism: print and electronic. Print journalism deals with written forms like newspaper, magazine, books, and handbills. Electronic journalism involves broadcasts like radio, television, Internet, and electronic billboards. Henry Townsend's determination to inform and educate a Yorùbá audience propelled him to start the newspaper *Ìwé Ìròhìn fún Àwọn Ègbá àti Yorùbá* (a newspaper for the Ègbá and Yorùbá nationals) in 1859. It became the first newspaper in Nigeria. Townsend said in his inaugural editorial, "My object is to beget the habit of seeking information by reading." Thus, Townsend had a mind-set of informing and educating the people. The colonial government used this mass medium to reach the Yorùbá audience. Similarly, Townsend used the newspaper to spread Christianity to Badagry and Ègbáland. Social and religious news dominated the news at the paper's onset. Nonreligious news followed later, such as news about Abèòkúta district, Lagos Colony, and other places in Yorùbáland. Later, it featured commercial events, prices of commodities like palm oil, announcements from local chiefs and the government of the Lagos Colony, the governor's movements, information on agricultural and craft exhibitions, and information on mission schools.

In January 1866, *Ìwé Ìròhìn* started publishing two separate editions: one in English and another in Yorùbá. The English edition was published on the fourth day of the month; the Yorùbá edition was published on the twentieth day of the month. The Yorùbá was essentially a four-page supplement to the English edition. Advertisements augmented sales revenue. *Ìwé Ìròhìn* ceased publication in 1867 as a result of civil disruption between the Ìbàdàn and Ẹ̀gbá traders.

Yorùbá print journalism began to develop in earnest. The following listed newspapers emerged, in chronological order:

Ìwé Ìròhìn 1859
Ìwé Ìròhìn Èkó àti Gbogbo Ilẹ̀ Yorùbá àti Ìlú Mìíràn 1888
In Leisure Hours (Nígbà tí Ọwọ́ bá Dílẹ̀) 1911
Èkó Akète 1922
Elétí Ọfẹ 1923
The Yorùbá News 1923
Èkó Ọ̀sọ̀ọ̀sẹ̀ 1925
Ẹ̀gbá National Harper 1926
Ẹ̀gbá Administration 1926
Èkó Ìgbẹ̀hìn 1926
Akéde Èkó 1931
Òṣùmàrè Ẹ̀gbá 1936
The Ìjẹ̀bú Weekly News (Ìwé Ìròyìn Ìjẹ̀bú) 1936
The Abẹ́òkúta Weekly Herald (Alóre Ẹ̀gbá) 1941
Ẹ̀gbáland Echo (Gboùngboùn Ẹ̀gbá) 1941
Ìròhìn Yorùbá 1945
The Ìjẹ̀bú Weekly Echo 1947
The Morning Star 1949
Oǹdó Provincial Pioneer 1952
Ìròhìn Ìmọ́lẹ̀ 1958
Gboùngboùn 1970
Ìlànà Yorùbá 1970
Ìṣọ̀kan 1980
Ọ̀kín Ọlọ́jà 1983
Aláròyé 1996
Alóre Ìpínlẹ̀ Ọ̀yọ́ 1996

Muslim News (Ìròyìn Àdínní) 1997
Ìwé Aláfẹ́ 1998
Òkìkí 1998
Akéde Àgbáyé 1998
Àlàyé (Baba Òrọ̀) 1998
Òtítọ́korò 1999
Yorùbá Ronú 1999
Àjọrò 1999
Alágbàwí 1999
Aṣojú-Odùduwà 1999
Alálàyé 1999
Ó Ṣẹlẹ̀ẹ̀ 1999
Al-Islam 1999
Atọ́ka Oòduà 1999
Òkèlè Ìrọ̀lẹ́ 1999
Àsọyé 2000
Káyégbọ́ 2000
Aláwííyé 2000
Alukoro 2000
Bójúri 2000
Ìwé Ìròyìn Sínágọ́gù 2001
Elétí Ọfẹ (New) 2002
Ìwé Ìròyìn Apostolic Faith 2007
Ọlọ́yẹ News 2005
Ìròyìn Òòjọ́ 2010

Magazine publishing also began in the late 1990s. *Aláròyé Newspaper*, *Aláròyé Magazine*, and *Ìrírí Ayé Aláròyé* are published by the same company. Other magazines include *Alálàyé Magazine*, *Akéde Àgbáyé Magazine*, *Akéde Odùduwà Magazine*. *Akéde Òdùduwà Magazine*, *Aláròyé Magazine*, and *Alálàyé Magazine* became very popular around 2007 and 2008. The magazines were well planned and featured columns on different topics such as politics, economy, sport, and culture. The covers featured similar structures, designs, and colors. The banner headlines and other headlines were displayed on the front page. All magazines from the *Aláròyé* family and *Akéde Odùduwà* magazine regularly feature the advertisements of 107.5 FM Radio Lagos and Eko FM 89.75 on their back covers. The content of most of the magazines are very similar: editorials, letters to the editor, creative writing, and stories about men's and women's issues, politics, entertainment, sports, health, divorce, crime, life experiences, and religion. Guest columnists also write for some of the newspapers and magazines.

Newspapers and magazines are written in modern Yorùbá orthography with or without full tone marking or diacritics. Only *Aláròyé* newspaper and three magazines, namely *Aláríyá*, *Akéde Àgbáyé*, and *Aláròyé*, are still in print as of today. Many Yorùbá newspapers and magazines are out of circulation for many reasons, ranging from lack of advertisements, poor financing, preference for English-language newspapers, poor reading culture, and lack of coverage of local and current events due to a lack of reporters. In the past, lack of journalistic training and practice were issues, but today it is different. Yorùbáland has well-trained journalists who work for newspapers and magazines. Yorùbá journalism has improved tremendously.

Radio and television journalism is firmly rooted among the Yorùbá. Radio services started early among the Yorùbá in the then Western Region of Nigeria. Television services started first in Ìbàdàn city. Western Nigerian Television (WNTV) was established in Ìbàdàn by the government of the Western Region under the leadership of the late Chief Ọbáfẹ́mi Awólọ́wọ̀ as a protest because he was denied airtime on the national radio services. A bill was then passed by the regional House of Assembly to establish a television station. WNTV started what could be regarded as a joint venture service with Overseas Radiovision services (ORL) on October 31, 1959. However, ORL pulled out of the partnership a year after Nigeria's independence. This event led to the birth of WNTV-WNBS (Western Nigeria Television and Broadcasting Services).

The cultural heritage of the Yorùbá, such as customs, institutions, dance, drama, drums, music, festivals, political issues, and traditional religious events are recorded, analyzed, and presented in the Yorùbá language on radio and television. Today, some radio stations use only the Yorùbá language, such as Radio Lagos FM and Fájì FM in Alágbàdo, Lagos. After independence, many radio and television stations were owned by the federal and state governments, but today there are more privately owned stations. Some exclusively Yorùbá-language radio and television stations are located in the states of Oǹdó, Ògùn, Kwara, Ọ̀ṣun, Ọ̀yọ́, Èkìtì, and Lagos.

See also **Media: Newsprint; Media: Radio and Television**

REFERENCE

Olúnládé, Táíwò. "Notes on Yorùbá Newspapers 1859–2002." In *The Yorùbá in Transition: History, Values and Modernity*, ed. Tóyìn Fálọlá and Ann Genova, 3–12. Durham, NC: Carolina Academic Press, 2006.

Táíwò Olúnládé

MEDIA: NEWSPRINT

As one of the three major indigenous languages in Nigeria, the contributions of Yorùbá to the country's print media cannot be overemphasized. The first newspaper in Nigeria, *Ìwé Ìròhìn fún àwọn Ẹ̀gbá àti Yorùbá* (newspaper for the Ẹ̀gbá and Yorùbá), was established in 1859 by Reverend Henry Townsend of the Church Missionary Society. The paper was originally printed in the Yorùbá language; an English supplement was added in 1860. As the first published Nigerian newspaper, *Ìwé Ìròhìn* inspired other newspapers. The first indigenous printers were trained by Townsend's printing press. The paper not only promoted literacy but also covered sociopolitical and cultural events in Nigeria. *Ìwé Ìròhìn* published great photographs depicting lifestyles of the people of Yorùbá in those crucial formative years of what would become the country of Nigeria.

Subsequently, English-language publications predominated. F. Omu points out that a short period of decline in cultural consciousness in the second decade of the nineteenth century was followed by a reawakening in the twentieth century, during which Yorùbá-language newspapers proliferated. Increase Coker listed the following newspapers from preindependence Nigeria: *Ìwé Ìròhìn Èkó, Yorùbá News, Èkó Àkéte, Elétí Ọfẹ, Èkó Ìgbẹ̀hìn, Akéde Èkó, Òsùmàrè Ẹ̀gbá, Ìròhìn Ìmọ́lẹ̀, Ìmọ́lẹ̀ Òwúrọ̀, Yorùbá Challenge, Ẹ̀gbá Echo*, and *Ìròhìn Yorùbá*.

These newspapers were established to promote the development of Yorùbá language and literature.

In addition, the founders established newspapers to enlighten and educate their fellow citizens and to champion causes important to the people. For instance, *Akéde Èkó* published a series of letters to the editor that described the story of its author, a young woman named Ṣẹ̀gilọlá. Her story was a stark social commentary on the position of women in colonial society.

After independence, the Sketch Group in Ìbàdàn established *Gbohùngbohùn*, and Concord Press Ltd. established *Ìṣọ̀kan*. However, the debut of *Aláròyé* in May 1996 marked a milestone in the history of the indigenous print media in Nigeria. After a brief period of instability, *Aláròyé* became a successful paper that fills the vacuum created by the demise of the previous Yorùbá print media that existed before it.

Olú Fáshèké has observed that, between 1960 and 1970, Nigerian newspapers used their photographers and the possibility of having pictures in print to promote their papers. They promoted headlines like "Peter Òbe Will Be There" or "Our Cameraman Alhaji Lateef Ọláyínká Will Be There." Between the late 1960s and early 1970s, then editor of the *Sunday Times* candid-camera section had a special documentary page in the paper.

See also **Media: Journalism**

REFERENCES

Coker, Increase. *Landmark of Nigerian Press*. Lagos (Nigeria): National Press Ltd., 1968.

Fáshèké, Olú John. *The Practice of Photojournalism, Photographic Techniques and Careers*. Lagos (Nigeria): Keystone (Books) Promotional Service, 2004.

Omu, F. *Press and Politics in Nigeria*. London: Longman, 1978.

Sunday Ọlọ́runtọ́lá

MEDIA: RADIO AND TELEVISION

A-sọ̀rọ̀-má-gbèsì is the Yorùbá descriptive name for radio. It means "one that speaks, and does not entertain a response." In 1932, the Radio Diffusion Service (RDS) in Lagos, under the British colonial government and the British Broadcasting Service, provided radio broadcasts over loudspeakers. In 1939, the RDS station in Ìbàdàn was commissioned, thereby setting the stage for radio broadcasts throughout Yorùbáland. With the creation of the Nigerian Broadcasting Corporation (NBC) in 1950, radio stations were created in Lagos and Ìbàdàn and then expanded to Abẹ́òkúta and Ìjẹbú-Òde in 1962. The transmitters—two shortwave and one medium wave—conducting all broadcasts were located in Ṣógúnlẹ̀ on the outskirts of the city of Lagos. Other than the several state-controlled radio stations, such as Èkó FM (Lagos State Radio Service) that broadcast solely in the Yorùbá language, numerous online Yorùbá radio stations currently stream worldwide to locations in the Diaspora. Ẹgbẹ́ Ọmọ Yorùbá's Voice-ofYorùbá.org in the United States and RadioPalmwine. com in the United Kingdom are a few examples. The 1990 establishment of Voice of Nigeria (VON) and the 1996 installation of three high-powered transmitters in Ìkòròdú, Lagos, provided access to worldwide transmission for radio in Yorùbáland.

A-móhùn-máwòrán, literally "a box that captures your voice and your image," is the Yorùbá word for television. The first television station in tropical Africa was established in Ìbàdàn on October 31, 1959, as the Western Nigeria Government Broadcasting Corporation (WNTV); the radio arm was WNBS. The Western regional government, under the leadership of Chief Ọbáfẹ́mi Awólọ́wọ̀, created WNTV in partnership with Overseas Rediffusion Limited. The initial five-hundred-watt transmitters were located in both Ìbàdàn and Abàfọn. The television station was set up to educate regional students and to entertain the regional audience. The Western Nigerian government managed the radio and television media houses under the umbrella of Western Nigeria Radio Vision Limited. By 1962 the Western Nigeria government would buy out the foreign Rediffusion Limited, taking full control of both WNBS/WNTV media houses.

Though not broadcasting primarily in Yorùbá, WNTV offered several Yorùbá-centered news programs and memorable entertainment shows, such as Moses Ọláìyá's *Aláwàdà*, Hubert Ògúndé's *Aṣọ Ẹbí*, and Oyin Adéjọbí's *Kóòtù Aṣípa*. In his *Nigerian Television:*

Fifty Years of Television in Africa, Olúyínká Èsan described the Southwest region of Nigeria—Lagos, Ìbàdàn, and Abéòkúta—as the hub of television industry in Nigeria that helped to establish the industry's trends. Most documentation about television in Nigeria tends to be restricted to television in this area, especially the premier station, WNTV.

At the present time, all Yorùbá state-controlled television stations offer a plethora of their programming in Yorùbá. On September 1, 2003, the late Prince Muyideen Àlàdé Arómiré in Lagos established Yòtòmì Television, which became the first twenty-four-hour television station to broadcast 100 percent of its programs solely in the Yorùbá language. Its audience base covers the entire Yorùbá territories of Southwest Nigeria and the Republic of Benin.

See also **Media: Journalism**

REFERENCE

Èsan, Olúyínká. *Nigerian Television: Fifty Years of Television in Africa*. Princeton: AMV Pub., 2009.

Níyì Coker, Jr.

MEDICAL PRACTITIONERS

Medical practice in traditional Yorùbá society is derived from the people's ontological conception of the dual composition of a person: the material and the spiritual. Thus, the medical practitioner must provide holistic care that addresses both aspects. Even in contemporary Yorùbá societies, this notion persists with some modifications in the nature and scope of indigenous medical practice.

Indigenous medical practitioners are called by different names depending on the scope of their practice. The herbalist (*onísègùn*) prescribes herbs to treat patients. The Ifá priest or priestess (Babaláwo) acts as a diviner to unlock the causes of illness and to prescribe the needed treatments, particularly when the illness transcends the physiological domain. In some instances, people combine the professional skills of the herbalist and the priest or priestess. That person may then be generically called *olóògùn*, a medical practitioner.

These various types of professional medical practitioners are required to be trained and initiated into the profession, usually through apprenticeship under the tutelage of either an outside master practitioner or a parent when the practice is a hereditary one. In addition, because of the spiritual dimension of the causes and treatments of illnesses and the perceived involvement of divinities, medical practitioners are usually devotees of Òsanyìn, who is regarded as the special consultant deity of medicine.

The main preoccupation of medical practitioners revolve around three main objectives: identifying the causes of the illness, getting rid of the symptoms, and achieving a holistic balance between the patient's physiological and spiritual well-being. The methods and processes of attaining these goals are approached in two stages. The first is the diagnostic stage in which the practitioner unravels the mystery behind the illness, usually through Ifá divination. Once the source of the illness has been revealed and the solution identified, the practitioner proceeds to the treatment stage. The treatment generally occurs at two levels, particularly if the illness is a serious one requiring ritual sacrifices or offering. The first either wards off or appeases supernatural or human agents responsible for the illness or protects the healer from those who caused the illness. The second level of treatment is the application of herbal preparations that involve preparations of plants and animal parts that may be cooked, uncooked, taken orally, or rubbed on the body.

Today, while individual medical practitioners are still very common in Yorùbá societies, two dynamics have emerged. First, the *olóògùn*, who belongs to a guildlike society, is hidden within a locality. Potential members obtain knowledge in medical practice through being initiated into one of these societies. Second, the new group of medical practitioners and organizations, who believe solely in physiological causes of illnesses, employ only herbal treatments. The most prominent of such organizations is the Yem-Kem Center for Alternative Therapy, founded by Akíntúndé Ayeni.

See also **Medicine; Medicine: Indigenous Therapeutic System**

REFERENCES

Abímbọ́lá, K. *Yorùbá Culture: A Philosophical Account.* Lagos (Nigeria): Ìrókò Academic Publishers, 2005.

Fálọlá, Tóyìn, and Matthew Heaton, eds. *Traditional and Modern Health System in Nigeria.* Trenton, NJ: African World Press, 2006.

Ìbígbọ́ládé S. Adéríbigbé

MEDICINE

In the Yorùbá worldview, medicines and drugs are referred to *òògùn*. The herbalist who prepares the *òògùn* is called *oníṣègùn* or *olóògùn* (the producer of medicine). Medicine (*òògùn*) encompasses the use of herbs and the act of combining herbs with incantations and/or sacrifice. The Yorùbá cosmology influences therapeutic methods. In this sense, Yorùbá therapeutics and cosmology are interrelated. The scope of medicine (*òògùn*) is strongly influenced by the Yorùbá perception of disease and healing. Healing (*ìwòsàn*) presupposes sickness and diseases. Sickness attests to an individual out of tune with nature and the supernatural world. The outward manifestation of sickness or disease, in the worldview of the Yorùbá people, is part of the story but not the full story.

The practice of traditional medicine embraces a number of different forms of treatment, such as herbal medicine, therapeutic fasting and dieting, hydrotherapy, radiant heat therapy, surgery and bonesetting, therapeutic occultism, psychiatry, and preventive medicine. Nature is the only perfect and supreme healer, and on it all healing depends. Nature provides *egbòogi, àgúnmu, àgbo,* and antidotes used to treat and prevent any form of diseases.

Egbòogi literally means "root of a tree." There are many *egbòogi* used for healing. Many are used especially for fever (*àìsàn ibà*) and typhoid (*ibàa jẹ̀dòjẹ̀dọ̀*). For example, the roots of bitter leaf (*ewúro*) and of *dóńgóyárò*, if peeled and soaked in water for about two days, are a very good medicine for malaria (*àìsàn ibà*).

Àgúnmu is a powdery substance derived from bark of trees (*èèpo igi*), roots (*egbòogi*), leaves (*ewé*), and some fruits and seeds (*èso*). *Àgúnmu* is taken with hot pap early in the morning, afternoon, or evening depending on the type of sickness. For a faster reaction, it is taken with warm water. It is used to cure fever and as a pain reliever.

Àgbo is made by combining or mixing a variety of components, such as bark, leaves, roots, fruits, vegetables, seeds, and so on. Sometimes the juice of fresh leaves is extracted. *Àgbo* is used for different ailments such as malaria (*àìsàn ibà*), typhoid (*ibàa jẹ̀dòjẹ̀dọ̀*), diabetes (*ìtọ̀ọ súgà*), and asthma (*ikọ́ ẹ̀gbẹ*).

Antidotes are, generally speaking, remedies that stop or control the effects of a poison. In relation to Yorùbá therapeutic system, medicine is both therapeutic and prophylactic, curative and preventive. The purpose of medicine is essentially to help the body help itself. The curative function helps the body return to its normal state; the preventive function builds up resistance against infection. Antidotes are much more than remedies to control the effects of a poison: "prevention is better than cure." Antidotes, therefore, serve more of a prophylactic than a therapeutic purpose. They are also called *àjẹsára* (immunization). The Yorùbá have the knowledge of preventive measures for diseases such as the following:

> *Mágùn*—when a woman is laced with venom
> *Májèlé*—to warn against eating poison
> *Arọ́bi*—to ward off spiritual attacks
> *Ìlasè*—to protect the feet from poisoned grounds
> *Àpèta*—to ward off spiritual missives and arrows
> *Ayẹta*—to prevent germs from entering the body

Consequently, the Yorùbá often look with disdain at anything that threatens their health. They recognize the various diseases that attack people and provide various means by which these diseases can be prevented, treated, and eliminated.

See also **Medical Practitioners; Medicine: Indigenous Therapeutic System**

REFERENCES

Jégédé, C. O. "From Disease Etiology to Disease Treatment: An Inquiry into Religion and the Yorùbá Therapeutics." *Orita: Ìbàdàn Journal of Religious Studies* 30.8 (2006): 12–23.

Voeks, Robert C. *Sacred Leaves of Candomble: African Medicine and Religion in Brazil.* Austin: University of Texas Press, 1997.

Ọbáfẹ́mi Jégédé

MEDICINE: INDIGENOUS THERAPEUTIC SYSTEMS

Generally speaking, we can speak of medicine in two ways: as a profession and as a cure to a disease. In discussing medicine as a profession, it is a learned vocation or career that is mastered during graduate training in a medical school. It is devoted to preventing, alleviating, or curing diseases and injuries. Medicine also refers to curing, treating, preventing, or alleviating symptoms of disease. Medicine includes substances that can prevent, cure, or relieve symptoms of diseases and preserve life. Medicine preserves and restores health by helping the body return to its normal state after a period of illness and by building the body's resistance against infections.

However, medicine in African epistemology differs from in Western epistemology. Unlike the Western world, where usually only medical doctors are concerned with health-related issues, Yorùbá cosmology is preoccupied with the means of combating ill health. Hence, medicine can be described as a constituent part of social institutions. Medicine is both therapeutic and prophylactic, curative and preventive. For African medicine, the purpose of medicine is essentially to help the body to help itself. It is curative in that it helps the body to return to its normal state; it is preventive in that it builds up resistance against infection.

Some traditional medical practitioners specialize in only mental diseases, others in setting bones, still others in women's diseases, and some are traditional birth attendants. Any person can be a medical practitioner provided he or she has the knowledge of therapeutic medicine and uses that knowledge to treat pathological conditions. Such a practitioner may be a professional, like a herbalist, or a lay person, but his or her practice brings health to people.

Traditional medicine falls broadly into two categories: physical and metaphysical. The physical category uses natural plants such as roots, stems, leaves, flowers, vegetables, and the like. It also makes use of animals, such as snails, chameleons, snakes, tortoises, and rats. The metaphysical category is concerned with the invisible world of the spirits. Here, prayers, invocations, incantations, and rituals are offered to the spiritual entities that are believed to cause disease in order to pacify or appease them. In the treatment of diseases, either category can be used alone or in combination with the other.

The Yorùbá often reject anything that threatens their health, and they combat ill health in various ways using òògùn (medicine). In this regard, the people recognize the various diseases that attack people, and they also know the various means by which these diseases can be cured.

See also **Medical Practitioners; Medicine**

REFERENCE

Ọ̀ṣúnwọlé, S. A. "From Religion to Medicine: Arts in the Service of Traditional Medicine." *African Notes: Journal of the institutes of African Studies* 5.2 (1998): 25–38.

Ọbáfẹ́mi Jégédé

MEMORIAL ARTS

Ojọ́ a kú làá d'èrè;
Ènìyàn ò sunwọ̀n láàyè

It's after death that we become well-carved memorial sculptures;
A living person has flaws

Memorial arts, as in the reference to the well-carved *èrè* above, are meant to honor in perpetuity memories of deceased relatives. Memorial arts ensure the immortality of deceased relatives. The burial rites, *àkó* and *ìsìnkú*, and *ìpà ọdẹ* are some examples of Yorùbá ritual and artistic responses to death (*ikú*).

Burial rites occur in two parts. Ìsìnkú (interment of a corpse) is usually accompanied by celebrations, especially if the deceased grew to old age. If the deceased belonged to an Egúngún family, at least one Egúngún masquerade, representing the lineage of the deceased ancestor, is performed at the deceased's ìsìnkú. The second burial rite centers on memorial arts, the àkó effigy sculpture. Among the Ọ̀wọ̀-Yorùbá community, the second burial rite is called àkó; in other parts of Yorùbáland, it is called àjèjé.

The Africanist art scholar Rowland Abíọ́dún, a native of Ọ̀wọ̀, describes àkó as a carved effigy of the deceased. Because it must be fully dressed in fine and expensive clothes during the ceremony, the wood carver carves only the unclothed parts—the head, hands, and legs (àyàjọra). The remaining body parts are left rudimentary. To prepare the deceased, it is customary that the holder of a chieftaincy title, or his or her surviving children, perform the àkó ceremony, an effigy ritual believed to provide an assurance of a pleasant transition into the afterlife (ẹ̀hìn-ìwà).

Àkó also allows the deceased's relatives, who did not attend the ìsìnkú, to see the deceased for the last time through his or her symbolic image to pay their final respects and wish the dead a happy transition to ẹ̀hìn-ìwà. An example of a eulogy delivered in the presence of the àkó effigy is Ó di gbéré; ó tún d'ojú àlá. Bí o bá délé bá mi kí bàbáà mi (Good-bye until we meet only in dreams. When you get to the afterlife help me greet my father). At the conclusion of the àkó, the effigy is buried like a corpse or simply discarded in the forest.

Ìpà Ọdẹ (also Ìpadẹ) is another second burial ceremony, traditionally performed for any deceased hunter (ọdẹ or ọlọ́dẹ). This rite centers on the memorial art called ìpadẹ (or ìpà), an effigy sculpture that represents the symbolic final appearance of the deceased hunter to his earthly guild of hunters (ẹgbẹ́ ọdẹ). The primary purpose of the ìpà ọdẹ ceremony is to formally separate the deceased's soul from his mortal ẹgbẹ́ ọdẹ, thereby preparing him for his final journey to the afterlife (ẹ̀hìn-ìwà). The Yorùbá believe that without this separation rite, the deceased hunter's soul will not rest but will continue to roam the forests.

The following hunters' dirge, collected by Ọláwọlé Fámulẹ̀ in 1991 at Òkè-Igbó town, gives credence to this thought:

Ọdẹ yówù ó kú, báa bá ṣí'pà a rẹ̀, ọrun olúmọkin ló ń lọ. Ọdẹ yówù ó kú, bá ò bá ṣí'pà a rẹ̀, tòun t'egbére ní ó máa jẹ kiri.

Any deceased hunter whose ìpà ọdẹ ceremony is performed goes straight to the afterlife. But the one without the ìpà ọdẹ ceremony would be roaming the woods with the wandering forest spirits.

As with àkó, ìpadẹ effigy is also a wooden sculpture. It is set up in the forest wearing the deceased hunter's hat (fìlà) and a large robe (agbádá). Unlike the àkó, the ìpadẹ bears no semblance to the deceased's physical features. After the ceremony, the effigy along with all the associated ritual items, such as the deceased hunter's charms (oògùn), hunting bag (àpò ọdẹ), scabbard (apó ọdẹ), foods he liked to take with him when he went hunting, the calabash with which he used to drink palm wine (ẹmu ọ̀pẹ) and herbal medicines (àgbo), and the carcass of a sacrificed chicken are hung on the effigy's shoulder. All of these items are left in the forest, where they decay over time.

See also **Art: Indigenous; Burial and Funeral; Carvers; Death, Mourning, and Ancestors; Reincarnation**

REFERENCE

Abíọ́dún, Rowland. "A Reconsideration of the Function of 'Ako,' Second Burial Effigy in Ọ̀wọ̀." *Africa: Journal of the International African Institute*, 46.1 (1976): 4–20.

Ọláwọlé Fámulẹ̀

METALS AND MINERAL RESOURCES

Metals and mineral resources serve three basic needs: they provide raw materials for creating and making the tools for physical survival needs (food, shelter, and warmth); they provide occupations for the makers and the users of the tools; and they provide explanation and meaning for the ubiquitous, lethal, and fiery legendary god of metals and war, Ògún.

Iron (*irin*), is the primary and the most important raw material for making farming, hunting, war weapons, household tools, and machines and equipment. Some examples include the hoe (*ọkọ́*), cutlass or machete (*àdá*), axe (*àáké*), sickle knife (*akọ́rọ́*), sword (*idà*), gun and gunpowder (*ìbọn àti ẹ̀tù ìbọn*), knife (*ọbẹ*), toys (*ṣaworo*), and metal musical instrument (*agogo*). Iron is present everywhere. All lives are dependent on it; it is an all-powerful giver of life. Yet iron is dangerous and lethal, capable of inflicting injury and causing death.

Consequently, smiths, farmers, hunters, warriors, and others whose occupation, business, or lifestyle involves the use of metals or products of metals (e.g., vehicles with metal components) idolize and fear iron (*irin Ògún*). The specialist artisan worshippers of the Ògún deity include smiths who make metal tools and weapons of war (*alágbẹ̀dẹ*), surgeons who perform circumcisions and facial marks (*olóòlà*), and barbers (*onígbàjámọ̀*). They recognize Ògún not only as a deity (*òrìṣà*) but as the first of all the deities (*ọṣìn mọlẹ̀*) to descend to the earth (*ilé ayé*).

Hence, Ògún is known as the omnipresent ruler of all of the earth (*Ògún lákáayé*). Ògún is fearfully glorified as the one who had water at home but preferred to bathe with blood (*ò-lómi-nílé-fẹ̀jẹ̀-wẹ̀*) and who had clothes but preferred to cover himself with palm fronds (*ò-láṣọ-nílé-fi-màrìwò-bora*). In legend, Ògún was known to have fought for the people of Ìrè town and to have served as the king of Ìrè (*Ògún Onírè*). Ògún and his brother Ṣàngó are the two most feared legendary deities of the Yorùbá.

Copper, the red-brown (*idẹ*) metal, was the etymological or historical source of the word *kọ́bọ̀* (the bronze coin): the old penny and primary unit of the Nigerian currency. Copper became widely used with the introduction of the British monetary units at the turn of the twentieth century. Before the colonial era, however, well-established Yorùbá households had gold (*wúrà*) and silver (*fàdákà*) jewelry, and copper (bronze) and alloy—such as brass (a mixture of copper and zinc)—metal artworks and ornamental treasures. They were also part of house furnishings, the decoration

industry, and the exclusive ceremonial outfits for the royals (*àwọn ọba*), chiefs (*àwọn ìjòyè*), and famous people. The Yorùbá say *ẹni igba ojúmọ̀* or *gbajúmọ̀* (anyone whom two hundred people could recognize).

The modern Yorùbá are less dependent on metals in making tools. They are, however, more ostentatious with the use of alloy, gold, and silver jewelry during all sorts of occasions, including weddings, funerals, college graduations, chieftaincy, and professorial inaugurations. They may be more discrete in their superstitions and worship of Ògún than the traditional Yorùbá, but they definitely fear his potent destructive powers. Some secretly consult the Babaláwo (Ifá priest), and they will always offer the prescribed sacrifices to the god of iron. They keep vigil in churches and mosques to pray for protection against metal accidents, and they engage in long sessions of prayers. Some who are Christians even invoke the blood of Jesus for protection when they travel in vehicles or operate metal machinery.

REFERENCE

Adéníji, D. A. "Iṣẹ́ Irin Wíwà àti Sísun." In *Iṣẹ́ Ìṣẹ̀nbáyé*, ed. T. M. Iléṣànmi, 2–16. Ilé-Ifẹ̀ (Nigeria): Ọbáfẹ́mi Awólọ́wọ̀ University Press, 1989.

Bọ́lá Dáúdà

MODERNITY AND MODERNIZATION

Modernity refers to a particular vision of the world together with a set of institutional and cultural formations that actualizes that vision. Modernization refers to the processes by which modernity is achieved. Thus, to modernize implies gradual adaptation to the processes that enable a transition to the modern period. The Yorùbá experienced European modernity and modernization as a result of colonialism in Africa. Their experiences are captured in the term *ọ̀làjú*. *Ọ̀làjú*, in Yorùbá, simply means "the opening of the eyes to see." It derives from two key words: *ojú* (eyes) and *lílà* (opening). Thus, when the Yorùbá say *ọ̀làjú ti dé* (*ọ̀làjú* has come) or *ọ̀làjú ti pọ̀ sí i* (*ọ̀làjú* has increased), they reference simultaneously both the signifiers of modernity (electricity, transportation, health care, paved roads, piped water, and the like) and the experience of collective enlightenment. Worldly progress, for them, translates as a progressive enlightenment through the gradual opening of the eyes to see. Thus, we can have the statement: *gbogbo ayé ti yí padà nítorí ọ̀làjú ti dé* (there are all sorts of changes in the world as a result of ọ̀làjú).

The term ọ̀làjú was first used to denote the imported colonial package, introduced by the missionaries. In a broad sense, however, it can represent the sociological experience of the Yorùbá with trade, migration, travels, education, and religion. Ọ̀làjú illuminates a space of enlightenment deriving from multilateral confrontations and compromises between old and new, local and foreign, good and bad—contrary to the enlightenment assumption of a cultural rupture with the past and with tradition. When the Yorùbá use the concept, it is meant to convey both the negative and the positive consequences of enlightenment. Thus, the people have the sayings, *Kò sí ìbọ̀wọ̀ fún àgbà mọ́; àwọn ọmọ ti lajú sí òdì* (there is no longer adequate respect for the elders because the children are now excessively enlightened), and *Ọ̀làjú ti sọ ayé di dídára ju ti àtijọ́ lọ* (Ọ̀làjú has made the world better than before).

The positive and negative understanding of ọ̀làjú indicates that the assumption of the modernization theory as to the erasure of tradition from modernity had only limited success. The experiences of Christianity and Islam provide cogent examples of how the Yorùbá cultural adaptability enabled a creative transformation of the offerings of modernity and modernization. The Christian missionaries were the first purveyors of ọ̀làjú, and the indigenous religion and kinship ties were the first indigenous items to come under siege. The fundamentalism of Christianity contrasted sharply with the cultural flexibility of Islam, especially with regard to marriage and materialism. Both fundamentally brought large-scale and ambivalent changes to Yorùbá sociocultural life. For example, the kinship system became unraveled under the onslaught of individualism and rabid urbanization as markers of modernity. Education also had far-reaching positive

impacts on economic and political developments. However, both were adroitly interrogated in manners that give the Yorùbá culture the ability to take charge of the elements of power and knowledge involved in social change. Thus, ọ̀làjú initiated, for the Yorùbá, a multilateral cultural perception of enlightenment as a culture's own ability to make progress without losing its internal cultural responsibility to enter into a critical dialogue with itself and others.

REFERENCES

Afọláyan, Adéshínà. "Is Postmodernism Meaningful in Yorùbá?" *Journal of Social Philosophy* 39.2 (Summer 2008): 13–26.
Peel, J. D. Y. "Ọ̀làjú: A Yorùbá Concept of Development." *Journal of Development Studies* 14.2 (1978): 1–21.

Adéshínà Afọláyan

MONEY

In hierarchical Yorùbá society, money (*owó*) is traditionally understood as one of the three most important achievements for individuals. The other two achievements are numerous children and longevity and good health. Money confers high status and, by implication, influence in the community by virtue of its currency as a stock of values at the disposal of the rich. Yet given the prevalent ọmọlúàbí ethic, the process of wealth acquisition was closely governed by a code of ethics or an unwritten code of honor, such that the source of wealth had to be transparent to the larger society. The honor and influence associated with wealth was thus contingent on the community's satisfaction that the wealth was not *owó-igbó*—money acquired through immoral or dubious means. This mediated the tendency of unbridled struggle for wealth. Accordingly, there is the saying *olówó kì í ṣe Ọlọ́run* (the rich man cannot play God). As such, social mores clearly controlled the process by which money was acquired. Adherence to social mores, along with the code of ethic, legitimized the manner of the deploying the wealth acquired. The traditional society's insistence on probity in the process of acquiring wealth is supported by the teachings of Ifá that everyone would have relative successes at different points of the life cycle; however, everyone is not destined by his or her *orí* or the *ẹlẹ́dàá* to be very wealthy.

In Yorùbáland, as in the rest of West Africa, cowries served as the medium of value and were imported and distributed throughout the region. West African cowries were not primitive money but a sophisticated currency that adapted to the peculiar demands of the West African economic environment. Cowries spread and became acceptable, thus facilitating trade from various areas. Cowries were the foundations of precolonial financial institutions, including the traditional banking systems that later emerged. These included the *àjọ*, a communal saving scheme, and *èsúsú*, the savings institution and credit association scheme. Although modest in its scale, these institutions formed the basis of the process of capital formation and accumulation in precolonial times.

Contact with the West affected the concept of money and its role in transforming attitudes in the society—resulting in the decline of the traditional system. Westernization introduced the Yorùbá to the global capitalist ethic, which erodes the restraint imposed in close-knit traditional society. The breakdown of traditional Yorùbá communities as a result of urbanization also exacerbated the situation. The influence of money in modern society and, in the absence of the ethical restraints imposed by tradition, the emergence of the concept of *òògùn owó*, unethical means of acquiring wealth, reflects the pervasive moral turpitude afflicting Yorùbáland.

See also **Cooperative Associations; Economic Systems; Market**

REFERENCE

Fádípẹ̀, N. A. *The Sociology of the Yorùbá*. Ìbàdàn (Nigeria): University Press, 1970.

Adémọ́lá Àràoyè

MUSEUMS

Museums were established in Nigeria as a part of the range of institutions meant to replicate and entrench Western hegemonic practices, especially Western culture. They were grafted onto an existing sociocultural fabric that, in colonial Nigeria, had a different conception of and approach to the display and preservation of artifacts. Museums represent that aspect of Western culture that favors the acquisition, study, classification, preservation, and display of artifacts. In this, museums cultivate the support of collectors, donors, scholars, and others whose expertise is essential to the survival of the institution and its embrace by the public. In colonial Nigeria, Kenneth Murray pioneered the survey of antiquities in the early 1940s, which was a precursor to the establishment of the Department of Antiquities. The notion of collecting diverse living cultural objects from individuals, families, and households, and then sequestering them in a public space for others to view, was as strange as it was new.

The Yorùbá, with their 401 deities, certainly had a system for caring for their artifacts premised on a custom that recognized cultural items as living and active. The avenues for preserving them were remarkably different from those transplanted by the British to Nigeria. The closest equivalent to the modern museum among the Yorùbá was shrines. While individuals may have special corners or designated stands in their private spaces for keeping and consulting with art objects specific to their individual families or patron deities, household collectives (*agbo ile*) often have shrines where, at specific times, the group supplicates its ancestors and performs annual ceremonies and rituals of gratitude and appeasement.

Preservation, an idea central to museums, is accomplished through a different set of practices and thought systems. Preservation deals more with sustaining practices and undergirding philosophies than with keeping works of art, which are regarded as manifestations of specific ideals. This philosophical principle accounts for the predictability and association of styles with specific deities. This explains why, for example, *ère ìbejì, osée Ṣàngó, ọpọ́n Ifá*, or *ọ̀pá Ọ̀sanyìn*, to mention a few, are expected to meet certain iconological criteria when they are being carved. It is also responsible for the willingness to repair a damaged mask, to reconstruct an Egúngún costume where feasible, or to discard them altogether and create new ones using an existing prototype.

The National Commission for Museums and Monuments has several branches across Nigeria. Notable among these are those in Lagos, Ilé-Ifẹ̀, and Ọ̀wọ̀. In addition, there are other public sites, such as the Institute of African Studies at the University of Ìbàdàn, the Ọ̀ṣogbo Sacred Grove, and the Center for World and Black and African Arts and Civilization, which continue to bridge the gap between museums as repositories for artifacts and living institutions. The threat to museums comes from several sources, including inadequate funding, security, preservation, and acquisition. The threat posed by religious zealotry and the belief that some artifacts are synonymous with idol worship comprise another challenge to museums in Yorùbáland.

See also **Heritage, Cultural: Management and Preservation; Heritage, Cultural: Sites**

REFERENCE

Ndoro, Webber, and Herman Kiriama. "Management Mechanism in Heritage Legislation." In *Cultural Heritage and the Law: Protecting Immovable Heritage in English Speaking Countries of Sub-Saharan Africa*, ed. Webber Ndoro, Albert Mumma, and George Abungu, 53–64. ICCROM Conservation Studies 8. Rome: ICCROM, 2008.

délé jẹ́gẹ́dẹ́

MUSIC: AFROBEAT

Afrobeat, a genre of popular music that has become a global musical phenomenon, was originated by Fẹlá Aníkúlápó-Kútì, the late Nigerian musician who used his music to address the crisis of leadership in postcolonial Africa. Afrobeat, which became a distinct genre in the mid-1970s, is defined by an organic synthesis of multicultural musical forms, notably, traditional Yorùbá music, highlife, jazz, and funk.

Specific features of Afrobeat include the use of Yorùbá folklore and drum language, as well as improvisational techniques that simultaneously reflect jazz and traditional Yorùbá influences. Abandoning the use of *oríkì* (praise poetry), which distinguishes other Yorùbá popular music genres, Afrobeat is marked by the performance of *yabis*: musically conveyed commentary targeting the autocratic political leadership in Nigeria and Africa as a whole. Western instruments used in Afrobeat include keyboard, guitar, woodwinds, and brass.

The social activism of Afrobeat was inspired by the politics of the civil rights movement in the United States, the politically charged bebop styles of Charlie Parker and Dizzy Gillespie, and the experimental works of Sun Ra, Ornette Coleman, and Cecil Taylor. The song "Jẹun Kó(o) Kú" from the album *Open & Close* is often considered the first major example of Afrobeat music. Released in 1971, "Jẹun Kó(o) Kú" illustrates Fẹlá's experimentation with mixing highlife music, jazz, Yorùbá drumming, call-and-response, and a form of musical storytelling reminiscent of the Yorùbá *àlọ́* tradition.

The effectiveness of Afrobeat's political themes derives significantly from the coherent style of the music. The cultivation of a fast tempo, an engaging groove, and a dense instrumentation powered by brass and woodwind punctuation provides an effective musical context for charged political messages. It is also important to note that the employment of Nigerian Pidgin as the main language of Afrobeat music—signaling a rejection of the colonial language of English—helped Aníkúlápó-Kútì to communicate across ethnic and social boundaries within and outside Nigeria. The social and political themes of Fẹlá's Afrobeat are diverse, including imperialism (*ITT International Thief Thief*, K203554, 1979), religious servitude (*Shuffering and Shmiling*, PMLP 1005, 1980), slavery and colonization (*Why Black Man De Suffer*, EMI, 1971), inept political leadership (*Zombie* and its flip side, *Mr. Follow Follow*, CRLP 511, 1976), and corruption (*Beast of No Nation*, Barclay Records, 1989). Fẹlá died in 1997 after a protracted illness.

See also **Aníkúlápó-Kútì, Fẹlá**

REFERENCE

Veal, Michael. *Fẹlá: Life and Times of an African Musical Icon*. Philadelphia: Temple University Press, 2000.

Bọ̀dé Ọmọ́jọlà

MUSIC: CHRISTIAN

Christianity, which started in Yorùbáland in the first half of the nineteenth century, brought European religious forms that were translated to the Yorùbá language. Various indigenous African churches evolved as early as 1902 with the aim of "indigenizing" the liturgy. These churches' strategy included composing indigenous song forms that employed folk tunes and introducing traditional musical instruments and dance for worship. The process led to the evolution of Yorùbá native hymns and native anthems, which flourished between the 1920s and the 1950s.

Christian music among the Yorùbá is broadly categorized into liturgical and nonliturgical forms. The latter evolved out of the desire to supply music to entertain worshippers during festive occasions and social functions. However, it should be noted that, stylistically, Yorùbá Christian music is similar to Western church music, traditional church music, and hybrid forms of these. All the forms are used either in isolation or in different combinations.

Church Liturgical Music

The Roman Catholic Church in Nigeria has incorporated the Yorùbá language and indigenous musical instruments for in Mass to curtail the defection of their members to other churches. The Anglican Church makes use of the Yorùbá Hymn Book, which contains translations of English hymns and some native arias; in addition to translated versions of psalms, introits, and versicles and responses. Native anthems and lyric arias are also used in the Anglican Church. The Baptist and Methodist churches make use of lyric arias in addition to their translated hymnals. The Seventh-Day Adventist Church employs the use of its own hymnal, Yorùbá a cappella songs, and lyric arias.

Indigenous churches use forms that are more traditional, including songs and chants. Indigenous Nigerian Pentecostal churches, such as Christ Apostolic Church, have their own Yorùbá hymns. These hymns are a mixture of translated hymns and indigenous ones. Classical Pentecostal (Holiness) churches, like Deeper Life Bible Church and Apostolic Faith, use more foreign forms such as Western classical, Western hymns, anthems, and gospel hymns. Also, the Gospel Faith Mission make more use of gospel hymns and lyric arias. Some other Pentecostal churches that are more liberal in approach make use of foreign gospel forms and lyric arias.

Gospel Music

The bulk of Yorùbá nonliturgical church music is gospel music. It differs in some ways from the Euro-American version in concept, history, and practices. As a result of borrowing elements from other sources, the form now has several styles, which include the native style, as performed by S. O. Akínpẹ̀lú, Bísí Adéoyè, Olú King, and Mrs. D. A. Fásọnyìn (of Good Women fame); the spiritual style of Shọlá Rótìmí, Níyì Adédòkun, and Òjó Adé; the *jùjú* gospel of Evangelist Ebenezer Obey; the gospel-*fújì* of Folúkẹ́ Awóléyẹ; the gospel-*wákà* of Serah Kòkúmọ́; and the eclectic style of J. A. Adélakùn (Áyẹwá of *Amọ̀nà tètè wá* fame), Bọ́lá Àrẹ, Tìmí Ọ̀súnkọ́ya, Tóún Sóẹ̀tán, and Tọ́pẹ́ Àlàbí. Foreign styles include the a cappella of the Ambassadors, the instrumental of Kúnlé Àjàyí, and the gospel-pop of Panam Percy Paul, Midnight Crew, Fọláké Umosen, and more.

Praise and Worship Music

Praise and worship music is dedicated to the praise and worship of God, including giving thanksgiving to him. It has been borrowed from the contemporary Western church and incorporated into Yorùbá church musical practices by youth of various denominations since the 1980s. It employs lyric arias from both Western and African sources. The praise and worship style is both liturgical and nonliturgical, and it is a popular feature of church services and youth programs such as praise nights, concerts, and music festivals.

Functions

Music in Yorùbá Christianity is essentially functional. Apart from adding to the identity of each church, it is used for the praise and worship, invocation, deliverance, and exorcism. It is also used to pray, evangelize, admonish, educate, entertain, and fight spiritual battles. It is important to state that music has been very instrumental in the radical spread of Christianity and church growth in Yorùbáland.

Today, Christian music accounts for a significant amount of music aired on local radio and television stations and on Internet radio. It is used as ringtones on mobile phones and in sound tracks in Christian films. The music industry has also benefited immensely from Yorùbá Christian music, as many producers, studio engineers, Christian artists, marketers, promoters, label owners, and record companies earn large amounts of money.

See also **Music: Islamic; Music: Popular; Musical Instruments**

REFERENCES

Adédèjì, 'Fẹ́mi. "Nigerian Contemporary Church Music Forms: A Preliminary Survey." *JANIM: Journal of the Association of Nigerian Musicologists* 6 (2012): 206–23.

Adédèjì, S. O. "Nigerian Gospel Music Styles: A Study of Its Styles." Unpublished doctoral dissertation, University of Ìbàdàn, Ìbàdàn (Nigeria), 2004.

Fẹ́mi Adédèjì

MUSIC: ISLAMIC

The spread of Islam in Nigeria was accompanied by the introduction of Arabic-Islamic musical instruments and vocal practices. Although Islam was introduced to northern Nigeria as far back as the eleventh century, Arab-Islamic elements did not manifest in Yorùbá traditional music until the fourteenth century, before Islam became widely accepted in western Nigeria. The indigenization of Arabic musical elements illustrates how the Islamic culture helped create new intercultural African musical forms. Examples of Islamic popular music genres in western Nigeria are the *àpàlà*, *sákárà*, *wàkà*, and *fújì*. These musical idioms are defined by a common set of performance and stylistic elements—notably, the use of traditional instruments, call-and-response vocal form, declamatory and melismatic singing, the projection of Islamic messages, and a process of continuous performance in which multiple songs are joined together. The musical antecedent to these Islamic genres was *wéré* music, a type of music performed during Ramadan to wake up Muslims for their early morning prayers. But in spite of these similarities, each genre is marked by a particular stylistic identity.

Sákárà is known for the use of the *gòjé* (one-string fiddle), which is employed to provide florid and microtonal interludes between vocal passages. The sound of this instrument contrasts with the percussive rhythms of *igbá* (calabash drums) and *sákárà* (single-headed, animal-skin frame drums)—the musical instrument from which the name of the genre derives. Other features of *sákárà* music include its philosophical lyrics and a sparse texture that contrasts with the heavy percussion of *àpàlà* and *fújì*. These stylistic features are illustrated in Ọlátúnjí's album *Yusuf Ọlátúnjí (Baba L'Ẹ́gbàá) and His Sákárà Group* (Zaresco OSRL 1729, 1976). *Àpàlà* music features a more diverse instrumentation through the use of the *dùndún* (hourglass drum), *ṣẹ̀kẹ̀rẹ̀* (gourd shakers), *agogo* (metal gong), *àgídìgbo* (lamellophone), and *àkúbà* (upright membrane drums). While the *gòjé* is the main instrument of *sákárà*, the *dùndún* is the distinctive instrument of *àpàlà*. As illustrated on Hárúnà Ìshọ̀lá's album *Late Ọba Adébóyè—Orímolúsì of Ìjẹ̀bú Igbó* (LP, Star Records SRPS 49, 1955), praise songs mixed with deep philosophical messages are commonly featured in *àpàlà* music.

Unlike *sákárà* and *àpàlà*, *wàkà*, which means "song" in Hausa, is exclusive to the female gender. The two most popular performers of *wàkà* music in the late twentieth century were and Sàláwà Àbẹ́ní and the late Bàtílì Àlàkẹ́. In its earlier form, according to Akin Euba, *wàkà* was "a type of socio-religious song used by

Muslims on ceremonial occasions such as marriage, child naming and the return of pilgrims from Mecca. It was initially performed without accompaniment." Àbèní's *wákà* is greatly influenced by the music of Kólawọlé Àyìnlá, a prominent *fújì* musician who was Àbèní's husband in the early 1980s. Àyìnlá's *fújì*, noted for the use of a heavy Yorùbá percussion, populist lyrics, and energetic dance provided a model for Àbèní's transformation of *wákà*.

Àbèní's album *Queen Salawa Abeni* (Leader Records LRCLS 44, 1983) demonstrates the transformation of *wákà* from a religious performance into a commercial urban and popular secular idiom. *Fújì*, which has been very popular in western Nigeria since the early 1980s, epitomizes the development of Islamic popular music in western Nigeria and the maturation of the socio-stylistic and performance elements displayed in the other three genres: *sákárà*, *wákà*, and *àpàlà*. The two most important pioneers of *fújì* in the late twentieth century were Kólawọlé Àyìnlá and the late Síkírù Àyìndé (alias Barrister), who named the music after Japan's Mt. Fuji, out of his love for the name. *Fújì*'s instrumentation approaches orchestral proportions, featuring multiple batteries of *dùndún* and *bàtá* drums, a row of high-pitched *agogo* (metal gongs), *sèkèrè* (shakers), Western drums, a synthesizer, and heavy amplification. *Fújì* lyrics often combine religious themes, Yorùbá folklore, fear of an unknown enemy, and trifling themes of love and romance. Some of these features are illustrated in Àyìnlá's album, *Ibi ẹ rí ẹ kígbe mi lọ* (LP, EMI NEMI 0145, 1979).

See also **Musical Instruments**

REFERENCE

Euba, Akin. *Essays on Music in Africa 2: Intercultural Perspectives.* Bayreuth, Germany: Bayreuth African Studies; Lagos (Nigeria): Elékóto Music Company, 1989.

Bòdé Ọmójọlà

MUSIC: MODERN COMPOSERS OF ART MUSIC

One of the major musical developments of the colonial era in Nigeria was the emergence of a new tradition of art music characterized by a synthesis of Western classical music forms and indigenous African musical elements. This new tradition has departed from traditional Yorùbá music in two major ways. First, the music is often written down in the European music notation system. Second, it is conceived as a form of contemplative music performed in a Western-type concert setting. Pioneering Yorùbá composers of this tradition in the twentieth century included Ẹkúndayọ̀ Philips (1884–1969), Fẹlá Ṣówándé (1905–1984), Ayọ̀ Bánkọ́lé (1935–1976), and Akin Euba (1936–). The younger generation of Yorùbá composers includes Christopher Ayọ̀délé, Ayọ̀ Olúrántí, and Bòdé Ọmójọlà.

Akin Euba, now emeritus professor of music at Pittsburgh University, remains the most prominent composer of art music in Africa, combining a rigorous research career with creative activities. Born in 1936, Euba was educated at Trinity College of Music in London and the University of California, Los Angeles. He later conducted ethnographic fieldwork in western Nigeria as part of his doctoral studies at the University of Ghana in Legon. He developed a number of theories about African art music. His concept of Africa pianism, for example, focuses on the use of the European piano as a medium for conveying rhythmic, percussive, melodic, and structural elements of African instrumental music. His notion of intercultural music analyzes salient issues related to the interaction of European and African elements in modern African music forms. Many of his works, including the 1953 album *Igi Ñlá So* and "Scenes from Traditional Life" (1977), illustrate the use of the piano to convey traditional Yorùbá drum language.

Euba also coined the phrases "creative musicology" and "creative ethnomusicology," both of which discuss the significance of orality in modern African art music and the process of incorporating research-derived musical material into modern notation-based composers. According to Euba:

> Composers around the world (especially those from non-Western countries) are producing music in which resources derived from traditional and folk music (normally the province of ethnomusicology) are combined with Western

techniques of composition (normally the area of specialization of historical musicologists and music theorists).

The phrase "creative ethnomusicology," though coined by Akin Euba, is conceptually reminiscent of the folk-inspired compositions of European composers like Béla Bartók, Modest Mussorgsky, and Zoltán Kodály.

Akin Euba's opera *Chaka*, which builds on the folk opera tradition of Yorùbá composer-dramatists like Hubert Ògúndé and Dúró Ládipọ̀, demonstrates how European and Yorùbá musical elements have been integrated to create a new tradition of Yorùbá music theater. The opera's libretto is based on the epic poem *Chaka* by the former Senegalese president Leopold Senghor. The opera, like the poem, is in two sections: chants 1 and 2. The central character of the work is Chaka, a nineteenth-century Zulu leader who courageously and vigorously resisted European domination in South Africa. In addition to Senghor's poem, Euba incorporates a Yorùbá praise poem, *oríkì*, into the second part of the opera, where it functions as a praise poem in honor of Chaka. The instrumentation of the opera is equally intercultural, combining Western instruments like the flute, clarinet, bassoon, trumpet, horn, bass trombone, and amplified double bass with African instruments like the *agogo* (bell), *ekwe* (Igbo slit drum), *ṣẹ̀kẹ̀rẹ̀* (gourd rattle), *dùndún* (hourglass membrane drum), *gúdúgúdú* (*bàtá* kettle drum), and the *atenteben* (Ghanaian bamboo flute) ensemble. In the opera, each of these instruments is assigned melodic and rhythmic functions that are idiomatic of their cultural origins and roles.

See also **Musical Instruments**

REFERENCES

Euba, Akin. *Essays on Music in Africa 2: Intercultural Perspectives.* Bayreuth, Germany: Bayreuth African Studies; Lagos (Nigeria): Elékóto Music Company, 1989.

Ọmọ́jọlà, Bọ̀dé. *Nigerian Art Music.* Ìbàdàn (Nigeria): Institut Français de Recherche en Afrique (IFRA), 1995.

Bọ̀dé Ọmọ́jọlà

Modern Yorùbá popular music forms, in spite of reflecting foreign influences, rely significantly on indigenous elements, notably instruments like the *dùndún* and *bàtá*, traditional forms such as *orin* (song) and *oríkì* (praise poetry), and performance contexts modeled on the festival tradition. Islamic genres like *àpàlà*, *sákárà*, *wákà*, and *fújì* often combine Islamic themes with deep Yorùbá philosophy while often rejecting an idiomatic use of European tonal and harmonic resources that define Christian-affiliated genres like highlife, *jùjú*, and Afrobeat.

Highlife was the music of the emerging elite of the colonial era in Nigeria. The word *highlife*, probably first used by Ghanaian musicians of the mid-1950s, designates a pan–West African genre popular in countries like Ghana, Nigeria, and Sierra Leone. It was brought about by similar cultural and social factors in these former British colonies. Bobby Benson played a leading role in the development of Nigerian highlife music. He introduced the first electric guitar to Lagos in 1948, released a chart-topping album *Taxi Driver* (Philips P 82019, 1960), and trained many Nigerian highlife musicians, including Roy Chicago and Eddy Okonta. Highlife music is noted for its clave patterns, European-style harmonic progressions, topical social themes, laid-back groove, and modest improvisation. Its main instruments are the guitar, European woodwind and brass instruments, and a Western drum set and conga drums.

Jùjú music is best defined in the works of Ebenezer Obey and King Sunny Adé. According to Christopher Waterman, its origins have been linked to "an interaction between social habits and musical concepts and the need for social interaction among a group of rascals or area boys in the old Sàró (Ọlọ́wọ̀gbọwọ́) quarter of Lagos." The genre evolved from *àsìkò*, notable for its use of Brazilian *samba* elements (like the *pandeiro* frame drum) and the *banjo*, as well as the guitar style of Kru sailors from Liberia. *Àsìkò* was later transformed into *jùjú* music by Túndé King. Born in 1910,

King and other musicians like Àkànbí "Ège" Wright, J. O. Àràbà, Daniel Òjògé Alésinlóyé, and Òjó Babájídé added the *dùndún* drum, electric guitars, and more vocalists, in the process creating *jùjú* music. In 1949, Àyìndé Bákàrè replaced the *agídìgbo* with the acoustic guitar, paving the way for greater use of modern technology and the emergence of a distinct sound quality that derives from the use of modern amplification system to enhance the sounds of traditional percussion instruments.

Until the early 1960s, *jùjú* was restricted to Lagos and performed mainly in the Òyó dialect. By the late 1960s, however, it had become popular across Yorùbáland, notably through the music of Isaac Kéhìndé Dáiró. Dáiró incorporated other Yorùbá dialects and folklore, notably those from Ìjèsà and Èkìtì. He also gave his *jùjú* music a unique identity through his use of the accordion. The incorporation of traditional themes like fate and destiny, fear of God, antics of the unknown enemy, and the simulation of a festival celebration helped to make *jùjú* music popular across class and religious divides.

Afrobeat, a musical genre developed almost exclusively by Fèlá Aníkúlápó-Kútì, departed significantly from *jùjú* and other forms of Yorùbá music in significant ways. Afrobeat music is notable for its strong political and antiestablishment themes; an intercultural musical language that builds on indigenous Yorùbá, highlife, and jazz elements; and the abandonment of praise poetry (*oríkì*).

Strikingly different from *jùjú* is a form of hip-hop music that emerged within the last two decades of the twentieth century, a reflection of the popularity of American rap music in Nigeria. Prominent hip-hop and rap musicians in western Nigeria include Olú Maintain (Olúmidé Edwards Adégbolú), Tony Tetuila (Anthony Olánrewájú Awótóyè), and 9ice (Àbòlorè Adégbolá Àkàndé). Yorùbá hip-hop music illustrates how Nigerian musicians have interpreted global forms to generate local varieties. For example, in 9ice's *Gbamú Gbamù*, a *fújì*-inflected musical language provides the medium for performing traditional Yorùbá folklore.

See also **Music: Afrobeat; Music: Popular; Musical Instruments**

REFERENCE

Waterman, Christopher. "Yorùbá Popular Music." In *Africa: The Garland Encyclopedia of World Music, Volume 1*, ed. Ruth M. Stone, 23–29. London: Routledge, 1998.

Bòdé Omójolà

MUSIC: TRADITIONAL

Traditional music refers to musical practices that predated colonial rule. This category of music is, however, not static and should not be defined in oppositional terms to modern practices. Indeed, the strength of this category of music lies in the ways it has constantly adapted to emerging social and political spaces, and in its capability to integrate foreign musical elements. Traditional music is distinct for its embrace of the Yorùbá language as a means of expression; its attachment to deities and rituals; its use of traditional instruments like the *bàtá*, *dùndún*, and *agídìgbo*; and its strong attachment to Yorùbá dance forms. Notable musical elements include call-and-response vocal forms, improvisational techniques, and a strong relationship between melodic forms and the inflectional quality of the Yorùbá language. Yorùbá music is particularly noted for its utilitarian value; it functions as a means of promoting group solidarity and the authority of traditional rulers, as well as a medium for narrating history. The song *Láyé Olúgbón* reminds us of the prosperous reigns of Olúgbón, Arèsà, and Àtàndá, three famous kings of the ancient kingdom of Òyó:

Láyé Olúgbón, mo ró'borùn méje;
E ò máa fiwé lórin.
Láyé Arèsà, mo ró'borùn méfà;
E ò máa fiwé lórin.
Láyé Àtàndá, mo ra kókò, mo rà'rán, mo ra sányán baba
*   aso*
Àfòle ló lè peé'lè yí ò dùn, àfòle.

During the reign of Olúgbón, I owned seven shawls; Please, take note of the facts as I sing them.

During the reign of Arèsà, I owned six shawls;
Please, take note of the facts as I sing them.
During the reign of Atanda, I ate good food and
    bought expensive clothes like àrán and sányán.
Only a lazy one would say those times were not
    good times.

Musical instruments can be grouped into four categories devised by Eric Von Hornbostel and Curt Sachs: membranophones (animal-skin drums like the dùndún, ìgbìn, and bàtá), aerophones (wind instruments like the tòròmọgbè and fèrè), chordophones (stringed instruments like the móló and gòjé), and idiophones (percussion instruments, excluding skin drums, like the agogo and ṣẹ̀kẹ̀rẹ̀).

Dùndún and bàtá ensembles are today the most popular of all instrumental ensembles. Both are to be found in use at rites of passage, religious festivals, and in educational institutions that integrate traditional music into the curriculum. Drums, especially the dùndún, are noted for their capability to imitate the tonal and rhythmic features of Yorùbá words to generate a drum language that is socially engaging and musically compelling. Although drums dominate Yorùbá instrumental music, the significance of other categories of instruments must be acknowledged. Kàkàkí (valveless trumpets), for example, are emblems of royal authority, and the orò (bull-roarer) represents the voice of ancestral spirits. The organization of instrumental ensembles illustrates some key features of Yorùbá music: the significance of improvisation, instrumental layering and ostinato patterns. In dùndún and bàtá ensembles, for example, the lead drum, the ìyáàlù, is the main instrument of improvisation and the medium for generating text-based passages that praise individual persons or religious deities. All the other instruments (omele) play cyclical phrases and generate polyrhythmic groves in support of the part of the ìyáàlù.

Vocal performances are of two main types, namely orin (songs) and oríkì (recitative praise poetry). Orin are often performed to drum accompaniment, whereas oríkì are generally unaccompanied. Oríkì are identified by their thematic focus, including oríkì idile (family praise poetry), oríkì ìlú (praise poetry of specific town), and oríkì iṣẹ́ (professional guilds' chant). Perhaps the most prominent guild chant is ìjálá ọdẹ (hunters' chant), which often contains potent narratives that form part of hunters' rituals.

Hereditary membership plays a key role in the practice of music in Yorùbáland. Traditionally, Yorùbá drummers usually hail from the àyàn hereditary family. The àyàn prefix, as in names like Àyánwálé and Àyándòkun, refers to families of drummers who trace their ancestry to Àyàngalú, the man generally believed to have been the first ever Yorùbá drummer. Àyàn families are responsible for the training of new musicians within the family, thus ensuring the sustenance of the tradition in Yorùbáland.

See also **Bards: Old and New; Lineages and Cognomen (Oríkì Orílẹ̀); Musical Instruments; Music: Islamic; Music: Popular; Praise Poetry and Eulogy (Oríkì)**

REFERENCES

Ọmọ́jọlà, Bọ̀dé. "Ìgbádùn in Yorùbá Performance: History, Social Discourse and Indigenous Aesthetics in the Music of Lágbájá." *Journal of Popular Music Studies* 21.2 (2009): 170–91.
———. *Yorùbá Music in the Twentieth Century: Identity, Agency and Performance Practice.* Eastman/Rochester Studies in Ethnomusicology. Rochester, NY: University of Rochester Press, 2012.

Bọ̀dé Ọmọ́jọlà

MUSICAL INSTRUMENTS

A notable element of Yorùbá musical culture is the use of indigenous traditional musical instruments. Unfortunately, there have been several misrepresentations of musical instruments in literature by non-Yorùbá authors.

Categories and Technology

Yorùbá musical instruments principally consist of membranophones of different categories. These are followed by idiophones and aerophones. Popular drum ensembles include bàtá, bàtákoto, àgèrè, àràn or *ìpèsè, ìgbìn, gbẹ̀du, dùndún, bẹ̀nbé, òsírígì, sákárà, ukoko,* and *apíńtì.* Some of the drums are upright, with or without pedestals, like *àràn* or *ìpèsè, ìgbìn, gbẹ̀du,* and *àgẹ̀rẹ̀.* Other types include double-membrane, cylindrical types, including *bàtá, bàtákoto, bẹ̀nbé,* and *dùndún.* Most of these drums are played with specially designed sticks. Popular idiophones include *sẹ̀kẹ̀rẹ̀* (used in *àpíìrì* and *èwọ* Ensembles), *agogo* (used in *aro* ensemble), and the *abẹ̀bẹ̀* (hand fan). *Kàkàkí, fàmí-fàmí,* and *tìyakọ-fífẹ́* are Yorùbá aerophones.

The Yorùbá classify musical instruments based on gender and the mother-child relationship. These gendered classifications are reflected in the musical aesthetics. For instance, the *omele abo* (female child) is the high-pitched rhythmic drum, and the *omele akọ* (male child) is the low-pitched drum. The *ìyá ìlù* (mother drum) is the master drum used for improvisation, direction, and communication.

In the traditional setting, drums are constructed by families of drum makers and devotees of the gods and goddesses. It is an established fact that drum construction involves both physical and metaphysical dimensions. For instance, there are specific woods and animal skins for different drums. Traditional hunters also confirm that there are spirits and gods dwelling inside the trees and animals. Only those who are endowed with spiritual powers could subdue or appease them before they can fell the trees or kill the animals. It is also believed that when used, the materials are more than mere objects, as they possess special spiritual potencies.

Ensemble Members

The *bàtá* ensemble consists of four members: *ìyá ìlù, omele abo, omele akọ,* and *kúdi,* whereas *àgẹ̀rẹ̀* has three members: *àgẹ̀rẹ̀, fèrè,* and *afèrè. Àràn* or *ìpèsè* consists of *ìpèsè, afèrè, àràn,* and *agogo,* whereas *gbẹ̀du* (*ọba Ògbóni*) has *afèrè, àpèrè* or *òpèrà,* and *ọbadan. Ìgbìn* has *ìyá ńlá, ìyá gan, keke,* and *afèrè,* whereas *dùndún* has *ìyá ìlù, kẹríkẹrì, gángán, ìsaájú, kànnàngó, gúdúgúdú, agogo,* and *sẹ̀kẹ̀rẹ̀. Apíńtì* has *ìyá ìlù, omele,* and *agogo,* and *àpíìrì* has *ìyá aje, omele,* and *aje. Òsírígì* has *òsírígì* drum and three *agogo: agbè, ojo,* and *konkolo.*

Functions

Yorùbá musical instruments perform musical, symbolic, communicative, and therapeutic functions. The musical functions include rhythmic, accompaniment, leading, and improvisation. Some drums symbolize specific spiritual and social phenomena. For instance, *àgẹ̀rẹ̀* symbolizes Ògún, and *gbẹ̀du* symbolizes royalty. In addition, drums are used for direct and indirect communication. For instance, the *ìyá ìlù* and *aguda* or *kẹríkẹrì* of *dùndún* are used as surrogates for communication.

Current Trend

Many Yorùbá instruments are becoming extinct today. While interested foreign "makers" try to reproduce some of the instruments with advanced technology, the original Yorùbá makers now compete with new instruments to communicate with the gods and truly serve their original purposes.

See also **Music: Traditional**

REFERENCES

Adédèjì, Fémi. "Traditional Music and Dance: An Appreciation." *Lagos Notes and Records* 17 (2011): 207–18.
Dáramọ́lá, Olú, and Adébáyọ̀ Jéjé. *Àwọn Àsà àti Òrìsà Ilẹ̀ Yorùbá.* Ìbàdàn (Nigeria): Oníbọn-Òjé Press, 1967.

Fẹ́mi Adédèjì

MYTHS

Myths (*ìtàn ìwásẹ̀*) are anonymous stories, presented as history, that deal with cosmological and supernatural traditions of a people, their gods and goddesses, culture, heroes and heroines, religious belief, and so on. The Yorùbá hold certain supernatural beings in high esteem and perceive them as gods or divinities, spirits or ancestors. Nevertheless, they still believe that Olódùmarè (the Almighty God) is the Supreme Being. From time immemorial, myths have become ingrained in the Yorùbá culture so much that the people use them to illustrate their religion and philosophical thoughts, as well as to preserve their history and support their institutions—more often than not, they employ them to strengthen their beliefs in the gods.

Myths are accepted on faith, taught as factual events, and can be cited as authority in answer to ignorance, doubt, or disbelief. In essence, the sum total of all Yorùbá myths, songs, histories, and other cultural components is called *ìtàn* (story, narration, or tale). Thus, it is not surprising that the Yorùbá consider mythological narratives or accounts about their primordial divinities and deified ancestors, such as Ọbàtálá (Òrìṣà-Ńlá), Ọ̀rúnmìlà (Ifá), Èṣù, Ògún, Ṣànpọ̀nná, Ṣàngó, Ọya, among the host of others, to be truthful and reliable.

People turn to the myths to decide which should be adopted as a personal, preferred divinity. For instance, if one adopts the archdivinity Ọ̀rúnmìlà as his or her preferred god, he or she is either trying to ensure happiness or address an unhappy situation. Another name for Ọ̀rúnmìlà is *òkítíbìrí, a-jí-pa-ojọ́-ikú-dà* (the great changer, who alters the date of death). If one chooses Èṣù, he or she seeks his protective and benevolent capabilities. Choosing Ògún is a way to tap into material and spiritual prosperity. It is believed that Ògún clears the paths of his devotees with his sharp machete, reminiscent of how he cut his way through the wilderness in the beginning of days.

To the Yorùbá, differences between different versions of myths do not negate their truthfulness. Such variation, some argue, is a result of the incursion of European colonial powers, who later became masters of the land and sought to displace the indigenous cult with their own version of narratives.

Efforts to "prove" myths are fruitless; myths do not set out to be logical accounts of events. Their authenticity or correctness cannot be verified. Their primary purpose is mainly to answer the requests of the devout followers who seek answers from the oracle. Although myths can seem absurd, they help the Yorùbá answer questions about existence and security in life, among other things.

See also **Deities (The *Òrìṣà*); Diaspora: Deities (*Òrìṣà*)**

REFERENCES

Awólàlú, Ọmọ́sadé F. *Yorùbá Beliefs and Sacrificial Rites*. London: Longman Group, 1981.

Ìdòwú, Bọ́lájí E. *Olódùmarè: God in Yorùbá Belief*. London: Longman Group, 1975.

Kazeem A. Ọmọ́fóyèwá

N

NAGÔ

Nagô was a term generally assigned to Yorùbá-speaking slaves arriving from ports in the Bight of Benin to the Portuguese colony of Brazil, as well as the British and French Caribbean between the eighteenth and nineteenth centuries. The term likely originated as a self-appellation by a southwestern Yorùbá subgroup, known as Ànàgó, and adapted by Fon speakers in Dahomey to *anagonu*, to refer to the Yorùbá in general. By the nineteenth century colonial authorities and slave owners in Brazil often made distinctions among different types of Nagô using subclassifications indicative of different Yorùbá kingdoms and subgroups, including Ọ̀yọ́, Ẹ̀gbá, Ìjẹ̀bú, Òwu, Ànàgó, Ẹ̀gbádò, and so on.

The word *nagô* is still in use in Brazil as a form of identity for practitioners of the Afro-Brazilian religions generally known as Candomblé. Names given to some of the devotees are *povos de santo* (people of the saint), and priests and priestesses are known as *pai-de-santo* or *mãe-de-santo* (father or mother of the saint), which refers to the syncretism of *òrìṣà* with Roman Catholic saints, among other West African and indigenous belief systems. There are regional differences in the association between *òrìṣà* and Catholic saints. For example, Xangô (Ṣàngó) is equated with St. Jerome in Bahia and Pernambuco, while Xangô is associated with St. Michael Archangel in Rio de Janeiro. Yemaja or Yemaya (Yemọja) is Our Lady of the Rosary in Bahia, but Our Lady of the Conception in Rio de Janeiro.

The Afro-Brazilian religions tied to *òrìṣà* worship are varied and known by different names in different regions of Brazil. For example, Xangô de Pernambuco (or Xangô do Recife or Nagô-Ba) refers to a type of Candomblé unique to northeastern Brazil, where Ṣàngó is the principal *òrìṣà* of worship. In Bahia, Candomblé de Nagô is similar to the Xangô religious groups in Pernambuco and Recife. In Rio Grande do Sul, *batuque* (a word for drum) relates to religious groups of Nagô ancestry who also worship the *òrìṣà*. Other Candomblé and *batuque* religious groups, however, have no connection with *òrìṣà* worship, rather with *voduns*, gods generally associated with Dahomey and *nkisis*, spirits associated with West Central Africa more generally.

The devotees of Candomblé revolving around *òrìṣà* worship believe that everyone has their own tutelary *òrìṣà*, or guardian angel, which acts as their protector and controls the individual's destiny. Determining one's guardian *òrìṣà* requires certain levels of initiation. *Òrìṣà* worship in Brazilian Candomblé shares much iconography, music, and dance that are clearly linked to West Africa, while others are unique to Brazilian cultural beliefs and practices. Brazilian syncretic religions are closely related to the Lucumí religion practiced in Cuba.

Nagô culture and influence is mostly found in Brazilian Candomblé but has spread to other Latin American countries, including Argentina, Uruguay, Venezuela, and Colombia. Because of other migrations, Candomblé is also found in other places in North and

South America, Europe, and—to a lesser extent—Africa and Asia.

See also **Deities: The Òrìṣà; Diaspora: Deities (The Òrìṣà); Diaspora: Impact of Yorùbá Culture; Diaspora: Yorùbá in North America; Diaspora: Yorùbá in South America and the Caribbean; Lucumí; Ọ̀yọ́túnjí: The Yorùbá Community in the United States**

REFERENCES

Fálọlá, Tóyìn, and Matt D. Childs, eds. *The Yorùbá Diaspora in the Atlantic World*. Bloomington: Indiana University Press, 2004.

Herskovits, Melville J. "African Gods and Catholic Saints in New World Negro Belief." *American Anthropologist* 39.4 (1937): 635–43.

Law, Robin. "Ethnicity and the Slave Trade: 'Lucumí' and 'Nagô' as Ethnonyms in West Africa." *History in Africa* 24 (1997): 205–19.

Reis, João José. "African Nations in Nineteenth-Century Salvador, Bahia." In *The Black Urban Atlantic in the Age of the Slave Trade*, ed. Jorge Canizares-Esguerra, Matt D. Childs, and James Sidbury, 63–84. Philadelphia: University of Pennsylvania Press, 2013.

Henry B. Lovejoy

NAMES AND NAMING

As a culturally homogeneous society, the Yorùbá's value system is reflected in their naming practices. The names (orúkọ)—whether they are personal, social, or local—are meaningful and more than identifying appellations. All names contain culturally relevant historical and aspirational information. Weighty rumination goes into bequeathing a name to a person, group of people, or place. It is possible to piece together the perspectives and historical circumstances of individuals and families from names. Likewise, the antiquated and contemporary narratives of Yorùbá residents and communities can be deduced from their names. This signification and emerging patterns of information is remarkable considering that the Yorùbá ethnonym is an exonym from a neighboring society. Whereas ọmọ-oòduà and ọmọ-káàárọ̀-oòjíi-re are the preferred endonyms.

Yorùbá naming practices are intricate and thoughtful. Conscious and careful efforts are made to give evocative names that not only are relevant to the circumstances of conception and birth but also capture the family's aspirations for the child. It is strongly believed that the name affects the bearer's destiny. The thoughtful intentionality within the naming system testifies to the saying, orúkọ ọmọ níí ro ọmọ (the child's name affects the child). The impact of a name is all encompassing; it is, therefore, intended to reflect multiple concerns. As the child is conceived, the circumstances of conception and the mother's natal experiences are noted and encapsulated in the names.

Equally important are the age-old customs of the naming ceremony, ìkómọjáde (act of presenting the child), which references the baby's first public appearance, and ìsọmọlórúkọ (act of naming the child). Previously, the kind of ceremony and when it is performed after the birth depends on gender (seven days for female and nine days for male) and multiple births (eight days for twins). The purpose of the ceremony includes welcoming the child, congratulating the parents, and thanking God, family deities, and ancestral spirits for the heavenly gift.

It is safe to say that all Yorùbá names have extant meanings and contain sentiments about the bearers or the immediate family. There are a few traditional names whose meanings are lost or have been affected by changes in the religious and societal structures. Some names are reinterpreted or completely removed from their applicative meaning to reflect values of modern society. No limit exists in the number of personal names emerging from two sources: orúkọ àbísọ (personal names given at birth) and orúkọ àmútọ̀runwá (commemorative heaven-given personal names).

Orúkọ àbísọ signifies the importance of names, especially considering the meaning of the constituent morphemes. A child's place in the family, the significance of his or her birth, the circumstances of his or her birth, and the vocation, religion, and social status of his or her family are some of the factors that may be reflected by the child's orúkọ àbísọ. Examples include the following:

Adéwálé	adé	wá	ilé	the crown came home
	crown	come	home	
Dúrójayé	dúró	jẹ	ayé	stay and enjoy the world
	stay	enjoy	world	
Fọlárìn	fi	ọlá	rìn	walk with wealth
	use	wealth	walk	

Orúkọ àmútọ̀runwá are names with which a child is believed to be born. These names reflect the situation of the child's birth and concretely illustrate belief in the spiritual realm. They are shared by people born with similar birth situations. For example, people born breech are referred to as Ìgè, and those children born with the placenta over their faces like masks are called Amúsàán. Children with such notable births are regarded as special and treated with reverence. Examples include Táíwò (*tọ́-ayé-wò*, taste the world) for the first and youngest of twins; Kẹ́hìndé (*kín-ẹ̀yìn- dé*, bear the rear) for the second and oldest of twins; Erinlẹ̀ (name of a river) for a child born with the umbilical cord around the arms or waist.

Two other categories of names are *oríkì* (praise names) and *orúkọ ìnagijẹ* (nicknames), which are acquired later in life. *Oríkì* function to recognize and commend achievements of the bearer. There are two forms: personal (*àdáni*) and lineage (*orílẹ̀*). *Oríkì àdáni* are used as personal names according to the circumstances of conception and/or birth or the parents' choice. *Oríkì* are also used for identity (each person or lineage has one), solidarity (with family or lineage), pride (of ancestry), and encouragement. A commendable action leads to praise names being called and the personal or lineage *oríkì* chanted. Examples include Àkàndé (a male child conceived as a result of a single sexual relation between parents) and Àbẹ̀kẹ́ (a female child whom people will be pleased to pamper).

Over time, the growing child is given other names, known as *ìnagijẹ* or *àlàjẹ́* (nicknames), that might point to physical features, emotional state, or complimentary or unflattering aspects of the bearer's personality or life. There are also situations in which an individual may choose to use an alias. For instance, a married woman does not refer to her in-laws by their given names. Another instance is when an *àdàpè* (avoidance name) is used. The following are examples of phrases derived from exploits of important previous bearers of the names:

apọ́nbéporẹ́   red as the relative of the palm oil (descriptive *ìnagijẹ* for a light-skinned person)

ìbíkúnlé   birth fills the house (for a big and tall person)

For example, bearers of the personal name Ìbíkúnlé get two *àdàpè*:

olókè   lord of the hill

agbàǹgbà ààsẹ   owner of a strong large door

These are in reference to Balógun Ìbíkúnlé, the great Ìbàdàn ruler and warlord.

As cultural elements, these names express gender divisions in the society. Interestingly, Yorùbá onomastics has focused more on anthroponyms, particularly their classification and analysis. Another grouping is Yorùbá toponyms. They are meaningful and full of referential information about different locations. These can be classified according to many factors, including nature (trees, hills, forests and so on), historical events, and historical figures.

See also **Lineages and Cognomen (*Oríkì Orílẹ̀*); Livestock: Domestication and Species; Praise Poetry (*Oríkì*)**

REFERENCE

Odùyọyè, Modúpẹ́. *Yorùbá Names: Their Structure and Their Meanings*. Ìbàdàn (Nigeria): Daystar Press, 1972.

Akinloyè Òjó

NARRATION TECHNIQUES

As in any human culture, the Yorùbá use language to narrate and project their identity diachronically and synchronically. They use multiple narration techniques to communicate the affective, cognitive, and ethical aspects of being. These techniques are rooted in the notion of speech as sacred. Indeed, in Ifá sacred literature, an entire *odù*, or chapter, is devoted to *ọ̀rọ̀*, or speech, to emphasize its primordial and metaphysical power in their people's life and identity. The spoken word is particularly potent; it has creative and destructive powers.

Two broad categories of narration techniques are available in the culture: nonverbal and verbal. Nonverbal narration techniques include the emic (mirroring the interlocutor's state of mind, mood, or body gestures) and proxemic (haptics and kinesics). Proxemics use the body to engage or challenge one's interlocutor to signal emotional closeness or distance, reverence or irreverence, respect or disrespect. Verbal narration techniques run the gamut of linguistic resources available to the speaker. These are very context specific. The occasion determines the choice of technique(s). Thus, the Yorùbá use invocations (curses and blessings), incantations (encomiums and panegyrics), folktales (to shape behavior), proverbs, aphorisms, riddles, puns, jokes, and satire, to cite a few examples.

The most versatile narration tool is the unlimited variety of proverbs in Yorùbá culture. As bearers of meaning, these proverbs are powerful and poignant signifiers, constantly adapted and reappropriated as needed. As rhetorical devices and flourishes, they cut to the heart of the matter in various situations that may require an intuitive but brief discursive grasp of what is at stake. The use of proverbs requires acute linguistic, verbal, and mental dexterity, such as the ability to pun, rhyme, and play on words to create aesthetics. It also requires a person to have some (if not deep) knowledge of the folklore: the pantheon of deities, family lore, community traditions, and the like. Some proverbs are told in riddle form to maintain polite conversation. Others are used to communicate bitter truths more tactfully. Conversely, the Yorùbá also deem silence as a form of narration, since it can communicate reticence, wisdom, maturity, and reluctance to engage. For example, there is the story of the garrulous squirrels that lost their offspring to curious and hungry humans because they talked too much!

These and other narration techniques attest to the richness and viability of Yorùbá material culture. They are indicative of wisdom, creativity, and intellect. The Babaláwo, or traditional priest, is the guardian of the language. His role is both sacerdotal and cultural. He is the repository of communal and ancestral memory. The defining feature of his training is mnemotechnics, or the art of memory. The Babaláwo's ability to memorize the Ifá sacred corpus and all manner of knowledge and wisdom contained therein for the benefit of his community. He possesses *àṣẹ*, or the power to make manifest that which is invisible and inexistent, through his mastery of speech. He is comparable to the griots of Guinea and Senegambia and the rabbis of the Jewish tradition.

See also **Communication: Nonverbal; Divination: Ifá; Invocation; Proverbs; Stories, Storytelling, and Storytellers; Urban Folklore; Words: Ọ̀rọ̀**

REFERENCES

Bascom, William. *African Folktales in the New World.* Bloomington: Indiana University Press, 1992.

Okpewho, Isidore. *African Oral Literature: Backgrounds, Character, and Continuity.* Bloomington: Indiana University Press, 1992.

Bíọ́dún J. Ògúndayọ̀

NATIONALISM

Nationalism presents the amalgam of twenty-two distinct Yorùbá subgroups into a nation with a common language, history, belief, politics, and economic agenda. It developed in three phases. The first phase was in the precolonial period, marked by group consciousness based on the expression of cultural pride and the creation of an imagined unity among diverse subgroups. Such a consciousness helped end the then-prevalent intertribal warfare between Yorùbá kingdoms and chiefdoms.

The second phase began in the 1880s, when the new intelligentsia and clerics, elevated by their connection to colonial power, engaged in a project of cultural nationalism. They created a myth of common origin, language, ideology, religion, belief, craft, and popular cultures. During the period, the early intellectuals and clergy wanted European missionaries and the British colonial administration to recognize their ideational culture and language and to acknowledge the superiority of the Yorùbá people in colonial Nigeria.

The third phase started in the 1940s, with colonial political elite who translated the cultural nationalism into a political project that involved appropriating the legacies of cultural nationalism. It sought to negotiate inclusion in the colonial politics and to gain political superiority in colonial and postcolonial Nigeria. During this period, the origin myth was changed and narrated as if all Yorùbá subgroups had always lived together as a political constituency. The elites created a collective consciousness centered on Western education, enlightenment (ọ̀làjú), politics, and infrastructural development. Yorùbá pride imagined its people as superior to other ethnic groups.

All these efforts translated into political action, such as the formation of political parties and sociocultural associations useful for accessing political power and negotiating political dominance in Nigeria. At first, Yorùbá nationalism rested on a fraternal relationship with other ethnic groups. However, since 1964 Yorùbá nationalism has been marked by political confrontation and violence in response to the marginalization the Yorùbá claim to have experienced under the British colonial government and in postcolonial Nigeria. This contemporary version of Yorùbá nationalism supports a strong attachment to mythological as well as actual power. It is based on the people's well-developed literacy and their perception of being enlightened.

The use of actual power here refers to the Yorùbá belief that there has been the successful introduction of welfare programs that are the real cause of human development in Nigeria. As part of their Yorùbá cultural pride, they often refer to the country's free primary education system, free health-care system, establishment of the first television station in Africa, and the unprecedented urbanization and industrialization in

western Nigeria between the 1950s and 1970s, which spread to other parts of Nigeria as a result of Yorùbá ingenuity in governance.

Nationalism has not led to the creation of a Yorùbá autonomous state. Nationalism occurs both culturally and politically among the people as an ideology and as an instrument some elite wield to preserve traditions and cultural values. At the same time, nationalism is mobilized for political control of the sociopolitical space and in the struggle to allocate more political power to the Yorùbá in Nigerian politics.

REFERENCE

Àjàlá, A. S. *Yorùbá Nationalism: Culture, Politics and Violence in South-Western Nigeria.* Cologne (Germany): Ruddiger Koepel, 2013.

Adérèmí Suleiman Àjàlá

NONGOVERNMENTAL ORGANIZATIONS

There are two broad groups of nongovernmental organizations (NGOs) in Nigeria. The first group consists of organizations with overt political orientations, such as the original Afénifére Group, Afénifére Renewal Group (ARG), Oòduà People's Congress, Oòduà National Congress, Àpapọ̀ Ọmọ Oòduà, Yorùbá Unity Forum, Àgbájọ Yorùbá Àgbáyé (or the Yorùbá World Congress), and Atáyése. These organizations tend to act as pressure groups on local, regional, and national politics. They are bound by a strong determination to fight perceived Yorùbá marginalization in federal public service and political appointments. They regularly lament the perceived lack of cohesion among the Yorùbá political elite, and they frequently call on the central government to address the apparent absence of the Yorùbá in the top echelons of political power.

Their goals include regional autonomy, self-determination, and the creation of a Yorùbá nation; Atáyése has proposed a referendum to create a Yorùbá nation. Some of these overtly political NGOs also espouse the need for political change. For instance, on its website, the ARG describes itself as "a group of the younger elements within the core progressive camp in Yorùbáland, who have been meeting and organizing for change in the direction of politics in Yorùbáland and, ultimately, in Nigeria."

The second group consists of cultural, nonpartisan, and philanthropic organizations whose goals include the economic, educational, civic, and cultural development of the Yorùbá nation and people. Organizations in this genre include the Yorùbá Indigenes Foundation (YIF), including Fún Ìṣọkan, Ìdàgbàsókè, and Ìlọsíwájú Ọmọ Yorùbá; Change Movement of Nigeria; youth-oriented NGOs including the Youth Initiative for Advocacy, Growth, and Advancement (YIAGA), the Youth Alliance on Constitutional and Electoral Reform (YACER), and Partners for Electoral Reforms (PER); and the Assembly of Yorùbá in the Diaspora (AYD).

According to its website, the YIF seeks to "institutionalize the inculcation of good values, positive behaviors, bordering on honesty, integrity, hard work and good neighborliness, as a cultural creed that will bring honor and respectable treatment to the average Yorùbá person within the global community." Change Movement of Nigeria translated the 1999 Nigerian constitution into the Yorùbá language. According to its website, its goal was to empower "the truly disenfranchised, the oppressed and the voiceless to be able to critically engage in participatory democracy and open governance."

The three youth-oriented NGOs—YIAGA, YACER, and PER—share the short-term goal to register all citizens, but young people in particular, to vote in Èkìtì and Òṣun gubernatorial elections and in general national elections. In the long term, their aim is to enhance the capacity of youth civil service organizations in southwestern Nigeria to monitor the distribution of voters' registration cards (or permanent voters' cards, PVCs) and to promote continuous voter registration in the states of Èkìtì and Òṣun. The AYD conceptualizes Yorùbáland as a kingdom of unity and progress, with traditional rulers spearheading development and caring for those in need.

See also **Afẹ́nifẹ́re, Ẹgbẹ́; Oòduà People's Congress**

REFERENCES

Afẹ́nifẹ́re Renewal Group, "Afẹ́nifẹ́re Renewal Group, Yorùbá Socio-Political and Economic Organization." http://www .afenifererenewalgroup.org.
Obike, Grace. "Youth NGOs to Launch Thumb It Right Campaign." *The Nation*, March 5, 2014. http://thenationonlineng .net/new/youth-ngo-launches-thumb-it-right-campaign/.

Kúnlé Amúwò

NOLLYWOOD: FILMS AND CINEMA

Nollywood refers to the Nigerian video industry of the 1990s. The name emulates those of other recognized and established film industry locations around the globe, such as Hollywood in the United States and Bollywood in India. Although the term *Nollywood* became popular during the 1990s, Nigeria's film industry began decades before. Prior to the 1990s and the popularization of video, celluloid films were produced in Nigeria. The Yorùbá in southwestern Nigeria paved the way for the establishment of a film industry in the country. The first indigenous feature film produced in Nigeria was *Kongi's Harvest* in 1973, which featured Nobel laureate Wọlé Ṣóyínká in the lead role as President Kongi. The film, based on Ṣóyínká's play of the same title, was written and produced in English.

The practitioners of the popular and highly successful indigenous Yorùbá traveling theater known as *alárìnjó* soon used celluloid film to advance their craft. They used film to produce dramas infused with songs and dance that expressed Yorùbá aesthetics and cosmology. These productions would be exclusively written and produced in the Yorùbá language.

Bíọ́dún Dáwódù's book *Three Decades of Yorùbá Movie Industry: Challenges and Prospects (1976-2006)* examines the emergence of the Nigerian film industry, including a focus on Yorùbá cinema. According to Dáwódù, the first films produced in Nigeria in the 1970s were Yorùbá films produced on 16mm and 35mm celluloid reel formats. Pre-Nollywood films include *Àjàní Ògún* by Ọlá Balógun (1976), *Ìjà Òmìnira* by Adéyẹmí Afọláyan (Adé-love) (1977), *Aiyé* (1978) and *Jáiyésimi* (1981) by

Chief Hubert Ògúndé, and Ọrun Móoru (1982), Ààrẹ Àgbáyé (1983), and Moṣebọ́látán (1985) by Moses Ọláìyá. Balógun would go on to be very instrumental and consequential in the development of the Nigerian film industry in its nascent stages; he directed a majority of the cinema productions for entertainment industry leaders such as Chief Hubert Ògúndé and Adéyẹmí Afọláyan.

The recession experienced in Nigeria in the late 1980s made production of films in the celluloid format an expensive venture. Economic pressure combined with the emergence and accessibility of the video recorder ushered in a new development in the local video production industry. Film stock was no longer imported for purchase and then exported for processing and postproduction editing. The video camera was easy to operate, and videotapes were inexpensive, easy to edit, and could be edited locally.

The earliest Yorùbá video productions occurred in the late 1980s. Controversy swirls around the first Yorùbá film produced on video. With the support of Babátúndé Adélùsì, the publisher of Ayé Àkámarà (This Strange Life), Adé Ajíbóyè produced Ṣóṅṣó Méjì (Two Pointed Ears) in 1988. The film premiered at the Tinúadé Cinema in Òwòròṅsòkí, Lagos. However, the following year, Àlàdé Arómiré, founder of Yọ̀tọ̀mì Television, premiered Ẹkún at the National Theatre in Lagos. Arómiré claimed that the film was shot in 1986, but the censors' board delayed official approval of the film for release to the public for three years.

The success of both films paved the way for a multitude of new films and for the emergence of Yorùbá film production companies such as Jídé Kòṣọ́kọ́ Productions, Báyọ̀wá International Films, and Mainframe Productions under the leadership of Túndé Kèlání. Mainframe has received acclaim for the finest technical production quality. Kèlání works with seasoned and established writers. He has produced and directed scripts by the preeminent Yorùbá scholar Professor Akin Ìṣọlá. Their partnership has produced Kòṣeégbé, Ṣaworoidẹ, Agogo Èèwọ̀, and Ó Le Kú. Other well-known Kèlání films are Ti Olúwa ni ilẹ̀, which features popu-

lar actor Kareem Adépọ̀jù (aka Bàbá Wándé); Arugbá; and Màámi, which features Funkẹ́ Akíndélé. Màámi was adapted from a novel with the same title, authored by renowned playwright Professor Fẹ́mi Ọ̀ṣọ́fisan.

The films by Yorùbá filmmakers can be found all over Africa and throughout the Diaspora. Many titles are available for viewing online. Several distribution companies for these films have been established by businesses primarily in Ìdúmọ̀tà, Lagos, which has become the marketing and dissemination outlet for the national and international distribution of Yorùbá-based Nollywood films.

See also Ògúndé, Hubert Adédèjì; Ṣóyínká, Wọlé

REFERENCE

Dáwódù, Bíọ́dún. Three Decades of Yorùbá Movie Industry Challenges and Prospects (1976-2006). http://www.nigeriafilms.com/news/3607/12/three-decades-of-Yorùbá-movie-industry-challenges-.html.

Níyì Coker, Jr.

NUMERALS

For a non-Yorùbá person, learning the Yorùbá number system can be a dizzying experience. Despite clamor from some groups for the system to be modified to meet the computer age, it still enjoys a large measure of popularity among the people. For this reason, a change to a decimal-based system is not likely forthcoming any time soon.

The Yorùbá use a modified vigesimal number system, which means that 20 (ogún) is its base. After the first unit numbers (1 through 10), other numbers are derived by adding or subtracting from multiples of 20. The first ten numbers have distinct names: ení, ejì, ẹta, ẹrin, àrún, ẹfà, eje, ẹjọ, ẹsán, and ẹwá for one to ten, respectively. Values from 11 to 14 are derived from additions to ten. Thus, 12 is ẹjìlá, an elided form of ẹjì lé ẹwá, which translates to "two in excess of ten." However, the names of numbers 15 to 19 result from subtracting the corresponding amounts from 20. For example, 16 is ẹrìndínlógún, which means "20 less 4." With the exception of the number 30, other numbers that are multiples of 10 but are not divisible by 20 are named by subtracting 10 from their succeeding numbers that are divisible by 20. In which case, 50 is àádọ́ta, ẹ̀wá-dín-lọ́gọ́ta (ogún mẹ́ta), which translates to "20 times 3 less 10." The number 30 bears the special name ọgbọ̀n. Thus, the number 27 is ẹ̀tàdínlọ́gbọ̀n, or "30 less 3," while 57 is as ẹ̀tàdínláàádọ́ta "20 times 3 less 3."

The numbers 200 (igba), 300 (ọ̀ọ́dúnrún), and 400 (irinwó) are justifiably given special names because of their commercial significance. Presumably, these numbers appear frequently enough in daily transactions, like calling the number of yam heaps made by a farmer or even piles of yams that are meant for sale or for storage.

With the exception of 400, other numbers divisible by 200 derive their names as multiples of 200. Numbers divisible by 100 but not by 200 are named by subtracting 100 from the succeeding number that is divisible by 200. Thus, 500 is ẹ̀ẹ́dẹ́gbẹ̀ta, ẹ̀wá dín ní igba mẹ́ta, or "200 times 3 less 100." The number 733 is ẹ̀ẹ́dẹ́gbẹ̀rin lé mẹ́talélọ́gbọ̀n, or "200 times 4 less 100 with an excess of 30 and 3." The number 2,000 bears the name ẹgbàwá

(igba mẹ́wàá), which translates to "200 times 10." This is another milestone in the counting process. Other four-digit numbers divisible by 200, such as 4,000 and 6,000 are ẹgbàajì and ẹgbàata, respectively. The number 200,000 is ẹgbàawá (igba mẹ́wàá, lọ́nà mẹ́wàá, or "200 times 10 times 10"), and 400,000 is called ẹgbàawá méjì (200,000 times 2).

A logical addition to the number system is ẹgbẹgbẹ̀rún (ẹgbẹ̀rún lọ́nà ẹgbẹ̀rún) for 1 million. Thus 1 billion naira can be called ẹgbẹgbẹ̀rún lọ́nà ẹgbẹgbẹ̀rún naira. This makes it easier to explain the magnitude of the national budget or the amount slated for some project to a layperson. These kinds of discussions are commonplace; thus, colloquial numbering expressions, like mílíọ́nù and bílíọ́nù (indigenized forms for million and billion), have found their way into the Yorùbá number system.

REFERENCE

Adéoyè, C. Láògún. Àṣà àti Ìṣe Yorùbá. Oxford: Oxford University Press, 1979.

Julius Fákínlẹ̀dé

ỌBÁSANJỌ́, OLÚṢẸ́GUN (1938–)

General Olúṣẹ́gun Ọbásanjọ́ ruled Nigeria for more than three decades, first as military head of state from 1976 to 1979 and then as civilian president for two terms from 1999 to 2007. In 1976 and 1999, he was the Yorùbá leader preferred by the northern Nigerian political class. He was second in command to Murtala Muhammad (1938–1976), who was assassinated in February 1976. General Ọbásanjọ́ was perceived as a person who could be manipulated by the northern political elite. It was therefore argued that he should succeed Muhammad. General Ọbásanjọ́ organized a presidential election in 1979, and he supported Alhaji Shehu Shagari (1925–), the political candidate from the north. He handed power to Shehu Shagari in 1979 and retired to his farm in Òtà near Abẹ́òkúta.

During retirement, Chief Ọbásanjọ́ did not take his eye off the affairs of Nigeria. As the first African head of state to hand over power voluntarily to a civilian government, he was a favorite of polite society. President Shagari and his government depleted the coffers of the country faster than they could be filled. The military organized a coup d'état on December 31, 1983, and asked Ọbásanjọ́ to return as leader of the country. Ọbásanjọ́ turned down the military's request. Ọbásanjọ́ gained even more support for rejecting power.

He criticized all subsequent governments. General Sani Abacha (1943–1998) tried Ọbásanjọ́ for treason in 1995 and put him in prison for life. Abacha worked to stay in power but died in 1998. The same year, Chief M. K. O. Abíọ́lá (1937–1998), who had won the annulled elections of June 12, 1993, also passed away. Ọbásanjọ́ and Abíọ́lá had been classmates at Baptist Boys High School in Abẹ́òkúta. Ọbásanjọ́ was released and supported by the northern political elite, both military and civilian, to stand for election in May 1999. In 2003, he ran for a second time. Support from the northern elite was not forthcoming at this time, but the Yorùbá of southwestern Nigeria helped him win a second term as president.

Assessments of Ọbásanjọ́'s political career differ. He believes himself a greater politician than Chief Ọbáfẹ́mi Awólọ́wọ̀ (1909–1987). Whatever one may think, he is a decisive player in Nigerian political history.

See also **Abíọ́lá, Moshood Káṣìmawò Ọláwálé; Awólọ́wọ̀, Ọbáfẹ́mi**

REFERENCE

Ọmọ́tọ́ṣọ̀, Kọ́lé. *Just Before Dawn.* Ìbàdàn (Nigeria): Spectrum Books, 1988.

Kọ́lé Ọmọ́tọ́ṣọ̀

ODÙDUWÀ

The Yorùbá-speaking people constitute one of the major ethnic groups of Nigeria. While a majority are found in southwestern Nigeria, others live in present-day Republic of Benin and Togo. As a result of the transatlantic slave trade, people of Yorùbá ancestry form a significant part of the contemporary African Diaspora. Inside and outside of Nigeria, the Yorùbá believe that their historical consciousness began at Ilé-Ifẹ̀. They claim common origin through their ancestor, Odùduwà. According to Samuel Johnson, "The origin of the Yorùbá nation is involved in obscurity," but he contends that "Odùduwà the reputed founder and ancestor of the [Yorùbá] race is really a mythical personage."

Two strands of tradition explain the origins of the Yorùbá people. One is migratory and the other is mythical, but both refer to Ilé-Ifẹ̀ as the source of origin. The first version narrates that they migrated from the east, probably from Egypt, Meroë, or Yemen, under the leadership of Odùdùwà, the son of Lámúrúdu. After a long migration, they finally settled in Ilé-Ifẹ̀. The settlement in Ilé-Ifẹ̀ suggests that the land was vacant when the Yorùbá people occupied it. The migrants must have established an urban community with a monarchical form of government and a high degree of cultural development.

The second tradition states that the earth was merely a watery and marshy waste, and divinities (possibly human beings) used to descend from heaven through spider's web to hunt on the vast expanse of water. To create solid earth, Olódùmarè (the Supreme Being) gave Ọbàtálá (Òrìṣà-Ńlá) a handful of earth, a cockerel, and a palm nut, and he created solid earth. At a spot on the water (now identified as Ilé-Ifẹ̀), Ọbàtálá released a pigeon that spread sand to create dry land. The palm kernels explain how trees came into being. Another strand of this tradition claims that Ọbàtálá began his journey from heaven (descending through a mystical chain) with a snail's shell filled with sand, a white hen, a black cat, five pieces of iron, and a palm nut. Ọbàtálá became drunk, and Odùduwà seized the instruments of authority, led the divinities to the world, and landed on a hill called Òkè-Ọ̀ràmfẹ̀ in Ilé-Ifẹ̀. Thus, Ilé-Ifẹ̀ became the cradle of the Yorùbá. This tradition has been criticized by many scholars particularly for its unscientific nature.

From these two versions, historians believe that a community of people existed and a monarchical form

of government with a high degree of sociocultural stratification had developed at Ilé-Ifẹ̀ before Ọbàtálá or Odùduwà and their groups arrived. Historical facts point to a kingdom with a titled ruler, Olókò of Òkò, who performed political and religious functions and wore a crown. The rivalry between Ọbàtálá and Odùduwà therefore represents the struggles between the old and new political order. Ọbàtálá (as the old order) was defeated and Odùduwà (as the new order) assumed political leadership. According to J. A. Àtàndá, Odùduwà ordered that "a constitution be drawn up and a government established, with himself at the head" (17). Although Ọbàtálá challenged Odùduwà, he was defeated.

Then there is Àgbọnmìrègún, who practiced Ifá divination. He was presumably the leader of the autochthonous society that succumbed to Odùduwà's political authority. Furthermore, Ifẹ̀ traditions revere Mọrèmi, a woman who saved her people from extermination at the expense of her only son. In any case, it seems plausible that Odùduwà struggled with the indigenous people and used the instruments of authority taken from Ọbàtálá to subjugate the preexisting community. He also used his charisma and political acumen to rule and to establish a new dynasty. With the new development, Odùduwà became the cultural hero of the Yorùbá, and his emergence gave the Yorùbá people a cultural and political identity.

After taking control of Ilé-Ifẹ̀, Odùduwà had to consolidate his hold and legitimize his political power by contending with his formidable neighboring communities. His military success enhanced his political hegemony. Odùduwà had lasting political achievements, not only by establishing a strong monarchical government and himself as the first king of Ilé-Ifẹ̀ but also by instituting a dynasty with a sustainable process of succession. Rulers of Ilé-Ifẹ̀ and other Yorùbá kingdoms trace their ancestry to Odùduwà to justify their claim to the throne.

Odùduwà's role extended to the culture of the people, especially language and religion. It is believed that Odùduwà spoke the Yorùbá language, and all who identified with him spoke the same language.

Encyclopedia of the Yorùbá

However, because of the political expansion and divergence from Ilé-Ifè, there are now many dialects of the language. Because Odùduwà landed in Ilé-Ifè and was a priest-king, the town became a sacred place for the Yorùbá people. Odùduwà was deified after his death, and Ilé-Ifè has been recognized since as the religious center of the Yorùbá people. Adébánjí Akíntóyè states that even long after his death, "the collective imagination of the masses began to represent him as larger than life" (12).

Odùduwà was not "a mythical personage," as Samuel Johnson suggested. He was indeed a real human being who brought significant cultural and political change to the Yorùbá people. Odùduwà should be viewed as a conquering hero, a visionary, and a transformational figure, whose era marked the end of a decentralized arrangement and the beginning of a centralized political system. Many traditional rulers trace their origin and authority to rule directly or indirectly to Odùduwà and Ilé-Ifè. Because of his contributions to the development of the Yorùbá people, Odùduwà is acknowledged as a cultural hero, a central figure, and a force of cultural and political unity whose name remains conspicuous in Yorùbá history. The Odùduwà factor led to the formation of an ethnocultural association known as the Ẹgbẹ́ Ọmọ Odùduwà (Association of Odùduwà Descendants), founded in London in 1945. It transformed into a political party (Action Group) in 1951. Odùduwà continues to be a rallying point among the Yorùbá people for cultural, political, and social reasons.

See also **Awólọ́wọ̀, Ọbáfẹ́mi; Politics and Political Parties since 1945**

REFERENCES

Akíntóyè, Adébánjí S. *A History of the Yorùbá People*. Dakar (Senegal): Amalion Publishing, 2010.

Àtàndá, J. A. *An Introduction to Yorùbá History*. Ìbàdàn (Nigeria): University Press, 1980.

Johnson, Samuel. *The History of the Yorùbás*. Lagos, Nigeria: C.S.S., 1921.

Julius O. Adékúnlé

ỌDÚNJỌ, JOSEPH FỌLÁHÀN (1904–1980)

Joseph Fọláhàn Ọdúnjọ was the son of Chief Ọdúnjọ, the Ẹ̀kẹrin of Ìbarà, Abẹ́òkúta. He attended St. Augustine's Catholic School, Ìtésí, Abẹ́òkúta (1914–1920), the Catholic Teacher Training College Òkè Àrẹ, Ìbàdàn (1920–1924), and the Institute of Education, London University (1946–1947). From 1924 to 1951, he worked in the education sector as teacher, headmaster, senior tutor, and supervisor in the old Western Region of Nigeria. He was a music teacher; he composed *Àkànṣe Orin Ìbílẹ̀*, a collection of church hymns in Yorùbá traditional tunes.

He was also the founder and first president of the Federal Association of Catholic Teachers (1936–1951) and assistant secretary of the Nigerian Union of Teachers (1942–1951). As a unionist, he was involved in the struggle for independence. He was the Western Nigerian minister for lands and labor (1952–1956) and later agriculture director of Western Nigerian Development Corporation. In addition, on the religious front, Ọdúnjọ was the president of the Ìbàdàn Catholic Diocesan Council (1963–1976).

J. F. Ọdúnjọ's fame was, however, not directly derived from all these activities but primarily from his authorship of the Aláwíyé series of Yorùbá textbooks for primary and secondary schools. He took up the challenge when, during World War II, there was a serious shortage of the supply of Yorùbá-language reading materials. The first in the series of primary school textbooks, *Ìwé Kínní A. B. D. Aláwíyé*, was published in 1943. The six textbooks in the primary series and the two in the secondary series have been reviewed and reprinted many times. He also published his collection of poems, *Àkójọpọ̀ Ewì Aládùn*; most of the poems had first appeared in the Aláwíyé series. The collection included a very long poem titled "Májẹ̀mú Láàrin Ẹ̀gbá àti Ẹ̀gbádò," about the unity among the two Yorùbá subgroups. Very popular among his poems are "Tójú Ìwà rẹ," "Iṣẹ́ ni òògùn Ìṣẹ́," "Ìjà Ẹlédè àti Ìjàpá," "Bí orí ìjàpá ṣe pá," and the song "Kí ni Ng ó Folè ṣe." Ọdúnjọ also wrote two novels, *Ọmọ Òkú Ọrun* (1964) and *Kúyẹ* (1964), and coauthored the novel *Kàdárà àti Ẹ̀gbọ́n Rẹ*

(1967). He has one play to his credit, *Agbàlówómèrìí Baálè Jòntolo.*

His literary works, though primarily geared toward the school-aged audience, also have relevance for general audiences. The Yorùbá ethical values of *omolúwàbí* are a recurring theme in all his literary works, which make use of simple yet apt imageries and explore oral literary traditions. Odúnjo made notable contributions as an active member of both the 1966 and 1969 Orthography Committees.

In 1976, in recognition of his immense contributions, he was awarded the honorary degree of doctor of letters by the University of Ifè, now Obáfémi Awólówò University. He was also conferred with chieftaincy titles in appreciation of his contributions to society: Asíwájú of Ègbáland, Lémo of Ìwórò, and Olúwo of Irówò-Ìbàràpá.

See also **Literature: Modern and Written; Omolúwàbí; Prominent Scholars; Writers**

REFERENCE

Odúnjo, J. F. *Aláwíyé (Ìwé Kerin).* Lagos (Nigeria): Longman Nigeria Ltd., 1958.

Philip Adédòtun Ògúndèjì

ÒGÚNDÉ, HUBERT ADÉDÈJÌ (1916–1990)

Ògúndé, Hubert Adédèjì, the doyen of Nigerian theater, was born in 1916 at Òsòsà near Ìjèbú-Òde to the family of Jeremiah Dèhìnbò and Eunice Owátúsàn Ògúndé. Ògúndé grew up in a rich oral tradition, an experience that was to become an asset in his theater career later in his life. His grandfather, an *àràbà* (Ifá chief priest), raised him in the cultic traditions. While growing up around Ìjèbú, he occasionally performed with Eégún Aláré, Dáramójó Atete, and Èkùn Oko as a dancer and drummer. He attended St. John's School, Òsòsà; St. Peter's Fájì, Lagos; and Wásinmi African School, Ìjèbú-Òde. He started his carrier as a teacher and organist in 1933 before joining the Nigeria Police Force in March 1941. He worked in Ìbàdàn and Èbúté-Méta, Lagos, as a third-class constable.

On June 12, 1944, he produced his first opera, *The Garden of Eden and the Throne of God,* at Glover Memorial Hall in Lagos. In March 1945, he founded the African Music Research Party and resigned formally from the Nigeria Police Force. A year later, Ògúndé produced *Tiger's Empire.*

Ògúndé was a nationalist who employed theater as a tool for fighting colonialism. A number of his plays, such as *Worse Than Crime, Strike and Hunger, Tiger's Empire,* and *Bread and Bullet,* were acerbic satires of the colonial administration. The administration punished him with fines and detained and incarcerated him at various times. After independence, in March 1964, his theater company was banned by the government of the Western Region for staging *Yorùbá Ronú,* a satire of the political situation in the region. Ògúndé traveled with his plays to different parts of Nigeria and West Africa. He also performed in Canada, United States, and Great Britain.

A multitalented and dynamic actor, singer, composer, drummer, dancer, dramatist, director, and theater manager, Ògúndé frequently changed his corporate name, revised and modernized his performance styles, and adapted available media in his performances to boost his image. A pioneer in many respects, he was the first indigenous dramatist to perform his play on radio when he appeared on the Lagos Radio Rediffusion Service in July 1945. His was also the first play to be aired on the Western Nigeria Television. Songs from his opening and closing glees were among the first of their kind to appear on Phonodisc. In 1967, when the *Atóka* photoplay magazine was established, *Yorùbá Ronú* was featured on the first cover. His celluloid films *Aiyé* (1979), *Jáiyésinmi* (1980), *Àròpin n Tènìà* (1981), and *Àyànmó* (1988) were also popular.

Ògúnde founded the Union of Nigerian Dramatists and Playwrights in 1971. He established a drama village in Òsòsà. The Obáfémi Awólówò University, Ilé-Ifè awarded him an honorary doctor of letters degree in 1988. Posthumously, he was honored as one of the one hundred eminent Nigerians during the centenary celebration by President Jonathan in 2014.

See also **Drama; Prominent Scholars**

REFERENCE

Clark, Èbùn. *Hubert Ogunde: The Making of Nigerian Theatre.* Oxford: Oxford University Press, in association with University Press Limited, 1979.

Philip Adédòtun Ògúndèjì

ỌMỌLÚWÀBÍ (ỌMỌLÚÀBÍ)

In folk etymology, Ọmọlúwàbí or *Ọmọ tí Olú Ìwà bí* means one the god of character gave birth to. *Ọmọ inú ìwà* means a child from the bosom of Ìwà. Odùduwà, believed to be the grand progenitor of the Yorùbá, is linked to the creation of Ìwà. He is *Odù tí ó dá ìwà sí lẹ̀* (the god who brought character into existence). Thus, the culture is anchored on the principle of *ọmọlúwàbí,* clean character and good behavior. Hence, a ladylike or gentlemanlike quality is *ìwà ọmọlúwàbí,* and the person who manifests such character is an Ọmọlúwàbí.

There are two main anthropomorphic characterization of Ìwà. One refers to Ìwà as *ọmọ bíbí inú Olódùmarè* (the natural child of Olódùmarè), the Supreme Deity. Thus, anyone who lacks *ìwà* cannot have any meaningful relationship with Olódùmarè in life and in the afterlife because such a person has rejected Olódùmarè in his or her blood and flesh. Another characterization focuses on Ìwà, the wife of Ọ̀rúnmìlà, the oracular divinity. She abandoned her husband because of his constant physical abuse. She returned to the home of her father, Sùúrù (Patience), who was thought to be the son of Olódùmarè. In either tradition, Ìwà is a female figure directly related by blood to Olódùmarè.

The corollary is that the Yorùbá see a divine connection, or a form of divinity or godliness, in being a person of good character. All of life's attributes are transient except Ìwà. Thus, it is said *ìwà níí bá ni dé sàréè, owó kò dé'bi kankan* ([One's] character is what accompanies one to the grave; wealth does not go any far). Ìwà can be broken down as *Ì* (the act, fact or totality of) and *wà* (being or existing), and so it means "the act of being, the fact of existence, wholeness, and the totality of humanness." *Mo wà bí ẹ̀wà* (I am as I can be) is a common utterance, akin to René Descartes's phrase "cogito ego sum." Thus, when a Yorùbá person says *mo wà* or *wọ́n wà,* he or she makes a declarative confession of wholeness and existence, the corollary of which implies both physical and moral wholeness and existence. Yorùbá people believe that the confession or profession of any faith, religion, or creed is of no value if the individual is a person without moral character. In other words, the sanctity of any religion manifests in good character. Thus, the saying, *ìwà lẹ́sin* (Ìwà is another name for religious devotion) is a truism. Indeed, reference to the virtue of *ìwàpẹ̀lẹ́* (gentleness), is common among the people. There is nothing a person possesses that has any value without good moral character. Thus, it makes sense to look for *ìwà* rather than anything else. A common Ifá verse says:

Owó lo ní tóò ní'wà, owó olówó ni
Ìwà, Ìwà là ń wá, Ìwà.
Ọmọ lo ní tóò ní'wà, ọmọ ọlọ́mọ ni,
Ìwà, Ìwà là ń wá, Ìwà.

If you have money without character, it's other people's money,
Character: character is what we should look for, character.
If you have children without character, they are other people's children,
Character: character is what we should look for, character.

See also **Children's Folklore: Education and Development; Education: Traditional; Ethics**

REFERENCES

Abímbọ́lá, Wándé. "Ìwàpẹ̀lẹ́: The Concept of Good Character in Ifá Literary Corpus." In *Yorùbá Oral Tradition: Poetry in Music, Dance and Drama,* ed. Wándé Abímbọ́lá, 389–420. Ilé-Ifẹ̀ (Nigeria): Department of African Languages and Literatures, University of Ifẹ̀, 1975.

Awóníyì, T. A. "Ọmọlúwàbí: The Fundamental Basis of Yorùbá Education." In *Yorùbá Oral Tradition: Poetry in Music, Dance and Drama,* ed. Wándé Abímbọ́lá, 357–88. Ilé-Ifẹ̀ (Nigeria): Department of African Languages and Literatures, University of Ifẹ̀, 1975.

Michael Ọládẹ̀jọ Afọláyan

The Oòduà People's Congress (OPC) was formed in 1994 as a sociocultural organization to protect and advance the interests of the Yorùbá people. Named after Odùduwà, the mythological progenitor of the Yorùbá race, it was founded by Dr. Fredrick Fáṣehun, a medical practitioner whose professional base was in Lagos State. The OPC was one of the various militant organizations that came into existence during General Sanni Abacha's reign of terror in Nigeria. The organization operates a hierarchical structure, with cells at the local level and zones at the national levels. Members are made to take oaths, vowing not to become involved in criminal activities.

Against the backdrop of state-sponsored assassination and persecutions of the Yorùbá in the aftermath of the annulment of June 12, 1993, presidential elections, the agitation for reinstating the election results, especially in southwestern Nigeria, OPC became a group to protect the Yorùbá from further harassment, intimidation, and destruction. Its goals were to protect, preserve, and advance Yorùbá cultural heritage, values, and interests in Nigeria and in the Diaspora. It boasts of seven million members at home and abroad. Membership in the organization also cuts across social, religious, political, and economic divides. There are two factions within the OPC, the first controlled by the founder Chief Fáṣehun, and the other controlled by Ọ̀túnba Gàní Adams.

The arrest and incarceration of OPC's founder led to a violent turn in the modus operandi of the organization. Cases of violent clashes of OPC members and Hausa communities in Lagos and Ògùn States in 2004 and 2006 left many casualties in its trail. OPC has also attempted to reclaim the traditional positions of the Yorùbá in Ìlọrin, Kwara State, from descendants of the Fulani.

The relevance of the OPC as a mass movement, sociocultural organization finds expression in the failure of the Nigerian state to provide adequate security for the citizens. The centralization of the high command of the police makes effective policing an extremely difficult task at the state and local government levels. Consequently, armed robbery, ritual killing, kidnapping, and other forms of threat to peaceful existence have been rampant in different parts of Nigeria. The mass appeal that the OPC had and still commands to a reasonable extent can then be located in the security that they provide in different parts of the Yorùbáland.

In its bid to project Yorùbá cultural values, OPC has been involved in organizing various festivals across most of the Yorùbá states that make up the Nigerian nation, including the Ọ̀ṣun Òṣogbo festival in Ọ̀ṣun State, Olókun festival in Lagos State, Òkòtà festival in Oǹdó State, Òkè'Bàdàn festival in Ọ̀yọ́ state, Olúmọ and Lísàbi festivals in Ògùn state, Òrànmíyàn festival in Ọ̀yọ́ state, and Oya festival in Kwara state.

REFERENCE

Adébámwí, Wálé. *Yorùbá Elites and Ethnic Politics: Ọbáfẹ́mi Awólọ́wọ̀ and Corporate Agency.* New York: Cambridge University Press, 2014.

Samuel O. Ọlọ́runtọ́ba

Ò̤NI OF IFẸ̀

The Ọọni of Ifẹ̀ is the spiritual and political title of the traditional monarch of Ilé-Ifẹ̀. Mythology suggests that the creation of the world begun from Ilé-Ifẹ̀. Odùduwà, the acclaimed founder of kingdom settled first at Ilé-Ifẹ̀ as the first Ọọni of Ifẹ̀. His palace was built in this ancient city of southwestern Nigeria, in present-day Ọ̀ṣun State. There is evidence that urbanization was present in the city around 500 CE.

Seniority of Ọọni of Ifẹ̀ in Yorùbáland

All the Yorùbá kingdoms maintain connections with Ilé-Ifẹ̀, although this is often from a spiritual than a political point of view. It is also common that all sons and grandsons of Odùduwà and the succeeding kings of their various tribal kingdoms have preserved this kinship through periodic renewal of contacts with the ancestral spirit at Ilé-Ifẹ̀. Not surprisingly, even the disputed recent version of the Bini history, which claimed that Odùduwà hailed from Bini and was a fugitive prince at Ilé-Ifẹ̀ where he made home, alludes to the fact that Odùduwà was a king in Ilé-Ifẹ̀ and that he reigned as a leader of Yorùbá people.

Nevertheless, the reputed seniority of Ilé-Ifẹ̀ being the cradle of the Yorùbá people conferred similar honor to the Ọọ̀ni on the Ifẹ̀ throne but did not suggest its supremacy over above other Yorùbá rulers. Each ọba (king), as a son of Odùduwà, is sovereign in his own kingdom; kings wear the beaded crown from Ilé-Ifẹ̀ and have military and political powers over their territory. Ifẹ̀, however, had no such political or military influence on them; it is only regarded as the cradle of the race. The list of the names of Ọọ̀ni of Ifẹ̀ from Odùduwà to the incumbent include the following:

1. Odùduwà
2. Ọsángangan
3. Ọbamakin
4. Ògún
5. Ọbalùfọ̀n Ògbògbòdirin
6. Ọbalùfọ̀n Aláyémọrẹ
7. Òrànmíyàn
8. Ayétiṣe
9. Lájàmìsán
10. Lajodoògùn
11. Láfogídò
12. Òdìdìmọdẹ̀ Rógbeeṣin
13. Aworokolokin
14. Ẹkùn
15. Ajímúdà
16. Gbooníjió
17. Ọ̀kánlàjọsin
18. Adégbálù
19. Ọ̀sínkọ́lá
20. Ògboòrú
21. Gíẹ̀sì
22. Lúwoo
23. Lúmodi
24. Agbẹdẹgbẹ́dẹ̀
25. Ọjẹ̀lokunbìrin
26. Lágùnjà
27. Lárùnká
28. Ọmọgbogbo
29. Àjílà-Ororun
30. Adéjinlẹ̀
31. Ọlọ́jọ́
32. Okiti
33. Lúgbade
34. Aríbiwọṣo
35. Ọ̀sínlade
36. Adagba
37. Òjígìdiri
38. Akínmóyèré (1823–1835)
39. Gbanlare (1835–1839)
40. Adégúnsẹ̀ Adéwẹlá (1839–1849)
41. Dẹgbinsókun (1849–1878)
42. Ọrarigba (1878–1880)
43. Derin Ọlọ́gbẹ́ńlá (1880–1894)
44. Adélẹ́kàn Olúbùṣe I (1894–1910)
45. Adékọ́lá (1910–1910)
46. Adémilúyì Ajagun (1910–1930)
47. Adésọjí Adérẹ̀mí (1930–1980)
48. Okùnadé Ṣíjúadé Olúbùṣe II (1980–2015)
49. Adéyẹyè Ẹnitàn Ògúnwùsì (2015–)

See also Ifẹ̀ Kingdom; Ilé-Ifẹ̀

REFERENCE

Fádípẹ̀, N. A. The Sociology of the Yorùbá. Ìbàdàn (Nigeria): University Press, 1970.

Samson O. Ìjàọlá

ORAL TRADITION

Oral tradition describes oral cultural materials such as ballads and chants, folktales and songs, and witty sayings that are transmitted by word of mouth from one generation to another. As cultural material, all members of a community shared in the oral tradition. Oral tradition documents, preserves, and transmits knowledge and culture, history, literature, law, and ethos. Although oral tradition is more common in societies without any system of writing, oral tradition is a feature of both literate and nonliterate societies.

Although various forms of writing existed in different parts of Africa before colonial rule, it was not until the colonial period that writing developed in Yorùbáland. Before the nineteenth century, the Yorùbá people documented, preserved, and transmitted their cultural materials from one generation to another orally. Among other things, histories of origin are preserved in oral materials.

Two general traditions existed among Yorùbá people regarding their origin. In one account, the people were said to have been created by God (Olódùmarè) and sent down from heaven to populate the world. It was from Ilé-Ifẹ̀ that the entire Yorùbá race originated. In yet another tradition, the people were believed to have migrated from somewhere in the east to Ilé-Ifẹ̀. Odùduwà, in the two traditions, was at the head of this celestial band or migrant group. In addition to these traditions, folklores, stories, songs, and the like abound, attesting to how Yorùbá people documented and shared both secular and esoteric knowledge through its oral tradition. For instance, a number of enactments at Ilé-Ifẹ̀ celebrated both the coming of Odùduwà and his band of celestial beings and Odùduwà and his groups of migrants.

Oral traditions are used to teach moral lessons, valor, and life lessons. Given the importance of oral tradition to the Yorùbá people, efforts have been made to ensure veracity of the traditions. Hence, in Ọ̀yọ́, a group of trained local historians (arọ́kin) were associated with the royal court. Their duty was not only to document and preserve oral traditions but also to make available these cultural materials when needed and then transmit them across generations.

Criticism of oral tradition ranges from human's inability to recall information after a long time, bias, embellishment, and exaggeration. Notwithstanding these inherent weaknesses, historians have argued that, by combining oral traditions with evidence from other sources such as archaeology, oral stories can reveal dependable historical truths. Notwithstanding its weaknesses, the richness of oral tradition has helped historians correct the popular Eurocentric impression that Africa had no history until the arrival of the Europeans.

See also **Bards: Old and New; Culture; History; Odùduwà**

REFERENCE

Johnson, Samuel. *The History of the Yorùbás.* Lagos (Nigeria): C.S.S., 1921.

Bùkọ́lá Oyèníyì

ORALITY AND LITERACY

Yorùbá language has been in use across the West African coast as a language of trade since before colonization. Today, it is an international language spoken in òrìṣà religious worship in Brazil, Argentina, Cuba, the West Indies, and the United States. At least twenty-two dialects of the language are spoken in Nigeria, where people engage in interpersonal communication, greetings, moral and skill education, traditional religious and passages rites, governance, adjudication, and entertainment.

The language has expanded through contact with outside cultures and through efforts at standardization. Today, its oral and written forms are used for worship in the new religions (Islam and Christianity), democratic government (for campaigns and for business in houses of assembly), for formal education (from primary school to university), and mass communication (print and electronic media). Its use in the contemporary entertainment industry has reached an enviable level in the performing arts of music and drama, especially video movies.

Yorùbá rhetoric relies on rich literary tropes based on cultural cues from Yorùbá traditions. In general, most greetings, honorific pronouns, and other terms of respect, particularly regarding elders, are obligatory. Other aspects of Yorùbá rhetoric include phonoaesthetics and other types of wordplay, stylistic repetitions, parallelism, lexical matching, and sense balancing. In addition, oral poetry (in speech, chants, and song modes) and oral narrative types are explored in oral and written communications.

The language was first committed to writing in 1817 by Thomas Edward Bowdich. A serious study of the language began in Sierra Leone by freed slaves and non-African missionaries and scholars. Of great significance was the contribution of the Church Missionary Society (CMS), under whose auspices many missionaries made contributions to developing the written Yorùbá language. Prominent participants in the fashioning of its orthography and, by implication, its literacy include Hannah Kilham, John Raban, Henry Venn, Henry Townsend, A. C. Gollmer, David Hindrer, Àjàyí Crowther, Max Mubler, John Bowen, R. Koelle, D. Schon, Carl Lepsius, and Edwin Norris. Their robust discussions on how properly to script the language culminated in the 1875 conference in Lagos, precursor to the 1966, 1969, and 1974 committees that reviewed Yorùbá orthography.

Production of reading materials and teaching in the Yorùbá language started in Sierra Leone and continued in Yorùbáland when the missionaries and the freed slave community finally settled in Nigeria. Crowther took the lead in translating the Bible; he also wrote primers, grammar books, and vocabularies that served as foundation of a dictionary published by the CMS. Many other literary works and newspapers were published in Yorùbá, which played a prominent role in popularizing reading culture. Many of the literary works were first serialized in newspapers before they were published. Today, a huge library of Yorùbá literature exists. Yorùbá is studied in graduate schools in Nigerian universities.

See also **Language: Government and Mission Policies; Language: Standardization and Literacy; Translation**

REFERENCES

Ògúnṣínà, Bísí. *The Development of the Yorùbá Novel c. 1930–1975.* Ìlọrin (Nigeria): Gospel Faith Mission Press, 1992.

Ọlábímtán, Afọlábí. "A Critical Survey of Yorùbá Written Poetry, 1848–1948." Unpublished PhD dissertation, University of Lagos, Lagos (Nigeria) 1974.

Philip Adédọtun Ògúndèjì

ÒṢOGBO: ÒṢUN AND THE ART SCHOOL

Òṣogbo is known as the town of dyes (*ìlú aró*) because indigo-dyed cloth is the predominant traditional craft there. Òṣogbo is a historically significant town in Yorùbáland; it is the capital of Òṣun State. It is the sacred site of Òṣun, the river and fertility goddess, whose followers can be found throughout Yorùbáland and the Diaspora. According to tradition, in the 1840s, Òṣun and her sacred river saved Yorùbá territory from being overrun by invading Fulani Islamic jihadists.

Òṣogbo is also home to a rich tradition of art and creative endeavors, both traditional and modern. The traditional crafts of cloth dyeing, metal smithing, beadwork, mud and wood sculpture, calabash carving, and leather work coexist with modern crafts such as cement and stone sculpture, mural decoration, and art forms in various media. The history of Òṣogbo art, as in other African countries, was shaped by colonial experiences and European contact, reflecting rebirth, renewal, and innovation. Change and transformation were inevitable, resulting in a remarkable artistic renaissance and growth in artistic endeavors.

The traditional culture of the town coupled with the efforts of art enthusiasts, both local and international, coalesced in the creation of the Òṣogbo Art School. In 1962, Ulli Beier and Susanne Wenger opened the first art school at the suggestion of Dúró Ládipọ̀ who offered his bar as a space for the experiment. Having started a successful venture with the Mbárí-Mbáyọ̀ Artists and Writers Club at Ìbàdàn, Beier teamed with Georgina Bretts (later Georgina Beier), a British artist, in 1964 to run a second art school in the town. Dennis Williams joined the duo and facilitated an experimental workshop at Òṣogbo. Important artists in that workshop include Jacob Afọlábí, Rufus Ògúndélé, Táíwò Ọláníyì (Twins Seven Seven), Bísí Fábùnmi, Jimoh Bùráímọ̀h, and Múráínà Oyèlámì. Later, others such as Áṣírù Ọlátúndé, the aluminum smith, and Níkè Davies-Òkúndaiyè, a batik artist, joined the experimental art workshop. Many of these artists became quite accomplished and were celebrated both at home and abroad. Some, like Níkè Davies-Òkúndaiyè, went on to open other institutions, establishing art centers, galleries, and workshops in Lagos, Òṣogbo, Ogidi, and Abuja.

As the years went by, the school expanded to include father and son Yínká and Kọ́lá Adéyẹmí, Adéníji Adéyẹmí, Isaac Akíndélé, Prince Láyí Orogún Adémọinọrẹ, Tòròmádé Fàtáì, Tóyìn Fọ́lọ́runṣọ́ (grandson of Áṣírù Ọlátúndé), Àrèmú Jimoh, Adémọ́lá Oníbọnòkúta, Túndé Ọdúnladé, Adémọ́lá Oyèlámì, Báyọ̀ Ògúndélé, Jìnádù Ọládépọ̀, and Phillip Olúfẹ́mi Babárìnlọ. Others students include Yẹ̀kínì Fọ́lọ́runṣọ́, Rahmon Olúgúnnà, Bàshírù Ọpábọ́lá, and David Osevwe. All these artists and others emerged from the Òṣogbo art movement. The convergence of local and foreign artists, artisans, dramatists, and writers transformed Òṣogbo into the symbolic capital of multicultural communion.

Artists at the Òṣogbo Art School drew some of their creative inspiration from Yorùbá culture, especially folktales and deities. Cornelius Adépégba describes much of the school's artistic production as "raw art" that reflects uninhibited creativity and a naive vision. Artists there worked with different media including oil colors, ink, beads, cloth and local dyes, cement, metal foil, and aluminum. Supporters and patrons provide avenues for the display of the artists' works, and they facilitate local and international recognition for the artists in the art world. The school's first exhibition was held at the Goethe-Institut in Lagos in the 1960s. Beier used his political capital to get the works of the artists exhibited in other locations, including the Thursday Show, held in the home of Jean Kennedy and Dick Wolford, and other exhibitions at the Ìwàlẹ̀wà Haus, Bayreuth, Germany. Consequently, local and international patrons and collectors began to seek out the artists. Beier's book *Black Orpheus* was one of the earliest published works on artists at the school. Scholars and critics have published other works, and biographical and autobiographical works have been written about individual artists of the school. Beier also helped document Yorùbá history, culture, arts, and religion through photographs and collecting other materials. Much of his collection is held at the Centre for Black Culture and International Understanding in Òṣogbo.

The works of the Òṣogbo artists can be found in private and institutional collections, including Yẹ́misí Shyllon, who claims to have the largest collection of the works from the Òṣogbo Art School, Ìwàlẹ̀wà-Haus, Universität Bayreuth, and the Institute of African Studies, University of Ìbàdàn.

One artist who made significant contribution to Òṣogbo art is Susanne Graz Wenger. She graduated from the Vienna Academy and moved to Òṣogbo in the 1950s with Ulli Beier, her former husband. She was skilled in ancient fresco technique and had produced several landscape studies, pottery, and animal sculptures before coming to Òṣogbo. She became famous for her impressionistic cement sculptures used to decorate the Òṣun Òṣogbo groove. The sacred site that sits on several acres of land became both Wenger's artistic and spiritual space. Wenger became an *Ajagemọ*, an Òṣun priestess. In her role as priestess, she formally became a custodian of the grove and was committed to

beautify it, a task that she took on with religious intensity until her death in 2009. The artisans who collaborated with her in the transformation and restoration of Òṣun grove include Adébísí Àkànjí, Làmídì Arúìsá, Rábíù Adéṣù, and Sàká and Bùráímọ̀h Gbàdàmọ́ṣí. The shrines and the house that she built were declared national monuments by the Nigerian Government in 1987. In 2005, UNESCO declared the grove a World Heritage Site.

Contemporary Nigerian artists of Yorùbá origin influenced by the Òṣogbo Art School include members of the Ọnà Art Movement and graduates of Ifẹ̀ Art School, namely Moyọ̀ Òkédìjí, Bọ́lájí Campbell, Kúnlé Fìlání, Túndé Náṣírù, Tọ́lá Wẹ́wẹ̀, Wọlé Lágúnjú, and Múfú Onífádé. Onífádé created the art movement Àràism.

REFERENCES

Adépégba, Cornelius, ed. *Òṣogbo: Model of Growing African Towns.* Ìbàdàn (Nigeria): University Press, 1995.
Probst, Peter. *Òṣogbo and the Art of Heritage: Monuments, Deities, and Money.* Bloomington: Indiana University Press, 2011.

Adérónkẹ́ Adéṣọlá Adésànyà

OTHER NIGERIAN GROUPS AMONG THE YORÙBÁ

The ecology of Yorùbáland, according to J. A. Àtàndá, is quite favorable for human settlement, movement, and development. Hence, Yorùbáland is home not just to the Yorùbá-speaking people but also to other African groups who have settled, in the course of time, in various towns and cities in Yorùbáland. Immigration by other African groups has been encouraged by economic need, strategic location of a particular town or city, infrastructural development, and a favorable ecology and climate, among other factors. Developments in rail and road networks and other infrastructure facilities also contributed immensely to rural-urban migration of skilled and semiskilled workers, traders, and students searching for opportunities in Yorùbá-speaking cities like Abẹ́òkúta, Ìbàdàn, Lagos, and Àkúrẹ̀.

Other Nigerian ethnic groups who live among the Yorùbá are the Igbo, Hausa, Fulani, Idoma, Tiv, Edo,

Ebira, Esan, Bini, Urhobo, Itsekiri, and the Ijaw people. These ethnic groups have made their home among the Yorùbá for a variety of reasons. For instance, the Igbo people, who are from southeastern Nigeria, are renowned for their entrepreneurial interest; they migrate to other lands to advance business opportunities. The Igbo are found in virtually every part of southwestern Nigeria, where they have invested resources in various business enterprises. The Hausa and Fulani from northern Nigeria have also established communities among the Yorùbá, where they are able to operate cattle ranches that provide meat and dairy products. Their settlements are known as *sábó*, an indigenous Hausa structure. *Sábó* can be seeing in various towns and cities. M. M. Gatawa notes that relations between the Hausa and Yorùbá people began in the eighteenth century in the Agege area of Lagos.

The Ijaw people are a prominent group from the Niger-Delta region of Nigeria, and they have settled near bodies of water in southwestern Nigeria, which reflects their maritime lifestyle. Although they are originally from the delta states, Bayelsa, Akwa-Ibom, and River of Nigeria, they have been assimilated into the coastal regions of Lagos and Ondó States where they engage in fishing and other water-based ventures. In southeastern Ondó State, the Ijaw are further divided into the Apoi and Arogbo ethnic subgroups.

Migration from countries outside of Yorùbáland is also prevalent, especially since the oil boom that boosted the economy of Nigeria. Thus, migrants from Côte d'Ivoire, Cameroon, Ghana, Togo, Senegal, and other places have come to settle in various Yorùbá towns and cities.

REFERENCES

Àtàndá, J. A. "The Yorùbá People: Their Origin, Culture, and Civilization." In *The Yorùbá: History Culture and Language*, ed. O. O. Olátúnjí, 1–33. Ìbàdàn (Nigeria): University Press, 1996.

Gordon, A. A. *Nigeria's Diverse Peoples: A Reference Sourcebook*. Santa Barbara, CA: ABC-CLIO, 2003.

Chinyere Ukpokolo

Òwu is the name of a precolonial state as well as a sub-Yorùbá group with deep roots. According to traditions, Ajíbósìn, the father of Òwu, was a son of predynastic Obàtálá in Ilé-Ifè. The ascendancy of the Odùduwà group led to the exodus of Ajíbósìn and his group to found a new settlement at Òwu Ìpólé, which eventually became the chief town of the Òwu Kingdom.

Traditions record nothing about Òwu after its defeat around the fifteenth century by Òyó until its reemergence in the southern forest as major player in Yorùbá sociopolitical and economic life. At Òwu Ìpólé, the state soon developed a reputation for prowess in warfare and for plundering weaker neighbors. Òwu soldiers became famous for their skill with the *agédéńgbé*, then the best-known weapon of contact warfare. Imbued with legendary fighting spirit, Òwu had, by the sixteenth century, emerged as the strongest southern Yorùbá state, with claims over some Òyó territories.

Òwu Settlements

By the 1830s, the Òwu kingdom had been destroyed by a combined army of Ifè, Ìjèbú, and Òyó refugees in war provoked by a combination of economic and political factors. The Òwu War touched off a series of interstate wars in the nineteenth century. A major consequence of the defeat of Òwu in 1826 was the dispersal of Òwu people into different parts of Yorùbáland. Indeed, an interdict was placed on the capital, Òwu Ìpólé, that it must never be rebuilt or reoccupied. However, the capital was eventually reoccupied ninety-two years later.

At present, Òwu remains distinct as a Yorùbá subgroup in spite of their presence in virtually all Yorùbáland. Òwu settlements exist in five states in southwestern Nigeria, and the largest concentration of the people can be found among the Ègbá in Abéòkúta. In Ògùn State, there are Òwu Abéòkúta, Akínhalè, Lápeléke, Òwu Ìjí, Apòmù Òwu Ewékorò, and Òwu Ifò among the Ègbá. The Òwu settled in the midst of Ìjèbú are Òwu Ìjèbú (Òwu Ìkijà), Òmù Èléní, Odòlówu Ìjèbú,

Odòlówu Ayépé Ìjẹbú, Òkè Sọpẹ́n (Òwu Ìjẹbú Igbó), and Òwu Òkè Olówu. Òwu settlements in Ọ̀sun State include Orílé Òwu, Òwu Ilé, Òwu Ẹ̀pẹ́, Kúta, Telemù, Ilémòwu, Ọ̀gbaáàgbà, Òwu Ilé Ogbó, Òkè Òwu in Gbọ̀ngán, Òkè Òwu in Modákéké, Òwu quarters in Ìwó, Òwu quarters in Èjìgbò, Òwu Àjáwà, and Olú Òwu compound in Ọdẹ Òmu.

In Ọ̀yọ́ State, Òwu quarters are located within Ọ̀yọ́ town, Oníkèkẹ́ near Ògbómọ̀ṣọ́, Ańlẹ̀ Wọlà compound in Ṣakí, Òwu quarters in Ìlerò, Òwu in Ẹ̀rùnmu, and Òwu quarters in Ìbàdàn. Similarly, among the Ìgbómìnà in Kwara State, three major Òwu settlements exist: Òwu Ìsin, Òwu Ọbalóyan, and Igbó Òwu. Three others are located within larger communities in Òwu Sàó, Òwu Òkèìyá Ìpo, and Òwu Òkè Ọdẹ. Lastly, Òwu Ìkọsí, Òwu Gbáwójọ, Òkè Olówu Mushin, and Òwu Ishẹ́ri are in Lagos State.

Òwu are particular about group identity and in 1992, the Diaspora's consciousness led to the establishment of Òwu National Union as a platform to negotiate Òwu's stake in the allocation of resources and opportunities in Yorùbáland.

REFERENCES

Àlàó, Akin. "Òwu an Early Yoruba State, 1600–1826." *Ifẹ: Annals of the Institute of Cultural Studies* 6 (1995): 60–74.
Johnson, Samuel. *The History of the Yorùbás.* Lagos (Nigeria): C.S.S., 1921.

Akin Àlàó

Ọ̀YỌ́ EMPIRE

Odùduwà, the ancestor of all the Yorùbá people, had many children, but one of his grandsons, Ọ̀rányàn, is credited as the founder of the Ọ̀yọ́ Empire. Samuel Johnson described Ọ̀rányàn as "a very brave and warlike Prince, and of an indomitable courage." The Yorùbá established numerous kingdoms, but the Ọ̀yọ́ Empire was the largest, strongest, and wealthiest. It reached the zenith of its power and glory in the eighteenth century. Other kingdoms were located in the forest region; the Ọ̀yọ́ Empire was the only one in the savanna, which enabled its expansion through the development of agriculture and trade. By participating in the trans-Saharan trade with the Hausa people to the north, the Ọ̀yọ́ Empire was able to procure horses to develop its cavalry. In the process of political expansion, the Ọ̀yọ́ Empire was engaged in military encounters with contiguous non-Yorùbá kingdoms, such as Borgu, Dahomey, and Nupe, and extracted tribute from them. Ọ̀yọ́ Empire's territory was contiguous, its people were heterogeneous, and their language was mutually intelligible.

The political organization of the Ọ̀yọ́ Empire was based on monarchical, hierarchical, and bureaucratic arrangement. The *aláàfin*, whose position was hereditary and sacred, and whose success depended largely on his bravery in wars, charisma, and wit, headed the centralized government. The position of the *aláàfin* was sacred. Therefore, he was regarded as inviolate, and his words and decisions were authoritative, final, and irrevocable. He ruled through courtiers, a council of chiefs (Ọ̀yọ́ Mèsì), and the Ògbóni society. Theoretically, the *aláàfin* was an absolute ruler and loyalty to him by his administrative officials and subordinate rulers was imperative. In practice, there was a constitutional arrangement of checks and balances that prevented the *aláàfin*'s use of arbitrary powers. The Ọ̀yọ́ Mèsì also held hereditary positions. They were kingmakers who, like the *aláàfin*, resided in the metropolis. They represented "the voice of the nation," and the *aláàfin* had to consult them on important matters of state. In the subordinate areas were chiefs who were responsible for maintaining law and order, contributing contingents of soldiers for the imperial army, and paying tribute to the *aláàfin*.

Kàtúngà, the capital, was strategically located for commercial purposes. With the openness of the region, commercial enterprise flourished and revenue was derived from taxes on trade. The most important articles of trade were slaves of divergent origin. Indeed, the empire's economy was dependent on domestic slave labor. As a result of trade, Muslim merchants from the north created a community in Kàtúngà and the provincial town of Ìlọrin. The Ọ̀yọ́ Empire, according to I. A. Akínjógbìn, "was a great deal more adventurous from the start." Military campaigns against neighbors such as the Borgu and Nupe peoples required strong leadership and called for the development of a formidable army. During the second half of the fifteenth century, the Nupe sacked Kàtúngà (Ọ̀yọ́-Ilé or Old Ọ̀yọ́), forcing Aláàfin Onígbogí to abandon it to take refuge in Borgu. S. O. Badà, the Ṣakí local historian, attributed the defeat of the Yorùbá by the Nupe to the maladministration of Aláàfin Onígbogí, which prompted his subjects to not only revolt but to also invite the Nupe for military assistance to overthrow him.

The period of the aláàfin's exile led to extensive Borgu-Yorùbá interethnic relations. According to R. C. C. Law, Onígbogí married the daughter of a Borgu king. Thus, with the abandonment of Ọ̀yọ́-Ilé, he and his followers sought refuge with his father-in-law. Onígbogí was allowed to establish himself in the Borgu town of Gbẹrẹ or Gbẹrẹgburu (on the Teshi River). According to Johnson, Onígbogí died at Gbẹrẹ, and Òfinràn, whose mother was the Borgu princess, succeeded him. This royal marriage alliance strengthened the Yorùbá-Borgu relations only within the period of the aláàfin's stay.

After leaving Borgu, the aláàfin and his entourage founded Ìgbòho, which became a temporary capital of the Ọ̀yọ́ Empire. The Borgu people organized several raids leading to the construction of three strong safety walls around Ìgbòho. At Ìgbòho, Ọ̀rọ̀mpọ̀tọ̀, a female ruler, succeeded to the throne as the aláàfin, reorganized the army, and introduced a number of military tactics. She introduced the use of gbájù leaf to obliterate the footprints of the infantry and cavalry soldiers in order to prevent enemies from trailing them, and she introduced the use of a cavalry. With one thousand infantry and one thousand cavalry soldiers, for the first time since the evacuation of Ọ̀yọ́-Ilé, the Yorùbá prevailed over the Borgu at the battle of Ìlayì. Eventually, Kàtúngà was reoccupied during the reign of Aláàfin Àbípa.

The Ọ̀yọ́ Empire was at the height of its power during the reign of Aláàfin Abíọ́dún (1774–1789). After him, weak rulers succeeded the throne, and the empire declined. The aláàfin's power waned, the military

became weak, the slave-based economy collapsed, and there were challenges from powerful neighbors. The most damaging factor was Àfọ̀njá's revolt, which led to the intervention of Muslim jihadists. Àfọ̀njá was the Ààrẹ-Ọ̀nà-Kakànfò (army commander); in an attempt to create a kingdom for himself, he asked the Fulani Muslim Álímì for help. The invitation was quickly accepted, since the Muslims saw it as an opportunity to spread Islam to the south. The Ọ̀yọ́ Empire could not withstand the onslaught of the militant and determined jihadists. Thus, in 1837, the Ọ̀yọ́ capital was sacked and the aláàfin had to relocate in the present site of Ọ̀yọ́ town. Abandoning the capital meant the reestablishment of the empire's power and restoring the authority of the aláàfin over his subjects. Since the attack by the Muslims, Ọ̀yọ́ could not recover its erstwhile power and dominance and by the nineteenth century the whole of Yorùbáland was engulfed in a series of civil wars.

REFERENCES

Akínjógbìn, I. A., and E. A. Àyándélé. "Yorùbáland up to 1800." In Groundwork of Nigerian History, ed. Obaro Ikime, 121–40. Ìbàdàn: Heinemann, 1980.

Johnson, Samuel. The History of the Yorùbás. Ìbàdàn: C. S. S., 1921.

Law, R. C. C. The Ọ̀yọ́ Empire, c. 1600–1836: A West African Imperialism in the Era of the Atlantic Slave Trade. Oxford: Oxford University Press, 1977.

Smith, Robert. "The Alafin in Exile: A Study of the Ìgbòho Period in Ọ̀yọ́ History." Journal of African History 6.1 (1965): 51–62.

Julius O. Adékúnlé

Ọ̀YỌ́TÚNJÍ: THE YORÙBÁ COMMUNITY IN THE UNITED STATES

Founded in 1970 by Walter Eugene "Serge" King, Ọ̀yọ́túnjí African Village is located near Sheldon, Beaufort County, South Carolina. King was a black nationalist who found in separatist ideology the solution to his fervent search for a black cultural identity in the 1960s. While this separatist ideology was rooted in the black national identity movement of the turbulent 1950s and 1960s, its uniqueness lies in the fact that King eschewed mere rhetoric. He planned carefully, traveling in the mid-1950s to Egypt, where he was introduced to Kemetic antiquities, and thereafter to Cuba and Haiti, where he was introduced to West African indigenous cultures and New World Vodou religion. King was steadfast in his conviction that the healing balm to assuage the battered social identity of blacks in America could be only the rejection of the enslaving cultural baggage of Western civilization and the donning on of the mantle of a reinvented West African culture. It would take him many years of travel abroad in the 1950s and 1960s to study the mores, values, and cultures of West Africa as well as to undergo a formal initiation into Yorùbá religion, endeavors he undertook in order to realize his separatist vision.

In contrast to the integrationist vision of the Reverend Martin Luther King Jr. and what he believed was the violent, anti-American credo of the Black Panther Party, Serge King founded Ọ̀yọ́túnjí African Village in fall 1970. He hoped that it would become part of the resolution to the issue of black ethnic and cultural identity. King had been initiated into the cult of Ifá in Abẹ́òkúta, Ògún State, Nigeria, and was crowned Ọba (King) Ẹfúntọ́lá Oseijeman Adélabú Adéfúnmi I of Ọ̀yọ́túnjí African Village in 1972. Residents of the ten-acre, innovative community numbered between 200 and 250 practitioners of black nationalist ideology; Ọ̀yọ́túnjí flourished as the first authentic, independent Yorùbá village outside the African continent. However, by Adéfúnmi I's death in 2005, its population had dwindled drastically. Nonetheless, his son, Ọba Adéjuyìgbé Adéfúnmi II, has kept the village going until the present.

The name Ọ̀yọ́túnjí, which literally means "Ọ̀yọ́ reawakens and rises again," derives from the ancient and powerful Old Ọ̀yọ́ Empire. The village is an eclectic mélange of northeastern and West African borrowings and influences mainly from Beninese (the former Dahomey Empire), Egyptian, Ashanti, Fon, and other African cultures. As a political outgrowth of a separatist community during the civil rights and Black Power movements, Ọ̀yọ́túnjí emerged as an invented alternative New World "African" culture, committed to the invocation and reclamation of West African ancestry, specifically of Yorùbá traditions and the reinvention of traditional African religion, replete with Yorùbá deities, shrines, and religious rituals and festivals.

The village's origin bears the marks of twenty- and twenty-first-century black nationalism, as King envisioned it: a place where blacks in the Diaspora could come to venerate sacred Yorùbá deities through dance, chants, ritual sacrifice, and where novices could be initiated into priesthood. Indeed, many people throughout the Diaspora have visited Ọ̀yọ́túnjí to venerate Yorùbá deities and their ancestors or to complete initiation rites into priesthood.

See also **Diaspora: Yorùbá in North America; Lucumí; Nagó**

REFERENCE

Clarke, Kamari. *Mapping Yorùbá Networks: Power and Agency in the Making of Transnational Communities.* Durham, NC: Duke University Press, 2004.

Pamela J. Olúbùnmi Smith

P

PALACE

The palace, *àfin*, is an architectural manifestation of the physical and philosophical ideals that inform Yorùbá social and political order. These ideals include splendor, majesty, dominance, plenitude, reverence, grandeur, wealth, and social order. Two of the pervasive sociocultural characteristics that inform the Yorùbá worldview are urbanism and divinity. The penchant to congregate in relatively large populations resulted in conurbation, coupled with the intensity and spread of Yorùbá spiritual experience, predicated on the existence of numerous *òrìṣà*—deities and divinities—make the *àfin* the epicenter of their religious and relational activities. The occupant of the *àfin* is the *ọba*, a divine personage who is revered because he personifies the collective desire and excellence of his people. As the most imposing edifice in town, the *àfin* is thus a prime example of architecture as the spatial articulation of a people's inspirations and aspirations.

To understand the *àfin* is to appreciate the complexity of the Yorùbá religious, social, and political system. Variations in the design and utilization of the *àfin* exist among the various subgroups of Yorùbá, numbering more than thirty-five million. However, the specificities of design, which address local organizational schemas, are only variations on the larger theme. Regardless of the peculiarities of each locality, the *àfin* is a beehive of activity. On the one hand, these activities are centered on Yorùbá private and domestic lives; the

activities involve the *ọba*—regarded as a divinity—and all of his *olorì* (wives), children, domestic servants, pages, and extended family. On the other hand, the *àfin* is the central space for public events. The original conceptualization of the *àfin*, which predated colonialism and has persisted despite several iterations of military and democratic governance, accommodated the needs of numerous groups from pages to chiefs and artisans to attendants.

The plan and social organization of a town typically revolves around the *àfin*, which is often surrounded by a defensive wall. The smallest familial unit of a town is the *ìdílé*, or *agbo ilé*, with an *olorí ilé* as the head. Typically, a town comprises quarters, each of which is a subdivision that is in turn an aggregation of many *ìdílé*. Presiding over the cultural and social administration of each quarter is a hereditary chief. All hereditary chiefs in a town are members of the *ọba*'s council. In effect, the *àfin* is a complex of buildings with many rooms, courtyards, and chambers designed to handle the many layers of activities. These activities emanate from, go through, or terminate at the *àfin* and include rituals, rites, and sacrifices; pageantry and annual festivals; diplomatic conferences with fellow kings; cultural and political meetings; and arbitration, conflict resolution, and counseling—among other activities.

As the most imposing architectural presence in the town, the *àfin* is intended to project an opulence that reflects the people's perception of their ruler. The impluvium of the central courtyard often reflects the impressive stateliness of the *àfin*. In addition to the variety of wall murals that are a common feature on porches and verandas, beautifully carved house posts complement doors with high reliefs. Of course, the architecture of most *àfin* has undergone changes in response to the sweep of modernity, just as the social organization has been influenced by postindependence military and democratic dispensations. For these and other reasons, the look and utilization of the *àfin* has continued to change.

Architecture relies on the visual arts to assert its dominance and proclaim its status as a monument to a town's worldview. No one knows this better than the *ọba*, who takes on the task of embellishing the palace by commissioning artists to produce impressive sculptures. The *ọba*'s palace usually doubles as a gallery and museum, with private shrines where sacrifices are offered to ancestors. Courtyards are resplendent, with an array of narrative and commemorative sculptures. One of the most popular *àfin* belongs to the Ògògà of Ìkéré-Èkìtì, where the sculptures of Ọlọ́wè, generally acknowledged as a master artist, abound. The *àfin* features a carved throne and doors that represent the history of European contact with the people of Ìkéré and house posts with carvings of the *ọba* and his household. The *àfin* is often more than a building. The corpus of bronze, brass, and terra-cotta sculptures from Ilé-Ifè, which date from the twelfth century, reflect the ancientness of the Yorùbá concept of a divine ruler. They also reflect the relevance of architecture and the arts as accoutrements of power. As the Yorùbá continue to find themselves in a swirl of constant change, it is safe to expect that the *àfin*, as a monument to a city's dynamism, will also reflect such change.

See also **Architecture: Domestic**

REFERENCES

Òjó, G. J. Afọlábí. *Yoruba Palaces: A Study of the Afins of Yorùbáland*. London: University of London Press, 1966.
Vlach, John Michael. "Affecting Architecture of the Yorùbá." *African Arts* 10.1 (October 1976): 48–53.

délé jẹ́gẹ́dẹ́

PAWNING AND PAWNSHIP

Pawning (known as *ìwọ̀fà* system) developed as a form of financial contract during the precolonial period. The practice allowed for a debtor to pledge human labor to a creditor as security for a loan. Pawns were sometimes expected to work for only a short period of time, until they were able to cover the interest on a loan. In some circumstances, pawns were engaged for a lengthy period of time; they were expected to provide services to the creditor until the debtor was able to make payments. A debtor could choose to pawn himself to his creditor from time to time. This form of pawnship was less frequent than the variant under which parents gave up their children or young family members as security for loans.

During the colonial period, European officials and missionaries described the *ìwọ̀fà* system as an economic transaction that promoted child abuse and servitude. This opinion was held mainly because many debtors saw the economic arrangement as a way to ignore paying their debts. There were instances in which pawns were left permanently in the hands of creditors and totally forgotten. Missionaries described the evils associated with the system mainly because children constituted majority of pawns. Young females, especially unmarried ones, were the most prized pawns. Debtors believed they could easily get out of debt should the creditor choose to marry the pawn. Anglican Missionaries in Lagos, Ọ̀tà, Òsíẹ̀lẹ̀, and Abẹ́òkúta raised funds to secure the release of many female pawns.

It is difficult to deny that the system was manipulated to the advantage of creditors and to the disadvantage of pawns. However, one aspect of pawning that Europeans failed to acknowledge is the fact that many aged members of the society considered the practice a way of training adolescents and youths. Pawnship was seen as a means of training children in a skill or trade and in learning the value of hard work. Suzanne Miers argued in her study that pawning served security purposes. For instance, during the Yorùbá wars of the nineteenth century, many parents pawned their children to keep them in the safe enclaves or houses of rich Yorùbá warlords.

Samuel Johnson noted in his study on the history of the Yorùbá that pawning operated differently than the institution of slavery. Unlike slaves, pawns were considered free members of the society; they retained their rights and social status. In some communities, pawns were allowed to live in their own homes. Unlike slaves, pawns were treated more humanely. They were not subjected to corporal punishment nor were they compelled to work. In addition, unlike slaves, who worked from sunup to sundown, pawns provided labor only for a specific number of days. In some communities, pawns were expected to report for work during the early morning hours. African scholars have debated at length the relation between slavery and pawnship system in Yorùbáland as well as in other African communities, such as among the Benin, Efik, Ijaw, Igbo, and Edo people. Pawning was eradicated after the colonial government launched a campaign against the practice in the mid-1920s.

See also **Debt and Debt Management; Slavery**

REFERENCES

Fálọlá, Tóyìn, and Paul Lovejoy. *Pawnship in Africa: Debt Bondage in Historical Perspective* Boulder, CO: Westview Press, 1994.

Johnson, Samuel. *The History of the Yorùbás*. Lagos (Nigeria): C.S.S., 1921.

Miers, Suzanne. *The End of Slavery in Africa*. Madison: University of Wisconsin Press, 1988.

Oróge, Adéníyì. "Ìwọfà: An Historical Survey of the Yorùbá Institution of Indenture." *African Economic History* 14 (1985): 71–88.

Tósìn Abíọdún

PHILOSOPHY

Philosophy is essentially when philosophers and cultures attempt to critically and systematically reflect on the universe, their experiences of it, and their sociocultural dynamics. The etymology of *philosophy* derives from the Greek word *philosophia*, literally "the love of wisdom." Wisdom, in this sense, refers to the comprehensive sets of ideas and beliefs with which an individual or culture makes sense of their existence. An appreciation of the uniqueness of Yorùbá philosophy in all its ramification derives from the fact that, like all cultural reflections on life and existence, it has evolved in line with the two dominant conceptions of philosophy in its evolution over the past three hundred years. These conceptions are philosophy as worldview and philosophy as critical reconstruction of ideas (or simply critical thinking). Philosophy as worldview provides an intellectual framework of ideas and beliefs by which individuals or cultures make sense of the universe and their existence within it. Philosophy in this sense is a guide to life. As a critical reconstruction of ideas, philosophy ensures that the ideas and beliefs that constitute the wisdom for living are subjected to critical analysis that makes sense of new and challenging realities.

Yorùbá philosophy, therefore, refers to philosophical discourse—traditional and contemporary—regarding assumptions, principles, worldviews, and attitudes that have been developed, interrogated, and refined over millennia. The philosophical activities generated by the Yorùbá reflect their confrontation with the universe and their cultural and existential predicament. This philosophy is divided into two parts: traditional and contemporary. Traditional Yorùbá philosophy constitutes the reflective and critical interrogation of culture and the full range of implications for human existence that flourished before colonialism. It reflects the ideas humans live by as moderated by the cultural framework: values, knowledge and beliefs (ìmọ̀ or ìgbàgbọ́), moral conduct (ìwà/ ìwàpẹ̀lẹ́), justice, spirituality, law, being and personhood (ènìyàn), the cosmos and ultimate reality (ayé or ọ̀run), diseases, sickness and health (àrùn, àìsàn, or ìlera), destiny (àyànmọ́), government (ìjọba), society (àwùjọ), death (ikú), and so on. All these constitute the ontological, axiological, epistemological, and political assumptions about existence that underlie the daily existence of the people.

Traditional philosophical rumination on the universe and existence was carried out as an extratextual enterprise in the sense that it was mediated by oral tradition. It occurred within a communalistic context that made it difficult to identify a single philosopher or the singular source of a philosophical text. Cultural artifacts and oral literature, including sculpture, folklore, proverbs, legends, songs, myths, dynastic poems, and epics, encode the philosophical wisdom of the Yorùbá. The Ifá corpus also constitutes a significant repository of wisdom, a practical guide accumulated through countless generations of Yorùbá existence, that serves as a "text" of literary, religious, and philosophical insights and reflection on how the people interpret their world and existence.

Contemporary Yorùbá philosophy has three interrelated dimensions. The first refers to the philosophical interest in the traditional thought system exemplified in the worldview and orature, conceptual systems, political systems, religion, culture, and so on. The second dimension involves how modern, professionally trained Yorùbá and non-Yorùbá philosophers come to terms with modern postcolonial realities in the prism of a cultural framework. For instance, a germane philosophical question for contemporary philosophers concerns the configuration of Yorùbá identity in a global world: how do we make sense of modernity and modernization, as well as migration to the Diaspora, without relinquishing Yorùbá identity in the process? Another question concerns how the dynamics of the traditional thought system can provide insights into current postcolonial realities of poverty, unemployment, corruption, leadership, social deprivation, political instability, injustice, economic exploitation, and so on. In this regard, the contemporary philosopher will be interested in how the traditional kinship principle (and the dynamics of social reciprocity it engendered) can assist in the evolution of an egalitarian society in Nigeria.

The third dimension of contemporary Yorùbá philosophy is the various contributions of professionally trained philosophers to philosophical thinking in the different branches of philosophy: metaphysics, epistemology, ethics, logic, political philosophy, aesthetics, philosophy of language, and the like. In this context, a contemporary Yorùbá philosopher can juxtapose

Descartes's conception of the human person to the Yorùbá conception of èníyàn, and explore how the consequences of such a comparison can affect the philosophy of personhood. The Ifá divination corpus features prominently in the three dimensions of philosophical reflections.

See also **Cosmology; Culture; Divination: Ifá**

REFERENCES

Gbádégẹsin, Ṣẹgun. *African Philosophy, Traditional Yorùbá Philosophy and Contemporary African Realities.* New York: Peter Lang, 1991.

Hallen, Barry. *The Good, the Bad and the Beautiful: Discourse about Values in Yorùbá Culture.* Bloomington: Indiana University Press, 2000.

Adéshínà Afọláyan

PIDGIN

Nigerian Pidgin, popularly called broken English or "brokin," is perhaps Nigeria's unofficial lingua franca. Although the official language is Standard English, Pidgin exists alongside the many indigenous languages of various ethnic communities, believed to number hundreds. Nigerian pidgin is a sociolinguistic response to using an official language imposed by colonialism and Westernization. Scholars widely acknowledge that Pidgin emerged to facilitate trade between Europeans and Africans who lived along the coastal areas of Nigeria.

Pidgin, as used in Nigeria, is largely oral and heterogeneous. It has been divided into three sets of social lects: acreotal (de-creolized) varieties that are largely influenced by Standard English; basiclectal (pidginized or repidginized) varieties that show heavy influence from other Nigerian languages; and mesolectal (creolized) varieties that Nigerians use as a primary or first language. Nigerian Pidgin speakers switch between the different lects according to context. Various regions in Nigeria speak Pidgin using the local language of their individual region for flavor. Scholars have identified several subvarieties of Nigerian Pidgin:

- Northern, heavily influenced by the Hausa language, and spoken in northern Nigeria
- Southwestern, spoken among Yorùbá and very close to the Bendel (Edo or Benin) Pidgin. Bendel (Edo or Benin), regarded by some scholars as the standard Pidgin
- Rivers, noticeably colored by languages spoken around Bayelsa and Rivers states
- Southeastern, spoken in southeastern Nigeria and influenced by the Igbo language
- Cross River, also colored by Cross River languages, especially Efik-Ibibio

Some common words in Nigerian Pidgin include the following:

pikin—child

chook—poke (with a sharp object)

sabi—to know (and *over-sabi* translates to acting like one knows everything)

vex—to be angry

chop—to eat

Abeg—please (I beg you)

Some general usages are:

How una dey?
How are you?

Wetin be your name?
What's your name?

Make una no vex
Do not be angry (or annoyed)

Who get this pikin?
Whose child is this?

Wetin dey happen?
What's happening?
What's going on?

I take God beg una . . .
I plead with you in God's name . . .

Pidgin English is spoken among Nigerians of all socioeconomic classes and can be grasped by anyone regardless of their years of formal education. This flexibility and relative ease of mastery differentiates it from Standard English. Pidgin is believed to be a linguistic unifier in a country with such diversity of languages. Although pidgin is hardly used in official communication, it is a popular language that is used to reach local populations for various campaigns. Pidgin is used widely in Nigerian popular culture, especially in hip-hop music. The late musician and activist Fẹlá Aníkúlápó-Kútì consistently used Pidgin in his music.

See also **Aníkúlápó-Kútì, Fẹlá; Music: Popular**

REFERENCES

Elugbe, Ben. "Nigerian Pidgin English: Phonology." In *Africa, South and Southeast Asia*, ed. Rajend Mesthrie Mesthrie, 55–64. Berlin (Germany): Walter de Gruyter, 2008.
Faraclas, Nick. *Nigerian Pidgin.* New York: Routledge, 2013.

Abímbọ́lá Adélakùn

PILGRIMAGE: CHRISTIAN

The term *pilgrimage* describes a journey or trip to visit a shrine or a sacred place. The term derives from the Latin word *peregrinus*, which referred to a free, provincial subject of the Roman Empire. Attempts have always been made to differentiate between pilgrimage and tourism, which derives from the Latin word *tornus.* The two differ according to the intent of the traveler and his or her activities associated with the journey or travel. A person traveling with a religious intent is regarded as a pilgrim; a person traveling for leisure, pleasure, or cultural adventure is considered a tourist. However, V. E. Smith argues that this demarcation is nothing more than "a culturally polarity that blurs travelers' motives." Indeed, it is important to note that it was not until the 1970s, as studies in the field of tourism became more popular, that pilgrimage and tourism began to be approached as two separate subjects warranting little interrelated or comparative treatment. Before that time, according to D. J. Timothy and D. Oslen, "the development of leisure, and therefore tourism, is incomprehensible without an understanding of religion and the practice of pilgrimage in ancient times."

From the understanding of pilgrimage as a religious journey based on the traveler's intent and his or her activities, the Christian pilgrimage can be described as a journey undertaken to visit sacred places recognized by Christians as fundamental to spiritual development. Ordinarily, Christian pilgrimage is not required as mandatory religious practice—in contrast to Islam, in which it is one of its five pillars. However, Christians have always been passionate about going on pilgrimages and regard such journeys as crucial for spiritual growth and personal fulfillment. This attitude is clearly discernable from the fact that pilgrimage became part of Christian practice very early in its history.

Historically, Christian pilgrimage began with visits made to sites connected with the ministry of Jesus. For example, the second-century scholar Origen went in search of places connected to Jesus, his disciples, and the prophets. By the fourth century, Christian pilgrimages to the Holy Land and Jerusalem had become quite popular. Indeed, by the latter part of this century, literature such as the "Bordeaux Itinerary" describing the stages of Christian pilgrimage, had become available. In addition, early church fathers like St. Jerome encouraged pilgrimages to locations such as Rome; sites associated with the apostles, saints, and martyrs; and places where sightings of the Virgin Mary had occurred.

In contemporary times, places, scenes, or sites of pilgrimage cut across different Christian denominations. These include, but are not limited to, Jerusalem and other parts of the Holy Land and Santiago de Compostela, a city in Spain. However, pilgrimages to Rome attracts Christians from all denominations, but predominantly by Catholics. Numerous other sites that attract Christian pilgrims are scattered across the Christian world. These places are considered unique because of the spiritual experiences and phenomena identified with them.

See also **Pilgrimage: Islamic; Tourism and Leisure; Travel and Exploration**

REFERENCES

Smith, V. E. "Introduction to Quest in Quest." *Annals of Tourism Research* 19 (1992): 1–17.

Timothy, D. J., and D. Oslen, eds. *Tourism Religion and Spiritual Journey.* London: Routledge, 2006.

Ìbígbóládé S. Adéríbigbé

PILGRIMAGE: ISLAMIC

The Muslim pilgrimage called the Hajj is one of the five fundamental pillars of Islam. It is the last pillar of Islam, and it is obligatory on all Muslims as long as they are able to do it. The conditions for the Hajj include being a Muslim, an adult, of sound mind, free, and capable (financially and physically). Muslims perform two types of pilgrimages. The first is the Hajj, which is usually held from the eighth to twelfth of Dhu al-Hijjah, the twelfth and last month of the Islamic calendar. The second type is called Umrah (or lesser Hajj), which is performed many times in the year. Although there are a number of differences between both types, they nonetheless have similar spiritual essence, goal, and benefit.

The Hajj is more popular among the Yorùbá people than Umrah, although many people also perform Umrah. In either case, Islamic pilgrimages can be discussed from two perspectives: religious and sociocultural. In terms of the religious aspect, the Muslim Yorùbá share similar orientation with all Muslims across the globe in that they regard Hajj as a religious duty, a spiritual retreat, and a response to a divine call to the sacred house of Allah in Mecca. For this reason, they usually take a lot of time to prepare spiritually and psychologically for the possibly once-in-a-lifetime spiritual journey. More specifically, Yorùbá Muslims consider Hajj the peak of religious devotion, observance of which could serve as a spiritual turning point in life. Many return from Hajj completely reformed in character and advanced in spiritual consciousness.

The social significance of Hajj for the Yorùbá takes unique dimensions. To many, performing the Hajj is a marker of social prestige and evidence of financial strength, both of which often result in creating a new cultural identity. Some pilgrims commonly return from the Hajj with one of their front teeth plated in silver or gold. Upon their return, they add the title of

Alhaji or Alhaja for a male and female, respectively, as a prefix to their names. These titles, are derived from the word *Hajj*, an Arabic word that roughly translate to "pilgrim" or "someone on a journey." Besides the title, returning from the pilgrimage could lead to a change in the pilgrim's social status, such as earning them religious titles in their community mosques. There might also be modification in the pilgrim's wardrobe, as some retuning pilgrims will begin to dress in Southeast Asian and Arab-style clothing, especially hats and scarfs. Last, a successful pilgrimage and safe arrival is often celebrated by many pilgrims with a party, during which gifts and souvenirs from the journey are distributed to families, friends, and relatives.

See also **Pilgrimage: Christian; Tourism and Leisure; Travel and Exploration**

REFERENCE

Ahmad, Khurshid, ed. *The Holy Quran: An Introduction.* Karachi (India): Jamiyat-ul-Falah Publication, 1968.

Kazeem Kẹ́hìndé Sanuth

PLANTS

The ancient Yorùbá were mostly farmers who depended on plants for their basic existence. Plants, therefore, were central to all livelihood survival needs and activities. Plants play a significant role in the survival, growth, and development of the Yorùbá nation. Virtually all the primary Yorùbá occupations use plants. First, medicinal trees and herbal plants are used for health and well-being, healing, cures, antidotes, and preventive charms and medications. Supernatural plants for self-defense and martial defense, and for warfare. Before the advent of writing and printing that arrived with Islam and Christianity, the Yorùbá depended solely on oral communication to record and transfer culture across generations. As an oral society, incantation, chanting, oratory, and songs are important. The Yorùbá have discovered that there are plants that have potential to aid memory, to help the vocal cords, and plants whose names can be invoked to cast a spell on enemy, move from one place to another, for clairvoyance, or to dis-

appear from points of danger. Thus, some plants have mystic qualities and are idolized.

Second, some plants serve an economic purpose, such as trees and plants for subsistence and cash crops. Today, staple foods for different Yorùbá ethnic subgroups—such as the Ọ̀yọ́, Èkìtì, Oǹdó, Ìjẹ̀bú, Ẹ̀gbá, Ìjẹ̀ṣà, and Ọ̀ṣun—reflect each group's indigenous plants, grains, shrubs, and herbs. The village settlement pattern and land ownership systems were also derivative of the habitat of the indigenous vegetation available in different parts of the Yorùbá territory. For example, grains, vegetables, palms, and tuber crops are more prominent in the northern savanna parts of the Yorùbáland, and tropical plants are more prominent in the rain forest of the south.

Third, plants provide the materials and tools for building and constructing shelter, artifacts, hunting, musical instruments for ceremonial entertainments, religious festivities, and rituals. For example, different plants are used for carving; for making boats, musical instruments, *ọpọ́n ayò* (wooden board for the *ayò* game); and for building pillars and roofing materials. *Ewé akòko* (the leaves of *akòko*) is an important part of the chieftaincy installation.

Fourth, since the British occupation of Yorùbáland in the 1880s to the rise of the oil industry in the 1970s, the Yorùbá economy shifted from subsistence food crops to cash crops, especially cocoa, kola nut, and palm products. Fifth, the drawbacks to using plants as alternative medicine are mainly a lack of knowledge about safe dosage, unhygienic processing and preservation, and the panacea problem—that is, the offering of an all-purpose-elixir that would cure all ailments. Not enough definitive or scientific proof of the efficacy of the properties of a particular plant to cure a given disease or illness existed in many cases. However, in the postindependence era, a new nationalist drive for the use of indigenous plants has gained popularity. Consequently, hybrid plants are being developed and hardier seeds and seedlings are being introduced to farmers, such as cyanide-free cassava.

While Christianity, Islam, and modern Western medicine have prevailed over the primordial use of supernatural and incantation use of plants, nationalists are employing modern research and using public and private investment to look into and promote the economic, nutritional, and medicinal values of indigenous plants. Public health departments in Nigerian universities are getting involved in researching into scientific analysis of the nutritional and medicinal properties of plants and herbs. They also look into safe dosage and advise on the hygienic processing and packaging of alternative medicine. The public is also learning more about indigenous vegetables and fruits as necessary for adequate diet, good health, and well-being.

See also **Medical Practitioners; Medicine; Medicine: Indigenous Therapeutic System**

REFERENCE

Verger, Pierre. "The Use of Plants in Yorùbá Traditional Medicine and its Linguistic Approach." *Seminar Series Department of African Languages and Literatures, University of Ifẹ̀* 1.1 (1976–1977): 242–97.

Bọ́lá Dáúdà

POLICE

Traditional systems of policing, intelligence gathering, and maintaining law and order were all interwoven and discretely enforced with beliefs, values, and settlement patterns. In precolonial times and through the rapid growth of towns in the 1950s and self-government in the 1960s, most Yorùbá lived in households in villages and small towns. Nothing portrayed the state and sense of safety and security better than the saying *Ìwó ò ní ààṣẹ* (the city of Iwo's houses has no doors). Life was simple and trusting not only because everyone knew everyone else but also because everyone was related in some way to everyone else. The elders ruled with a seemingly simple but rather sophisticated separation of powers among ruling functionaries: the Babaláwo (Ifá priest), the Ògbóni (elders), the kingmakers, the village head or town ruling king-in-council, and the general populace. No one dared cross the boundaries of this hierarchy. Sanctions and penalties were swift and severe; even the king could be dethroned.

Five informal, unobtrusive, self-regulatory, and effective traditional Yorùbá police functions existed. First was the controlling power of personal conscience. A guilty conscience was enough to haunt any culprit to insanity and/or to death, while a clear conscience gave the innocent the most cherished peace of mind. Thus, an ordinary oath of innocence (*ìbúra*) on one's life or the lives of one's children or an invocation of the spirit of the gods—either Ògún, the god of iron, or Ṣàngó, the god of thunder and fire—was enough to set free anyone arraigned before the household or village head or king. Second, nemesis (*àdàbi*) was the most powerful type of police, though unseen. The Yorùbá wholeheartedly trusted and believed (and many still do, regardless of religious faith) in the saying *ẹní bá ṣebi, bí ọba ayé kò bá rí i, ti ọ̀run á dá a léjọ́* (If one was clever enough to escape human justice and oversight of the earthly king, one cannot escape the god of retribution). No one ever joked about the swift retributive justice and fairness of the gods, especially the god of iron (Ògún), the god of thunder and fire (Ṣàngó), and the god of smallpox (Ṣànpọ̀nná).

Third, placing an *ààlè*, a piece of iron or palm frond (both symbols associated with Ògún), on one's property was enough to keep out intruders and trespassers or to get a suspect to surrender himself to relevant authorities. Fourth, community watch was very effective. The Yorùbá would say *etí ọba nílé, etí ọba lóko, ènìyàn ní jẹ́ bẹ́ ẹ̀,* (the king has ears), which implied that there were informants or secret agents everywhere. Fifth, the Yorùbá routinely solicited the help of the Babaláwo (Ifá priest) to find lost property, to invoke a curse on the culprit, or to solve any puzzling breach of the law.

Although modern policing has been part of governance since the turn of the twentieth century, the Yorùbá seldom use the police and the court system for two reasons. First, many believe that *a kì í ti kóòtù bọ̀, ká tún ṣọ̀rẹ́* (we cannot go to court and come back friends). They also believe that there is no quarrel, dispute, or conflict that cannot be reconciled: *kò sí àjàtúká* or *kò sí ajàmárẹ́, bẹ́ẹ̀ ni kò sí arẹ́májà.* Therefore, they avoid any recourse to litigation because most conflicts involve only members of the same household or community. Second, even before politicians deployed the local police against their opponents in the late 1950s and early 1960s, the public did not trust the police. The police were perceived as agents of government rule and oppression. The police are also known to be mischievous and capable of roping one in, and using one to get a promotion: *ọlọ́pàá kò ṣeé bá ṣọ̀rẹ́, wọn á parọ́ mọ́ ọ, láti fi ọ́ gbokùn.*

See also **Communication: Nonverbal**

REFERENCE

Tamuno, Tekena N. *The Police in Modern Nigeria, 1861-1965: Origin, Development, and Role.* Ìbàdàn (Nigeria): University Press, 1970.

Bọ́lá Dáúdà

POLITICAL PARTIES AND POLITICS IN YORÙBÁLAND SINCE 1945

Because of their early exposure to Western education, the Yorùbá are very enlightened, critical minded, and culturally refined. The sense of nationalism among the Yorùbá has defined and continues to define their political orientation, mobilization, and engagement with the larger Nigerian federation. Political activities that are culturally oriented toward the placement of Yorùbá people within the wider political context of Nigeria started with the formation of Ẹgbẹ́ Ọmọ Odùduwà by the late chief Ọbáfẹ́mi Awólọ́wọ̀ in 1947. This cultural association transformed into a political party called the Action Group in 1951. Ideologically, the party was progressive; welfare socialism comprised its core platform. The party won in all the elections conducted in the region, and it dominated the political space from 1951 to 1964. A conflict broke out in the Action Group between Chief Ọbáfẹ́mi Awólọ́wọ̀ and his deputy, Chief S. L. Akíntọ́lá, over the control of the party. Their conflict created avenues for other political parties with dominant political bases in the eastern and northern part of Nigeria, such as the National Council of Nigeria

Citizens and the Northern Peoples Congress (NPC), to make inroads in Yorùbá-speaking western Nigeria. A series of crises ensued with the population census of 1963, the general elections of 1964, the imprisonment of Ọbáfẹ́mi Awólọ́wọ̀ by the NPC-controlled federal government in 1965, and the unwarranted imposition of emergency rule in the Western Region that same year led to the military overthrow of the civilian government on January 15, 1966.

The military government lifted the ban on political activities in 1978; old members of the defunct Action Group formed the Unity Party of Nigeria under the leadership of Chief Ọbáfẹ́mi Awólọ́wọ̀. As in the First Republic, the Yorùbá people formed the nucleus of the Unity Party of Nigeria. The party won in all the states in the region in the general elections of 1979. In 1983, an attempt by the ruling National Party of Nigeria to rig the elections for governor in Oǹdó and Ọ̀yọ́ states was met with serious violence, reminiscent of the 1964 "operation *wẹ́tìẹ̀* syndrome," during which homes of political opponents were soaked in gasoline and burned. This tendency to react violently to cheating and imposition of unpopular candidates in elections is a distinctive characteristic of the Yorùbá political culture. The criminal annulment of the June 12, 1993, presidential election, won by late chief M. K. O. Abíọ́lá, a Yorùbá man from Ògún State, further drew the ire of the Yorùbá who felt that the northern oligarchy deliberately denied one of their own to occupy the highest office in the country. Although the late Abíọ́lá did not support the progressively inclined Unity Party of Nigeria in the Second Republic, his membership of the Social Democratic Party, his rapprochement with the old guards of the defunct Unity Party of Nigeria, and—most important—the absence of any alternative candidates from the region in that election translated into maximum support for Abíọ́lá. Protests, coupled with the local and international campaigns that followed the annulment of the June 12 elections, led to withdrawal of the military from politics in 1999.

When civil rule was restored in 1999, the Yorùbá political elite formed the Alliance for Democracy (AD)

to run in the general elections. Some of the old guards in the defunct Unity Party of Nigeria, such as the late Bọ́lá Ìgè, the late Adébáyọ̀ Adéfaratì, the late Abraham Adésànyà, Olú Fálaè, Ayọ̀ Ọ̀pádòkun, Ayọ̀ Adébánjọ, and Ṣégun Ọ̀ṣọbà, and emergent elite like Ahmed Bọ́lá Tinúbú, Níyì Adébáyọ̀, Ìbíkúnlé Amósùn, Gbénga Daniel, and others, were charter members of AD. To a great extent, Nigeria's Fourth Republic severely altered the political balance of the Yorùbá as their core principle of maintaining an oppositional stance and remaining regionally rooted to the people has been severely tested. Although the AD remained true to the principle of Action Group and the Unity Party of Nigeria in not forming alliances with conservative elements from northern Nigeria in 1999, they were hard-pressed to do so in 2003, as many members of the AD who felt short-changed in the selection process left the party for the ruling Peoples Democratic Party (PDP). The top echelon of the party also reached a gentlemen's agreement with then president Olúṣẹ́gun Ọbásanjọ́ and the PDP for them to not field a presidential candidate in the 2003 presidential elections. As a result of this agreement, the PDP won not just the presidential election but also the governorship elections in all states of southwestern Nigeria, with the exception of Lagos.

Yorùbá politics is being gradually redefined under the leadership of Ahmed Bọ́lá Tinúbú, who was governor of Lagos State between 1999 and 2007. Unlike his predecessor, Chief Awólọ́wọ̀, Bọ́lá Tinúbú has his eyes on the control of the central government. Consequently, he has been forming political alliances across the Niger, the latest being the fusion of his Action Congress, a party with strong base in western Nigeria, with political parties in the eastern and northern Nigeria to form the All Progressives Congress (APC). How this unfolds and affects the politics of the Yorùbá depends on the success or failure of the APC-led federal government in its four-year term from 2015 to 2019.

See also **Abíọ́lá, Moshood Káṣìmawò Ọláwálé; Action Group; Akíntọ́lá, Samuel Ládòkè; Awólọ́wọ̀, Ọbáfẹ́mi; Ọbásanjọ́, Olúṣẹ́gun**

REFERENCES

Awólọ́wọ̀, Ọbáfẹ́mi. *The Autobiography of Chief Ọbáfẹ́mi Awólọ́wọ̀.* Cambridge: Cambridge University Press, 1960.
———. *Path to Nigerian Freedom.* London: Faber, 1947.

Samuel O. Ọlọ́runtọ́ba

POLITICAL SONGS

Music is a powerful force for political mobilization, and political songs are used for promoting and advertising political parties, candidates, and party manifestos during election campaigns. Political songs fall under what O. B. Jẹ́gẹ́dẹ́ describes as political folklore; they are a form of oral, poetic communication and are artistic, eloquent, and informative in nature. The songs portray the ideology of political parties and the manifestos of individual contestants. They also tell the story of conquests of past and future opponents.

Political songs are sometimes used as a kind of modern-day duel. In the 1960s, for instance, the Yorùbá voters who defected from the Action Group (AG) to the Nigerian National Democratic Party (NDP) used to sing the song below to spite their former political associates in the AG:

Bóo rójú mi, oò rínú mìi,
Dẹmọ ni mo wà

My appearance may not reflect my intention
I am for Democratic Party [even though you may think I am a member of AG]

In another example, members of the National Council of Nigerian Citizens (NCNC) lampooned the AG by using the AG's logo, the palm tree, as a weapon of mockery:

Inú igbó lọ̀pẹ̀ ń gbé,
A kì í kọ́lé adẹ̀tẹ̀ sígboro.
Inú igbó lọ̀pẹ ń gbé.

The palm tree resides in the forest,
A leper's house is not built in the city.
The palm tree resides in the forest.

In recent times, political songs have drawn inspiration from religious hymns and choruses. In the following example, the tune of a song from the Christian Hymn Book was adapted for the campaign of the gubernatorial candidate of Peoples Democratic Party (PDP) of Nigeria in Èkìtì State during the June 2014 gubernatorial election:

Wọ́lé, wọlè wọ́le ní isísìnyí.
Ayọ̀ Fàyosé ń pè ọ́ pé ma bọ̀.
Ayọ̀ Fàyosé ń pè ọ pé ma a bọ̀.
Dìbò fún Ayọ̀délé Fáyóòsé
Lábẹ́ àsíá ẹgbẹ́ òṣèlú
People Democratic Party (PDP) Power.
Ayọ̀ Fayose, yes o o.

Enter, enter, enter now.
Ayo Fáyóse is calling you to come.
Ayo Fáyéṣe is calling you to come.
Vote Ayọ̀délé Fáyóṣe
Under the political platform of
People Democratic Party [PDP] Power
Ayọ̀ Fáyóṣe is the one, yes.

Another prominent feature of political campaign songs in Yorùbáland is the use of contemporary musicians such as *fújì* and *jùjú* musician to compose and sing political songs as jingles on radio and television. The following example is a song composed by a popular gospel *jùjú* musician, Yínká Ayéfélé, for the former governor Káyọ̀dé Fáyẹmí of Èkìtì State during his second term of electioneering in 2014:

Governor Fáyẹmí for second term
Governor Fáyẹmí ń bọ̀ wá sẹ̀ẹ̀kan si
Ṣé kí n ma ṣọhun tó ṣe?
Gbogbo iṣẹ́ tó ṣe fún wa l'Ékìtì ko lónkà
Gbogbo iṣẹ́ tó ṣe fún wa l'Ékìtì,
Ó ṣojú gbogbo wa.

Governor Fáyẹmí for second term
Governor Fáyẹmí is coming for the second term
Should I list all what he did?
All he did for us in Èkìtì are immeasurable
All what he did for us in Èkìtì,
We all witnessed it.

Although political songs are still used in political campaigns, more of them are broadcast on radio and television as jingles. They are also recorded on CDs or cassettes and sold to party supporters. Yorùbá political songs are quite interesting and have remained a major part of urban folklore passed down from one generation to the other.

See also **Advertisement**

REFERENCE

Jẹ́gẹ́dẹ́, O. B. "Folklore and Politics: Narrative Strategies of Political Songs as Advert for Electioneering Campaign in Ọ̀yọ́ State, Nigeria." *Ọ̀pánbàtà: LASU Journal of African Studies* 5 (2012): 227–45.

Adékẹ́mi Adégún Táíwò

POLITICAL SYSTEMS

A political system is the institutional arrangement of formal and informal structures and processes, including rules of engagement. For the Yorùbá, it represents the historical evolution of the institutions by which they defined and redefined their political experience with organizing their societies. The nineteenth century was a time of great political ferment. Between 1813 and 1893, about fifty different wars were fought among various Yorùbá subgroups: Ọ̀yọ́, Ẹ̀gbá, Àwórì, Ìjẹ̀bú, Àkókó, Ìgbómìnà, Èkìtì, Okun Yorùbá, Ọ̀wọ̀, Ẹ̀gbádò, Ìjẹ̀ṣà, Ifẹ̀ and others. Ironically, it was within this period also that the Yorùbá's unique political systems were consolidated. The predominance of wars inevitably led, in most Yorùbá societies, to the evolution of large and centralized political organization headed by a monarchy with typical and atypical reference to common descent or tradition of origin.

Three representative political systems exist in traditional Yorùbáland. The first is the military republicanism associated with some of the splinter states that evolved from the ruins of the Old Ọ̀yọ́ Empire in the nineteenth century. Founded in 1829, Ìbàdàn developed a form of state building founded on military meritocracy. This was mainly a result of its origin as a war camp for displaced refugees and a significant military outpost. Ìbàdàn's political system evolved into two nonhereditary spheres, the military and the civil, which resolved into four chieftaincy offices. The chief (baálè) was the civil head of the town; the balógun headed the military; the séríkí was the military second in command; and the ìyálóde was in charge of women's affairs. The safeguard against unbridled political ambition is an intricate promotion system that made ascension to the highest offices a slow but steady affair.

The second category of political system is represented by the Ègbá subgroup. They developed a federated republicanism marked by the absence of political centralization that includes the military. The founding of Abéòkúta (literally, "among the crevices of the rock") in 1830 references the Ègbá's forced flight from the rampant wars. The Ègbá communities were grouped into four autonomous divisions—Ègbá Gbágùrá, Ègbá Òwu, Ègbá Òkè-Ònà, and Ègbá Aké. The four divisions, each with its own "president," had similar political structure. The Ògbóni (the elite legislative council), the Ológun (the military chieftaincy), the Pàràkòyí (leadership of the trade and craft guilds), and the odè (the hunters who maintained law and order) constituted the dynamic representation of the constituent pluralistic forces around which the stability of the Ègbá communities depended.

The most dynamic and ubiquitous of the political systems was the constitutional monarchy. This system evolved constitutional dynamics to safeguard its boundaries and to guard against the emergence of wanton dictators. Constitutional procedures for power sharing that ensured easy succession were also instituted. The basic sociopolitical unit of the Yorùbá town is the lineage or kinship group (ebí) headed by the baálé. This group is then enlarged into an àdúgbò (or ward headed by olórí àdúgbò). Due to the centralized nature of the Yorùbá constitutional monarchy, the political structure has a pyramidal framework of hierarchies with the oba at the top, assisted by the traditional chiefs usually (s)elected from within the several olórí àdúgbò. The designation of the oba varies from one Yorùbá subgroup to the other—aláàfin (Òyó),

òòni (Ifè), aláké (Ègbá), èwí (Èkìtì), awùjalè (Ìjèbú), and so on.

The oba was assisted in administrative matters by aristocratic courtiers or eunuchs (èfà): the Òsì Èfà dealt with political issues, the Òtún Èfà with religious matters, and the Ònà Èfà with the judicial. There were also various titled functionaries who presided over various duties from divination and music to the maintenance of building and the execution of offenders. Finally, a varied number of palace attendants, messengers, and guards, called the Ìlàrí (or Odi in Ìjèbú and Emèsè at Ifè, Ìjèsà, or Èkìtì), assisted the oba.

The constitutional dynamics of the chieftaincy vary from one subgroup to the other. In Òyó, the Council of Chiefs is represented by the eight-member Òyó Mèsì, or kingmakers. Amongst the Òyó Mèsì, the Basòrun was the de facto prime minister who presided over the constitutional boundary that limits the oba. Although the oba is often regarded as the aláse-èkejì-òrìsà (the next in command to the gods), the Basòrun served as a sort of ambivalent balance between the will of the ruled and the will of the ruler. Following the Council of Chiefs, in terms of nobility, is the èsó or military class headed by the Ààre-Ònà-Kakanfò, or generalissimo. The Ògbóni cult (or Òsùgbó in Ìjèbú) constitutes the next, even more powerful element in the multifunctional constitutionality that supervises the Yorùbá political system and within which the oba functions.

The centralized political structure did not always guarantee stability and order. For instance, there was the prevalent problem created by power and hegemonic dynamics between the king, the chiefs, and the people. The checks and balances failed, in the final analysis, to constrain unbridled personal aggrandizement and succession ambition. The final counterpoint to the strength of the political systems was the often violent intrusion of colonialism that distorted their cultural and ethnic boundaries and foisted an artificial dynamics serving exploitative logic.

See also **Government: Historical Political Systems**

REFERENCE

Ojigbo, Anthony Okion. "Conflict Resoltion in the Traditional Yorùbá Political System." *Cahiers d'Études Africaines* 13.50 (1973): 13–21.

Adéshínà Afọláyan

POPULAR CULTURE

The Yorùbá have a lively, exuberant, and extroverted popular culture corresponding somewhat to the expansive and laid-back topography of their towns and cities, which are invariably dominated by markets. The markets and town squares are the locations of intense commercial activities, political meetings, festivals, and fierce outspokenness, evoking a tradition in which rebellious masquerades criticize oppressive rulers and berate widespread social abuses. Popular culture is conceived here as the arts, artifacts, customs, and rituals of everyday life located at the interstices of the traditional worldview and institutions and the influence of Christianity, Islam, and Western civilization. The infrastructure of traditional popular culture that survives in attenuated forms speaks to such cultural repertoire as *ewì* (poetry), *oríkì* (praise poetry), *ẹkún ìyàwó* (bridal chanting or weeping), *èsà* (the chanting of masquerades), *ìjálá* (hunters' songs or chants), *rárà* (a form of incantatory singing usually deployed by palace singers), and *odù ifá* (a collection of 256 oral poems dealing with the adventures of Ọ̀rúnmìlà).

Didactic oral narratives, such as ancestral legends, folktales, riddles, and proverbs, perform socialization functions. Suffused by a religious worldview that encompasses liturgies, evocations rituals, and religious songs, traditional Yorùbá culture emphasizes the use of the talking drum with its capacity for mischievous ambiguity, praise, or ridicule, as the occasion may demand. Names are not just carriers of identities; they purposely evoke circumstances of birth or embody narratives that remind one of the past and carry portents of future aspirations. In times of protest, for example, insurgent groups and poets give themselves names that resonate with the essence of the struggle.

For example, *àgbẹ̀kòyà* (farmers' revolt) was the name adopted by a widespread peasant movement in the then Western Region, populated by the Yorùbá people. The mechanisms of popular culture include neo-traditional forms such as songs and poems composed on CD by poets such as Ọlátúnbọ̀sún Ọládàpọ̀, Adébáyọ̀ Fálétí, Ọlánrewájú Adépọ̀jù, and Kúnlé Ológundúdú.

The modern Yorùbá theater has evolved from stage to television and from the radio to the movie screen. Nollywood, the nickname for the Nigerian movie industry, is a global industry. Prominent names in the development of the industry include Hubert Ògúndé, Dúró Ládipọ̀, Akínwùmí Ìsọlá, Kọlá Ògúnmọ́lá, and comedian Moses Adéjùmọ̀. Yorùbá theater is a modification of the famous *alárìnjó* (mobile theater), which evolved from the *egúngún pidán pidán* (masquerades who entertain by sorcery and magical arts). It later metamorphosed through home videos into its current global format, captured in the popularity of *Africa Magic Yorùbá* on DSTV Cable Television Network.

Popular culture is also reflected on television by such programs as *Lágbo Video*, *Kọnsọligbádùn*, and *Ojú Ọjà*, which are regularly featured on Lagos Television. Radio, the preeminent medium for entertainment and news among the lower classes, also features a variety of programs that cater to the entertainment, information, and educational needs of a large portion of the public. Yorùbá-language newspapers include *Akéde Àgbáyé*, *Aláròyé*, and magazines with romantic stories. Furthermore, the explosive growth of cities and towns resulted in part from the Christian Church's incorporation of different aspects of Yorùbá popular culture, such as festive drumming and traditional dance styles. These elements of popular culture combine with Christian modes of worship to produce a unique version.

Jùjú, *fújì*, *àpàlà*, and *dadakúàdà* are some of the influential music varieties that combine traditional culture as reflected in proverbs and riddles such as *lówe lówe l'à ń lùlù àgídìgbo* (it is by proverbs and riddles that we bring out the best melodies from the musical instrument). The Yorùbá have made an impact on imported musical varieties such as highlife, jazz, and country music. As fun loving people, Yorùbá are known for throwing parties and feasts, a carryover from the tradition of various festivals in traditional society. Festivals are the flip side of Yorùbá admonitions to work hard, as seen in the saying *isé loògùn isé* (hard work is the remedy for poverty). Noticeable, too, is a protest epistemology dating back to the free speech festivals of traditional society: *n ó wí, oba kì í pòkorin* (I will have my say, as the king does not slay singers). This tradition resurfaced in the Àgbékòyà movement, Hurbert Ògúnde's theater, and the protest against the annulment of the presidential election results from June 12, 1993. It must be said, however, that such values and motifs exist in contention with other tendencies in popular culture.

See also **Àgbékòyà Rebellion; Drama; Literature: Oral; Media: Newsprint; Media: Radio and Television; Music: Islamic**

REFERENCE

Barber, Karin, ed. *Readings in African Popular Culture*. Bloomington: Indiana University Press; Oxford, UK: James Currey, 1997.

Ayò Olúkòtún

PRAISE POETRY AND EULOGY (*ORÍKÌ*)

Oríkì, according to Karin Barber, "are attributive epithets . . . that are central in the social, religious, and political life of the Yorùbá people. They are vocative in address and name-like in form, disjunctive both in relation to each other and internally, and condensed and allusive in reference." A text or performance of *oríkì* is an assemblage of potentially separate and diverse units that can be performed in varying orders and combinations. These diverse units are held together by their common application to a specific subject. The goal of the *oríkì* is not to tell a complete story but to allude to incidents about the heroic deeds and qualities of the subject being praised. It is the accumulated meaning of the attributes and the significance of the deeds that build up the heroic structure of *oríkì*. The meaning of *oríkì* does not reside in the story line but in the litany of names, epithets, and attributes.

Several types of *oríkì* can be recognized on the basis of the subject matter. The *oríkì* of individuals and lineages, towns and places, chiefs and kings, divinities, and plants and animals. *Oríkì* is not necessarily panegyric. While the *oríkì* poet tries to characterize the subject, the poet inevitably touches on the subject's shortcomings, which he or she does in a euphemistic, pleasant manner. No matter how pleasantly the truth is couched, it is always said. Thus, *oríkì* is used to define its subject, usually by maximizing those attributes which the society consider good qualities and playing down, as much as possible, the unflattering ones.

For instance, when a new child is expected, the circumstances of the baby's conception, the expectant mother's experiences during pregnancy and delivery, and the circumstances of the child's birth are closely observed and encapsulated in a one-word *oríkì* known as *oríkì sókí* or *oríkì àbíso*. Consider the following male *oríkì* that reflects the circumstances of conception of a child: Àkànní or Àkàndé means "child conceived after a single physical relation between parents," and Àjàmú or Àjàní means "child conceived after prolonged arguments between between parents." Female *oríkì* also reflect the same circumstances or the hopes of the parents on the child: Àbèní means "child conceived after her mother has been begged," and Àdùké means "child whom people shall contest to pet."

As the child grows into adulthood, he or she acquires another form of *oríkì* known as *ìnagijé* or *àlàjé*, phrases that point to the person's emotional or physical characteristics. For instance, a dark person may be called *adúmáadán* (one who's skin is dark and smooth) or *igbó-fi-dúdúsolá* (the forest is resplendently dark). An irascible person may be referred to as *òjò-pa-gbòdògì-ró-pòròpòrò* (the rain beats the *gbòdògì* leaf and it sounds noisily). A generous but extravagant person may be called Màmíná (the one who does not know how to spend wisely), while someone who is not cheerful is called *akíni-gán-in* (the one who greets briefly). An accumulation of several phrases of *ìnagijé* over a period of time may result in *oríkì bọ̀rọ̀kìnní*, praises in honor of important personaltes such as war-lords, chiefs, kings, and the wealthy.

Apart from the *àlàjẹ́*, or *ìnagije*, which usually points to the flattering aspects of its bearer, the Yorùbá have other *oríkì* phrases that are attached to personal names as appellation. These are the phrases that are derived from important people who have borne those names before the current bearers. They are called *oríkì àdàpè*, avoidance epithets. For instance, anybody whose *àbísọ* name is Ìbíkúnlé usually has added to his name *olókè, àgbàngbà ààsẹ̀* (lord of the hill, owner of a strong large door), which was applicable to Balógun Ìbíkúnlé (1851–1964), the famous Ìbàdàn ruler. Adéyẹmí has *alówólódù-bí-ìyere* (one who has money in large pots like locust bean) as his *àdàpè*, which was also appli-cable to Aláàfin Adéyẹmí (1876–1905). Adéníjì and Ògúndípẹ̀ have *àpáta* (rock) and *arápásọwú* (one who has a powerful arm to wield a heavy iron hammer), respectively.

A category of *àdàpè* also exists for personal names known as *orúkọ àmútọ̀runwá*, which are usually given to children with an unusual birth condition. For instance, all that are born breech bear the name Ìgè and have the appellation *adùbí* (one for whose birth people con-test), and all Àjàyí are referred to as *ògídí-olú-oníkànga-àjípọn* (special-titled person, owner of a well from which water is drawn at dawn).

When an individual is being praised, his or her personal *oríkì* is usually accompanied by the *oríkì orílẹ̀* (lineage *oríkì*) if the praise singer is familiar with the subject of praise. The individual is referred to by all the names and epithets he or she bears, along with the avoidance phrases usually attached to important people who have borne such names before. His or her physical makeup and characteristic behavior are encapsulated in the *àlàjẹ́* or *ìnagije* phrases, while he or she is traced to the ancestors and activities for which they have become notable. The *oríkì* of divinities are performed by their various devotees, and those of plants and animals occur mainly in the repertoire of the *ìjálá* chanters.

Oríkì can be spoken, chanted, or sung, depending on the situation of performance. When a child greets the parents in the morning, the *oríkì* is generally spo-ken, but on festive occasions the *oríkì* may be chanted or sung. *Oríkì* can also be played on the drum (espe-cially the *dùndún* talking drum) as the speech tones are reproduced with the drum in a kind of language. In the official residence of kings and important chiefs, the *oríkì* of the predecessors of the present incumbent are beaten on the drum everyday; while drummers coin new *oríkì* for the incumbent.

Oríkì is not private property but a traditional mate-rial that its owners know and others, especially bards, poets, drummers, and raconteurs, learn for their own use. Today, however, the freelance poets in urban cen-ters have not only turned *oríkì* into the personal prop-erty of the rich but they concentrate more on the flat-tering aspects of these individuals, hoping for reward for doing so. These modern, materialistic bards are able to describe only physical and emotional prop-erties of people to the neglect—usually due to igno-rance—of the *oríkì* of towns and lineages. Hence, *oríkì* and the life of the genre is in danger.

See also **Lineages and Cognomen (*Oríkì Orílẹ̀*); Names and Naming**

REFERENCES

Barber, Karin. "Praise Poetry: Yoruba Oríkì." In *African Folklore: An Encyclopedia*, ed. Philip M. Peek and Kwesi Yanka, 364–65 New York: Routledge, 2004.

Ọlátúnjí, O. Ọlátúndé. *Features of Yorùbá Oral Poetry*. Ìbàdàn (Nigeria): Unversity Press, 1984.

Akíntúndé Akínyẹmí

PRISON

Most precolonial African societies did not erect and maintain prisons to confine offenders and social devi-ants. However, available historical evidence suggests that different precolonial Yorùbá kingdoms built and maintained prisons. These kingdoms were able to establish and maintain prisons mainly because they possessed a centralized political system headed by a monarchical ruler, a standing army, and sufficient economic and capital resources. Yorùbá kingdoms operated under the rubric of a centralized political system. Under this arrangement, the king (ọba) shared political authority only with heads of kin groups and appointed chiefs. The king held the right to appoint adjudicators to manage disputes and see to the maintenance of law and order. In addition, the king's court served as the highest court of appeal; any decision made and pronounced at the court was considered final and binding on all disputing parties.

Indigenous prisons were founded mostly by kings and local chiefs. European anthropologists who visited different Yorùbá communities in the nineteenth century confirmed in their accounts that every politically important man or chief kept a cell in which criminals were kept for offenses such as drunkenness and disobedience. Indigenous prisons not only received criminals but also welcomed different categories of offenders, such as slaves, debtors, witches, and political opponents. In some Yorùbá kingdoms, secret societies or fraternities administered local prisons. For instance, the Ògbóni cult society held prisoners and social deviants in a place known as the Ògbóni House.

Another important feature of the culture of confinement among Yorùbá people is the fact that imprisonment did not serve as punishment per se. Local prisons served mainly as transitional sites; they were places where offenders were confined for only a short period of time, at least until their cases were reviewed and decided upon by appointed judicial bodies. Like other precolonial African societies, indigenous customary laws and penal procedures adopted by different kingdoms did not make room for the idea of keeping offenders out of sight for a lengthy period of time. Yorùbá indigenous laws emphasized restorative justice and reconciliation. In as much as punishment was meted out on offenders, measures were also put in place to ensure that offenders were fully reintegrated into the society. Punishment procedures such as the payment of fines and compensation, imposition of supernatural sanction, and the application of corporal punishment were discretely and widely applied to foster mutual relations between the offender and the victim.

From the fifteenth century onward, new cultures of confinement developed. This era was marked by the growth and expansion of the Atlantic slave trade. New architectures of confinement developed in several Yorùbá states, especially in states established along or close to coastal areas and trade routes. These architectures of confinement included staging posts, enclosures, compounds, and barracoons, and they were used mainly for the confinement of slaves until they were sold to Europeans. Initially, local slave traders built barracoons beside beachfronts or close to creeks and estuaries, where they were easily located by European ships and local slave dealers. However, following the abolition of the slave trade, local slave dealers and merchants began to situate their barracoons in hidden locations, where they could not be easily discovered by British naval ships patrolling the West African coast. Many of these hideouts were later discovered and destroyed by British naval officers.

The first colonial prison in Nigeria emerged in Lagos after the territory was declared as a British colony. In 1862, H. S. Freeman set up a prison to function as part of the British-style criminal justice system. Available evidence shows that the Yorùbá people strongly resisted the carceral domination that came with colonialism. Therefore, the people constituted a significant part of the colonial prison population throughout the colonial period. In the early phase of colonial rule in Nigeria, many local Yorùbá leaders were imprisoned for resisting imperial rule. In the period after World War I, many Yorùbá nationalists, such as Abdul Tinúbú, Herbert Macaulay, and Ọbáfẹ́mi Ṣóléyẹ, were imprisoned by the colonial government because they called for the termination of British rule.

See also **Police**

REFERENCES

Milner, Alan. *The Nigerian Penal System*. London: Sweet and Maxwell, 1972.

Abíọ́dún, Tósìn Fúnmi. "A Historical Study on Penal Confinement and Institutional Life in Southern Nigeria, 1860–1956." Unpublished PhD dissertation, University of Texas at Austin, 2013.

Tósìn Abíọ́dún

PROMINENT PENTECOSTAL PASTORS

Pentecostal churches are generally regarded as the epitome of African Christianity. This is particularly so in the context of their providing an African interpretation of the Bible and the Christian liturgy, known as "existentialist Christianity." Such a Christian paradigm combines the message of the eternal salvation of the soul with members' worldly prosperity. Consequently, the churches have witnessed phenomenal growth, not only across Yorùbáland but also in Nigeria, throughout Africa, and in different parts of the globe. Quite a number of Yorùbá Pentecostal pastors have become significant faces of this phenomenon.

Pastor Enoch Adébóyè

Enoch Adéjàre Adébóyè is the general overseer of the Redeemed Christian Church of God (RCCG). Adeboye was born in 1942 to Moses and Esther Adébóyè in Ifẹ̀wàrà, Ọ̀sun State, Nigeria. In spite of the difficulties arising from the poor economic status of his parents, Adébóyè beat all odds to purse a remarkable educational career and he ultimately obtained a doctorate in mathematics at the University of Lagos. He also became a member of faculty at the same institution, rising to the position of associate professor of mathematics before his retirement in 1980.

Adébóyè's spiritual journey and church leadership after years of "worldly living" began with his encounter with the founder of RCCG, Josiah Akíndayọ̀mí. This encounter resulted in Adébóyè becoming a "born-again" Christian in 1973. He immediately assumed the role of interpreter to Akíndayọ̀mí. He not only became fervent in his faith but also adopted Akíndayọ̀mí as his spiritual mentor. He was ordained a pastor in 1975.

The RCCG was founded by Josiah Akíndayọ̀mí in 1952. It is basically an apocalyptic church with belief in the end of the world which the Parousia would

herald. Moreover, the church adopted a classical format, with the majority of its parishes being in Lagos and its environs. The emergence of Dr. Enoch Adébóyè as general overseer of the church in 1980, after the death of the founder and leader, dramatically transformed the church. After initial controversy surrounding Adébóyè's election to the post, he introduced far-reaching measures that transformed the church from a little tribal church to an expanding and modern-day church. Indeed, the church transformed from a "world rejecting" church to a "world accommodating" church. Perhaps the chief architect of this transformation was the introduction of model parishes, a departure from the classical parishes that brought in people of different socioeconomic positions, thus stimulating social and economic mobility of the church. The model parishes' format became structured by the introduction of strategic and doctrinal positions.

The groundwork for the development and expansion of the church began with the establishment of the Redeemed Christian fellowships by Adébóyè in May 1998. These fellowships, which essentially were students' initiative on various university campuses, soon provided impetus for the founding of other groups such as the Redeemed Christian Campus Fellowship (RCCF) and Christ the Redeemers Friends Universal. All these groups became effective agents of evangelization of very important personalities, bringing them into the church's fold.

Today, the RCCG under Pastor Adébóyè has become a worldwide megachurch with a formidable presence and impact in all continents of the world. In the United States alone there are well more than one hundred parishes. In Nigeria, the church has established considerable numbers of social and educational institutions. There are primary and high schools run by the church in different parts of the country. Its university, Redeemer University—with its temporary campus at the Redemption Camp, Lagos-Ìbàdàn Expressway—has moved to its permanent site in Ẹdẹ, Ọ̀sun State, Nigeria.

Pastor Adébóyè's influence far transcends the pastoring of members of his church. He has become an acknowledged world personality who has significantly affected not only Nigerian society but also global communities spiritually, politically, socially, and educationally. For example, *Newsweek*, an American international news magazine, in its January 2009 edition listed Adébóyè as the forty-fifth most powerful person in the world. He was recognized not only for the huge population of his church but also for remaining above the fray by not faking supernatural powers and for showing honesty.

The pervading influence of Pastor Adébóyè as a foremost religious leader and the enormous strength of the membership of the church both in and outside of Nigeria have cast him in the limelight. Consequently, his favors, support, intervention, and blessing are sought by political office holders. Thus, the monthly Holy Ghost services, annual conventions, and congresses have become pilgrimage venues to pray for blessings and acceptance.

Bishop David Oyèdépò

Bishop David Ọláníyì Oyèdépò is founder and president of David Oyèdépò Ministries International (DOMI). This is the umbrella organization comprising Living Faith Church (or Winners' Chapel), Living Faith Church Worldwide (a global network of churches), and World Mission Agency (WMA), the global missionary arm of the church's operations. Today, Oyèdépò presides over the Winners' Chapel network, which has a presence in more than three hundred cities in Nigeria, thirty-two African countries, several countries in Europe, and the United States.

Oyèdépò was born in Òsogbo in 1954, to a mixed religious family from Òmù-Àrán, Kwara State, Nigeria. His mother was a Christian and belonged to the Eternal Order of the Cherubum and Seraphim Movement (C&S). His father was a Muslim. However, Oyèdépò was raised by his grandmother, who introduced him to Christian life. Oyèdépò became "born again" in 1969, when he was in high school, through the influence of his teacher, Betty Lasher, who had taken an interest in his spiritual development. After high school Oyèdépò attended the Kwara State Polytechnic and studied

architecture. He then worked briefly with the Federal Ministry of Housing in Ìlọrin. He later resigned to become a full-time missionary.

Oyèdépò's pastoral journey began with the claim of a mandate he received from God during an eighteen-hour vision in May 1981 to liberate the world from all oppression of the devil by preaching the word of God. This led to the founding of Liberation Faith Hour Ministries, later Living Faith Church Worldwide. In 1983 Oyèdépò and his wife were ordained pastors by Pastor Enoch Adébóyè, general overseer of the Redeemed Christian Church of God. In 1985 Oyèdépò was ordained bishop and officially commissioned his new church, located in Kaduna. However, the church moved to Lagos in 1995.

Under Bishop Oyèdépò, the church has witnessed such phenomenal growth that today it has grown beyond a church ministry into an expansive conglomerate, with properties including four private jets, estates, restaurants, shopping stores, bakeries, processing plants, educational institutions, and other commercial properties all over the world. The educational institutions include elementary schools, high schools, and two universities, Covenant University, located in Canaan Land, Ọ̀tà, Ògùn State—which is also the headquarters of Ministry and Landmark University, located in Òmù-Àrán, his hometown. Construction of the third university is under way in Calabar, Cross Rivers, Nigeria.

Bishop Oyèdépò has written and published more than seventy titles on Christian literature and inspiration. He is the chair and publisher of Dominion Publishing House (DPH), a publishing arm of the ministry. DPH has more than four million books circulating to date. Bishop Oyèdépò is generally regarded as a pastor, author, educator, and industrialist with personal fame and wealth. Indeed, Forbes in 2012 named him as the wealthiest pastor in Nigeria with a net worth of more than US$150 million. He is also very much engaged as an influential spiritual leader with a large followership in the Nigerian body politic. In 2014, he accompanied the Nigerian president, Goodluck Jonathan, to Jerusalem on Christian pilgrimage. There was also a major controversy on the visit of the president to his church on Sunday, January 25, 2015. The visit sparked accusations of Oyèdépò's involvement in partisan support for the president in the approaching 2015 presidential election.

Pastor William Kúmúyì

William Fọ́lọ́runṣọ́ Kúmúyì is founder and general superintendent of the Deeper Life Bible Ministry. The church headquarters is situated at KM 42 Lagos-Ìbàdàn Expressway, Nigeria. The church has experienced phenomenal growth, and its branches can be found not only in different parts of Nigeria but also across the globe.

Kúmúyì was born in 1941 to Christian parents from Ẹ̀rìn-Ìjẹ̀sàa, Ọ̀sun State, Nigeria. He completed his secondary school education in 1961. In 1967, he proceeded to the University of Ìbàdàn, from where he graduated with a first-class honors degree in mathematics. Kúmúyì's Christian life led him to become "born again" in 1964, while teaching at Mayfair College, Ìkẹ́nẹ́, and he later ultimately became a world-renowned Pentecostal pastor. However, it was while he was working as a mathematics lecturer at the University of Lagos in 1973 that he started a Bible study group with fifteen university students who had approached him for training in Scripture. By 1980 the small Bible study group had attracted thousands of followers. This led to the formal establishment of the Deeper Life Bible Church.

By 1988 the church's congregation was estimated to have grown to fifty thousand people. Today, the church has well more than a thousand churches in Lagos State alone, five thousand across Nigeria, and branches in more than forty countries in Africa and other parts of the world. The phenomenal growth of the chuch has been attributed to divine intervention and to the singular dedication of Pastor Kúmúyì. Members of the church bear testimonies of Christ's miraculous intervention in changing lives in response to prayer and the proclamation of the Gospel. Kúmúyì himself has described this phenomenon as the work of God, who has strategically and prudently used miracles to attract all people to God through the church. This growth is also attributed to the down-to-earth spirituality of Pastor Kúmúyì. He is dedicated to both reading and studying the Bible. Also, he delivers his messages clearly, captivating both illiterate and highly literate listeners. Kúmúyì was named one the five hundred most powerful people on the planet by *Foreign Policy* magazine in 2013.

In recent years two major controversies developed in relation to Kúmúyì and his ministry. The first was in 2011 when he, at age seventy-one, married Esther, the sixty-five-year-old national and international women's coordinator of the church, based in London. This was just eighteen months after the death of his first wife. The second controversy surrounded the elaborate wedding of his son in Dubai, which caused outrage within and outside the church. The couple was actually suspended from the church and it took the intervention of church elders for the couple to be reinstated.

See also **Christianity: The Aládurà and Pentecostal churches**

REFERENCES

Adogame, Afe, and Cordula Weissicoppel, eds. *Religion in the Context of African Migration.* Berlin (Germany): Bayreuth African Studies, 2005.

Bible-Davids, Rebecca. *Enoch Adeboye Father of Nations.* London: Biblos Publishers, 2009.

Korieh, Chima Jacob, ed. *Religion, History, and Politics in Nigeria: Essays in Honor of Ogbu U. Kalu.* New York: University Press of America, 2005.

Ìbígbọ́ládé S. Adéríbigbé

PROMINENT SCHOLARS

Yorùbá scholarship involves those who have turned the light of their scholarship on the theoretical and practical interrogation of cultural production, creative practices, and historical evolution. Yorùbá scholarship is unique in its inclusive disciplinary dynamics. First are the creative writers in whose hands the traditional past has become the powerful source of a creative and literary efflorescence of the human experience. Dúró Ládipò, together with Hubert Ògúndé and Kọ́lá

Ògúnmọ́lá, was part of an artistic revolution in the late nineteenth and early twentieth centuries that led to a deliberate introduction of indigenous cultural forms into Christian entertainment. Ládìpọ̀'s *Mọrèmi*, for instance, dramatizes this traditional experience. Daniel O. Fágúnwà and Amos Tutùọlá are two authors who pioneered a nontheatrical genre that explored Yorùbá folklores as a site for understanding modern existence. Fágúnwà pioneered the Yorùbá-language novel with the publication of *Ògbójú Ọdẹ nínú Igbó Irúnmalẹ̀* (1938); Tutùọlá took that literary form to a uniquely inventive level in *The Palm-Wine Drinkard* (1946), written in ungrammatical, "broken" English.

From these followed the flowering of the Yorùbá literary form in English and the mother tongue, including Adébáyọ̀ Faleti's *Baṣọ̀run Gáà* (1972), Akínwùmí Ìṣọ̀lá's *Ẹfúnṣetán Aníwúrà* (1971), and Ọlábímtán's *Kékeré Ẹkun* (1967). J. F. Ọdúnjọ's *Aláwìyé* series pioneered popular engagement with the Yorùbá language and literary forms—stories (ìtàn), poems (ewì) and idioms—for juveniles, serving as an early introduction to the Yorùbá tradition for young minds. Yorùbá literary scholarship also comprises contemporary academic literary critics and creative writers.

Rowland Abíọ́dún is a pioneering scholar of Yorùbá art and aesthetics; his many works explore the evolution of the Yorùbá artist at the juncture of history, rituals, and morality.

In the hands of Akínwándé Olúwọlé Ṣóyínká, Oyinadé Ògunbà, and Òyékàn Owómóyèlá, the Yorùbá culture achieved the height of sophisticated literary analysis. Ògunbà specialized in festival drama, beginning his scholarship with a dissertation on the Ìjẹbú Agẹmọ Ritual. His later scholarship was, quite naturally, founded on a mutually beneficial intellectual confrontation and exegesis on Ṣóyínká's dramaturgy. Ṣóyínká's *Death and the King's Horseman* (1975) represents his highly motivated intellectual embrace of Yorùbá worldview, mythology, and culture in an attempt to forge a unique theatrical and artistic reality and philosophy. Along with Ṣóyínká, Owómóyèlá explored the boundaries of cultural experience in oral literature and literature, language, and philosophy. In

Yorùbá Proverbs (2005), his massive and definitive compilation and annotation of proverbs, Owómóyèlá provided a singular paroemiographic framework around which Yorùbá thought can be engaged. In this regard, his intellectual service to Yorùbá culture is similar to that of Ayọ̀ Bámgbóṣé and Ọládélé Awóbulúyì in the Yorùbá language and grammar. Bámgbóṣé's *A Grammar of Yorùbá* (1966) and Awóbulúyì's *Essential of Yorùbá Grammar* (1978) constituted linguists' recognition of the significance of the Yorùbá language in educational advancement. What Bámgbóṣé and Awóbulúyì outlined as the basics of Yorùbá language proficiency, Babátúndé Fáfúnwá experimented with in an attempt to prove the significance of Yorùbá in pedagogical learning.

In philosophy, Ṣẹ́gun Gbádégẹsin and John Olúbí-Ṣódípọ̀ have both demonstrated, beyond Owómóyèlá's paroemiology, the versatility of the Yorùbá philosophical reflections and worldviews. Olúbí-Ṣódípọ̀'s interests lay in a conceptual clarification of Yorùbá terms such as witchcraft (àjẹ́), causality, knowledge (ìmọ̀), belief (ìgbàgbọ́), and the like, especially in works like "Notes on the Concept of Cause and Chance in Yorùbá Traditional Thought" (1973) and *Knowledge, Belief and Witchcraft: Analytical Experiments in African Philosophy* (1997), coauthored with Barry Hallen. Gbádégẹsin's interest lies in the scrutiny of the conceptual foundation of Yorùbá philosophical thought as well as a rigorous critique of African postcolonial realities. This interest is represented in his major work *African Philosophy: Traditional Yorùbá Philosophy and Contemporary African Realities* (1991).

Yorùbá sociological experience constitutes the focus of Nathaniel Akínrẹ̀mí Fádípẹ̀. *The Sociology of the Yorùbá* (1970) remains perhaps the most detailed and comprehensive sociological inquiry into the Yorùbá people. In *Àjọbí and Àjọgbé: Variations on the Theme of Sociation* (1983), Akínṣọlá Akìwọwọ extended the sociological line of inquiry into Yorùbá life. Akìwọwọ was concerned with establishing an indigenous sociological framework on Ifá oracular narratives. The concepts of àjọbí (consanguinity) and àjọgbé (cohabitation) are the essential concepts around which one can achieve the understanding of the human society as an organismic system (àṣùwàdà). In *Yorùbá Towns* (1962), Akin Mábògùnjẹ́ laid out his abiding concern with the morphological structure of the ìlú as well as the evolution of Yorùbá urbanism. Oyèrónkẹ́ Oyèwùmí, in *The Invention of Women* (1997), and Bọ́láńlé Awé, in *The Ìyálóde in Ìbàdàn Politics and Society, c. 1850-1997* (1998), research the conceptual dynamics of gender relationship in the traditional Yorùbá society, especially as it enables us to confront patriarchal systems in contemporary times.

Bọ́lájí Ìdòwú and Wándé Abímbọ́lá are instrumental in expounding the intricacies of the traditional religion. Abímbọ́lá, more than any other scholar, remains prominent in his study of the oral tradition as manifest in the Ifá divinatory framework as a mirror on the Yorùbá thought system. *Ifá: An Exposition of Ifá Literary Corpus* (1979) illustrates the centrality of Ifá in the Yorùbá religious framework. The theological underpinning of Yorùbá religion, especially its confrontation with Christianity and colonialism, has drawn the attention of Bọ́lájí Ìdòwú in *Olódùmarè: God in Yorùbá Belief* (1962).

Yorùbá study has benefited the most from various historical analyses, reconstructions, and interrogations by historians fascinated with the evolution of the Yorùbá as a people. Samuel Johnson's pioneering study *The History of the Yorùbás* (1921), as well as the anticolonial historiographical struggle of the Ìbàdàn School of History, paved the way for a serious reconsideration of the complexities of Yorùbá cultural practices, social manifestations, artistic expressions, inter- and intracultural relationships, trading, wars, sociopolitical dynamics, and so on. In *The Origin of the Yorùbá* (1971), Sàbúrì Bíòbákú moved from the general advocacy of the Ìbàdàn School to a specific historical research focusing on oral tradition as a legitimate means for reconstructing history. J. F. Adé-Àjàyí, a colleague of his at the Ìbàdàn School, has advocated for a research scholarship that de-emphasizes the dominance of colonialism in Africa's historical dynamics. In *Yorùbá Warfare in the Nineteenth Century* (1964), Adé-Àjàyí attempted to reconsider the chaotic internal dynamics of nineteenth-century Yorùbáland. This emphasis on the internal evolution of the Yorùbá,

as well as their interaction with their neighbors, is what also defined Isaac Akínjógbìn's and J. A. Àtàndá's research on Yorùbá history.

Tóyìn Fáláọlá occupies a status in historical scholarship that straddles a deep and critical conversation between the older and younger generations of Yorùbá historians. For instance, in "A Research Agenda on the Yorùbá in the Nineteenth Century" (1988), Fáláọlá attempts to redirect the path of historical research on Yorùbá historiography, especially in its most turbulent century. For him, given the abundance of the materials available on the evolution of the Yorùbá over time, Yorùbá history ought to be a dynamic enterprise not restricted by static assumptions.

See also **Fádípẹ̀, Nathaniel Akínrẹ̀mí; Fágúnwà, Fáláọlá Olọ́runtóyìn Ọmóyẹni; Daniel Ọlọ́runfẹ́mi; Johnson, Samuel; Ládipọ̀, Dúró; Ọdúnjọ, Joseph Fọláhàn; Ògúndé, Hubert Adédèjì; Ṣóyínká, Wọlé; Translation; Tutùọlá, Amos; Writers**

REFERENCE

Fáláọlá, Tóyìn. *Yoruba Gurus: Indigenous Production of Knowledge in Africa*. Trenton, NJ: Africa World Press, 1999.

Adéshínà Afọláyan

PROSTITUTION

Prostitution is the act of purchasing sexual services. A prostitute is any active participant in the voluntary act of commercialized sexual services. In traditional society, prostitution was rarely known. While adultery and sexual pervasion such as rape were not alien to ancient Yorùbáland, prostitution appears to be a more recent phenomenon. Various terms for prostitution include *panságà obìnrin, ọ̀dọ́kọ, kárúwà,* and *alágbèrè.* However, these words do not in themselves mean "prostitution" but "adultery." As language itself is generative, the word *aṣẹ́wó* is now used to refer to a prostitute.

The reasons for becoming a prostitute are diverse, such as financial challenges, war refugees, defection in moral character, lack of education, loose parental background, and psychological and social influences. These reasons may not necessarily justify the practice or inform our judgment about the agents involved in the practice.

In the West, dominant liberal and individualistic attitudes seem to foster the perceptions of prostitutes as competent and autonomous individuals with rights to their bodies. Rather than being seen as an immoral or unnatural act, prostitution is socially regulated to avoid abuse, oppression, and disrespect. The Yorùbá-African disposition, however, stands contrary to such opinions. The Yorùbá attitude toward prostitution views it as antithetical to fostering communality. Although sex is traditionally considered an act to be decently conducted with the rightful person (husband and wife), at the rightful place, and for the rightful purpose, some people in society still practice and engage in prostitution.

The people's worldview frowns on sexual misconduct such as prostitution, rape, and adultery, which are considered not only condemnable and detestable but also a taboo that requires ritual purification. Prostitutes are not only looked down upon with cultural and moral repugnance, the act of prostitution is perceived as an objectification of women and men's dignity, honor, and worth. Given the social and moral prohibition against prostitution, there are measures to prevent people's engagement in prostitution. These range from whipping and public ridicule to the spiritual stricture of *mágùn* (thunderbolt). The use of *mágùn* (do not mount) is a traditional mechanism against sexual promiscuity designed to prevent, expose, or punish a promiscuous people. *Mágùn* can be destructive or preventive, but its main purpose is to guard against sexual immorality.

Although the rationale of placing *mágùn* on someone's body has been questioned in recent times as an anachronistic, punitive measure, the extent to which contemporary alternatives have been effective remain questionable. Some of the contemporary ways of addressing the menace of prostitution include arrest and prosecution of men soliciting for illicit sex by law enforcement authorities, feminist advocacy, emphasis on education of the girl child, and social and economic empowerment policies focused on women.

See also **Ethics; Sexuality and Sexual Behavior; Superstitions; Taboos**

REFERENCE

Fálọlá, Tóyìn. "Prostitution in Ìbàdàn, 1895-1950." *Journal of Business and Social Studies*, n.s., 6.2 (1989): 40–54.

Adémọ́lá K. Fáyẹmí

PROVERBS

Òwe is a virtual memory bank for all of the Yorùbá way of life and living, including philosophy, values, beliefs, ethics, and political economy. The Yorùbá say *ó ní ohun tí adìẹ ń jẹ kí àgbàdo tó dáyé* (before the advent of grains, chickens had something to eat). Thus, before the invention of Internet search engines, encyclopedias, Wikipedia, dictionaries, and thesauruses, òwe as a genre was the "search engine": *òwe lẹsin ọ̀rọ̀, bí ọ̀rọ̀ bá sọnù, òwe la fi ń wá a*. Òwe is the oral equivalent of a database for storing, retrieving, processing, and using Yorùbá literature and oral history.

There is no equivalent word for òwe in the English language. Yes, as truism, aphorism, or adage, òwe does everything a proverb does as a condensed statement of truth or principle. However, the body of oral genre called òwe is more than a pithy dictum or maxim. While most proverbs in English literature have been reduced to cliché and have, therefore, lost their value, òwe continues to be cherished among the Yorùbá as a measure of perceptive intelligence and wisdom. Thus, honor, respect, and high esteem are accorded to anyone who has a good knowledge, understanding, and ability to use and interpret òwe appropriately and effectively—in a certain way, at the right time, and for the right occasion.

As codes of ethics and civic responsibilities, òwe exist for all aspects of public and private affairs. For example, to rebuke an overdressed guest, they say *sìn mí relé àna, tó lọ gbé ẹwù ẹtù wọ* (an escort on a visit to one's in-laws' house is not expected to dress better than the the person who invited him or her). To solicit cooperation between the young and old, one might say *ọwọ́ ọmọdé kò tó pẹpẹ, bẹ́ẹ̀ ni t'àgbà ò wọ akèǹgbè* (while a child may not easily reach out to the ceiling, the elderly may also find it difficult to dip his or her hand in a gourd). To ensure elder's humility, one might say *àgbà tó jẹ àjẹìwẹ̀hìn, ni yóò ru igbá rẹ̀ délé* (the elder who ate without thinking to leave anything for the young ones would have to carry his or her load home alone). To sanction a rude son-in-law, there is the saying *báyòówù kí ó rí, ẹnì kan kì í bá àna rẹ̀ yan odì* (whatever the situation is, no man refuses to greet his in-laws).

The Yorùbá is a hierarchical society with a special regard for the elders. Consequently, *òwe* that act as unwritten codes of behavior and as sanctions and rewards exist for every one according to their place (status and age) in the hierarchy.

See also **Body Language and Idioms**

REFERENCE

Owómóyèlá, Oyèkàn. *Yorùbá Proverbs*. Lincoln: University of Nebraska Press, 2005.

Bọ́lá Dáúdà

PSYCHIATRY

Psychiatry and the treatment of psychological disorders is a field with deep cultural roots in Yorùbá communities. The Yorùbá identify several different causes of mental illness, including heredity, witchcraft, violation of taboo or other disturbance of supernatural forces, and physical and psychological injury. Ultimately, all of these causes are related to an imbalance between body, mind, and spirit that the Yorùbá see as central to maintaining both physical and mental health. In the traditional Yorùbá healing system, the nature of mental illnesses is most frequently defined in terms of its perceived cause rather than its particular symptoms.

Determination of the cause of mental illness is most commonly undertaken through divination by a trained diviner (Babaláwo). According to Yorùbá beliefs, an individual receives his or her *orí,* or destiny, from Olódùmarè, the supreme god, before birth. However, by the time of birth the person has forgotten their *orí.* Psychological disturbance may be a manifestation of a person's *orí* or it may be evidence of an imbalance in a person's life, which must be rectified in order to put him or her back on the correct path of his destiny. The diviner has the power to communicate with the gods through deep understanding of the mystical knowledge of Ifá. By performing rituals involving a set of instruments, including a divining board, a tapper, and palm nuts, the diviner is directed to the appropriate verse of the Ifá canon, which he can interpret to identify the cause and proposed treatment for the individual's psychological turmoil. Treatment might come in a variety of forms, including ritual sacrifices, herbal remedies, anti-witchcraft measures, or initiation into the cult of a particular *òrìṣà,* such as Ṣànpọ̀nná, who is responsible for smallpox and some mental illness.

In addition to the divination and indigenous treatments for mental illness, Yorùbá individuals have engaged in a variety of other means of diagnosing and treating psychological disorder. Most Yorùbá people today identify religiously either as Christians or Muslims, and these religious beliefs often play a role in how people conceive of and treat mental illnesses. In addition to consulting the Babaláwo, Christian Yorùbá, particularly those who ascribe to charismatic churches such as the Aládurà, might consult a faith healer, whereas Muslims might turn to a local *malam* (imam) to help them with a psychological problem.

The Yorùbá region has also played a significant role in the development of Euro-American psychiatric medicine in Africa. Several of the first Western-trained psychiatrists to conduct research and clinical work in Nigeria were Yorùbá. Adéoyè Thomas Lámbò and Tọ́lání Asúni were the first European-trained Yorùbá psychiatrists. Both worked at Arò Mental Hospital in Abẹ́òkúta, bringing Western psychiatric care to Nigerian patients. Lámbò, in particular, worked to integrate his training with that of indigenous medical practitioners in a local cultural setting. Their work helped produce several major works in cross-cultural psychiatry, including *Psychiatric Disorder among the Yorùbá* (1963) and the World Health Organization's *International Pilot Study of Schizophrenia* (1973).

See also **Lámbò, Adeoye Thomas**

REFERENCE

Fálọlá, Tóyìn, and Matthew M. Heaton, eds. *Traditional and Modern Health System in Nigeria*. Trenton, NJ: Africa World Press, 2006.

Matthew M. Heaton

PSYCHOLOGY

Four key concepts form the basis of Yorùbá psychology: predestination (*orí*), journey (*ìrìn àjò*), community (*ẹbí, ará, ọ̀rẹ́*), and character (*ìwà*). These help us understand how the Yorùbá have created a self-sustaining culture across time. They also explain how the Yorùbá mind-set wrestles with challenges of the human condition, from banal, quotidian events of life to the most traumatic events. Yorùbá psychology is one of resilience, ambition, creativity, and adaptability. Thus, it is possible to postulate an infrastructure of Yorùbá psychology from these concepts. It is located in spirituality and the value systems promoted by both of these across time. In turn, both are regularly and consistently expressed through traditional religion, Christianity, and Islam in their various iterations.

The Yorùbá believe that each soul has a choice (*àkúnlẹ̀yàn*) in his or her destiny (*orí*). The individual has his or her *orí* from birth to death. Thus, *orí* encompasses the twin notions of predestination and personal responsibility. A saying goes *orí ẹni l'àwúre ẹni* (a person's good fortune results from his or her choice). Since life's journey is replete with opportunity and adversity, the individual can negotiate life's circumstances and challenges in several ways. All Yorùbá share a belief in the Supreme Being (Olódùmarè, Ọlọ́run) and a pantheon of deities and ancestral spirits (the *òrìṣà* who act as intercessors in the journey through life—even though each individual and community claims affinity and devotion to its own versions of Yorùbá spirituality. Indeed, there is no such thing as an atheist Yorùbá. Life and its attendant challenges can also be managed through rites of passage, sacrifice, rituals (*ìrúbọ, ẹbọ, ètùtù*), and other psychosomatic tools (potions, amulets, talismans, prayer beads, totems, tattoos) that offer psychic and material resources during one's existence. Language—in the form of expiatory and propitiatory prayers (*ọfọ̀, àṣẹ*), proverbs, and aphorisms—also helps Yorùbá to cope with life's crises and challenges.

In addition, in Yorùbá psychology, the community, family, kinship ties, and other kinds of social interaction and connectedness are part of a holistic approach in facing mental stressors during one's life. Since one is never alone, strong community and kinship ties provide emotional and spiritual succor in times of crises. In addition, a multiplicity of professional healing specialists—versed in traditional and in Western mental health protocols—are available for individuals and families to resolve and overcome life's painful moments. Chief Olúṣọlá Lámbò and his brother Professor Adéoyè Lámbò were pioneering Yorùbá mental health experts who exemplified the openness to both traditional (ethnobotany and ethnopsychiatry) and Western (psychiatry) approaches to mental health challenges among the Yorùbá. Therefore, Yorùbá psychology is a holistic system whose ultimate goal is total well-being, and it encompasses the gamut of choices in healing the mind, body, and soul.

Yorùbá also emphasize the importance of character, or *ìwà*, which connotes attitude, behavior, mood, thought, action, and speech. It is the ethical component to other aspects of being. Thus, an individual is expected to live a life of balance and self-control in harmony with his or her community, nature, and the divine. Here, the Greek philosopher Heraclitus's maxim about character being destiny best describes that idea in Yorùbá culture. The importance of character in Yorùbá life cannot be overstated. A plethora of proverbs mention character as the essence of a person's moral rectitude. The concept of beauty and goodness is encapsulated in *ọmọlúwàbí* (a child or person of character), a broad and deep concept that stresses balance, self-control, humility, generosity, endurance, mindfulness, knowledge, and wisdom, among many other virtues.

Two proverbs illustrate the importance and necessity of character in the Yorùbá mind-set: *ìwà l'ẹ̀sìn* (a person's character is his or her true religion, not which faith that person preaches or confesses) and *Ìwà rere l'ẹ̀ṣọ́ ènìyàn* (good conduct and/or character is the true mark of a person's beauty). The Yorùbá concept of beauty is a deeply metaphysical concept. It is akin to classical (Aristotle, Plato, and Plotinus) Greek philosophical notions of beauty in that it emphasizes balance, order, symmetry, grace, and exemplary behavior. When the Yorùbá say *ó gún regé*, they mean everything about the named person, or object, is perfect and in harmony—symbolically and actually.

Finally, the general attitude is one of measured optimism and intense awareness of one's limitations and that of the gods—even when faith is challenged by fate. For example, the Yorùbá say *òrìṣà, b'ó ò le gbè mí, fi mí sílẹ̀ bi o ṣe bá mi* (if the gods cannot help, they can at least leave us alone). Thus, the Yorùbá can be quite realistic when facing life's challenges. Yorùbá culture recognizes individuality, not individualism. Each person is part of a continuum whose life is subsumed in networks of phenomenological, ontological and cultural relationships. Thus, the family is part of the clan, the clan part of the community, and the community part of the larger society. The society is part of a larger universe of humans, nature, and other beings. Yorùbá psychology emphasizes a humanistic outlook on life encompassing the maxim "we are all our brothers' keepers." The proverb *ènìyàn l'aṣọ mi* (people are like clothing) aptly summarizes the ecology of life in Yorùbá psychology. The clothing metaphor describes two key roles of human interaction: to protect against enemies or inimical situations (such as shame and indignity) and to enhance and dignify a person's efforts in the journey of life and living. For the Yorùbá the goal of life may be material success and well-being. However, the purpose of life is to live right, do right, and die right.

See also **Lámbò, Adéoyè Thomas; Ọmọlúwàbí; Psychiatry; Sacrifice; Words: Ọ̀rọ̀**

REFERENCES

Béwàjí, John A. I. "Ethics and Morality in Yorùbá Culture." In *A Companion to African Philosophy*, ed. Kwasi Wiredu, 396–403. Oxford (United Kingdom): Blackwell Publishing, 2004.

Gbádégẹsin, Ṣégun. *African Philosophy: Traditional Yorùbá Philosophy and Contemporary African Realities*. New York: Peter Lang, 1991.

Bíọ́dún J. Ògúndayọ̀

Ω

To the average Yorùbá, queerness conjures a series of perceived anomalies and discomforting attitudes toward sexual deviance as they relate to homosexuals and effeminate males. As an academic discipline, queer theory is yet to be generally received in the Yorùbá cultural context as a socially acceptable mode of thinking or behavior. The height of homophobic sentiment in Africa in general—masked, of course by religious and cultural beliefs—is the promulgation of a January 13, 2014, Nigerian law that criminalized same-sex relationships. People convicted under the law can face up to fourteen years of imprisonment. Nigeria is not alone in this. Uganda proposed a law in 2009 recommending the death sentence for "aggravated homosexuality." Homosexuality is illegal in at least thirty-six African countries.

Yorùbá society's homophobic beliefs draw from the millennial Ifá divination system, which proscribes that it is better for a man to make love to a woman than to a man. Some scholars, such as J. L. Matory and G. O. Ajíbádé, have argued that the issue is less one of the existence of same-sex relationships and more about preconceived prejudices against such sexual orientations. Research on the topic is thus minimal among scholars in Nigeria. Most academics, especially among the Yorùbá of southwestern Nigeria, see this area of research as suspicious and a consequence of colonial obscenity, corruption, and immorality—hence, it is an affront to core Yorùbá traditional values. Contrary to popular stereotypical assumptions, G. O. Ajíbádé argues that homosexuality did exist in Yorùbá societies before colonial intrusion.

In examining traditional Yorùbá religious practices, homosexuality did in fact exist among the Yorùbá of the southwestern Nigeria but was never considered a legitimate social institution. Ajíbádé identifies three forms of homosexual behavior among the Yorùbá: transgenerational (that which goes beyond any generational specificity), transgender (that which transcends a given gender), and egalitarian relationships (relates to respecting choices made by individuals on their choice of emotional or conjugal partnerships). These various forms display a distinctiveness determined by the customs and historical experiences peculiar to each community. Of significant import is the statement credited to Wándé Abímbọ́lá, the ultimate authority on Yorùbá oral tradition, who asserted, "Homosexuality was never part of our [Yorùbá] traditional culture; though it can be found today in urban areas such as in Lagos." In summary, the question is no longer one of the perception of social stigma and aberration associated with homosexuality in Yorùbá society but of whether a society has the political or cultural authority to impose subjective morality on its citizenry. In 2005, Bísí Álímì, a Yorùbá man from southwestern Nigeria announced his homosexuality on Nigerian television and almost lost his life. He escaped to England, where he secured asylum. It is hoped that through consciousness raising, the larger African community can become gradually more open to the fact that sexuality is part of human life and should be considered an essential ingredient of human expressiveness, whether we morally agree with it or not.

See also **Sexuality and Sexual Behavior**

REFERENCES

Ajíbádé, G. O. "Same-Sex Relationships in Yorùbá Culture and Orature." *Journal of Homosexuality* 60 (2013): 965–83.

Matory, J. L., ed. *Sex and the Empire That Is No More: Gender and the Politics of Metaphor in Ọ̀yọ́ Yorùbá Religion.* New York: Berghahn Books, 2005.

Níyì Afọlábí

R

REGENCY

Even though the Yorùbá culture recognizes that only male children sit on the royal stool and serve as kings, in a few towns, the death of a king allows a female heir to temporarily succeed her father until a new male king can be chosen. Examples of towns where females can become temporary leaders are Adó-Èkìtì, Àkúrę́, Àkùngbá, Apoi, Ìdó-Àní, and Ọ̀bà-Ilé. Regency is common among the eastern Yorùbá people domiciled in the Nigerian states of Èkìtì and Oǹdó. Two things perhaps led some towns to choose women as their temporary kings. One is the fear that if a man is chosen for the temporary task, he may seize power and attempt to make himself a permanent king. Another is the assumption that women prefer to be with their husbands instead of occupying a position that will place too much restriction on them. As regents, they are confined to their palaces or whatever places their towns recognize as official quarters, have occasional public appearances, and less freedom to do their personal transactions in their normal or ordinary lives. The restrictions that guide the conduct of a regent are to make sure that the dignity of a leader is preserved and respected.

As the acting king, a regent enjoys the benefits of office the way a king does. She is installed as an acting leader; she goes through the ritual of installation befitting her office. Her installation is usually done more quickly and is less involved than that of a king. Recognized as a ruler, she lives in the palace, wears a crown, dresses as a man, presides over traditional cabinet meetings, performs all other services expected of a king, and—under normal circumstances—receives the respect a king should have.

A regent is expected to vacate the throne immediately once a new king has been selected. However, history has revealed that at times, regents, obsessed with power, succeeded in their attempts to make themselves permanent on the temporary leadership task. Wùmí Akíntidé reports that two regents in Àkúrę́ refused to quit the throne after their tenure of office, and they continued to rule:

> [They] were both powerful women of substance with a lot of medicinal power. One of them became the 13th Déjì of Àkúrę̀. Her name was "Ẹyẹarò." She reigned for 26 years from 1393 to 1419. The second one became the 25th Déjì. Her name is "Ẹyẹmọin." She reigned for 30 years from 1705 to 1735. We are able to talk about them today because their reigns were properly documented.

In the towns that have regents, the message about women is that they are as capable of leading as men are. Even though their position is supposed to be temporary, regents still pass through the installation rituals and experience other aspects of kingship on the throne.

See also **Royalty and Chieftaincy; Succession**

REFERENCE

Akíntidé, Wùmí. "The Role of Regents in Yorùbá Tradition." *Sahara Reporters Online*. January 24, 2014. http://saharareporters.com/2014/01/25/role-regents-Yorùbá-tradition-dr-wumi-akintide.

Báyọ̀ Ọmọlọlá

REINCARNATION

Reincarnation is variously described as rebirth of the soul in another body, reappearance after death, or beginning a new cycle of death and rebirth after spending some time in the spiritual sphere. The Yorùbá have two predominant notions of reincarnation: *àkúdàáyà*, reappearance of a dead person in a different location, and *àtúnwá*, rebirth of an ancestor. *Àkúdàáyà* describes the experience of someone who died but is physically seen in other locations before or after burial, usually by those who are not yet aware of the death of the person. Indeed, the reincarnated person may be encountered living a normal life with a wife or husband and with children, which reinforces the Yorùbá belief that people who die before attaining old age can continue their earthly lives in another location.

The second manifestation is derived mainly from belief in the ancestral cult. Here the concept of reincarnation centers on the notion of the human features or characters of the ancestors being reborn in some children. This partial form of reincarnation allows the ancestors to continue to have their separate existence. Thus, their being reborn in their descendants does not terminate their continued "personal" existence in the ancestral world. The analogy commonly been used to represent this dynamic is that of the sun giving out energy but remaining hot. The Yorùbá think that this form of reincarnation is experienced by people who die in old age and become ancestors through their exemplary, righteous living on earth. It is considered a form of rebirth, as exemplified in terms such as *yíyà-ọmọ* (turning into a child) or *àtúnwá* (another coming). The names given to such children are usually gender based. Ìyábọ̀ or Yétúndé (mother has come back)

denotes a female ancestor, and Babátúndé or Babáwálé (father has come back) denotes a male ancestor.

Certain procedures help identify both the occurrence of reincarnation and the ancestors involved. First, potential reincarnation is restricted to the paternal lineage. Consequently, reincarnated children are named after ancestors from the father's lineage. Second, the identity of the reincarnated ancestor can be known by consulting the Ifá oracle. Other means of identification consist of close observation of the looks, mannerisms, and activities of a child at birth or as the child grows into adulthood. Other indicators include recognition of identical bodily marks on the child as those of an ancestor, the child's recalling or exhibiting traits of an ancestor, the child's ability to recall the ancestor's past existence, and a child's display of characteristics or skills that suggest the child is older than his or her age. Overall, belief in reincarnation reflects the Yorùbá philosophy of cosmic harmony. It is the recognition of the unity of existence subsumed in the circle of birth and rebirth.

See also **Names and Naming**

REFERENCES

Awólàlú, J. O. *Yorùbá Beliefs and Sacrificial Rites*. London: Longman Group, 1979.

Ìdòwú, E. B. *African traditional Religion*. London: S.C.M. Press, 1973.

Ìbígbọ́ládé S. Adéríbigbé

RELIGION AND COMMUNICATION

There has never been a people that did not have some form of religion: every group has a religion. Religion often determines people's way of life, as there is no culture without religion. The Yorùbá ethnicity is not an exception; rather, it is awesomely endowed with religious ecology. The Yorùbá religion comprises the traditional religious and spiritual concepts and practices of the people. Also, every religion and its conviction are expressed in different communicative forms—simple teaching, living, celebrations, rituals, charms, songs (dirges), incantations, ritual prayers, sacrifice, libations (as seen in the *Schnapp* advert), invocation, trance and hysterics, and forms of communication between the supernatural and living beings—otherwise classified as extramundane communication, which can be bottom-up or top-down communication.

While it is easy to send and understand messages sent through other modes of communication, extramundane communication is not as easy. In some cases, for someone who wants to be involved in the use of the extramundane, it might require certain rituals of initiation, because the extramundane involves communicating with supernatural beings: ancestors, spirits, gods, and the Supreme God. Thus, the Yorùbá religion is associated with the sacred realm of the gods. It is believed that the continuation of life is guaranteed through well-determined and periodic contact with the deities, when the people renew their faith by communicating in the form of charm, songs, incantations, ritual prayer, sacrifices, libations, invocations, trances, and hysterics.

It may also take the form of cultural and individual performances that invoke an intensity of emotion leading to temporary spiritual rituals. It is a multidimensional communication that manifests in cultural celebrations such as festivals, consummation of marriages, and naming and housewarming ceremonies. Again, religion involves intrapersonal processes such as incantation, physical revelation, magical otherworldly verbalization, spiritual transmigration, dedication, and consecration. These characteristics and elements can be neatly grouped into bottom-up (e.g. festivals, ceremonies, divination, and ancestral worship) and top-down (e.g. potent speech, dreams, and telepathy) communication within the extramundane mode. In essence, it is expressed in various forms.

Festivals ordinarily are seen as a form of entertainment or used for merriment. Festivals are celebrated periodically, sometimes annually, as part of Yorùbá religion to communicate different periods in the annual calendar or to celebrate planting or harvest seasons, among other things. The period for the celebration is clearly marked out in the calendar. For instance, Egúngún (Masquerade) festival is one of the festivals brought by some Yorùbá ancestors about four hundred years ago when they migrated south of the river Niger after the fall of the Old Ọ̀yọ́ Empire to a place known as Modákẹ́kẹ́ in Ilé-Ifẹ̀, in Ọ̀sun State.

Apart from entertainment, the festival also portrays the people's belief in reincarnation. As such, the festival is used to link up with the departed souls and to receive blessings from them annually. For this reason, the festival is very popular among the Ọ̀yọ́-speaking people of Yorùbáland. Egúngún festival is a seven-day event that takes place in the month of July every year. This month was chosen because the planting season is over and expectations for a bumper harvest are high, as July is noted for its heavy rainfall.

On the first day of the event, all the descendants of the Egúngún family converge in a sacred place, usually in the grove called *igbó ìgbàlẹ̀*. It is at this grove that Egúngún priests perform prayers and commune with their deity, as is the usual practice. It is forbidden for strangers to witness this. The arrival of the chief Egúngún signifies the commencement of the year's festival. He then proceeds to the ọba's palace to pay homage and offer prayer for the peaceful coexistence of his subjects. The king in turn gives the Egúngún a certain amount of money and kola nuts.

This event marks the first day when young masquerades would be noticed in some parts of the town. Subsequent days witness the outing of traditional masquerades like Ẹlẹ́bitì, Ọgbabù, Ológbojò, and Iyekiye, to mention a few, converging at the town center called Ojà-Ọba, where they test new discoveries of their latest occult powers by laying curses on one another through incantations.

This is an interesting aspect of the event where visitors and interested people keep watch on the one who will emerge as the year's strongest Egúngún. Young masquerades, most of them children of adept worshippers called the ọlọ́jẹ̀, move around the town beating people with a whip (*pàsán*); citizens who do not like to be beaten give them money, gifts, or ransom. Some of the big masquerades visit people's homes to offer prayers while women kneel before them in adoration as their "fathers from heaven" and respond to prayers from the masquerades by saying àṣẹ. The seventh day marks the end of the festival, when the masquerades called Ayinlẹ̀ proceed to the market center. After pouring libations, Ayinlẹ̀ removes his top regalia and rolls on the ground seven times. The event is then declared closed for the year, and no Egúngún is seen in the town again until the following year's festival.

Among the communication items used in the festival are native chalk, palm frond, calabash, pigeon or white dove, kola nut, lantern, ram, statue of Ògún, paddle, hoe, cutlass, palm wine, dog, snail, shrine, masquerade dress (white garment), songs. The festival is characterized by the use of drums, gin and palm oil; pouring of libations; and performing of rituals. These items and activities signify various things.

Thus, clearly among the Yorùbá religion communicates, and it is expressed in various forms. Egúngún festival as exemplified here is religious, as it structures the way of life of the Yorùbá people just as Buddhism, Confucianism, Hinduism, Islam, and Christianity shape the lives of their believers.

See also **Invocation; Libation; Religion and Ritual; Sacrifice**

REFERENCES

Momoh, C. S. "Global Principles of Religious and Ethnic Tolerance." *Journal of Contemporary Studies* 1.3 (2003): 27–53.

Ogwezzy, A. O. *A Functional Approach to African Communication Systems.* Lagos (Nigeria): Concept Publication, 2008.

Abigail Odozi Ogwezzy-Ndisika

RELIGION AND RITUAL

The works of scholars like J. O. Awólàlú and E. B. Ìdòwú suggest that religion permeates almost all aspects of the Yorùbá world. Ìdòwú asserts that "in all things they are religious; religion forms the foundation and the all governing principle of life for them." The statement resonates to this date. Indeed, this assertion suits the traditional worldview of the Yorùbá since they are committed to the divine guidance of Olódùmarè (the Supreme God) and a plethora of other gods and deities on diverse matters. Yorùbá oratory (oral tradition of myths, legend, and history) accords to Olódùmarè the creation of heaven, earth, humans, divinities and deities of diverse forms of life (tree, earth, water and sea, animals, and the like), and Ilé-Ifẹ̀, the ancestral home or holy city of the Yorùbá.

In most oratory, the arch-divinities of Òrìsà-Ńlá (the molder of human heads) and Ọ̀rúnmìlà (divinity of wisdom) play complementary roles with Olódùmarè in the theocratic ordering of the world and the world beyond. Ọ̀rúnmìlà is particularly embraced as the source of the systematic theogony or corpus known as Ifá. Ifá constitutes the scriptural codes of belief for the Yorùbá. Ifá is central to religious beliefs about happenstances, events, and other phenomena. It serves interchangeably as a divinity system and sometimes as a god. The Ifá corpus constitutes about 256 permutations of *odù*.

Odù could be conceived as the nucleus of the entire Ifá corpus, which comes in a 4-by-4 combination to produce 16 major chapters of Ifá, starting with Ogbè (the minimum unit of *odù*). Each of these 16 major *odù* can also combine with one another (16 times 16) to produce 256 minor *odù*. These possible 256 permutations of *odù* are often interpreted as emissaries or subdivinities of Olódùmarè. They also represent the possible range of combinations of the original 16 *odù*. The original 16 *odù* are Ogbè, Ọ̀yẹ̀kú, Ìwòrì, Òdí, Ìrosùn, Ọ̀wọ́nrín, Ọ̀bàrà, Ọ̀kànràn, Ògúndá, Ọ̀sá, Ìká, Òtúrúpọ̀n, Òtúrá, Ìrẹtẹ̀, Ọsẹ́, and Òfún. These *odù* are conceived as divine instructions and insight on all matters and are only accessible to the Ifá Priest, initiates, or diviners (known as Babaláwo). These *odù* are also interpreted as possible 4,096 (256 times 16) sentences, stories, myths, and proverbs. The *odù* prescribes measures to be taken on the matter about which the clients seek consultation. Prescriptions may take the form of admonition, forbearance, obedience, appeasement, penitence, sacrifice, or observation of rituals. Ritual and its nature is of keen interest here.

Ritual is only one mechanism for establishing regulations that emerge from community consciousness. This suits the nature of ritual among the Yorùbá since it emanates from the religious credo of Ifá on matters. Rituals are observed for upholding established traditional rites and for the sake of piety, averting repercussions from the wrong actions and behaviors of the members of the society or the whole society, and suppressing the impact of perverted practices, taboos, and other social vices. Rituals are usually administered by qualified priests known as àwòrò, ìwòrò, or aborè, and rituals have specific requirements that must be adhered to and not be mistaken in the course of a particular desire or the invocation of the gods or òrìṣà on matters. For this reason, the Yorùbá attach taboos to diverse ritual processions. For instance, in the invocation or consultation of Èṣù, palm nut oil is prohibited to avoid incurring the wrath of Èṣù; in the ritual offered to Ọbàtálá white and black cloth is required but palm wine is prohibited. Ritual requirements exist for the supreme divinity, Olódùmarè, and other divinities, cults like Egúngún, coronations for chiefs and kings, festivals, and other domains of the Yorùbá world.

In view of this brief insight, one can assert that the saying ẹ jẹ́ ká ṣe é bí wọ́n ti ń ṣe é, kí ó lè baà rí, bí ó ṣe yẹ kí ó rí (let us do it the way it is usually done so that we may have the usual result) summarizes ritual among the Yorùbá.

See also **Invocation; Libation; Religion and Communication; Sacrifice**

REFERENCES

Awólàlú, J. O., *Yorùbá Beliefs and Sacrificial Rites*. London: Longman Group, 1979.

Ìdòwú, E. B. *African Traditional Religion*. London: S.C.M. Press, 1973.

Wálé Owóṣéní

ROYALTY AND CHIEFTAINCY

Gbogbo nǹkan l'ọmọ ọba kò ní;
Bí i ti dàńsákì kọ́.

If a person from a royal family does not have anything,
He (she) still deserves being constantly praised.

This expression sums up the social expectations for people with royal blood. No matter what the situation is, under normal circumstances, people from royal families are celebrated, respected, and given priority or favorable treatments in traditional settings. The traditional system of government is headed by a king (ọba) who has chiefs (olóyè) as his cabinet members. A king resides in a palace (àfin), where he presides over the government of his territory, which usually has subordinate towns and villages.

Only people with royal blood can become kings in most towns and cities, and their installation (ìfijoyè or ìwúyè) is usually observed through a traditional rite. Most kings and their royal families trace the history of their origin or town to Odùduwà, the founder of the Yorùbá nation. However, an exception is Ìbàdàn, a war settlement or camp where a leader is chosen by promotion and seniority of chiefs. Another exception is in Àkúrẹ́, where a female daughter of a late king may become a regent until a new king is chosen. No matter the method of selecting a king, the Yorùbá regard a king as ranking next to the gods (aláṣẹ, ẹkejì òrìṣà). The selection of a king is done through a traditional process that involves Ifá consultation and the approval of chiefs who have the responsibility of filling the vacant stool after a king has passed away or has been deposed. Once chosen and installed, as royalty, a new king is at the top of the social hierarchy.

As the exclusive reserve of the king and his family members, royalty involves different opportunities in dress, homage, public image, word choice, authority, assertion, access, security, and entertainment. For example, a king puts on gorgeous dress; wears a crown; uses a fly whisk; uses royal bracelets made of beads (ẹjìgbà ìlẹ̀kẹ̀) around his neck, wrists, and ankles; and holds a staff of office. He receives constant respect from chiefs and other subjects. He enjoys the luxury of the palace and the entertainment provided by drummers and poets who praise him and offer him information to appease and direct his sense of administration. Males prostrate and females kneel when they greet him; they may not stand up until someone says ọba ní

Encyclopedia of the Yorùbá

ẹ dìde (the king says you should get up). The act is to recognize him and respect his high status.

Considered as the most powerful human being, a king is unquestionable; his subjects (chiefs and other people) often respond to his messages with *ọba làṣẹ* (the king has the final say). His authority extends over his territory. When he steps out of the palace, he receives a great deal of respect from his subjects who, by tradition, must obey his commands. Robert Thompson sums up how powerful kings are: "the king . . . incarnates the most awesome powers a mortal can possess."

In precolonial days, a king would appear in public only on special occasions, such as festivals. He would sit on his royal stool (usually made of decorated wooden objects) and occasionally walk around to see things in his domain. Today, kings use modern furnishings such as cushioned stools or chairs with artistic designs carved in them that reflect different royal objects, such as a crown, fly whisk, and staff of office. Their palaces are often well furnished, and most kings demonstrate their royalty in the carved images in their palace doors at the entrance and inside.

Royalty includes the immediate family of the king and his extended family, particularly the members of the patrilineal side; consequently, a king's family enjoys the privilege that accrues with their connection to royalty. For example, the wives of a king are treated with respect by chiefs and the town's people. They are seldom seen outside of the palace. Traditionally, the wives remain in the palace most of the time and rely on servants to run errands. Their royal status is expressed in their dress, jewelry, and grooming. They are called *olorì ọba* or *ayaba* and accompany their husbands, especially on special occasions such as during festivals. A typical Yorùbá king has many wives with whom he shares the advantages of the office.

As royalty, the king indirectly attends to the needs of his town through his administrators, and he receives tributes from his subjects. In most cases, chiefs preside over the affairs of their quarters, and their appointment, after the nomination by a would-be chief's

family, which is always subject to the approval of the king. Certain chiefs have different assignments in the palace. They are supposed to discharge their services to ensure that the king succeeds in his administration. They are like liaison officers because they serve as the interface between their quarters and the palace. Chiefs also dress elaborately and use bracelets made of beads (*iyùn* or *èjìgbà ìlèkè*). They usually wear bracelets around their necks and wrists.

Chiefs are classified as traditional or honorary chiefs. Most chiefs with traditional titles hold the titles because they are historically connected to the people who first held the titles. Honorary titles are bestowed on people when a king notices certain commendable qualities in them. This category is very common today. For example, the Olúbàdàn has created the title of Onígègé-wúrà (the writer with golden pen) and the Eléjìgbò has added Babalájé (rich man). The people who hold the titles do not have regular palace meetings with the kings who honored them.

Some chiefs have received traditional titles because of their personal qualities and influence, not because they are traditionally linked to the pioneers of their titles. For example, Moshood Káṣìmawò Ọláwálé Abíọlá became an Ààrẹ-Ọ̀nà-Kakaǹfò, not because of his historical connection with Oníkòyí, the first general marshal of the Yorùbá army. Abíọlá was a successful businessman with political influence in Nigeria. His personal accomplishments led the *aláàfin* of Ọyọ́ to confer the title on him. Other titles are reserved for females, such as Ìyálójà and Ìyálájé.

Traditional chiefs who control land sometimes sell plots and receive gifts from people. They report to the king and offer the king part of the money collected (known as *ìsákọ́lè*) from the sale of any land in their jurisdiction. Chiefs also serve as a check on the power of the king. A king is subject to a system of checks and balances. If a king misuses the privileges of his office, particularly in glaring abuses of power, chiefs may ask the king to abdicate the throne or commit suicide. Even though chiefs exercise a check on the king's power, they must prostrate themselves before the king and always show him respect. A king loses respect and tributes if he violates the rules and norms his town.

See also **Abíọ́lá, Moshood Káṣìmawò Ọláwálé; Kingship; Regency; Succession**

REFERENCE

Thompson, Robert Farris. "The Sign of the Divine King: An Essay on Yorùbá Bead-Embroidered Crowns with Veil and Bird Decorations." *African Arts* 3.3 (1970): 74–80.

Báyọ̀ Ọmọlọlá

S

SACRIFICE

In a culture with strong beliefs in fairies and mystical causation, protective rituals and sacrifices are regularly performed. People must be protected from the wrath of fairies, and fairy-human social relationships must be harmonized. Therefore, whenever any misfortune occurs in Yorùbá society and the source remains unknown, both humans and invisible spirits are subjects of divination by the people concerned. To complete any divination process, there is always a prescribed sacrifice. Whether the prediction of the divination is good or bad, the client must always offer a sacrifice. If the prediction is good, a sacrifice will quicken a positive outcome; if the prediction is evil, a sacrifice will help dispel the ill effects.

The corpus of Ifá divination includes a wide variety of genres like anecdotes, wits, dilemma poems, and tales. These genres are connected in their reflection of patterns of conflicts and resolution through sacrifices. Ẹṣẹ ifá verses contain statements of human problems, wishes, and hopes, and they are a testimony to how different people have reacted to these problems. Some of these desires are universal human needs, and others are pertinent to Yorùbá life. The following statistics attest to the frequency of occurrence of some of the desires: Of the 128 ẹṣẹ ifá listed by Wándé Abímbọ́lá, 27 deal with the desire for children, 20 with victory over enemies who may cause death, 18 regarding attempts to escape death, and 33 with the desire

for blessings. Of the 186 ẹṣẹ ifá discussed by William Bascom contain various themes, for example, 36 contain the theme of death, 28 with the desire for children, and 24 with the desire to have wives. The themes reflect the values the Yorùbá attach to the things they desire and wish to avoid.

Certain significant aesthetic phenomena emerge from this Ifá complex. One finds that the basic function of poetry in this oral mode of production is to resolve everyday human problems. In actual divination, the Ifá priest continues to chant until the client tells the priest he or she has found the verse that relates to his or her own problem. Therefore, after completing the long process of divination, the diviner will advise the client specifically about what type of sacrifice to make. The client then buys the necessary articles required for the sacrifice and brings them to the diviner. According to Abímbọ́lá, diviners believe that the psychological function of sacrifice is critically important: "They maintain that sacrifice helps to unite all the forces both natural and supernatural [including the fairy spirits] that operate in Yorùbá society."

Broadly speaking, four forces are at play in Yorùbá ritual: gods, ancestors, witches and other supernatural powers, and human beings. The function of sacrifice is to enlist the support of these four forces to achieve the desired ends and to ensure that none of the forces work against one's purpose. It is apparent in divination texts that human beings play an essential role in making a sacrifice successful. The importance of the human factor in the success of a sacrifice is encapsulated in the use of the mouth as a metaphor for the consumption of objects of sacrifice in Ifá verse cited by Abímbólá:

> The story is that of a farmer who wanted to go and take possession of a piece of farmland. He was warned to make sacrifice to Orí [head], Earth [Ilè], Egúngún [ancestor god] and Òòsà-Ńlá [creation god]. He offered the sacrifice but he did not call his neighbors to take part in the sacrifice. He discovered later that things were not all right for him on his farm. He then went back to his Ifá priests and told them his plight. His Ifá priests asked him whether he offered all the required sacrifice and he answered in the affirmative. But when they asked him whether he made sacrifice to *olúbòbòtiribò, baba ebo*, he said that he did not know what was so called. Then, his Ifá priests told him that people's mouths are meant by the term *olúbòbòtiribò, baba ebo*. (37)

Thus, during the offering of any sacrifice in Yorùbáland, people are invited to the shrine of the god to whom sacrifice is being made, not only to watch the ritual but also to eat part of the food used for the sacrifice.

See also **Divination: Ifá; Divinatory Systems; Religion and Ritual**

REFERENCES

Abímbólá, Wándé. *Ifá: An Exposition of Ifá Literary Corpus*. Ìbàdàn (Nigeria): Oxford University Press, 1976.

——. *Ìjìnlè Ohùn Enu Ifá (Apá Kejì)*. Glasgow: Collins, 1968.

Bascom, William R. *Ifá Divination: Communication Between Gods and Men in West Africa*. Bloomington: Indiana University Press, 1969.

Akíntúndé Akínyemí

SÀRÓ AND ÀGÙDÀ

Their family names stand out and set them apart from the local populations: Medeiros, de Souza, da Silva, dos Santos, Pereira, Campos, Amaro, Paraiso, d'Almeida, da Rocha, and the occasional Hernández, Rodríguez, and Fernández. These are names that evoke transatlantic legacies and long family traditions associated with the Afro-Brazilian returnees, who are referred to as the Amaros or the Àgùdàs. Names like Williams, Taylor, Coker, Ransom, Johnson, Cole, Savage, Thomas, and other English names are the trademarks of the returnees from Sierra Leone, popularly referred to as the Sàró. With particularly high concentrations of Sàró and Àgùdà families, colonial Lagos and other Yorùbá coastal towns have their fair share of cosmopolitan African subjects.

Unlike the Sàró, the Àgùdà group were not found exclusively in Yorùbá-Nigeria but also in most of the coastal towns and cities along the Bight of Benin, which stretches from the Gá region of modern-day Ghana to the Aneho region of Togo. It passes through the Grand and Petit Popo regions of the modern-day Republic of Benin to the Badagry-Lagos axis in Nigeria and as far as Calabar and the Fernando Pó region (present-day Bioko), where Anglophone Nigeria meets Spanish-speaking Equatorial Guinea.

The Àgùdà are mostly of Afro-Brazilian origin. They returned to Africa in massive successive waves mostly from the states of Bahia, Pernambuco, and Maranhão in northeastern Brazil in the aftermath of the 1835 Malê Rebellion in Bahia. Apart from the Afro-Brazilians, a sizable number of those who came to be known as Amaro or Àgùdà in Nigeria, Benin and Togo, or Tabom (*tá bom*) in Ghana, were also returnees from Cuba, mostly from the Yorùbá-dominated regions of Havana and Matanzas. The Sàró came mostly from the Freetown region of Sierra Leone. They emanated mainly from the Akú segment of the Sierra Leonean population. Akú, which became the collective ethnic name and identity of Yorùbá-speaking people in Sierra Leone, derived directly from the copious Yorùbá philosophical mode of greetings that invariably start with *a kú* to fit any time of day, context, or circumstances.

The reverse exodus from Latin America (Brazil and Cuba) of formerly enslaved Africans and their descendants represents an essential chapter in the collective agency of enslaved Africans, particularly the Nagô and Lucumí, as the Yorùbá-speaking groups were collectively referred to in Brazil and Cuba, respectively. The oppressive regimes of slavery in the Americas led enslaved Africans to resist racial discrimination and oppression and to spearhead various antislavery revolts, like the 1812 Apunté Revolt led by Yorùbá carpenter José Apunté in Cuba and the deadly Malê Rebellion of Bahia in 1835. The Bahia rebellion was very well organized and almost succeeded, shaking the Brazilian slave oligarchy. Historians attribute the use of the Yorùbá language by charismatic leaders of the rebellion such as Alufa Likutan as an important factor in the rebellion's near success. In the aftermath, Bahian authorities instituted massive repression of Africans, especially Yorùbá freedmen, subjecting them to drastically stringent laws that dispossessed them of their status and rights to own property, to wear shoes, and aspire to social and material mobility. However, instead of subjecting themselves to such restrictions, the Àgùdà families organized themselves into groups and financed their return to their African homeland, initiating a movement aptly referred to by French ethnographer Pierre Verger (Fatumbi) as *flux et reflux*, a back-and-forth movement between the two coasts of the Yorùbá Atlantic.

By virtue of their origin and formation in the Diaspora, both the Àgùdà and the Sàró became key actors in the local politics and British administration of Lagos from the beginning of the twentieth century to the independence of Nigeria in 1960. The Sàró brought with them from Sierra Leone the Western education they had received from the British, which made them well suited for clerical and lesser administrative posts within the British colonial administration. The Àgùdà brought their expertise as craftsmen, traders, masons, smiths, and other categories of professional know-how to build a new and emerging nation. Àgùdà professionals soon found themselves in a pitched battle against the Sàró returnees, who felt they were too submissive to the colonial masters, and against British colonial administrators, who refused to treat them as their professional and social equals. The Àgùdà created defiant, popular sayings like *Àgùdà ò je lábé Gèésì, isé owó wa ni àwa ń je* (The Àgùdà are not waiting on the British for their daily bread; they are able to take care of their needs themselves).

Indeed, whatever rivalry existed between the Sàró and the Àgùdà of Lagos was subordinated to what became known as the Yorùbá cultural renaissance, which eventually birthed new political formations with clear leanings toward independence and anti-colonialism. These formations represented the collective efforts of both groups; leaders from both sides, such as Sir Adétòkunbò Adémólá and Sapará-Williams, were examples of political progressivism.

See also **Lucumí; Nagô**

REFERENCES

Ayoh'Omídire, F. "Àgùdà and Jagùdà: Afro-Brazilian Returnees, Cultural Renaissance and Anticolonial Protagonism in West Africa." In *Back to Africa, Volume 1: Afro Brazilian Returnees and their Communities*, ed. K. K. Prah, 193–209. Cape Town: CASAS, 2009.

Guran, M. "The Returnees of Benin, Nigeria and Ghana: Àgùdà and Tabom." In *Back to Africa, Volume 1: Afro-Brazilian Returnees and Their Communities*, ed. K. K. Prah, 181–91. Cape Town: CASAS, 2009.

Felix Ayoh'Omídire

SCIENCE

Any discussion of science, particularly in a non-Western context, must begin with an examination of exactly what is meant by the term *science*. This term came into common usage in the West in the wake of the Enlightenment as part of an effort to differentiate the growing field of empirically based natural philosophy from the more deductive enterprises normally associated with philosophy and from other subjective methods of physical interpretation, such as religion or myth. Thus, science in this context is a rational, observation-based system of knowledge for interpreting the natural world. Under this definition, the Yorùbá can be said to have developed a rich and effective corpus of scientific knowledge before extensive contact with the West, despite the fact that they did not share the concern of post-Enlightenment Westerners with insulating science from philosophy and religion.

A systematic, empirical approach to the natural world is evident in myriad aspects of precolonial Yorùbá life from divination to architecture. Perhaps nowhere is Yorùbá scientific methodology more immediately apparent than in the practice of traditional medicine. Though often dismissed by practitioners of Western medicine as unhygienic, imprecise, secretive, and ultimately unscientific, traditional medicine is, in fact, quite rational and empirical in its methods. Practitioners draw upon a massive corpus of natural knowledge and remedies, derived from centuries of observation and trial, to systematically diagnose and treat patients. In fact, the oníṣègùn (healer or herbalist) brings an accumulation of medical, botanical, and zoological knowledge to bear that often rivals that of even the most elite Western specialists. Traditional medicine is regularly marginalized because it operates outside of the Western medical community, because its practitioners value proprietorship and are thus hesitant to share their knowledge openly, and because it is often and unapologetically employs "alternative" practices like divinatory methods to diagnose disease and to prescribe treatment and prevention. Yorùbá traditional medicine is a sophisticated and scientifically based system of healing that incorporates aspects of counterintuitive principles such as germ theory with the role of psychology in recovery, a system utilized by millions of people to this day.

Focusing on the precolonial scientific achievements of the Yorùbá risks creating the impression that Yorùbá scientific achievement was forever interrupted by Western influence and colonial domination, that what remains of precolonial Yorùbá thought represents the shattered roots of what might have grown into a great Yorùbá rival to Western science. To accept such an image, however, is to ignore the perseverance and dynamism of the Yorùbá people. When Western scientists arrived in Yorùbá territory, it was to local experts whom they turned for the collection, classification, and even interpretation of data. In fact, the climatic challenges of West Africa often meant that Western researchers were heavily dependent on more acclimatized Yorùbá personnel. Further, many aspects of precolonial Yorùbá science, particularly in the area of medicinal knowledge, have been incorporated into the Western scientific corpus. Given that Yorùbá people, and Africans in general, have contributed—and continue to contribute—to the Western scientific tradition since the term science came into popular use, one might be tempted to ask whether there is any distinction between Western and Yorùbá science.

REFERENCES

Dòpámú, Adé P. "Traditional Medicine in Healthcare Delivery." In Understanding Yorùbá Life and Culture, ed. Níkẹ S. Lawal, Matthew N. O. Sádíkù, and P. Adé Dòpámú, 427–40. Trenton, NJ: Africa World Press, 2004.

Èésúọlá, Olúkáyọ̀dé Ṣégun. "Scientific and Technical Knowledge and Practices among the Yorùbá before Colonialism." In Perspectives on African Environment, Science and Technology, ed. Tóyìn Fálọlá and Maurice Amutabi, 57–68. Trenton, NJ: Africa World Press, 2012.

Daniel Jean-Jacques

SCULPTURE

The practice of sculpture is widespread among the Yorùbá, who have been described as the most prolific art-producing group in Africa. Sculpture is practiced in a variety of media, including stone, wood, wrought iron, cast metals, molded clay, and mixed media. In their final form, sculpture may be freestanding as a three-dimensional object or in low or high relief as a two-dimensional object. Before Nigeria's independence, sculpture was an exclusively male genre. It was men who, as blacksmiths, wrought and forged iron works. They carved, sculpted, and cast sculpture from diverse media. Women specialized in pottery and undertook two-dimensional works such as weaving and wall decorations for shrines. In considering sculpture among the Yorùbá, it is helpful to distinguish between its practice in colonial and postcolonial times.

Since precolonial times, sculptures have served several purposes. House posts, which are often carved of wood, express the affluence of the wealthy or designate social importance. In the ọba's palace, house posts bear the load of the impluvium, a central architectural feature of most palace squares. Several examples abound among the Yorùbá in which the proverbial 401 deities are symbolized through three-dimensional iconology. Among these are the *ère ìbejì* (twin figure), the *osé Ṣàngó* (Ṣàngó dance staff), and the Ọ̀sanyìn staff.

The earliest body of sculptures, which is from Ilé-Ifẹ̀, has been dated between the eleventh and sixteenth centuries. Rendered in terra-cotta, copper, bronze, or brass, the sculpted figures of men and women, some from royalty or the religious class, are stunning for their realism or pure abstraction. Beyond being artworks, the Ifẹ̀ sculptures reveal the synergy between creative enterprise and political institutions. Sculptors of the postpavement period in Ifẹ̀—between 800 and 1600 CE—served as reflectors of aesthetic tastes and recorders of the prevailing social and political order. The sculptors of the Ifẹ̀ genre had supreme mastery of the lost wax-casting process.

From the second half of the nineteenth century through the first half of the twentieth century, a substantial body of Yorùbá sculpture in wood was burned by European missionaries. In the 1940s, there was an attempt by some missionaries to redress what they realized was an unjust demonization of Yorùbá sculpture with the establishment of a workshop in Ọyẹ́-Èkìtì, through which George Bámidélé Àrẹ̀ògún and Làmídì Fákẹ́yẹ came to prominence. Perhaps the greatest sculptor from the African continent is Ọlọ́wẹ̀, sculptor to the Ọba of Ìṣẹ̀-Èkìtì and other royalty in Yorùbáland. In terms of the complexities of his composition and the dexterity with which he executed his works, Ọlọ́wẹ̀ was a virtuoso. Among his clients was the Ọ̀gọ̀gà of Ìkẹ́rẹ́-Èkìtì, whose palace door was exhibited in London in 1924 but was never returned.

The introduction of art at the university level has led to the diversification of sculptural expression. Artists have taken advantage of exposure to diverse media and technology to produce sculptural works that reveal individual subjectivities. Whereas Yorùbá sculptors in preindependence Nigeria produced sculptures mainly on commission, artists now routinely hold solo or group exhibitions to promote their work.

See also **Art: Indigenous; Art: Contemporary; Carvers**

REFERENCES

Fákẹ́yẹ, Làmídì Ọlọ́nàdé, and Bruce M. Haight, with David H. Curl, eds. *Làmídì Ọlọ́nàdé Fákẹ́yẹ: A Retrospective Exhibition and Autobiography*. Kalamazoo, MI: Oak Woods Media, 1996.
Pemberton, John, III. "Introduction: In Praise of Artistry." In *The Yorùbá Artist*, ed. R. Abíọ́dún, H. J. Drewal, and John Pemberton III, 119–36. Washington, DC: Smithsonian Institution Press, 1994.

délé jẹ́gẹ́dẹ́

SECRET SOCIETIES

Secret societies (*ẹgbẹ́ awo*) can broadly be divided into two types: religious and nonreligious. Although the nonreligious societies may have a guardian relationship with a spirit being or deity, they were instituted not primarily for worship but for fraternal purposes. All the *òrìṣà* (deities) have a cult in charge of each of them, such as the *awo egúngún, awo orò, awo gẹ̀lẹ̀dẹ́, awo oníṣàngó, awo olóòṣàálá*, among others. However, it is the *awo ifá* (the divinatory cult) that is prominently followed by Egúngún. In traditional Yorùbá, Ògbóni (Òṣùgbó in Ìjẹ̀bú) is the most widespread of the nonreligious secret societies that have direct involvement in governance. Other secret societies, like the *awo ọpa*, were not widespread and not much is known about them. Although Ifá classifies *àjẹ́* and *oṣó* (witches' or wizards' cult) with the *ajogun* (malevolent forces), some believe in the existence of *àjẹ́ funfun* (white witches) who are not malevolent.

Members of secret societies are bound by strong oaths, and so the societies are also known as *ẹgbẹ́ ìmùlẹ̀* (oath-bound associations). The sacredness of oath taking makes the guardian relationship with the deity or spirit obligatory even for the nonreligious cults. Therefore, the hunters' guild, whose guardian deity is Ògún, can be considered a secret society. Officials of the cults constitute the executives of the societies and are the primary custodians of cultic mysteries and other tangible and intangible customs. *Olúwo* or *olúáwo* (lord of the mysteries) is usually the leader or deputy as in the Ifá cult. The grand master in the Egúngún cult is, however, the *alágbàáà*. Regular meetings are held and there are special emblems, coded languages, and special greetings and dress identified with each cult. Whereas all these elements are apparent in many secret societies, those of witches and wizards are not.

The traditional òdbóni or òṣùgbó may be seen as a Freemason-style cult that plays significant roles in the societal governance. High chiefs, who constitute the ọba's (king) cabinet, and priests of deities in the community are usually members of the òdbóni. In Ọ̀yọ́, the aláàfin was represented in the cult by a palace female. Elsewhere when the ọba participates directly, he is just a member. The apènà (the way maker) is the deputy of the olúwo who directs adjudication in matters of misunderstanding among members. Male members are generally called ológbòóni and female members erelú. Meetings are held at an ilédì (bond lodge or cult house). The òdbóni take Ilẹ̀ (Mother Earth) as its guardian deity. It has two pieces of metallic images, ẹdan akọ (male) and ẹdan abo (female), joined by a chain signifying the fraternal cultic bond.

Ajàgbó, ikúkú-oró, and ẹrú-òdbóni are other such images, either in brass or wood, that represent spiritual forces controlling affairs in the cult. The level of the involvement of òdbóni in polity differs from place to place. In Ẹ̀gbá and Ìjẹbú, the òdbóni constitutes the kingmakers and is very prominent in adjudication and governance. In Ọ̀yọ́, the òdbóni served a checks-and-balances purposes for the Ọ̀yọ́ Mèsì and the king before it was disbanded by Aláàfin Adéyẹmí II in 1948. Today a modern version of the òdbóni is known as the Reformed Ògbóni Fraternity, but it has no direct political function and has adjusted its rituals along Christian tenets.

REFERENCE

Fádípẹ̀, N. A. The Sociology of the Yorùbá. Ìbàdàn (Nigeria): University Press, 1970.

Philip Adédọtun Ògúndèjì

SEXUALITY AND SEXUAL BEHAVIOR

The centrality of traditional family values and the privileged position of children in the family suggest that heterosexuality is the sexuality of preference for Yorùbá culture. The ritual of courtship and marriage, the elaborate nature of the naming ceremony, and the view of childless persons as not having lived a fulfilled life all result in the primary place given to children and the belief that a sexual relationship between adults should be between a man and a woman. In instructional books for teaching Yorùbá culture in secondary schools in the 1980s and 1990s, the issue of sexuality is not discussed explicitly, which implies that male-female sexual relationships are considered "normal."

However, even though textbooks do not address sexuality, Yorùbá people are not ignorant of sexuality beyond male-female sexuality. The Ifá corpus makes reference to male-female sexual relationship, which is the privileged sexuality, but it does include references to female-female sexuality and male-male sexuality. Ifá is quite categorical in its rejection of sexualities other than male-female sexuality. It is for this reason that female-female sexuality is portrayed as dirty and disgusting and male-male sexuality is abhorred and represented as an act that can lead to diseases. The media in the past ten years have reported different cases of male-male and female-female sexuality, which may indicate that some small fraction of the population of the Yorùbá people engage in homosexual intimacy even though this it is widely considered abnormal in Yorùbá society.

Sexual behavior among the Yorùbá people is guided mainly by moral considerations. Although the Yorùbá people privilege male-female sexuality, they equally think the act should take place between married adults. The Yorùbá people discourage young people from engaging in sex before marriage. It is for this reason that if a bride has sex before her wedding it is a shameful thing that results in public condemnation. While there are measures to determine and punish premarital sex for women, no similar sanction exists for punishing men who may be guilty of the same thing.

The Yorùbá also condemn incest, as do many societies around the world. The saying adánìkàn pèrò, níí bá ìyá rẹ̀ sùn (which literally means "it is someone who does not share his thoughts with other people that contemplates having sex with his mother") supports this claim. Therefore, only a person who fails to learn the rudiments of the culture commits incest. The Yorùbá people usually advise potential couples to visit their family homes before getting married so that they can find out whether they are related by blood. Precisely because the Yorùbá emphasize good character, the rigorous ritual of marriage constitutes avenues to express acceptable sexual behavior, which is the reason that rape is condemned.

See also **Marriage and Marital Systems; Queerness**

REFERENCE

Fádípè, N. A. *The Sociology of the Yorùbá*. Ìbàdàn (Nigeria): University Press, 1970.

Káyòdé Ọmọniyì Ògúnfọlábí

SLAVERY: CAUSES

The Yorùbá consider *ẹrú*, slaves, as people who have been captured, used, sold or bought, to serve, and forced to be obedient to their masters. Slaves were usually strangers. In general, slaves were prevented from returning to their own people. Only a few people, such as Bishop Samuel Àjàyí Crowther was able to return to his home country of Nigeria from Sierra Leone, where he was freed. Three factors led to widespread enslavement among the Yorùbá: territorial expansion, internal and intertribal wars, and the transatlantic slave trade.

Before the European and Arab slave traders had contact with Yorùbáland, slavery was not prominent but had been in existence. However, internal wars to expand Yorùbá territory and the land of towns and cities were common. If a town captured another in a war, the captured people would be taken away from their territory and might become slaves to their captors. Most of them would be given to powerful people, who used them for farm cultivation, clearing land, or other personal purposes. When contact with Europeans, Americans, Indians, and Arabs was established, slavery became popular. Warriors, powerful kings, chiefs, and wealthy people began to engage in the trade because it became a source of valuable income.

At the height of the trade, foreigners who made their way to Yorùbáland bought many slaves from slave traders. This practice continued for many years. The local slave traders who benefited materially and financially from the practice became more aggressive in their search for more slaves. Foreign slave traders provided their Yorùbá business partners with powerful weapons to target and fight their enemies. They then sold their vanquished enemies into the slave trade. One of the signs of being a good warrior and rich or influential person was the ability not only to defeat enemies but also to capture and own slaves. Also, a few Yorùbá engaged in selling their own people and others to foreign slave traders until 1893 when slavery was officially abolished.

Today, the involvement of Yorùbá and the consequence of the effect of slave trade on the people reflect in the diasporic culture in places live Brazil, Cuba, Americas, Venezuela, Haiti, Trinidad and Tobago, Gambia, and Sierra Leone. In these countries, Yorùbá culture has survived even though the slave trade ended decades ago. For example, Tóyìn Fálọlá cites an example of the impact of the Yorùbá on the Americas and other places as "the emergence of distinctive Yorùbá òrìṣà traditions in the Americas; the physical presence, in various parts of the world, of the descendants of Yorùbá people taken as slaves." Society expected masters to treat their slaves as they would treat their family members. The cultural expression that conveys this idea is *bí a ṣe bí ẹrú ni a bí ọmọ* (a child and a slave are delivered through same birth process).

See also **Pawning and Pawnship; Slavery: Types**

REFERENCES

Fálọlá, Tóyìn. "Atlantic Yorùbá and the Expanding Frontiers of Yorùbá Culture and Politics." 2012. Yourubaland.net, http://Yorùbánation.net/atlantic-Yorùbá-and-the-expanding-frontiers-of-Yorùbá-culture-and-politics/.

Miers, Suzanne. *The End of Slavery in Africa*. Madison: University of Wisconsin Press, 1988.

Báyò Ọmọlọlá

Slavery is understood broadly as a state or a condition whereby an individual loses his or her freedom and becomes the property of another person or a state. As a property, a slave serves his or her master and owes his or her existence to the master or owner. Although differences existed in how slaves were treated in different communities, slaves generally served their masters for the length of their enslavement or for life. Slavery has been around as long as human history. It is difficult, if not impossible, to trace the origins of slavery among Yorùbá people. However, slavery existed in Yorùbáland until 1893, when it was officially abolished.

Before its abolition, there were three categories of slaves in Yorùbáland. The first were detained for debt, known as *ìwọ̀fà*. The second describes people who were captured in wars and then enslaved (*ẹrú*). The last category includes criminals serving terms for punishment for their crime. *Ìwọ̀fà* differs remarkably from the general understanding of slavery, mainly because the *ìwọ̀fà*'s family voluntarily hands over an *ìwọ̀fà* to a master unlike the other categories. This was a system of credit whereby a family took a loan and offered up one of their children to serve as collateral for the loan and to work in lieu of paying interest. The child served his or her master for as long as the loan remained unpaid. While serving the master, an *ìwọ̀fà* could own property and visit his or her parents. His or her liberty was, however, curtailed to the extent that his or her master would allow. In spite of being in a servile position, an *ìwọ̀fà* was a free person and could not be tasked beyond his or her ability or what reason demanded.

War victims were treated differently from an *ìwọ̀fà*. The treatment meted out to victims of war was usually determined by the need to foster peaceful settlement; the victor was recognized as superior, and the loser was subject to the disposition of the victor. Still, it was a common practice among warriors to allocate war victims to important chiefs and kings of the communities. These state officials deployed these slaves on their farms and in trades. The severity of their treatment depended largely on the personality of the state officials and the behaviors of the slaves themselves. Ẹfúnṣetán Aníwúrà, the Ìyálóde of Ìbàdàn, was reputed to be harsh in her treatment of slaves. Her notoriety for maltreating slaves earned her not only expulsion from Ìbàdàn but also unconditional release of her slaves.

In some situations, slaves emerged as heads of households, especially in Èkìtì, Ìjẹ̀sàland, and Oǹdó during the Yorùbá civil war. In Ìbàdàn, slaves became important in the state administration, not only in providing unpaid services to their respective owners but also in fighting for Ìbàdàn warlords in Ìbàdàn's war of expansion. In the case of Ìbàdàn, slaves helped their masters obtain additional slaves. In many instances, slaves earned their freedom and became important members of the state by sheer enterprise.

In precolonial Yorùbáland, criminals were either used locally as slaves or sold to other communities as slaves. By implication, Yorùbáland also must have received slaves, especially prisoners of war, from other communities. No matter how they were acquired, slaves were not treated kindly. However, like other slaves, they could gain their freedom through hard work or the grace of their masters.

Arab and European contacts introduced an entirely different system of slavery in Yorùbáland. While slaves were transferred abroad, a large majority ended up in local communities and production centers after the abolition of slave trade by the British in early nineteenth century. These slaves received completely different treatment from those who were serving to pay off loans or those who were criminals. For the most part, a large number of slaves obtained through wars fell into this category. When slavery was abolished in 1893, the abolition applied to all three forms of slavery.

See also **Pawning and Pawnship; Slavery: Causes**

REFERENCES

Miers, Suzanne. *The End of Slavery in Africa*. Madison: University of Wisconsin Press, 1988.

Oróge, Adéníyì. "Ìwọ̀fà: An Historical Survey of the Yorùbá Institution of Indenture." *African Economic History* 14 (1985): 71–88.

Bùkọ́lá Oyèníyì

SOCIAL CONTROL

Every society, premodern and contemporary, usually has had means for regulating individual and group behavior to promote conformity to acceptable societal norms, traditions, and beliefs. Among the Yorùbá, mechanisms of social control have been ingrained in the process of socializing individuals to the acceptable norms, cultures, practices, and beliefs of society. The family, which in most cases transcends the nuclear family structure to include extended family, exists as the primary agent of socialization. It plays a significant role in making individuals internalize relevant social control measures, especially the younger members of the family. The dos and don'ts of society are usually passed down to younger family members by elders in the immediate extended family and by the larger community through engaging tales and storytelling. For instance, when individuals contradict certain rules and regulations of society, they face repercussions. Ostensibly, the younger ones are dissuaded from following in the footsteps of earlier dissidents.

Equally, traditional religions and gods provide models of conformity to the acceptable way of life of the society. For instance, the power of such gods as Ògún (god of iron) and Ṣàngó (god of thunder and lightning) are shared with children through stories as models of conduct. For example, if an individual steals a metal item, the god of Ògún is consulted; the usual punishment is sudden death. If someone commits an offense and the god of Ṣàngó is consulted, the repercussion is often death by thunderstorm.

It should be noted that the vagaries of modernity and contemporary administrative system have largely affected the continued relevance of related social control mechanisms, especially in urban and semiurban communities. Nevertheless, the activities of most social organizations, such as hometown associations and vigilante groups, be it in urban or rural areas, are still considerably guided by extant Yorùbá social controls.

See also **Superstitions; Taboos**

REFERENCES

Fálọlá, Tóyìn. "A Research Agenda on the Yorùbá in the Nineteenth Century." *History of Africa* 15 (1988): 211–27.
Trager, Lillian. *Yorùbá Hometowns: Community, Identity and Development in Nigeria*. London: Lynne Rienner Publishers, 2001.

Adébùsúyì Isaac Adéníran

SOCIAL STRATIFICATION

It was often believed that the precolonial Yorùbá societies were simple communalistic, conflict-free, egalitarian societies. While it is true that in Yorùbá communities, at least at the level of the extended family, members strived to be their brothers' and sisters' keepers, group antagonisms, inequalities, and exploitation were familiar features of their communities. It was the communal spirit that prevailed among the people during and after the era of the Pax Britannica (1815–1914), which overshadowed the social inequalities, violence, and insecurity that enveloped Yorùbáland before the British conquest.

Like all feudal societies of the era, the Yorùbá's monarchical institutions were hierarchically structured into three basic groups. At the apex of the hierarchy were kings (rulers) and their family members, officials of the state or the kings' courts and council, and wealthy and outstanding members of the respective communities. Below these categories of persons were the freeborn commoners of the communities. At the bottom of the hierarchy were people of varying degrees of servitude, such as serfs and slaves, who were usually strangers and captives, respectively.

A special category of people in Yorùbá communities were iron workers or smelters—and these occupied distinct abodes within their respective communities. The distinct position and abodes of iron smelters were on account of the reverence and fear of Ògún, the god associated with iron making and power. So all iron smelters and workers and their family members, regarded as descendants of Ògún, were to be revered and viewed with awe. The economic value of iron products, hoes, cutlasses, axes, and knives in taming nature also conferred an enhanced status on iron workers.

Social mobility among members of Yorùbá groups was limited. However, successful farmers, hard-fighting individuals (warriors), and hunters of big game like elephants, buffalo, lions, leopards, hyenas, and warthogs were accorded enhanced status and prestige in Yorùbáland, no matter the group or class they hailed from. However, no matter the successes and failures of individuals, members of their families shared in their glories and tribulations. This communal orientation and behavior among the people limited individual as well as group mobility.

Although these different groups enjoyed varying degrees of rights and privileges, a feature of Yorùbá feudalism was that every freeborn, through their clan and lineage heads, could secure land for cultivation. It was this feature of the Yorùbá socioeconomic system that masked social inequalities among the people. In essence, Yorùbá people had evolved from a conflict-free, egalitarian, communal socioeconomic and political practice into their own unique style of feudalism.

REFERENCES

Fádípè, N. A. *The Sociology of the Yorùbá*. Ìbàdàn (Nigeria): University Press, 1970.

Forde, D. *The Yorùbá-Speaking People of South-western Nigeria*. London: International African Institute, 1962.

Adémọ́lá Babalọlá

SOCIOLOGY

While various ethnic subgroups of the Yorùbá have distinct patterns for devising and regulating social conduct, interactions, and relationships, an astonishing development is that a common sociological orientation has routinely served as the springboard for related forms of societal disposition, that is, communalistic cleavage or a "shared" way of life. Rather than seeing the individual as independent in his or her decisions or choices, inherent traditions of the Yorùbá have emphasized the individual's function an integral component of the group's functioning. Put differently, individuals or personalities are traditionally perceived through the image of a subsisting group. Against this background, individuals' realities are better mirrored through the lens or imagery of their extant groups, which often includes the larger social space.

Extant age-group (cultural) practices among the Yorùbá include the notions of àjọjẹ (joint subsistence), àjọgbé (joint residence), and àjọṣe (joint work or conduct). These all give credence to the veracity of the group taking the preeminent role in constructing acceptable patterns of social relations or interactions among the people. In the age-group system, any individual's private or public responsibilities and/or social expectations are considered group roles. For instance, if a mature male or female desires to get married, the remaining members of his or her group are actively involved in measures of finance, logistics, and moral assistance.

Another interesting issue in understanding the "sociology of the Yorùbá" is the communal nature of the process of socializing individuals into their respective social roles. While the family acts as the primary agent of socialization, the larger community usually plays a significant role in molding individuals into acceptable members of their community by means of internalization of basic norms, values, beliefs, and practices of the society.

Ostensibly, vagaries of the modern era have had a huge impact on the nature of traditional social interactive patterns. Few of the sociological frameworks for social relation within the traditional Yorùbá social system are still tenable in most of the rural settlements, and in a considerable number of urban centers, the impacts of globalization, technology, new media, and Westernization are quite visible. What used to be "Yorùbá sociology" has paved the way for a kind of "Western sociology"; that is, European and American ways of social interaction, which are essentially individualistic in orientation, unlike the traditional Yorùbá pattern, which is routinely communalistic.

See also **Social Stratification**

REFERENCE

Trager, Lillian. *Yorùbá Hometowns: Community, Identity and Development in Nigeria.* London: Lynne Rienner Publishers, 2001.

Adébùsúyì Isaac Adéníran

SORCERY

Sorcery, known as *oṣó*, *ìwà oṣó*, and *ìkà ẹbọra*, is widely recognized and accepted as a cultural phenomenon by the Yorùbá and in the Diaspora. Sorcery can be conducted as a stand-alone act or part of a wider conglomeration of religious practices premised on the concepts of cause and effect. The belief in sorcery to affect everyday life is evidenced in a number of expressions. The prevalence of sorcery is dealt with through divination, remedies, charms, and other means of neutralizing and protecting a person from harm. Within the complex of Yorùbá religious and spiritual beliefs, sorcery is focused on negatively affecting a person's *orí*, the spiritual head that holds the possibility of good destiny and good, balanced character.

While the *term* sorcery in English is not inherently neutral, the idea of consulting and working with supernatural forces can be used for both negative and positive outcomes. Sorcery can be practiced to exert negative impacts on the person's *orí*, such as a curse, *èpè*, that misaligns a person with his or her destiny and negates prosperity, health, and intellect. An example of sorcery being used for positive outcome is to make rainfall and to provide protection in court proceedings. An example given with the Ifá divination Odù Ogbè Òtúrá, is the pun *Ogbè, kò séjó*, which translates as "there is no case in court."

The religious belief takes the form of an henotheistic schema with a distant God, Olódùmarè, whose intermediaries (*òrìṣà*) are closer to humanity and are capable of manipulating spiritual power (*àṣẹ*) for and on behalf of the devotee, ultimately aligning the person's *orí* with the will of *òrìṣà*. The *òrìṣà*, deities, and ancestors are positive powers that help protect a person and guide him or her to optimal destiny, interceding by way of divination and offerings and sacrifices to ward off unwarranted sorcery and *ibi*, misfortune.

Agents employed in sorcery include *ajogun*, the "belligerent enemies of man," and the *eníyán* or *ẹlẹyẹ*, the witches. The *ajogun* are an anthropomorphized army of potential negative and fatal powers that include *ikú* (personified death), *àrùn* (sickness or disease), *òfò* (loss), and *ìyà* (treachery). An *olóògùn* (owner of medicine) is one who is prepared through initiation and training to deflect sorcery.

See also **Sacrifice; Witchcraft**

REFERENCES

Abímbọ́lá, Wándé. *Ifá: An Exposition of Ifá Literary Corpus.* Ìbàdàn (Nigeria): Oxford University Press, 1976.
Verger, Pierre Fatunmbi. "Poisons (Oró) and Antidotes (Èrò): Evil Works (Àbìlù) and Protection from Them (Ìdáàbòbò). Stimulants and Tranquilizers. Money—Wives—Children." *Seminar Series Department of African Languages and Literatures*, ed. Ọlásopé O. Oyèláràn, 298–353. Ifẹ̀-Ifẹ̀ (Nigeria): University of Ifẹ̀, 1976.

Martin A. Tsang

ṢÓYÍNKÁ, WỌLÉ (1934–)

Born on July 13, 1934, at Abẹ̀òkúta to Samuel Ayọ̀délé and Grace Ẹ̀niọlá Ṣóyínká, Akínwánde Olúwọlé Ṣóyínká is one of the most distinguished African playwrights and dramatists. His father was the head teacher at St. Peter's Primary School, Aké, Abẹ̀òkúta, where Ṣóyínká had his primary education between 1938 and 1944.

Childhood

After completing his primary education, Wọlé Ṣóyínká spent one year at Abẹ̀òkúta Grammar School under the tutelage of his uncle, Reverend Israel Olúdọ̀tun Ransome-Kútì, an Anglican priest and a school principal, and the first president of Nigerian Union of Teachers. Between 1946 and 1950, Ṣóyínká was a student of Government College, Ìbàdàn, where he began to win prizes for his poems. Before gaining admission to University College Ìbàdàn, he worked as a clerk at the government pharmaceutical store in Lagos and had his short stories read on national radio. From 1954 to 1957, he attended University of Leeds, England, where he recorded lectures and short stories for the British

Broadcasting Corporation (BBC). After receiving his bachelor of arts with honors, he worked for two years at the Royal Court Theater in London as a play reader and actor. There, he had his first plays produced, including *The Invention*, a satire on racism in South Africa.

Academic and Writing

Ṣóyínká returned to Nigeria on the eve of independence from British colonialism as a Rockefeller Research Fellow. The period 1960–1970 became the most important in the life of the new writer. He was involved in the development of the School of Drama at the University of Ìbàdàn, and he formed two theater groups: the 1960 Masks to produce *A Dance of the Forests*, commissioned by the Nigerian government for the independence celebrations, and later Orisun Theater Company, to stage political satires for the stage and radio.

Ṣóyínká wrote many plays, novels, and poems and produced films during this period. He became increasingly political and was detained for twenty-two months (August 1967–October 1969) during the Nigerian Civil War; he was exiled to the United Kingdom and Ghana after the war. He published his seminal collection of essays, *Myth, Literature and the African World* (1976), and wrote *Death of the King's Horseman* (1976), for which he won the Nobel Prize for Literature in 1986. He has written more than twenty-five major plays, including *The Lion and the Jewels* (1959), *Kongi's Harvest* (1965), *Madmen and Specialists* (1970), *A Play of Giants* (1984), and *The Beatification of Area Boy: A Lagosian Kaleidoscope* (1994). His novels include *The Interpreters* (1965) and *Season of Anomy* (1973). His poetry collections include *A Shuttle in the Crypt* (1969) and *Samarkand and Other Markets I Have Known* (2002). He has also written memoirs: *The Man Died* (1972), *Aké: The Years of Childhood* (1981), *Ìsarà: A Voyage around Essay* (1990), and *Ìbàdàn: The Penkelemes Years* (1994).

Politics

Ṣóyínká's involvement in politics began with his return to Nigeria after his education in England. He criticized the Nigerian military government for annulling the presidential election of Chief Moshood Káṣìmawò Ọláwálé Abíọ́lá in 1993, and he formed the United Democratic Front of Nigeria with other political exiles. In 1997, he was sentenced to death in absentia by the government of General Sani Abacha. He is today one of Nigeria's foremost writers and leaders of opinion.

See also **Fágúnwà, Daniel Ọlọ́runfẹ́mi; Prominent Scholars; Translation; Writers**

REFERENCE

Ọláyẹbí, Bánkọ́lé. *WS: A Life in Full*. Ìbàdàn (Nigeria): Bookcraft, 2004.

Ṣọlá Adéyẹmí

SPIRIT POSSESSION

Most spirit possessions are considered religious experiences because of the Yorùbá belief in òrìṣà. Most of the time, the òrìṣà are believed to possess the devotee for purposes like allowing the devotee to perform extraordinary feats or to give blessings. In addition, spirit possession affirms the presence of the òrìṣà during the celebration. Ṣàngó is the god associated with thunder and lightning. He is ruthless and does not forgive wrong deeds. It is also believed that he is so powerful that, when provoked, he breathes fire and throws thunderbolt (ẹdùn ààrá). The ẹlẹ́gùn Ṣàngó is usually a Ṣàngó devotee who, when possessed by Ṣàngó, will enter a trance that makes him oblivious to pain. While in the trance, the ẹlẹ́gùn Ṣàngó may cut himself with a knife, swallow hot coals, breathe fire, or dance vigorously until the spirit of Ṣàngó dismounts him. The Ṣàngó festival is not complete without the ẹlẹ́gùn Ṣàngó.

The Yorùbá believe in life after death. It is believed that in the event of a young person's untimely death, he or she lives the remainder of years in another place. However, when older relatives die, they become ancestors who watch over the ones they left behind. Egúngún is believed to be the spirit of ancestors who have come to give blessings. Likewise, the Arugbá Òṣun (votary maid) is the person people look to during the Òṣun celebration. Òṣun is the river goddess, and she blesses worshippers with the things they desire, such as health, wealth, and children. According to a myth, Ọ̀sun, Ọbà, and Ọya were the wives of Ṣàngó until rivalry drove them into the forest, where they all became bodies of water.

The Ọlọ́ya are devotees of the water goddess Ọya (one of Ṣàngó's wives). Spirit possession among Ọya devotees happens as with other gods, with the exception that the person possessed by Ọya does not necessarily have to partake in the event. An onlooker, who is a devotee but not a participant in the proceedings, can be possessed by the spirit. Spirit possession is an assurance that Ọya is pleased with the gathering in her honor and will bestow blessings like good health, the blessing for which she is most famous.

Of all the deities in Yorùbá cosmology, none has power over traditional medicine like Ọ̀sanyìn; he is knowledgeable in the use of roots and herbs that cure illness, particularly illness caused by malicious spirits. During an Ọ̀sanyìn festival, singing and dancing are customary. When the euphoria reaches its peak, at least ten per cent of those present become possessed by Ọ̀sanyìn, the god of traditional medicine, which confirms the presence of the god at the proceedings.

Although the Yorùbá consider the different forms of spirit possession discussed here temporary—meaning the devotees return to their normal physical state after a while—the Yorùbá also believe in a permanent type of spirit possession such as with witches (àjẹ́), wizards (oṣó), and the born to die (emèrè or àbíkú). Once possessed, the spirit stays permanently with the concerned individuals, who choose either to be virtuous with their powers or to afflict people with various kinds of evil.

See also **Deities: The Òrìṣà; Diaspora: Deities (Òrìṣà); Sorcery; Witchcraft**

REFERENCES

Adéoyè, C. L. Àṣà àti Ìṣe Yorùbá. Ìbàdàn (Nigeria): University Press, 2005.

Fádípẹ̀, N. A. Sociology of the Yorùbá. Ìbàdàn (Nigeria): University Press, 1970.

Tópẹ́ Olúwabùnmi Akíndípẹ̀

The Yorùbá people have their own games and sports that enhance the teaching and learning of their culture. Through games and sports, the Yorùbá people develop the physical assets they need to carry on in life. They engage in games or sporting activities after their daily work. There are two types of sports: indoor and outdoor. While some sports happen in broad daylight, others are moonlight sports. Examples of daylight sports are ayò, ààrin, and òkòtó. The moonlight sports include ẹkùn mẹ́ran, bojúbojú, ìjàkadì, àlọ́ àpamọ̀, and àlọ́ àpagbè, which usually involve children.

Wrestling (ìjàkadì or ẹkẹ) is a sport that involves physical combat between two people. Adults and children take part in wrestling; as the child grows up, he or she will watch and consequently imitate the adults. Through wrestling, one's physical development is enhanced.

Ayò aids counting. It teaches addition, subtraction, multiplication, and division. By participating in ayò, one is expected to be good at counting; otherwise, one will be disgraced by the other players. Ayò game is an intellectual exercise involving skill and mental exertion. It is on a level with chess. Experts can play it at great speed. The Yorùbá play ayò for amusement and for the prestige that is attached to being skilled at the game.

The ayò board (ọpọ́n ayò) is generally fifty by twenty centimeters and about 8 centimeters deep. Two rows are dug in a surface and each has six cuplike hollows large enough to allow the insertion of four bent fingers. The hollows are about five centimeters in diameter. The hollows are variously referred to as pits, holes, or houses. The players use forty-eight seeds (ọmọ-ayò) from the plant Caesalipinia crista (igi ayò). The ọmọ-ayò are distributed evenly in groups of four into the twelve holes. Ayò is played by two persons who squat or sit facing each other. The players alternate their turns. Seeds are captured either from one's own side or from the opponent's side. The game is concluded when the seeds left in both rows of holes are too few for the game to be continued. The winner of the ayò game is the player who has the highest number of captured seeds. The tactics of the game involve calculated moves that entail considerable concentration, anticipation, and intellectual exertion.

The essence of sports among the Yorùbá people is to develop people's physical skills, intellectual skills, and healthy attitude toward honest labor. Sports among the Yorùbá help develop a sense of belonging and an appreciation of cultural heritage.

REFERENCE

Adéoyè, C. L. Àṣà àti Ìṣe Yorùbá. Oxford: Oxford University Press, 1979.

Abídèmí Bólárìnwá

STIMULANTS AND INTOXICANTS

Stimulants are substances that increase levels of physiological or nervous activity in the body. They make one feel more active and full of energy. Stimulants can be broadly divided into three categories: fruit, leaf, and weed. Among the fruits are kola nut (obì), bitter kola (orógbó), sweetening fruit (àgbáyun), and alligator pepper (ataare). The leaves and weeds include tobacco (tábà) and marijuana (igbó), respectively. Marijuana is categorized as drug dangerous to human health.

Kola nut is the fruit of kola tree that grows in the forest. Kola nut is found in a pod, and it possesses either two or three lobes. The matured pods are plucked or fall from the branches, then preserved for eating. A ripe kola nut is usually white or reddish brown in color. It keeps the eater awake and active. Bitter kola is in the form of an oval pod and has a light yellow color. It is bitter, as the name implies, and keeps the eater awake, but it is also has medicinal properties.

Tobacco leaves are ground, usually with potash, into a powder called aásà. Aásà is prepared in two ways: for snuffing (aásà fífín) and for placement on the tongue (aásà mímu). Sweetening fruits (àgbáyun) are fruits that turn red when ripe. The fruit consists of three parts: the skin, a whitish cream, and the seed. When the cream is licked, it makes other foods and drinks taste sweet and sugary.

Intoxicants are substances that cause one to lose self-control. Some traditional intoxicants are ọtíkà, (made from Guinea corn), ògógóró (distilled from fermented palm wine), ṣẹ̀kẹ̀tẹ̀ (made from maize), àgàdàgídí (made from ripe plantain), ẹmu (palm wine), and ògùrọ̀ (tapped from date palm). Intoxicants are broadly divided into two categories: naturally occurring and distilled. The naturally occurring intoxicants include ẹmu, ògùrọ̀, and àgàdàgídí; the distilled ones are ọtíkà, ṣẹ̀kẹ̀tẹ̀, and ògógóró.

Ọtíkà is a by-product of Guinea corn that is soaked for three days, ground, and sieved to ferment it. The fermented liquid is then boiled for several hours. The resulting wine is then filtered. Ṣẹ̀kẹ̀tẹ̀ is produced from dried maize. The dried maize is soaked for three days, ground, and left for seven days to ferment. It is run through a sieve, and the liquid product is boiled along with fried maize. After some hours, the liquid is filtered for consumption. Àgàdàgídí is produced from ripe plantain that has been soaked for four or five days. The fermented liquid is filtered and then it is ready to drink. Palm wine (ẹmu) is tapped from palm tree. The tapped liquid is diluted with water and then it is ready to drink. Wine tapped from the date palm is called ògùrọ̀.

See also **Alcohol; Kola Nut**

REFERENCES

Adéoyè, C. L. Àṣà àti Ìṣe Yorùbá. Ìbàdàn (Nigeria): University Press Limited, 1980.
Ilésànmi, T. M., ed. Ìṣẹ́ Ìṣẹ̀nbáyé. Ilé-Ifẹ̀ (Nigeria): Ọbáfẹ́mi Awólọ́wọ̀ University Press, 1989.

William Ọládélé Ṣàngótóyè

STORIES, STORYTELLING, AND STORYTELLERS

Traditionally, stories are narratives relayed in every culture primarily as means of transferring mores, history, and cultural values through entertainment. These narratives instruct and indoctrinate and are often made up of structured plot and story lines, characters, and narrative points of view that best convey the theme of the story. Stories possess universal elements that bridge national, ethnic, cultural, linguistic, and sociolinguistic divides.

Transfer of knowledge among humans is predominantly based on stories, and the human brain consists of cognitive machinery empowered to understand, remember, and narrate. The art of storytelling predated the art of writing among the Yorùbá. The art of storytelling was more important than the originality or authenticity of the stories. Subsequently, documentation of stories and their narration in written form began to define and redefine the story as a type and a form of literature.

Thematic and archetypical stories cover countless issues. In particular, stories of nomadic hunters and gatherers are told with mystery to the fascination of the audience. Several of these have been collected for the preservation of folk traditions. Essentially, narratives make up a great part of the archetypal and universal language ingrained in the minds of people that consciously and unconsciously regulates and molds the psyche of peoples across the universe.

The ability to recount series of events and institute a link between them is regarded as the act of storytelling. Traditionally, the act of storytelling comprises piecing together events in words and images, often through dramatic improvisation and embellishments. Storytelling is a means for sharing and interpreting experiences, particularly because the teller's art and the audience participation create the bond, an emotional tie between the teller and the audience.

During the performance, key aspects to observe critically include the posture and gesticulations of the performer, the dancelike gyrations of the body, and the tempo and timbre of the narrative voice. Together, these elements concretize the emotional tie between the storyteller and the audience. Contemporary storytelling is necessarily extensive in scope and form. It has "graduated" from the orally transmitted forms to the documented or translated form of collections of stories to the more recent form of the story as a literary genre. This encompasses fairy tales, folktales, mythology, legends, and fable, among others, with a comprehensive representation of history, personal narrative, political commentary, and evolving cultural norms.

Contemporary storytelling is also widely used to address educational objectives. Although one acknowledges the painstaking efforts of story collectors and translators, storytelling in written form suffers certain limitations despite its ability to preserve and circulate stories to a wider readership. For instance, the atmosphere of extemporaneity in narration, the critical participation and vibrancy of an audience, the dynamic suspense created by an unfinished performance, the consistent unraveled maze of tension between the artist and the audience, the diffusion of the sound from the oral performance, and the automatic shift of the perception of the narration or narratives from the auditory to the visual senses are all lost in the written form. Storytelling is adaptable; age and other factors are irrelevant in the transference of people's identities.

Irrespective of the elements of narration, written or performed, narrators are the souls of stories. Sources and influences on tellers reflect their social, cultural, and spiritual experiences and exposure. This rich background provides the canvas upon which myths, history, and cultural identities are painted. Typically, a storyteller employs the cultural identity of his or her nation as the vehicle of narration. The identity of the Yorùbá with respect of social and physical setting, institutions, and religious and other core beliefs make up a great influence. Geographical settings portrayed by early storytellers were greatly influenced by agrarian communities.

D. O. Fágúnwà, an early leader of the Yorùbá storytelling form, has outstanding narratives to his credit. Establishing Fágúnwà's tradition are portraits of dense forests surrounding his town Òkè-Igbó, which doubtlessly influenced the creation of his heroic characters, who were mostly hunters, wandering heroes, questers, and supernatural beings who inhabited luxuriant trees and eerie elements that inhabited extraordinary forests. The Yorùbá rites of passage and identity celebrate, among other things, kingship and chieftaincy institutions. They are portrayed in narratives that employ the storyteller as a dominant character type in the storytelling.

Closely following Fágúnwà in Yorùbá storytelling is Amos Tutùọlá, a renowned teller who borrowed extensively from the Fágúnwà narrative framework. Tutùọlá's exemplary engagement of Yorùbá folktales is portrayed in his narration of seven tales in his *Yorùbá Folktales*. They are an expression of an artist who translates stories in a short and exact manner. Tutùọlá's first internationally acclaimed narrative employs at least nine traditional folktales in its plot.

The international community is aware of the significance of Yorùbá storytelling. National associations, international storytelling centers, and societies for storytellers and listeners are brought together periodically. The most instructive is the international celebration of the art on the World Storytelling Day, which is celebrated annually on the spring equinox in the Northern Hemisphere and the first day of autumn equinox in the Southern Hemisphere. Events like these continually celebrate stories, the tellers, and the tellers' art.

See also **Fágúnwà, Daniel Ọlọ́runfẹ́mi; Narration Techniques; Translation; Tutùọlá, Amos**

REFERENCES

Bámgbóṣé, Ayọ̀. *The Novels of D. O. Fágúnwà*. Benin City (Nigeria): Ethiope Publishing Corporation, 1974.

Tutùọlá, Amos. *The Palm-Wine Drinkard and My Life in the Bush of Ghosts*. New York: Grove Press, 1984.

Doyin Àgúorù

SUBGROUPS

The Yorùbá are divided into many different ethnic subgroups, such as Okun, Ìgbómìnà, Ìbọ̀lọ́, Ọ̀yọ́, Oǹdó, Ẹ̀gbá, Ifẹ̀, Àwórì, Ọ̀wọ̀, Ìjẹbú, Èkìtì, Ìjèṣà, Àkókó, Ẹ̀gbádò, Ìbàràpá, Ìlọrin, Ìlàjẹ, Itsekiri, Kétu, Sábẹ, Ìfọ̀nyìn, Ìdásà, Pópó, Ifẹ̀ (or Aná, in the Republic of Togo), Àhọ̀rí, Itsha, and Màhi. Each of the subgroups of the Yorùbá inhabits a particular region. In the savanna grassland region of the north, particularly near the Niger-Benué confluence, are the Okun Yorùbá subgroup, who are further divided into Owé, Ọ̀wọ́rọ̀, Gbẹdẹ, Ìjùmú, Ikiri, Búnú, and Yàgbà village units.

The Ìgbómìnà subgroup occupies the west of Okun in north-central Yorùbá. They are further divided into Ìlá, Ìpo, Èrèsé, Èsìsá, Ìyàngbà, Ẹkùmẹ́sáán-Òró, Ìlere, Ìsin, and Ẹkù-Apa village groups. Northwest of Ìgbómìnà are the Ìlọrin people, a small Yorùbá subgroup who largely inhabit the town Ìlọrin. Southwest of the Ìgbómìnà are the Ìbọ̀lọ́, the southernmost group of northern Yorùbá. The Ọ̀yọ́ subgroup, one of the largest, are located west of Ìgbómìnà.

The territory of the Ọ̀yọ́ subgroup extends from the border with the Ìgbómìnà in the east to the border with the Kétu in the west. To the south of Okun are Èkìtì and the Àkókó subgroups, who occupy the hilliest region of Yorùbáland. To the west of the Èkìtì are the Ìjèṣà subgroup, and west of the Ìjèṣà are the Ifẹ̀ of central Yorùbáland. The Ẹ̀gbá subgroup is located west of Ifẹ̀, and to the north of Ẹ̀gbá lives the Ìbàràpá subgroup. This is the middle belt of Yorùbáland and mostly tropical forest, with the grasslands intruding into the Èkìtì and Àkókó territories. South of Èkìtì and Àkókó are the Ọ̀wọ̀ subgroup, and west of Ọ̀wọ̀ are the Oǹdó, and then the Ìjẹbú, and the Àwórì subgroups. The territory occupied by these subgroups is in the very thick-forested part of Yorùbáland. The Ìjẹbú and Àwórì extend further south to the coast and inhabit large expanses of the coastal lagoon.

The Itsekiri, the easternmost Yorùbá subgroup, occupies the Atlantic coastland, which consists of mangrove swamps interspersed by creeks and lagoons. The Yorùbá subgroup next to the Itsekiri are the Ìlàjẹ, and immediately north of the Ìlàjẹ are the Ìkálẹ̀ subgroup, who occupy a thin territory of partly forests and partly swamps. To the west of the Ìlàjẹ and Ìkálẹ̀ subgroups are the coastal Ìjẹbú, and west of them the coastal Àwórì. The coastal Ìjẹbú comprise the southernmost tip of the large Ìjẹbú subgroup. A number of small Yorùbá subgroups—the Kétu, Ìdásà, Sábẹ, Àhọ̀rí, Mahí, Sha (or Itsha), and Ifẹ̀ (or Aná)—are located in the farthest western region of Yorùbáland, which includes central and southern Republic of Benin and the western provinces of the Republic of Togo.

Each of the subgroups speaks some dialect of Yorùbá. The many local Yorùbá dialects form three main families: (1) northwestern Yorùbá, spoken in the Ọ̀yọ́, Ọ̀sun, Ìbàdàn, and northern Ẹ̀gbá; (2) southeastern Yorùbá, spoken in the Oǹdó, Ọ̀wọ̀, Ìkálẹ̀, and Ìjẹ̀bú; and (3) central Yorùbá, spoken in Ifẹ̀, Ìjẹ̀sà, Èkìtì, and Ìgbómìnà. The various dialects are clearly distinct from one another and help to define the internal differentiation among the subgroups present today. Some subgroups located in close proximity are able to understand one another. For instance, an Ìlọrin Yorùbá man would find it difficult to understand an Èkìtì but would consider that an Ìgbómìnà speaks merely with a different accent. Also, Ìgbómìnà and Okun Yorùbá may find it harder to understand each other's dialect than would, say, Ìgbómìnà and Ìlọrin or Ìbọ̀lọ́, who are closer to each other.

Also, local variations exist in the dialect of every subgroup. For example, while all the Ìgbómìnà subgroup speaks a dialect called Ìgbóònà, in terms of intonation and pronunciation of specific words, they differ slightly from each other. Because of these dialectical differences, the Ìgbómìnà people have been classified into two groups: Ìgbómìnà *mo yé* and Ìgbómìnà *mo sàn*. The *mo yé* group includes Ìgbómìnà in Èsìsá, Esa, Ilere, and Ìyàngbà village groups, and the *mo sàn* group is made up of Erèsé, Ìpo, Ìsin, Ẹkùmẹ́sàán-Òró, Èsìẹ́, Ṣáárẹ́, and Ìlá village groups. Among the Ìjẹ̀bú subgroup, the variation in dialect has resulted in the emergence of four provinces of the subgroup, with each province identified with a variant of the subgroup dialect. These are the western Ìjẹ̀bú known as Rémọ, the central Ìjẹ̀bú (around Ìjẹ̀bú-Òde), the coastal Ìjẹ̀bú, and the northeastern Ìjẹ̀bú (around Ìjẹ̀bú-Igbó). The Oǹdó subgroup had four dialects: the area around the Orósùn Hill or Ìdànrè Rock of eastern Oǹdó territory, the northeastern group (around Ilẹ̀-Olújì), group in the deep southern Oǹdó forests near Ikale and Ilaje, and the populations occupying the rest of the Oǹdó forests (around Òde-Oǹdó). The Ọ̀yọ́ subgroup in the mostly open savanna was homogeneous in dialect, although the region was roughly divided into two provinces: the northern and central Ọ̀yọ́ territory and the province of Èpò to the south.

Despite the several subgroups of Yorùbá and the differences among them, the subgroups share considerable cultural characteristics. Some features or cultural traits that unite the subgroups are the following: the claim that their ancestor was Odùduwà; that Ilé-Ifẹ̀ is their cradle or dispersal center to other places; their praise songs, cognomens, or *oríkì* about themselves; that their greetings commence with *ẹ kú, a kú*, or *o kun o*; that they were traditionally agriculturist; that they formed monarchical governments; that they are highly urbanized; that they believe in Ifá and Ògún deities and in the concept of destiny, or *orí*; that their dress is very distinct from other non-Yorùbá speaking people; that they practice certain customs such as greeting elders by prostration and kneeling, as well as wedding and burials rites; and that there is geographical contiguity of the lands occupied by the different groups.

REFERENCES

Adétúgbọ̀, A. "The Yorùbá Language in Yorùbá History." In *Sources of Yorùbá History*, ed. S. O. Bíòbákú, 176–204. Oxford: Clarendon Press, 1973.

Akíntóyè, S. A. *A History of the Yorùbá People*. Dakar (Senegal): Amalion Publishing, 2010.

Aríbidésí Usman

SUCCESSION

The Yorùbá system of government formation is rooted in an age-old procedure that results in the emergence of kings and chiefs. The procedure for choosing a king is more elaborate than that for chiefs. The filling of both positions, however, includes rituals. Only those from the royal family can become kings. In every city, the historical founder is the one recognized to be the root of kingship. It is common to have a number of *ìdílé ọmọ ọba* (royal families) who trace their roots to the founder of the place. The process of choosing a new king begins after the passing away of a king (*ọba wọ àjà* or *ọbaá wàjà*).

The first step involves chiefs (*afọbajẹ*) being assigned with the task of holding a meeting; there they decide who should fill the vacant stool. Such a meeting usually takes place in the palace or at the home of the most senior chief (depending on the situation in their town or city). At the meeting, chiefs suggest possible candidates. The second step involves royal families who are entitled to the throne; they hold their own meeting and nominate their candidates. After receiving the names of nominees, the chiefs ask a leading Ifá priest (Babaláwo) to cast the divination instrument (ikin), which will reveal a suitable or better prince (ọmọ-ọba) to fill the position. The practice is sacred even though manipulation cannot be ruled out because of human factors, such as the personal interest of chiefs.

Once Ifá has chosen a king, the next step is to announce the name of the person to the public. After that, the king-elect is put in a secluded place (barà), where initiation into the leadership position begins. The new king is exposed to full information about the town, his position, societal expectations, and rituals. Samuel Johnson wrote that it was "during this time [the new king] remains strictly in private, learning and practicing the style and deportment of a king, and the details of the important duties and functions of his office."

After the orientation and associated sacrifices, the official installation occurs, which is open to the public. A chief, senior king, or official authorized to supervise the ceremony officially presents the king to the people. The crowning of a king is the final step. Before akòko leaf is used as a mark of recognition and the new king is crowned, townspeople are asked if they accept him as a king. At this stage, though, nobody opposes a new king. The coronation offers a new king his crown (adé), fly whisk (ìrùkèrè), bracelet (èjìgbà), and staff of office (ọ̀pá àṣẹ). The new king's dance and public address are part of his succession. Eulogizing for old kings and the new king are also part of the ceremony.

The succession to a royal stool is accompanied by ceremony, as is the succession to a vacant chieftaincy position. A traditional chief is nominated by his family and is approved if the king feels comfortable having the person in his cabinet. After the death of a chief, the king will invite the families who are entitled to the vacant office to the palace and ask them to present their candidates. Where more than one candidate is nominated, the king often has the final say. Occasionally, the choice may be made through Ifá divination. If more than one person or families are interested in a position, the king decides who will be his chief and may use Ifá divination to guide him in his choice. Usually, the choice is often based on rotational history of the position (if the position is rotational). Once a chief is chosen and approved, the official installation is done. Usually, a new chief is presented to the public and told his or her assignment at the palace, where the king places ìyẹyè, a leaf, under his cap or her veil. Once installed, a merriment ceremony (ìwúyè) follows.

See also **Royalty and Chieftaincy**

REFERENCE

Johnson, Samuel. *The History of the Yorubas*. Lagos (Nigeria): C.S.S., 1921.

Báyọ̀ Ọmọlọlá

SUPERSTITIONS

Superstition is a positive or negative belief in subjects that contradict natural science. Most of these superstitions in the Yorùbá context are taboos. These taboos are the people's cultural dos and don'ts that attract supernatural punishment if violated. They are like dogmas that can never be argued with. They are called èèwọ̀ in Yorùbá.

For the Yorùbá, according to superstition, every literary creation is prompted by gods and directed by them. The Yorùbá believe that there are gods and goddesses who preside over various areas of human life. Some writers even say that superstition means "the institutions of the super beings." This means that superstitions are laws that people cannot question because they are from the unknown superiors. Some of the superstitions in Yorùbá context are the following:

- A pregnant woman must not walk outside when it is sunny for fear of a demon replacing the baby in her womb.
- No one must use his or her hands or palm to collect rainwater from the sky. One's fingers can be crippled.

- Parents must not see the burial ground of their children. It may lead to incessant death in the family.
- A husband and his wife's lover must never eat together and then shake hands. It may lead to the death of one of them.

These examples are universal to Yorùbáland. There are some superstitions that are tribal or for some families. Some situations may arise in families that bring up some taboos for generations in that family, so that whoever does something within the family from a particular point in time will have to appease the family god; otherwise, he or she will be afflicted with a particular disease or ailment.

Research has shown that the presence of the gods in Yorùbá philosophy of life is a framework for a society's morality. An aspect of this morality comes in the form of rituals that elevate the cordiality between men and the gods. For example, any woman who decides to walk in the sun must tie a pin or needle around her cloth in obeisance to Ògún, whom the Yorùbá believe to be the god of iron. With a pin or needle around the woman's cloth, it is believed that Ògún will guard against any evil occurrence to the baby in the womb.

Similarly, the taboo that a husband and his wife's lover must not eat together and shake hands is just to prevent the woman from having a lover at all—she is to be completely faithful to her husband. In conclusion, superstitions are laws regulating offenses that cannot be legally taken to the court of law for judgment.

See also **Taboos**

REFERENCE

Fádípè, N. A. *The Sociology of the Yorùbá.* Ìbàdàn (Nigeria): University Press, 1970.

Paul Olúwọlé Àsáwálé

SYMBOLS AND SYMBOLISM

Yorùbá people live in a symbolic world. Even the most literal minded among them constantly make use of and recognize symbols. Greeting, eating, wearing clothes, and exchanging gifts are all represented by symbolic actions. While symbols and symbolism are common across cultures, the Yorùbá people believe that symbols are cultural constructs and know that most do not have universally recognized meanings. Thus, they say, *Báyìí ni à ń ṣe ni ilé wa, èèwò ni ní ibòmíràn* (how we do this in our home is a taboo in another home). In Yorùbá society, a particular symbol can be understood only in relation to other symbols that form part of the larger cultural complex.

Taking the culture of greetings as an example, purged of its cultic meaning, most Yorùbá shake with their right hands; it is considered an insult to greet with a left hand. However, in the Ògbóni cult, members greet with their left hands and use certain signs that differentiate their greeting from ordinary day-to-day greetings. Young people greet the elderly by bowing down (young men prostrate and young women kneel) as a mark of respect. The crown, fly whisk, and beads are symbols of royalty. When certain beads are worn in other contexts, they carry different meanings entirely. For instance, beads worn by a maiden on her waist symbolize beauty.

Foods are categorized into different symbolic classifications; *iyán* (pounded yam) is regarded as *oúnjẹ* (real food), *àmàlà* (yam flour) is considered *òògùn* (medicine), *ẹ̀kọ* (corn paste) is an alternative in the absence of the first two, and *gúgúrú* (popcorn) is good only for snacking. Yorùbá people also believe that certain ritual actions are not only symbolic but also necessary for the sanctification of the society. For example, certain ritual actions are symbolic rather than ordinary practice. Most traditional Yorùbá people bury their dead (especially elderly men and in certain instances elderly women) inside the house or in a family compound to symbolize continuous relationship of the dead with the living (ancestral worship).

In their religious experience, Yorùbá use representations of symbolic imagery for their divinities, except for Olódùmarè, who cannot be represented by any image. Different images are made by artists to depict a particular divinity and distinguish it from others. A short, double-blade axe represents one of Ṣàngó's weapons; thunder and lightning are considered two other symbolic weapons Ṣàngó fights with. A laterite rock with palm oil on top symbolizes Èṣù's shrine. Ifá is symbolized by items such as ọ̀pẹ̀lẹ̀ (a sixteen-stringed cowrie chain), *ikin* (sixteen palm nuts), *ìrọ́kẹ́* (tapper), and *ọpọ́n ifá* (Ifá tray). It is also believed that each *odù* symbolizes a compass direction and a particular divinity. Òrìṣà-Ńlá's (Ọbàtálá) white dress symbolizes purity, cleanliness, and holiness on the part of his worshippers. On the whole, the Yorùbá worshippers represent the divinities through symbols and images not as an end in themselves but as a means to cast their minds on the objects of their worship.

See also **Color Symbolism; Secret Societies**

REFERENCES

Adélọ́wọ̀, E. Dàda. "Rituals, Symbolism and Symbols in Yorùbá Traditional Religious Thought." *African Journal of Theology* 4.1 (1990): 162–73.

Ìdòwú, E. Bọ́lájí. *Olódùmarè: God in Yorùbá Belief.* London: Longman, 1963.

Enoch Olújídé Gbádégẹsin

T

TABOOS

Taboos (*èèwọ̀*) and superstitions (*àìwọ̀*) are forbidden aspects of everyday life, sacred "rules" that invoke sanctions. Their purpose is to enforce norms and values in the society. In folk etymology, taboos and superstitions are known as *ohun tí kò wọ̀* (things that are not convenient) and *ohun tí kò wọ inú ara* (things that do not connect, add up, or dare not agree). They moderate moral, social, and psychological behavior. They even serve some medical purposes. They are collective or individualized. Some things are forbidden by virtue of the family history. For example, one family's *oríkì* says *ọmọ òrìjẹ ẹfọ̀n, tí ó ń jẹ ẹran erin* (offspring of those who eat elephant meat in the absence of buffalo meat). Today, we know that heavy consumption of red meat has health repercussions, including high cholesterol and cancer. Also, if members of a family have historically shown allergic reactions to some food, over time, it could become a family taboo to eat that food.

Sometimes, taboos are a protective social device. The taboo against children not eating in a doorway avoids collisions with someone rushing inside and prevents dust from getting in the food. In addition, taboos protect against activities that could hurt another person or actions perceived in the culture as unacceptable. For example, it is taboo to hit one's parent. Another taboo forbids a pregnant woman to walk alone on a sunny day. Although this may be to forestall medical emergencies, it is believed that some paranormal phenomena like evil spirits could replace the fetus with a demonic child. Taboos thus guide and guard social life and daily behaviors.

The indigenous method of teaching good character includes learning about the repercussions for breaching the taboos associated with them:

Òfófó níí pẹrú.
Èpè wọn a sì polè.
Ilẹ̀ dídà níí pọ̀rẹ́
Alájọbí níí pa ìyekan tó bá ṣe ibi.
A jọ gbórí ilẹ̀, a jeku
A jọ gbórí ilẹ̀, a jeja
A jọ gbórí ilẹ̀, a jẹ'koko ìgbín
Àṣẹ dọwọ́ ilẹ̀ a jọ mu.

Perfidy is what kills the slave of the house;
Verbal curse kills the thief.
Betrayal is what kills the bosom friend
The sacred blood of family ties is what kills the relative that does evil.
[Because] we lived on mother earth and ate rats together,
We lived on Mother Earth and ate fish together,
We lived on Mother Earth and ate whole snails together.
[Therefore,] justice shall flow by virtue of the allegiance with which we swore together to Mother Earth.

In other words, the emphasis is in the rule of natural justice that accompanies the violation of each taboo.

See also **Superstition**

REFERENCE

Fádípè, N. A. *The Sociology of the Yorùbá.* Ìbàdàn (Nigeria): University Press, 1970.

Michael Ọládèjọ Afọláyan

TECHNOLOGY

The technological history of Yorùbá begins, as in most regions of the world, with the relatively crude hand axes and scraping tools of the early Paleolithic Era. Around two hundred thousand years ago, these simple tools were supplanted in the archeological record by more delicate tools produced from skillfully struck stone flakes. Archeological sites dating from this period also yield the first evidence of implements with hafts, such as axes and thrusting spears. About fifty thousand years ago, finely worked microliths appeared, and these allowed for advanced projectile systems such as the bow and arrow.

The earliest ceramics found in Yorùbáland date to circa 4000 BCE, which—in combination with more numerous axes and adzes—suggests that agriculture began to propagate across the region at that time, a process that was completed by roughly 1000 BCE. Over time, the Yorùbá developed advanced agricultural techniques, including shifting cultivation, crop rotation, manure fertilization, irrigation, and erosion control. Ceramics heralded the coming of agriculture, but they would also come to be celebrated for their aesthetic value in their various forms: pottery, sculpture, or potsherd paving along ceremonial paths in great centers such as Ilé-Ifẹ̀.

Domesticated animals reached Yorùbá territory after 3000 BCE from further north in the Sahel. The arrival of horses was delayed until after the first century BCE as a result of the desiccation of the Sahara. Once horses were introduced, they were significant only in the northernmost regions of Yorùbá country and had little impact on agriculture. These limitations were associated with the difficulties of equine maintenance presented by tropical disease and parasitism. Despite the expense and difficulty of maintaining horses in the region, a number of Yorùbá polities, most famously the Ọ̀yọ́ Empire, maintained elite cavalry forces.

It is strongly suspected that iron working was independently developed in the region around the sixth century BCE and likely spread with the migration of skilled iron workers. Closely associated with the deity Ògún, these craftsmen came to occupy a distinguished position in the society. They organized into guilds and produced high-quality weapons, tools, and ceremonial implements through both casting and forging techniques. Work in copper and its alloys emerged later, during the ninth century CE, but eventually achieved an astounding level of excellence, as evidenced by the world-famous Ifẹ̀ bronzes.

Much later in the nineteenth century, contact with the West, and ultimately colonial occupation, had a dramatic impact on the technological landscape of Yorùbáland. The introduction of large numbers of firearms revolutionized and intensified warfare, and cheap Western manufactured goods threatened the livelihood of many craftsmen. The onset of colonialism saw the widespread introduction of foreign technologies but at the price of political oppression and socioeconomic marginalization.

Despite these consequences, it is essential to bear in mind that the Yorùbá are not helpless victims, overcome by the juggernaut of Western technology. In fact, the Yorùbá have played a significant role in the development of many "Western" technologies, most famously in the field of pharmacology with the development of medication from local herbs for the treatment of sickle-cell anemia. Today, Yorùbá people can be found developing and interacting with technologies all over the world.

See also **Science**

REFERENCES

Fálọlá, Tóyìn, and Matthew M. Heaton. *A History of Nigeria.* Cambridge: Cambridge University Press, 2008.

Usman, Aríbidésí. *The Yorùbá Frontier: A Regional History of Community Formation, Experience, and Changes in West Africa.* Durham, NC: Carolina Academic Press, 2012.

Daniel Jean-Jacques

TEXTILE ARTS (USAGE)

A consideration of textile arts among the Yorùbá must account for the variety of fabrics used and consider the specific purposes and occasions that warrant such use. Wedding ceremonies are some of the most common occasions that call for a calculated and impressive display of colors in an astonishing variety of combinations. At weddings the groups associated with the groom and bride have their own specific colors. The groom and bride emerge wearing identical colors. All other members of the group also wear identical colors, which are not the same as those of the bride and groom. Typically, a Yorùbá wedding conjures a carnival: a spectacle for the display of high fashion by both men and women. The fabrics may be made of aṣọ òkè or lace, the two most popular fabrics. (These are also known as aṣọ ẹbí, or "family wear," and aṣọ òkè, which literally means "fabric from the hinterland," and is a hand-woven fabric of the Yoruba.) Depending on the status of the families, Guinea brocade or even àǹkárá (wax print) may also be used.

Other occasions that warrant the use of distinguished and expensive dress include the naming of a newborn, conferring a chieftaincy title, coronation, and the burial of an important person. The most impressive, and often the most expensive, dress is the aṣọ òkè, which is woven solely by men on a double-heddle horizontal loom in strips of about five inches wide that are then sewn into the desired dress. Aṣọ òkè comes in three distinctive types: sányán, woven from silk and cotton in shades of umber; àlàárì, a combination of cotton and synthetic threads with a distinctive rich crimson color; and ẹtù, indigo with streaks of white. Notable centers of production for aṣọ òkè are Ìṣẹ́yìn, Ọ̀yọ́, and Oǹdó. In recent years, the aṣọ òkè has undergone a remarkable makeover in fabric content and design. The new aṣọ òkè is woven with softer industrial yarns in a much broader range of colors than was previously available. As a result, the stiffness that characterized the old aṣọ òkè has given way to a much more pliable fabric. This development has made aṣọ òkè more popular among younger Yorùbá men and women. Aṣọ òkè has become the indisputable fabric of choice during formal events and weddings.

Other types of fabrics are woven locally. These include the kíjìpá and the ìtagbe, which are woven exclusively by women on an upright, single-heddle broad loom, with dimensions that range from one foot to three feet wide. While kíjìpá is woven in several homesteads across Yorùbáland, ìtagbe, which is exclusive to the Ògbóni society, is woven in Ìjèbúland.

The production of a resist-dyeing technique, known as àdìrẹ (tie-dye) and batik, has enjoyed considerable circulation because of its relatively ease of production and affordability. Abẹ́òkúta, Ìbàdàn, and Òṣogbo are acknowledged as important cities for the design and marketing of àdìrẹ. The classic version of àdìrẹ was the àdìrẹ ẹlẹ́kọ, which employed cassava starch to create design patterns that were stenciled on the fabric before it was immersed in indigo dye. Hand-painted or stenciled designs were often a combination of figurative images, symmetric designs, short phrases, and Yorùbá maxims, such as Ìbàdàn dùn (Ìbàdàn is enjoyable); Ọmọ lèrè (child is beneficial); and Gbé jẹ́ẹ́ kí o níyì (modesty begets dignity). Today, Níkẹ̀ Òkúndayè, a celebrated artist and art entrepreneur, has turned the production of multicolored wax-resistant àdìrẹ into a sustainable industry and trained scores of apprentices who in turn have popularized the craft in their respective domains.

During major political events, it is customary to see supporters of a particular candidate turn out by the hundreds, all wearing identical, factory-manufactured fabrics bearing the image and slogans of a candidate. Mass-produced printed fabrics can be commissioned by anyone to celebrate a desired event, advertise a belief, or commemorate wedding or death anniversaries, cooperative activities, or religious festivities.

An expressive but inexpensive fabric is the àǹkárá, a wax print that originated in Holland but has become identified with West Africa. It particularly became popular from 1999 to 2007, when the administration of President Olúṣẹ́gun Ọbásanjọ́ enjoined Nigerians to embrace it as alternative to expensive, machine-made lace fabrics, which are still a favorite of the Yorùbá. In the hierarchy of fabrics, àǹkárá serves multiple roles: it can be used as a high-fashion fabric or as daily wear. The same cannot be said of lace or, for that matter, highly expensive damask, an import that appears to have lost the luster that it once had as a cherished fabric for major events. Whether produced locally or imported, the Yorùbá are adept at imposing their own aesthetic on textiles in ways that affirm their penchant for endless social events, known otherwise as *ó wàńbẹ̀* parties.

See also **Body Adornment and Cosmetics; Dress**

REFERENCE

Òjó, E. B. "Printing Contemporary Handwoven Fabrics (Aṣọ-òkè) in Southwestern Nigeria." *Design Issues* 23.2 (Spring 2007): 31–39.

délé jẹ́gẹ́dẹ́

TIME RECKONING AND CALENDARS

Although the Yorùbá have adopted the Western calendar and system of reckoning time, they had their own calendar before the Europeans arrived on the African continent. In contrast to the Western system's seven-day week, the traditional week comprised four days in predictable pattern. Not unlike the Gregorian calendar, in which days of the week are named for Roman gods, the four days in the Yorùbá week are named for the major deities (òrìṣà). The first day is for Ọbàtálá (*Ọjọ́ Ọbàtálá*), the second for Ọ̀rúnmìlà (*Ọjọ́ Ọ̀rúnmílà, Ọjọ́ Ifá,* or *Ọjó Awo*), the third for Ògún (*Ọjọ́ Ògún* or *Ọjọ́ Ọṣọ́ọ̀sì*), and the fourth for Ṣàngó (*Ọjọ́ Ṣàngó* or *Ọjọ́ Jàkúta*). Some of these days also overlap with the worship days dedicated to other lesser deities, such as Sànpọ̀nná (day one); Ọ̀sun and Èṣù (day two); Ọya (day four), and so on. The Yorùbá later on adopted an economic system based on the market-day cycles within the community. It is important to underscore here that there are

some Yoruba communities where the week consists of eight, or even sixteen days rather than four days.

The Yorùbá monthly calendar (also known as *Kọ́jọ́dá*), like many other ancient ones, was based on the lunar cycle and consisted of twenty-eight days, reckoned from the intervals between two consecutive new moons. Thus, there were thirteen lunar months in a year. In contrast to the Gregorian calendar, which begins with January 1 and ends December 31, the Yorùbá calendar, begins on June 3 and ends on June 2. Stemming from influences on Yorùbá culture by the Arabs and the West, time measurement was subdivided into *wákàtí* (an Arabic word meaning "hour") and *ìṣéjú* (second, literally "the blink of an eye"). Thus, there are sixty *ìṣéjú* in one *wákàtí*. The year (*ọdún*) is further subdivided into *osù* (month), *ọ̀sẹ̀* (week), and *ọjọ́* (day). The names of the months of the year are based on festivals: *Sẹ́rẹ́* (January), *Ẹ̀rẹ́lẹ́* (February), *Ẹ̀rẹ̀nà* (March), *Igbe* (April), *Ẹbìbí* (May), *Okúdù* (June), *Agẹmọ* (July), *Ògún* (August), *Ọwẹ́rẹ̀* (September), *Ọ̀wàrà* (October), *Bélú* (November), and *Ọpẹ́* (December).

Names of the days of the week are as follows: *Ọjọ́ Àìkú* (Sunday), *Ọjọ́ Ajé* (Monday), *Ọjọ́ Ìṣẹ́gun* (Tuesday), *Ọjọ́rú* or *Ọjọ́ rírú* (Wednesday), *Ọjọ́bọ̀* (Thursday), *Ọjọ́ Ẹtì* (Friday), and *Ọjọ́ Abámẹ́ta* (Saturday). Arabic influences on the Yorùbá can also be observed in alternative names for some of the days of the week (mainly direct loan words from the Arabic language): *Ọjọ́ Atàlátà* (Arabic: *al-thalāthāʾ*, Tuesday), *Ọjọ́ Alàrùba* (Arabic: *al-arbaʿāʾ*, Wednesday), *Ọjọ́ Alàmísì* (Arabic: *al-khamīs*, Thursday), and *Ọjọ́ Jímọ̀* (Arabic: *al-jumuʿah*, Friday). The alternate name for Sunday is *Ọjọ́ Ìsinmi* (day of rest), based on Christian and Western influences.

REFERENCE

Zaslavsky, Claudia. *Africa Counts: Number and Pattern in African Cultures.* 3rd ed. Chicago: Chicago Review Press, 1999.

Timothy T. Àjàní

TOURISM AND LEISURE

There are five main points to consider with respect to the growth and development of tourism and leisure among the Yorùbá. First, the foreign perception of Nigeria as not being a safe, secure, or comfortable place to visit affects tourism to the country. Foreigners' perception of endemic corruption in Nigeria in general and the Yorùbá market haggling system in particular not only make tourists vulnerable to being cheated but also make them wary of choosing to visit Nigeria. Second, the Yorùbá tend to visit friends and relatives rather than tourist attractions or locations in the conventional sense. The Yorùbá culture, values, and beliefs place a high premium on work as expressed in the saying *iṣẹ́ l'òògùn iṣẹ́* (work is the solution to poverty). Hence, they perceive leisure, particularly recreation, holidays, and pastimes, as a waste of time. Even a modern Yorùbá as a tourist abroad is more likely to be a businessperson on a trip than a tourist on holiday.

The leisure industry is a fast-growing industry among the Yorùbá, behind transportation, gas stations, and educational institutions. Event centers have sprung up across the country. Families often have an obligatory friends and family "do," or party, that involves traveling. Elaborate celebrations of life include naming ceremonies, birthday parties, funerals and memorial services, weddings, celebrations of professorial or household chieftaincy titles (*oyè jíjẹ* and *ìwúyè*, respectively), matriculation and convocation ceremonies, and induction ceremonies for newly qualified lawyers, pharmacists, and medical doctors. Although some see such things as a waste of time, the Yorùbá are never short of ideas for celebrations that involve leisure activities, such as taking a break from work, making traveling arrangements, arranging hotel and lodging requirements and catering, hiring music from disc jockeys or live bands, engaging in media and social networking, and buying gifts.

Third, local and state governments are promoting themselves as tourist destinations, highlighting their historical cities and seasonal festivals, as well as mystical and sacred sites of legendary heroes and heroines. For example, Ọ̀ṣun festival in Òṣogbo, Agẹmọ festival in Ìjẹ̀bú, Ògún festival in Ìrè and Oǹdó, Òkè'Bàdàn and Egúngún festivals in Ìbàdàn, and the Ojúde Ọba (a large horse-riding carnival on the third day of the Muslim festival Id el Kabir) in Ìjẹ̀bú are popular among tourists.

Fourth, the Yorùbá crafts industry also attracts tourists. For example, tourists visit the *ọlọ́nà igbá* (calabash carvers) in Ọ̀yọ́, the *aládìrẹ* (print textile and tie-dye industry) at Abẹ́òkúta, *ẹní ìko* (the raffia-mat makers) at Badagry, and *ìkòkò amọ̀ mímọ* (clay pottery) at Ìmọ̀pé in Ìjẹ̀bú.

Fifth, since Nigerian independence in 1960 and the 1977 International Festival of African Arts and Culture in Lagos, there has been a cultural revival of the Yorùbá tourist resources by all levels of government. For instance, many local and state governments have engaged in developing, modernizing, and promoting historical sites. For example, the government has built restaurants, constructed steps, and installed an elevator at Olúmọ Rock at Abẹ́òkúta and at the Bower Tower in Ìbàdàn. Ìkọgòsì Warm Springs, Òkè Ìdànrè, Bílíkísù Sugbó in Ìjẹ̀bú, and the lagoon beaches in Lagos, have also been developed to attract both local and foreign visitors. Before these developments, those sites enjoyed only the patronage of school visits and excursions.

See also **Heritage, Cultural: Sites; Heritage, Cultural: Management and Preservation; Museums; Pilgrimage: Christianity; Pilgrimage: Islamic; Travel and Exploration**

REFERENCE

Nash, D. *The Study of Tourism: Anthropological and Sociological Beginning.* London: Elsevier Science, 2005.

Bọ́lá Dáúdà

TOWN HISTORIES

Yorùbáland is a heterogeneous society; hence, Yorùbá people are divided into many subgroups, each with its own peculiar history, dialect, and culture. A subgroup comprises many villages and towns. The following are major Yorùbá subgroups: Abinu, Àkókó, Àwórì, Ẹ̀gbá, Ẹ̀gbádò, Ègùn, Èkìtì, Ìbàràpá, Ìbọ̀lọ́, Ifẹ, Ìfọ̀nyìn, Ìgbómìnà, Ìgèdè, Ìjẹ̀bú-Rémọ, Ìjẹ̀bú, Ìjẹ̀sà, Ijùmú, Ìkálẹ̀, Ìkiri, Ìlàjẹ, Kétu, Ọ̀họ̀rí, Oǹdó, Ọ̀wọ̀, Ọ̀yọ́, and Yàgbà.

The histories of these and other Yorùbá communities are different, although considerable overlap exists. For the most part, nearly all these communities share in the belief that they originated from a common source, Ilé-Ifè, and that Odùduwà, the famed father of the Yorùbá race, was their father.

In addition, there is uniformity among various cultural and sociopolitical institutions. Yorùbá communities owe this uniformity to efforts of ancient leaders who deliberately forged unity and cultivated mutual relations despite their diversity. Also, this unity has resulted from the missionaries who established a formal school system and a standardized, written Yorùbá language. Since the nineteenth century, political leaders have pointed to linguistic unity and a shared belief in a common ancestry as strategies to unite the people.

The earliest writers and chroniclers of the histories of the different communities in Yorùbáland have documented myths of origin and the founding of the different dynasties. Some of these earliest efforts showcased activities of different leaders to establish territories, expand frontiers, and consolidate power. Some of these leaders, including Odùduwà, Òrànmíyàn, and Lísàbi were regarded as the founders and fathers of their different communities.

The nineteenth century, however, witnessed a number of significant developments that altered Yorùbáland and played a fundamental role in documenting the histories of different communities. Notable among these are the abolition of the transatlantic slave trade, the return of liberated slaves to their Yorùbá homeland, the introduction and spread of Christianity, and the imposition of colonial rule in Nigeria. Works about Yorùbáland written in Arabic existed before the nineteenth century, but these nineteenth-century events stimulated the writing of histories of origin, peoples, and communities.

The first set of writings was essentially concerned with the histories, cultures, and peculiarities of the different communities. This set of writings was followed by works that focused primarily on the various events of the nineteenth century, such as the Yorùbá civil war. A number of them also examined postwar efforts by the victors to dominate others, and others encouraged fighting for independence.

Owing to the spread of Christianity and the acceptance of Western education, histories of towns and peoples soon emerged. Following this development was the establishment of the University College, Ìbàdàn (now University of Ìbàdàn), which paved the way for the development of an indigenous, university-trained intelligentsia. These new crop of chroniclers were well trained and methodical in their approach to writing histories of Yorùbáland's peoples, events, and communities and to codifying Yorùbá orthography. Books, journals, newspaper articles, and other writings created a growing body of work about every aspect of Yorùbá life, culture, and society.

One of the most notable individuals to emerge during these early efforts was Samuel Àjàyí Crowther, a rescued slave who later became an Anglican bishop, a popular administrator, and an author; he is best known for translating the English Bible into Yorùbá. Together with Crowther, C. A. Gollmer, Henry Venn, and John Raban played important roles in developing Yorùbá orthography. Other notable writers include Emmanuel Moses Líjàdù, Josiah Ṣówándé, Àjàyí Kómọláfẹ́ Ajíṣafẹ́, John Lósì, G. O. George, and Adénrelé Ọbasá. Líjàdù authored *Yorùbá Heathenism*, with a focus, like Johnson, on religion. Samuel Johnson used oral accounts collected largely in Ọ̀yọ́ and Ìbàdàn to write *History of the Yorùbás*.

The popularity of these initial efforts led to a flowering of ethnohistories. For example, Chief Òjó, the Badà of Ṣakí, wrote on the Ṣakí; J. D. Abíọ́lá wrote about Ilésà; and N. D. Oyèrìndé wrote *Ìwé Ìtàn Ògbómọ̀ṣọ́*. A. K. Ajíṣafẹ́ compiled Yorùbá laws and customs as well as a book on religion in Yorùbáland. Joseph Odùmósù focused on traditional medicine, compiling lists and techniques published under the titles *Ìwé Egbòogi* and *Ìwé Ìwòsàn*. Odùmósù pioneered a community newspaper with his publication of *Ìwé Ìròhìn Ìlú*. Other writings included those of David Ọnàdélé Ẹpẹ̀gà who wrote *Ìtàn Ìjẹbú àti Ìlú Míràn* and *Ṣónibárẹ́* in 1919 as well as *Ifá: Amọ̀nà Àwọn Baba Wa* in 1948. Moses B. Òkúbọ́tẹ̀ wrote *Ìwé Ìkékúrú ti Ìtàn Ìjẹbú* in 1934. J. O. Ajíbọ́lá wrote *Òwe*

Yorùbá, Ìtòjọ, and *Oúnjẹ Ilẹ̀ Wa* in 1947. Like Crowther, Seth Rúnsèwé Kalẹ́ was also an Anglican bishop. He wrote *Tibi Tire* and *Ìkíni L'Édè Yorùbá* in 1943. Henry Townsend founded the first pan-Nigerian newspaper, *Ìwé Ìròhìn fún Àwọn Ẹ̀gbá àti Yorùbá,* in 1859. Robert Campbell published the *Anglo-African,* an English newspaper based in Lagos in 1859. Between 1859 and 1950, there were about twenty newspapers in Yorùbáland alone.

A few common trends in all these efforts were the use of Yorùbá language in documenting histories or cultural practices of the different communities and the collection and use of local materials. The use of Yorùbá gave way to the English language with the widespread acceptance of Western education and the establishment of the first university in Nigeria in Yorùbáland. This not only stimulated the institutionalization of historical writing but also spearheaded the spread of ethnohistories, as several scholars began to criticize the initial literature, especially for their narrow consideration of materials and wide-ranging claims. For instance, Samuel Johnson was criticized for his use of Ọ̀yọ́ and Ìbàdàn narratives in writing the history of Yorùbáland. This criticism was one of the underlying reasons for the proliferation of written works on other communities and subgroups across Yorùbáland. These books, reports, and newspapers focused essentially on ethno-political and socioreligious developments and practices across Yorùbáland.

See also: **Crowther, Samuel Àjàyí; History and Historiography**

REFERENCES

Johnson, Samuel. *The History of the Yorùbás.* Lagos (Nigeria): C.S.S., 1921.

Ọlábímtán, Afọlábí. "A Critical Survey of Yorùbá Written Poetry 1848–1948." Unpublished PhD dissertation, University of Lagos, Lagos (Nigeria), 1974.

Bùkọ́lá Oyèníyì

TRADE: NATIONAL AND INTERNATIONAL SYSTEMS

The Yorùbá-speaking people of southwestern Nigeria are very enterprising. This quality is evident in their involvement in trade, craft, and agricultural activities since precolonial times. Agriculture was the main occupation of the people, and women sold farm produce at market. The involvement of women in the sale of food products and other petty trade is a reflection of the gender balance in the construction of economic activities among the people since precolonial times. Income from trade provided the means for Yorùbá parents to send their children to schools both within and outside Nigeria before the introduction of free education in the region. Such incomes also provided a reliable and predictable means of social mobility.

In the precolonial economy, markets were organized in various forms to accommodate the needs of the people. There were village markets, night markets, daily markets, weekly markets, and periodic markets. As the names imply, the various markets were conducted on different days and times. These markets attracted buyers and sellers from various nearby communities and sometimes from long distances. Food items were the major commodity sold in the markets. These precolonial market arrangements continue in various forms today. A major difference is the diversity in the kinds of products and people that are found in the markets.

The trans-Saharan and transatlantic slave trades as well as colonialism altered the structure of the economy of the Yorùbá; these experiences affected the configuration of communities, economic activities, migration patterns, and relationships with other nations within and outside Nigeria. Because of their location near the coast, the Yorùbá were very much involved in the slave trade, both as victims and as accomplices. As victims, they were hunted by African, Portuguese, and other European slave traders for centuries. As accomplices, the powerful kings and merchants served to further Europeans' unbridled demands for able-bodied men and women from the region.

Colonialism and Trade

Colonialism also changed the structure of the economy of the Yorùbá through the introduction of cash crops such as cocoa, rubber, cotton, kola nut, and palm oil. With the higher financial gains that resulted from trade in cash crops, many farmers in the states of Oǹdó, Ògún, Ọ̀yọ́, Ọ̀ṣun, and Èkìtì concentrated on cash-crop farming. The introduction of the wage economy under colonialism led to rural-urban migration. Although this boosted trade by increasing the wage earners' purchasing power, it also led to a shift in attention away from food production. Colonial infrastructure such as railways and ports further boosted intra-Yorùbá trade and led to the establishment of new settlements along railway lines. The railway line from Lagos to Kano, which was completed in 1912, helped boost trade activities in cities such as Ìdó, Abẹ̀òkúta, Ìbàdàn, and Ìlọrin. The Lagos ports also helped boost import and export trade in Yorùbáland.

Over a long period, a merchant class emerged who engaged in exports and imports of various semi-manufactured and fully manufactured goods. Such imported goods were distributed through a network of wholesale and retail outlets in various parts of the Yorùbáland and other parts of the country. The Yorùbá people are also involved in craftwork such as weaving, smithing, wood carving, and so on—and they sell these products at the various markets and in other parts of the country and throughout the West African coast.

Trade and Migration

Yorùbá traders have traditionally moved to other parts of Nigeria and West Africa to engage in buying and selling; then they either return home on a regular basis or settle permanently to establish their own businesses. Consequently, Yorùbá, especially the Ògbómọ̀ṣọ́ from the current state of Ọ̀yọ́, are found in different parts of Nigeria, especially in the north. Yorùbá are also found in neighboring African countries such as Ghana, Cameroun, Côte d'Ivoire. In contemporary times, Yorùbá are actively involved in the huge informal trade network spanning from Òkè-Àrín in Lagos through the Seme border and Cotonou to other countries in West Africa.

Trade and the Yorùbá in Diaspora

The international dimension to trade in Yorùbáland finds expression in the huge Yorùbá population found in other parts of the world. While the slave trade contributed to the huge Yorùbá Diaspora in many countries such in Brazil, Jamaica, Cuba, and Venezuela, globalization has further intensified the migration of Yorùbá people to different parts of the world. This diasporic population has created a unique trading opportunity, as it provides markets for films and videos, music CDs, clothes, food items, and other products. In this context, trade becomes not just a process of exchange but also a form of cultural expression. Yorùbá in the Diaspora are engaged in the acquisition and display of products made by continental Yorùbá and exported to them through various official and unofficial channels.

Conclusion

Trade is central to the overall economic well-being of the Yorùbá people. The gender dimension of trade shows that women are active agents in facilitating economic activities. Migration has played an important role in fostering trade among the Yorùbá. Trading activities have not been limited to the geography of southwestern Nigeria; rather, the Yorùbá ply their trades in different parts of the world. It is significant that although the trade patterns of the Yorùbá have been diversified and modernized, they retain some elements of the pre-colonial times. The Yorùbá have long been involved in trade both within and outside of Nigeria.

See also **Economic Systems; Diaspora: Impact of Yorùbá Culture; Markets**

REFERENCES

Fálọlá, Tóyìn. "Trade and Markets in Pre-colonial Economy." In *An Economic History of West Africa since 1750*, ed. G. O. Ògúnremi and E. K. Fáluyì, 61–71. Ìbàdàn: Rex Charles in association with Connel Publications, 1996.

Smith, Robert H. T. "Periodic Market-places and Periodic Marketing: Review and Prospect II." *Progress in Human Geography* 4 (March 1980): 1–31.

Samuel O. Ọlọ́runtọ́ba

TRANSLATION

When Christian missionaries arrived in Yorùbáland in the nineteenth century, they soon realized that their evangelical work would be tremendously aided if they made use of the enfranchised Yorùbá Christians from Sierra Leone and used the language of the people, to communicate with them directly. This explains the instruction given by the Church Missionary Society (CMS) to Samuel Àjàyí Crowther during his ordination in 1843 that he start conducting services of Christian worship in the Yorùbá language. This practice of using the language as medium of expression for Christian worship services compelled the missionaries to embark on urgent translation into Yorùbá of select portions of the English Bible and to intensify their interest in the language. The consequence of this interest was the series of activities undertaken by missionaries for the purpose of establishing a written language. In the year 1875, the first conference of experts under the chairmanship of Bishop Crowther reached an agreement on Yorùbá orthography. The intention of the missionaries in evolving a workable orthography for the language was to make the written language useful not only for the evangelists but also for the speakers of the language themselves. They wished the people to be able to read the Holy Bible in their own language. In the mid-1880s, the translation of the Bible to Yorùbá (*Bíbélì Mímọ́*), which Samuel Àjàyí Crowther initiated and supervised, was completed. Crowther also published the Yorùbá version of the Anglican Book of Common Prayer.

Simultaneously, translations of English poems were being published by missionaries in weekly Yorùbá newspapers. It is noteworthy that the translations of English poems in *Ìwé Ìròhìn* in particular usually were published in one issue of the newspaper, with their Yorùbá translations following in succeeding issues. For example, in the June 1, 1867, issue of *Ìwé Ìròhìn* the following poem by Bonar was published:

Be True
Thou must be true thyself,
If thou the truth wouldst teach,
Thy soul must overflow, if thou
Another's soul wouldst reach.
It needs the overflow of heart
To give the lips full speech.

Think truly, and thy thoughts,
Shall the world's famine feed;
Speak truly, and each word of thine
Shall be a fruitful seed;
Live truly, and thy life shall be
A great and noble creed.

And on June 21, 1867, the Yorùbá translation appeared in the same newspaper, as follows:

Jẹ́ Òtítọ́
Ìwọ jẹ́ òtítọ́ fúnrarẹ,
Bí'wọ ó bá kọ́ni l'ótìítọ́,
K'ọ́kàn rẹ k'ó kún, b'íwọ
O bá dé ọkàn ẹlòmíràn,
O ń fẹ́ ọkàn kíkún
Láti fi ọ̀rọ̀ s'ẹ́tè lí sísọ.

Ro l'ótìítọ́, èrò rẹ,
Kí ó ò sì jẹ onje ayé
Sọ òtítọ́, gbogbo ọ̀rọ̀ rẹ
Yóò jẹ igi eléèso;
Wà l'ótìítọ́, ayé rẹ ó sì
Jẹ́ ìrántí ìgbàgbọ́ ńlá.

Furthermore, from the end of the nineteenth century until the beginning of the twentieth century, the educated elite established a number of sociocultural organizations charged with the collection, translation, and publication of folkloric materials. For instance, the Ẹgbẹ́ Onífẹ̀ Ilẹ̀ Yorùbá organized periodic lectures on issues relating to history and culture, and Ẹgbẹ́ Àgbà Ò Tán established a publications committee for works of history and philosophy. Some of the committee's prominent titles with extensive oral data translated to English are Ajíṣafẹ́'s *History of Abẹ́òkúta* (1921) and *The Laws and Customs of the Yorùbá People* (1924), D. O. Ẹpẹ́gà's *Ifá* (1908) and *The Mystery of the Yorùbá Gods* (1932); E. M. Líjàdù's *Ifá* (1897) and *Ọ̀rúnmìlà* (1907), J. B. O. Lósì's *The History of Abẹ́òkúta* (1924), and J. Òjó-Cole's *A Collection of Yorùbá Thoughts* (1931).

From the 1930s, the wind of the Negritude literary movement that encouraged the enthusiastic collection of African folklore and oral tradition by native scholars themselves got to the Yorùbáland. The effort dovetailed with the anticolonial resurgence of the 1940s, which generated further recordings of materials concerning oral poetry, epic narratives, and associated genres. A pioneer of this new wave was the scholar Professor Adébóyè Babalọlá, described by Okpewho (1992) as one of the first African scholars to revolutionize the study of oral literature, especially in his book *The Content and Form of Yorùbá Ìjálá* (1966). That book has a 250-page appendix of ìjálá chants in Yorùbá and English translation. The standard set by Babalọlá in the translation of oral poetry into English was later followed by other scholars such as William Bascom and Wándé Abímbọlá on *ifá* poetry, Olúdáre Ọlájubù on *iwì egúngún* chants, Bádé Àjùwọ̀n on *ìrèmọ̀jé* and *ògbérè* funeral dirges, and Afọlábí Ọlábímtán on *ofọ̀* and *àyájọ́*, to mention just a few.

With the sudden death of Chief Daniel Ọlọ́runfẹ́mi Fágúnwà, a prominent writer and novelist, on December 9, 1963, Professor Wọlé Ṣóyínka decided to translate the author's most popular published novel *Ògbójú Ọdẹ Nínú Igbó Irúnmalẹ̀* (1938) into English as *The Forest of a Thousand Daemons* (1968). Other translators have followed in Ṣóyínká's footsteps by translating two other titles of Fágúnwà's novels into English: *Igbó Olúdùmarẹ̀* (1949) as *The Forest of God* and *Ìrìnkèrindò Nínú Igbó Elégbèje* (1954) as *Expedition to the Mount of Thought*. More recently, another scholar, Pamela Smith, has taken the bold step of translating the works of two notable contemporary writers—Akínwùmí Ìṣọlá and Adébáyọ̀ Fálétí—into English, with her publication of *Ẹfúnṣetán Aníwúrà, Ìyálóde Ìbàdàn and Tinúubú, Ìyálóde Ẹ̀gbá: Two Yorùbá Historical Dramas* (2008) and *The Freedom of Fight: A Novel of Resistance and Freedom* (2010). Smith's translation of Akínwùmí Ìṣọlá's biographical novel *Ogún Ọmọdé* (1990) as *A Treasury of Childhood Memories* is due for publication in 2016. Karin Barber collaborated with Ọládèjọ Òkédìjí to publish excerpts from his personal translation of his play *Aájọ Ajé* (1997) into English as *Running after Riches* (2000). The translation of Òkédìjí's most popular play, *Rẹ́rẹ́ Rún* (1973), by Bọ̀dé Ọ̀sanyìn also has appeared in English as *The Shattered Bridge*.

Similarly, works of some prominent Nigerian creative writers who write in English have been translated into Yorùbá. For instance, Akínwùmí Ìṣọlá has translated two of Wọlé Ṣóyínká's English titles: *Aké: The Years of Childhood* (1982) as *Aké: Ní Ìgbà Èwe* (2001) and *Death and the King's Horseman* (1975) as *Ikú Olókùn-ẹsin* (1994). Following that trend, Adémọ́lá Àrèmú and Dọtun Ògúndèjì translated Fémi Ọ̀ṣọ́fisan's *Red Is the Freedom Road* 1982) and *Who Is Afraid of Ṣólàrín?* (1978) into Yorùbá as *Ọ̀nà Ọmìnira, Ọ̀nà Ẹ̀jẹ̀* (1997) and *Yéèpà, Ṣólàrìn Ń Bọ̀* (1982), respectively. Wálé Ògúnyẹmí also published *Ìgbésí Ayé Okonkwo* (1997), a translation of Chinua Achebe's first novel *Things Fall Apart* (1959). The issue that begs further discussion is whether this last set of works should be referred to as translation or "cultural retrieval," on the basis of Akínwùmí Ìṣọlá's (2006) argument that the works were African ideas in the first place, "translated" into English by their authors, but retrieved back into the culture by translators.

See also **Crowther, Samuel Àjàyí (1807–1891); Literature: Modern and Written; Literature: Translation; Prominent Scholars; Ṣóyínká, Wọlé (1934–); Tutùọlá, Amos (1920–1997)**

REFERENCES

Ìṣọlá, Akínwùmí. "Not Translation but Retrieval: On Translating Ṣóyínká into Yorùbá." Unpublished paper, 2006.

Òkédìjí, Ọládèjọ. "Translating *Aájọ Ajé* (with Extracts from the Play in Both Yorùbá and English Translation)." In *Kiss and Quarrel: Yorùbá/English Strategies of Mediation*, ed. Stewart Brown, 172–80. Birmingham University African Studies Series 5. Birmingham, UK: Center for West African Studies, 2000.

Okpewho, Isidore. *African Oral Literature: Background, Character, and Continuity.* Bloomington: Indiana University Press, 1992.

Ọlábímtán, Afọlábí. "A Critical Survey of Yorùbá Written Poetry, 1848–1948." Unpublished PhD dissertation, University of Lagos, Lagos (Nigeria), 1974.

Akíntúndé Akínyẹmí

TRANSPORTATION

Transportation is an integral part of every human society. The need to move goods and people from one place to another underlies human society, and advances in transportation have had considerable effects on socioeconomic interactions. Transportation systems include roads, waterways, railways, and airplanes. In the nineteenth century, transportation was primarily done by human carriers, except in the coastal and riverine areas, where canoes were used. Animal transport was not common then. Both human and animal modes of transportation were constrained by weight, speed, distance, and climate. They were also unreliable, and they could be costly for long-distance journeys.

The imposition of British rule on Yorùbáland, starting with the Lagos conquest in 1861, followed by that of the inland states, led to expansion in existing transport facilities. The British interest was to exploit the forest products and minerals in Yorùbáland. The British considered the provision of modern transport for water, road, and rail as prerequisites for the effective exploitation of agricultural and minerals. In addition, modern transport opened up Yorùbáland to the modernizing influence of modern commerce. Lagos Harbor was improved to facilitate export trade even though the many states were far removed from the harbor.

The opening of the Lagos Railway in 1896 and its further extension inland had tremendous effects on trade and mobility in Yorùbáland. The line traversed the Yorùbá cities of Ọ̀tà, Ìbàdàn, Ìkìrun, and Ìlọrin and crossed the north. The railway increased long-distance journeys and trade, and for many years it remained the main transport mode. Yorùbá towns far removed from the line were connected with feeder roads to the railway. The earliest roads were narrow and unpaved but adequate for the transport of goods by human carriers.

The first motor road was built between Lagos and Ìbàdàn in 1905; by 1914 the number of such roads had increased. The railway also operated road transport service to the railway, although this was stopped in the 1920s because of competition from indigenous private transporters. Air transport was not common until the establishment of the airport in Lagos in the 1940s; this was limited, as the inland states were not connected to the air route until after independence. These transportations combined facilitated trade and

social contacts within Yorùbáland and other part of the country as well as Europe.

Since independence, the transport system has undergone tremendous transformation. Road transport became the most popular, while the railway declined, although it has started operating again after many years of inactivity. In most Yorùbá towns and cities, road transport such as taxi, buses, and motorcycles (ọ̀kadà) and tricycles (kẹ̀kẹ́ Napep) are popular intracity transport, and lorries and trucks are commonly used for interstate traffic. Air transport is also popular, although among people with high income. Most Yorùbá cities are served by airports, even though many operate only domestic flights.

REFERENCES

Akínjógbìn, I. A., and S. O. Ọ̀ṣọbà, eds. *Topics on Nigerian Economic and Social History*. Ifẹ̀ (Nigeria): University of Ifẹ̀ Press, 1980.
Ẹkúndáre, R. O. *An Economic History of Nigeria, 1860–1960*. London: Methuen, 1973.

Shehu Tìjjání Yusuf

TRAVEL AND EXPLORATION

Curiosity and the quest for knowledge are some of the underlying factors driving travel, tour, and exploration. Other factors include trade and commerce, religion, hunting and pleasure. It is difficult, if not impossible, to ascribe a beginning date for travel and exploration in Yorùbáland; however, oral accounts among different subgroups and archeological evidence show that travel and expedition have a long history.

From the two oral accounts of Yorùbá origin, the people were said to have migrated from the east to settle at Ilé-Ifẹ̀, the famed cradle of the Yorùbá people. In yet another account, the Yorùbá people were said to have descended from the heavens and landed at Ilé-Ifẹ̀. The need to cope with an increasing population, among other factors, later resulted in dispersal from Ilé-Ifẹ̀ to other locations where the Yorùbá live today. Common to these three events is travel and expedition. Without a doubt, the Yorùbá people were migrants, moving from one place to another until they settled in different places that would become kingdoms. As told in oral accounts, Odùduwà, the famed father of the Yorùbá people, commissioned his children to seek new land and establish communities there.

Besides histories of origin, archeological evidence attests to the fact that the Yorùbá, at different times, embarked upon travel and expedition for secular activities like trade and commerce, hunting and also for religious worship. For the former, different Yorùbá communities are known for their expertise in producing specific crops, their dexterity in making specific things, and in trading activities. For instance, Òṣogbo, Ọ̀yọ́, Ìgbómìnà, and Abẹ̀òkúta are reputed for cloth making, and Ekìtì, Oǹdó, Ìjẹ̀sà, and Yàgbà for their farming, including hunting, practices. Different markets where products from one part of Yorùbáland are exchanged for others abound across Yorùbáland. Hence, trade-related travel, either short or long distance, is common. Besides trade trips within Yorùbáland, trading activities have also taken Yorùbá people to other communities outside of Yorùbáland.

Religious-related travel and expedition is also an important feature of Yorùbá life. Before the introduction of Islam and Christianity, religious worship and festivals drew traditional religious worshippers from different communities in much the same way as Islam and Christianity today draw worshippers from different communities to different centers of religious worship.

In many oral accounts, references are made to reputable hunters. Tìmì of Ẹ̀dẹ is described as àgbàlé ọlófà iná—a sharpshooter whose arrows emit fire. Stories of hunters who, in the course of expedition, lost their ways and became residents in other towns for years are also told. The history of Òṣogbo, like Ìrèsì and Ọ̀yọ́-Ilé, cannot be dissociated from a hunting expedition that went awry. Tìmẹ́hìn, a great hunter and the mythical founder of Òṣogbo, was said to have been commissioned by the Ọba Ọlárọ̀óye at Ìpólé-Omu to find urgent solutions to incessant dryness and diseases that plagued his kingdom. Tìmẹ́hìn assembled other notable hunters, and together they found a new place near the Ọ̀sun River. The cases of Ìrèsì and Ọ̀yọ́-Ilé are similar. In the first, a hunter, having consulted with

Ifá, fled Ilé-Ifẹ̀ and followed a horse to a place where it could no longer move (because of exhaustion). In the case of Ọ̀yọ́-Ilé, Ọ̀rànmíyàn, at the instance of the oracle at Nupe, was said to have followed an alligator to where the alligator disappeared. Stories of great hunters such as these are common across Yorùbáland.

Irrespective of motivations for travel and expedition, both advance knowledge; hence, a traveler is assumed to be more experienced and more knowledgeable than, for instance, a trained professional without connections to other places. This belief, though, which underscores the importance of knowledge and experience that accrue from travel and expedition, should not be misconstrued as privileging travel and expedition over training and skill acquisition.

Notwithstanding difficulties associated with tracing the origin of travel and expedition, it could be argued that motivations for travel and expedition include trade and commerce, hunting, religious worship, and pleasure. Geography plays important role in travel and expedition associated with trade and commerce, and intergroup relations—for instance, marriage, training, and skill acquisition—have also played important roles.

While evidence abounds in oral accounts and archeological excavations on travel and expedition for trade, commerce, and religion during the precolonial period, not much evidence has survived on travel and expedition for pleasure during the period. Two plausible reasons for this are the nature of precolonial society and the impermanent nature of most items related to pleasure.

Precolonial Yoruba society was a purely agricultural society that concentrated its efforts on production, harvesting, and marketing. Despite this, enormous resources were devoted to social events like marriages, naming ceremonies, and funerals. At these and other outlets for pleasure, performances ranging from ìjálá and ìrèmọ̀jé to ìjàkadì or ẹkẹ and ẹ̀ṣẹ́ (wrestling and boxing) competitions offered pleasure to the people. While the indigenous society provided for kingship and other festivals, as well as markets and religious centers, individuals and families devoted their resources to the possession and regular maintenance of masquerades, as well as acquisition of the necessary skills and materials associated with dancing, wrestling, and boxing. Whether owned and maintained by individuals or the state, masquerades, *ìjálá*, *ìrèmòjé*, *ìjàkadì* or *ẹkẹ*, and *èṣẹ́*, as well as the materials required for their performance, provided for occasional spectacles with which rulers, their guests, and society at large were entertained. Moonlight stories, parables, riddles, and the like were sometimes organized into competitions, as part of spectacles or as side attractions in secular and religious worships to entertain rulers and guests at festivals. Given the impermanent nature of these festivals and spectacles, little or no permanent structures were constructed in their honor. Kings and chiefs had different games and sports competitions that drew people from far and near. For instance, the Bẹẹrẹ festival celebration in Ọ̀yọ́ often drew neighboring kings and chiefs as well as other people to the city of Ọ̀yọ́. At such games, competitions were held, and participants come from different parts of Yorùbáland both to participate in the spectacle and to demonstrate their loyalty to the *aláàfin*, king of Ọ̀yọ́.

In general, three types of tourism have developed in contemporary Yorùbáland. Cultural tourism, which describes tourism that focuses on the specific lifestyle and history, art and architecture, religion(s), and other (cultural) elements that shape the way of life of a particular people, are found in different parts of Yorùbáland. Notable examples include dungeons used during the transatlantic slave trade in Badagry, Lagos, the Ọ̀sun-Ọ̀ṣogbo Sacred Grove, which has become a UNESCO World Heritage Center, and the Ọ̀rànmíyàn staff site and other sites at Ilé-Ifẹ̀, Ọṣun State. Safaris and ecotourism continue to flourish at Old Ọ̀yọ́ National Park in Ìgbòho, Ọ̀yọ́ State; the soapstone in Èsìẹ́, Kwara State; and the warm springs at Ìkọgùsì and the Ìdànrè hills, both in Oǹdó State. Ecotourists also visit the waterfall at Ẹ̀rìn-Ìjẹsà in Ọṣun State and Olúmọ Rock at Abẹ́òkúta, Ògùn State. In addition to these sites, there are numerous zoological and botanical gardens in different cities and universities across Yorùbáland.

Although cultural tourism and ecotourism have developed across Nigeria in general, Yorùbáland, in particular, has a great variety of cultural and ecotourism sites. Moreover, a new development in travel and expedition in contemporary Yorùbáland today is religious tourism. While this is not a totally new development, as oral accounts abound of Yorùbá Muslims who trekked to Mecca for holy pilgrimage before the colonial period, there is a higher number of religious centers in Yorùbáland today that draw tourists from near and far. Notable centers include the camps of the Redeemed Christian Church of God and Mountain of Fire and Miracle Ministry along the Lagos-Ìbàdàn Expressway, the camp of the Christ Apostolic Church, Ìkeji-Arákeji, and that of the Living Faith Church Worldwide, also known as Winners' Chapel, at Ọ̀tà.

The burgeoning landscape of travels and expedition in contemporary Yorùbáland cannot be dissociated from the introduction and spread of Christianity and Islam, which facilitated religious and job-related movements as well as movement for pleasure. Just as a guild of hunters from one community would join their fellow hunters in another community at an annual festival during the precolonial period, members of different churches and mosques occasionally join their fellow Christians and Muslims at services with different games and sports competitions today. These games and sports continue to draw people from one community to another. Unlike the situation in the precolonial period, a number of permanent structures are built today to commemorate sports and games.

Except for sites or structures that are owned by individuals and religious organizations, most sites with touristic value have been taken over by the government, marking Yorùbáland as an important destination for tourists. Visitors to these various sites include Yorùbá and non-Yorùbá people from different parts of the world. As never before in Yoruba history, travel and expedition in Yorùbáland today is driven by trade, religion, curiosity, and pleasure.

See also **Festivals and Carnivals; Heritage, Cultural: Sites; Heritage, Cultural: Management and**

Preservation; Literature: Oral; Markets; Odùduwà; Pilgrimage: Christianity; Pilgrimage: Islamic; Sports; Tourism and Leisure

REFERENCES

Àrèmú, D. A. "Preservation of Archaeological Resources in Old Ọ̀yọ́ National Park." Ìbàdàn Journal of Humanistic Studies 9.10 (2000): 110–20.

Clapperton, H. Journal of a Second Expedition into the Interior of Africa from the Bight of Benin Soccatoo. London: John Murray, 1829.

Clarke, J. D. "Carved Posts at Old Ọ̀yọ́." Nigerian Magazine 15 (1938): 248–49.

Harunah, B. Hakeem. Nigeria's Defunct Slave Ports: Their Cultural Legacies and Touristic Value. Lagos (Nigeria): First Academic Publishers, 2000.

Bùkọ́lá Oyèníyì

TUTÙỌLÁ, AMOS (1920–1997)

In 1920, Amos Tutùọlá was born to Charles and Esther Tutùọlá, Christian cocoa merchants in Abẹ́òkúta, Nigeria. Tutùọlá was a servant to F. O. Monu, an Igbo man. He attended Salvation Army Primary School in lieu of wages at age seven and Anglican Central School in Abẹ́òkúta at age twelve. When his father died in 1939, his education ended. Young Tutùọlá left school and moved to Lagos after an unsuccessful attempt at farming. He trained as a blacksmith and worked for the Royal Air Force from 1942 to 1945 during World War II. Subsequently, he engaged in selling bread and acted as messenger for the Nigerian Department of Labor, among other vocations.

The nature of his work gave him some free time, which he spent writing stories in English. His first long narrative, The Wild Hunter in the Bush of the Ghosts, influenced by D. O. Fágúnwà's Ògbójú Ọdẹ Nínú Igbó Irúnmalẹ̀, was bought by Focal Press, an English publisher of photography books. Tutùọlá completed his first full-length book The Palm-Wine Drinkard in 1946 in just a few days. The next year, he married Victoria Àlàkẹ́; they had four sons and four daughters.

Despite his humble formal educational background, Tutùọlá wrote his novels in English. After he had written his first three books and became internationally acclaimed, he joined the Nigerian Broadcasting Corporation in 1956 as a storekeeper in Ìbàdàn. It was at Ìbàdàn that Tutùọlá started to adapt his work for the stage. He became also one of the founders of the Mbárí Club, the writers' and publishers' organization in Ìbàdàn. He was a research fellow at the University of Ifẹ̀ in 1979 and then an associate of the International Writing Program at the University of Iowa. In the late 1980s, Tutùọlá moved back to Ìbàdàn.

The most famous of Tutùọlá's novels are The Palm-Wine Drinkard and Dead Palm-Wine Tapster in the Deads' Town, which was written in 1946 and first published in 1952 in London by Faber and Faber. It was then translated into French by Raymond Queneau and published in Paris as L'ivrogne dans la brousse in 1953. Other Tutùọlá works that continued to explore the rich Yorùbá traditions and folklore include My Life in the Bush of Ghosts (1954), Simbi and the Satyr of the Dark Jungle (1955), The Brave African Huntress (1958), Feather Woman of the Jungle (1962), Àjàyí and His Inherited Poverty (1967), The Witch-Herbalist of the Remote Town (1981), The Wild Hunter in the Bush of the Ghosts (1982), Yorùbá Folktales (1986), Pauper, Brawler and Slanderer (1987), and The Village Witch Doctor and Other Stories (1990). Tutùọlá died at the age of seventy-seven on June 8, 1997.

See also Fágúnwà, Daniel Ọlọ́runfẹ́mi; Pidgin; Prominent Scholars; Stories, Storytelling, and Storytellers

REFERENCE

Owómóyèlá, Oyèkàn. African Literatures: An Introduction. Waltham, MA: Crossroads Press, 1979.

Adéníyì Àkàngbé

U

URBAN FOLKTALES

The postcolonial Yorùbá nation is highly fertile territory for folk stories, especially those alluding to the political and economic behavior of people in and surrounded by power. These modern-day stories are excellent examples of the reuse and adaptation of folk narratives. Specifically, telling tales and riddles is an objective modern experiment in hegemonic politics. In bars, restaurants, on buses, at parties, even in offices and political meetings, people enjoy narrating old stories with contemporary images. A major iconographic shift in this class of modern tales is the absence of animal characters, especially tortoise, the traditional protagonist in Yorùbá folktales. Instead, the characters are primarily human. This new genre of stories, according to Rópò Şekóní, started circulating in urban centers during the corrupt civilian administration of 1979–1983 and has steadily gained popularity—especially given the growing levels of socioeconomic uncertainty, which is threatening the material well-being of the people.

The following is an example of a contemporary urban folktale that references the theme of social inversion: An elected state governor asks his driver to deliver some cartons of beer to his father in his native village. Midway, the driver stops to check the cargo, loaded into the trunk by the governor himself. He finds that the four cartons are actually bursting with new currency notes. Quickly driving to his native village, the driver stashes the money in his mother's hut, then fills the cartons with bottles of beer and proceeds to deliver them to the governor's father. A few days later, the governor's father sends his governor-son a thank-you note for the beer, asking why he did not send whiskey, his favorite drink, instead. The governor quickly summons his driver, who swears that he delivered exactly what he found in the trunk: cartons of beer.

The driver is arrested and put in police custody. While in custody, his house is thoroughly searched, but no incriminating evidence is found. After his release, the driver relocates to his parent's village, becomes a farmer, and—unlike before—successfully clothes and feeds his seven children and sends them all to private schools in the city. Quite unexpectedly, however, a military coup takes place; the governor is arrested and thrown in jail on corruption charges.

This urban folktale focuses on the reversal of a corrupt political ethos that ordinarily exploits and victimizes ordinary working-class people. Similar to tortoise in traditional folktales, the driver serves the role of trickster, achieving a just and equitable outcome for the underdog, even though the odds are clearly stacked against him. The driver is depicted as a wily individual willing to take major risks to make an unfair system answerable to his needs. The driver's appropriation of the governor's loot is a way of using urban folktales to call attention to the need for social reform, allowing the masses to dispossess (if only symbolically) the exploiters and redistribute the nation's wealth more equitably. In several of the urban folktales, dual themes became clear: antagonism exists between the socioeconomic elite and the citizens they exploit, and there is always an underlying desire by the latter to avenge inequities at the expense of the former.

Since the 1990s, Nigeria's federal government policies toward the press were increasingly liberal. This liberalization has resulted in the proliferation of private FM radio stations and cable television networks, which offer programming not only in English but also in various Nigerian languages. This has proved a catalyst for many private radio and TV stations to allocate airtime to shows that feature storytelling. Therefore, the narration of urban folktales is a common occurrence on radio and television in all seven Yorùbá-speaking states in southwestern Nigeria. An excellent example is the weekly session of riddles and folktales entitled *Ààlọ́ Ìyá Àgbà* (Folktale Session with Grandma) on DSTV, a leading cable television network provider in Nigeria, and *Storyland*, created by ace storyteller Jìmí Ṣólàńkẹ́, on the network Nigerian Television Authority International.

These radio and TV productions inform young people about their native language, culture, and history. As a result, they promote appreciation in these young people of their rich heritage. Therefore, media presentations underscore the value of Yorùbá culture, serve as platforms for individual artists to develop verbal art performances, and build their plots around local customs and institutions. This process passes invaluable information to the listener, contributes to cultural continuity, and preserves invaluable knowledge for future generations.

See also **Narration Techniques; Stories, Storytelling, and Storytellers**

REFERENCE

Ṣẹkọní, Rópò. *Folk Poetics: A Sociosemiotic Study of Yorùbá Trickster Tales.* Westport, CT; London: Greenwood Press, 1994.

Akíntúndé Akínyẹmí

URBANISM AND URBANIZATION

An urban center is a settlement with a substantial population whose sustenance is inextricably linked to a contiguous countryside. Furthermore, its economy has grown beyond substituent level. Urbanization involves spatial, social, and temporal phenomena. Urbanization is a process, and according to Ayọ̀dẹ̀jì Olúkòjú, urbanism is the "factual and spatial expression of the ever changing urbanization."

The origin of the development of urban areas in Yorùbáland can be traced to before the seventeenth century. Urbanization in the precolonial Yorùbáland seems to have reached its zenith in Ilé-Ifẹ̀, which is regarded in Yorùbá mythology as the cradle of civilization. Archaeological findings and other materials in Ilé-Ifẹ̀ have revealed very sophisticated development of township system, evident by the intricate and complex art works, sculptures, handicrafts, and metalwork found there.

Apart from Ilé-Ifẹ̀, other large towns included Ọ̀yọ́, Iléṣà, Ìgbómìnà, Kétu, Abẹ́òkúta, and Òwu. These urban centers were usually administrative headquarters of the kingdoms in which they were located and contained the symbols and paraphernalia of power, authority, and economy. The growth of these centers was facilitated by different factors, the most important of which was trade. Before colonial rule, cities and towns were actually centers of commerce; market centers served not only people in the immediate vicinity but also those in the surrounding areas and beyond. The major items of trade were agricultural produce, agricultural implements, game and birds, pottery, textiles, war weapons, ivory, and slaves. Some of these were exchanged for imports from the savanna areas of West and North Africa, the Middle East, and Europe. Agricultural production was the cornerstone of the economy of urban centers; it fed the trade and was the largest sector of the economy. Other contributors to trade were arts and crafts. In some Yorùbá urban centers in the savanna, there were professionals totally devoted to the production of arts and crafts, including carvers, blacksmiths, goldsmiths, artisans, dyers, tanners, and potters.

In precolonial Yorùbáland, markets were usually located very close to the seats of power, such as palaces and religious and ritual centers; they were strategically located at junctions on trade routes; and they were linked to local and international trade. These trade networks in turn linked urban centers together in networks covering wide geographical areas.

Furthermore, there were other important factors in the development of Yorùbá cities. First was the decline and fall of the Old Ọ̀yọ́ Empire between the eighteenth and nineteenth centuries. These developments were partially brought about by the invading Sokoto Caliphate. In the attendant chaos, many people migrated south into many towns there, increasing those towns' population. Linked to this were the civil wars among the southern Yorùbá states. These wars created a large body of war refugees who fled into new areas to seek safety. For instance, the Ẹ̀gbá were displaced from their permanent settlement close to modern Ìbàdàn to their present location. The wars led to the creation of new urban centers out of hitherto unremarkable villages and then further developed existing urban centers. Some of the centers created included Abẹ́òkúta, Ẹ̀dẹ̀, Èjìgbò, Ìbàdàn, Ìjàyè, Ìwó, Ògbómọ̀sọ́, Òkèihò, Òṣogbo, and Ọ̀yọ́. Consequently, the massive movement of people across Yorùbáland in the nineteenth century made the cities ethnically, religiously, and occupationally diverse. Due to the jihadists' invasion of northern Yorùbáland and the settlement of Muslim scholars and traders there, some embraced Islam and proceeded to convert others to it.

Second, the abolition of the transatlantic slave trade in the nineteenth century freed from the civil wars captured slaves who were destined for the Americas. Instead, they settled in the communities where they were liberated from and increased their populations. Freed slaves from the United States, Canada, and Brazil and recaptives from Sierra Leone also returned to Yorùbáland. Although their numbers were small, they contributed to the urbanization of Yorùbáland.

They were the vanguard of the spread of Western education in Yorùbáland. Some of them were highly skilled artisans: masons, carpenters, bricklayers, builders, tailors, bakers, cooks, and dressmakers. Thus, they contributed to the physical development and the social and cultural life.

Third, the advent of Christian missionaries to Nigeria, especially from the 1840s, also contributed to urbanization. The Christians began their work by first settling in major towns along the coast. From there, they moved into the hinterland and settled in Ìbàdàn, Abẹ́òkúta, Badagry, Ìjẹ̀bú-Òde, and so on. They contributed to their population through the establishment of educational institutions; hospitals, clinics, and health centers; vocational training centers; and the construction of architecturally noteworthy church buildings. All these became magnets that drew people from the rural areas to the urban centers.

The urbanization of Yorùbáland did not end with the British. Some of the socioeconomic development programs of the colonial state led to further expansion of cities. The construction of railways and stations, road networks, sea and air ports, hospitals, and administrative headquarters led to the rise or further expansion of towns like Lagos, Abẹ́òkúta, Ìbàdàn, Òṣogbo, Ẹ̀dẹ̀, and Òta. The most developed of these was Lagos, which was the site of a new seaport, the southern terminus of the Nigerian railway network, and the location of the foremost international airport in Nigeria. In addition, some cities were made administrative centers by the colonialists, including Lagos, Ìbàdàn, and Abẹ́òkúta. In addition, local, regional, and international trade assisted in the expansion and creation of new urban centers. For instance, Lagos became a great hub of commerce in West Africa.

With all these infrastructural developments and the relative security provided by colonial rule, many people from the rural areas felt secure and migrated to the urban centers. In Lagos, Ìbàdàn, and Abẹ́òkúta, and other places, they sought jobs and other opportunities. Starting from the interwar years and extending into the postcolonial period, Yorùbá urban centers became melting pots for many ethnic, social, religious, cultural, and political groups and interests. In addition, some the cities became notorious for problems associated with urban areas: crime, prostitution, pollution, overcrowding, ethnic conflict, and religious conflicts.

See also **Cities**

REFERENCES

Fálọlá, Tóyìn, and Steven J. Salm, eds. *Globalization and Urbanization in Africa.* Trenton, NJ: Africa World Press, 2004.

Mábògùnjé, Akin L. *Urbanization in Nigeria.* London: University of London Press, 1968.

Tòkunbọ̀ Ayọ̀ọlá

V

VEHICLE SLOGANS AND GRAFFITI

Slogans on commercial vehicles are more than mere catchphrases or political manifestos; they advertise particular sensibilities and express general aphorisms. Slogans are windows into Yorùbá cosmology. Slogans and graffiti grace vehicles across Yorùbáland. The vehicles that yield the richest harvest of slogans and graffiti are those owned by men. The Lateef Jákàndè administration streamlined the public transportation business in Lagos State in the 1980s; it imposed a uniform yellow color that considerably minimized sloganeering on buses. Public buses in Lagos of the móòlùè (mold it) and dáńfó (loner) varieties display an array of slogans and graffiti, which were made more memorable for sheer quaintness. Popular slogans include the motivational and the instructive: "No Moless" (No Bothering), "Stand By," "No Retreat," "No Surrender," "Old Soldiers Never Die," and "Let My People Go." Clearly, an imaginary battle line has been drawn and these slogans are barking orders at the fictional enemy.

It is important to have a visual register of commercial vehicles plying the roads in Nigeria. Two distinct categories are identifiable. The first category includes corporate or municipal buses, as in the Bus Rapid Transport or the Young Shall Grow in Lagos, which have a structured regimen complete with corporate colors, logos, and operational principles. Other than the emblazoned corporate names, approved banners, and delightfully crafted advertisements, vehicles in this category are generally devoid of any social aphorisms. The second category includes local, wood-bodied trucks, móòlùè, and dáńfó that are owned and run by cooperatives or individuals. These vehicles provide the bulk of slogans and witty sayings; they add color and spice to a public transportation system characterized by disorder, incivility, and utter disregard for basic traffic etiquette.

While trucks focus on interstate transportation, the móòlùè and the dáńfó are seen on intra- and interstate roads. The trucks are often festooned with paintings that may include wild animals, martial arts fighters, superheroes, and other Western heroes. Among slogans that are common in, though by no means exclusive to, are "Safe Journey," "No Condition Is Permanent," and "Never Say Die." The dáńfó is, by design, an eleven-passenger van, although its operators see this as the minimum number of passengers needed to make a trip. A dáńfó is on the road once the basic conditions—a driver's cabin and reconceptualized passenger seats—are met. Headlights, side mirrors, and dependable tires are often regarded as accessories. It is not inconceivable to see inscriptions such as Tìẹ Dà? (Where Is Yours?) and Ṣéjú Ẹ! (Blink! Or, Stop Steering!) on them.

In a society saturated by the externalization of religious beliefs, commercial vehicles provide a good sampling of man's invincibility and God's infallibility: "Man Pass Man," "God Pass Them," "God Is Aware,"

Baba Dárí Jì Wọ́n (Lord Forgive Them), *Alhamidulillahi* (Glory Be to Allah), *Olúwa Ṣèyí* (God Did This), "Power Belong [*sic*] to Jesus," *El Shaddai* (God Almighty), and finally, "God's Case No Appeal." For those who aspire to own a *dáńfó*, there is the following advice: "Play Cool," *Láì Dákẹ́ Àdúrà* (Ceaseless Praying), and the classic "God's Time Is the Best."

See also **Cartoons**

REFERENCE

Láwuyì, Ọlátúndé Báyọ̀. "The World of the Yorùbá Taxi Driver: An Interpretive Approach to Vehicle Slogans." *Africa: Journal of the International African Institute* 58.1 (1988): 1–13.

déle jégédé

VILLAGES

Villages derive their names from their founder. The founder must be responsible enough to have control over several acres of land that will accommodate future growth and development. This founder, known as the *baálẹ̀*, is the apex of decision making. There is no limit to the number of years the *baálẹ̀* may occupy the position of leadership. If there is evidence of misdeeds, the *baálẹ̀* can be relieved of the position. The fundamental role of the village is to be receptive to all newcomers. Villages normally engage in different skill development programs, including housing, agriculture, socialization, apprenticeship, health behavior, and education.

Villages are good places to see how houses are developed and built in a rural setting. These houses are built close to each other in an old-fashioned form. There are no specifications. The number of windows and doors is determined exclusively by the owner. In nearly all cases, they do not meet any standard. The houses are built of mud and in many instances are not plastered. The poor conditions of these houses encourage lizards to run up and down the walls and rats to take solace. In the past, the roofs of houses were made of leaves; today iron sheets have replaced the leaves.

Villages are deprived of many amenities like public water systems, electrification, and paved roads.

People rely on vigilante justice as a security system to prevent theft of any magnitude. In most cases, villagers know one another and consider themselves members of the same family. Yorùbá villages are, to a large extent, homogeneous, but if there are a few who are not Yorùbá-speaking people, they often learn the language quickly. Examples are people from Ghana, Benin Republic, and other parts of Nigeria. Everyone is welcomed into a village's life.

Agriculture is the primary occupation in villages. It is through agriculture that villagers raise food to eat and earn money to live. Agriculture determines their future. This is why it is commonly said, "Live in the village and bury your laziness." People are engaged in different aspects of agriculture and animal husbandry, such as farming, fishing, hunting, herding animals, and raising poultry. Two kinds of crops exist in villages: permanent and seasonal. Permanent crops include cocoa, palm kernel, coffee, tea, oranges, and timber. Seasonal products include cassava, yam, rice, banana, plantain, other fruits, and vegetables. People living in villages see it as a shame to buy food because they feel that they have the capability to produce for their need and make money from the excess. People in villages engage themselves in self-sufficiency. Farmers also say that if money is not available in quantity, food is available in abundance.

Socialization is an interesting aspect of village experience. Socialization may take different approaches, like playing together, farming together, telling stories, and attending places of worship, if available. Youth play together and run around the village even at night. While playing, they are socialized into the social norms of the community and learn to respect their culture, traditions, and customs.

Everyone is taught to be friendly, open, accommodating, and respectful. Disagreement over religion is uncommon. Humans are respected on the basis of performance, not necessarily on the ability to impose a particular direction on others. The concept of democracy prevails and is inculcated into the children. Children are taught that going to bed early makes a person healthy for the next day's work.

A key problem in villages is access to adequate health care. People who live in villages suffer from diseases that many nations have overcome, such as waterborne diseases. Malaria is one of the highest killers of children. Stagnant water that breeds mosquitos is common. People have been advised to pour kerosene on standing water to prevent mosquito eggs from developing, but mosquitos still kill. Governments at the federal, state, and local levels have not met the challenges of meeting rural health needs. However, very simple sanitation, if it becomes part of the culture, will solve many health problems.

At the village level, education is considered an important tool to shape the lives of youth. A common saying is that if the parents missed education, education must not miss the children. Primary schools are available. Some governments provide free mandatory education, and others choose to levy a minimal amount of education. Villages combine their efforts to start primary schools. Actually, though, learning begins at home. Village children learn how to count by playing games together, and by helping their parents to carry cocoa, they learn counting and responsibility.

See also **Cities; Political Systems; Town Histories**

REFERENCE

Abórìṣàdé, Ọládiméjì, ed. *Local Government and the Traditional Rulers in Nigeria.* Ilé-Ifẹ̀ (Nigeria): University of Ifẹ̀ Press, 1985.

Ọládiméjì Abórìṣàdé

VISIBLE AND INVISIBLE FORCES

The Yorùbá people believe in the Supreme Being who is called Ọlọ́run, which means "the Owner of Heaven" or Olódùmarè. The Supreme Being is also the creator of a pantheon of other divinities and spirits, referred to as òrìṣà or imọlẹ̀. Prominent among these divinities are Ọbàtálá or Òrìṣà-Ńlá, who is considered the archdivinity because of his role in the creation of the universe. Ọ̀rúnmìlà, gifted with knowledge, is the oracle divinity and so functions in the capacity of a counselor since he has knowledge of humans' lives and can help in rectifying misfortunes. They worship Ọ̀rúnmìlà and consult him for the solutions to various problems. This worship and consultation is done via the office of a Babaláwo, an Ifá priest who performs divination using a divining tray and other emblems. Other prominent divinities include Ògún (the god of iron and war), Ọ̀sanyìn (the god of medicine), Ṣàngó, Ṣànpọ̀nná (the god of smallpox), Òrìṣà-Oko (the patron god of farmers), and others, all of whom act on behalf of the Supreme Being in the administration of the world. From conception to death, life is marked by consultations of oracles and the performance of prescribed sacrifices, or ẹbọ. Events and seasons like marriage, erecting a building, health care, and planting and harvest seasons are founded and sealed by means of communing with the relevant invisible deity who has charge of the particular affair at hand.

An inextricable link exists between visible and invisible forces in Yorùbá culture because divinities and spirits administer *every* phenomenon and aspect of creation in which human beings, flora, and fauna interact. For instance, the earth (ilẹ̀), which serves various purposes in nature, is believed to be inhabited by a spirit. According to A. A. Lawal, land is "the sacred soil of the ancestors, the channel of communication between the dead and the living. It is the origin of royal power and the basis of health and prosperity." Sacrifices and libations are offered at planting seasons, or whenever a corpse is to be interred, in the event of desecration of the earth caused by the flouting of established taboos, and other events. Various elements of the earth, like rivers, lagoons, seas, mountains, hills, trees, and wind, are assigned to the care of various deities and spirits. The Yorùbá think that, in this way, harmony is maintained among the forces of nature.

The theocentric worldview of the Yorùbá extends to the relationship between living people and deceased relatives, whom they believe influence world affairs in their capacity as invisible forces. They are, in the words of J. S. Mbiti, "living dead" who, through their spirits (ẹ̀mí), continue to commune with their living familiars in a temporal world. This belief rests on the African conception of time as a boundless continuum in which the past and present are united into a single phenomenon. The Yorùbá, therefore, hold that the family is composed of both living and dead members. Hence, a Yorùbá person is expected to offer food and drinks to his or her ancestors in supplication and veneration.

The practice of medicine in a traditional setting combines the use of nature with the invocation of divinities and spirits. The oníṣègùn, or medicine man, is a diviner, priest, and manufacturer of charms. The medicine man performs diagnosis and provides therapy and prophylaxis by beginning with physical examination of the patient, yet he or she introduces element of religion into ascertaining the cause of ailments (àìsàn) and their required remedies. His or her materials that often include herbs, leaves, animals, bark, and other items, are all procured from nature but not without the performance of some rituals to invoke Òsanyìn the divinity whose responsibility is to order medical care. Yorùbá medical care is a practice in which medicinal materials from nature are combined with spiritual powers that actually assure effective treatment of diseases. The witches and wizards (egbé àjé) are believed to possess supernatural powers with which they exert influence on the physical world. The belief in the existence of witches (àjé) is so strong that all misfortunes, such as strange diseases, accidents, untimely deaths, and crop failures, are often attributed to the malevolent powers of the witch. In summary, the Yorùbá outlook on life is such that humans, the earth, animals, the environment, and spiritual entities relate with one another in harmony.

See also **Deities (The Òrìṣà); Divination: Ifá; Sacrifice; Sorcery; Witchcraft**

REFERENCES

Lawal, A. A. "Agriculture in Yorùbá Society and Culture." In *The Yorùbá in Transition: History, Values, and Modernity*, ed. Tóyìn Fálọlá, and Ann Genova, 361–76. Durham, NC: Carolina Academic Press, 2006.

Mbiti, J. S. *African Religions and Philosophy*. London: Heinemann Educational Books, 1969.

Chinyere Ukpokolo

The visual arts encompass those aspects of creative expression that stimulate the aesthetic senses or capture perceptional interest. On any given day, people are confronted with a barrage of images, sites, and enactments that compete for our attention. These could include the quaint, three-dimensional cement sculptures of colonial sentries, with their fez caps standing at attention and one hand on its long rifle standing on the balcony of the ọba's palace. Such expressive elements of visual culture offer insights about Yorùbá architecture that could be revealing in the extent to which they codify local history, taste, and indigenous masonry. The ọba's palace, àfin, for example, is often central to Yorùbá political and sociocultural cosmology both metaphorically and physically. In its grandeur, the àfin captures the elevated social status of the ọba at the same time that it reflects the collective wealth of his subjects.

In any given township or village, there most certainly will be signage, produced often by the local sign writer. From street signs, some with illustrations that give unabashed graphic illustrations, the inquirer is directed to the "native doctor" whose specialty covers an impossibly wide range of ailments from urology to gynecology: the treatment of erectile dysfunction is handled by the same "doctor" who also treats infertility in women in addition to a host of other diseases, including cancer.

An iconic and unmistakably Yorùbá clothing is the àdìrẹ, which entails tying and dying a piece of fabric, usually in indigo dye. In recent years, the visionary enterprise of Níkẹ̀ Davies-Òkúndayè has turned this popular textile into an international asset. She diversified the range of colors, broadened the repertoire of designs, and took advantage of color-fast dye to obviate the initial bleed of traditional indigo àdìrẹ. In Abẹ́òkúta, a thriving àdìrẹ industry exists. Added to this is the extraordinary inventiveness of weaving aṣọ òkè or aṣọ òfì, which is now favored dress among the Yorùbá on major occasions, such as wedding or chieftaincy ceremonies.

Visual arts are not the monopoly of educational institutions, where this is a distinctive area of study that focuses on the tremendous contributions of artists, painters, sculptors, printmakers, and designers in this regard. Two pioneers of the visual arts in Nigeria were Chief Àìná Ọnàbólú (1882–1963) and Akinọlá Láṣèkan (1916–1972). Ọnàbólú single-handedly introduced the teaching of art into secondary education curriculum and Láṣèkan pioneered cartooning in Nigeria. In the 1960s, Ulli Beier and Susanne Wenger turned the city of Ìbàdàn and Òṣogbo into vibrant centers of creative enterprise with the establishment of the Mbárí Club in Ìbàdàn and then the Mbárí Mbáyọ̀ Club in Òṣogbo, which produced eminent visual artists such as Twins Seven-Seven and Jimoh Buraimoh. Among Nigeria's distinguished visual artists are Yusuf Grillo, Kọ́ládé Ọ̀shínọ́wọ̀, and Làmídì Fákéyẹ. Grillo's cerebral paintings, stained windows, and mosaic murals are notable for their unmistakable poise and elegance and for the range of cool colors—mauves, magentas, and alizarins—that he favors. The visual arts have brought Nigeria into international limelight, not least for its corpus of stunning bronze Ifẹ̀ heads and terra-cotta figures that date to the eleventh to sixteenth centuries.

See also **Art: Contemporary; Art: Indigenous; Cartoons; Dress; Palace; Textile Arts (Usage)**

REFERENCES

Lent, John A. *Comic Art in Africa, Asia, Australia, and Latin America through 2000: An International Bibliography*. Westport, CT: Praeger Publishers, 2004.

Òjó, E. B. "Printing Contemporary Handwoven Fabrics (Aṣọ̀òkè) in Southwestern Nigeria." *Design Issues* 23.2 (Spring 2007): 31–39.

délé jẹ́gẹ́dẹ́

W

Warfare is a major theme of Yorùbá history. Warfare featured prominently in the foundation and subsequent development of many Yorùbá kingdoms and in relations between the Yorùbá and their neighbors. In Ile-Ifẹ̀, as in other nascent Yorùbá kingdoms, the Odùduwà group fought with indigenous groups to establish its authority. The rise and expansion of the Ọ̀yọ́ Empire led to wars with neighboring groups such as Nupe, Baruba, Edo, Aja, Fon, and other peoples brought under its imperial sway. Leadership in war was exercised by military or *ológun* chiefs, known as the Balógun or the Ààrẹ-Ọ̀nà-Kakaǹfò as was the case in Old Ọ̀yọ́, which had the most developed system.

The army was made up of all able-bodied men, slaves and free, in the state. Women were involved at every stage of warfare, though they rarely featured in actual combat until the nineteenth century, and even then only to a limited extent. The seriousness of the war determined how many war chiefs and soldiers would be enlisted, voluntarily or otherwise, to fight. The size of the army varied from a few hundred in the smaller kingdoms to several thousand "that could wear out a hole marching over a hide," as in the Old Ọ̀yọ́ Empire. Weapons of war consisted of cutlasses (*àdá*), daggers (*ọ̀bẹ*), single- or double-bladed swords (*idà*), bows and arrows, thrusting and throwing spears (*ọ̀kọ̀*), as well as knives, slings, fighting bracelets, and clubs of all types. Soldiers' attire consisted, for the most part, of padded jackets sewn with charms. Taking advantage of its location in the grassland, Ọ̀yọ́ was able to build a cavalry using horses obtained from Hausaland. Naval warfare on the lagoon and coastal waters, with fleets of war canoes, occurred among the Àwórì of Lagos and Badagry. For added security, many towns were encircled by walls, some of which were as high as twenty feet, and surrounded by outer ditches planted with thorns.

Though known to the Yorùbá by the early sixteenth century, firearms entered Yorùbá warfare only during the 1840s, when they were first used during the Òwu war. Thereafter, they became a key element of warfare, giving the name *kírìjì* (from the sound of cannon mortar) to the key battles of the sixteen-year war between the Èkìtìparapọ̀ and their Ìbàdàn opponents. The collapse of the Old Ọ̀yọ́ Empire at the beginning of the nineteenth century, and the struggle for supremacy among successor states threw the Yorùbá into a century of fratricidal civil wars that crippled and destroyed many states, led to the rise of new ones, intensified slavery and the slave trade, allowed for the emergence of a professional military class, and militarized society. In general, these wars were fought over serious issues of politics and power, undertaken after careful deliberation and exhaustive diplomacy, and executed through the use of seasoned and varied tactics and strategies. They left in their wake far-reaching demographic upheaval, economic dislocation, and sociopolitical transformation of Yorùbá society.

See also Èkìtìparapò War; Òwu War; Warriors; War Songs

REFERENCES

Àjàyí, J. F. A, and Robert S. Smith. *Yorùbá Warfare in the Nineteenth Century*. Ìbàdàn (Nigeria): University Press, 1971.

Fálọlá, Tóyìn and Dáre Ògúntómisìn. *The Military in Nineteenth Century Yorùbá Politics*. Ile-Ifẹ̀ (Nigeria): University of Ifẹ̀ Press, 1984.

Fúnṣọ́ Afọláyan

WARRIORS

In Yorùbáland, the term *warrior* refers to two important categories of people. First, warriors were men of valor and exceptional courage, whose devotion and passion was to protect the state from internal and external aggression. Second, certain deities (*òrìṣà*), especially Èṣù, Ògún, Ọṣọ́ọ̀sì, and Ọ̀sun, were regarded by most worshippers of Yorùbá traditional religion as warriors. These deities were believed to protect their worshippers, who could be individuals, group of individuals, or a community. They were also believed to be responsible for breakthroughs and for providing opportunities to their worshippers.

Men of valor and exceptional courage abounded in different communities. During the precolonial period, sports and games provided each community with the opportunities to identify and develop these individuals. They grew under the tutelage of reputable warriors who were responsible for their training and development. These individuals formed the corps of soldiers or warriors the community depended on for its defense.

In peacetime, they engaged in common occupations like other people—and a large majority of them were either hunters or herbalists. In wartime, they temporarily abandoned these pursuits to defend their communities. In exceptional circumstances, such as during the nineteenth century, when a large portion of Yorùbáland was engrossed in warfare, wars could lead to situations in which warriors were permanently engaged in warfare. In the case of the nineteenth-century Yorùbá war, a class of youth emerged who knew no other jobs other than warfare, because the war lasted for close to seventy years. Situations such as these were very rare in Yorùbá history.

Warriors were respected and generally sought after, especially by young girls, who preferred them as husbands. Societies bestowed great respect on warriors. Notable warriors in Yorùbá history include Ògèdèǹgbé of Iléṣà, Fábùnmi of Òkè-Mèsí, Òjó Aburúmákú, Tìmì Àgbàlé Ọlọ́fà Iná, and Baṣọ̀run Ògúnmọ́lá.

In Yorùbá religious worship, Èṣù, also known as Ẹlẹ́gbára, the primordial trickster, was believed to have existed since the beginning of the world. Èṣù, often depicted as a child—and sometimes as an old man—was regarded as the first of the warriors. He was regarded as the great gatekeeper who could open doors of opportunity or of trouble to individuals. As such, in religious thought, people first offered Èṣù his portion of any sacrifice. It was believed that failure to offer Èṣù the first offering might lead to a situation in which other deities reject such sacrifice. As a warrior, Èṣù was regarded as protecting dutiful worshippers while endangering the lives of erring worshippers. Èṣù was also believed to have control over material and spiritual progress.

Ògún, as a deity, is believed to be the god of iron and steel. He is the patron deity of blacksmiths, drivers, farmers, and others who use tools made of iron and steel. Ògún is believed to be ever ready to protect diligent worshippers while imposing stiffer punishment, sometimes destruction, on delinquent ones. Ògún was a hunter and a warrior in his lifetime. He was brave, courageous, and forceful. His warrior worshippers, therefore, hold him in great awe and respect on and off the battlefield.

Ọ̀sun, like Èṣù and Ògún, was also a warrior. A small metal staff with a metal rooster represents Ọ̀sun. Ọ̀sun is believed to warn and ward off danger from her warrior worshippers and to provide for their needs. Her staff must not fall over, as this is regarded as symbolizing a great evil. As such, it is placed in a conspicuous place within the house.

See also Èkìtìparapò War; Òwu War; War Songs; Warfare

REFERENCES

Àjàyí, J. F. A., and Robert S. Smith. *Yorùbá Warfare in the Nineteenth Century.* Ìbàdàn (Nigeria): University Press, 1971.

Fálọlá, Tóyìn, and Dáre Ògúntomisin. *The Military in Nineteenth Century Yorùbá Politics.* Ilé-Ifẹ̀ (Nigeria): University of Ifẹ̀ Press, 1984.

Bùkọ́lá Oyèníyì

WAR SONGS

War songs were performed at times of war to boost morale of the warriors and to celebrate victories. In the distant past, especially during the internecine Yorùbá wars, war songs were usually accompanied by different drums depending on the war and the subgroup. These types of drums were called war drums (*ìlù ogun*). In most cases, they were not ordinary drums but were usually ritualized for effectiveness. Yorùbá war songs fall into three types. The first instills fear and dismay into the hearts of their opponents. The second type encourages the warriors. The third type is a song of victory after the conquest. The following is an example of the first category:

LEAD: *Wèrèpè ni Balógun—*
Wèrèpè ni Balógun—
Ẹni tó bá kọlù ú
Á yúnra dójú ikú.
CHORUS: *Wèrèpè ni Balógun—*
LEAD: *Ẹni tó bá kọlù ú*
Á yúnra dójú ikú.
CHORUS: *Wèrèpè ni Balógun.*

LEAD: Balógun is an itching seed—
Balógun is an itching seed—
Anyone who falls on him
Will itch his body until she [or he] dies.
CHORUS: Balógun is a itching seed—
LEAD: Anyone who falls on him
Will itch his body until he dies.
CHORUS: Balógun is a itching seed.

This war song instilled fear in the hearts of opponents that the war chief Balógun was an untouchable seed that made people itchy (*ẹwẹ* or *wèrèpè*). This metaphor reveals that the war chief is unconquerable; if he falls on the enemies, they will die, and if the enemies try to touch him, they will die.

The two songs below are examples of the second category of war song that instill confidence in the hearts of the warrior:

LEAD: *Àwa là ó borí àwọn wọnyí o—*
CHORUS: *Àwa là ó borí àwọn wọnyí o—*
LEAD: *Ológun má mà ṣojo—*
Àyà gbogbo ènìyàn ló ń sọ kúlẹ́kúlẹ́—
CHORUS: *Ológun má mà ṣojo— . . .*
LEAD: *Ológun mọ́kàn ṣakin—*
Àyà gbogbo ènìyàn ló ń sọ kúlẹ́kúlẹ́—
CHORUS: *Ológun mọ́kàn ṣakin—*

LEAD: We are going to overcome these ones (the opponents)
CHORUS: We are going to overcome these ones (the opponents)
LEAD: Warrior, do not panic
The heart of every warrior reels
CHORUS: Warrior, do not panic . . .
LEAD: Warrior, take heart
The heart of every warrior reels
CHORUS: Warrior, take heart.

These two songs are of admonition to the warriors. The first song encourages the warriors to be confident of victory, and the second encourages the warriors that all warriors have similar feelings of doubt, but all should take heart.

The third category of war song celebrates victory after the war:

LEAD: *Ọwọ́ ti talásẹjù, a sì ti pa á—*
CHORUS: *À ó fi jẹyán lọ́la—*

LEAD: We have captured the stubborn person and we've killed him (her)
CHORUS: We shall use it to eat pounded yam tomorrow

The warriors would have been jubilant as they sang the song of victory. The warriors exaggerated in their song; it is not that they ate human flesh, but it was a way to show that they were superior to their enemies. In contemporary Yorùbá society, war songs are not commonly found except during reenactments in movies.

See also **Ceremonial Songs; Political Songs; Warfare; Warriors**

REFERENCE

Finnegan, Ruth. 1970. *Oral Literature in Africa Oxford*: Oxford University Press.

George Olúṣọlá Ajíbádé

WEALTH

Wealth (ọrọ̀) to the Yorùbá needs to be understood within the people's indigenous economic activities. In precolonial times, economic activities were predominantly agricultural: animal husbandry, hunting, fishing, and cultivating such crops as yam, cocoa, kola nut, and oil palm. They also traded ornaments, mats, and other items. The wealthy man in this setting was a stakeholder in the agrarian economy, and his wealth was reckoned according to the vastness of his farmland and the numbers of his livestock, slaves, wives, and children. Wealth was considered the product of industry, that is, as evidence of hard work, commercial acumen, and sound organizational skill.

W. R. Bascom identifies three levels of socioeconomic status: the ọlọ́rọ̀ (wealthy man) or olówó (man of money, rich man), the mẹ̀kúnnù (one who is able to care for his or her immediate needs but does not have property like the typical wealthy man), and the òtòṣì (destitute). Wealth was thought of primarily as a bequest from the Supreme Being, Olódùmarè. Bascom notes that the Yorùbá insisted on hard work and rejected indolence. Yet they believed that there were other factors that determined wealth or prosperity, that accounted for why some hardworking people remained poor while some people who did not work very hard became rich. This was attributed to luck, which was not a chance occurrence but a real or physical manifestation of phenomena predetermined before a person was born.

To the Yorùbá, the human person is a composite of *ara* (body) and a collection of other spiritual entities—hence the belief that the possession of wealth or lack of it is a matter of destiny, which can inform a person's luck and economic success. An individual is believed to have been conferred with either good luck or ill luck in the extraterrestrial world before his or her birth. The personal choice of good or bad luck is referred to as àkúnlèyàn (to kneel [before the deity] and choose), which implies that one gets only what he or she chooses upon coming to life. The Supreme Being can bequeath good or ill luck before an individual's birth. This is called àyànmọ́, or fate, in which the financial success or failure has been affixed by the gods.

The idea of predestination accounts for the reference to the wealthy man as an olórí ire (the successful one or the fortunate one). *Olórí ire* is derived from the Yorùbá designation of the orí (head) not merely as a tangible physical and physiological entity but also as the spiritual point at which the Supreme Being relates with the human person. Predestination in Yorùbá belief is open ended and can be affected by sacrificial supplication (ẹbọ). Harsh economic conditions, regardless of hard work, can therefore be mitigated by appeasing the gods through an individual's orí. The Supreme Being may then amend previous ill luck.

The Yorùbá also believe in the lesser deity Ajé (the goddess of the marketplace) who is responsible for ordering profits in the market place. She takes charge of whatever has to do with money. Her prominence in Yorùbá economy and social thought is often expressed in prayerful wishes like ajé á wá ooo (wealth will come). In summary, wealth in Yorùbá worldview can be achieved through divine appeasement (as with ajé) and predestination (as in àkúnlèyàn, àyànmọ́), as well as human handiwork or industry.

See also **Agriculture and Farming; Debt and Debt Management; Economic System; Markets; Sacrifice**

REFERENCE

Bascom, W. R. "Social Status, Wealth and Individual Differences among the Yorùbá." *American Anthropologist* 5.1 (1951): 1–12.

Chinyere Ukpokolo

Western medicine is the science of diagnosing and healing the sick. It is rooted in biomedical science and germ theory approaches that espouse that every disease has an organic origin that can be unmasked and removed. It rejects celestial factors and divine forces. It is "orthodox" medicine as compared to "indigenous" medicine. It has evolved from many sources and is transmitted from one culture to another. It embodies both material and nonmaterial components of culture in the same way as indigenous medicine, which is holistic and considers both the physical/organic and celestial factors in the etiology of diseases and treatment of the patients. The latter, as epitomized in indigenous healing methods, affirms that the celestial influences the terrestrial and the physical; practices and behaviors in the latter have repercussions for the celestial. In the simplest sense, the knowledge, values, norms, prescriptions, and proscriptions for healing the sick and wounded are not restricted to Western nations.

It is indisputable that Western medicine has borrowed much from Africa, but the orientation and training of "Western medicine" practitioners tend to undermine Yorùbá healing arts. Western medicine has been criticized as elitist, expensive, and bureaucratic in nature. In contrast, indigenous medicine is client-friendly and often cheaper and environmentally sensitive. For example, consider an example of a fruit with many medicinal properties: ọ̀gẹ̀dẹ̀ (banana). *Musa sapientum* has two major kinds: ọ̀mìnì and àgbagbà. The first is sweeter and smaller than the latter.

Bananas contain three natural sugars—sucrose, fructose, and glucose—and fiber. Bananas give an instant, sustained, and substantial boost of energy. Research has proved that just two bananas provide enough energy for a strenuous ninety-minute workout. They can also help overcome or prevent a number of illnesses and conditions. Bananas have been found to help with depression because of the protein called tryptophan. Bananas can resolve anemia and high blood pressure, as they are rich in iron and potassium. They relieve constipation because of their fiber content and soothes heartburn and ulcer by neutralizing acidity.

It is believed that with increased enlightenment, much can be achieved using indigenous healing methods. *Adáhunṣe, oníṣègùn, ìyá eléwé ọmọ*, and *babaláwo* should be respected and encouraged to share their knowledge. Cases of traditional midwives called *agbẹ̀bí* abound in the communities. Yorùbá indigenous healers know the plants and fruits that are edible, poisonous, and those that have medicinal properties without the aid of an exotic electron microscope or advanced pharmacological techniques. Many have learned the art of healing from their parents and grandparents who were healers as well as Ifá diviners.

Herbal medicine is gaining ground, as many people both in urban and rural areas become increasingly aware of its inherent benefits and become dependent on medicinal plants to cure many diseases.

See also **Healing; Health Care; Plants**

REFERENCES

Badru, F. A. "Sociology of Health and Illness Relations." In *Sociology for Beginners*, ed. L. Olúrodé and O. Ṣóyọmbọ̀, 326–55. 3rd ed. Lagos (Nigeria): John West Publications, 2003.

Badru, F. A. "On the Viability of Indigenous Health Care System in Nigeria: Insights from the Yorùbás." In *An Interdisciplinary Discourse on the Human Condition*, ed. A. M. A. Nínálowó, F. A. Badru, and R. Akínyẹmí, 174–200. Lagos (Nigeria): Faculty of Social Sciences in conjunction with Department of Sociology, University of Lagos, 2010.

Fàtáì Adéṣínà Badru

WIDOWS AND WIDOWHOOD

Married women whose husbands die remain widows if they do not remarry. In Yorùbá society, a husband's death may lead to a great deal of emotional, physical, mental, and spiritual problems for the widow. The culture and customs subject women to oppressive, humiliating, and dehumanizing funeral rites on the deaths of their husbands. Wives become the primary suspects in their husband's death. They are subjected to varying degrees of unpleasant treatment in the name of rites, sanctions, and practices during the period of widowhood, especially during the first year. Some of these rites include the following:

- Passing through certain shrines for oaths to verify the killer of the deceased husband or, in some very rare situations, drinking part of the water used to bathe the corpse
- Appearing with unkempt hair or having her head shaved to sever the bond with her late husband and to deflect attention from other suitors
- Keeping vigil for the first forty days after the burial
- Being confined for days and not allowed to bathe or go to the toilet unless accompanied by another woman
- Mourning for three months without looking in a mirror
- Losing the right of inheritance

Widowhood can last for life if the woman does not marry again. However, it is the first year that is most significant and when some of the aforementioned rites are performed. In addition, during widowhood, a widow's health suffers as she is pressured to conform to widowhood practices and to the loneliness resulting from the death of her husband.

During the period of widowhood, a widow is watched critically in all of her actions. She must not be seen with another man. To the Yorùbá, the wife is part of the inheritance of the deceased husband; as part of the inheritance system, a brother-in-law can "inherit" or marry his deceased older brother's wife. Traditionally, whoever takes the widow of a deceased relative is permitted to have children with her, which ends her widowhood. This practice of wife inheritance (levirate union) shortens the period of widowhood. With the popularity of Christianity and Islam and changes in modern customs, the occurrence of wife inheritance has reduced, which has resulted in more instances of widowhood for life.

The experiences of male widowers are different from those of widows. A widower is not castigated but pitied after the death of his wife. He also undergoes no rites like the widow does. In fact, he is free to have a sexual relations with another woman within days of the death of his wife so that the dead wife will not attempt to sleep with him, according to Yorùbá belief.

See also **Gender; Marriage and Marital System; Women: Traditional**

REFERENCES

Adéoyè, C. L. Àṣà àti Ìṣe Yorùbá. Oxford: Oxford University Press, 1979.
Fádípè, N. A. The Sociology of the Yorùbá. Ìbàdàn (Nigeria): University Press Ltd., 1970.

Láídé Sheba

WILDLIFE: PRESERVATION, HUNTING, AND DESTRUCTION

It is a paradox that the Yorùbá people, who were passionate about the domestication of animals, also relish the hunting and consumption of wild game. The early Yorùbá probably domesticated animals that strayed into their communities or were purchased from Nupe, Fulani, and Hausa traders. Animals and birds such as goats, chickens, and turkeys were usually domesticated for social and economic exchange. Highly valued and respected individuals were given domesticated animals and birds as gifts to mark the occasion of their visits to Yorùbá households, and sick domesticated animals and birds were slaughtered for consumption by owners, most often during special ceremonies.

Aside from the domestication of animals and birds, the Yorùbá also preserved them by their ritual "deification" or symbolism. Stories abound among some Yorùbá subgroups about how some animals, birds, and reptiles provided their ancestors succor or help during perilous times. As a demonstration of gratitude to such animals, reptiles, and birds, the descendants of such ancestors were never to hunt or consume such wild game.

Hunting in Yorùbáland

Hunting, particularly in the wild, was traditionally a specialized vocation among the Yorùbá. While seasonal group hunting during the dry season was practiced by almost all Yorùbá, individuals on their farms also set traps and dug holes to capture animals such as rodents, snakes, and rats. Wild animals, birds, snakes, and reptiles were highly valued and prized for their better nutritional value compared to domesticated ones. The enormous energy and risk exerted to get these game animals made them being highly valued and prized. The Yorùbá people say *t' ọ́dẹ bá r'ọ̀ṣẹ́ r'ọ̀yà, tó bá p'ẹran, kò níí fún ẹnìkankan l'ẹ́ran jẹ* (the hunter that counts or consider the cost incurred in hunting a wild game would not share his hunt with others).

Except for rodents (such as rats), birds, and snakes caught on farms and in neighborhoods, wild game hunts were not an activity that the common person could engage in. Only Yorùbá of means could afford to buy or acquire wild game for consumption. The consumption of wild game was a luxury for people of means. The game was specially cooked and kept for their consumption. Most of the time, the woman of a wealthy household would cook the game to avoid the prying eyes of children and other wives.

See also **Hunting; Livestock: Domestication and Species**

REFERENCE

Babalọlá, Adéboyè. *The Content and Form of Yorùbá Ìjálá*. Edinburgh, K: Edinburgh University Press, 1966.

Adémọ́lá Babalọlá

WITCHCRAFT

Belief in witchcraft persists in Yorùbáland despite modernization, although fear of witches has decreased. The prescientific understanding of natural events or diseases that was beyond ordinary daily experiences was explained by the mysterious circumstances of witchcraft. The Yorùbá ontology of witchcraft is an esoteric science that belongs to the generation of beings in the cosmos of humans created by Olódùmarè, the Supreme Deity of the Yorùbá. According to oral traditions, belief in witches reminds people of their religious devotion to the deity and explains good and evil in moral theology. It also explains misfortunes, illnesses, death, and prosperity in life. For instance, if a child has malaria and is not responding to treatment, parents and relatives will begin to look inward to find out why the illness continues. If a witch cries in the night when the cause for the child's persistent illness is being sought and the child dies the following morning, his parents and relations will not hesitate to conclude that the crying witch caused the death of their child.

A witch (*àjẹ́*) is someone with mysterious powers to do good and evil. A good witch uses his or her witchcraft to protect her or his children, relatives, and spouse. He or she also uses it to make his or her family prosper. An evil witch has a diabolical spirit with the intention of punishing members of his or her family and extended family. Generally, old women were believed to be witches having diabolical powers or evil machinations to wreak havoc in society. Yorùbá use traditional means to overcome the menace of witchcraft, including relying on the Babaláwo's secret knowledge and power over witches. His house is always a haven of deliverance and hope for a troubled soul who is under the yoke of witchcraft.

Modern science has provided more precise explanations for illnesses, misfortune, hope, and confidence in modern people's ability to overcome challenges. The development of medical science and improvements to hygiene have unraveled the secret of longevity. In contemporary society, the word *àjẹ́* does not always have the old connotation of witchcraft. It is also slang to describe someone who is outstanding in his or her profession.

See also **Sorcery**

REFERENCE

Washington, Teresa N. *Our Mothers, Our Powers, Our Texts*, Bloomington: Indiana University Press, 2005.

Ṣẹ́gun Ògúngbèmí

The imposition of British colonialism in Yorùbáland brought about a drastic change to the original culture of the Yorùbá people of southwestern Nigeria, including gender relations. The colonial encounter provided a watershed moment for women's participation in sociopolitical, religious, and economic life in Yorùbáland. The British colonial administration's attitude about women in public space was informed by a Victorian notion of womanhood, which it imported to Africa. This was a turning point at which Yorùbá women who were until then politically active in the society began to be less involved in the day-to-day running of their society. The colonialists ignored the social, economic, religious, and political structures that gave women power. They imposed new political, economic, and religious structures that excluded women. The British administrators, informed by the Western male-centered attitude, preferred to deal only with men in state matters. African men were easily incorporated into public service, the emerging capitalist economy, and religious structures.

The colonialists' refusal to recognize that precolonial Yorùbá women enjoyed certain rights and privileges also reflected in their denying higher education for girls until much later in the colonial era. The exception was professions that emphasized women's domesticity, such as catering, tailoring, and housekeeping. J. S. Ọdéyẹmí argues that the missionaries who collaborated with colonial administrators also advanced gender disparity in religious spaces through the arrangement in churches that men sat to one side and women and children to the other. Unlike precolonial times, when women participated in traditional religion as priestesses and some deities were women, women were not admitted to the clergy in the Christian churches on the basis of a theological position that viewed the ministerial priesthood as an office for men only.

Despite the unfriendly disposition to women in the public space during the colonial era, Yorùbá women continued to distinguish themselves in various ways. These women included Fúnmiláyọ̀ Ransome-Kútì, who formed Abẹ̀òkúta Ladies' Club (ALC), a group of Christian-educated women, teachers, and traders who carried out charity work, formed sewing circles, and catered events. According to Nina Mba, the aims of the ALC included raising the standard of womanhood in Abẹ̀òkúta and encouraging learning among the adults to wipe out illiteracy. The ALC later expanded to include market women in its membership. The group took an interest in the problems of the market women and eventually saw the women in Nigeria as an oppressed group. The ALC protested taxation of market women. Their agitation for women's inclusion contributed to the dethronement of the king of Abẹ̀òkúta, Aláké Adémọ́lá, and resulting in women's integration into the executive organ of Ẹ̀gbá Central Council. Under the leadership of Ransome-Kútì, women resisted what they perceived to be oppressive and aberrant conditions in Yorùbáland.

One major offshoot of women's engagement with traditional rulers designated as sole native authorities during the colonial era was that women such as Ransome-Kútì and others in the ALC corrected erroneous assumptions about the position of women in the political hierarchy, family, and economic life.

See also **Widow and Widowhood; Women: Contemporary; Women: Traditional; Women in Politics**

REFERENCES

Fádípè, N. A. *The Sociology of the Yorùbá*. Ìbàdàn (Nigeria): University Press, 1970.

Ọdéyẹmí, J. S. "Gender Issues among the Yorùbás." *International Journal of African Catholicism* 4.1 (2013): 1–22.

Chinyere Ukpokolo

WOMEN: CONTEMPORARY

For women in contemporary Yorùbáland education and social change undoubtedly have increased the level of literacy among Yorùbá women. However, the general problems of unemployment and unstable economic conditions have adverse effects on young women. In politics and political participation, Yorùbá women have been engaged and involved, especially as compared to the challenges of exclusion in the past. Since 1999, women have been active participants in the electoral process and have been elected to positions. These efforts were fraught with challenging conditional ties associated with patriarchy and inadequate empowerment, but women were still able to take bold steps to move into the political arena. However, the institutional and systemic problems challenging women's participation in politics has continued to strengthen the involvement of women.

In the twentieth century, Yorùbá market women were active in the political process of the colonial era. They raised funds for the political party activities of the Action Group (AG) and the National Council for Nigeria and Cameroons (NCNC). They also engaged in political mobilization to win elections. Despite the fact that many were not educated, they understood the political economy of the colonial era, which they effectively used to address developmental issues germane to the economic survival and sustainability of market women.

The foremost historian of women's studies in Nigeria is Professor Bọ́lánlé Awẹ́. Her work reconceptualized Western biases in women's studies and has addressed misinterpretations of the relevance of women in society. Furthermore, scholar Oyèrónkẹ́ Oyěwùmí rejects the interpretation of Western feminists of African women's experiences in her scholarly work *The Invention of Women*.

Since the 1960s, Western-educated Yorùbá women had access to leadership positions in governance and civil service. Tẹjúmádé Alákijà (nee Adérẹ̀mí), a princess from Ilé-Ifẹ̀, became the first female head of service in Western State. Other highly placed civil servants have included Fọláyẹgbẹ́ Akíntúndé Ighodalo, Rónkẹ́ Doherty, and Fọlákẹ́ Ṣólànkẹ́. As business professionals, Yorùbá women have been prominent entrepreneurs and merchants contributing to the establishment of industries. Examples include Chief Bísóyè Téjúoṣọ, Ọ̀túnba Bọ́lá Kúforíjì-Olúbí, and Alhaja Sùlìá Adédèjì. More recently, Yorùbá women have become prominent chief executives of banks and other sectors,

including Ṣọlá David-Borha, Fúnkẹ́ Ọ̀pekè, Fúnkẹ́ Ọ̀síbódù, and Bọ́lá Adéṣọlá.

Wúràọlá Èsan, a law professor, was the first female vice-chancellor of a university in Yorùbáland, Lagos State University. She was the daughter of a chief, a politician during the nationalist era, and the first female proprietor of a school in Ìbàdàn, Yéjídé Girls Grammar School.

See also **Widow and Widowhood; Women: Colonial; Women: Traditional; Women in Politics**

REFERENCE

Oyěwùmí, O. *The Invention of Women: Making an African Sense of Western Gender Discourses* Minneapolis: University of Minnesota Press, 1997.

Mutiat Títílọpẹ́ Ọládèjọ

WOMEN: TRADITIONAL

Women in precolonial Yorùbá society enjoyed many rights and privileges. Eurocentric scholarship on women in Yorùbáland suggests that women are oppressed and suppressed in the culture. Such representations have received criticism from more critical studies on women in indigenous Yorùbá culture. Scholars like Oyèrónkẹ́ Oyěwùmí maintain that the concept of gender never existed in precolonial Ọ̀yọ́ Yorùbá society. In *The Invention of Women*, Oyěwùmí insists that the Yorùbá designations *ọkùnrin* (male) and *obìnrin* (female) were employed merely to denote anatomical differences between males and females, not to preclude either sex from attaining certain social status or to indicate the superiority of one, namely male, over the other. Western notions of social thought, with its fixation on the body as an instrument of selfdefinition and an indicator of destiny, are absent in the Yorùbá worldview.

For Oyěwùmí, biologicism, defined by Heinrich Rommen as "'a purely biological concept of human nature' . . . [that] dismisses the efficacy of 'reason and free will,'" is a Western invention that pervades postcolonial Yorùbá society and other African societies. In Yorùbá language, both *he* and *she* can be rendered as

/o/ or /wọn/, depending on whether the subject is singular or plural. *Wọn* could also be honorific to represent seniority, and seniority is given a premium rather than sexual identity. An elderly woman may earn more reverence than a younger man; he defers to her because of her age. Yorùbá women's agency is predicated on the belief *k'ọ́kùnrin r'éjò, k'obìnrin p'ejò, k'ejò ṣaa ti kú* (if a man sees a snake, and a woman kills it, the most important thing is for the snake to be dead). Realization of collective goals takes precedence over the anatomy of the individual.

Yorùbá cosmology has definite roles for men and women in society. Women play key roles in religious ceremonies as priestesses and prophetesses. Some important deities are female. For instance, several cults, including Ọ̀ṣun, Ògún, and Ṣàngó, have women priestesses who are known as Ìyá Ọ̀ṣun, Ìyá Ògún, and Ìyá Ṣàngó, respectively. The Yorùbá people, like many Africans, believe in the duality of human existence, and this has a physical application, reflected in the people's belief that, according to Kenniston McIntosh, "all undertakings needed to include and harmonize the qualities associated with such parings as land and water, natural and supernatural forces, and male and female characteristics." Yorùbá religion is anchored in the belief that symbols of calm and peace (èrọ̀) represent female principles, whereas toughness represents male principles.

Hence the prayer *k'ọdún ó y'abo fún wa o* (may this year bring us all that the female principle stands for). This prayer is a metaphor for the people's conception of female (*abo*) and male (*akọ*). A "female year" in this context is blissful; a "male year" is very unpleasant. Maleness or femaleness were prescribed by nature and, as such, were seen not as dialectically opposed attributes but rather as complementary ones. They are also indispensible. The prominence of female deities in the Yorùbá pantheon is a reflection of the fact that maleness or femaleness does not automatically imply exclusion from certain social statuses.

Women in Yorùbáland can be Ifá priestesses. They are better known as Ìyánífá. Tádé Adégbindin, an Ifá scholar, noted that Ifá corpus has several verses that acknowledge the indispensability of women in the progress of humanity. In the Yorùbá worldview, both men and women must work together to achieve societal goals, not only in procreating but also in providing the values that complement the qualities inherent in men and women. Ifá corpus advocates Òtúrúpọ̀n Méjì as a panacea for human progress, which demonstrates that wisdom is not inherent in solely one person. The need to harness the wisdom and capabilities of both sexes for human progress includes gender inclusiveness. Indeed, Yorùbá women in precolonial Nigeria were admitted into sacred knowledge (*awo*). As initiates, such women could participate as leaders in high religious ritual practices from which uninitiated men and women were precluded. The admission of women into sacred knowledge translated into religious powers for those women. They went on to serve as diviners (Ìyánífá).

With the domestic arrangement, married life represents a space in which the Yorùbá woman possesses and wields social, economic, and political power in her capacity as wife and mother. In the home, J. S. Ọdẹ́yẹmí describes the woman as "the harbinger of new life, of kings, and noble men. She is the nurturer and the care giver who sustains life until maturity." As the king's wife (*olorì*), she is the power behind the throne, surreptitiously contributing to the decisions of the king. Generally, although the role of the woman in the home was crucial in Yorùbá society, women were not confined only to the domestic space. They were able to exercise freedom and engage in diverse trades.

The precolonial Yorùbá woman's active participation in economic activities allowed for accumulation of wealth, through which she accessed sociopolitical space. Prominent examples of women who achieved socioeconomic power and subsequently wielded great political influence in their societies and environs include Ẹfúnṣetán Aníwúrà, the Ìyálóde (woman leader) of Ìbàdàn and Mọ́gàjí of her lineage, and Madam Ẹfúnróyè Tinúbú, the first Ìyálóde of Ègbáland. Other women became *adelé ọba* (regents) to fill leadership vacuums in their communities, and some became the *ọba* of their communities, such as in old Oǹdó kingdom.

Yorùbá people also believe that some women have extrasensory, celestial powers. Some of these powers are intended for destruction, and these women are referred to as ìyá ayé (women of the world). Women were often regarded as atúnnídá, or women who have the ability to affect one's destiny and possibly change such an individual. As indigenous Yorùbá society is predominantly polygynous, acrimony in households is common. To consolidate one's power in such a home, a woman must bear children; motherhood is highly valued by the Yorùbá people. A proverb states ọlọ́mọ ló l'ọkọ (the one who bears children is the owner of the husband). Thus, a barren woman does everything humanly—even spiritually—possible to have a child, which may result in the children of cowives becoming possible targets of attack from a barren woman or other enemies. The issues of having children and the struggle to attract their husband's admiration contribute to rivalries among cowives.

See also **Regency; Widow and Widowhood; Women: Colonial; Women: Contemporary; Women in Politics**

REFERENCES

Adégbindin, Tádé. Personal communication (interview conducted November, 8, 2013).

McIntosh, Keniston Marjorie. *Yorùbá Women, Work, and Social Change.* Ìbàdàn (Nigeria): Book Craft, 2009.

Ọdéyẹmí, J. S. "Gender Issues among the Yorùbás." *International Journal of African Catholicism* 4.1 (2013): 1–22.

Chinyere Ukpokolo

WOMEN IN POLITICS

The postcolonial state structures were products of colonial encounters, and they represent a departure from the mode of governance in the indigenous sociopolitical system in which men and women participated in diverse sociopolitical, economic, and religious structures. Although the number of women in governance was not equal to that of men, women had a voice in decision making on issues that concerned them and the general populace in precolonial times. Following independence in the 1960, women in Nige-

Table W.1   Women elected to political offices by region in Nigeria in 2011

Office	Governor	Senate	House of Representatives	State House of Assembly
North-central	0	1	2	15
North-east	0	1	4	4
North-west	0	1	1	2
South-east	0	2	6	21
South-south	0	1	4	12
South-west	0	1	8	15

Source: British Council Gender Report, 2012.

ria have continued to play peripheral roles in state governance.

During independence, Nigerian women have not enjoyed equitable participation in governance. The table here reflects women's representation in elective positions following the 2011 Nigerian general election by region.

Male domination carried over from the colonial period into the postcolonial era—and Yorùbá women, just like women from other ethnic groups in Nigeria, despite their academic qualifications and numerical strength, continue to struggle for participation in leadership and recognition in public spaces such as politics, academia, civil service, and the like. In Islam and Christian churches, leadership as clergy, to a large extent, remains a male preserve. In Pentecostal churches, however, women increasingly function as ordained ministers and take up other duties in the churches.

Although the postcolonial era holds opportunities for the Yorùbá woman, the home still plays a crucial role in defining her character, including her ability to realize her full potential. Yorùbá culture still preserves certain domestic and social expectations regarding the place of the woman in the home, particularly with Christian expectations for her to be a Christian mother. Society still expects women to perform certain culturally prescribed domestic roles.

Therefore, the portrait of the Yorùbá woman in postcolonial Nigeria depicts a female who seeks to balance traditional conventions with the demands of modernity. Nevertheless, women continue to employ diverse platforms to engage with oppressive systems and marginality. What has changed is the context of engagement, which has resulted from a paradigm shift in how oppressive structures manifest. Depending on the context and the nature of the subject of contestation, many women, literate, nonliterate, and even academics, have remained at the vanguard of influencing their society to shape people, to promote those changes necessary for women's inclusion, and to agitate for equal opportunities for men and women.

The underlying principle remains women's quest for inclusion, in the writing of history and in demanding the rewriting of history. Activism and scholarship have often been employed in agitating for change and inclusion. Educated Yorùbá women increasingly break new ground in gaining positions hitherto perceived as men's preserve. Among these women are Professors Bólánlé Awé, Abíólá Odéjídé, and Àrinolá Sànyà. In diverse ways, they depicted women's capacity to break new ground in the public space of postcolonial Nigeria.

See also **Widow and Widowhood; Women: Colonial; Women: Contemporary; Women: Traditional**

REFERENCES

Adégbindinin, Tádé. Personal communication (interview conducted November, 8, 2013).
Oyèwùmí, Oyèrónké. *The Invention of Women: Making African Sense of Western Gender Discourses*. Minneapolis: University of Minnesota Press, 1997.

Chinyere Ukpokolo

WORDS (ÒRÒ)

Words (òrò) in Yorùbá worldview extend beyond oral or written text. They are multifaceted, complex, and cryptic. Words are part of the oral culture, which involves myriad genres, including ofò, àyájó, ògèdè, àásán, àbìlù, èpè, and ìwúre. In the case of predominantly oral cultures, oral tradition is an indispensable source of history, an indicator of deep thought, and a transmitter of cultural and religious values. Nonliterate culture still allows for the exploration of historical being, contributions to philosophy and knowledge,

and existence (ìwàláàyè). Words are complex phenomena among the Yorùbá people. Here this entry is limited to a discussion of incantatory words in the Yorùbá worldview.

When a word is spoken, it is believed to carry power, or àsé. The Yorùbá people claim that àsé is activated by the spoken word, hence the saying àìlèsòrò ni ìpìlè orí burúkú (the inability to voice words is the beginning of bad luck). Words are linked to Èlà, a prominent deity, as illustrated in the following Ifá orature:

Ta ló kó wí?
Ta ló kó so?
Èlà ló kó wí.
Èlà ló óo so.
Taa ni e ń pè ní Èlà?
Hòò tó rò náà ni à ń pè ní Èlà.

Who was the first to speak?
Who was the first to talk?
Èlà was the first to speak
Èlà was the first to talk.
Who were you calling Èlà?
It was the Hòò that descended that we call Èlà.

Many incantations fall under the category of prayers, especially ìwúre and àyájó. Prayer, of course, can be understood in the narrow sense of requesting favors from supernatural beings. Prayers can be appeals or pleas to spirits, ancestors, deities, and/or the Supreme God. At times, many incantations are combined with medical ingredients to make the medicines more effective. Prayers and incantations help make life worthwhile and easier to bear despite hardships and catastrophes. Thus, the existence and vitality of the Yorùbá people hinge mainly on the power of words.

To the Yorùbá, certain words are regarded as sacred. Therefore, no word should be spoken carelessly. It is a difficult task to delineate the various incantatory words among the Yorùbá, but the most important parameter to separate them is the context of use, which helps determine the dialectal variations of these genres. For example, the ofò or ògèdè is potent, and sacred words are spoken to make a prepared medicine work better. In this regard, the attributes or power of herbs that were combined to make a particular medicine are recited. In the case of *àyájọ́*, the power of myth and history are employed to appeal to the spiritual forces believed to be present in the air. In the case of *ìwúre* (blessings), natural truths or phenomena and history or myths are combined in prayer. *Àásán*, *àbìlù*, *èpè*, and other genres are mainly used for evil, especially in times of war. Basically, most of these special words in Yorùbá cosmology accompany certain materials. In addition, each of them has a context of performance.

None of these genres has disappeared in modern times, and they are increasingly heard in the liturgies of mainstream religions. For example, either consciously or unconsciously, Yorùbá Christians use the word *àyájọ́* in their prayers, such as *gbọgbọgbọ lọwọ́ ń yọ ju orí, o ó yọ ju ọ̀tá rẹ lọ lórúkọ Jésù* (hands are always on to and higher than the head [when they are raised], you will triumph over your enemies in Jesus' name). Even *èpè* (curse)—highly derided by Christians, Jews, and Muslims—is technically discernible in some of their songs. For example, a gospel singer sings *ẹni ó bá rokú rò mí, á fọmọ rópò, ènìyàn ò lè rokú rò mí kí ó mú un jẹ gbé o!* (anyone who thought that I will die, that person will pay for it dearly with his or her own child, no one can think that I will die scot-free!). This portends that the space and place of these scared words is changing but remains important in contemporary society.

See also **Homage (Ìbà); Libation**

REFERENCE

Ọlátúnjí, O. Ọlátúndé. *Features of Yorùbá Oral Poetry*. Ìbàdàn (Nigeria): University Press Limited, 1984.

George Olúṣọlá Ajíbádé

WORK SONGS

A work song is a piece of music closely connected to a specific form of work. It is sung while conducting a task or song associated with a task or trade. The culture of work songs is old, and anthropological evidence suggests that all agrarian societies tend to have them.

Work songs are sung by individuals or groups of people. Work songs mobilized people, calling members of a community together for a collective task. Thus, they were extremely important. Mainly, group work songs created connection and familiarity between workers, which was intended to increase productivity, reduce boredom, raise morale, and keep people working.

Work songs function to stimulate workers, alleviate hardship, and increase the tempo of individuals and groups of workers. If a particular work song involves rhymes, one worker raises the song and others echo it. In this context, any worker can raise any song as he or she is inspired. The verses in work songs are often improvised and sung differently each time. Improvisation provided singers with subversive form of expression. Before industrialization, farming was the most common occupation among of the people, which is why most work songs are linked to farming activities.

In many instances, songs about farming themes or crops are evident in agricultural work songs. The cassava and pawpaw are very common subjects of work songs. Because of the place of the two foods in Yorùbá society, farmers would often sing about them, regardless of whether they were being harvested. For example:

> *Iṣẹ́ oko pé;*
> *Bébi ń pa mí ma jẹ̀bépẹ;*
> *Iṣẹ́ oko pé.*
> *Bébi ń pa mí ma sùngẹ́ jẹ;*
> *Iṣẹ́ oko pé.*

> Farming is profitable;
> I will eat pawpaw whenever I am hungry;
> Farming is profitable.
> I will roast cassava whenever I am hungry;
> Farming is profitable.

Work songs among the Yorùbá are fluid. Many songs can be used as work songs because they are primarily sung to reduce or remove boredom and increase productivity. Ruth Finnegan noted that "work songs can also comment on life in general, on local events or local characters and can express ideas of life, friendship or even obscenity. In short, work songs lighten the labor and give an opportunity, however limited, for poetic and musical expression in the midst of work."

Work songs can be sung by an individual or a group of people. Different types of songs, ranging from social, political to religious songs, boost worker's morale. It has been noted from experiential participation that the Yorùbá *ìjálá*, hunter poetry, is a notable genre among farmers and hunters, and a majority of hunters were also farmers.

See also **Ceremonial Songs**

REFERENCE

Finnegan, Ruth. *Oral Literature in Africa*. Oxford: Oxford University Press, 1970.

George Olúṣọlá Ajíbádé

WORLDVIEW

Yorùbá people construct their reality in many forms: religious, ethical, philosophical, psychological, and sociological. The majority of Yorùbá are religious and theistic. Their cosmos consists of the Supreme Being (Ọlọ́run or Olódùmarè), who is believed to govern the affairs of human lives. Though remote, invisible, and hidden from view, Olódùmarè directs and controls the affairs of people through titular divinities and other lesser spiritual beings, such as ancestors charged with the day-to-day running of affairs. Olódùmarè does not act unilaterally like the Christian God and Muslim Allah.

In their philosophical thought, there are two important realms of existence: *òrun* (heavenly abode) and *ayé* (earthly abode). The *òrun-ayé* distinction is important in understanding Yorùbá concepts of life, death, destiny, reincarnation, and the soul. The world is believed to be made up of both good and evil; these are the principles by which human society is organized. For example, engagement with the problem of evil reveals itself through definitions of evil, sources of evil, and attitudes about evil and their implications for interpersonal and social relations. Evil is not perceived as a negation of good. Rather, calamities, misfortunes, and other occurrences defined as evil necessarily organize the human universe.

Thus, the Yorùbá have different philosophical thinking than the West in their approach, content, and context—though that approach may be shared with other indigenous communities. While believing in this coexistence of good and evil, they nevertheless possess a mechanism for resolving the complexity of such coexistence in the world without the perceived contradiction that characterizes Western philosophical thought. Their theological understanding hinges on the process of negotiation through certain ritual practices between benevolent and malevolent forces that dominate the human and spiritual universe.

Yorùbá religious thought makes a distinction between the physical body (*ara*) and the spiritual elements that inhabit it and give it life and individuality. Still, there is the conception that the two are inseparable entities that make up human personality. The spiritual elements consist of both the head (*orí*, the inner head) and breath (*èémí*), which are the vital components without which the body dies. *Orí*, which is more than a physical head that carries human brain, controls one's destiny and direction through the use of one's *ẹsẹ̀*. *Orí* also guides one's deeds and actions; a bad and good choice depends on one's choice of *orí*. In essence, *orí* is the element that predetermines a person's success or failure in the world. The relationship of *ara*, *èmí*, and *orí* is illustrated by an Ifá verse in which the body is molded by Òrìṣà-Ńlá, the *èmí* is provided by Ọlọ́run (Olódùmarè), and the *orí* is provided by Àjàlá.

In Yorùbá sociological thought, life cannot be lived in isolation without an adverse consequence. Consider the proverb *ẹni tí ó bá dá ayé jẹ, yóò dá ìyà jẹ* (he or she who lives alone suffers alone). The widespread acceptance of positive attributes such as generosity (*ìfifúnni*), hospitality (*ìkónimọ́ra*), kindness (*ìṣoore*), truthfulness (*ìsòtítọ́*), respect for life (*ìbọ̀wọ̀ fún ẹmí ènìyàn*), and self-lessness (*àìmọ ti ara ẹni nìkan*) are common motifs in Yorùbá folklore. *Àlọ́* (folktales) particularly serve as a medium through which children are taught how to cultivate and embrace good virtues.

Good virtues can also be learned through proverbs (òwe), Ifá corpus (odù), and some mythical stories and parables. Generosity, hospitality, and kindness are interconnected and closely related. The Yorùbá expect that a person who possesses a virtuous moral character, such as kindness, ought to be generous and hospitable. All virtues are intrinsically connected with and relevant to individual and communal peace. When these qualities are in abundance, the Yorùbá consider the society to have abundant life. However, they consider a person who is selfish and unkind to have a flawed moral character. Thus, he or she is not a person in a normative sense. Yorùbá will say kì í ṣé ènìyàn (he or she is not a normal person, not in an anatomical and physiological sense but in a moral sense).

In their cultic worldview, the number of òrìṣà worshipped by the Yorùbá is very high, although they range in importance from those worshipped by only a single descent group in a single town to those whose cult is found throughout Yorùbáland and beyond. The nature and origins of òrìṣà are varied. Some are personifications of natural features, such as hills or rivers, or of natural forces. Others are deified heroes with cosmic attributes, such as Ṣàngó, the divinity of thunder and, by tradition, an early aláàfin of Ọ̀yọ́. The important divinities lead hierarchies of minor ones with similar characteristics, symbols, and functions. Mythically speaking, the òrìṣà were led by Ògún, the divinity of iron, hunting, and war, while the benign "white" òrìṣà, particularly important to women, were led by Òrìṣà-Ńlá, the Yorùbá creator. The parallels between these hierarchies and the Yorùbá political system are obvious.

The major òrìṣà have shrines and priests with their own distinctive dress and insignia. Each òrìṣà has its favorite sacrificial offerings, and its followers observe a distinctive set of food taboos. Each òrìṣà cult has rituals, music, oral literature, dances, and divination techniques. To their followers, the òrìṣà bring the benefits of health, wealth, and children, but they punish neglect, impiety, and the breaking of taboos. The ruler (ọba) plays an important unifying role in cultic life in the town, and major festivals involve a procession to the palace to greet him and bestow on him the blessing of the òrìṣà. Rulers are expected to participate in annual festivals on behalf of their community.

See also **Cosmology; Deities (The Òrìṣà); Diaspora: Deities (Òrìṣà); Sacrifice; Worship**

REFERENCES

Drewal, Henry John, John Pemberton III, and Rowland Abíọ́dún. "The Yorùbá World." In *Yorùbá: Nine Centuries of African Art and Thought*, ed. Henry John Drewal, John Pemberton, Rowland Abíọ́dún, and Allen Wardwell, 13–43. New York: Center for African Art in association with Harry N. Abrams Inc., 1989.

Ìdòwú, Bọ́lájí, *Olódùmarè: God in Yorùbá Belief*. London: Longman Publishing, 1963.

Enoch Olújídé Gbádégẹsin

WORSHIP

The religious symbols of Yorùbá worshippers of òrìṣà and ancestors are grounded in natural associations. As such, respect and devotion are important values. Worship requires a fundamental attitude of strict discipline and reverence. In Yorùbá society, ancestors and òrìṣà are believed to continue as active spirits in the families and society; they have a great deal to do with the well-being of the worshippers. Worshippers constantly adore and venerate them. Because ancestral spirits and òrìṣà are believed to play important roles in this society, the Yorùbá worship them spontaneously rather than through coercion. For example, òrìṣà who were delegated on behalf of Olódùmarè (Supreme Being) were held in high esteem because they were believed to be benevolent to the worshippers and all inhabitants in society.

Worship is a religious exercise that involves the performance of devotional acts in honor of the òrìṣà and ancestral spirits. Yorùbá consider worship a matter of ultimate importance, which, if neglected, is at one's own peril. Because worship is considered an opportunity to communicate with the Supreme Being through the òrìṣà, it is expressed in both words and deeds. These words and deeds take the form of holy rites and ceremonies and include bodily gestures such as prostration, praying, invocation, hailing the òrìṣà, offering sacrifices, singing, drumming, and dancing. Worship can be a private affair whereby an individual venerates his or her personal òrìsà or deity, or it can be a public one, which is very common.

With a public form of worship, the ruler of each family, quarter, village, and town is an active participant; he ensures the provision of all symbolic materials needed for proper veneration and worship. There are also cultic functionaries: officiates and attendants at worship. Worship is carried out at sacred places of worship such as shrines, temples, and altars. Sacrificial materials such as kola nuts, palm oil, palm wine, bitter kola, and important animals, depending on the preference of a particular òrìsà, are always made ready. The Yorùbá engage in liturgical practices such as prayers, music, and dancing. All these distinct elements are packaged together to make worship interesting and acceptable to the òrìsà and ancestors.

Yorùbá people believe that before one can approach any òrìsà in worship, he or she must observe certain rules and regulations, such as bodily cleansing and or purification. Worshippers and officiating ministers do not approach their òrìsà or ancestors carelessly; there are taboos to be observed and restrictions imposed on the uninitiated. In this society, òrìsà and ancestral worshippers believe that if worship is properly conducted, there are many benefits to gain, namely, spiritual enlightenment, mystical experience, physical and material blessings, and sanctification of society.

See also **Cosmology; Deities (The Òrìsà); Diaspora: Deities (Òrìsà); Sacrifice; Worldview**

REFERENCES

Ìdòwú, E. Bólájí, *Olódùmarè: God in Yorùbá Believe*. London: Longman Publishing, 1963.
Awólàlú, J. Omósadé, *Yorùbá Belief and Sacrificial Rites*. New York: Athelia Henrietta Press, 2001.

Enoch Olújídé Gbádégesin

WRITERS

Yorùbá writers can be divided into three distinct groups: those who write in English, French, or Arabic; those who write in Yorùbá and any of the previously mentioned languages; and those who write only in Yorùbá. Each of these groups writes from particular points of view and with particular aims. Those Yorùbá writers who write in languages other than Yorùbá tend to write from the point of view of a larger political constituency than the Yorùbá homeland. Their points of view are usually pan-African and pan-Nigerian. More specifically, they are concerned about the image of Africa and the Africa contained in the writings of Europe and the Arab world. Writers such as Wolé Sóyínká, Amos Tutùolá, and Olá Balógun (who writes in French) belong to these groups of Yorùbá writers.

The second group of writers consists of those who write in Yorùbá and in English, French, or Arabic—these do not seem to write with any particular ideological axe to grind. Rather, they seem to use whichever language seems convenient for them as they approach each subject. The best-known practitioner of this group is Akínwùmí Ìsòlá. He has published novels, plays, and anecdotes in both Yorùbá and English. Although he studied French and uses it, there is no record of a publication of his in French. Those of his plays written in English have always been purposely targeted at a Nigerian and African audience.

The most interesting, perhaps, of the three groups are those who write in Yorùbá. They are completely at home in their Yorùbá skin and unapologetic in their Yorùbá-centric worldview. This worldview, briefly, accepts that the British conquest of Yorùbáland was a mere historical point in the history of the two peoples. The Yorùbá must use whatever tools they have not only to make their situation better but also to make the British a better people as well. This sentiment is well expressed in the final pages of Samuel Johnson's *History of the Yorùbás*.

This sentiment informs the decision of D. O. Fágúnwà's characters (the hunters) in *Ògbójú-Odẹ Nínú Igbó Irúnmalè* to take over the administration of the city of Èdìdàrẹ after they had overpowered and conquered the residents of the city. To teach the Èdìdàrẹ Yorùbá behavior and norms, the hunters did not replace the

Èdìdàrẹ's king but appointed one of their members as the town's leader to oversee the behavior of the people of Èdìdàrẹ and to ensure that by the time the hunters were on their return journey, the people of Èdìdàrẹ would have learned the civilized way of doing things.

Yorùbá writers have brought into Yorùbá writing a greater variety of genres than what has been available in the English language literature of Nigeria. Police procedural thrillers, private detective stories, and investigative crime novels exist in Yorùbá literature, whereas none of these exists in the English literature of the country. Writers using the Yorùbá language write for stage, radio, film, and television. The world that the writers using Yorùbá language have created is sufficient unto itself.

See also **Colonial Politics; Fágúnwà, Daniel Ọlọ́runfẹ́mi; Literature: Women Writers; Literature: Written and Modern; Ọdúnjọ, Joseph Fọláhàn; Prominent Scholars; Ṣóyínká Wọlé; Translation; Tutùọlá, Amos**

REFERENCES

Johnson, Samuel. *The History of the Yorùbás*. Lagos (Nigeria): C.S.S., 1921.

Ọmọ́tọ́sọ̀, Kọ́lé. "The Nigerian Federation in the Nigerian Novel." *Publius: the Journal of Federalism* 21.4 (January 1991): 145–53.

Kọ́lé Ọmọ́tọ́sọ̀

Y

YORÙBÁ COUNCIL OF ELDERS

The Yorùbá Council of Elders (YCE), also referred to as Ìgbìmọ̀ Àgbà Yorùbá, was founded in 2001. Its mission is to advance the welfare of the Yorùbá race and its descendants, wherever they may be across the globe. Among the leading members of the council at its founding were late Pa Emmanuel Aláyàndé, Justice Adéwálé Thompson, and Chief Bọ́lá Ìgè. The current national secretary is Chief Ìdòwú Ṣọ́fọlá, a senior advocate of Nigeria. The YCE was created to counterbalance the influence of the Afẹ́nifẹ́re group, a sociocultural organization of senior Yorùbá who had a mandate similar to the YCE. It was led by prominent Yorùbá personalities, especially those associated with leading the National Democratic Coalition (NADECO), which spearheaded the opposition against the Abacha dictatorship. The YCE included the leader Abraham Adésànyà and deputy leader Chief Bọ́lá Ìgè, as well as Chief Reuben Fáṣọ̀ràntì, Fẹ́mi Òkúróunmú, Dáwódù, Ọláníhún Àjàyí, and Ayọ̀ Adébánjọ.

When the Alliance for Democracy (AD) was formed in 1998, its adoption of the Afẹ́nifẹ́re agenda as its manifesto confirmed suspicions that the AD was a Yorùbá vanguard party. The YCE sought to integrate the Yorùbá into the mainstream of the national process on the basis of its historical marginalization and role as the center of national opposition. The YCE's positions are opposed to Afẹ́nifẹ́re's puritanical perspectives on Yorùbá interests and have tended to be aligned with the thinking of the federal government on critical developments in the country. The tension between the YCE and Afẹ́nifẹ́re reenact the two poles of clashing historical perspectives on the most effective strategic approach to protect and advance Yorùbá interests. This tension was reflected in the ambivalent position of late Chief Bọ́lá Ìgè—a staunch disciple of late Yorùbá iconic leader Chief Ọbáfẹ́mi Awólọ́wọ̀—whose activities straddled both the YCE and the Afẹ́nifẹ́re. Futile attempts were made to suspend his membership in the Afẹ́nifẹ́re group as a result of his association with the YCE. Some have insinuated that the YCE was also Ọbásanjọ́'s instrument to build a base constituency in Yorùbáland to sustain his relevance in mainstream Nigerian political life

In 2008 the more youthful Afẹ́nifẹ́re Renewal Group, led by the Honorable Wálé Òṣún, and with the active participation of Ayọ̀ Afọlábí, was established to reunite the many strands of Yorùbá cultural leadership organizations into one body and to transfer leadership to a younger generation. These developments reflect the fractious character of the internal dynamic of the Yorùbá and were expressed by the resignation of YCE's secretary-general Justice Adéwálé Thompson, who described the murder of Chief Bọ́lá Ìgè as the handiwork of an Afẹ́nifẹ́re man.

The YCE has launched a Yorùbá Village in the United Kingdom as a center of learning of Yorùbá language and culture as well as a rallying forum for Yorùbá descendants in the United Kingdom.

See also **Aféníféré, Egbé; Associations for Promoting Yorùbá Culture; Awólówò, Obáfémi; Politics and Political Parties since 1945**

REFERENCES

Adébámwí, Wálé. *Yorùbá Elites and Ethnic Politics: Obáfémi Awólówò and Corporate Agency.* New York: Cambridge University Press, 2014.

Olátúnjí, Dáúdà. "Why We Built Yorùbá Village in London— YCE, the Vanguard (Nigeria)," March 17, 2013. http://www.vanguardngr.com/2013/03/why-we-built-Yorùbá-village-in-London-yce/.

Adémólá Àràoyè

YOUTH AND YOUTH CULTURE: MODERN

Western education, evangelism, gender equality movements, working mothers, globalization, the Internet, and media technology have all jointly and independently revolutionized, transformed, and wholly integrated traditional Yorùbá villages and towns into the modern global village. Government educational and religious bureaucratic functionaries have encroached upon many of the responsibilities of close-knit family households and communal villages and towns. In particular, the conventional and nonmonetized parental upbringing and home training duties and responsibilities of the household and domestic group members have been commercialized and transferred to helpers, nannies, teachers, day-care centers, and private and public boarding schools. Boarding schools and facilities operate for nursery school–aged children. Consequently, as all of the Yorùbá values and beliefs are changing, so are modern youth and youth culture, mirroring the emerging global village lifestyle and worldview.

Children imbibe culture, and the home is best positioned as the primary agent of socialization. However, non-Yorùbá speaking "surrogate mothers" (housemaids and nannies) from neighboring countries raise Yorùbá youth. Men were never much involved with child rearing, and modern market women do not have time to be with their children. Many children grow up without much interaction with their parents. They are in bed before their parents come home from work, and they are not awake before the parents leave home for work. Hence, the greatest significant impact of these new trends on youth culture is that most of youth do not speak Yorùbá. Because language is critically important for the storage, retrieval, processing, and use of culture, the modern youth are literally adopting the culture of their foreign counterparts.

The Yorùbá have evolved a treasury of ethics, proverbs, parables, taboos, legends, fables, and coded nonverbal communication for everyday public and private interactions and relationships. Every member of a household and village or town community, especially the elders, village head (*baálè*), or town chiefs or king (*oba*) in council, is responsible for the rule of law, including dissemination, monitoring, and compliance with the unwritten codes of behavior that all members. However, modern youth have a taste of freedom even before they could differentiate between the right and wrong. They become independent before they understand the full consequences of their actions. They have freedom without the responsibility that often serves as a check on freedom. They leave home early, either to day or boarding schools, colleges, and universities. Many graduate from universities as teenagers with little or no experience of what life entails.

Consequently, they are no longer under traditional parental control. Youth today operate by what the Yorùbá would describe as *ojú olómo kò tó o* (beyond the oversight of parents). They are anonymous dwellers of both real and virtual (Internet) cities. The Yorùbá say *orúko tó wuni ni à ń jé léhìn odi* (we bear whatever name we like when we live beyond the borders). They have access to mobile phones, Internet and social networks, and twenty-four-hour cable television networks. These things are beyond the supervision and control of adults.

The modern youth culture of violent protest, rebellion, and thuggery began in the early 1960s. The landmarks of that period were the worldwide student power movements, economic austerity, the *àgbékòyà* riots, politics, and the constitutional crisis in the old Western Region of Nigeria, and eventually the coup d'état and civil war of the mid-1960s and early 1970s. Armed robbery, drug abuse, and licentiousness became more pronounced with the demobilization of more than 120,000 soldiers (mostly youth) at the end of the civil war in early 1970. Since then, youth have also joined the rest of their counterparts with the youth culture of binge sex, drug and alcohol abuse, cyber fraud and Internet crime, violent cults, and occultism, especially in high schools and on college and university campuses.

The career aspirations of youth have also changed. While traditional youth changed from farming and family occupations into pursuing professional courses in engineering, law, medicine, and accounting, modern youth pursue media studies, business and public administration, fashion design, and event management.

Perhaps the most prominent expression of youth culture is fashion and recreation. The modern youth fashion and recreation culture, especially their leisure and engagement in sports, music, films, and clothing, is varied and differentiated. The main differentiating factor is religion. Unlike traditional youth, most modern youth, especially Christians and Muslims, wear their religions overtly in public. They are more publicly unequivocal and fundamentalist in their dress codes and their attitudes toward other faiths. Modern films, such as those shown on Africa Magic Cable Network in particular, and hip-hop and rock music are common and popular among youth. While traditional youth took part in athletics and sports, modern youth are mostly interested in music, video games, television, and social networking.

See also **Children and Childhood; Children's Folklore: Education and Development; Gang, Gangster, and Gangsterism; Music: Popular; Youth and Youth Culture: Traditional**

REFERENCE

Peel, J. D. Y. *Religious Encounter and the Making of the Yorùbá*. Bloomington: Indiana University Press, 2003.

Bọ́lá Dáúdà

YOUTH AND YOUTH CULTURE: TRADITIONAL

Youth and youth culture are entwined with the primary Yorùbá beliefs and values. Reincarnation and the continuity of life, protection of the family name and honor, and the desire to leave a memorable legacy of integrity or good name (ọmọlúwàbí) are core Yorùbá beliefs and values. Procreation is crucial to upholding these beliefs and values. Therefore, the Yorùbá not only believe in having children but also have faith in the youth (èwe or ọ̀dọ́). They often invest all of their resources in them. For example, they say *torí ọmọ la ṣe ń ṣiṣẹ́* (we work for the children). In addition, to emphasize priority in the child's education over personal wealth, the Yorùbá say *ọmọ tí a kò kọ́, ni yóò gbé ilé tí a kọ́ tà* (it is the untrained and uneducated child would sell the house we built). An unhappy woman would endure and go the extra mile for her children. She would say *mi ò ní kọ ọkọ̀ọ̀ mi, màá dúró tójú àwọn ọmọ mi* (I would not divorce but would stay to look after my children).

The growth and development of youth and youth culture is not left to chance; adults shape, guide, and monitor them. At birth, the first step is that parents carefully select the name of their children. They know that both real and nicknames influence the behavior of the child (orúkọ ń roni, ìnagijẹ ń rònìyàn). The name is the rein or instrument of self-control and self-discipline: *orúkọ ẹni ni ìjánu ẹni*. Therefore, parents examine their own circumstances in choosing meaningful names for the child.

Culture is imbibed from childhood, and the first agent is the home. The phrase *ilé ni a ti ń kọ́ ẹ̀ṣọ́ ròde* (charity begins at home) has deep meaning among the Yorùbá. To them, the home encompasses more than one's immediate nuclear or extended family. Home is the household and the entire community. The Yorùbá say *oyún nìkan ni a kì í báni gbé, tẹrú tọmọ níí báni wo ọmọ* (it is only pregnancy we cannot help the expectant mother to carry; both the freeborn and slave helped to bring up the child). The youth belong to the entire community, and it is the responsibility of everyone, especially elders, to ensure their appropriate upbringing and good behavior. A youth who refused to respond positively to home training would be labeled as *ọmọ asa* (outcast) or *ọmọ àlè* (bastard). The Yorùbá are quick to sound the warning that *ọmọ tí kò gba èkọ́ ilé, aráyé á kọ́ ọ níta* ("life" will teach and tame such an unruly child in a hard way).

Apprenticeship played a great role in the lives of youth and in the evolution of the youth culture. Ordinarily, male and female youth learned the trade of their parents. For example, a farmer would apportion part of his farmland to a youth who was old enough to be independent. Hence, as families become larger, small landholdings become a major problem of the land ownership system. Occasionally, a family might assign one or two of the children to learn trades outside the family occupation.

Recreation and leisure were important for the youth. The Yorùbá youth culture evolved from interactions with adults and among other youths. For example, on a sunny day, the youth would gather under the tree to play games, and in the evening, under the moonlight, they sat around the elders to listen to stories with moral lessons. Youth played with toys in courtyards. Male and female youth formed entertainment bands. They went on hunting and fishing expeditions. However, the youth operated under the strict guidance, control, and supervision of adults. They did not operate any cults on their own. They only participated in seasonal cultural carnivals or events such as *egúngún, orò, gèlèdé,* and *agẹmọ.* Even when they were of courting age, the family arranged the marriage after fully investigating the respective bride and groom because *kò sí ẹni tí ó fẹ́ ọmọ láti ìdílée wèrè* (no one wants to marry into a mad family).

The traditional Yorùbá youth culture was unlike the modern youth culture of drug abuse, violent films, hip-hop and rock music, violent cults and occultism, and licentiousness. It was the parents' pride for the bride to be a virgin on her wedding day, and a thing of shame to the family if she had sex before marriage. Therefore, youth culture was an extension of the adult culture of uprightness, communal rights and responsibility, and work ethic. The youth who had been well grounded in the wisdom and experiences of the adults would be acknowledged and appreciated as *ọmọ àgbà.* In Ìjèbúland, for example, an age cohort of youths often celebrated their rite of passage by appearing before the king to receive a name.

See also **Apprenticeship; Children and Childhood; Children's Folklore: Education and Development; Ethics; Music: Popular; Ọmọlúwàbí; Youth and Youth Culture: Modern**

REFERENCE

Fádípè, N. A. *The Sociology of the Yorùbá.* Ìbàdàn (Nigeria): University Press Limited, 1970.

Bọ́lá Dáúdà

CONTRIBUTORS

Ọláyíwọlá M. Abégúnrìn, Howard University

Tósìn Abíọ́dún, Hillsboro, Oregon

Ọládiméjì Abórìṣàdé, University of North Carolina at Charlotte

Olúfadékẹ́mi Adágbádá, Ọlábísí Ọnàbánjọ University (Àgọ́ Ìwòyè, Nigeria)

Wálé Adébánwí, University of California–Davis

Àkànmú Adébáyọ̀, Kennesaw State University

Fẹ́mi Adédèjì, Ọbáfẹ́mi Awólọ́wọ̀ University (Ilé-Ifẹ̀, Nigeria)

Ọmọ́tádé Adégbindin, University of Ìbàdàn (Nigeria)

Àrìnpé Adéjùmọ̀, University of Ìbàdàn (Nigeria)

Julius O. Adékúnlé, Monmouth University

Abímbọ́lá Adélakùn, University of Texas at Austin

Babáṣẹhìndé A. Adémúlẹ̀yá, Ọbáfẹ́mi Awólọ́wọ̀ University (Ilé-Ifẹ̀, Nigeria)

Adébùsúyì Isaac Adéníran, Ọbáfẹ́mi Awólọ́wọ̀ University (Ilé-Ifẹ̀, Nigeria)

Harrison Adéníyì, Lagos State University (Nigeria)

Ìbígbọ́ládé S. Adéríbigbé, University of Georgia, Athens

Adérónkẹ́ Adéṣọlá Adésànyà, James Madison University, Harrisonburg, Virginia

Olútáyọ̀ C. Adéṣínà, University of Ìbàdàn (Nigeria)

Olúṣẹ̀yẹ Adéṣọlá, Yale University

Lérè Adéyẹmí, University of Ìlọrin (Nigeria)

Ṣọlá Adéyẹmí, University of Greenwich (London)

Ọlátúndé Adéléyẹ Adéyẹmọ, Ọlábísí Ọnàbánjọ University (Àgọ́ Ìwòyè, Nigeria)

Níyì Afọlábí, University of Texas at Austin

Adéshínà Afọláyan, University of Ìbàdàn (Nigeria)

Fúnṣọ́ Afọláyan, University of New Hampshire

Michael Ọládèjọ Afọláyan, M&P Educational Consulting International, Springfield

Ọláyínká Àgbétúyì, Indiana University

Doyin Àgúorù, University of Ìbàdàn (Nigeria)

Adérẹmí Suleiman Àjàlá, University of Ìbàdàn (Nigeria)

Timothy T. Àjàní, Fayetteville State University

George Olúṣọlá Ajíbádé, Ọbáfẹ́mi Awólọ́wọ̀ University (Ilé-Ifẹ̀, Nigeria)

Adéníyì Àkàngbé, University of Ìbàdàn (Nigeria)

Tọ́pẹ́ Olúwabùnmi Akíndípẹ̀, Ọbáfẹ́mi Awólọ́wọ̀ University (Ilé-Ifẹ̀, Nigeria)

Tósìn Akínjọbí-Babátúndé, Elizade University (Ìlárá-Mòkín, Nigeria)

Akínbíyì Akinlabí, Rutgers University

Ṣọlá Akínrìnádé, Ọbáfẹ́mi Awólọ́wọ̀ University (Ilé-Ifẹ̀, Nigeria)

Akíntúndé Akínyẹmí, University of Florida, Gainesville

Fenda A. Akíwùmí, University of South Florida

Adétáyọ̀ Àlàbí, University of Mississippi

Akin Àlàó, Ọbáfẹ́mi Awólọ́wọ̀ University (Ilé-Ifẹ̀, Nigeria)

Kúnlé Amúwò, Covenant University (Ota, Nigeria)

Ayọ̀ọlá Ọládùnkẹ́ Àráńsí, Kwara State University (Màlété, Nigeria)

Adémọ́lá Àràoyè, Independent Scholar, Monrovia (Liberia)

Nurudeen Ọlátóyè Arógundádé, Ọbáfẹ́mi Awólọ́wọ̀ University (Ilé-Ifẹ̀, Nigeria)

Ṣọládoyè S. Asà, Ọbáfẹ́mi Awólọ́wọ̀ University (Ilé-Ifẹ̀, Nigeria)

Paul Olúwọlé Àsáwálé, Ọbáfẹ́mi Awólọ́wọ̀ University (Ilé-Ifẹ̀, Nigeria)

Abímbọ́lá Aṣòjò, University of Minnesota

Dàmọ́lá Àyánṣọlá, Adélékè University (Ẹdẹ, Nigeria)

Gabriel Ayọ̀ọlá, University of Georgia, Athens

Tòkunbọ̀ Ayọ̀ọlá, Elizade University (Ìlárá-Mọ̀kín, Nigeria)

Wahab Adémọ́lá Azeez, Federal College of Education (Lagos, Nigeria)

Abídèmí Babátúndé Babalọlá, Rice University

Adémọ́lá Babalọlá, Ọbáfẹ́mi Awólọ́wọ̀ University (Ilé-Ifẹ̀, Nigeria)

Emmanuel Gbádébọ̀ Babátúndé, Lincoln University

Túndé Babáwálé, University of Lagos (Nigeria)

Fàtàì Adéṣínà Badru, University of Lagos (Nigeria)

Olúyẹmisí Bámgbóṣé, University of Ìbàdàn (Nigeria)

John Ayọ̀túndé Ìṣọ̀lá Bẹ́wàjí, University of the West Indies, (Kingston, Jamaica)

Abídèmí Bọ́lárìnwá, University of Ìbàdàn (Nigeria)

Níyì Coker, Jr., University of Missouri, St. Louis

Adémọ́lá Dasylva, University of Ìbàdàn (Nigeria)

Bọ́lá Dáúdà, Early Years' Education Foundation (Ìbàdàn, Nigeria)

Ayọ̀ Fádáhùnsi, Ọlábísí Ọnàbánjọ University (Àgọ́ Ìwòyè, Nigeria)

Tèmítọ́pé C. Fágúnwà, University of Ìbàdàn (Nigeria)

Julius Fákínlẹ̀dé, Federal University of Technology (Àkúrẹ́, Nigeria)

Tóyìn Fálọlá, University of Texas at Austin

Ọláwọlé Fámulẹ̀, University of Wisconsin–Superior

Adémọ́lá K. Fáyẹmí, Lagos State University (Nigeria)

Stephen Fọlárànmí, Ọbáfẹ́mi Awólọ́wọ̀ University (Ilé-Ifẹ̀, Nigeria)

Enoch Olújídé Gbádégẹsin, Ọbáfẹ́mi Awólọ́wọ̀ University (Ilé-Ifẹ̀, Nigeria)

Abọ́sẹ̀dé George, Bernard College, Columbia

Stephen D. Glazier, University of Nebraska, Lincoln

Matthew M. Heaton, Virginia Tech

Samson O. Ìjàọlá, Samuel Adégbéyẹ̀ga University (Ogwa, Nigeria)

Daniel Jean-Jacques, University of Texas at Austin

délé jégẹ́dẹ́, Miami University, Oxford

Ọbáfẹ́mi Jégẹ́dẹ́, University of Ìbàdàn (Nigeria)

Adépéjú Johnson-Bashua, Lagos State University (Nigeria)

Fẹ́mi Kọ́lápọ̀, University of Guelph (Ontario, Canada)

Henry B. Lovejoy, University of Texas at Austin

Moses Mábayọ̀jé, Rutgers University

Insa Nolte, University of Birmingham

Ṣẹ́gun Ọbasá, University of Texas at Austin

Kọ́léadé Odùtọ́lá, University of Florida, Gainesville

Olúkọ̀yà Ogen, Ọ̀sun State University (Ìkirè Campus, Nigeria)

Bíọ́dún J. Ògúndayọ̀, University of Pittsburgh

Philip Adédọ̀tun Ògúndèjì, University of Ìbàdàn (Nigeria)

Akínwùmí Ògúndìran, University of North Carolina at Charlotte

Káyọ̀dé Ọmọniyì Ògúnfọlábí, Ọbáfẹ́mi Awólọ́wọ̀ University (Ilé-Ifẹ̀, Nigeria)

Àdìsá Ògúnfọlákàn, Ọbáfẹ́mi Awólọ́wọ̀ University (Ilé-Ifẹ̀, Nigeria)

Ṣẹ́gun Ògúngbèmí, Adékúnlé Ajásin University (Àkùngbá-Àkókó, Nigeria)

Abigail Odozi Ogwezzy-Ndisika, University of Lagos (Nigeria)

Akinloyè Òjó, University of Georgia, Athens

Mutiat Títílọpẹ́ Ọládèjọ, University of Ìbàdàn (Nigeria)

Olúwatóyìn M. Ọláìyá, Èkìtì State University (Adó-Èkìtì, Nigeria)

Samuel O. Ọlọ́runtọ́ba, University of South Africa

Sunday Ọlọ́runtọ́lá, University of Lagos (Nigeria)

Ayọ̀ Olúkọ̀tún, Lead City University (Ìbàdàn, Nigeria)

Táíwò Olúnládé, Lagos State University (Nigeria)

Felix Ayoh'Omídire, Ọbáfẹ́mi Awólọ́wọ̀ University (Ilé-Ifẹ̀, Nigeria)

Kazeem A. Ọmọ́fóyèwá, University of Ìbàdàn (Nigeria)

Bọ̀dé Ọmọ́jọlà, Mount Holyoke College/Five Colleges

Báyọ̀ Ọmọlọlá, Howard University

Kọ́lé Ọmọ́tọ́sọ̀, Africa Diaspora Research Centurion (South Africa)

Sànyà Ọshá, Tshwane University of Technology (Pretoria, South Africa)

Wálé Owóṣéní, University of Ìbàdàn

Adébáyọ̀ Oyèbádé, Tennessee State University

Bùkọ́lá Oyèníyì, Missouri State University, Springfield

Akin Oyètádé, SOAS, University of London

William Ọládélé Ṣàngótóyè, University of Ìbàdàn (Nigeria)

Kazeem Kẹ́hìndé Sanuth, University of Wisconsin–Madison

Láídé Sheba, Ọbáfẹ́mi Awólọ́wọ̀ University (Ilé-Ifẹ̀, Nigeria)

Pamela J. Olúbùnmi Smith, University of Nebraska at Omaha

Adékẹ́mi Adégún Táíwò, Èkìtì State University (Adó-Èkìtì, Nigeria)

Martin A. Tsang, Florida International University

Chinyere Ukpokolo, University of Ìbàdàn (Nigeria)

Aríbidésí Usman, Arizona State University, Tempe

Olúfẹ́mi Vaughan, Bowdoin College

Shehu Tìjjání Yusuf, Bayero University (Kano, Nigeria)

INDEX

Tóyìn Fálọlá, PhD, recent former President of the African Studies Association, is the Jacob and Frances Sanger Mossiker Chair in the Humanities and a Distinguished Teaching Professor at the University of Texas at Austin. He was recently appointed by the Library of Congress to the Kluge Chair of Cultures and Countries of the South. He is a Fellow of the Historical Society of Nigeria and a Fellow of the Nigerian Academy of Letters. Professor Fálọlá has received various awards and honors, including honorary doctorates from Monmouth University, City University of New York, Staten Island, Lead City University (Nigeria), Adékúnlé Ajáṣin University (Nigeria), Táí Ṣálàrìn University of Education (Nigeria), and the University of Jos (Nigeria). Professor Fálọlá is author and editor of more than one hundred books. For his singular and distinguished contribution to the study of Africa, his students and colleagues have presented him with five *Festschriften*: Adébáyọ̀ Oyèbádé, *The Transformation of Nigeria: Essays in Honor of Tóyìn Fálọlá*, and *The Foundations of Nigeria: Essays in Honor of Tóyìn Fálọlá*, and one edited by Akin Ògúndìran, *Pre-Colonial Nigeria: Essays in Honor of Tóyìn Fálọlá*. Two of his memoirs have been published by the University of Michigan Press: *A Mouth Sweeter than Salt: An African Memoir* and *Counting the Tiger's Teeth: An African Teenager's Story*. An extensive elaboration of the impact of his scholarship is presented in Abdul Bangura's *Tóyìn Fálọlá and African Epistemologies*.

Akíntúndé Akínyẹmí is Professor in the Department of Languages, Literatures, and Cultures, and an affiliate faculty at the Center for African Studies, University of Florida in Gainesville. His research interests include Yorùbá as well as African-language literature, popular culture, and diaspora studies. Between 1999 and 2001, he was a postdoctoral research fellow of the Alexander von Humboldt Foundation at the Institute of African Studies, University of Bayreuth in Germany and the Center for West African Studies, University of Birmingham in the United Kingdom. He is the author of *Yorùbá Royal Poetry: A Socio-historical Exposition and Annotated Translation* (2004) and *Orature and Yorùbá Riddles* (2015); co-author of a French–Yorùbá dictionary, *Dictionnaire usual Yorùbá-français* (1997); and editor/co-editor of *African Creative Expressions: Mother Tongue and Other Tongues* (2011), *Ṣàngó in Africa and the African Diaspora* (2009), *Emerging Perspectives on Fẹ́mi Ọṣọ́fisan* (2009), and *Emerging Perspectives on Akínwùmí Ìṣọ̀lá* (2008).

www.ingramcontent.com/pod-product-compliance
Lightning Source LLC
Chambersburg PA
CBHW080129270326
41926CB00021B/4401